The Study
of
Sociology

An Introduction

The Study of Sociology

An Introduction

JOSEPH S. HIMES
North Carolina College

WILBERT E. MOORE
Russell Sage Foundation
Consulting Editor

SCOTT, FORESMAN and COMPANY

The author gratefully acknowledges the authors and publishers who gave permission to use their materials in this book.

American Foundation for the Blind, Inc.: From *The War Blind in American Social Structure* by Alan G. Gowman. Copyright 1957.

American Geographical Society: Table 1 adapted from "A Functional Classification of Cities in the U.S." by Chauncey D. Harris, from *The Geographical Review*, January 1943.

American Sociological Association: Table 1 adapted from "Channels of Communication in Small Groups" by Robert F. Bales et al., from *American Sociological Review*, August 1951; from "A Portrait of the Farm Family in Central New York State" by Howard W. Beers, from *American Sociological Review*, October 1937; adapted from "Social Disorganization and Reorganization in Harlan County, Kentucky" by Paul F. Cressey, from *American Sociological Review*, June 1949; Table 1 from "A Preliminary Study of Size Determinants in Small Group Interaction" by John James, from *American Sociological Review*, August 1951; Table 1 from "Social Stratification and Mobility Patterns" by Carson McGuire, from *American Sociological Review*, Vol. 15, 1950; adapted from "Stratification in a Prairie Town" by John Useem et al., from *American Sociological Review*, June 1942.

Appleton-Century-Crofts: From *Social Psychology* by Kimball Young. Copyright 1956 by Appleton-Century-Crofts.

Morroe Berger: Adapted from "The Political Process in Trade Unions: A Theoretical Statement" by Seymour Martin Lipset, from *Freedom and Control in Modern Society* edited by Morroe Berger et al. Copyright 1954.

Bureau of Applied Social Research: Adapted from *Mass Persuasion* by Robert K. Merton. Copyright 1946. By permission of the author and the Bureau of Applied Social Research, Columbia University.

The Journal of Criminal Law, Criminology and Police Science: From "A Strategy for Research on Social Class and Delinquency" by Frank R. Westie and Austin T. Turk, reprinted by special permission from *The Journal of Criminal Law, Criminology and Police Science*, Copyright © 1965 by the Northwestern University School of Law, Volume 56 Number 4.

Thomas Y. Crowell Company: Condensed and adapted from Ruth S. Cavan, *The American Family*. Copyright © 1958 by Thomas Y. Crowell Company.

William H. Form: Figure 5.1 from *Industry, Labor and Community* by William H. Form and Delbert C. Miller, copyright 1960. Reprinted by permission of the authors.

Funk & Wagnalls and Bertha Klausner: Adapted from *A Maine Hamlet* by Lura Beam, by permission of the publishers, Funk & Wagnalls, N.Y., and Bertha Klausner, N.Y.

Harcourt, Brace & World, Inc., and Routledge & Kegan Paul Ltd.: Condensed and adapted from *The Human Group* by George C. Homans, copyright, 1950, by Harcourt, Brace & World, Inc., and reprinted with the permission of Harcourt, Brace & World, Inc., and Routledge & Kegan Paul Ltd.

Harper & Row, Inc.: Figures 127 and 128 (pp. 853-854) *Industrial Sociology* by Delbert C. Miller and William H. Form (Harper & Row, 1951); Abridgment of pp. 737-739 by Morris L. Stein et al., in *Clinical Studies of Personality*, Vol. 2 (Torchbook edition) edited by Arthur Burton and Robert E. Harris. Copyright © 1955 by Harper & Row, Publishers, Incorporated; Condensed and adapted from pp. 4, 5, 9, 23, 24, 100-103 *The Tastemakers* by Russell Lynes. Copyright 1949, 1953, 1954 by Russell Lynes. Reprinted by permission of Harper & Row, Publishers, and Russell Lynes.

Holt, Rinehart & Winston, Inc.: Adapted and condensed from *An Introduction to Cultural Anthropology* by Robert H. Lowie. Copyright 1934, 1940 by Robert H. Lowie. Copyright © 1962 by Luella Cole Lowie. Reprinted by permission of Holt, Rinehart and Winston, Inc.; Adapted and condensed from *The American Community in Action* by Jesse F. Steiner. Copyright 1928 by Holt, Rinehart & Winston, Inc. Copyright © 1955 by Jesse F. Steiner. Reprinted by permission of Holt, Rinehart & Winston, Inc.

Journal of Human Relations: Condensed and adapted from "The Soviet Man" by Max Oppenheimer, Jr., from the *Journal of Human Relations*, Vol. 7. Used with permission of the author and the *Journal of Human Relations*, Central State University, Wilberforce, Ohio.

Mrs. Manford Kuhn: Adapted from "American Families Today" by Manford H. Kuhn from *Family, Marriage and Parenthood* edited by Howard Becker and Reuben Hill. Copyright 1955.

H. K. Lewis & Co. Ltd.: From *"Collective Behavior,"* by Ralph H. Turner and Lewis M. Killian, reproduced by courtesy of Dr. L. S. Penrose from *The Objective Study of Crowd Behaviour,* London, H. K. Lewis & Co. Ltd.

Little, Brown and Company and William Collins Sons & Co. Ltd.: From *Point of No Return,* copyright, 1947, 1948, 1949, by John P. Marquand, with permission of Little, Brown, and Company and William Collins Sons & Co. Ltd. of London.

The Macmillan Company: Adapted from *Our Primitive Contemporaries* by George Peter Murdock. Copyright 1934.

Margaret Mead: Adapted from "The Kwakuitl of Vancouver Island" by Irving Goldman from *Cooperation and Competition Among Primitive Peoples* edited by Margaret Mead. Copyright 1937.

William Morrow and Company and Laurence Pollinger Ltd.: From *Coming of Age in Samoa* by Margaret Mead. Copyright © 1928, 1955, 1961 by Margaret Mead.

Princeton University Press: From *The Invasion from Mars* by Hadley Cantril. Reprinted by permission of Princeton University Press. Copyright 1940.

Public Opinion Quarterly: Adapted from "Cohesion and Distintegration in the Wehrmacht in World War II" by Edward A. Shils and Morris Janowitz, from *Public Opinion Quarterly,* Summer 1948.

Russell Sage Foundation: Tables 4 and 5 from *The Education of Sociologists in the U.S.* by Elbridge Sibley. Copyright 1963. Reprinted by permission of the publisher, Russell Sage Foundation.

The Society for the Psychological Study of Social Issues: Condensed and adapted from "Industrial Conflict in Detroit" by Dwight W. Chapman, from *Yearbook of the Society of the Psychological Study of Social Issues,* edited by Theodore W. Newcomb et al. Reprinted by permission of the author.

Time: Condensed and adapted from "Dispute in Dubuque" courtesy *Time;* Copyright Time Inc. 1951.

The University of Chicago Press: Reprinted from *Street Corner Society* by William Foote Whyte by permission of The University of Chicago Press. Copyright 1943; Reprinted from "Social Psychological Conception of Human Freedom" by William L. Kolb from *Ethics,* Volume 63; Reprinted from *Mind, Self, and Society* by George Herbert Mead. Copyright 1934. By permission of The University of Chicago Press.

The author also wishes to acknowledge those who provided the photographs used in this book:

Jesse Alexander from Nancy Palmer Agency: 279 (top); American Community of Builders, Inc.: 462 (top); Peter Amft: 246 (bottom); James Ballard: 275 (bottom); William Barksdale from Nancy Palmer Agency: 19; Charles Biasiny: 364, 365 (top right), 365 (bottom); Blue Ridge Aerial Surveys: 462-463 (bottom); Henri Cartier-Bresson from Magnum Photos: 318 (top); Todd Cazaux: 276 (center right), 278 (top); CBS News: 22; Chicago Police Department: 18, 20 (top right); Communications Satellite Corporation, Washington, D.C.: 392 (bottom); Gordon Coster: 459; James Foote, Office of Economic Opportunity: 21 (top); Ford Motor Company: 276 (bottom); Stephen Frisch: 276 (top); George Gardner: 277, 278 (bottom), 392 (top); William A. Graham from Nancy Palmer Agency: 463 (top and center); Bob Grant: 122, 123, 124 (bottom left), 125 (top); Copyright © 1963, Martin J. Dain, *Faulkner's County:* 176, 177, 178; Elliot Erwitt from Magnum Photos: 208; Richard Harrington from Three Lions: 275 (top); Hedrich-Blessing, architecture by Bertrand Goldberg: 460 (bottom); Heilman from Monkmeyer: 67 (top); Iron Workers Local Union #40 NYC: 95 (bottom); Peter Larsen from Nancy Palmer Agency: 284; Jane Latta from Photo Researchers: 66, 67 (bottom), 68 (bottom), 69 (top), 70 (bottom); Charlotte Livingstone from Photo Researchers: 71 (bottom); John Loengard, *Life* Magazine, © Time Inc.: 23; Leonard McCombe: 95 (top); Fred W. McDarrah: 460 (top); Vernon Merritt from Black Star: 21 (bottom left); Wayne Miller from Magnum Photos: 318 (bottom); Monkmeyer: 246 (center left); Office of Economic Opportunity: 20 (center left); Port of New York Authority: 301; Maurie Rosen: 20 (bottom); Ann Zane Shanks: 244, 245, 246 (top and center right), 274; Art Shay: 141; Gerry Souter: 365 (top left); David Strickler from Monkmeyer: 69 (bottom), 70 (top); Michael Sullivan, Office of Economic Opportunity: 21 (center right); Tass from Sovfoto: 393; United Press International: 71 (center), 124 (top), 124-125 (bottom), 196; Urban Renewal Administration: 461; Wheaton from Monkmeyer: 68 (top); Wide World Photos: 71 (top), 279 (bottom); WLS-ABC Radio: 276 (center left).

PREFACE

Many people have contributed to this book—some very directly, others quite inadvertently. This is only natural. Space permits me to single out only a few for mention here. However, I express my deep gratitude to them all; to any who should be named but are omitted, my apologies.

My primary debt is to my students, who have taught me much—perhaps most of all how to write this book. I am especially obligated to Mrs. Christine Totton, Mrs. Ruth Johnson, Miss Margaret L. Hamlett, and Mrs. Frances Ransom, who worked with me in writing, refining, and rewriting the original manuscript. I have thanks also for my wife, Estelle, who encouraged me through the long process of writing and who helped in the tedious task of final writing and polishing of the manuscript. I owe a professional debt to Dr. Michael Schwartz, co-author of the accompanying *Study Guide*, and to Dr. Wilbert E. Moore, author of the Foreword, for their critical comments and suggestions. Finally, I am obligated to my colleagues at the North Carolina College for their assistance and encouragement. Again, to all these people, named and unnamed, my sincere thanks.

Joseph S. Himes
Madras, India, 1967

TABLE OF CONTENTS

FOREWORD

Sociology today is growing at a pace that leaves some of us, long in the field, more than slightly breathless, and indeed a little anxious about our competence. The growth is not just in numbers of highly qualified scientists, which Professor Joseph S. Himes discusses in an early chapter of this book; these relatively new recruits to the discipline are also contributing to the growth in sociological knowledge in the form of verified propositions, based in considerable measure on refinements in the techniques of observing and analyzing social behavior.

The time is long past when an adult could safely assume that he knew all important features of a social order simply on the basis of experience. Social reality has become too complex and too changeful for such an assumption, and it is not just *our* social world, or our segment of it, that affects our lives and welfare. A radical reorganization of the social system in Communist China, the painful quest for political stability in new African nations, the attempt to modernize archaic regimes in Latin America—these social phenomena affect American national policy and, in some degree, virtually every citizen.

It is the aim (and sometimes the performance) of sociology and other social scientific fields to detect relationships among complex structures and complex sequences of events. It is the plain fact, however, that the need for sophisticated knowledge about social behavior often exceeds the capacity of the social sciences to perform. Since we can foresee no future time in which matters will be simpler, the demand for skilled social scientists is likely to grow. In this book Professor Himes has written with a lively awareness of these issues, drawing materials from cultures other than our own, and showing how sociological concepts help to illuminate complex intercultural and inter-societal relations.

The utility of economics has been recognized for some decades, and psychology too has highly developed fields of application. Political science has had to compete with practical politicians, and sociology sometimes has been confused with social work. Now, however, those who seek practical answers to very complex social questions are increasingly turning to sociologists for help. This is flattering to the sociologist, who long felt rather unloved; but the trend also may prove awkward, since we do not always have those answers.

It is important to recognize, of course, that many sociologists do not seek to be practical, just as many physicists or biologists are engaged in "pure" research. Yet it is also true that verified propositions or scientific laws are likely to be found useful for human goals, sooner or later. Our social values do permit the pursuit of knowledge for its own sake; all I am saying (as a sociological generalization) is that scientific knowledge, at least, is likely to be put to use.

The student entering upon the study of sociology comes to a segment of the world that has elements of familiarity but also elements of novelty. At first glance it may appear that the novelty is merely a matter of vocabulary—that familiar groups or customs or beliefs are being discussed in unfamiliar language. Critics of sociology have even charged that it is "the art of saying what everybody knows in terms nobody can understand." As a sociologist I plead "not guilty." Much of sociology, I have been arguing, is not common knowledge, and our vocabulary is on the whole less formidable than that of other technical fields. It is true that some sociologists, like some physicians or biologists or physicists, are needlessly pretentious and obscure; but technical concepts, when properly used, add precision and often constitute a kind of shorthand by avoiding elaborate descriptions. They have the additional, secondary function of reminding the user that he is approaching an intellectual problem technically, not casually.

The text that Professor Himes has written is conspicuously free from pomposity and pointless jargon. The basic concepts that sociologists have found useful in analysis and in formulating generalizations about social behavior are here, but they are introduced and illustrated in a way that demonstrates their utility. Professor Himes brings to the writing of this book a rich experience in teaching sociology to the uninitiated, and a highly developed sense of the relevance of sociology to a liberal arts curriculum. Professors of sociology would, perhaps, like to have all students in an introductory course go on to more advanced studies, and indeed to become sociologists. They know this is not possible, but they still feel that sociology has an important place in college education. In fact, we feel that the study of sociology is part of the civilizing mission of higher education. The mastery of a set of social facts (some of which will be amended by later evidence) is far less important than acquiring the habit of mind common to all the sciences: the habit of dispassionate inquiry and observation. Facts spoil quickly. And in the decades to come it will be increasingly recognized that the value of formal education is not in the use of the mind for "data storage and retrieval," to use current computer language, but in the development of skills and attitudes appropriate for continuous learning.

Many of the topics to be covered in an introductory text in sociology are fairly standardized, though, as the author points out, we are not immune to accelerating specialization, and thus to the growing problem of selectivity. Professor Himes has found a clear path through the thickets of special sociologies by attending to central issues. Unlike some texts, there is here a clear and sensible order to the topics. This order may reduce the freedom of teachers to shuffle the chapters and deal them out anew, but it has the advantage for students that the book *progresses*. Human personality, for example, appears fairly late in the proceedings, for the sensible reason that it is mainly a social product, rather than in an early chapter, on the spurious grounds that it is an independent building block of social systems. Moreover, the author links social change and social planning, under the correct perception that much of contemporary change is deliberate rather than mindlessly mechanical. And that, to reiterate, reminds us that sociology is sometimes practical. The sociologist may not have clearly superior talents in identifying social goals, but he should have a somewhat better than average capacity to identify means for their achievement.

I envy the student getting his first glimpse of a scientific field that is certain to develop with great and exciting rapidity in the decades to come. Mastery of the field will of course be increasingly difficult and, for any individual, necessarily partial. Yet the discipline as a whole will, I believe, justify the prophetic vision of Auguste Comte, the man who gave our discipline its name over a century ago. To Comte, sociology was destined to be the "queen of the sciences." And so it is. Welcome to the approaches to the court!

Wilbert E. Moore

Part I

INTRODUCTION TO THE STUDY OF SOCIOLOGY

Our study of sociology begins with an overview of the field as a scientific discipline and as a modern profession. Chapter 1 defines sociology and relates it to the other behavioral sciences. The approach and methods of sociological study and the various forms of sociological knowledge are described; the nature and place of theory in sociological study are explained; and the methods of sociological explanation are examined. The chapter concludes with a brief description of the book's organization.

Chapter 2 discusses sociology as a profession. First, it traces the growth and stabilization of the field. The chapter then describes sociologists and their activities: the number of sociologists; their training; the variety of jobs and occupations they fill; and the nature and activities of their professional associations.

Chapter 1

SOCIOLOGY AS
A SCIENCE

WHAT SOCIOLOGY IS

In a preliminary way, sociology may be defined as the systematic study of human social relations. The initial image created by this definition is one of an active process of inquiry. The tangible evidence of systematic study is the accumulating body of published reports, which both describe the methods of systematic study and present the information gained thereby.

Inquiry in sociology employs the scientific method as adapted to the characteristics of social phenomena.[1] As scientist, the sociologist is interested in understanding and explaining the phenomena under study. Certain specialized techniques of controlled empirical (sensory) observation are used to secure information about the social world. These observations, or data, are then classified and organized on the basis of their type and nature. The data are next examined to discover similarities, contrasts, connections, influences, trends, and other relationships that may help to describe or explain the phenomena being studied.

For example, a sociologist may study the family at different times, say 1900 and 1960. He may observe marriage practices, number of children per family, rights and duties of husband and wife, methods of child-rearing, modes of budgeting and financial control, and the like at the two dates. By classifying and analyzing these data he can both describe the family at the two time periods and reveal trends and directions of change.

Sociology is that vast and accumulating body of knowledge of human relations that has resulted from scientific study. This knowledge covers a bewildering range of facets of human life. In a later chapter it will be shown that sociologists have accumulated knowledge of human social life in fifty-five different identifiable areas.

It is neither possible nor necessary to present all the accumulated sociological knowledge in this book. Instead, we will summarize and synthesize the basic knowledge of the field in a limited number of core areas. First, we will examine sociological knowledge of human society in being, i.e., social organization. Next, we will study socialization and personality as product and producer of human society. Another part of basic sociological knowledge will treat human society in becoming, i.e., social change. Each of these broad areas of sociological knowledge is described more fully in the last section of this chapter and presented in some detail in the following chapters of this book.

The dual nature of sociology is illustrated in many ways. Whenever a student writes a term paper for a sociology course, he is expected to use a simplified version of the scientific method and to report some information gained through this activity. Numerous articles in journals and monographs in the library describe the methods used and report the knowledge gained in the scientific study of a wide range of sociological topics. Some studies have had profound and lasting influence on the course of sociological development. One of these is the "Yankee City Series" by W. Lloyd Warner and associates.[2] This illustration is useful in the present context for two reasons. First, Warner and his collaborators were social anthropologists, and their work demonstrates the close connection between neighboring behavioral sciences. This point is discussed further in the following section of this chapter. Second, some of Warner's conclusions, particularly those relative to social class in the United States, set in motion a chain reaction of sociological research.

Published between 1941 and 1948, the "Yankee City Series" includes six volumes and describes the method of study and the findings of the investigation of a New England city of some 17,000 inhabitants. In the first volume, Warner and Lunt describe the scope and method of the six-volume series in the following way.

> The "Yankee City series," . . . will be complete in six volumes. Each will deal with a significant aspect of the life of a modern community as it has been recorded and analyzed by the combined and co-operative labors of a group of social anthropologists. The same techniques and viewpoints applied by them to the study of societies of simpler people are here subjected to empirical testing in a concrete case study in modern American society. . . .[3]

From one perspective, sociology comprises an interrelated and interlocking series of studies like the one sketched above. These studies reveal a continuous process of investigation that utilizes numerous adaptations of scientific method and approaches organized social life from many standpoints. As a result, the fund of methodological adaptations, empirical data, and generalizations grows steadily.

How Sociologists Collect Information ♦ Sociologists collect information, i.e., make scientific observations, in several different ways. For some purposes the investigator may join a group or activity and observe social behavior while participating in it. At other times the sociologist may stand apart, observing a group or activity from the outside. In certain situations it may be more desirable to secure information from people directly by interviewing them in their homes, at work, or elsewhere. A great deal of important sociological information can be secured from public records, such as the juvenile court, the welfare department, or the marriage bureau, where it has already been collected and recorded.

Both anthropologists and sociologists collect information about people by living among them, i.e., by "participant observation." In this way William Foote Whyte studied the boys and young men in a poor, crowded section of an eastern metropolis. The report of his method, findings, and conclusions, *Street Corner Society,* is now a sociological classic. Howard S. Becker described the experience of a participant-observer team that studied medical students in the following way:

> They attended lectures with the students in the first two years of medical education. They followed the students to the laboratories where they spent most of their time, watching and engaging in casual conversation with them as they dissected cadavers or examined pathology specimens. The observers sat around with them in fraternity houses while they discussed their school experiences. They accompanied the clinical students on rounds, observed them examining patients in clinics and wards, and sat in on oral exams and discussion groups. They had meals with the students and accompanied them on night calls. The observers followed residents and interns through their busy schedules of teaching and medical practice.[4]

Sometimes it is not possible or necessary to participate in the behavior that is being observed. The investigator stands outside, so to speak, and watches the social drama unfold before him. If he is trained, has a plan of work, and possesses good research tools, he can make accurate scientific observations. In this way sociologists have studied mental hospitals and prisons, delinquent gangs and labor strikes, street crowds and lynch mobs, and industrial factories and business offices.

At other times the research plan may require detailed information from each individual observed. In this event interviewing is the method of collecting information. The sociologist must decide which individuals are to be interviewed (choose a sample), determine the questions to be asked (construct an interview schedule), and secure the cooperation of the people (respondents) being interviewed. The largest—and perhaps the most important—research activities using the interview method are the decennial census of the United States and other studies conducted by the Bureau of the Census. Public opinion agencies such as the Institute of Public Opinion (Gallup Poll) or the National Opinion Research Center (University of Chicago) also secure social information by interview.

Often the information the sociologist needs has already been collected and recorded. It is stored up in the official records of juvenile court or police station, welfare department or marriage bureau, and so on. The investigator simply has to copy the specific facts that he needs. However, he must have a plan of study, know which facts he wants, and have appropriate instruments for recording the information. Equally important, he must decide whether he wants information on every individual in the records, or on selected individuals (a sample).

SOCIOLOGY AND THE OTHER BEHAVIORAL SCIENCES

All the behavioral sciences are related in their common origin in the general social life of man. Moreover, all overlap as regards data and approaches. Yet each has a different focus, techniques of observation, and body of knowledge, and hence each constitutes a different field of study. It is important therefore to distinguish sociology from the other main divisions of behavioral science. For this purpose an analogy may be employed. As shown in Figure 1-1, the behavioral sciences may be likened to the six main limbs of a large tree, whose trunk consists of the study of the entire social life of man. The limbs all stem out from the trunk in different directions. Each therefore provides a different perspective or angle for approaching the trunk, which, in the final analysis, is the foundation of them all.

All the specific behavioral sciences are branches of the six main limbs. On the first limb one can locate the branches of economics, political science, and geography. These disciplines approach the study of human social relationships in terms of some specific end or factor. For example, economics is concerned with the investigation of those collective activities that are related to the creation, use, acquisition, transfer, and exchange of economic values and materials. Geography is the study of social behavior as it is conditioned by significant features of the natural physical environment. Political science investigates the nature, source, organization, and administration of power and control in human society.

Another limb of the behavioral sciences includes social or cultural anthropology, ethnology, and ethnography. These are the sciences of culture. They emphasize inquiries into the origins, nature, and functions of culture and culture systems.

History constitutes a limb by itself. It differs from the other behavioral sciences in certain respects. In this field of study emphasis is laid on the temporal sequences in human affairs and on recounting and cataloging the events and experiences of a society. History seeks to describe how the present has grown out of the past and is likely to unfold into the future.

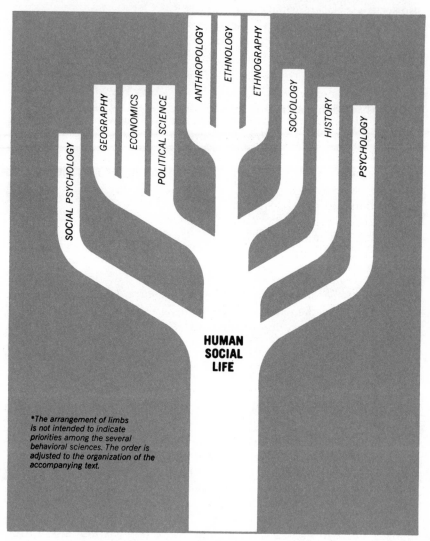

*The arrangement of limbs
is not intended to indicate
priorities among the several
behavioral sciences. The order is
adjusted to the organization of the
accompanying text.

FIGURE 1-1

The fourth limb of the tree, the field of psychology, is concerned with the sensory, motor, thinking, and feeling processes in individual human behavior. Stress here is laid on investigation of the mechanisms and processes of psychic behavior within the individual.

Closely akin to individual psychology and sociology is the field of social psychology, the next limb on the tree. It investigates individuals as participants in social relations and focuses attention on the individual's behavior as it affects and is affected by the actions of others.

Many sociologists are also social psychologists, and sociology draws heavily on this field of behavioral science.

Sociology constitutes the last limb on the tree. Its core task, as noted above, is the systematic investigation of organized human social relations.

The analogy of a tree of human behavioral studies indicates that the notion of neatly separate and easily distinguishable behavioral sciences is a fiction. Each of the main limbs has its origin in the common trunk of human social life. As they grow out and spread, the limbs tend to overlap, interlace, and become increasingly indistinguishable. For example, as sociology pursues the study of personality, it overlaps and draws upon psychology, anthropology, and social psychology. When the sociologist investigates the problem of social organization and social structure, he must draw upon the findings of the anthropologist, economist, and political scientist. And so it goes. Sociology is kith and kin to the other behavioral disciplines, since all have common parentage and interbreed their offspring.

SOME FORMS OF SOCIOLOGICAL KNOWLEDGE

The study of sociology usually begins with a systematic review of the basic knowledge of the field. It is already evident from a reading of the foregoing pages, however, that sociological knowledge is not all of one kind. Words like principle, concept, generalization, data, and theory testify to the variability of the forms and levels of sociological knowledge.

At the outset we must distinguish fact, or empirically verified knowledge, from theory, or empirically unverified statements. Although, strictly speaking, theory cannot be called knowledge, it constitutes an important and substantial part of the content of sociology. In the present section we will discuss forms of sociological knowledge that vary in scope of applicability to social reality. In the following section the nature and uses of theory are discussed.

Knowledge of Universal Reference ❯ Some sociological knowledge applies to all or almost all societies. This form of knowledge is variously called sociological concepts, principles, or laws. The term law, however, seems too absolute and sacred for our purpose. Knowledge of universal reference can be illustrated from many spheres of life. Every human society prohibits sexual contacts between close blood relatives (the incest taboo). Almost everywhere individuals and families are ranked to form a stratification or layer system of some kind. All peoples assign different tasks, rights, and privileges to individuals according to sex, age, family connection, education, and the like.

These are elements of sociological knowledge that have been verified under all or almost all possible conditions. One basic aim of sociology as a science is to expand this form of knowledge. Yet it is recognized that at present no sociological knowledge is so universal and sacred that it may not be challenged by new evidence and insight.

Knowledge of Limited Reference ♦ Many elements of sociological knowledge apply only to limited social phenomena. Such knowledge results from the application of the scientific method in the study of specific social units or phenomena. In the scientific research process this kind of knowledge is referred to as findings, generalizations, or conclusions. For example, studies of the family reveal that the so-called "independent family" is typical of the United States, while in India the "joint family," or father-controlled unit, is the prevailing type. Although virtually all human societies are known to be stratified in some way, the research reveals many different types of stratification systems. In some communities six layers or classes have been identified, while in others only three or even two could be discovered. Or again, although division of labor in terms of sex is universal in human society, the studies reveal many different ways of allocating tasks to men and women. In some societies women are restricted to household activities, while in others they engage in gainful occupations in business and industry.

This form of sociological knowledge has been verified as applicable to limited situations or phenomena. In some instances generalizations of limited reference have not been tested for applicability to situations different from those in which they were derived. In other instances, testing has shown that the generalizations can have only limited applicability. One major aim of sociology as science is to test, refine, and stabilize the great body of knowledge of limited reference. Ideally, the aim of science is to transform knowledge of this type through repeated verification under all possible conditions into knowledge of universal reference.

Sociological Data ♦ A prodigious amount of sociological knowledge refers only to a single social phenomenon; it is thus concrete and nontransferable. This knowledge, which results from empirical observation, is called data. For example, a study of families produces a considerable fund of information about each of the families interviewed. This information is true only of the one family from which it was secured and has no reference to any other family in the sample of families that may have been studied. Data, or specific information of this type, is the raw material for the scientific process.

Sociological data may be either quantitative or nonquantitative. The sociologist seeks to state his data in numerical or quantitative form, since this enables him to make more precise generalizations and easier comparisons. The greatest fund of quantitative data available to the sociologist is found in the reports of the decennial census of population. One important step in the scientific process involves the classification and organization of data. A basic task of scientific analysis thus is to extract from data the generalizations of limited reference that the data permit. For this purpose a number of precise techniques and skills have been developed. Thus it will be seen that sociology as a scientific discipline follows an uneven but inexorable course from data to generalization of limited reference to principles of universal reference.

Visible and Invisible Facts ▶ Some social phenomena are visible; that is, they can be directly observed. For example, when one walks down a street in Madras, India, he can *see* that women wear saris, that automobiles pass on the left-hand side of the road, and that people do not shake hands when they meet. Certain socially important physical facts are also directly observable. One can see, for instance, that the members of a certain group are adolescent Negro girls.

However, many important social phenomena cannot be observed directly, i.e., they are invisible. One can "feel" or "sense" the presence and variation of such phenomena, but he cannot observe them directly. Some invisible phenomena can be brought to light and observed by talking to people, i.e., by interviewing them. For example, in this way it is possible to ascertain the attitudes of older people toward medicare, certain childhood experiences of the city dweller, or the vocational aspirations of teen-agers. To observe some other invisible social phenomena, such as morale or social organization, the sociologist uses devices called "indicators."

An indicator consists of one or more directly observable and measurable phenomena that are so closely linked to an invisible phenomenon that amounts and variations of the former equal (indicate) amounts and variations of the latter. A thermometer is an indicator. Temperature is the invisible variable phenomenon whose presence and change can be felt but not directly observed. A thermometer is so constructed that the position and variations of the height of the column of mercury in the glass tube equal (indicate) amounts and variations of temperature.

To observe morale, an invisible social phenomenon, a sociologist needs an indicator. The social components of morale include obedience to orders, confidence in leaders or supervisors, and participation in the life of the organization. Variations of morale are indicated by qualifying adjectives attached to these components, e.g., cheerful, enthusiastic, or willing for high morale, and grudging, indifferent, or unwilling for low morale. Among the kinds of directly observable phenomena that can be used in constructing an indicator of morale are rates of absenteeism, rates of rule infractions, rates of disobedience, rates of reported sickness, and frequency of volunteering for extra duty. One of the continuing tasks of sociology is to test, refine, and improve the empirical indicators that are in regular use. Often, in order to avoid possible errors, a sociologist may use several indicators to observe and measure a single phenomenon.

THEORY IN THE STUDY OF SOCIOLOGY

What Theory Is ♦ The term theory often repels or frightens people. It calls to mind impractical schemes and ideas, or it conjures up images of abstract, incomprehensible verbiage. As a matter of fact, though, such a view of the matter is neither correct nor justified. A great deal of theory is really quite simple and commonplace. For example, in a discussion of contradictory theories of juvenile delinquency, Frank R. Westie and Austin T. Turk identify the following very commonplace theoretical proposition. "Among the three social class levels, the middle class has the lowest rates of delinquent behavior."[5]

Theory may be defined as a statement (proposition) or logically connected series of propositions that purport to describe a segment of reality. Theory is always based on evidence. Yet, by its very nature, theory is not a conclusion from careful analysis of all the relevant evidence. It is therefore partly a statement of fact, partly an informed guess. The propositions predict that when the evidence is analyzed, reality will correspond to the description contained in the theory.

Often only a thin or blurred line separates theory from fact. It is not always clear how much or how thorough verification is required to transform a theory into a fact. For example, is the Darwinian doctrine of evolution still a theory, or is it now so thoroughly substantiated that it must be regarded as a scientific fact? All of us from time to time refer to theories as though they were fact and neglect to recognize that they are not yet fully verified.

It is important to recognize that theory constitutes a substantial part of the subject matter of sociology. Many of the ideas presented and examined in the following chapters of this book are theories. For example, in Chapter 7 on communities we examine and compare three celebrated theories of the organization and use of geographic space in large urban places. In Chapter 16 we review and comment on several well-known theories of social change. The plurality of theories in the same area, e.g., juvenile delinquency, urban space, and social change, indicates that reality is envisaged in different and contradictory ways.

One distinctive feature of theory is its tentative character. It is always being tested, refined, and revised in the crucible of empirical research. In the onward march of science, new evidence is always being brought forward to question, challenge, or even reject old theories. There are dramatic instances of the tentativeness of theories in the behavioral sciences.

For example, the "instinct theory" provided the basis for explaining human social behavior for many years. The theory held that individuals were equipped by heredity with fully developed patterns of social behavior. The automatic operation of these nonmodifiable patterns produced the systems of orderly social relations observed in human societies. The instinct theory was employed by William McDougall, Sigmund Freud, Floyd Allport, and others in the explanation and interpretation of many kinds of social behavior.[6]

All the while, however, the theory was being tested in empirical research. A steadily accumulating body of reports tended to indicate that the instinct theory failed to fit the facts produced by empirical observation. Luther L. Bernard summarized and synthesized the findings of this research into a complete and logically consistent rejection of the instinct theory.[7]

Some Uses of Theory ❯ From one perspective the scientific process involves continuous interaction between data and theory. Data are collected, analyzed, and interpreted within a framework established by relevant theory. Speaking of the dynamic role of theory in science, Talcott Parsons writes: ". . . [S]cientific theory most generally defined as a body of logically interrelated general concepts of empirical reference is not only a dependent but an independent variable in the development of science. . . ."[8] For our purpose it will be enough to indicate three uses of theory in sociology.

First, theory guides the process of sociological research. It is the prime source of hypotheses (the statements of expected relationships and outcomes to be tested by empirical observation). Theory dictates the proper questions to be asked and the correct observations to be made in the test of hypotheses. Once the data are gathered, theory establishes a framework within which to classify and analyze them. Finally, theory constitutes the frame of reference for the interpretation of the research findings.

These uses of theory in the research procedure are illustrated in the research methodology of studies reported in the journals and monographs. As Frank R. Westie and Austin T. Turk point out, however, often researchers fail to make their theoretical positions clear and neglect to take account of contradictory or inconsistent theory in the field of investigation.[9] Such failures tend to limit the empirical validity and sociological usefulness of their findings.

Second, theory is a unifying force in sociology. Talcott Parsons writes that ". . . [T]he body of theory in a given field at a given time constitutes to a greater or less degree an integrated system."[10] The degree of unity may be limited by such factors as unevenness of development, internal contradictions, inconsistencies of statements, and the like. For example, Westie and Turk point out that although there is agreement in theory that social-class level is an important variable in the explanation of juvenile delinquency, there are serious contradictions regarding the nature and direction of that influence.[11] In their judgment, the identification of spheres of unity and sources of disunity establishes a basis for movement toward greater unity of theory.

On the other hand, disunity of theory tends to affect the nature and quality of empirical research. For example, Westie and Turk point out that contradictory theory about juvenile delinquency has tended to limit the scientific usefulness of a great deal of research.[12] Karl Marx and W. Lloyd Warner constructed basically different theories of the nature of social classes.[13] Marx based class differences on variations of a single factor, "ownership of the means of production," while Warner used a multifactor theory including such variables as ownership of property, income, education, place of residence, family connection, and evaluation of social participation. While both men confirmed the existence of social classes, the particulars of the social-class systems that they developed vary widely and are largely noncomparable.

Sociological theory constitutes a thread on which various and succeeding studies are strung together to form a continuous and cumulative process. The theoretical framework of one study can provide the point of departure of numerous others, some to verify findings of the original inquiry, others to test subordinate or correlated propositions. For example, W. Lloyd Warner's study of social classes in Yankee City provided the theoretical springboard for numerous other investigations of social stratification.

The rich legacy of the great contributors to the field is not so much the data that they collected, however important these may be. It lies rather in the almost inexhaustible theoretical systems that they originated. In this respect the link between Emile Durkheim, George Simmel, Max Weber, Franklin Giddings, William Graham Sumner, Charles Horton Cooley, and the contemporaries remains fresh and vivid.

Robert K. Merton presents an illustration of how Emile Durkheim's theory of suicide has provided a unifying force in many areas of sociological study. Merton restates Durkheim's theoretical scheme as follows.

1. Social cohesion provides psychic support to group members subject to acute stresses and anxieties.

2. Suicide rates are functions of unrelieved anxieties and stresses to which persons are subjected.

3. Catholics have greater social cohesion than Protestants.

4. Therefore lower suicide rates should be anticipated among Catholics than among Protestants.[14]

Merton notes that this formulation has provided the point of departure for investigations in such related fields as obsessive behavior, morbid preoccupations, and other maladaptive conduct. Such theory has also been fruitful in studies of delinquency, mental illness, sex deviation, drug addiction, alcoholism, and other forms of social and psychic deviation.

Third, theory provides a logical basis for sociological prediction, one of the important goals of sociology. That is, theoretical schemes make it possible to predict in general terms expected relationships, sequences, and outcomes that have been demonstrated in the past through empirical observation.[15]

The most adequate applications of theory to the problem of prediction deal with success or failure of individuals entering marriage and of prisoners released on parole.[16] For example, the theoretical framework of the Burgess-Cottrell-Wallin marriage prediction system can be restated as follows:

1. The term marital adjustment refers to variable states of spousal relations and individual satisfaction that form a continuum with success and failure as extremes.

2. The degree of adjustment of a given marriage can be measured and indicated on the success-failure continuum, and constitutes a function of a complex of intervening factors whose influence can be calculated.

3. It is therefore possible to predict the degree of adjustment to be expected in a given marriage after calculating the influence of the intervening complex of factors.

Scientific predictions not only state the anticipated outcome as a class of possible outcomes; they also indicate the degree of probability that the stated outcome will actually occur. For instance, Burgess and Wallin have a hypothetical premarital counselor state the following scientific marriage prediction: "According to the expectancy table your combination of background, attitudes and personality traits places you in a group where 90 per cent of marriages are successful."[17]

METHODS OF SOCIOLOGICAL EXPLANATION

Sociological study is not limited to the classification of observations and the description of social phenomena. These activities answer the question "What?" Study in sociology is also interested in answers to the question "Why?" That is, we want some explanation of the social phenomena that we have recognized and described.

Sociological study employs three principal methods of explanation. First, the nature of some social phenomena can be explained in terms of their origins, changes, and survivals. Second, the appearance and existence of some social forms are explained by their association with supporting or conditioning factors and circumstances. And third, the utility of social phenomena is explained in terms of their consequences for social life.

Historical Development ◗ The nature of many social phenomena can be explained, in part at least, in terms of their historical development. A study of the historical evidence will show how the social item has changed over time. It is possible to reveal how component elements have been lost, modified, or added, or have survived unchanged in the life history of the phenomenon. Developmental analysis will draw attention to internal and external forces that have shaped and altered the phenomenon in the course of its life history. Such historical study will thus reveal the present form of the social phenomenon as a configuration of elements from past and present that is more or less adjusted to the surrounding social milieu.

Historical development is employed to explain the nature of many existing social phenomena and conditions. One of its major applications is in the study of the family. Much light is thrown on the forms and problems of the contemporary American family by tracing its development from colonial and frontier times. In this study we give attention to the growth of land area; the increase, dispersion, and differentiation of population; the transition from an agrarian to an industrial economy; the growth of urbanism; mobility and the concentration of people; and so on. We trace the development of the family in adjustment to these changes by noting the loss, addition, modification, and retention of elements in relation to its form at an earlier time. From this perspective we can explain, in part at least, the present form and problems of the American family.

Correlation ◗ For some purposes, however, historical development is not an adequate or applicable explanation. For example, although we may explain the nature of the contemporary juvenile court in historical terms, this method does not explain why it was created in the first instance. That is, the method of historical development cannot explain the factors and conditions that are meaningfully associated with the appearance of a social phenomenon. For this task of explanation the method of correlation is employed.

Correlation is a method of explanation that identifies the social factors and conditions associated with the appearance or existence of a social phenomenon. For example, one might ask: Why did the modern Negro protest movement begin in the mid-1950's instead of some years earlier or later? Or, one might ask: Why is juvenile delinquency more prevalent in slum areas of cities than in middle-class sections? Social explanation by correlation may also be used in making predictions. For example, as was pointed out above, when the engagement of a couple is associated with certain known conditions of background, personality, and experience, it is possible to predict the chances of success of the marriage that follows.

Explanation of social phenomena by the method of correlation involves two related steps. First, it is necessary to identify the factors and conditions that exist in the milieu surrounding the phenomenon under study. Second, it is necessary to measure by mathematical procedures the degree and regularity of the association of these factors with the phenomenon being studied.

The reader is cautioned that correlation does not mean causation. It means only that a certain social phenomenon is found associated to a specified degree of closeness and regularity with a series of surrounding factors and conditions. For example, juvenile delinquency is correlated with deteriorated housing, congested living, economic deprivation, limited education, family disorganization, psychic frustration, and the like. This cluster of correlated factors explains the circumstances under which juvenile delinquency exists. It does not, however, explain what causes delinquency.

Functionalism ▶ In sociological study we seek still another explanation. For example, the correlation method can tell us the circumstances under which the modern Negro protest movement originated. It is possible to trace the brief history of the movement and thus explain its present form. However, neither of these methods can explain the effects of the Negro protest on American life. For explanation of the social consequences of a social phenomenon, sociologists employ the method of functionalism.

Any given social phenomenon is an operating part of a larger dynamic system of parts. As it works, well or badly, it affects the rest of the system and the people who live within the system. In sociological study we seek to identify these consequences and to evaluate them for the system within which they occur.

Some of the social consequences of a social form are the same as its stated purposes. For example, the Negro protest movement has actually gained some of the civil rights and social opportunities for Negroes that it set out to attain. Some of the consequences of an operating social form are, however, neither intended nor recognized. For example, contrary to its aims, the Negro protest movement has precipitated an increase of interracial violence in American communities. We have observed in retrospect that the movement has contributed to the social and emotional maturity of Negro college students. Some other consequences of an operating social form are harmful both to the social system and to the individuals concerned. For example, the increase of interracial violence is one harmful, dysfunctional consequence of the Negro protest movement. There is little doubt also that the movement has interrupted traditional communication between Negroes and whites in many places.

The identification and analysis of social consequences is an important part of sociological study. Kingsley Davis asserts that functional analysis, or the study of social consequences, is sociological analysis.[18] It is through these approaches to explanation that sociology transcends mere description and becomes significantly scientific.

PLAN OF THIS BOOK

This book is an introductory text for the beginning study of sociology. Although it discusses methods of sociological study, it is not a research manual. It surveys and summarizes much of the general knowledge of the field, yet it is not a sociological encyclopedia. The principal aim of this book is to help steer the beginning student through the maze of accumulated sociological knowledge, indicating what seems to have lasting importance and demonstrating how the materials can be arranged into a coherent system. With such an introduction, the beginning student should be able to move confidently into advanced or independent study in any of the subdivisions of the field of sociology.

Three basic issues—social organization, personality, and social change—dictate the structure of the book. The organization of human society is approached from several perspectives in Parts II, III, and IV. The key concepts of social organization and culture are analyzed and illustrated in Part II.

Part III treats social groups as the basic and universal form of human social organization. The analysis covers small groups, extended or large-scale organization, and communities. In Part IV social institutions, population, and social stratification are examined as structural aspects of social organization.

Personality is viewed in Part V as both product and producer of social organization. This subject facilitates the shift of study from social organization to social change. In this part of the book we analyze the formation and organization of personality and its relationship to structured social life.

Part VI of the book is devoted to a study of social change. Collective behavior, or relatively unstructured social activity, is viewed as a precipitate of changing social organization. Crowds, publics, mass phenomena, and social movements are also treated in this part. The book concludes with an examination of the issues of social change, social problems, and social control.

FOOTNOTES

1. See Claire Selltiz *et al., Research Methods in Social Relations* (New York: Holt, 1959).
2. W. Lloyd Warner and Paul S. Lunt, *The Social Life of a Modern Community* (New Haven: Yale University Press, 1941).
3. *Ibid.,* p. xix.
4. Howard S. Becker, "Problems of Inference and Proof in Participant Observation," in *American Sociological Review,* 23:652-660 (December 1958).
5. Frank R. Westie and Austin T. Turk, "A Strategy for Research on Social Class and Delinquency," in *The Journal of Criminal Law, Criminology and Police Science,* 56:459 (1965).
6. See William McDougall, *An Introduction to Social Psychology* (Boston: J. W. Luce, 1918); Sigmund Freud, *Civilization and Its Discontents* (New York: Norton, 1961); and F. H. Allport, *Social Psychology* (Boston: Houghton, 1924).
7. Luther L. Bernard, *Instinct: A Study in Social Psychology* (New York: Holt, 1924).
8. Talcott Parsons, *The Structure of Social Action* (Glencoe: Free Press, 1949), pp. 6-7.
9. Westie and Turk, *op. cit.,* p. 454.
10. Parsons, *op. cit.,* p. 7.
11. Westie and Turk, *op. cit.,* pp. 454-462.
12. *Ibid.,* pp. 454-455.
13. See Karl Marx, *Capital* (London: Sonnenschein, 1903); and Warner and Lunt, *op. cit.*
14. Robert K. Merton, *Social Theory and Social Structure* (Glencoe: Free Press, 1957), p. 98.
15. See Joseph S. Himes, "Prediction," in Julius Gould and William L. Kolb, eds., *A Dictionary of the Social Sciences* (New York: Free Press, 1964), p. 525.
16. See Daniel Glazer, *The Effectiveness of a Prison and Parole System* (Indianapolis: Bobbs-Merrill, 1964); and E. W. Burgess and Paul Wallin, *Engagement and Marriage* (Chicago: Lippincott, 1953).
17. Burgess and Wallin, *op. cit.,* p. 507.
18. Kingsley Davis, "The Myth of Functional Analysis," in *American Sociological Review* 24:767 (February 1957).

CAREERS IN SOCIOLOGY

VOCATIONAL OPPORTUNITIES for trained sociologists are growing in a nation increasingly concerned with educating and assisting its citizens to understand and solve their pressing social problems. Sociologists may choose occupations and careers from a wide range of specialties. Photographs on the next six pages show a sampling of the fields that will provide rewarding careers for professional sociologists.

A member of the police department's Human Relations Commission speaks to officers in seminar.

TEACHING
Universities, with or without research
Colleges and junior colleges
High schools
Medical and nursing schools
Schools of social work
Departments of education

CRIMINOLOGY
Parole and probation officers
Policemen and policewomen
Police training officers
Superintendents of penal institutions

A social worker in Harlem talks with a teen-ager . . .

FAMILY RELATIONS
Churches
General and mental hospi-
tals
Public or private welfare
agencies
School systems
Public park systems
Unions and industries
Agencies for counseling on
marriage, children's prob-
lems, vocations, the aged
and retired
Recreational agencies

. . . works with a street gang . . .

. . . and advises a family.

INTERGROUP RELATIONS
Fair employment commis-
    sions
Fair housing commissions
Public employment agencies
Many federal agencies
Employers' associations
Large industries
Advertising councils
National unions
Civil rights organizations
Religious organizations

Job Corps members meet with leader.   *Community workshop discusses issues.*

City Council meeting takes up problems of mutual interest.

VISTA volunteer works in poverty areas.

Head Start worker tutors student.

Worker eases urban renewal problems.

COMMUNITY RELATIONS
Housing agencies
Urban renewal agencies
Anti-poverty agencies
Peace Corps, VISTA
Community organization
    projects
Rural community consult-
    ants
UNESCO, other international
    agencies
Foreign Service of U.S. State
    Department

21

PUBLIC OPINION RESEARCH	Research designers and administrators
	Interviewers
	Data processors
	Computer specialists
	Researchers for private companies or university agencies

Vote Profile Analysis system attempts to select victors from early election returns.

INDUSTRIAL SOCIOLOGY	Consultants, personnel managers and staff, counselors, research workers for business, industry, and labor

MEDICAL SOCIOLOGY	Members of research teams
	Consultants to director of hospital or other agency

Sociologist exhibits scale model of Columbia, Maryland—a completely planned city.

DEMOGRAPHY
AND ECOLOGY

City planners
U.S. Census Bureau
Actuaries for insurance
    companies
Population projections for
    business firms and public
    agencies
International agencies

Source: Adapted in part from Caroline B. Rose, The Study of Sociology (Columbus: Charles E. Merrill, 1965),
pp. 80-83.

Chapter 2

SOCIOLOGY AS
A PROFESSION

Sociology developed rapidly after it was introduced in the United States almost a hundred years ago. The emphasis shifted from philosophical to scientific, and from deductive to empirical; and the number and competence of practitioners increased phenomenally. At the same time, the position of sociology in the academic world and the social utility of the discipline grew apace. One consequence of these developments was the emergence of the modern profession of sociology.

DEVELOPMENT OF SOCIOLOGY

The study of sociology must look backward to the history of the field and outward to the current state of specialization. In this chapter we will try to orient the student to inquiry in both directions.

Historically, the field of sociology as it now exists in the United States has developed through a series of identifiable stages. Writing in 1936, Floyd N. House asserted that "Sociology originated in Europe rather than in this country; however, at the present time, it is much more strongly established as an academic subject in the United States than anywhere else."[1] Sociology has been taught continuously in some two or three American universities since the early 1880's. The subject is now a standard of the curriculum of virtually every college in the country.

System Building ▶ The earliest activities of American sociologists can be characterized as "system building." That is, these early scholars devoted themselves to the construction of inclusive logical systems of explanation of social phenomena. They often engaged in great controversies among themselves, criticizing opposing systems and defending their own schemes.

The distinguished American sociological system builders include such scholars as Lester F. Ward (1841-1913), Albion W. Small (1854-1926), Edward Alsworth Ross (1866-1958), William Graham Sumner (1840-1910), Charles Horton Cooley (1864-1929), and Franklin H. Giddings (1855-1931). These men wrote the opening chapters of sociological thought in the United States. Perhaps of even more importance is the fact that their insights and judgments provided an almost inexhaustible fund of theories and hypotheses for empirical testing by later sociologists.

The method of the system builders was nonempirical. That is, they did not engage in field research for the testing or formulation of theories. Instead, they deduced from reading, casual observation, and meditation the "basic principles" of human social life. By deduction from these key principles or major factors, they constructed systems of general propositions that purported to explain human social life in all —or almost all—its manifestations. The system stood or fell not on its relevance to observed fact, but rather on the defensibility of its key principles and the logical consistency of the superstructure of its deductions and general propositions.

William Graham Sumner is today one of the best known of the early single-factor system builders. Sumner represents a school of sociological thought called "Social Darwinism." In the latter part of the nineteenth century, Social Darwinism was debated; the adversaries included, in addition to Sumner, such distinguished scholars as Lester F. Ward in the United States and Herbert Spencer in England.

Sumner was concerned with the problem of social control—the ways in which societies inculcate their values into the minds of their members and prevent deviant or disruptive behavior. He argued that social control produced social consensus, which was crucial in social organization.

From a reading of the descriptions of a vast number of societies, primitive and civilized, ancient and modern, large and small, Sumner reasoned that human beings are impelled by four basic "motives of human action" (social forces), viz., hunger, love, vanity, and fear.[2] Each of these motives issues through "interests" into the specific actions of individuals. The efforts and actions issuing from interests "fall into parallel lines, because the conditions and interests are the same."[3] Reasoning further, Sumner asserted: "The result is mass phenomena; currents of similarity, concurrence and mutual contributions; and these produce folkways."[4] In critical life situations, folkways harden into mores, and when collective activity represents responses to basic and universal needs, folkways and mores become structured into social institutions.[5] Sumner conceptualized social organization in the following way.

> . . . The relations of men to each other . . . consist in mutual relations . . . from which result societal concatenations and concretions, that is,

more or less fixed positions of individuals and subgroups toward each other and more or less established sequences and methods of interaction between them, by which the interests of all members of the group are served. . . . The structure thus built up is not physical but societal and institutional; that is to say, it belongs to a category in which custom produces continuity, coherence, and consistency, so that the word "structure" may properly be applied to the fabric of relations and prescribed positions with which societal functions are permanently connected. . . .[6]

Sumner regarded the operation of control in this social system as an automatic and inevitable process. He believed that the individual was formed and controlled by "natural" social forces and laws. The science of sociology focused on ascertaining and describing these natural social laws as revealed in systems of folkways, mores, and institutions.

The early scholars made substantial contributions to our basic fund of general knowledge. In the following pages we will make frequent references to the work of Sumner and Cooley. These early scholars staked out the main boundaries of the field and laid its foundation of concepts and theory.

By the outbreak of the First World War, these pioneers had identified some of the major subfields of sociology. Writing of these developments, Floyd House listed the following subfields: social evolution and progress, social psychology, social pathology and criminology, urban and rural sociology, population and race relations, the family and school, statistical and case methods, and sociological theory and research.[7] Many of these titles appeared in the names of course listings in college and university curricula and in texts and treatises of the time.

The Chicago Period ❱ Just after the First World War, Robert E. Park, Ernest W. Burgess, William Isaac Thomas, and their associates at the University of Chicago initiated a new and distinct epoch in American sociology. Alvin Boskoff points out that by 1921, when Park and Burgess published their *Introduction to the Science of Society*, progress toward stabilizing leading concepts and unique perspectives gave sociology its basic scientific orientation.[8] Park, Burgess, Thomas, and others crystallized the focus of sociology on systematic human relations and sorted out the concepts that still constitute the basic tools for analyzing those relations.

These were men of considerable personal magnetism and force, and they attracted a group of brilliant students to the University of Chicago. Their impact upon American sociology, therefore, resulted as much from the disciples that they sent out into the academic world as from the force and importance of their ideas. As a result, for a whole generation, sociology in the United States was identified with the University of Chicago.

The Chicago group converted sociology into an empirical, research-oriented discipline. They defined the urban community as the main locus of investigation and formulated a theoretical model for empirical study.[9] Utilizing their graduate students as investigators, they tested and refined the propositions of the model in Chicago and built up a systematic series of empirical studies.[10] By the time of the Great Depression of the 1930's the Chicago group had transformed sociology into a body of organized knowledge, established a perspective and method of study, and accumulated a growing body of empirical observations of one large urban community.

From these developments, a series of new subfields emerged and became increasingly well defined. The urban community was established as a prime area of sociological concern, and the sociology of urban life was defined in contrast to the sociology of rural communities. The concepts and approaches of ecology (the relations between organisms and their environment) were borrowed from biology and applied to human situations as a new tool in the analysis of urban social organization and change. In time, human or social ecology emerged as a subfield with a recognized place in university curricula.

Studies in the Chicago metropolitan area drew increasing attention to deviant and abnormal aspects of social life. As a consequence, much of the theoretical and factual content of criminology issued from these developments. In similar manner social disorganization, collective behavior, and the sociology of mental illness were either defined or presaged as subfields of sociology in the work of the Chicago group.

The rich legacy of valid generalizations from the Chicago period is well represented in the following chapters of this book. For example, much of the discussion in Chapter 7 on communities rests on verified findings in Chicago and other cities. Park and Burgess and especially Herbert Blumer defined and stabilized the field of collective behavior. Their generalizations are an important part of the material presented in Chapter 15. The lasting contribution of the Chicago group is the stress of social relations as the focus of sociological inquiry. These thinkers worked in terms of a process model of society and were concerned with social interaction and social change.

Influence of the Europeans ▶ It was said above that sociology originated in Europe. Auguste Comte (1798-1857) first used the word sociology and directed scholars to the study of human social relations. However, it was not until the second half of the nineteenth century that sociology developed significantly in Western Europe. In the years prior to the First World War, many American sociologists went to Europe to complete their educations. When they returned, they brought back the theories and ideas of the great German, French, and Italian sociologists.

From Germany, as translated and interpreted by Talcott Parsons, C. Wright Mills, Kurt Wolf, Lewis Coser, Charles Loomis, and others, came the imaginative and sophisticated work of Max Weber, Ferdinand Tönnies, and George Simmel. Although the works of a number of French scholars have been well received in the United States, the ideas of Emile Durkheim have had the most solid and lasting influence. Gabriel Tarde and Gustave Le Bon have also had some influence on thought in American sociology. The Italian philosopher-sociologist Vilfredo Pareto had a vogue prior to World War II and left some contributions.

The impact of the Europeans on American sociology is marked by contributions to the repertory of basic concepts. For example, Max Weber is associated with such concepts as bureaucracy, ideal-type, and caste. Ferdinand Tönnies introduced the paired concepts *Gemeinschaft* and *Gesellschaft.* Simmel is best known for the terms "dyad" and "triad" and his studies in small group relations and social conflict. Emile Durkheim contributed such basic concepts as division of labor, collective representations, and anomie. Pareto is best known for his concepts of residues and derivations.

The Europeans made substantial contributions to the clarification and refinement of sociological theory. A good illustration is Max Weber's work in the development of pluralistic causal theory. In a series of celebrated studies on the role of religion in social development, he helped to discredit the doctrine of economic determinism that Karl Marx popularized. In these studies, particularly *The Protestant Ethic and The Spirit of Capitalism,* Weber not only showed that Protestantism, with its emphasis on individual rights and responsibilities, was a forerunner of modern European capitalism, but also established a congenial atmosphere for its growth. In this work, as in his other studies, Weber demonstrated the validity of multifactor theories of sociological explanation.

The European sociologists also made substantive contributions to general knowledge in the field. In doing so they provided an almost unlimited fund of theoretical propositions for empirical testing by the research-oriented American scholars. Weber, Durkheim, and Simmel have been especially fruitful in this respect.

Structural-Functionalism ▶ From an early date some sociologists were preoccupied with issues of social structure. For example, as shown above, Sumner's sociological system rested upon a conception of the structure of society. Social control, as the leading social consequence (function), issued from this structure through the working of natural forces and laws. This perspective was further exploited by Sumner and Keller in their systematic treatise on sociology.[11]

Many other scholars, both in the United States and abroad, utilized a "structural-functional" approach to analysis and explanation. For example, Cooley's remarkable insights on socialization and personality represent conceptualizations of important functions of primary social structures.*[12] In Europe Emile Durkheim, Bronislaw Malinowski, Vilfredo Pareto, Leopold Von Wiese, and others, to one degree or another, implicitly or explicitly, utilized a structural-functional approach in the interpretation and explanation of social phenomena.

Structural-functionalism was the conceptual opposite to the process model that the Chicago group espoused. Interaction was viewed as one consequence of the operations of the working parts of the structure. Change was neglected or treated as pathological or abnormal. The focus of inquiry was the integrity or "equilibrium" of the operating system or structure. The central problem of sociological study consisted in identifying and analyzing the conditions (functions) that affected the integrity of the on-going system.

Writing of this strain in modern sociology, Walter Buckley observed in 1957: "Notwithstanding an increasing volume of criticism, structural-functional analysis continued to develop and, to a great extent because of the criticism, it has become quite highly refined."[13] Most of the recent sophisticated structural-functional theory and analysis have come from a few major contributors, viz., Talcott Parsons, Marion Levy, and Robert K. Merton.[14]

Parsons at Harvard and his brilliant student Merton at Columbia developed the leading centers of structural-functionalism. They attracted a galaxy of competent students to whom they transmitted the new sociological approach. These students not only accepted and transmitted the structural-functional approach; some of them made important criticisms and refinements of the theory. By the late 1950's this coterie of scholars had established structural-functionalism as the reigning sociological approach.

Structural-functionalism holds that integrated social wholes should be analyzed into constituent structures and functions. The focus of research is primarily on the consequences (or functions) of the operation of structures for the survival or maintenance of a certain state of the social whole. Comprehensive dynamic analysis of an on-going social system (or structure) with its complex of numerous interrelated variables requires continuous and systematic reference of every problem to the state of the social system as a whole.

However, the present stage of sociological development requires some simplification of elements and factors. Groups of variables are removed, so to speak, from the system, treated as generalized categories, and viewed as constants within the system. Thus simplified, the empirical social system can be described in terms of a set of structural categories. Linkage between these rather static elements and the dynamically variable elements of the system is made through the concept of function, whose role is to provide criteria of the importance of dynamic factors and processes within the system. "Thus," writes

*See the extended discussion of socialization in Chapter 12.

Buckley, "an additional requirement is a set of 'dynamic functional categories' that describe the important process by which particular structures are maintained or upset and the relations of the total system to its environment."[15]

The structural-functional group gave further impetus to the empirical thrust of modern sociology. Investigators ranged far beyond the urban community that had been the main locale of study for the Chicago group. Virtually every aspect and facet of social life came under the scrutiny of sociological research. The literature reporting this research accumulated rapidly and now forms a great fund of empirical knowledge.

However, in recent years structural-functionalism has come under increasing criticism, partly because many of its propositions were couched in excessive jargon and obscure language. At the same time, there has been a compensatory revival of interest in social process and other neglected aspects of sociological inquiry. Under the impact of these developments, structural-functionalism has lost much of its doctrinaire character and promises to leave certain lasting contributions to sociological theory, knowledge, and methodology. This debate has brought clearly into view the two conceptions of society. Ralf Dahrendorf observes that this is an old problem in social thought and suggests that the duality of basic themes is the distinguishing feature of sociological theory today.

> Throughout the history of western political thought, two views of society have stood in conflict. Both of these views are intended to explain . . . how is it that human societies cohere? There is one . . . school of thought according to which social order results from a general agreement of values, a *consensus omnium* or *volonté générale* which outweighs all possible or actual differences of opinions and interests. There is another equally distinguished school of thought which holds that coherence and order in society are founded on force and constraint, on the domination of some and the subjection of others. To be sure, these views are not at all points mutually exclusive. The Utopian (as we shall call those who insist on coherence by consensus) does not deny the existence of differences of interest; nor does the Rationalist (who believes in coherence by constraint and domination) ignore such agreements of value as are required for the very establishment of force.[16]

SOCIOLOGY TODAY

Trend Toward Synthesis ◗ Within these crisscrossing lines of development, perhaps the most significant characteristic of American sociology today is the trend toward synthesis and integration. The discipline has recovered from excessive involvement in schools of theory and interpretation. There are no longer any dominating system builders to involve the discipline in heroic controversies of theory and doctrine. In many quarters the call goes forth for synthesis and integration of the accumulated theory and knowledge. Thus, for example, after a review of some of the "ambiguities" and "contradictions" of juvenile delinquency theory, Frank R. Westie and Austin T. Turk offer the following comprehensive proposal for the synthesis and integration of theory in this field.

The research task implied by the proposed strategy is indeed formidable. While a dedicated effort might establish in detail the empirical relationships between class and juvenile delinquency, no one investigator could expect to pursue, in one lifetime, all of the theoretical and research leads contained in the many interpretations attached to these relationships. Thus, the task is of necessity a group one. If the strategy is to bear fruit, atomistic, individualistic research must be de-emphasized in favor of large-scale coordinated research programs involving many researchers with varied skills and interests. The contemplated research program on delinquency in relation to social class would involve the use of specialized teams operating at successive cycles in the implementation of the strategy. Team A would be concerned with the first cycle of the program: establishing precise relations between class and delinquent behavior. Upon completion of their work, which would be expected to have at the same time provided some indication of which explanatory propositions might later prove most useful, other teams—B, C, and so on—would concentrate upon each of the interpretations in the surviving lists, i.e., those attached to the established empirical relationships. In most cases the various surviving interpretations imply empirical knowledge, often knowledge we do not have. Accordingly, these can be formulated as new presupposed empirical relationships, along with others then logically implied, to which strings of possible interpretations would be attached. On the basis of such cycles of coordinated research, students of delinquent behavior will be in a position to develop theories that link specific, empirically supported propositions which have been found to hold under certain determinate conditions. Provocative theoretical discussions and insights can then be superseded by the logical construction of propositional systems grounded in interlocked research findings.[17]

Already the trend toward synthesis has made substantial progress. There is no longer any question about the canons of science and the necessity for sound methodology. Almost without exception, sociologists are in agreement regarding the nature of the "sociological perspective" and the "sociological problem." These are no longer issues for either debate or defense. Less progress, however, has been made in the synthesis of theory and the harmonizing of noncomparable empirical findings. As a consequence, proposals like that of Westie and Turk quoted above are both timely and relevant.

Specialization ▶ Traditionally it has been said that sociology includes three major subdivisions: social organization, social psychology, and methodology. The basic knowledge of the field and the methods of gaining that knowledge can be classified under these headings.

From a somewhat different perspective, the branches of sociology may be classified as general and specialized. Within this scheme of classification, social organization, social psychology, and methodology are regarded as general branches. Areas like the family, criminology, medical sociology, and the sociology of knowledge illustrate the specialized subfields.

General theory and methodology are adapted to the nature of phenomena and the particular problems of a limited sector of social life. In time a body of data and generalizations is built up that has special relevance for workers in this field. All the specialized branches, however, remain firmly anchored in general sociology as the trunk of the tree of human relations.

Another distinctive characteristic of American sociology today is the proliferation of specialized subfields. The extent of this development can be demonstrated in several ways. By reference to the annual meeting programs of the American Sociological Association it is possible to gain a picture of the nature and extent of specialization. Figure 2-1 presents a listing of the subfields that appeared in the annual meeting programs for the years 1955, 1960, and 1965.

This exhibit reveals several aspects of the current state of sociology. At the outset it will be seen that a total of 39 different areas were included in the programs. That is, evidently sociological research and activity goes on in these 39 areas. Unfortunately, however, a study of these annual meeting programs provides no rationale for the categories represented and gives no indication of how exhaustive the listing is considered.

It will also be seen that such a listing does not differentiate among the areas in terms of importance or any other criterion of priority. For example, the programs do not distinguish between general and specialized fields. Moreover, a study of these programs fails to reveal any way of subgrouping or classifying the specialized subfields.

An inspection of the titles in the figure will communicate to the reader some sense of the range of facets of human life that have come under scrutiny by sociologists. Scholars and researchers, trained in the field of sociology and armed with sociological tools of investigation, have studied all these phases of human society. In fact, research and publication have proceeded far enough in each of these areas to justify establishment of a program section at an annual meeting of the national professional association.

Another, and perhaps more definitive, picture of the subfields of sociology is contained in the 1966 National Register of Scientific and Technical Personnel. This classification of subfields and professional specialties, presented in Figure 2-2, gives a clearer picture of the proliferation of the field of sociology.

First, eight major subdivisions are listed. These include sociocultural theory; methodology; demography and population; rural-urban sociology; social change and development; social organization, structure, and institutions; social problems and social disorganization; and social psychology. Under these eight major divisions of the field are listed 55 specialties.

Some Specialties of Sociology as Listed in Annual Programs of the American Sociological Association, 1955-1965

Sociology of Industry
Sociology of the Family
Sociology of Communication and Opinion
Sociology of Racial and Ethnic Relations
Social Psychology
Sociology of Education
Sociology of Popular Culture and Recreation
Sociology of Religion
Sociology of Demography and Population
Sociology of Mental Health
Sociology of Small Groups
Sociology of Social Structure
Sociology of Knowledge and Science
Sociology of Politics
History of Sociology
Sociological Methodology
Sociology of Social Change
Sociology of Occupations and Professions
Sociological Theory
Sociology of Differentiation and Stratification
Sociology of Medicine
Sociology of the Community and Locality Relations
Sociology of the Graphic and Plastic Arts
Sociology of Complex Organizations
Sociology of Social Disorganization and Deviation
Sociology of Planning for Development in Underde-
    veloped Areas
Sociology of Law
Sociology of Literature
Sociology of Urban Life
Sociology of Rural Life
Sociology of International Relations
Sociology of Crime and Juvenile Delinquency
Statistics and Quantitative Sociology
Sociology of Age Statuses (i.e., adolescence, middle
    age, old age)
Collective Behavior
Sociology of Military Life
Sociology of Music
Sociology in Action (welfare)
Sociology of Mass Society

FIGURE 2-1

THE PROFESSION OF SOCIOLOGY

There is no exact census of sociologists in the United States. Officials of the American Sociological Association estimated that by the end of 1966 there were some 10,000 members. With the exception of students, most of these persons are professionally committed sociologists. This number, however, is significantly smaller than the total number of professional sociologists in the country. Many professionally trained and committed sociologists do not belong to the national association.

In addition, there are tens of thousands of individuals who have undergraduate and/or graduate training in sociology, but who are neither committed nor engaged in sociological activity. Other persons, not really trained in sociology, nevertheless claim to be sociologists. In a broad interpretation of the term, all such persons would be included as sociologists. The following discussion, however, is limited to persons who are trained in sociology and professionally committed to the practice of sociology.

The Education of Sociologists ▶ Training in sociology is inconsistent and often even confused. At the undergraduate level stress tends to be placed on the communication of the general knowledge of the field. Graduate training, however, tends to stress preparation for research. Many students enter graduate training in sociology from undergraduate experiences in fields unrelated to sociology.

In order to engage in the professional practice of sociology, an individual must have some graduate training. With a master's degree a person may teach lower-level sociology courses in junior colleges and four-year liberal arts colleges and engage in professional activities related to sociology. However, for the individual who wishes to engage in research, upper-level undergraduate instruction, graduate teaching, and various kinds of administrative activities, the Ph.D. in sociology is obligatory.

Elbridge Sibley has shown that the modern sociological specialties described above constitute the basis of graduate professional training. Students working for the Ph.D. in the field must specialize in two or more of these subareas. Writing in 1963, Sibley generalized regarding American universities.

> Departmental policies vary as to the number of different fields of specialization in which each doctoral candidate must qualify, and as to the range of choice open to the individual. The number of special fields required ranges from one to five, the modal department requiring three, . . . The number of different fields specifically listed in departmental prospectuses varies from 3 to 17; the actual range of choice is still wider, for many departments indicate that individual candidates may be permitted to offer specialties other than those named. . . .[18]

As noted above, the growing synthesis of the field is reflected in the content and emphasis of graduate training. In this connection,

Sociological Specialties as Listed in the National Register of Scientific and Technical Personnel

Socio-Cultural Theory	*Social Organization, Structure,*
General Theory	*and Institutions*
Symbolic Interactionism	Bureaucracy
History of Social Thought	Cultural—the Arts
Methodology	Educational
Computer Techniques	Family
Experimental Sociology	Industrial
Field Data Collection	Intergroup including Race,
Measurement and Index	and Ethnic
Construction	Legal
Model Building	Medical
Mathematical Sociology	Occupational
Social Survey Design and	Political
Methods	Religious
Statistical Analysis	Scientific
Demography and Population	Stratification
Migration	*Social Problems,*
Labor Force	*Social Disorganization*
Population Characteristics	Criminology
Population Trends	Deviance
Vital Statistics	Poverty and Dependence
Rural-Urban Sociology	Social Conflict and Accom-
Community Studies	modation
Human Ecology	*Social Psychology*
Rural Sociology	Attitudes
Urban Sociology	Collective Behavior and
Social Change and	Social Movements
Development	Cultural Deprivation
Invention and Innovation	Culture and Personality
Social Control	Group Interaction
Social Process	Leadership
Social Mobility	Public Opinion
Socioeconomic	Reference Groups
Development	Role Behavior
Sociopolitical Change	Social Perception
	Symbolic Communication
	Sociology of Language

Source: Specialties List, National Register of Scientific and Technical Personnel, American Sociological Association and National Science Foundation.

FIGURE 2-2

Sibley pointed out on the basis of his study of graduate education in the United States that there is some consensus regarding what should be studied. However, he found that the level of training was uneven and the content tended to be superficial. With reference to the consensus of content, he wrote:

> Published prospectuses of institutions offering the doctorate in sociology reveal some consensus on what every candidate must study. The various rubrics appearing in different catalogs can be subsumed under a few categories: general sociological theories, the structure and functions of social groups and organizations, the psychology of social interaction, and methods of empirical research both quantitative and nonquantitative. To these universal requirements, many if not most departments add the study of culture as developed by the adjacent discipline of anthropology. . . . Convergence of empirical and theoretical interests has been a significant trend in sociology in recent years; it represents progress toward maturity of the science. But it is not easy to devise a curriculum whereby beginning students come to comprehend this.[19]

It turns out in fact that in graduate training sociology is essentially an apprenticeship in empirical research. An important, often major part of experience consists in the actual practice of empirical research within some kind of university-based research institute or center. The graduate student experiences a discontinuity between this kind of professional training and undergraduate study that stresses acquisition of knowledge, sometimes in a field unrelated to sociology. After receiving the Ph.D. degree he experiences another discontinuity between research-oriented graduate training and initial employment as a teacher of lower-level courses in an undergraduate setting.

Academic Organization of Sociology ▶ The university structure for graduate training in sociology is typically a department of sociology or a department of sociology and anthropology. In some universities, general sociology is related to a department or division of rural sociology. In such university departments faculty members are expected to engage in research and are sometimes called "research professors."

The research activity of university departments of sociology is often structured as an "institute" or a "center." The institute or center is a bureaucratic instrument for connecting many independent and semi-independent research activities to the university. Typically, the full-time staff of the institute or center consists of a director and assistant director and a small clerical staff. The research staff is composed of the professors in the department and their graduate students. Salaries of professors are often paid in part by the university and in part from public and private research grants or contracts. The institute or center provides research stipends of various kinds to support graduate students and permit them to have actual research experience.

The research activities of the institute or center are supported in various ways. Appropriations to the department from regular university sources include some funds for research activities. In addition, professors acting individually or officially through the institute secure other funds through government contracts and grants or by contract with foundations and business firms. One main responsibility of the director and assistant director is to search out a continuous source of funds to support on-going and contemplated research.

The institute or center is more than an agency for training graduate students in empirical research methods. It is an important instrumentality through which university-based sociologists fulfill a prime obligation as scientists to the profession. In this setting and through this instrumentality they carry on a continuous systematic study of human social relations, which is the central concern of the discipline. More than this, though, the research carried out in such institutes and centers is of inestimable value to public and private agencies of social policy and planning.

What Sociologists Do ♦ Most sociologists are engaged in university and college teaching and research. A limited number of professionals give full time to research, either in academic settings or elsewhere. An even smaller number of practitioners with Ph.D. degrees are engaged full time in applied activities related to sociology.

From a study of 401 sociologists with the Ph.D. degree, Elbridge Sibley was able to report professional distributions. These findings are shown in Figure 2-3. The upper part of the exhibit indicates employment location and the lower part reveals type of activity.

It will be seen that almost three fourths of all the sociologists interviewed are employed by universities and four-year colleges to teach and/or conduct research. Sibley reports that although a quarter of the respondents were employed outside academic settings, no more than 5 per cent appears in any one category. On the other hand, although almost three quarters of the informants were engaged in teaching or teaching and research, 15 per cent were occupied full time in research. Negligible proportions were engaged in other professional activities.

When we consider the activities of non-Ph.D. sociologists, a much wider range of occupations is observed. The picture essay which appears on pages 18-23 shows some of the types of jobs that are now held by persons with training in sociology. There is no way to ascertain how many such persons there are in the country or what proportion of them are engaged in any given occupational category or occupation.

Most, though not all, of the occupations shown in this exhibit are available to people with bachelor's or master's degrees. Some of the occupations call for technical skills, e.g., computer techniques, interviewing skill, etc., in addition to basic training in sociology. The range of jobs is great enough to provide the prospective student of sociology considerable latitude of choice. A moment's reflection will show also

Primary Employment

Location	Per Cent
Universities and four-year colleges	74
Junior colleges, technical and other schools	3
Educational agencies except schools	2
Health, welfare and correctional agencies	5
Other government agencies	4
Business and industry	5
Other voluntary and nonprofit organizations	3
Miscellaneous and unspecified	4
Total	100

Principal Activities

Field	Per Cent
Teaching (including teaching combined with research and academic faculty positions not otherwise specified)	73
Research, including administration of research (excluding research combined with teaching)	15
Consulting and administration	7
Social work and related activities	1
Editing, writing, lecturing	1
Not employed (including retired and unspecified)	3
Total	100

Source: Elbridge Sibley, The Education of Sociologists in the United States, New York, Russell Sage Foundation, 1963, Tables 4 and 5, p. 48. Based on a sample of 401 respondents.

FIGURE 2-3

that most of the jobs listed in this exhibit involve direct relations with people who are being served in one way or another.

Professional Associations ◗ Associations provide major vehicles for giving expression to professionalism among sociologists. Probably every sociologist who is committed to the profession belongs to one or more such associations. Progression of a sociologist in the profession is marked in various ways by activities and services in these associations.

Figure 2-4 presents a list of the national, regional, and specialized sociological associations in the United States. The American Sociological Association is the parent organization of sociologists, and its purposes and programs set the pace for the entire profession. Among these purposes and programs the following can be identified:

1. Maintenance of communication among sociologists in the United States and abroad.

2. Exchange and advancement of research and knowledge in the field.
3. Establishment of criteria for membership in the profession.
4. Establishment and communication of codes of ethical practice for the profession.
5. Facilitation of contacts between job seekers and employers in the field of sociology.
6. Maintenance of contacts between sociologists and government, industry, labor, and other social organizations.
7. Maintenance of contacts and cooperation with sociologists and sociological organizations in other countries.

The professional associations perform some important functions both for their members and for the profession. First, associations are the prime agencies through which sociologists reveal their identification with the discipline and their standing in the profession. To be recognized as a professional sociologist an individual must be a member of the American Sociological Association and one of the regional or specialized associations. His class of membership, i.e., fellow, regular, associate, student, provides one clue to the individual's standing in the profession. A certificate of membership is usually a prized possession that the member may display proudly in his office.

Associations constitute the intellectual market place of the profession. At their annual meetings, members report their research. In both formal and informal situations they exchange ideas, discuss problems of common interest, seek assistance and advice, and the like. This traffic in the intellectual products of the profession functions to reveal the member's identity as a sociologist and his standing in the profession.

National, Regional, and Specialized Sociological Associations

NATIONAL	American Sociological Association
REGIONAL	Eastern Sociological Society District of Columbia Sociological Society Southern Sociological Society Ohio Valley Sociological Society Mid-West Sociological Society Southwestern Sociological Association Pacific Sociological Society
SPECIALIZED	American Catholic Sociological Society Rural Sociological Society Society for the Study of Social Problems

FIGURE 2-4

The associations also serve as the economic market place of the profession. They all operate an official placement service where job seekers and potential employers can be brought into communication. The annual meetings tend to generate a significant job traffic among the senior professionals. Representatives of government agencies, foundations, and industries visit the association annual meetings to bring research opportunities and funds to the attention of professionals. Publishing companies buy advertising space in annual meeting programs and rent exhibit tables in the headquarters hotel, where they carry on a lively book-selling business. The publishers' representatives also carry on a continuous dialogue with authors and potential authors.

The associations are prime agencies of fellowship within the profession. Friends and acquaintances get together to catch up on news and gossip. Some of the universities arrange informal breakfast or luncheon meetings of their alumni. Publishing companies give cocktail parties for authors and customers. Every professional sociologist recognizes that the opportunities for fellowship are among the more pleasant and important experiences of these annual meetings.

The professional associations constitute an arena wherein members can strive for prestige and power. The offices of the association constitute some of the most prized rewards of the profession. They are also important sources of power. As a result, in every association there is a continuous, often lively, political process. Occasionally, the succession to office or the amendment of the constitution generates a "great debate" that rocks the profession for months, sometimes for years.

Finally, the associations, especially the American Sociological Association, act in various ways to safeguard and advance the profession. As a preliminary to the effort to up-grade and standardize the training of sociologists, the Association sponsored the study of sociological education that was alluded to earlier in this chapter. Or again, the A.S.A. is currently sponsoring a project designed to improve sociology teaching in high schools and to harmonize such courses with sociology as taught in colleges and junior colleges. Several years ago the national association formulated and promulgated a code of ethical practice for American sociologists. All of the associations—national, regional, and specialized—promote useful relations between sociologists and various public and private organizations of social policy and social action. The associations also act in many other ways to protect and to enhance the "image" of sociology and sociologists in the American scene.

In this part of the book we have been describing the field of sociology, explaining what sociology is, tracing its development, and describing sociologists and what they do. In the remainder of the book we settle down to the study of sociology. In these chapters we will examine the perspective and approaches of sociology, the central problems of analysis, and the basic concepts and propositions of the field.

FOOTNOTES

1. Floyd N. House, *The Development of Sociology* (New York: McGraw-Hill, 1936), p. 219. See also Harry Elmer Barnes, ed., *An Introduction to the History of Sociology* (Chicago: University of Chicago Press, 1948).
2. William Graham Sumner, *Folkways* (New York: New American Library, 1906), pp. 32-33.
3. *Ibid.*, p. 33.
4. *Ibid.*, p. 33.
5. *Ibid.*, p. 61.
6. *Ibid.*, p. 46.
7. House, *op. cit.*, Table of Contents. See also Part V.
8. Alvin Boskoff, "From Social Thought to Sociological Theory," in Howard Becker and Alvin Boskoff, eds., *Modern Sociological Theory in Continuity and Change* (New York: Dryden, 1957), pp. 3-32.
9. See E. W. Burgess and R. E. Park, *The Urban Community* (Chicago: University of Chicago Press, 1926).
10. See Nels Anderson, *The Hobo* (Chicago: University of Chicago Press, 1923); Louis Wirth, *The Ghetto* (Chicago: University of Chicago Press, 1928); Clifford R. Shaw, *Delinquency Areas* (Chicago: University of Chicago Press, 1929); Harvey W. Zorbaugh, *The Gold Coast and the Slum* (Chicago: University of Chicago Press, 1929); E. Franklin Frazier, *The Negro Family in Chicago* (Chicago: University of Chicago Press, 1932); Walter C. Reckless, *Vice in Chicago* (Chicago: University of Chicago Press, 1933); Frederic M. Thrasher, *The Gang* (Chicago: University of Chicago Press, 1936); and Robert E. L. Faris and H. Warren Dunham, *Mental Disorders in Urban Areas* (Chicago: University of Chicago Press, 1939).
11. A. G. Keller, *Societal Evolution* (New York: Macmillan, 1915).
12. Charles Horton Cooley, *Human Nature and the Social Order* (New York: Scribner's, 1902).
13. Walter Buckley, "Structural-Functional Analysis in Modern Sociology," in Becker and Boskoff, eds., *op. cit.*, p. 248.
14. See among other sources: Talcott Parsons, *Essays in Sociological Theory, Pure and Applied* (Glencoe: Free Press, 1949); Talcott Parsons, *The Social System* (Glencoe: Free Press, 1951); Talcott Parsons and Edward Shils, *Toward a General Theory of Action* (Cambridge: Harvard University Press, 1951); Talcott Parsons, R. F. Bales, and E. A. Shils, *Working Papers in the Theory of Action* (Glencoe: Free Press, 1953); Marion Levy, *The Structures of Society* (Princeton: Princeton University Press, 1952); and Robert K. Merton, *Social Theory and Social Structure* (Glencoe: Free Press, 1957).
15. Walter Buckley, *op. cit.*, p. 250. See also Max Black, ed., *The Social Theories of Talcott Parsons* (Englewood Cliffs: Prentice-Hall, 1961).
16. Ralf Dahrendorf, *Class and Class Conflict in Industrial Society* (Stanford: Stanford University Press, 1959), p. 157.
17. Frank R. Westie and Austin T. Turk, "A Strategy for Research on Social Class and Delinquency," in *The Journal of Criminal Law, Criminology and Police Science*, 56:461-462 (1965).
18. Elbridge Sibley, *The Education of Sociologists in the United States*, (New York: Russell Sage Foundation, 1963), p. 121.
19. *Ibid.*, pp. 32-34.

SOCIAL ORGANIZATION AND CULTURE

Part II examines social organization and culture as the two basic concepts of sociology. Chapter 3 explains the nature of social organization and describes its constituents, variations, and trends of change. The chapter ends with a definition of "society" and a description of the two main types, "communal" and "associational."

In Chapter 4 culture is defined and analyzed. The nature, characteristics, and functions of culture are discussed. Norms and values, the major components of culture, are examined at length. The chapter ends with a discussion of the functional relationship of culture and social organization.

Chapter 3

SOCIAL ORGANIZATION

Characteristically, man manufactures and uses tools. The factories, farms, air lines, and laboratories that we see around us testify to this fact. But man's major tool is social organization. This is not strange, for man is a social creature; he is uniquely endowed with the capacities for creating and utilizing social organization. His hereditary equipment for speech, symbolic communication, complex mental performance, and dexterous manual manipulation underlie organized social life.

Yet, unlike the social organization of animals such as ants or bees, human social organization varies profoundly from culture to culture. This variation shows that the forms of human social life are learned, not instinctive. Stripped of the instincts that promote survival in other animals, man must meet his needs nevertheless. He does this everywhere through one or another form of social organization. Organized social life is in the most natural sense the ordinary mode of human existence. Human beings not only learn to live under and to utilize social organization; they have been exposed to no other way of living. The hermit in his lonely cave, Robinson Crusoe shipwrecked on an island, and the children abandoned to life among wolves are novelists' creations or social oddities.

SOCIAL ORGANIZATION DEFINED

Social organization constitutes the framework of ordinary human behavior. This framework has six characteristic features. First, in every group there is a division of labor. Group tasks are broken up into individual assignments that are related both to each other and to group goals. For example, carpenters, masons, electricians, and plumbers combine and harmonize their work in order to complete the building of a house. These and other occupations are created by breaking down the total task of house building into component tasks.

Second, the division of labor produces a structure of interdependent roles and statuses. The term role or social role has two somewhat different, though related, meanings. On the one hand it refers to a pattern of expected behavior that is associated with a social position, e.g., the position of builder, foreman, or carpenter. The role tells the individual what he ought to do, to whom he owes obligations, and upon whom he may make rightful claims. On the other hand, a role is the way an individual performs the expected behavior pattern. It designates his unique style of acting as builder, foreman, or carpenter. The two meanings are interdependent, but they can usually be distinguished by the context in which the term is used.

The term social status also has two related meanings. On the one hand, it refers to the position to which a role is attached. In this sense a status is simply a part or unit of a social structure. On the other hand, in a more restricted sense status refers to the rank of a position in a hierarchical system of positions. Thus in house construction, the builder has a higher status (rank) than the foreman, who outranks (by higher status) the carpenter. As with role, these meanings are interdependent, but they can be distinguished by the context in which the term is used. Social organization emerges from the arrangement and hierarchizing of social statuses and from the meshing of the related social roles.

A third feature of social organization is a set of social norms, a body of agreements regarding the behavior that is expected of participants. Social norms are the rules of social action that govern the way individuals perform the roles they occupy. In some societies the norms are mutually consistent, and individual behavior closely conforms to their requirements. This condition of mutual consistency, or harmony, among norms is called normative integration, and is found most often among small isolated societies or groups.

Often, however, the social norms, or rules of behavior, are varied and inconsistent. This situation is illustrated in large cities or frontier localities. The lack of harmony or consistency among social norms indicates that normative integration is limited. For example, if the rules and schedules of work of the various craftsmen fit together harmoniously, work on the new house proceeds smoothly and rapidly. If, however, the work of electricians interferes with the performance of carpenters, or if plumbers have not finished their task before plasterers are scheduled to begin, there may be trouble. Conflict arises, the work is slowed, and the builder experiences problems of management.

Fourth, communication is another feature of social organization. The coordination of the behavior of individuals occupying interdependent roles and the achievement of collective goals depend upon the transmission of information and ideas. Mechanisms operate to guarantee that vital messages get to the participants and are understood by them. In some societies and groups these mechanisms are simple and involve direct contact among the participants. We call this primary communication. At other times and in large, complex societies the mechanisms may provide for the broadcasting of standardized messages to vast, dispersed, unseen audiences of social participants. This is called mass communication. Both forms of communication are essential to social organization.

By way of illustration, in the building of the house instructions of the builder, orders of foremen, reports of inspectors, and wishes of the owner must be received and understood by all the workmen. For these purposes blueprints, lists of specifications, and copies of building codes, as well as face-to-face conversations, are utilized. However, if a workman misreads the blueprint, misunderstands an order, or ignores a specification or code, an error results. A building error means that a role expectation has been missed, role coordination is interrupted, a social norm has been ignored or violated, and achievement of a group goal has been in some measure limited.

Fifth, social organization provides for orderly allocation of authority to participants, i.e., an authority structure. The right of each participant to command, or his obligation to comply, is consistent with his role and status, and is specified in the norms. As a result, each participant is protected from abuses, and available authority is used in an orderly way to insure performance of tasks and to facilitate attainment of collective goals. For example, the builder has authority over the foremen, who in turn exercise authority over the workers under their supervision. The rules, however, protect the participants, foremen as well as workers, against abuse of the authority of the builder or inspectors.

Finally, social organization involves some agreement upon collective ends and means. The ends of activity are both explicit and implicit in the division of labor, and the means for attaining these ends are specified in the social norms. What is characteristic of social organization is the fact that participants are in some measure of agreement, or consensus, regarding both ends and means. This consensus produces social cohesion, or solidarity, within the society or group. As a consequence, the business of life proceeds with determination and assurance. Thus, although consensus and cohesion seem to result from the other features of social organization, they are at the same time basic and indispensable to each of these features.

Consensus and cohesion can be illustrated by reference to the craftsmen and the new house. In order for the house to be built and for each man to derive satisfaction from his work, there must be considerable agreement as to what is to be done and how it is to be done, and some sense of team membership. These characteristics can be seen to grow as the men work successfully and harmoniously together over a period of some weeks.

In the following case, Conrad M. Arensberg and Alexander B. Horstall describe the social organization in a shoe factory studied in the

1940's. Job titles designate the social roles that emerge from the division of labor. Social norms exist as work rules and unofficial patterns of collective activity. Formal and informal communication involves all workers and facilitates basic consensus and cohesion. As a result, shoes get produced, the company makes a profit, workers earn a living, and people derive satisfaction from their work.

All work came from the Lasting Room and was first processed by the heel-lasters, sitting together on one side of the Bottoming Room. They were then ready for the four teams . . . [who] were two trimmers, a pounder, a rougher, a shanker and two cementers.

1. Racks were rolled to the stair-well at the head of the room by the bed-laster or toe-laster who had completed the work, and left there.

2. Racks were lined up at the stair-well by the floor boy for the heel-lasters to take when ready. If the racks were piling up, the floor boy might wheel them down to mid-floor, opposite the battery of heel-lasting machines. If the heel-lasters were "caught up" they would stand at the stair-well and take the racks from the bed or toe-lasters as delivered.

3. Racks completed by heel-lasters were pushed to mid-floor, whence they were taken by the rougher or pounder to his particular team's bench. . . .

4. Racks were brought to the trimmers of each team, who removed the shoes to their bench for the first of five main operations performed by the team. These operations prepared the shoe for the attachment of the sole.

(a) *Trimming.* Two trimmer girls started the shoe through each team by trimming off leather which had bunched up at the toe, or any excess at the shank. They removed tacks from the insole. Their two machines were a physical unit and the girls faced each other, one with her back to the window and the other with her back to the aisle. Completed shoes were placed on the pounder's bench.

(b) *Pounding.* The pounder, a man, pounded and ground toes and heels, smoothing the overlapping leather more successfully than had the knives of the trimming machines. He faced the windows, his back to the aisle. He passed his output to the rougher's table at his side.

(c) *Roughing.* A man used a revolving wire brush to roughen the overlapping leather at the bottom of the shoe, preparatory to cementing. He faced the windows. His output went to the shanker.

(d) *Shanking.* This was done by a girl who placed a thin metal strip, previously bent to fit the insole of the shoe, in the center of the instep and stapled it in place. Her output went to the two cementers, and she used the same large bench they did.

(e) *Cementing.* Two girls squirted a layer of cement around the margin of the shoe, which later glued the sole in place. Then a "filler," a small felt pad, was stuck in place at the ball of the foot, and the shoe was placed in a special type of rack having boxes to receive each shoe. These two girls faced the rest of their team, with their right sides to the windows. This work was considered by girls the most desirable in the room. Gaining [this] position was considered a promotion. The work required a nicety of skill and was less mechanical . . . and offered opportunity occasionally to do extra racks requiring a mere cementing operation.

5. In the final step, racks were pushed to the floor by the two cementers of each team, there to be inspected for completeness by the floor boy before being taken to the elevator and finally leaving the Bottoming Room. Incomplete racks were held until the missing shoe had been traced.[1]

THE ENDS OF SOCIAL ORGANIZATION

It has been said that social organization is man's most versatile tool. Human beings use social organization as the means for attaining many different kinds of social and individual ends. It may prove helpful to consider these social ends from two somewhat different perspectives. From one perspective it is seen that some ends people seek through organized activity are imperative. That is, human beings must attain these social ends in order to survive both as individuals and as collectivities. Other social ends, however, are not essential to survival. Such ends constitute desired conditions or qualities of existence.

From another perspective, social ends may be seen as the consequences, or functions, of social organization. That is, they are the results of social organization, whether imperative or not, intended or not, recognized or not.

Imperative Ends ▶ First, let us consider the uses of social organization as a means for attaining ends. D. F. Aberle and his associates have identified imperative ends—goals that every society must attain. The following list is based upon their conclusions.

1. Personnel Maintenance. Every society must guarantee reproduction of members and means for obtaining subsistence from the environment.

2. Division of Labor. Every society must work out a division of labor that guarantees that the available personnel do the necessary work.

3. Communication. In every society there must be modes of learned symbolic communication that permit and guarantee the effective function of socialization and role-differentiation.

4. Shared Ideas and Beliefs. The members of every society must be in basic agreement regarding certain central ideas and beliefs.

5. Shared Goals. Members of every society must be in agreement regarding the main goals of collective and individual effort.

6. Regulation of Social Activity. Each society must prescribe the approved means for attaining the shared goals.

7. Regulation of Emotional Expression. In every society emotions must be regulated—some suppressed and others insured.

8. Training New Members. Every society must train new members, infant and older, to become useful operating members.

9. Control of Disruptions. Every society must arrange to control disruptive behavior, such as force and fraud, both from within and from without.[2]

Non-Survival Ends ❯ No human group uses its social organization merely as the means for survival. Everywhere men strive through organized social life to attain ends that are related to the conditions or quality of their lives. Thus they seek power or wealth or prestige or knowledge or pleasure and so on almost without end.

Earlier sociologists made lists of social ends, both imperative and nonessential, which they called "social forces." William Graham Sumner identified hunger, love, vanity, and fear as the major social forces.[3] William Isaac Thomas produced a list that still has heuristic value. He spoke of the wishes for security, recognition, response, and new experience. [4] However, the ends that men seek through organized activity are too numerous and varied to be compressed satisfactorily into a single list. It may prove more useful to illustrate how human beings use social organization to attain certain non-survival social ends.

In the following material, John Seeley and associates discuss the ends that people in a middle-class suburban community seek through their clubs and associations. No one is faced with a survival problem. Rather, they act for philanthropic ends, to improve personal skills, to facilitate social relations, or to achieve or reflect individual and family status.

GOALS OF ASSOCIATIONS IN CRESTWOOD HEIGHTS

Clubs and associations in Crestwood Heights exist to relate people to one another and to their culture: they are means directed to ends—ends which also enter into the functioning of more formal institutions. . . . Thus, in any Crestwood club or association, only the most careful scrutiny can determine the balance which may be struck through membership between intimacy and some less sentimental utility. . . . It is perhaps inevitable that there should be many such external ties for each individual in a society which stresses independent activity dissociated almost entirely from the kinship system or other habitual primary ties.

In their "purposes" clubs and associations in Crestwood Heights represent a blend of philanthropic, utilitarian, and aesthetic elements. . . . Just as a Crestwooder cannot usually waste money without some trace of guilt, he is also generally unable to waste time. He must always be "doing something," but it is equally mandatory that his something be "useful," either to himself or to others. Self-improvement, self-promotion, both important for the Crestwooder, are goals eminently suited for realization through associations. The desire to help others less fortunate than oneself is also most easily fulfilled by joining some philanthropic group since opportunities for mutual aid on a personal and individual basis are extremely limited, even among kin.

Closely allied with the practices associated with this utilitarian, "rational," and, perhaps, Puritan concept of leisure, is the use of the club, association, and, to a less degree, the intimate friendship group, for the furthering of business or professional or other ulterior aims.

Clubs and associations also provide an outlet for the professional and organizing skills of married Crestwood Heights women. . . . For many of these women, the work satisfaction predominates over the social prestige accruing from the activity. . . .

The acquisition of valuable skills is also an enticement to membership. . . . The necessity to acquire the skill legitimizes and sanctifies what would otherwise be a mere exhibition of buying power. . . .

The number of clubs and associations to which Crestwood Heighters belong is legion. For some purposes, the distinction between "formal" and "informal" associations does not seem too important. . . . The Crestwooder who understands his environment chooses his human contacts somewhat as a painter mixes colors—a membership here, a patronage there, all blending into an acceptable, harmonious design which will cast due luster on its creator and serve as an enduring symbol of his taste and skill.

One primary function of these groupings is to assign status to individuals, or more often, to families, although many members may not be fully aware of the function. . . . Prestige depends more on wealth than lineage [in Crestwood Heights]. Since profound secrecy must surround the actual amount of income, other sure ways must be found to proclaim one's financial potency and hence one's claim to social status. Membership in exclusive and expensive clubs is a convenient and effective means of proclamation. . . . Occupation, also a highly important determinant of status, is not sufficient in itself to assure prestige.[5]

Social Functions as Social Ends ▶ From another perspective, the ends achieved by social organization may be viewed as its actual accomplishments, results, or consequences. When seen in this way, social ends are called social functions. Robert K. Merton has identified and described several types of social functions.[6]

"Manifest functions" are results of organized social activity that are both intended and recognized. They are defined in advance as the goals of activity and stressed as important by the people concerned. *"Manifest functions,"* writes Merton, "are those objective consequences [of social action] contributing to the adjustment or adaptation of the system which are intended and recognized by participants in the system: . . ."[7]

For example, in the United States the intended and recognized consequences of economic organization include the production of goods and services, profits, and adequate wages. In some circumstances one consequence of religious orthodoxy is the refusal to practice birth control.

"Latent functions" are the unintended and unrecognized consequences of organized social activity. For example, the same economic organization that produces goods, services, profits, and wages also creates consumer preferences in fashion, entertainment, and leisure activities, and produces waste of natural resources, differences of wealth and power, and unemployment. Or again, the wars that issue from international organization have created or abolished nations, shifted populations, improved the social position of minority groups, or otherwise modified the course of history in unanticipated ways.

"Dysfunctions" are those objective consequences of organized social activity that militate against the adjustment or adaptation of the system.

Dysfunctions are unintended and often, though not necessarily always, unrecognized. For example, the economic system in the United States produces such consequences as fraud and corruption, economic depression, mass unemployment, and waste of resources. The attention given recently to the "war on poverty" suggests that this dysfunctional consequence of organized economic activity long went partly unrecognized.

SOME DIMENSIONS OF SOCIAL ORGANIZATION

Units of Social Organization ♦ By reference to the boundaries that determine and separate areas of social solidarity and activity, social organization can be described in terms of its component parts or units. This approach is suggested by such familiar terms as *group, community, class,* or *institution.* As employed in sociology, such terms constitute useful concepts for classifying and analyzing the basic constituents of social organization. At this point it will be useful to identify and define five such components.

A *social group* includes two or more individuals engaged in symbolic communication and in direct contact with each other at least some of the time. This social unit shares a common past, perceives a common future, and behaves in accordance with norms peculiar to the relationship while seeking some end in common. A social group exhibits enough solidarity to be identified as a unit more or less distinct from other, similar units. Familiar examples include "pal" gangs, families, religious congregations, and labor union locals.

Large-scale or *complex organization* refers to large aggregations of dispersed individuals. Typical illustrations include national labor unions, political parties, religious denominations, national educational associations, and large industrial and business concerns. Large numbers of dues-paying, card-carrying members are united by common interests and systems of formal communication. Sometimes the patterning of specialized roles and relationships by formal rules produces a type of organization that is called bureaucracy. Any given member seldom engages in direct interaction with more than a few other members. Though dispersed and indirectly connected, members nevertheless share a sense of social solidarity, and the organization is capable of concerted action.

A *community* is a social group or complex organization with a delimitable geographical locale, which possesses a system of social relations capable of satisfying many of the needs and wants of its members. Delimitable urban and rural places—farming settlements, villages, towns, cities, and metropolitan areas—constitute the more common illustrations. Frequently, however, the term is applied to ethnic, religious, or class subdivisions within metropolitan areas, e.g., the Negro, Jewish, or working-class communities; to a field of shared values and communication, e.g., the business or scientific community; or to a cluster of nations with shared values and communication, e.g., the North Atlantic Community or the community of free nations.

The concept *social category* designates a number of individuals who are regarded collectively as a unit because of the possession of one or more identifiable and socially significant characteristics in common. Males and females, the aged and adolescents, and social classes are examples of some of the more significant social categories.

Social institution refers to a mode of viewing organization in social life that is revealed in all societies. It cuts across groups, complex organizations, communities, and social categories. In this sense social institution stresses binding social rules for achieving major societal goals, rather than a particular aggregation of individuals. The basic institutions are family, government, economy, education, and religion.

We also use the term in the discrete sense to designate a particular institution, when the social interest, the time period, or the locality are specified. When used in this way, institution indicates a pattern of thought and action of some importance and permanence, which is embedded in the habits of a particular group or the customs of a specific era. For example, we may speak of the institution of the contemporary American family, the medieval Roman Catholic Church, or the Mogul Empire in China.

Normative and Functional Organization ▶ Social organization can be subdivided into normative and functional. Normative organization arises from the established rules of social activity, while functional organization arises from the interplay and adjustment of actual behavior. The two are present and interrelated in all social situations.

The term normative organization refers to that pattern of commonly accepted and sanctioned rules of social activity that prescribes the division of labor, the allocation and performance of social roles, the evaluation and choice of collective ends, and the definition and arrangement of appropriate means for their attainment. This pattern of organized life is likely to be the one that is described in school books, portrayed in public speeches, or extolled in public relations brochures. For example, democratic government is described normatively as the rule of the majority, with respect for the individual and guarantees for the rights of citizens.

The concept of functional organization, in contrast, refers to the actually observed system of social activity. It reveals the understanding and fulfillment of social roles, and indicates the ends that people esteem and work for, and the modes of behavior that are accepted and followed. Functional arrangements tend to develop alongside the officially defined normative order. For example, it seems to many people that democratic government is not the ideal arrangement suggested by the normative order, but rather that government is controlled by competing special interests, that the will of the majority is often flouted, that the individual is often ignored, and that personal rights are regularly infringed.

The two aspects of social organization are interdependent. Functional schemes tend in time to become crystallized into normative rules. The nature and interrelationship of normative and functional social organization are illustrated in the bottoming room of the shoe factory. The excerpt presented earlier describes the official or normative organization of this department. With regard to the nature of the functional arrangement, Arensberg and Horstall write:

> Observation of activity in the Bottoming Room showed that in addition to the work operations there was activity related in some way to the starting of these work operations in a team. This was a method of allocating racks among the teams according to some order, which was different from the order in which they came from the heel-lasters.
>
> Further observation showed that for each type of shoe in the racks coming from the heel-lasters, there was a corresponding object on one of the four rougher's benches. These objects had come to serve as symbols in an unofficial record-keeping and exchange around the workers' own routing of racks-to-be-done. One might say they were the "coins" of a small economic system. When a rack came to mid-floor from the heel-lasters, only the rougher upon whose bench lay the associated object might take it for his team. The sooner he took it, the sooner he could pass the object to the next team and the sooner that team's rougher could take another rack of the same type of shoe. Since the racks were pushed to mid-floor in any part of the room, just as they left the heel-lasters, there was a continual signaling by the roughers of the type of rack which had come to mid-floor. This took the form of shouting the name of the associated object, e.g. "Who's got the bar?" At the signal, the rougher or pounder whose team had the symbolic tool went over and took the rack in exchange for the signal-object and brought it back to the trimmers of his own team. Such exchanges served to pass along the associated object to the next team in a well-defined order of allocation of work by the four teams. The order was: Team #4 to #3 to #2 to #1 to #4.
>
> Such signaling and exchange took place continuously between the roughers and pounders, the men members of the various teams. In the exchange, since no team in the person of its rougher or pounder took a rack for which it lacked the associated object, and since every team when taking a rack passed along an associated object, it followed that at the end of the day the number of cases done, plus the number of objects held, was the same for each team (within limits determined by the number of objects).
>
> But meanwhile, the racks to be worked on had been routed among the teams in a manner calculated to equalize pay for fast and slow teams alike, and assure that all the workers should score a uniform production of racks. Thus, when work came through rapidly, the exchanges might result in a condition where one team had several racks piled up at its trimmer's machines, together with several exchange objects on its rougher's bench standing for racks routed to other teams.[8]

Social System ◗ When we describe social organization in dynamic terms, we call it *social system*. Social relations and social structure are the components of social system. A social system is a patterned set of social relations that is adjusted to the structure of a specific collectivity and geared to a set of social ends. Social systems vary in inclusiveness and complexity. Some may involve only two or three individuals, as in a partnership or family. Others, however, may embrace thousands or even millions of participants, as in a labor union, nation-state, or international organization.

Illustrations of social systems may be found in such familiar groups and situations as work groups and ball teams, barber shops and beauty salons, railroad stations and airports, supermarkets and department stores, and street corner gangs and athletic cheering squads. A college class is a familiar example of a social system. In time and through repetition, the relationships among professor and students fall into a pattern, become orderly and predictable, and flow along day by day in a relatively smooth manner. The lecturing, question-answering, examination-giving activities of the professor become meshed and harmonized with reciprocating activities of the students. Eventually, the system comes to operate in a predictable way and requires little conscious effort for orderly performance.

Social structure is the framework of social system. It is reflected in the more or less stable and enduring arrangement and articulation of roles and statuses, lines of authority, and channels of communication. Social structures vary in form, complexity, and stability. Sometimes, as in a family, pal gang, or sports audience, structure is relatively flexible or undefined. In other situations, e.g., a government bureau, a Communist cell, or an army squad, social structure is explicit and relatively rigid.

A clan or tribe is an example of a social structure in which roles and relationships are arranged on the basis of blood and marriage ties. A bureaucracy is a formal, often rigid hierarchy of precisely defined social roles and statuses. In the college class the professor and students are included within a structure that positions them vis à vis one another and that allocates authority and channels communication.

Social structure and social system are illustrated in the following description of feudalism, particularly in the division of labor, the hierarchical arrangement of statuses, the organization of political control, and the system of customs. Within this formal and somewhat rigid social structure there existed a systematic network of social relations. Lords and serfs, ecclesiastics and warriors, men and women were all tied together in an orderly and predictable scheme of reciprocal and interdependent activities.

FEUDALISM AS SOCIAL STRUCTURE AND SOCIAL SYSTEM
Following the breakup of tribal society and the subsequent period of almost incessant warfare, Western Europe settled into a pattern of social

organization known as feudalism, which lasted almost a thousand years. The social organization embraced a set of units of political, economic, religious, and family life that reflected a series of rigid gradations of status. Within this structure, social activities came to be carried out in relatively stabilized ways adjusted to the various classes and groups, the geographic environment, and the cultural tradition.

Component Units. The main unit of social and economic organization of the feudal system was the *manor*—an estate or villa belonging to a lord with an enserfed village community attached to it. A lord with only one manor was lowest in the ruling class. Dukes, counts, and viscounts often had hundreds of manors. An episcopal manor or monastery sometimes had thousands of manors. When a noble or church held such a large number of manors, it was called a *domain*. Over all was the king, or supreme noble, to whom the various nobles owed their loyalty and service. The king thus united the domains and manors into the largest unit of organization. A generally accepted code of relationships bound the vast aggregation of kingdoms into orderly and systematic relationships.

Self-Sufficiency. The manor was an economically and socially self-sufficient unit of organization. It raised or manufactured practically everything it used. Food, clothing, tools, dwellings, furniture, and virtually everything else needed for its way of life were produced and consumed on the manor. Little surplus remained for exchange or sale. Such commerce as existed, however, took place within the confines of the manorial system, or between neighboring and friendly manors.

It was common for a rich noble or king to set aside a distant part of his castle for wives, concubines, and favorite servant girls. Known as the *gynaceum,* this part of the castle was a center of domestic handicrafts. Here the women wove and made cloth. These were the original centers of the domestic handicrafts in Europe and exerted considerable influence upon the guilds that developed later.

Status System. The feudal society was differentiated into two great status divisions with innumerable gradations in between. At the top was the ruling class of nobles, warriors, and ecclesiastical leaders. Below was a subject class of tillers of the soil and domestic workers, within which at least four subdivisions can be isolated.

As suggested above, the ruling class included the kings and princes along with the lesser gradations of nobles. Another distinct sector of the upper class was the leaders and princes of the Church. The professional soldiers, who became "knights in armor" when relative stability was established and warfare was limited, must also be included among the upper class.

At the bottom of the lower class were the slaves, chiefly domestics, who were not allowed to have family relations. Next to them were the serfs, who were bound to the land on which they worked and could marry only with the lord's consent. They lived in wretched cottages without either chimney or windows, owned but little personal property, and could be transferred from one lord to another when property changed hands. The serfs were forced to spend many weeks of the year working in the lord's *demesne* (share of the land).

The villeins, the third subdivision of the lower class, were somewhat better off. They lived on the borderline, the lowest of the freemen or the highest of the serfs. Still higher, at the top of the lower class, came the freemen, who owned land but also owed military service to the lord.

Though better off economically, the families of the freemen were more unstable because of the constant danger that the husband might be taken by war.

Social Activities. The circumstances of all levels of the system powerfully affected social behavior. Distinctive patterns of family organization developed. While polygyny was tolerated among the nobility, and the slaves had no family life at all, the church princes were generally bound by the rule of celibacy. Manners and morals also varied widely from one level to another. Although most people, nobles as well as serfs, were illiterate, scholarship developed as a monopoly of the church leaders. Meanwhile, numerous patterns of conspicuous consumption evolved to symbolize the status distinctions described above.

Sources of Social Integration ▶ Social integration, or cohesion and harmony among constituent elements, is another variable aspect of social organization. When the elements are consistent and unified, the level of integration will be high, and individuals will be able to act together smoothly and efficiently in the attainment of collective goals. Disintegration suggests the loss of harmony and cohesion among constituent elements and a consequent reduction of smoothness and efficiency in social action. Integration is never complete, for, as Kingsley Davis observes, ". . . [N]o system of norms is entirely consistent with itself or entirely adequate for all emergencies; . . ."[9] Yet, extreme or prolonged weakening of social integration threatens the survival of the system and the well-being of its members.

It has been observed that small, isolated societies of primitive people often tend to be highly integrated. Through long isolation and intimacy the social elements have worked themselves into harmonious adjustment and close unity. On the other hand, large, heterogeneous, open societies tend to be less well integrated. The introduction of new patterns and the rapidity of change prevent the harmonizing of elements and activities and the development of smoothness and efficiency of fit and function in social life.

One major problem of sociology is the search for the sources of social integration. Ralf Dahrendorf has pointed out that philosophers and social scientists have pondered this problem for a long time and have proposed two somewhat contradictory answers.[10] One group of scholars argues that social integration results from force. The powerful impose their will upon the weak and constrain them to submit to order and to control their impulses and actions. Another equally distinguished body of thinkers replies that integration results from voluntary agreements. People agree—sometimes because they recognize that they must, sometimes from preference—on what is to be done and how it should be done. The consensus thus achieved is the source of cohesion and harmony in society.

Dahrendorf calls these the "two faces of society" and notes that they are not altogether irreconcilable. In some situations, voluntary agreements establish the integration that permits the organization and imposition of force. Thus, because of patriotism, or hatred of an enemy, or collective lust for power, the members of one society may organize a great army to conquer a neighboring society, upon whom they impose a new social order.

On the other hand, social cohesion and harmony enforced by a superior power may in time become accepted and voluntary. For example, people may agree freely to the social arrangements that had many years earlier been imposed upon their ancestors by force of arms. Consensus, not force, then becomes the source of social integration, which may develop to a very high level.

The sources, variations, and consequences of social integration will be an issue of continuing concern in the following chapters of this book. From this perspective it will be possible to undertake useful analyses of many important sociological problems. There will be many occasions to recognize the two faces of society and to see how they are interdependent.

TRENDS OF SOCIAL ORGANIZATION

When we contemplate changes occurring in the world as a whole, certain broad trends of social organization come into view. Many modes of organized life that distinguished Western societies are now appearing at an increasing rate in other societies. At the same time, the patterns of social organization in the Western World are themselves in process of change. Five dimensions of change in modern social organization have been identified in recent research. First, kinship is declining as the major basis of social organization. At the same time, collective life tends to become increasingly ordered by specialized groups or associations. Second, social functions and implementing organizations tend to become more minutely differentiated. This trend is revealed particularly in the high degree of specialization of social institutions and social activities. Third, the steady rise of secularism and rationality as ideological bases of social life constitutes another trend. Fourth, the emergence of mass patterns of organization and function is more and more evident. And fifth, at the same time, a tendency toward centralization of organization and control, and intensification of the search for "togetherness" appear as characteristic counter-trends.

Decline of Kinship ◗ The kinship units of tribe, clan, and large family are declining in importance as units of social organization. In most of the "developing" societies of the world the tribe is giving way to the nation-state as the principal mode of organizing for social control and intersocietal relations. Meanwhile, specialized associations of many kinds tend to perform the functions that formerly belonged to the clan or the family. In the Western societies the major governmental, economic, educational, and religious functions have already been removed from the family and turned over to other nonkinship units of social organization. For example, from one point of view at least, the history of the American family can be told in terms of a reduction of basic functions and decline in influence in the general fabric of social life. This pattern of change is being repeated in the nonwestern countries of Africa, Asia, and the Middle East. As a consequence, in many parts of the world, tribe and clan are disappearing as meaningful units of social organization.

The functions, powers, and activities that are given up by the declining kinship organizations are taken up by an increasing number of specialized groups and associations. Some familiar illustrations include the nation-state, political parties, educational organizations, economic corporations, labor unions, trade groups, veterans' associations, farm bodies, and religious denominations. In turn, all these specialized units of social organization tend to subdivide into numerous subordinate units. Thus, for example, a labor union has national, regional, state, and local units, together with many specialized and short-term committees and boards.

Growth of Specialization ▶ Speaking of the simpler societies, Robert Redfield wrote: "There is not much division of labor in the folk society: what one person does is what another does."[11] In the course of a lifetime each man and woman would learn and perform all or almost all the activities and roles of adult members of the society. For example, a person would successively be infant, child, adolescent, man or woman, and elder. He became provider, family member, warrior, teacher, and religious votary. He was artisan and artist, playmate and counselor, soldier and peacemaker. By the time he became an adolescent and underwent the puberty rites, he had absorbed the knowledge and learned skills necessary to become an adult member of his society.

Everywhere, though, the major trend today is toward increasing differentiation of social functions, activities, and organization. The increased division of labor is illustrated by the fact that the current United States Labor Department *Dictionary of Occupational Titles* lists over 50,000 different jobs. The assembly line depends upon the subdivision, standardization, and specialization of manufacturing tasks. The body of knowledge, the different operations and social roles in almost any field of activity today are so vast and complex that no individual can hope to master them all in a lifetime.

This growing specialization of functions and activities is reflected in the growth of specialization in groups and associations. This fact can be corroborated by examining a telephone directory or noting the variety of organizations appearing in the news items of any metropolitan newspaper.

Increase of Secularism and Rationality ▶ Social organization has tended to become secular and rationalistic. The revolts against the authority of scholarship and religion, the spread of the spirit of science, and the ideological exaltation of the individual have brought sacred patterns of conduct and organization under increasing scrutiny. A popular inclination to pragmatism means that social organization and action are expected to work in the interests of the masses of individuals. Earlier, moral philosophy came to replace religious doctrine as the gauge and control of conduct. More recently, social policy has tended to replace moral philosophy.

These developments were an almost inevitable consequence of certain historical events. The Protestant Reformation of the fifteenth and sixteenth centuries unleashed a universal revolt against sacred authority. The individual, not the church, became the agent of his eternal fate and the church was reduced to a facilitating agency. The Renaissance directed men to the natural world, themselves included, for the answers that formerly were the exclusive property of scholastic authorities. The spirit of inquiry, testing, and proof was stirred and set loose upon man's organized social life. This line of development led to the institution of science and later to the several social sciences. More recently, "scientism," or the vulgarization of science, has fostered the notion that a gimmick or gadget can be fashioned for every problem and every situation.

The political revolutions of the eighteenth and nineteenth centuries transformed the individual into the ultimate source of social power and the major object of group policy. These revolutions relegated social institutions, especially government, to the role of servants of the people.

One consequence of these changes is the growing belief that people are justified in using social organization to attain secular ends. This trend is illustrated in the case of clubs and associations in suburban Crestwood Heights summarized above. There it was shown that in that suburban community social status constitutes a kind of social asset, much like money, that can be accumulated, deposited, exchanged, invested, and otherwise manipulated. Clubs and associations are the major instruments for accomplishing these secular ends.

Such a view of social organization differs radically from the sacred orientations of primitive societies. The rationalistic manipulation of status contrasts with the situation in medieval Western societies, when a man's lot was regarded as a matter of divine providence, and when one lived out his days in the web of life that extended from birth into the hereafter.

Tendency Toward Mass Character ▶ Social organization in many societies tends to reveal "mass" characteristics. Mass organization suggests vast numbers of more or less isolated individuals who participate equally in many aspects of the common life and come together under formalized and impersonal conditions. The phrase "mass organization" suggests arrangements that overlay the ordinary units of social organization—i.e., social groups, communities, and social institutions. Individuals are lifted out of these ordinary units of organization by means of mass communication and participate in a kind of impersonal social pageant. Social arrangements necessitated by the press, the movies, radio, and television are the typical units of mass social organization.

The decisive feature of mass organization is not solely large numbers. There have been in the past, and indeed exist at present, some societies with teeming populations which exhibit few evidences of mass organization. China and India in the recent past are obvious illustrations. In these societies the lives of many people are still encompassed exclusively within the traditional units of organization.

The trend toward mass society is linked to the spread of the media and experiences of mass communication, i.e., newspaper, radio, motion pictures, and television. With the spread of industries and cities people become separated from kinship and village groups and are more or less isolated and detached in great and growing cities. Loneliness, insecurity, anxiety, and restlessness tend to develop and become magnified. Those modes of organization and activity that are facilitated by mass communication and transportation, i.e., public audiences, crowds, fandoms, etc., tend to develop, and include large numbers of these isolated and lonely individuals.

Countertrends ♦ Two trends contrary in direction to those just discussed can also be identified and examined. First, social organization, while becoming more specialized, also tends to become centralized. Local units of organization tend to join together into national structures, and large-scale organizations merge into vast social monoliths. Existing central organizations grow larger by the accretion of functions and powers that are relinquished by smaller units. This centralizing trend is illustrated in American industrial corporations, religious denominations, professional associations, governmental organizations, and the like. As a consequence, some observers view the society as a loosely integrated aggregation of organizational giants engaged in reciprocal influence and struggle.

Though centralization of organization is contrary to the trend toward differentiation of tasks and proliferation of specialized units, both trends are sustained by the increase of rationality and secularism. These opposing trends are examined in greater detail in Chapter 6 in connection with the discussion of large associations.

The second countertrend is the quest for community, often expressed as the urge for "belongingness" or "togetherness." Shaken by the effects of mass living, modern man seeks new secular and rational schemes for social solidarity and cohesion. There is a kind of flight from the loneliness of the mass to the secure warmth of intimate associations like those of Crestwood Heights described above. It was noted that one important—although often implicit—function of such organizations is to produce the warmth and intimacy in human relations that were missing in family or job, the two most important connections of the Crestwooders.

TYPES OF SOCIETIES

The term *society* is used to mean many different things. Within the present context of analysis two such meanings are significant. In its broadest and most general sense, society is, according to R. M. MacIver and Charles H. Page, "a system of usages and procedures, of authority and mutual aid, of many groupings and divisions, of controls of human behavior and of liberties. . . . It is the web of social relationships."[12] This is the meaning that is expressed in such phrases as "human society" or "organized society"; it is equivalent to expressions such as "social life" or "human life." This use of the term is descriptive of the nature of human life in general, and need not detain us further.

The phrase *a society* is definitive and constitutes one of the key concepts of sociology. We need therefore to examine this concept and to note some of its heuristic implications for empirical analysis. D. F. Aberle and his associates define a society as "a group of human beings sharing a self-sufficient system of action which is capable of existing longer than the life-span of an individual, the group being recruited at least in part by the sexual reproduction of the members."[13] A society is the most inclusive and independent unit of social organization.

Most nations are societies, although the two concepts—nation and society—are not equivalent, for sometimes a nation may contain within itself one or more smaller societies. The Hopi of Arizona, for example, constitute a society lying wholly within the United States. In New Zealand the Maori, the aboriginal inhabitants, have been confined to reservations, where they reside as a societal enclave within the larger national society.

The contrasts in societies like those just mentioned suggest that human societies are of different types. This observation was also implied in our analysis of trends of social organization in the preceding section. As a matter of fact, the contrasts among societies have been recognized by behavioral scientists for a long time. They have proposed a number of schemes of classification.

Herbert Spencer, the celebrated English sociologist, differentiated "militant" and "industrial" societies. By stressing different criteria, Sir Henry Maine, an English anthropologist, distinguised between societies based on "status" and those based on "contract." Later, Ferdinand Tönnies, a German sociologist, identified *Gemeinschaft* (community) and *Gesellschaft* (society). The nineteenth-century French sociologist Emile Durkheim contrasted societies united by *mechanical solidarity* (social segments) with those united by *organic solidarity* (social organs). Howard Becker, a contemporary American sociologist, has differentiated the two types as "sacred" and "secular." One of the most celebrated pairs of types is that formulated by Robert Redfield, the American anthropologist, who speaks of "folk" and "urban" societies.

In the following passage, Redfield describes the method of study by which types of societies are identified. All the investigators who have formulated paired types have followed a procedure of the same general kind. The construction of "ideal-types" is an important scientific objective of sociological study. These constructs provide one way to conceptualize general knowledge in the field and serve as versatile tools of analysis.

> All societies are alike in some respects, and each differs from others in other respects; the further assumption made here is that folk societies have certain features in common which enable us to think of them as a type—a type which contrasts with the society of the modern city.

> This type is ideal, a mental construction. No known society precisely corresponds with it, but the societies which have been the chief interest of the anthropologist most closely approximate it. The construction of the type depends, indeed, upon special knowledge of tribal and peasant groups. The ideal folk society could be defined through assembling, in the imagination, the characters which are logically opposite those which are to be found in the modern city, only if we had first some knowledge of nonurban peoples to permit us to determine what, indeed, are the characteristic features of modern city living. The complete procedure requires us to gain acquaintance with many folk societies in many parts of the world and to set down in words general enough to describe most of them those characteristics which they have in common with each other and which the modern city does not have.

> In short, we move from folk society to folk society, asking ourselves what it is about them that makes them like each other and different from the modern city. So we assemble the elements of the ideal type. The more elements we add, the less will any one real society correspond to it. As the type is constructed, real societies may be arranged in an order of degree of resemblance to it. The conception develops that any one real society is more or less "folk." But the more elements we add, the less possible it becomes to arrange real societies in a single order of degree of resemblance to the type, because one of two societies will be found to resemble the ideal type strongly in one character and weakly in another, while in the next society strong resemblance will lie in the latter character and not in the former.[14]

In this book the two basic types of societies are called *communal* and *associational*. The term communal stresses strong identification and deep involvement of individuals in the common way of living that is structured largely by nonspecialized kinship organizations. Associational emphasizes specialization of means and ends and their implementation in a multitude of associations with restricted functions.

It must be pointed out that, although such concepts are mental constructs, they have real value in current sociological analysis. First, they suggest the critical features to look for when studying a society or some aspect of a society. Again, they help to reveal the meaning of specific cases of conformity and of deviation from decisive characteristics of the ideal-types. Further, these classificatory concepts provide keys for understanding and interpreting many general characteristics of societies. In research, the ideal-types suggest questions to be asked and hypotheses to be formulated in the study of a given society or social phenomenon.

The Communal Society ▶ The communal and associational types may be delineated by setting down the characteristics that distinguish each. (The reader is reminded that these types are mental constructs and that they actually describe no existing society precisely.) The communal type includes the following features.

1. As a rule, such societies tend to be small, isolated, and homogeneous.
2. The number and variety of groups in communal societies tend to be limited, while the division of labor is simple, being based mainly on sex and age.
3. The norms and values of communal societies are fused together into a sacred, relatively inflexible, and all-powerful traditional pattern.
4. The heritage of traditional norms and values is unwritten and uncodified.
5. In such societies there is a strong and pervasive sense of consensus.
6. In communal societies social relations tend to be limited in range and general or inclusive in character.
7. Such social relations tend to be intimate and informal.
8. Further, social relationships in communal societies tend to be nontechnical and noninstrumental.
9. The patterns of social relations in communal societies tend to be strongly sanctioned, i.e., enforced.
10. One consequence of these circumstances is the fact that social relations tend to be well integrated, i.e., consistent and harmonized.
11. In communal societies the number and variety of social roles that are performed by an individual tend to be limited.
12. These roles are inclusive in nature, i.e., nonspecialized, and rather well harmonized within personalities.
13. In communal societies social roles and statuses are structured through the kinship systems of tribe and clan and the locality system of village or town.

14. Therefore a distinctive character of communal societies arises from limitation and simplicity of social organization and from congruence, i.e., harmony of culture, social relations, and social roles.

The Associational Society ❯ Because of its great size and complexity it is risky to generalize about the associational type of society. Yet, some contrasts are so evident and well established that they may serve as useful keys in the analysis of social organization. The following list of characteristics specifies some of the typical features of associational societies.

1. Typically, associational societies are large and accessible to strangers, and include dispersed heterogeneous populations.
2. There are numerous specialized groups and associations, some of which are large, dispersed, and formal in organization.
3. The norms and values of such societies tend to be rational, utilitarian, expedient, and impersonal.
4. The inconsistencies of such norms and values are managed through formal hierarchical organization in which rank is determined by relative inclusiveness and importance.
5. Many of the norms of associational societies are written into systematic codes and documents.
6. The rules of social behavior are often inconsistent and not well harmonized and integrated.
7. Social contacts and relations in associational societies are numerous and varied and depend on both mass communication and face-to-face experiences.
8. Formal and impersonal social relations tend to be stressed, and informal personal contacts are limited to small groups and other face-to-face situations.
9. Many social relations tend to be casual and superficial and are typically technical, competitive, and instrumental in character.
10. These modes of social relationship tend to weaken or limit social solidarity and integration.
11. Individuals perform many varied, specialized, or segmental social roles.
12. As a consequence, personalities tend to be flexible and rather loosely integrated around such social roles.
13. Roles and statuses are arranged into complex, formal structures, often called bureaucratic, which are consistent with the heterogeneous populations; and specialized norms and values are adjusted to modes of rationalistic instrumental social relations.

FOOTNOTES

1. Alexander B. Horstall and Conrad M. Arensberg, "Teamwork and Productivity in a Shoe Factory," in *Human Organization* 8:14 (Winter 1949).
2. Adapted from D. F. Aberle, *et al.*, "The Functional Prerequisites of a Society," in *Ethics*, 60:104-111 (January 1950).
3. William Graham Sumner, *Folkways* (Boston: Ginn, 1906), pp. 18-19.
4. William Isaac Thomas, *The Unadjusted Girl* (Boston: Little, Brown, 1928), p. 4.
5. Condensed from John R. Seeley, *et. al.*, *Crestwood Heights* (New York: Basic Books, 1956), pp. 292-295.
6. Robert K. Merton, *Social Theory and Social Structure* (Glencoe: Free Press, 1957), pp. 19-84.
7. *Ibid.*, p. 51.
8. Horstall and Arensberg, *op. cit.*, p. 15.
9. Kingsley Davis, *Human Society* (New York: Macmillan, 1949), p. 246.
10. Ralf Dahrendorf, *Class and Class Conflict in Industrial Society* (Stanford: Stanford University Press, 1959), p. 157.
11. Robert Redfield, "The Folk Society," in *American Journal of Sociology* 52:297 (January 1947).
12. R. M. MacIver and Charles H. Page, *Society* (New York: Rinehart, 1955), p. 5.
13. Aberle, *et al.*, *op. cit.*, p. 101. See also Julian Gould and William L. Kolb, *Dictionary of the Social Sciences* (New York: Free Press, 1964), pp. 674-675.
14. Redfield, *op. cit.*, pp. 297.

THE AMISH: A COMMUNAL SOCIETY

AMISH COMMUNITIES exist in twenty states and in Ontario; their total estimated population exceeds 60,000. The Amish founders in Europe felt that the great Reformers did not go far enough in remodeling the medieval Church. As a consequence of their beliefs they suffered as heretics at the hands of Church and State alike, and many came to America to escape religious persecution. The Amish today are gentle, industrious farmers. Their greatest values are a devout religion, an agrarian way of life, and a cohesive family and community. Although their lives are spent largely in their own communal society, they are not able to avoid all contact with the associational society of the United States that surrounds them and continues to exert its pressures on them.

THE AMISH FAMILY is a strong social unit, noted for its stability.

◄ *AGRICULTURE provides a stable economy for the Amish; although horse-drawn implements are primitive by modern standards, Amish farms are known for their fertility and productiveness. Boys, introduced to farming at an early age, usually develop a strong interest in agriculture.*

► *BASIC SKILLS of reading, writing, and arithmetic are considered important for Amish children; but beyond that, parents emphasize farming and home management rather than theoretical learning in the schools.*

◄ *LEISURE ACTIVITIES of Amish children include tug of war, jumping rope, and high jumping. Here, spectators view a softball game like that to be found in any American schoolyard.*

► COMMUNITY LIFE is secure and self-sufficient. Hard work, love of the land, and a strong commitment to the teachings of the Bible unite members in a firm brotherhood. When a farmer's barn burns, for example, neighbors take time out from their own chores to help him build a new one (below). In the larger associational society such neighborliness would be unusual, but in the Amish community it is taken for granted.

◄ DISPLAY OF WEALTH and luxury is taboo in the Amish community, but members treasure objects they make themselves, especially in a group setting. Amish women are talented at quilting and at hooking and braiding rugs.

◄ **PRESSURE TO CONFORM**
*to the larger society is constantly
exerted on the Amish, particularly
on the younger members. Contacts
with the associational society ex-
pose young people to its "worldly
ways," as at this amusement park
(left). The Amish are not ignorant
of world events; some vote, and
many subscribe to local daily
papers. A few girls adopt lipstick,
permanents, and high heels—but
most preserve the Amish way of
dress (below).*

► **HORSE-DRAWN BUGGIES**
*are still the principal means of
travel for the Amish. Buggies are
dangerous on modern roads used
by high-speed vehicles; but the
Amish feel that to accept the
automobile would lead to the
breakdown of their community
life and open the floodgates of
social and cultural change.*

◄ PUBLIC SCHOOLING, many Amish believe, subjects children to undesirable secular influences. Here, an Amish father (center) is ordered to jail for violation of the compulsory school attendance law.

◄ CUSTOMS, DRESS, and handicrafts of the Amish subject their communities to exploitation as tourist attractions. Here, a restaurant near Reading, Pennsylvania, advertises "Pennsylvania Dutch Cooking."

Chapter 4

CULTURE

Social organization means that the members of a human group not only agree on *what* must get done; they also agree on *how* it should be done. They think up and try out together various ways of acting, adopting those they prefer. Sometimes they must also produce equipment—e.g., dibble sticks and boomerangs or disk plows and repeating rifles—to enable them to act in the preferred ways. Collectively, these thought-up, tried-out, and preferred ways of acting together are called *culture*. Culture thus appears as one of the products of organized human life.

Once the ways of acting have been adopted, they tend to become binding on the members of the group. This is so, first, because each person grows up with an intimate knowledge of the ways of his own culture, and so takes them for granted as the only possible ways of acting. Second, every culture is valued by its members as being right and desirable, and conformity is enforced by various means. Individuals are encouraged or required to do things in the preferred ways, and discouraged or forbidden to act in other ways. Culture thus portrays the preferred or *normative pattern* of social organization. Insofar as culture constrains people to act in certain ways, it may be regarded as a producer of social organization.

THE NATURE OF CULTURE

In his classic definition, E. B. Tylor, the celebrated English anthropologist, said that "culture is that complex whole which includes knowledge, belief, art, morals, law, custom, and any other capabilities and habits acquired by man as a member of society."[1] William F. Ogburn has emphasized the importance of material objects in the concept of culture.[2] The knowledge, belief, art, morals, law, custom, and other capabilities and habits acquired by man as a member of society are constituents of culture. The basic reference of this phrase is to ways of social action. That is, the action patterned by culture is interaction, or relationships among the members of society.

Patterned social relations or cultural action may take place at three levels. First, cultural action may be overt. For example, in the United States women curl and wave their hair, rouge their cheeks and lips, polish their fingernails, wear ornaments on ears, wrists, and necks, and walk in high-heeled shoes. In other societies, for similar reasons women may decorate their bodies with scars, distend their lower lips by inserting strips of wood, file or blacken their teeth, and tattoo their chests, arms, and legs. The skills involved in driving a car or throwing a boomerang also illustrate overt culture patterns.

Second, social action may take the form of mental action or cultural belief. For example, most American farmers would seek a natural cause for crop failure, relying on naturalistic or scientific explanations of the reasons for plant growth. A Dobuan farmer of New Guinea, however, thinks that spirits control human affairs and natural processes. If his yam vines wither and die, he believes it is because evil spirits have gotten into them. Again, many variations of the belief in life after death appear among the cultures of the world. Some people believe in the transmigration of the soul and its reincarnation in subhuman animal forms. Others believe in an eternal life in a "happy hunting ground" or a land flowing with milk and honey. Some people believe in one god, while others hold with equal fervor to faith in a pantheon of specialized deities.

Race relations in the United States are conditioned by cultural beliefs. For example, reporting an investigation of resistance and readiness for school desegregation among white residents of Guilford County, North Carolina, Melvin M. Tumin writes: "Of the 287 persons asked, the Negro was alleged to be inferior to the white,

in responsibility by	209 or 72.8%
in morality by	198 or 69.0%
in ambition by	191 or 66.5%
in intelligence by	170 or 59.2%"[3]

Such beliefs have a powerful influence on actual conduct, for they often lead to behavior which tends to maintain the beliefs and make them seem to be true.

Third, culture may reveal the patterning of feeling. For example, in some societies, light filtering softly through stained-glass windows, the muffled sound of an organ, and the sight of the crucifix will evoke reverence in a devout worshiper. Among some peoples, snakes cause fear, while to others they are objects of reverence.

Cultural Equipment and Products ❯ Many material objects are produced through the application of cultural skills and techniques to the physical environment. Trains, radios, desks, pencils, shoes, razors, and automobiles are familiar illustrations. Primitive man too had his man-made material objects, including such items as dibble sticks, boomerangs, bows and arrows, fist hatchets, tents, and so on. Some material objects constitute the equipment necessary for the performance of culture patterns.[4] Driving, for example, requires an automobile; flying, an airplane; and shooting, a gun. The human body is frequently an element in cultural behavior patterns: the hand becomes cultural equipment in hand shaking, and hair is necessary to create a coiffure.

As noted, material objects are produced by the application of cultural techniques and the use of cultural equipment. The relationship between raw materials and culture is illustrated in the process of manufacture—e.g., of automobiles, radios, and airplanes. From this perspective such man-made material objects are called cultural products.

Characteristics of Culture ▶ Culture possesses a number of distinctive characteristics.[5] First, it is socially created, rather than instinctive or biologically determined. Ways of social action arise from the association of individuals with one another in the business of living. At times the process of culture creation is deliberate and rational. For example, inventors work alone in garrets or collectively in modern laboratories to create the processes and equipment of modern technology. The republican form of government, social insurance, and the juvenile court are deliberate social inventions. Frequently, however, the process of culture creation is gradual and almost imperceptible. For example, it is difficult to determine when the practices of shaking hands, driving on the right-hand side of the road, or saluting the flag were initiated.

By its very nature, then, culture is *not* biologically inherited. To be sure, individuals do inherit some simple patterns of action. For example, the eye blinking, waste elimination, breathing, eating, and crying behavior observed in infants is based on inherited biological needs. However, even these patterns are conditioned by culture, which determines their meanings and specifies how, where, and when they may occur.

Second, culture is socially shared. That is, most members of a collectivity tend to do the same things in essentially the same ways. This is one reason that people in a given group appear similar to outsiders, and their behavior appears orderly and comprehensible. For example, in the United States most people share similar patterns of speech and political, recreational, and family behavior. However, in spite of this, many unique patterns of activity can also be observed. Although these may be created in the course of social experience, they are considered culture only when they are socially shared and generally practiced.

Third, culture is learned. Individuals acquire or learn culture through association with others. This learning refers to the reproduction or duplication of the ways of social activity that are shared by the members of a group. The learning of culture may be viewed from a number of perspectives, as expressed in such terms as social inheritance, assimilation, acculturation, borrowing, diffusion, socialization, and the like. But always, what is essential is a process of learning carried out in a group situation.

For example, as children grow up in their families and communities, they acquire through socialization the ways of acting, thinking, believing, and feeling that their parents, relatives, and neighbors reveal. Immigrants to a new society undergo acculturation or assimilation as they come to learn the ways of the people with whom they associate.

Fourth, culture is gratifying to the people who practice it. That is, ways of social activity lead to the achievement of desired goals. Such modes of social action are preferred because they fulfill a need or attain an end, and also simply because doing things in the preferred way itself is pleasant. For example, American farmers use tractors to perform many agricultural tasks because they are an efficient available source of power. Indian farmers find the use of bullocks gratifying, not only because they are the major source of available power, but also because their use is traditional.

For many Protestants, worship on Sunday is a satisfying, comfortable practice, but Jews and Seventh Day Adventists prefer to practice their religious ceremonies on Saturday.

Finally, specific cultural patterns tend to be linked together harmoniously, or integrated, because they work together in fulfilling social functions. In this way each specific pattern gains purpose and meaning. For example, balls, bats, gloves, and base pads are linked with throwing, running, catching, signaling, and other patterns of behavior in the culture pattern of baseball. Driving a car, eating a meal, writing a letter, or attending church illustrate other integrated clusters of culture patterns. Those ways of activity that cannot be harmonized with other ways tend to be neglected or rejected.

Culture and Communication ▸ Culture serves to implement communication. Both the means and the content of human communication are cultural. Familiar means include newspapers, radio, and television. What is more important, the elements of meaning—motives, judgments, ideas, and feelings—are packaged in symbolic form and exchanged by these and other means of communication in the course of social interaction.

For example, elements of culture like mathematical symbols, chemical abbreviations, musical notations, and the Morse code constitute a kind of international language that employs a variety of material equipment. These symbols contain and convey essentially the same meanings to all receivers who are familiar with them. Americans find it easy to communicate with other Americans because they share the same language, general ideas, historical traditions, and some common experiences. This is true even though they may be from different regions, social classes, occupations, and racial or ethnic backgrounds. Similarities in cultural background make it relatively easy for Americans to communicate meanings accurately to one another. When culture produces or accentuates similarities of content and meanings, it tends to facilitate communication. For example, Jews all over the world share many elements of culture in common. They practice the same religion, share a common historical tradition, entertain similar memories and aspirations, and communicate by means of a common classical language.

If, however, cultural differences tend to minimize or obliterate similarities of content and meaning and to stress differences, communication may be impeded. This cultural situation often has undesirable social consequences. For example, in the Jordan valley, where Jews and Arabs are in close contact, ancient cultural differences nonetheless establish an almost impenetrable barrier to communication. As a consequence, actions are misunderstood, gestures misinterpreted, motives miscalculated, and meanings misapprehended. The result is tension, distrust, and hostility instead of harmony and cooperation.

Ethnocentrism (the tendency of groups to interpret and evaluate the cultures of others by reference to their own patterns) functions to accentuate cultural differences and to impede communication. It directs attention to the dissimilarities, and cultural differences themselves become socially important. Group effort is devoted to the maintenance of cultural integrity, and the attempt to understand or harmonize divergent practices is therefore minimized. For example, Americans are often accused of disparaging the ways of the immigrant groups within the nation. Their language, customary practices, and ideas are considered undesirable, and little effort is made to understand these people or to communicate clearly with them. It may be noted also that many of these people respond with similar ethnocentrism to native Americans.

The meaning of an individual's actions or words is determined by his customary ways of acting, thinking, believing, and feeling. To understand him correctly and communicate with him clearly, one must keep these cultural patterns in mind. This point of view, called cultural relativism, means that social acts must be interpreted in terms of the culture of the actor.

For example, an Indian may be puzzled when he sees an American enter a cathedral with his shoes on, and an American cannot understand why an Indian worker refuses to begin a job on Tuesday (for him an inauspicious day). Kashmiri women think Western women are unfeminine, and Western women cannot understand how Arab women can bear to become a man's second or third wife. Each of these acts must be interpreted in terms of the culture where it is customary.

To do otherwise is to impede understanding and limit the possibilities of clear communication.

CULTURE ILLUSTRATED: THE PEOPLE OF RAMPUR

The following case illustrates the nature and characteristics of culture. Along with most Indians, the people of Rampur have learned to satisfy important needs through Hinduism, the caste system, the joint family, and communal living in villages. Some patterns, however, such as the *Jajmani* system of exchange, organization into factions, and gay costumes of the women, are characteristic of the region where Rampur is located. The gregarious, cheerful, secure manner of the people suggests mental and emotional culture patterns. All these patterns, and many others that are not described here, are woven and fused together into a systematic way of life.

When studied, Rampur was a village of some 1100 inhabitants situated on the great Gangetic Plain, about 15 miles from New Delhi. The people were Hindus speaking a Hindi dialect sprinkled with Punjabi expressions. As in the rest of India, both the people and the culture of Rampur were a mixture of ancient and modern strains. The culture was distinctly Indian, although it was not "typical" of the entire country in all respects. The people of Rampur practiced a way of life that illustrates the nature and functions of culture.

The houses were crowded together in a disorderly arrangement of streets, many of which were narrow dead-end alleys.[6] The preferred pattern of family living was two residences, one for women and children and another for men and cattle. There were two *caupals* (social houses) for the men of the village.

Of the 784 acres in the village, over 90 per cent were under cultivation and a fifth under irrigation, thus permitting two crops a year. The village had practically no grazing land and forest resources, and only 7 per cent of the area was communally owned. Just over half—53 per cent—of the 150 families were engaged directly in agriculture on holdings that varied from less than 5 to 50 acres, averaging .75 acre per individual. The other families engaged in nonagricultural occupations in keeping with the caste system and depended on farmers for their food. Crops raised, in order of importance, were wheat, millets, gram, sugar cane, and hemp. The little village supported a large number of livestock, mostly oxen, with practically no grazing resources.

Kinship played a major role in ordering human relations; it was the basis of such social and political groupings as the joint family, the caste, the faction, and the *panchayat*. The joint family formed the basic unit for individual identification. The caste system acted as both an integrating and a divisive force. The village was divided by factions based on kinship and organized politically into *panchayats*.

Through the joint family system, Rampur, like other north India villages, was part of an intervillage network. The people of other villages were often relatives, and entire villages were classified by kinship terminology as mother's brother, grandfather, or grandmother villages. This complicated kinship system affected marriage, which was controlled by a combination of factors, viz., caste endogamy, village exogamy, limited territorial exogamy, and clan exogamy.[7] Fathers or go-betweens had to go a long distance to find eligible mates for daughters. Wives of the village came from elsewhere and daughters all left when married.

The caste system organized life on hierarchical principles and stressed status differences between groups.[8] The Jats, who owned all the land and monopolized agriculture, were the dominant caste—dominant even over the Brahmins. The lower castes lived on the outskirts of the village and were not part of the formal caste organization. The various castes were bound by economic interdependence resulting from the specialization of occupations, which was formalized by the *Jajmani* system of reciprocal obligations. Each caste represented a distinct ethnic group with its own social identity, living in a separate section of the village and practicing the ancient taboos against intercaste contacts and relations. However, because of increased mobility, greater work opportunities, and rising education, along with legal changes, the caste system was weakening.

Factions constituted another major type of social organization in Rampur. They were small and relatively cohesive groups of varied lineage and clan composition. They acted as units in social, economic, and ceremonial undertakings. The quarrels between factions tended to develop around wealth, women, and land.

From an economic point of view Rampur was an isolable and self-contained community. Village boundaries were clear and contained within them the land and other resources upon which the villagers depended for their livelihood. Traditional local government was informal and consisted of caste *panchayats,* which cut across village lines. Recently the government established a system of local *panchayats* with power of taxation, but it had not become effective at the time of the research. In Rampur, leadership was a function of the factions and was primarily protective and defensive. Each faction or combination of factions sought to defend its family interests. The leader was essentially a spokesman for a family or group of related families and had little authority to make independent decisions or to exercise power over the group.

Children played in groups; men smoked and talked in groups; women went to the well or collected cow dung in groups; and a visitor was always surrounded and followed about by a crowd. Faces seemed secure, children were open-faced and laughing; old men were bland and peaceful; young men were restless but unrebellious; women were straight and proud. The women worked hard but did not appear drab and demeaned. They seemed strong, bold, gay, and sharp-tongued. Their skirts and head scarves were brilliantly colored with rhinestones and mirrors, and they wore heavy silver jewelry on their ankles, wrists, and necks.[9]

This description of Rampur life not only illustrates the general nature of culture; it also serves at least two other functions in the following analysis. First, it reveals the "pattern" and the "preference" dimensions of culture that were mentioned in the opening paragraphs of this chapter. These dimensions are examined below under the headings of cultural norms and cultural values. Second, this material exhibits the functional connection—the integration—of culture and social organization. This topic is examined at the end of this chapter.

CULTURAL NORMS

In attaining their ends, groups develop, stabilize, and sanction appropriate modes of action. These sanctioned patterns of activity are called cultural norms. Norms not only specify what should be done; they also define the rights and obligations of the individuals who participate in the activities.

For example, many social norms define and control the activities of individuals in seeking a job and earning a living. They must prepare and qualify for the job, follow an application procedure, and conform to the rules of the job after being employed. The rules of the job specify what an individual must do or may not do and indicate his rights and obligations in relations with fellow workers.

Cultural norms reveal the general characteristics of culture that were examined above. They are socially created, socially shared, socially transmitted, and gratifying to individuals, and they tend to become integrated through use. At least three additional characteristics should be mentioned. First, norms represent an ideal form of social behavior in a given situation. Second, because they are sanctioned, cultural norms seem to embody a force that constrains individuals to conform to the ideal. And third, they reveal group judgments of preference about modes of action, and hence embody cultural values.

These characteristics are illustrated in the rules of the job. Standards of punctuality, care of tools and equipment, safety regulations, and the like define the proper or ideal ways workers should behave in the shop or office. In one way or another, all workers deviate somewhat from these rules. However, they are under continuous pressure—sometimes clear and strong, sometimes only subtle and implicit—to comply with the rules. The sanctions range from the threat of loss of job to eyebrow raising or exaggerated expressions of shock. The rules, written and unwritten, reflect judgments of preference and desirability with reference to the possible alternatives existing in the work situation.

Types of Norms ❯ Cultural norms may be classified in terms of several different dimensions. They are differentiated by reference to the kind of sanctions applied. Norms are also classified in terms of the manner by which they came into being. Again, norms are distinguished with reference to their degree of prevalence in a given society. Each of these dimensions provides categories that are sociologically useful. In the following paragraphs four types of cultural norms are described briefly.

(1) *Folkways* are the ordinary forms of social behavior. They are the routine habits of daily social intercourse. In a real sense they are ways of the folk, for they arise from the context of interpersonal relationships, are unwritten and uncodified, and are transmitted down

through the generations. Such common activities as social courtesies, customs of the street and highway, table manners and food preferences, and certain modes of dress are folkways.

Some folkways are technical in nature and dependent upon the cultural equipment with which they are connected. They include the skills and techniques for manipulating tools, machinery, and other individuals in highly standardized social situations. Essentially technical rather than personal, such folkways arise from the rational adaptation of social action to the characteristics of technical equipment or activity. Often they are written and codified and consciously transmitted. For example, the norms connected with driving a car—steering, shifting gears, manipulating brake and accelerator pedals, operating the instrument panel, and giving hand traffic signals—illustrate this class of folkways.

(2) *Mores* are the norms regarded as essential to the welfare of the society. They mark off areas of necessary or required behavior. Mores reflect some measure of conscious appraisal by the society, and they therefore embody a group judgment of high value. Mores are enforced by powerful group sanctions, and their violation leads to punishment. In this respect they differ from folkways, whose sanctions are relatively mild and informal. Often only a fine or blurred line distinguishes mores from folkways.

In American economic life, private property, profits, contracts, and free competition are supported by mores. Among the Todas of southern India, on the other hand, land cannot be privately owned, for it belongs to the whole tribe. Premarital chastity, monogamous marriage, and marital fidelity are cardinal family-sex mores in Western societies. In contrast, the Todas practice fraternal polyandry (the marriage of two or more brothers to one wife), and their family mores forbid jealousy between brothers.

(3) *Taboos* are negative or prohibitive mores. They designate forbidden activities. Their enforcement is considered essential to the welfare of the group. Their violation may be severely punished, and may be thought to cause group disasters. Certain forms of incest are tabooed in every human society, and in the United States sexual promiscuity, interracial sex contacts, and violation of the Sabbath are usually associated with taboos.

(4) *Laws* are norms sanctioned by the authority of government. If unwritten, existing in customary practice, and sanctioned by tribal councils or other communal agencies, they are called common laws. When enacted by legislative bodies, written and codified, and enforced by an agency of formal government, they are statutory laws. Federal statutes in the United States, for example, require every person earning a designated amount during a calendar year to file an income-tax return. In some states, however, marriage may be contracted by common-law usage. Many of our most important mores and taboos,

such as those forbidding incest or theft, are also codified into laws and are enforced by governmental authority.

Universals and Alternatives ▶ Cultural norms are distinguished also in terms of their prevalence in a society. Some of each of the types of norms just described are practiced by almost all the members of a given society. For certain activities, however, a culture may have two or more possible norms which are similar in value and degree of preference. Ralph Linton has called these classes of norms "universals" and "alternatives," respectively.[10] Choice between alternative norms may be a matter of class, ethnic, regional, or other tradition, or of individual or family preference. This distinction among norms provides a key to the uniformity and variability of culture and aids in explaining the similarities and dissimilarities of social behavior. For example, in the United States the practice of shaving is very widespread, i.e., a universal pattern among adult males. Alternative norms, however, permit considerable variability in the frequency, time, and the manner of shaving. While a man may feel constrained to shave, he may choose a straight razor, a safety razor, or an electric shaver.

Organization of Culture ▶ Cultural norms never exist in isolation. They arise, function, persist, and disappear as integral constituents of normative orders. Within such orders their arrangement varies widely in degree of harmony. In some situations they are closely integrated; elsewhere, component norms may be only loosely harmonized or even in conflict. The organization of cultural norms can be analyzed in terms of the size and inclusiveness of the cultural units in which they function.

The *cultural complex* is the basic distinguishable unit of functionally interrelated elements. Cultural norms and values exist and function as constituent elements of cultural complexes. In this manner they are integrated into the total culture and gain functional significance. An occupation or craft may be cited as an illustration of a cultural complex. It is composed of a functional cluster of specific skills and pieces of equipment. For example, the *Dictionary of Occupational Titles* gives the following job description in which blacksmithing is described as a cultural complex:

Forges metal objects and parts for building, repairing, or manufacturing equipment. Heats metal in forge and hammers it into a desired shape on anvil, with steam, electric, or compressed-air-powered hammer. Forge-welds metals by heating parts and hammering them together. Sharpens hand and machine tools, such as chisels, drills, and picks, by heating them and hammering the cutting edges to proper shape, . . . tempers metal by heating it to proper temperature and then dipping it into a quenching medium; repairs or builds equipment, such as sleds, wheelbarrows, small tools and hooks.[11]

Cultural complexes are organized as functioning elements into larger units. *Subcultures, cultures,* and *civilizations* are the more important of such inclusive cultural units.

A *subculture* is an alternative and subordinate variation of a culture. Its foundation is composed of the normative universals of the basic culture. To these are added special adaptations of a particular subgroup. The whole is integrated and defines a way of life for the subgroup. Geographic regions, social classes, rural and urban localities, ethnic groups, and occupations constitute common bases of subcultures. Almost any group or category, however, may distinguish an identifiable subculture.

A *culture* is an autonomous and self-sufficient system of social usage. It is the order of patterned activity and social function that encompasses and distinguishes a society. It is composed of functionally interrelated cultural complexes. A culture is a total design for living: norms and complexes of all types exist for meeting all significant life problems. The system of cultural organization represented in the culture constitutes adaptations to the variable conditions of the society.

The names of nations and societies are also generally the names of cultures. Thus it is proper to speak of American, Mexican, or French culture. Most primitive peoples also possess distinct cultures. Reference has been made in the foregoing pages to the Rampur culture. Sometimes one culture may be found as an enclave within another; the people of Rampur illustrate this situation.

The term *civilization* denotes a constellation of basically similar cultures. The cultures included need be neither contiguous nor contemporaneous. What is essential, though, is the fact that a civilization is understood to include cultures that are basically similar in content and degree of development. Different civilizations embody different adaptive arrangements of cultures, subcultures, and cultural complexes.

Among the familiar illustrations of civilizations are Western and Oriental. Western civilization, for example, is understood to include many different specific cultures—Canadian, Swedish, Italian, Australian, and South African, to mention only a few. The similarities of these cultures result in a broad field of communication and interdependence.

The Universal Culture Pattern ▶ The differences among cultures and civilizations are immediately evident. However, the similarities among these cultural units are less apparent. For a long time anthropologists have been searching for the common elements in all cultures. One result of this search has been formulated as the hypothesis of a "universal culture pattern." It is argued that such a universal culture pattern exists because man is a single species of animal and everywhere he confronts the same basic problems. We cite two formulations of the universal culture pattern.

Clark Wissler first attempted to deduce a universal culture pattern from the studies of the American Indians. He concluded:

The same general outline will fit all cultures; thus, we say the.facts of culture may be comprehended under nine heads . . .; viz., Speech, material traits, art. mythology, religion, social system, property, government and war.[12]

The Least Common Denominator of Culture:
A Formulation of the Universal Culture Pattern

Age grading	Inheritance rules
Athletic sports	Joking
Bodily adornment	Kin-groups
Calendar	Kinship nomenclature
Cleanliness training	Language
Community organization	Law
Cooking	Luck superstitions
Cooperative labor	Magic
Cosmology	Marriage
Courtship	Mealtimes
Dancing	Medicine
Decorative art	Modesty concerning natural
Divination	functions
Division of labor	Mourning
Dream interpretation	Music
Education	Mythology
Eschatology	Numerals
Ethics	Obstetrics
Ethnobotany	Penal sanctions
Etiquette	Personal names
Faith healing	Population policy
Family	Postnatal care
Feasting	Pregnancy usage
Fire making	Property rights
Folklore	Propitiation of supernatural
Food taboos	beings
Funeral rites	Puberty customs
Games	Religious ritual
Gestures	Residence rules
Gift giving	Sexual restrictions
Government	Soul concepts
Greetings	Status differentiation
Hair styles	Surgery
Hospitality	Tool making
Housing	Trade
Hygiene	Visiting
Incest taboos	Weaning
	Weather control

FIGURE 4-1

George Peter Murdock has undertaken a more ambitious search for the universal culture pattern.[13] He examined the records of over 1000 separate cultures in the Human Relations Area Files at Yale University.[14] Murdock calls his statement the "common denominator of culture." The major categories of this model of the universal culture pattern are shown in Figure 4-1.

A MAINE HAMLET: NORMS AND VALUES OF AN AMERICAN SUBCULTURE

The following material illustrates several of the points examined above. First, it identifies and describes the norms that distinguished a New England subvariety of American culture. Second, it indicates the degree of sanction, or enforcement, that supports these practices in the way of life. Third, the terms "belief" and "code" suggest that these norms are preferred and therefore have great value for the people. In this respect the material introduces the discussion of cultural values that follows.

Attitudes toward church and school had been institutionalized for a long time. "Beliefs" and "codes" were equally influential. Two beliefs were held most firmly, viz., individualism and the continuity of customs.

Individualism. Individualism meant a person's right to be fully himself with the corresponding obligations of self-denial and self-control. The customary limitations to individualism most often under social scrutiny were orderliness, organization, cleanliness and the use of time and opportunity. An individual might depart from the standards without hurting anyone but himself since the norms were not compulsory. Honesty and sexual morality comprised the codes and no variation was permitted from the standards.

The passion for saving was one aspect of individualism. Thrift was the other side of the coin of independence. One saved to have more of himself, otherwise he might have to take directions from others. This stress on independence did not negate cooperation which was old-fashioned and hearty. Economy was tied to work and the lazy were thought to be just one step from the poor house.

The feeling for the individual in one's self was so strong that it protected all kinds of eccentricity in others. The hamlet sheltered its dreamers, its lazy man, its separated couples, its middle-aged widow with gigolos, its citizens who were just plain queer. Individualism showed in a good way in treatment of the handicapped and single women. Single women were as much at home in the hamlet as on college faculties or in metropolitan cities.

Self-Control. Self-control was a discipline, a principle of education, and a panacea. No matter what anyone wanted, doing without was thought to be better for him. Many people had never tasted spirits. Smoking was not considered in relation to health but as the indulgence of a useless habit. The town had two soda fountains but people in the hamlet did not know what an ice cream soda tasted like. Once a day was often enough for coffee.

Orderliness and Cleanliness. Order was a virtue related to organization. Organization was an essential of work. People were rated, even within their own families, on whether or not they were good organizers. Organization led into an almost excessive regard for time. In a day, the hours for meals, rising, retiring, and rest or play were fixed.

Cleanliness was in a way a component of order and organization. Not everyone could organize but everyone could clean. Washing woolens, silks and heavy clothes was a problem since they were not dry cleaned. The care of milk, butter, and other foods was extraordinary. Personal cleanliness was a matter of family habit.

Morality. Against the positive habits of industry, economy, prudence, and doing right for its own sake, instruction on what was bad or wrong was limited. Sin must not be shown except in connection with punishment. The hamlet did not have the obvious great sins. Murder was unknown. Crimes of violence against the person, theft, and graft were also unknown. The live issue, on which there was thought, instruction, and social judgment, was honesty. At this point the code began. People believed in their own local government, or else they stopped complaining the moment elections were over. The permitted defection from truth was in horse trading. It was not supposed to be honest; it was a game of skill played by two professionals set to do each other down. Suffering for the sake of doing right was a commonplace. Sexual continence and fidelity were unquestioned. Love was not much talked about as a theory, but it suffused spousal, parental, and sibling relations.

Courtship and Marriage. From about the fifteenth or sixteenth year girls and boys went around together in the evening in crowds of as many as twenty. When a couple began to go steady it was a kind of announcement. Marriage as an institution appeared to the young as permanent as the land. A man and a girl got married at the girl's house and had a wedding supper, a shower, and a party. After that they drove to their new house, a strip of land with a cow and some poultry. Perhaps the neighbors followed to give them a chivaree; but they had to be fed and were hard to get rid of. After the bride had cooked the first breakfast, the groom went away to his work in the field.

On the first Sunday after marriage, if there were services, they "appeared out" at church in the bridal clothing. Thereafter, except as the man worked in the woods in winter, they were hardly separated for a meal and never for a night. This couple rarely appeared in public except together. Their picture in the community eye was a twin picture, the woman silhouetted against the man.

The position of the sexes could be observed daily. Usually the woman had an inferior position in the marriage. Sometimes the man was subservient; sometimes the man and woman appeared equal and complementary. The total effect was a mysterious union, inevitable. If the functional balance of the sexes was changed by illness, adaptability was admired. Otherwise, it became grounds for criticism.

Classes. Regulations concerning social class were not part of the codes in the same sense that honesty and sexual morality were. But they still affected daily social behavior and could not be disregarded in marriage without heavy penalty. Class divisions were based on family money and character. Character and mentality were under review more continuously than is possible now even for one single family. Class lines could be observed in eligibility for marriage and in children's visiting.[15]

CULTURAL VALUES

Cultural values are a society's estimates of worth—its preferences and rejections. They arise from the social recognition and ranking of alternatives. They attach to virtually every individual, object, relationship, and experience of which people are aware. Responding preferentially or evaluatively, therefore, is one of the capabilities acquired by man as a member of society.

A college education, a satisfactory job, a comfortable home and automobile, and an economically secure old age are familiar illustrations of American cultural values. During the Second World War our men discovered that some Japanese soldiers preferred to be killed in battle rather than be captured by the enemy. In many societies men prefer full-busted, broad-hipped, buxom women over the slender, athletic type that Americans regard as desirable. The beatniks who haunt the streets and bars of free-thinking sections of American cities typify cultural values that contrast sharply with the materialism of the American middle class.

It is possible to identify a group's values through empirical study. For example, from an analysis of historical material and current experience Nathan Hurditz inventoried the leading cultural values of middle-class American Jews.[16] The major influencing variables were religious tradition, business ethic, urban psychology, and minority-group status. The resultant list of values included high regard for literacy and intellectuality, and the importance of study; cleanliness, sobriety, sexual morality, and family unity and solidarity; foresight, care, moderation, heightened awareness, punctuality, and exactness; and opportunism, anticipation of alternatives, flexibility, and calculability.

Characteristics of Values ▶ The characteristics of culture that were discussed earlier are also applicable to cultural values. They are, thus, socially created, socially shared, socially transmitted, gratifying to people, and inclined to become harmonized. Three additional characteristics of cultural values should be mentioned. First, every culture attributes relative preference or worth to their actual patterns of activity as well as to the goals of activity. Thus, both social means and social ends are invested with values. For example, in both America and China the enjoyment of adequate and well-prepared food is a value that individuals seek for themselves and their families. However, Americans prefer to sit on chairs at tables and eat with knives and forks, while the Chinese prefer to sit cross-legged on straw mats and eat with chopsticks. Americans like beef and potatoes, while the Chinese prefer rice and fish.

Second, since values often represent alternatives that cannot be attained simultaneously, they must be ranked in terms of relative worth or preference. The ranking of values is illustrated in many familiar situations. The female graduates of a high school may go to college, get married and not go to college, go to work and neither attend college nor get married, enter the military service in lieu of all these alternatives, etc. Since they cannot do all these things simultaneously they must rank these possible careers in order to make a choice. Planning by a newly married couple with limited income may involve the ranking and choice among such values as a new home, a new car, and a baby. Their income may not permit all these desired values in the first years of marriage.

And third, values differ in their effects upon the social organization and the individuals who entertain them. As was noted in the discussion of social functions in Chapter 3, some valued means and ends may contribute to the well-being of the social organization and of the participants. For example, in the Maine hamlet described above, hard work, economy, honesty, prudence, and sexual morality were essential to the way of life and contributed to the well-being of the people. In American sports, fair play is essential to the game and the safety of the players. The free enterprise system rests upon such values as private property, contracts, and free competition.

However, some values are harmful both to social organization and to individuals. The positive values of a subgroup may be disapproved of or harmful for the larger society. For example, in some groups theft, dope pushing, fraud, and collusion constitute desirable means to attain ends that have general approval.[17] In the general society, however, these practices have negative value and are regarded as dysfunctional. Poverty, waste, social conflict, and racial discrimination are negatively evaluated in the American cultural system.

Four brief cases have been selected to illustrate the nature and functions of values. Two primitive and two industrial societies are contrasted. The cases show how differently human beings evaluate the same ends of collective endeavor. They also demonstrate how values serve to shape and direct social activity. These cases will introduce the discussion of the organization of values that follows.

Hopi Values. In Hopi culture the main consideration seems to be the group. The individual is subordinated to the group, which serves to protect and sustain him.

Family life, farming, hunting, government, ceremonies, and the other collective activities stress nonassertive cooperation of group members. Ambition and striving for wealth, power, and prestige—even though these conditions are prized—are disapproved and viewed with suspicion. The collective pressure of the society supports conformity to group tradition and ways. Nonaggressiveness is favored, although the culture provides opportunities for the expression of hostility through gossip, female dominance, ceremonies, and the like.

The culture disapproves of self-assertive striving, yet maximizes individual security. Children are treasured, and every adult female relative functions as a mother. Childhood is marked by permissiveness, few routines, and great indulgence. The culture thus fosters strong dependence of the individual on the group for support and expression. The ideal Hopi individual is cooperative, conformist, dependent, nonassertive, nonaggressive, and secure.[18]

Kwakiutl Values. The culture of the Kwakiutls contrasts sharply with that of the Hopi. Inhabiting a narrow strip of Alaskan coast, these people have access to rich resources of sea and forest. They build houses and ceremonial halls of cedar planks, make wood carvings and totem poles without metal tools, and paint stylized animal designs on buildings, artifacts, and even their bodies. Their dances are ecstatic and tend to support the individualistic orientation of the culture.

The central value of Kwakiutl culture is individual prestige, which is established, maintained, and enhanced through extravagant competition. Suspicion and rivalry in interpersonal relations are stressed. The individual is trained to be aggressive and self-assertive. A man increases his prestige by putting his rivals to shame. As a consequence, the individual becomes defensive, tense, and insecure. His prestige can be maintained only by eternal rivalry and every man is a threat to every other.

Although virtually every life situation functions to produce prestige or shame, the main status-producing institution is the "potlatch." A potlatch is a great feast at which a man heaps his rival with gifts of etched copper sheets, cedar bark blankets, canoes, and shell money, or destroys these articles in great ceremonial bonfires. The greater the display, the greater the prestige that accrues. This display is accompanied by speeches of self-praise and scorn for the rival. The rival can escape the shame and retrieve his prestige only by a greater display of conspicuous waste.

Children are early introduced to this pattern by parents who stake them to articles to be lent under a system of obligatory reimbursement with interest. When a youth is ready, his parents help him give his first potlatch. Marriage is also used as the occasion for the exchange or destruction of wealth. Under the burden of inescapable shame individuals sometimes commit suicide. The typical Kwakiutl is therefore prestige-oriented, individualistically self-assertive, highly emotional, suspicious, tense, and insecure.[19]

Values of the American Economic System. Economic activity in the United States rests upon four cardinal moral values:
   The private ownership of the tools of production, trade, and service.
   Freedom of individuals, both singly and collectively, to risk private property in initiating economic activity.
   The conviction that "free competition" is the most desirable process of economic relations.
   The conviction that the chance to earn profits is a legitimate reason for risking private property in competitive economic activity.

In the United States, individuals participate in economic activity through four basic social roles which are differentially evaluated and ranked.
   As owners—stock-holders and policy-makers.
   As managers—policy administrators.
   As workers—production and service operators.
   As consumers of goods and services (include individuals in the three other roles).

Although in the last analysis the consumers determine the basic decisions in the process of economic activity in the United States, four major groups

exercise intervening control. In combination or in competition they decide who makes and gets what and in what proportions. The four groups are:
Business, both big and small.
Government, representing the public.
Organized labor.
Organized agriculture.

Although devoted to making profits, economic activity in the United States at present also assigns value to four intervening goals.
Production of goods and services and productivity, or efficiency of productive operations.
Promotion of consumer satisfactions through the use of goods and services.
The continuation of profits and power through conservation and expansion of such socioeconomic resources as good will, market reputation, public image, and the like.
Developing responsibility for the general welfare.[20]

Soviet Economic Values. In the Soviet Union, official economic values are distinguished from private values. Under the official Communist ideology there are four cardinal economic values.
Collective ownership of the major tools of production, trade, and service.
The conduct of economic activity for political and ideological ends.
Detailed planning and control of internal economic operations and external economic relations.
Economic motivation by collective incentives, such as the common good, national pride, and work-group prestige.

In achieving this Soviet collective goal, individuals participate in economic activity through three basic social roles that are differentially evaluated and ranked.
As officials, representing the Party, the government, and the society. Officials perform the functions of owner — policy-maker and manager — policy-administrator.
As workers, production and service operators.
As consumers of goods and services, including individuals in the other two roles.

In the Soviet system, economic decisions are official governmental policy. Trade unions are agencies of the government. There is very little private business and agriculture. Individuals are not free to decide whether or not to risk private capital in free competitive enterprise, nor does the consumer have the opportunity to select from among competing goods and services. The government decides who makes and gets what and in what proportions.

Within the official order there is a limited functional order based on private economic values of the same kind that are found in the United States. Insofar as the official structure permits, individuals own and risk private property in competitive enterprise, compete individually for economic advantage and values, and respond to individual economic incentives. This substratum of private economic valuation persists and expands because it tends to support the official system and because increasing relief from economic stringencies gives it living room.[21]

Types of Values ◗ Cultural values are functionally interdependent and tend to be arranged in orderly systems. In such systems three types of value elements can be identified.[22] First, there is a limited number of abstract, largely unattainable *ultimate* values. Second, ultimate values are rephrased into a more numerous series of reasonably attainable categories of *intermediate* values. And third, each category of intermediate values is further subdivided into an almost unlimited number of *specific* individual and group values.

Ultimate values express the general views of the group regarding the nature of the universe, the relations of man to the universe, and the relations of man to man. These views represent the group's definition of the ultimate meaning of human life.[23] They are taken as "given" and considered to be inherent in the "natural order" of things, or embodied in a powerful official ideology. Ultimate values constitute the core of the culture around which the consensus of the society is integrated.

Arnold J. Toynbee states that Western civilization "stands for the sacredness of the individual human personality."[24] The cases presented above, however, show that both the Hopi and the Soviet Union regard the collective whole as the major ultimate value. With the Hopi this view is embedded in the tradition, while the Soviets support it by an official ideology.

Intermediate values consist of reformulations of ultimate values into concrete and attainable terms. They are implemented by cultural norms operating in the major institutional structures of the society. In the United States there are broad systems of intermediate values in such areas as economic activity, government, family, education, religion, recreation, science, technology, welfare, and art. Within these broad systems such categoric goals as the following can be identified: adequate housing, freedom of speech, freedom of assembly, good physical and mental health, free public education, equality before the law, a living wage, law observance, the free ballot, the right to organize and seek opportunities, wholesome family life, equality of opportunity, religious freedom, and economic security. These values refer to obtainable objectives of individuals in such roles as member of society, citizen, worshiper, worker, family member, businessman, student, and so on.

Specific values are derived when individuals and groups make applications of the intermediate values. They are seen in the objects, experiences, and relationships that individuals and groups prefer in daily activity. Although the number and variety of specific values appears almost unlimited, they are qualified by the structure of the total value system.

For example, the intermediate value of religious freedom embraces all the multitude of specific preferences that are designated by the various faiths, denominations, sects, and cults in the United States. When stated in terms of specific values, adequate housing refers to more than mere shelter and sanitary facilities. For some people, adequate housing may be an urban apartment, while for others it is a single-family dwelling in the suburbs. It may be a ranch, functional, colonial, or some other style of building containing a family room, patio, split-level arrangement, and a host of other alternatives of personal taste and architectural style.

Some Leading American Values ▶ In every society, certain classes of things, relationships, or experiences are emphasized more than others. The four short cases presented above show that these value preferences tend to vary from one society to another. A number of studies have sought to identify the leading American values. The aim of all these studies has been to identify the typical themes to be found in the three types of values.

Figure 4-2 summarizes the findings of three recent studies of American values. An inspection of this table shows that a large number of items are regarded as important in the American value system. Despite the variety of detail, the investigators agreed upon a limited number of central values that are widely accepted. Seven items appear in all three lists and are indicated in the figure by parenthetical numbers. They include (1) some expression of effort and optimism; (2) moral purpose or control; (3) some manifestation of secular rationalism; (4) some form of individualism; (5) change or progress; (6) some expression of pleasure or comfort; and (7) some manifestation of humanitarianism or love.

This list of leading American values reveals the importance of the individual in the ultimate values of the society. It suggests also that the social whole or collectivity occupies a subordinate position in the societal value system. This value inventory provides a key to the ethos of the culture and gives some indication of the quality of life in the society.

Value Orientations ▶ The basic values of a society may not be interpreted in the same way by all people or at all times. Such variations of interpretation or expression are called value orientations. They reflect the tendency toward value styling and indicate the variable directions that values may take.

The concept of orientation permits us to recognize that although many values continue as important social elements, their interpretation or direction may change with the passage of time. Moreover, a value or group of values may be dominant in a society but differently interpreted and expressed in the several sectors and regions. Value orientations, then, constitute one dimension of cultural pluralism. Figure 4-3 lists some of the orientations (variable interpretations) of the seven leading American values.

An inspection of the table shows that there are three orientations of individualism as an American value. Some individuals, as in the Maine hamlet, emphasize the right, even the obligation, of people to express their special and unique characteristics, and to create at what-

Three Inventories of Dominant American Values

KLUCKHOHN AND KLUCKHOHN[1]	WILLIAMS[2]
View of Life (1) "Effort and Optimism" (2) (a) "Moral Purpose" (3) (b) "Rationalism" *The Individual in Life* (4) "Romantic Individualism" (a) Cult of the Average Man (b) Tendency to Personalize *Individual and Social Values* (5) Change a Value in Itself (6) "Pleasure Principle" "Externalism" "Simple Answers" Humor (7) Generosity	(1) "Achievement" and "Success" "Activity" and "Work" (2) "Moral Orientation" (7) "Humanitarian Mores" Efficiency and Practicality (5) Progress (6) Material Comfort Equality Freedom External Conformity (3) Science and Secular Rationality Nationalism-Patriotism Democracy (4) Individual Personality Racism and Related Group- Superiority Themes
GILLIN[3] (1) Personal Output of Energy (3) Pragmatic Ingenuity Mechanistic World View Mobility of the Person (5) Change and Novelty (1) Optimism (4) Individualism Competitiveness	(7) "Fair Play" Cooperation in the Com- mon Welfare Honesty or Frankness Prestige Power (6) Recreation Efficiency (7) Love (2) Inner-Regulated Morality

Reproduced from J. S. Himes, "The Organization of American Values: A Theoretical Model," Alpha Kappa Deltan, Autumn 1956, p.17.
1. Clyde and Florence Kluckhohn, "American Culture: Generalized Orientations and Class Patterns," in Conflicts of Power in Modern Culture, edited by Lyman Bryson, Louis Finkelsteine, and R. M. MacIver, New York, Harper, 1947, pp. 108-109.
2. Robin M. Williams, Jr., American Society, New York, Alfred A. Knopf, 1951, pp. 388-442.
3. John Gillin, "National and Regional Cultural Values in the United States," Social Forces, Vol. 34, No. 2, pp. 109-110.

FIGURE 4-2

ever cost a way of life out of their peculiar tastes, talents, opportunities, and decisions. This may be called "romantic individualism." It is said to have prevailed during the colonial and early national periods and is presently most often associated with New England.

Individualism is also expressed in accentuation of untrammeled freedom of the individual to attain whatever wealth, power, and prestige he can by all means at his disposal. Much is made of the opposition to restraining social control. This orientation may be called "rugged individualism." It is said to have distinguished the late nineteenth and early twentieth centuries and is today most often associated with the business and industrial communities.

In many quarters at present, social effort is heavily oriented toward individual security, especially economic. Limitation of personal risk and protection against hardships beyond the individual's control are emphasized. This has been called the "welfare orientation" in individualism and is associated with poor people in large cities.

Three orientations of the value of effort and optimism have been identified. At one time and in some places effort referred to individual, pioneering, and creative activity that may be called "frontiersmanship." Today, in many places effort is conditioned by large-scale bureaucracies, where the skillful manipulation of social relations is crucial and may be called "salesmanship." Many individuals channel

Some Changing and Variable Orientations of Leading American Values

I. *INDIVIDUALISM*
    A. Romantic Individualism
    B. Rugged Individualism
    C. Welfare Individualism
II. *EFFORT AND OPTIMISM*
    A. Frontiersmanship
    B. Salesmanship
    C. Conmanship
III. *SECULAR RATIONALISM*
    A. Non-spiritual, Non-mystical Approach
    B. Pragmatism
    C. Rational Vulgarisms—Scientism, Gimmickry
IV. *CHANGE OR PROGRESS*
    A. Natural Progress
    B. Planned Change
    C. Wish for Novelty
V. *MORAL CONTROL*
    A. Inner Direction
    B. Tradition Direction
    C. Other Direction
VI. *PLEASURE OR COMFORT*
    A. Avoidance of Pleasure as Sinful (Puritanism)
    B. Compensation for Effort
    C. Access to Pleasure as a General Right
VII. *HUMANITARIANISM OR LOVE*
    A. *Noblesse Oblige*
    B. Charity
    C. Service
    D. Activism, Reform

FIGURE 4-3

effort into the manipulation of people by morally dubious methods of a type that has been called "conmanship."

David Riesman's personality typology reflects the variable orientations of the moral purpose and control value.[25] The "inner-directed" man is said to depend upon internalized philosophical standards and moral norms for control. "Tradition-direction" expresses the dominance of the social heritage as the source of moral control and purpose. With the "other-directed" man, the source of moral control and purpose is said to be the responses of peers and associates. This model of cultural pluralism provides a favorite theme for those moralists who decry conformity and exhort people to return to control by character or conscience.

INTEGRATION OF SOCIAL ORGANIZATION AND CULTURE

In all societies, social organization and culture are harmonized in significant measure. The society is thus an operating system. The integration of social organization and culture can be revealed in two ways. From one perspective, social integration can be seen in the adjustment of cultural and organizational units of various types. Social integration is also produced by inclusive mechanisms, or integrative systems, that function to harmonize elements of social organization and culture.

Values, Social Organization, and Norms ♦ A society, as the most inclusive unit of social organization, is based upon and incorporates a total value system and a total normative system. Indeed, these systems are major dimensions of societal organization. At the same time, the consensus of the society is organized around the ultimate values and expressed in the unity of the culture. Each subunit of organization is associated with a corresponding type of value and norm. Thus intermediate values and subcultures are organizational dimensions of social categories, social institutions (including large-scale associations), and communities. Complexes of values and normative items are associated with groups, associations, and other small units of social organization.

Integrative Systems ♦ The concept of integrative system refers to the customary approach of a society to the problem of social harmony. The approach may be conditioned by many variables, such as history, prevailing ideas, degree of isolation, and level of cultural development. In time, the approach acquires social force and functions as a prime agency for harmonizing the elements of culture and social organization. The three general types of integrative systems are belief systems, rational systems, and social ideologies.[26]

There are two main types of belief systems. One type is fused into

*NAVAHO CHILDREN
are being taught to use
handkerchiefs, a product
of another culture, and
in this way are acquir-
ing a foreign cultural
pattern and a new value.*

*THIS MOHAWK
INDIAN is one of many
who have been attracted
to the dangers and em-
ployment offered by high-
steel construction, a job
paralleling the skill
and daring traditionally
required of the Mohawk
brave. Thus old values
are retained and new
skills acquired.*

the elements of an inclusive tradition. Within this tradition there are beliefs that explain the nature of the universe, the relation of man to the universe, and the relations between animate and inanimate objects. Other beliefs explain the origin of the society, prescribe its proper form, and indicate its earthly destiny.

Such explanations and interpretations are sacred and binding. In time, under their control and direction, the elements of culture and social organization become stably adjusted and harmonized. There are few outside influences and little social change to disrupt the integration of the society.

Social integration based on traditional belief systems is best illustrated in isolated, primitive societies. However, this type of belief system is sometimes also found in social enclaves in advanced societies, such as the American Appalachian mountain folk, sea island people, and the Louisiana bayou residents.

The other type of belief system is contained in a powerful religious doctrine. This type is exemplified by the early Christians, the Moslems under Mohammed, and some of the Oriental religious movements. In a sense, the society is captive to the religious faith and fervor. The whole way of life is an expression of the religious order. Strict rules prescribe the organization of the culture and the structure of groups, communities, and institutions. These elements are harmonized by the requirements of the sacred order and religious mission.

In the early stage of a messianic religious movement, the integrative force of the belief system results from the fervor of the faith. At a later time, however, religious belief may function to integrate the society through an all-powerful, inclusive institutional apparatus. This is illustrated in Medieval Europe, where the Church functioned as the integrative agency of a religious belief system.

On the other hand, rational systems employ secular pragmatism rather than sacred belief as the integrative principle. The approach to the social world is dictated by the skepticism and empiricism of science. The rational approach is exemplified in the schemes of organization and integration found in modern nation-states. Political organization is designed by a constituent convention and rationalized in the provisions of a constitution. Economic organization embodies the rationality of technology. To one degree or another, the approach of rationality has invaded every other sphere of social organization.

Under the spirit of rationality, the cultural and organizational elements are shaped and fashioned to design and fitted together with a view to harmony and efficiency of operation. The approach is pragmatic, and little weight is given to the traditional belief. As a consequence, social integration is a flexible, changing state, seldom as complete as in traditional systems.

In some societies, the approach and method of rationality are harmonized to a deliberate scheme of societal destiny. The controlling force is an ideological scheme that contains an interpretation of history, a prescription for social organization, and a judgment of societal destiny. The use of ideological systems as an integrative force is best exemplified in the modern totalitarian nations. Yet even in the co-operative and socialist countries of the "middle way," ideology serves as an integrative force.

An ideological system functions in two ways to facilitate social integration. On the one hand, the tenets of the ideology, much like religious doctrines, establish articles of faith around which elements of culture and social organization are unified and harmonized. On the other, the ideological system contains stringent prescriptions for constructing, arranging, and harmonizing elements of the social system. Because ideological systems contain elements of rationality, the social integration achieved is seldom complete and stable.

FOOTNOTES

1. E. B. Tylor, *Primitive Culture* (London: John Murray, 1871), p. 1. See also Clyde Kluckhohn and William H. Kelly, "The Concept of Culture," in Ralph Linton, ed., *The Science of Man in the World Crisis* (New York: Columbia University Press, 1945), pp. 78-106.
2. William F. Ogburn, *Social Change* (New York: Viking, 1922).
3. Melvin M. Tumin, *Desegregation: Resistance and Readiness* (Princeton: Princeton University Press, 1958), p. 34.
4. See John Gillin, *The Ways of Men* (New York: Appleton-Century, 1948), p. 179.
5. See George Peter Murdock, "Uniformities in Culture," in *American Sociological Review*, 5:361-369 (June 1940).
6. O. H. K. Spate, *India and Pakistan: A General and Regional Geography* (London: Methuen, 1954), suggests that this crowded village settlement pattern is rather typical of India.
7. Irawati Karve, *Kinship Organization in India* (Bombay: India Publishing House, 1965), reveals that marriages in India are controlled by complex kinship arrangements that vary from region to region, but everywhere depend on the joint family and caste systems.
8. See the discussion of caste in Chapter 11 below.
9. Condensed and adapted from Oscar Lewis, *Village Life in Northern India* (Urbana: University of Illinois Press, 1958), *passim*, especially Chapter 9, pp. 306-321.
10. Ralph Linton, *The Study of Man* (New York: Appleton-Century, 1936), pp. 272-273.
11. *Dictionary of Occupational Titles*, Volume I, Second Edition, Division of Occupational Analysis, U.S. Employment Service, March 1949, p. 69.
12. Clark Wissler, *Man and Culture* (New York: Crowell, 1923), p. 75.
13. George Peter Murdock, "The Common Denominator of Culture," in Ralph Linton, ed., *The Science of Man in the World Crisis* (New York: Columbia University Press, 1945), p. 123. See also Clyde Kluckhohn, "Universal Categories of Culture," in A. L. Kroeber, ed., *Anthropology Today* (Chicago: University of Chicago Press, 1953), pp. 507-522.
14. The Human Relations Area Files is a kind of library or depository where descriptions of all the cultures of which there is any record have been accumulated and are available to scholars.
15. Condensed and adapted from Lura Beam, *A Maine Hamlet* (New York: Wilfred Funk, 1957), Chapter 10.
16. Nathan Hurditz, "Middle-Class Values of American Jews," in *Social Forces*, 37:123 *et passim* (December 1958).
17. See Robert K. Merton, *Social Theory and Social Structure* (Glencoe: Free Press, 1957), Chapter 4.

18. See Robert H. Lowie, *An Introduction to Cultural Anthropology* (New York: Rinehart, 1955), Chapter 25.

19. Adapted from Irving Goldman, "The Kwakiutl of Vancouver Island," in Margaret Mead, ed., *Cooperation and Competition among Primitive Peoples* (New York: McGraw-Hill, 1937), Chapter 6.

20. In this connection see *Fortune*, February 1951, pp. 61-72; Robin M. Williams, *American Society* (New York: Knopf, 1952), pp. 136-199; and R. L. Bruckberger, *Image of America* (New York: Matson, 1959), especially Chapters 14 and 17.

21. See *Fortune*, February 1953, pp. 121-124 and 199 ff.; and Santha Rama Rau, *My Russian Journey* (New York: Harper and Row, 1959).

22. See J. S. Himes, "The Organization of American Values: A Theoretical Model," in *Alpha Kappa Deltan*, Autumn 1956, pp. 12-18.

23. Clyde Kluckhohn, "Values and Value-Orientations in the Theory of Action," in Talcott Parsons and Edward A. Shils, eds., *Toward a General Theory of Action* (Cambridge: Harvard University Press, 1951), p. 14.

24. Arnold J. Toynbee, "Freedom's Religious Foundations," in *Bulletin of America's Town Meeting of the Air*, Vol. 21, p. 3, November 1955.

25. David Riesman *et al.*, *The Lonely Crowd* (New Haven: Yale University Press, 1950).

26. See H. H. Bonner, *Social Psychology* (New York: American Book Company, 1953), Chapter 8.

Part III

GROUPS

Social groups, large associations, and communities are among the leading forms of social organization. All are called "groups" because they are collectivities of individuals that are capable of independent social action. In Part III, small groups are distinguished from large associations, and the characteristics, structures, and functions of both are examined. Modes of internal and intergroup relations are analyzed, and the concept of bureaucracy—one of the most important ideas in sociology—is introduced in connection with the discussion of large associations.

Part III concludes with a treatment of communities. The nature of communities is examined and their social and spatial structure is portrayed. The metropolitan community is described, and the chapter concludes with a discussion of the extension of the idea of "community" in the concept of "region."

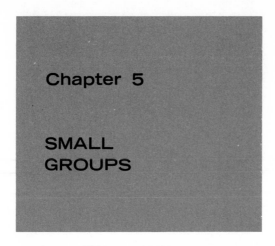

Chapter 5

SMALL GROUPS

THE NATURE OF SOCIAL GROUPS

Human life is group life. Everywhere people live in the company of their fellows. Ely Chinoy observes that "whether savage or civilized, hunters, fishers, or farmers, inhabiting desert, mountain or plain, men live together with other men."[1] Charles Horton Cooley believed that "the family, the play-group of children, and the neighborhood or community group of elders are found in all human societies."[2]

In communal societies, kinship groups like family and clan and locality groups like village and neighborhood are typical. Associational societies, on the other hand, are distinguished by the presence of specialized interest groups, large and small. Familiar illustrations include industrial and business corporations, committees, labor unions, athletic teams, political parties, staffs and squads, religious denominations, professional organizations, and agricultural associations.

Social Group Defined ▶ Werner S. Landecker notes that many different characteristics have been employed in defining social groups.[3] For present purposes, three are important. First, a social group is a collectivity of individuals (at least two) who are mutually oriented and who are aware of their distinctions from other collectivities of individuals. Second, shared values and beliefs serve to unite the individuals of a group into a more or less cohesive whole. And third, a social group possesses a system of patterned relations among the individuals.

The number of members of a group may vary considerably. Sometimes there are only two or three, as in a family, law firm, or tennis team. Other groups, such as country clubs, fraternity chapters, or garden clubs, may have many more members.

Individuals are members of social groups through positions (statuses) and participation (roles). That is, each individual as a member is located in the collectivity with respect to the others and acts in relations with them. Familiar words like brother, parishioner, or chairman suggest the status and role aspects of various group memberships. For example, brother as applied to the member of a fraternity chapter indicates the general place and the general pattern of activities that belong to all the members. As chairman of a committee, however, one brother has a special place and is expected to perform a somewhat specialized role.

Some Group Dimensions ▶ The difference between groups like families and friendship cliques and groups like professional associations and religious congregations can be stated in terms of a series of variable dimensions. Along one dimension, social roles may vary from inclusive, or all-embracing, to segmental, or narrowly specialized. Inclusive roles incorporate the individual as a total person within the activities of the group. For example, in families every member knows every other member intimately from long association, and almost nothing can be hidden from parents or siblings. However, in some other groups an individual has a role that utilizes only a segment of his total personality. He is a specialist and is not in long and intimate association with other members. This type of role is exhibited by a person in his professional association, work situation, or church connection. Fellow members know him only—or mainly— in terms of the segment or specialty appropriate to the group where they meet him.

Along another and related group dimension, statuses vary from unique to categoric. Unique statuses go with inclusive roles, and are particularized to fit the features of one specific person. The group position is a kind of personal, nontransferable possession of the member. Unique statuses are typical in families where only one particular person can occupy the place of father, grandmother, or "Tiny Tim." On the other hand, categoric or transferable statuses go with segmental roles. Many individuals could occupy the status since it is not fitted to a particular person. For instance, although only one particular man can be father in his family, almost any man with suitable qualifications could be a brother in his lodge, a member of his labor union, or a communicant in his church.

Along still another group dimension, participation may range from direct to mediated. In some groups, all members can participate personally in the consensus and activities. For example, in his family or friendship clique an individual acts for himself, relating face-to-face with others and communicating by sound of voice and sight of eye. He cannot be represented by another, for he has an inclusive role and occupies a unique status. In some groups, though, people participate by means of intermediaries. Because of size, dispersion, complexity, or the like, it is impossible for all members to participate directly in group action. A proxy, representative, or even an impersonal medium of communication mediates participation. Most people experience this situation in large groups like political parties, labor unions, or farm organizations.

Finally, groups vary in terms of the strength of member identifications. An individual identifies strongly with some groups; he may be relatively indifferent or detached toward others. As he passes from one group situation to another, he responds to the demands, pressures, appeals, and opportunities of each in terms of his variable identifications. Through such experiences, an individual develops an image of himself that is linked to the groups in which he participates. If this image is favorable, his identification with the group is likely to be strong. If his picture of himself as linked with the group is unfavorable, the individual may be inclined to dissociate himself from the group.

Membership and Reference Groups ♦ On the basis of variable identifications, it is possible to differentiate between membership and reference groups. A membership group is any group to which an individual belongs—in which he is a member by having one or more statuses and roles. His family, his fraternity chapter, and his church congregation are his membership groups. The discussion of groups thus far in this chapter has referred to membership groups only.

A reference group, on the other hand, is any group—whether an individual is a member of it or not—that influences his decisions and actions. The individual takes the group, real or imagined, into account. It is evident from this definition that all of an individual's membership groups are also reference groups, since they influence his decisions and actions. But many other groups, some he may aspire to belong to and some he may wish to avoid, also function as reference groups. For example, for a freshman a certain fraternity, to which he cannot yet belong, may be an important reference group. He controls his behavior and manages his relations in order to make himself acceptable as a prospective member. Harry M. Johnson states that a group functions as a reference group:

1. When an individual aspires to membership in the group.
2. When an individual strives to be like members of the reference group in some respect or to make one of his membership groups like the reference group in some respect.
3. When an individual derives satisfaction from being *un*like members of the reference group in some respect, and strives to maintain this difference.
4. When an individual appraises himself or his membership group in terms of the reference group as a standard, even though he may not strive to be either like or unlike members of the reference group.[4]

An individual makes decisions and initiates actions in terms of the standards and expectations of his reference groups. In any given situation, a decision or action may be more strongly influenced by one such group than by others. For example, a marriage choice may be more significantly determined by family than by political party, while voting behavior may be conditioned by political affiliation rather than by religious connection.

TYPES OF SMALL GROUPS

Social groups may be usefully classified as "small" and "extended." It is the social significance of group size that is decisive in distinguishing the two types. Typically, small groups depend upon direct participation of members, while in extended groups or large-scale associations, interaction is largely mediated. These groups also differ in the nature of their component roles and statuses, and in the strength of member identifications.

There is some difference of opinion on the upper limit of size of small groups. Some restrict the terms to dyads (two members) or triads (three members), while others include larger collectivities. However, as already noted, a limited number of members is only one characteristic of small groups. The decisive characteristic is direct interaction of members. Thus, any group is a small group if its size and situation permit and facilitate direct interaction among members. With this in mind, Robert F. Bales defines a small group as "any number of persons engaged in interaction with one another in a single face-to-face meeting or a series of meetings, in which each member receives some impression or perception of each other member distinct enough so that he can, either at the time or in later questioning, give some reaction to each of the others as individual persons, even though it be only to recall that the other was present."[5]

Formal Small Groups ◗ By reference to the group dimensions discussed above, two types of small groups can be identified. They are called informal or primary when, typically, (1) roles are inclusive, (2) statuses are unique, and (3) identifications are strong. Small groups are formal or secondary when, typically, (1) roles are segmental, (2) statuses are categoric, and (3) identifications are restricted. In this latter type, communication tends to be channeled, social relations formally patterned, and goals specific.

Familiar illustrations of formal small groups include committees, army squads, and work teams. Such small groups often constitute segments of larger units of social organization. They have been called the "building blocks" or "task forces" of the social structure. A study by John James illustrates the universality and range of size of formal small groups in large-scale organizations. Figure 5-1 summarizes his findings.

In such formal groups, patterned social relations are functionally organized around the specific external aims of the group and operate through a system of segmental social roles and communication chan-

Some Formal Small Groups in Government and Industry

Organization	Number of Groups	Range of Size	Mean Group Size
U. S. Senate Sub-Committees	46	2-12	5.4
U. S. House Sub-Committees	111	3-26	7.8
State of Oregon, Boards, Commissions, etc.	96	2-14	5.7
City of Eugene, Oregon, Executive Council, etc.	19	3-11	4.7
Sub-Groups in Officer and Board Organization in Four Large Corporations*	29	3-9	5.3

Source: John James, "A Preliminary Study of the Size Determinants in Small Group Interaction," American Sociological Review, 16:47 (August 1951), adapted from Table 1.
*Utilities, insurance, oil, chemicals.

FIGURE 5-1

nels. Thus, as Scott A. Greer has observed, sergeants and privates interact in terms of the manual of arms, for there is an external end in view, an army to be run, and a war to be won.[6] Dirty equipment cannot be tolerated. Obedience and deference are required of privates. Strict attention to military duty is expected of all squad members irrespective of rank. In these respects the army squad is a formal small group. However, as will be shown below, this group also reveals many elements of informality.

Informal or Primary Groups ▶ Small groups are informal or primary when roles are inclusive, statuses unique, and identifications strong. In such groups interpersonal relations tend to be stressed as the principal group aim. Charles Horton Cooley, who originated the concept of primary group, differentiated between primary and secondary social relations. In group research, the polar concepts of primary and secondary have been indispensable heuristic tools. Let us look at Cooley's classic characterization of the primary group.

> By primary groups I mean those characterized by intimate face-to-face association and cooperation. . . . The result of intimate association, psychologically, is a certain fusion of individualities in a common whole, so that one's very self . . . is the common life and purpose of the group. . . . One lives in the feeling of the whole and finds the chief aims of his will in that feeling.
>
> . . . It is always a differentiated and usually a competitive unity, admitting of self-assertion and various appropriative passions;. . . .

The individual will be ambitious, but the chief object of his ambition will be some desired place in the thought of the others, and he will feel allegiance to common standards of service and fair play. . . .

The most important spheres of this intimate association and coöperation—though by no means the only ones—are the family, the play-group of children, and the neighborhood or community group of elders.[7]

In such groups social roles are inclusive, statuses unique, and identifications deep and decisive. Social relations under primary group conditions are shaped by an understanding and acceptance of group norms. Although these characteristics are typical of primary groups, they also characterize all informal small groups in some measure. Thus formal and informal or primary and secondary are polar concepts denoting the extremes of a continuum. Actual small groups fall somewhere between the poles and represent some combination of formal and informal characteristics.

For example, in the army squad, the private and sergeant may forget their ranks and the manual of arms and interact intimately in a pal or filial relationship. Behavior which, in the official frame of reference, would be regarded as neglect of duty, is either ignored or accepted as a personal expression. Primary relations within formal small groups is illustrated in the excerpt below regarding the German army.

SMALL GROUPS IN THE GERMAN ARMY

In the following material about the German Army in World War II, Edward Shils and Morris Janowitz illustrate the nature and functions of small groups. It will be seen that the primary "buddy" groups of soldiers developed within the formal army squads and sections. Although squads and buddy groups are almost identical in membership, they are differentiated in terms of degree of formality of organization and relationships. Both types of small groups exist within the German Army, an extended group, and are connected with it through organization and consequences. The material describes the functions of small groups and thus introduces the next section of this chapter.

A German sergeant, captured toward the end of the second world war, was asked by his interrogators about the political opinions of his men. In reply, he laughed and said, "When you ask such a question, I realize well that you have no idea of what makes a soldier fight. The soldiers lie in their holes and are happy if they live through the next day. If we think at all, it's about the end of the war and then home."

. . . For the ordinary German soldier the decisive fact was that he was a member of a squad or section which maintained its structural integrity and which coincided roughly with the *social* unit which satisfied some of his primary needs. He was likely to go on fighting, provided he had the necessary weapons, as long as the group possessed leadership with which he could identify himself, and as long as he gave affection to and received affection from the other members of his squad and platoon. In other words, as long as he felt himself to be a member of his primary group and therefore bound by the expectations and demands of its other members, his soldierly achievement was likely to be good.

Modern social research has shown that the primary group is not merely the chief source of affection and accordingly the major factor in personality formation in infancy and childhood. The primary group continues to be the major source of social and psychological sustenance through adulthood. In the army, when isolated from civilian primary groups, the individual soldier comes to depend more and more on his military primary group. His spontaneous loyalties are to its immediate members whom he sees daily and with whom he develops a high degree of intimacy. For the German soldier in particular, the demands of his group, reënforced by officially prescribed rules, had the effect of an external authority. It held his aggressiveness in check; it provided discipline, protection, and freedom from autonomous decision.

Army units with a high degree of primary group integrity suffered little from desertions or from individually contrived surrenders. In the Wehrmacht, desertions and surrenders were most frequent in groups of heterogeneous ethnic composition in which Austrians, Czechs, and Poles were randomly intermixed with each other. In such groups the difficulties of linguistic communication, the large amount of individual resentment and aggressiveness about coercion into the German service, the weakened support of leadership due to their inability to identify with German officers— all these factors hampered the formation of cohesive groups.[8]

FUNCTIONS OF SMALL GROUPS

Some of the social consequences of small groups have already been suggested in the preceding excerpt. In a review of the research on small groups, Michael S. Olmsted summarizes their individual and societal functions.[9]

Individual Functions ♦ At least four individual functions of small groups can be identified. First, small groups serve to meet basic individual needs and to condition attitudes and sentiments. For example, the family provides the care and protection that are indispensable to infants. The primary groups in the German Army gave their members security, emotional response, and recognition.

As Cooley has shown, small groups, especially primary groups, equip individuals with basic attitudes and sentiments. He mentioned such sentiments as sympathy, loyalty, cooperation, fair play, ambition, and competition. The importance of the family in this connection is well known. In the excerpt above it is shown that primary groups in the German Army produced a number of basic attitudes and sentiments in the soldiers.

Second, small groups invest the individual with basic statuses and anchor him within the general social organization. For example, one's family gives one his basic social status. Memberships in playgroups, neighborhoods, teams, committees, work groups, and the like give him other qualifying statuses. In the German Army the soldier's status was determined by membership in a squad and a buddy group.

Social mobility, or change of group position and participation, is effected in part by alterations of small-group membership.[10] The individual gives up his part in one or more small groups and takes up or seeks to take up places in other groups. For example, when a man moves upward in the community, he may change church membership, withdraw from a lodge and join a country club, and cultivate pal relations with men of higher community rank. If a conscript in the army were promoted, he would withdraw from membership in his primary group as an initial act of upward mobility.

Third, small groups give the individual a picture of himself and of others. Direct contacts with others, whether intimate or formal, permit him to fashion an image of himself as a social actor in relation to others. Cooley has called this process the "looking-glass self."[11] The view of oneself that springs from primary relations may be inclusive and deep. In small formal groups, the image created is more restricted. The individual sees himself as official, technician, teacher, team member, or the like.

This function of small groups is illustrated in the experiences of men in the German Army. As squad, section, or platoon members they saw themselves in the segmental role of soldier. In the intimate experiences of the primary groups, however, the picture of self is more informal and inclusive. The looking-glass function of small groups is also illustrated in the case of Negroes, many of whom learn through repeated relationships to see themselves as inferior and disparaged. On the other hand, upper-class individuals gain quite a different self-image from their small-group experiences.

Finally, small groups, especially primary groups, tend to protect members. For example, one of the major functions of the primary groups in the German Army was both physical and social protection of the soldier members. This fact is especially evident in the case of defective or disabled members. The small group accommodates to the limitations or idiosyncrasies of the deviant member. The stream of group behavior tends to flow in adaptation around the deviation of the member and to absorb him naturally into the social fabric of membership.

Some Societal Functions ▶ Research has disclosed numerous contributions of small groups to the general social organization. Four such societal functions may be examined briefly. First, small groups form the "building blocks" of the larger social organization. In such large organizations as armies, industrial corporations, governmental bodies, labor union federations, religious denominations, and farm associations, most participants are members of committees, teams, squads, locals, cells, or other formal small groups. The articulation of such small formal units by some rational design constitutes one aspect of the formal social organization.

Many informal small groups, however, occupy no such rational position in an articulated or hierarchical structure. Like the primary buddy groups in the German Army, families, playgroups, friendship cliques, and neighborhoods, for example, are not rationally arranged. Nevertheless, such groups constitute building blocks in the general social organization. Their location in the general organization and their relationship to one another arise from and influence the ebb and flow of social relations.

Second, as Scott Greer observes, small groups constitute the "task forces" of society.[12] That is, both formal and informal small groups implement the performance of social tasks and the attainment of social ends. Sometimes small groups support the aims of the larger parent organization. For example, both the formal squads and informal buddy groups of the German Army aided the war effort of the military and governmental organization. Sometimes, however, small groups oppose the aims of the larger parent organization. In a celebrated study of a work group, the so-called "bank wiring room study," F. J. Roethlisberger and W. J. Dickson showed that the informal group of workers obstructed the aims of the factory by violating work rules, slowing down the work pace, assisting slow workers, and the like.[13] Every college and university administration has experienced the "obstructive" or "noncooperative" impact of some campus group.

Third, small groups are society's agents in the task of socialization. That is, they function to transmit the culture and initiate individuals into the roles and expectations of the society. Cooley long ago called attention to the importance of the family, playgroup, and neighborhood as agencies of socialization. As Shils and Janowitz emphasize in the excerpt quoted above, all small groups, both formal and informal, perform this societal task. Terms like initiation, indoctrination, and inculcation reveal popular recognition of the socialization function of small-group experience.

In small-group experience of direct close contact, the individual perceives the culturally defined and socially sanctioned models being acted out. He can identify directly with them and internalize the appropriate group expectations and self-images. For example, as Shils and Janowitz observe, squad and section leaders in the German Army facilitated identification and socialization in the context of primary group relations. In a similar manner, the culture of the factory or office is transmitted in the work group.

Finally, small groups facilitate communication. As a result of direct participation in group action, meanings can be exchanged without the intervention of intermediaries. Symbolic communication is supported and extended by peripheral gestures of face, body, voice, and the like. Everyone has experienced this direct, intimate communication in his family or pal group. It is also evident in a committee, fraternity, or staff meeting. The participation of members in the consensus of the small group further facilitates communication. The basis of meaning and the significance of symbols are already established and understood. This fact is illustrated in the experience of the soldiers in the German Army. In families, friendship cliques, or established neighborhoods, people "talk the same language" because they share a common culture and consensus.

Small groups also mediate communication between the larger organization and the individual. The stated aims or official ideology of the formal organization are translated through the small groups into meanings and motives that have validity for the individual. For example, the war ideology of the Nazi government, the National Socialist Party, and the Wehrmacht were translated into the determination to keep fighting and not to surrender by the communicative experiences of the primary groups of conscript soldiers. In a factory, the foreman provides the link between the corporation and shop organization and the small work group. In a college or university, administrative policy is discussed and interpreted in fraternity chapters, academic clubs, and pal groups.

Sometimes, however, small groups may impede communication between the larger parent organization and the individual. Value commitments, behavioral orientations, or aims of the small group may obstruct the understandings of or compliance with larger group aims. In the case of the German Army, the conscript soldiers in the field either ignored or failed to understand the ideology and formal aims of the governmental, party, and military organizations. In the bank wiring room referred to above, the workers rejected company aims and thus prevented effective communication between large organization and individuals. A campus group may misinterpret or disregard administrative policy and thus foster poor administration-student communication.

SOCIAL RELATIONS WITHIN SMALL GROUPS

Complexity of Relations ▶ We have seen that social groups reveal identifiable systems of social relations among members. In small groups such relations are typically direct and nonmediated. Informally defined roles and statuses foster primary relations, while formality of role and status support secondary relationships.

Social relations within small groups tend to be complex. Figure 5-2, for example, shows that at least fifteen possible lines of interpersonal relationship may exist within a group of six. The lines represent the channels of interpersonal relations. The flow of interaction proceeds along the lines continuously in all directions, and the streams of interaction crisscross, interlock, and fuse into a more or less stable system.

Main Lines of Interpersonal Relationships in a Six-Member Group

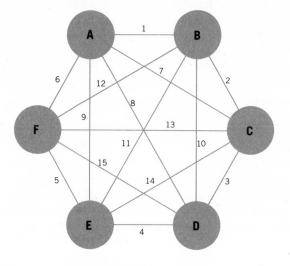

FIGURE 5-2

Complexity is also revealed in the variable, sometimes inconsistent content of social relations. For example, person A in the diagram may simultaneously cooperate with B, whom he treats as an equal, while opposing C, whom he regards as a rival. At the same time, D condescends toward E, whom he considers to be inferior, and shows deference to F, who is considered superior. The variable content of small-group relations is examined in a later section of this chapter.

Further complexity of social relations results from the tendency of small groups to develop subunits that interact among themselves. For example, persons A and B in the diagram may form a dyad and respond as a unit to the other members. Two members, such as C and F, may interact through a third member as an intermediary. Sometimes one member may act toward the entire group in the role of leader or agitator. Social relations among subunits of small groups are illustrated in the case of the "Corner Boys" presented later in this chapter.

In the course of ordinary activity, the members of small groups direct innumerable specific interactions along the interpersonal channels. Robert F. Bales and associates investigated the specific interactions that occurred in a series of small groups.[14] Their observations were made over a period of several years. Some of the groups were composed of students assembled in an experimental room to solve contrived problems. Some were nonstudent committees or work groups in their natural settings. Two therapeutic groups were also included. A large number were meetings of diagnostic committees to discuss cases in a research clinic setting. Most of the groups could be called decision-making, problem-solving, or discussion-oriented.

Each individual act in the intercommunication process was observed and recorded. The verbal unit was usually the simple subject-predicate combination. The nonverbal unit was the smallest overt segment of behavior that had "meaning to others," such as a laugh, a nod, or a fidget.

Total interactions for the eighteen six-member groups are shown in the accompanying figure. The members are ranked according to the frequency of initiation of interactions and the number of interactions received. These data illustrate some significant aspects of the complexity of social relations in small groups. First, a vast number of specific interactions takes place within such collectivities. Second, some members participate much more freely in the interaction chain than others.

Content of Relations ◗ Relations within small groups also vary in terms of their social content. In his concept of "pattern variables," Talcott Parsons provides a tool for analyzing and describing the social content of social relations.[15] Defining pattern variables, Guy E. Swanson writes: "The pattern variables are the dichotomous courses of action from each of which any actor must select explicitly or implicitly in order to formulate a choice among the alternatives open to him in any

Total Interactions by Rank of Initiating Member and by Receiving Member in Eighteen Six-Member Groups

INITIATING MEMBER	TO INDIVIDUALS						TOTAL TO INDI-VIDUALS	TO GROUP AS A WHOLE	TOTAL INITIATED
	1	2	3	4	5	6			
1	—	1238	961	545	445	317	3506	5661	9617
2	1748	—	443	310	175	102	2778	1211	3989
3	1371	415	—	305	125	69	2285	742	3027
4	952	310	282	—	83	49	1676	676	2352
5	662	224	144	83	—	28	1141	443	1584
6	470	126	114	65	44	—	819	373	1192
TOTAL	5203	2313	1944	1308	872	565	12205	9106	21311

Source: Adapted from Table 1, p. 463, in Robert F. Bales et al., "Channels of Communication in Small Groups," American Sociological Review, Vol. 16, No. 4, (August 1951).

FIGURE 5-3

relationship."[16] That is, pattern variables are opposites, e.g., cooperation or conflict, that describe the fields of choice for action and thus reveal the socially meaningful content of the social relationship. The five pattern variables identified by Parsons enable us to reveal the social content of social relations within small groups.

First, members of small groups may interact as equals or as unequals. They may be differentiated in status, authority, rights, responsibilities, etc. These criteria may be related to other characteristics, such as age, sex, education, and skill. For example, the sergeant and private interact as unequals in the army situation, although off duty in a canteen or bar they may see themselves as equals. In a patriarchal family husband and wife are unequals, but democratic family organizations show relative equality of authority and status between spouses.

The equal-unequal variable gives directionality to social relations. Between unequals relations flow up and down, i.e., from inferior to superior and the reverse; between equals interaction is horizontal, i.e., from one individual to another at the same social level. Moreover, the meaning and content of communication varies with its directionality. For example, the flavor and tone of relations between sergeant and private as equals in a bar will be very different from the content of their relations at drill or on maneuvers. Husband and wife in a patriarchal family may feel real affection for each other, but their relations will display elements of content that are lacking in the democratic family.

Second, social relations within small groups may vary with the extent of agreement among members regarding collective goals and means. Sometimes consensus in these matters is substantial. For example, conscript soldiers in the primary groups of the German Army manifested much agreement about what they wanted and how to get it. The members of a committee, work group, or athletic team may also reveal substantial ends-means agreement. Under such circumstances, relationships tend to be cooperative and satisfying.

In other situations, however, small-group members may not be in agreement regarding the ends and means of collective activity. For example, there may be discord in a family, or a pal group may be torn by dissension. Joint action is hampered and personal satisfaction curtailed.

Third, social relations within small groups may be relatively free or constrained. When participation is free, members feel few restraints to entering into all phases of collective activity. For example, in his family, friendship clique, or other primary group, an individual feels frèe to speak and act much as he pleases.

Groups sometimes impose restraint upon individual activity. Feelings must be inhibited, action guarded, and words carefully chosen. The rules of conduct and the group structure limit one's freedom of expression and action. Thus, in a committee, at a reception, or in a work team, an individual might hesitate to say things, reveal feelings, or manifest actions that would go largely unnoticed in one of his primary groups. The socially significant content of his behavior, therefore, is different in the variable group situations.

Fourth, social relations within small groups may be conditioned by specific, nontransferable or by general, categorical commitments to other group members. That is, one's obligations and actions may be directed to a unique individual, or they may be adjusted to a class or category of persons. For example, an individual has obligations to his father, his long-time pal, or his fiancée which cannot be transferred to anyone else. These commitments therefore qualify his behavior *vis à vis* these persons in a unique way.

Sometimes, however, the commitment is to a class of individuals. That is, a person may be committed to his co-workers, fraternity brothers, or relatives in general, but his relationship with any one may be equally applicable to any other. This mode of group behavior is typical of formal small groups.

Finally, social relations within small groups may define members as ends or means. The goal of interpersonal action may be some condition or effect that enhances another member. This mode of activity is typical of primary groups and is illustrated in the experiences of the German conscripts who thought constantly of each other and were prepared to make sacrifices for each other. Such a manner of action does not prevent personal ambition or competitiveness, for as Cooley observed, these ends may be consistent with the enhancement of another member or of the group as a whole. Thus a father may compete with his son in a ball game or assist the son to win some coveted place or prize in the life of the community.

Sometimes, however, members of small groups use other members as means to personal or exclusive ends. Gratification or enhancement of the other person is ignored or minimized. For example, a father may encourage or urge his son to excel in school or play to gratify his own wish for recognition or to fulfill a long-suppressed ambition. A member of a boy's gang may lie, letting another member take punishment for a mischievous act which the boy actually committed. Members of small groups, of course, may use each other as social instruments in more gross and direct ways. In all such instances the content or quality of social relations is affected by the degree to which the means variable is accentuated.

SOCIAL RELATIONS AMONG THE CORNER BOYS

William Foote Whyte studied the natural groups of boys in a large eastern metropolis. His analysis indicates how the endless flow of specific interactions achieved organization and gained meaning because they were patterned in certain more or less orderly ways. The pattern variables of group relations are illustrated in the following excerpt from Whyte's study.

Mutual Obligations. The stable composition of the group and the lack of social assurance on the part of its members contribute toward producing a very high rate of social interaction within the group. The group structure is a product of these interactions.

Out of such interaction there arises a system of mutual obligations which is fundamental to group cohesion. If the men are to carry on their activities as a unit, there are many occasions when they must do favors for one another. The code of the corner boy requires him to help his friends when he can and to refrain from doing anything to harm them. When life in the group runs smoothly, the obligations binding members to one another are not explicitly recognized. Once Doc asked me to do something for him, and I said that he had done so much for me that I welcomed the chance to reciprocate. He objected: "I don't want it that way. I want you to do this for me because you're my friend. That's all."

It is only when the relationship breaks down that the underlying obligations are brought to light. While Alec and Frank were friends, I never heard either one of them discuss the services he was performing for the other, but when they had a falling-out over the group activities with the Aphrodite Club, each man complained to Doc that the other was not acting as he should in view of the services that had been done him. In other words, actions which were performed explicitly for the sake of friendship were revealed as being part of a system of mutual obligations.

Not all the corner boys live up to their obligations equally well, and this factor partly accounts for the differentiation in status among them. The man with a low status may violate his obligations without much change in his position. His fellows know that he has failed to discharge certain obligations in the past, and his position reflects his past performances. On the other hand, the leader is depended upon by all the members to meet his personal obligations. He cannot fail to do so without causing confusion and endangering his position.

Relations Between Unequals. The relationship of status to the system of mutual obligations is most clearly revealed when one observes the use of money. During the time that I knew a corner gang called the Millers, Sam Franco, the leader, was out of work except for an occasional odd job; yet, whenever he had a little money, he spent it on Joe and Chichi, his closest friends, who were next to him in the structure of the group. When Joe or Chichi had money, which was less frequent, they reciprocated. Sam frequently paid for two members who stood close to the bottom of his group and occasionally for others. The two men who held positions immediately below Joe and Chichi were considered very well off according to Cornerville standards. Sam said that he occasionally borrowed money from them, but never more than fifty cents at a time. Such loans he repaid at the earliest possible moment. There were four other members with lower positions in the group, who nearly always had more money than Sam. He did not recall ever having borrowed from them. He said that the only time he had obtained a substantial sum from anyone around his corner was when he borrowed eleven dollars from a friend who was the *leader* of another corner gang.

The situation was the same among the Nortons. Doc did not hesitate to accept money from Danny, but he avoided taking any from the followers.

The leader spends more money on his followers than they on him. The farther down in the structure one looks, the fewer are the financial relations which tend to obligate the leader to a follower. This does not mean that the leader has more money than others or even that he necessarily spends more—though he must always be a free spender. It means that the financial relations must be explained in social terms. Unconsciously, and in some cases consciously, the leader refrains from putting himself under obligations to those with low status in the group.

Leader as Focus of Organization. The leader is the focal point for the organization of his group. In his absence, the members of the gang are divided into a number of small groups. There is no common activity or general conversation. When the leader appears, the situation changes strikingly. The small units form into one large group. The conversation becomes general, and unified action frequently follows. The leader becomes the central point in the discussion. A follower starts to say something, pauses when he notices that the leader is not listening, and begins again when he has the leader's attention. When the leader leaves the group, unity gives way to the divisions that existed before his appearance.

The members do not feel that the gang is really gathered until the leader appears. They recognize an obligation to wait for him before beginning any group activity, and when he is present they expect him to make their decisions. . . .

The leader is the man who acts when the situation requires action. . . .

When he gives his word to one of his boys, he keeps it. . . .

The leader is respected for his fair-mindedness. . . . [He] need not be the best baseball player, bowler, or fighter, but he must have some skill in whatever pursuits are of particular interest to the group. . . .

The leader is better known and more respected outside his group than are any of his followers. . . . One of the most important functions he performs is that of relating his group to other groups in the district. Whether the relationship is one of conflict, competition, or cooperation, he is expected to represent the interests of his fellows. . . . The leader does not deal with his followers as an undifferentiated group. . . .

[He] mobilizes the group by dealing first with his lieutenants. . . . The leadership is changed not through an uprising of the bottom men but by a shift in the relations between men at the top of the structure. . . . This discussion should not give the impression that the leader is the only man who proposes a course of action. Other men frequently have ideas, but their suggestions must go through the proper channels if they are to go into effect.

Role Structure. The actions of the leader can be characterized in terms of the origination of action in pair and set events. A pair event is one which takes place between two people. A set event is one in which one man originates action for two or more others. The leader frequently originates action for the group without waiting for the suggestions of his followers. A follower may originate action for the leader in a pair event, but he does not originate action for the leader and other followers at the same time— that is, he does not originate action in a set event which includes the leader. Of course, when the leader is not present, parts of the group are mobilized when men lower in the structure originate action in set events. It is through observation of such set events when the top men are not present that it is possible to determine the relative positions of the men who are neither leaders nor lieutenants.

Each member of the corner gang has his own position in the gang structure. Although the positions may remain unchanged over long periods of time, they should not be conceived in static terms. To have a position means that the individual has a customary way of interacting with other members of the group. When the pattern of interactions changes, the positions change. The positions of the members are interdependent, and one position cannot change without causing some adjustments in the other positions. Since the group is organized around the men with the top positions, some of the men with low standing may change positions or drop out without upsetting the balance of the group. . . .

Interactional Equilibrium. The actions of the individual member may also be conceived in terms of equilibrium. Each individual has his own characteristic way of interacting with other individuals. This is probably fixed within wide limits by his native endowment, but it develops and takes its individual form through the experiences of the individual in interacting with others throughout the course of his life.[17]

INTERGROUP RELATIONS

Processes ❱ As noted above, small groups form constituent parts of larger units of social organization. They are positioned laterally or hierarchically with relation to one another, like the building blocks in a wall. For example, an army is composed of several series of squads, sections, and platoons. At its grass roots, a political party contains a large number of precinct clubs. The larger units of social organization—extended groups—are themselves located with reference to each other to form still larger units or total societies. Thus, American society includes economic corporations, political parties, religious denominations, labor union federations, educational systems, professional associations, farm organizations, and so on. In a primitive society families, clans, and villages may be joined to make tribes, which are further federated into kingdoms.

Social groups thus placed in a social organization are in dynamic interaction with one another. The flow of these relations tends to shift and alter with changes of the positions and adjustments of the groups affected. The flow or process of intergroup relations forms a stream that has neither beginning nor end. The dynamic interrelations among small groups is suggested in the material about the German Army and more clearly revealed in the experiences of the corner boys. Many common words and phrases refer to the process of intergroup relations. Witness, for example, race relations, labor-management relations, Jewish-gentile relations, or international relations.

Social groups, both small and extended, touch and collide and separate and pass one another in the endless drama of social life. Their actions and interactions have far-reaching consequences for the nature and well-being of social organization. The dynamic processes of intergroup relations can be analyzed in terms of rivalry, competition, conflict, cooperation, accommodation, and assimilation.

Competition is distinguished by three characteristics. First, it is directed to goals that are limited and impersonal. Second, it tends to be expressed by continuous overt activity aimed only indirectly at competitors. And third, it enhances in-group solidarity while reducing intergroup communication and relations.

Competition is said to be nonviolent and culturally patterned. Rules prescribe the activities of competitors and impose legitimacy upon their efforts. For example, business competition is regulated by fair-trade practices of governments and voluntary agencies. The impersonal competition of wheat farmers in the United States, Canada, Australia, and Argentina is controlled and patterned by the rules and practices of the international market.

Rivalry refers to conscious competition among specific groups. For example, General Motors and Ford or Democrats and Republicans are rivals. Competition among rivals is direct, with mutual awareness and considerations of strategy and tactics, but it remains nonviolent and nondestructive.

Conflict is differentiated from competition in two main ways. First, it aims at coercing the opponent by limitation, injury, or annihilation. Second, it is expressed in intermittent overt activity. Like competition, conflict tends to enhance in-group solidarity while limiting intergroup interaction.

A labor strike, gang fight, or international war is a dramatic illustration of conflict. The methods and activities of conflict are revealed in considerable detail in the case of the sit-down strike presented at the end of this chapter. Our values dispose us to regard conflict as inherently undesirable. Much ordinary social behavior, however, seems to contradict this view, and research has shown that social conflict often has positive social functions.[18]

Accommodation refers to intergroup arrangements that facilitate joint effort and limit opposition. This process seems to depend upon three dimensions: (1) the structural arrangements among groups, (2) correlated psychic, social, and cultural characteristics of the groups involved, and (3) a system of social relations in which cooperation is maximized and conflict minimized. For example, at the outbreak of the First World War, Negroes and whites in the United States had achieved a significant accommodation. The Negro minority was fixed in subordinate status, and modes of mutual aid and acceptance had been developed. Both groups improvised many social and cultural devices to regulate antagonism and to accentuate indispensable cooperation.

Many common words suggest the process or condition of accommodation. "Victory" defines accommodation by reducing the opponent to inferior status. "Truce," "armistice," or "draw" designate agreements in which former antagonists retain relatively equal statuses. "Election," "verdict," and "adjudication" suggest accommodations through legal methods. "Negotiation," "arbitration," "mediation," and "conciliation" denote methods of communication aimed at achieving an accommodation.

Cooperation constitutes joint action for common or complementary goals. Groups are disposed to cooperate when they visualize themselves as allies, when they share similar or compatible values, when they possess attitudes and habits that favor joint action, and when the social rules permit or encourage collaboration. For example, the so-called Western democracies find encouragement and occasion for cooperation because their systems are grounded in such psychic, cultural, and social foundations.

In cooperation, groups may relate to one another in different ways. Division of labor, with different groups performing specialties, constitutes one mode of cooperation. Sometimes groups cooperate by performing the same actions, thus magnifying the total effort. In the United States the term cooperation is associated with a popular value. It cannot be argued, though, that cooperation is intrinsically more desirable or natural than conflict. Both are basic types of intergroup relations.

Assimilation refers to the process of merging and fusion through which accommodating and cooperating groups lose their separate identities and become one. The distinctive feature of assimilation is reciprocal and mutual adaptation and fusion at the cultural, social, and psychic levels. With sympathy and understanding, groups enter a new world of acting, thinking, and feeling.

The experiences of foreign-born groups in the United States are a familiar illustration. Terms like melting pot, naturalization, and Americanization refer to the accommodation-assimilation continuum. The urbanization of rural migrants and the absorption of upward mobile groups are other illustrations. In the assimilation of immigrants in the United States, Charles Marden and Gladys Meyer have identified the characteristics and goals of immigrants, the characteristics and goals of dominants, and the prevailing social structure as being major factors.[19] Within this frame of reference, recency, degree of cultural difference, geographic concentration, color, and permanence of residence are major variables.

The Individual and the Reference-Group ♦ Groups come into relations with each other when their members interact by performing appropriate reference-group roles. Each individual possesses a variety of roles that are defined and distinguished by the values (norms) of the group to which they refer. For example, a man may have simultaneously the roles of father, worker, union official, lodge brother, church leader, P.T.A. member, and citizen. Some of these are roles of small reference-groups, while others designate parts played in extended groups. Such reference-group roles commit him to certain standpoints and policies *vis à vis* individuals who are members of the same or other groups. For example, when the man speaks to the school principal as the father of his children or confers with the foreman of his plant as an official in his union, such relationships are both interpersonal and intergroup.

From the point of view of intergroup relations, an individual's membership or reference groups are called "in-groups." This term was originated by William Graham Sumner to differentiate an individual's membership reference groups from all the others, both small and extended, of which he is not a member and with which he does not identify.[20] This latter category is called "out-groups." In this perspective, intergroup relations may be seen as interactions among in- and out-groups. Thus from the point of view of organized workers, labor-management relations are intergroup relations between the union as the in-group and industrial management as the out-group. From the standpoint of Negro demonstrators, the Negro minority is the in-group and dominant whites are the out-group.

It is rare indeed that all members of one group are simultaneously in contact with all members of another. Rather, intergroup relations are normally carried on by delegated members (often officials) who act out appropriate reference-group roles of their respective in-groups. Often, however, intergroup relations are enacted by ordinary (nondelegated) members who incidentally come into contact with one another in the usual business of life. Their relations are intergroup insofar as they act out appropriate reference-group roles in these contact situations. The other members, usually the majority, behave as in-group members in respect to the intergroup situation insofar as they know about it and react to it.

The mass demonstrations of Negroes for civil rights in recent years illustrate the phenomenon of intergroup relations. Dr. Martin Luther King and other organizational officials act out appropriate in-group roles in contacts and communication with white officials and leaders. In addition, thousands of "lay" Negroes also act out in-group reference roles in the demonstrations, marches, sit-ins, and so on. They act and think and feel like members of the Negro minority group *vis à vis* visible or invisible whites. Beyond all this, however, every individual who identifies as a member of the Negro minority group responds to the demonstration events in terms of appropriate in-group reference roles. It is therefore possible and correct to speak of "race relations" to designate a process of interrelationships between the Negro minority and the white dominant groups.

Group Relations Illustrated ▶ Dwight W. Chapman's account of the famous sit-down strike in the automotive industry illustrates many characteristics of intergroup relations. Leading participants include the union, company management, city and state governments, press and radio, and an assortment of large and small groups that constitute "the public." Each of the large organizations involved, e.g., the union and the companies, is composed of numerous small formal and informal groups. Much of the tugging and hauling between union and management takes place against varying sets of legal and nonlegal rules governing intergroup relations.

The behavior of union members within the barricaded plant illustrates the nature and functions of primary relations. The case is particularly useful in demonstrating how group relations are mediated and enacted by group members who perform reference roles. Chapman also shows how intergroup relations progress unstably from one form to another in a time sequence. Conflict, cooperation, and accommodation are among the forms of social interaction illustrated.

Overt Activity. On December 28 the organized workers in the Cleveland Fisher Body Plant quit work but remained in the building, and the next day the Fisher Body Plants in Flint were similarly struck. The occupation of factories making these key parts thus brought the whole General Motors system to a virtual standstill. The strike, meanwhile, spread to General Motors plants in other communities: Cleveland, Anderson (Ind.), Kansas City.

There followed a series of antagonistic maneuvers and tactics and counter-activities by both company management and the union. The General Motors management offered to negotiate, but refused to consider certain basic demands of the union. The workers rejected negotiation on these terms. Next, the company obtained a court injunction against the union. The sheriff, however, was unable to serve the necessary papers on the occupying workers. Meanwhile, it was revealed that the sheriff owned a large block of General Motors stock. The newspapers generally condemned the strike as illegal and irresponsible and pressured the governor to call out state troops. In Flint, the company-backed Flint Alliance urged forceable ejection of the workers, reopening of the plant by force, the return of the workers to their jobs. Company and city police were defeated by the occupying workers in a skirmish when the police tried to turn off heat and electricity in the plant. Meanwhile, even under tremendous public pressure, Governor Frank Murphy refused to call out the militia, rebuked management for truculence in dealing with both government and the union, and made a powerful appeal to human sentiments in an effort to prevent physical injury and loss of life.

In-Group Solidarity. Life inside the plant was organized in vigorous support of the strike. The activity of occupation was determined and disciplined. Each building housed several hundred laborers and each had its commanding committee. The men stood guard in shifts. Ready at hand to repel attack were piles of hinges or automobile door handles to serve as missiles. Fire-doors communicating with other parts of the plant still held by company police were welded shut and reënforced by conveyor trucks backed up against them. Fire hoses under pressure to the nozzle were stretched from hydrants toward every entrance. Every man wore around his neck a scarf which, when dipped in a nearby bucket of water, could serve as an emergency gas mask. Appointed individuals served as police charged with maintaining a strict set of rules: there must be no damage to company property, no smoking except in restricted quarters, no liquor or firearms introduced into the building by union visitors or occupants returning from overnight leaves. Life within the building was organized to avoid monotony and to maintain morale. The cafeteria prepared and served generous meals at regular hours. Each man had the privilege of an occasional twelve hours away from the plant, a device which not only helped maintain spirit within the building, but also permitted the growing number of union members outside to hear at first hand of the solid and military determination that prevailed within.

Intermittent Activity. The maneuvers and tactics of both sides continued for several weeks longer in a series of intermittent skirmishes. Early the following year Governor Murphy was able to announce that a mutually acceptable agreement had at last been reached. The agreement represented a compromise of the demands of both sides in the dispute. The union, however, gained status and became the officially recognized bargaining agency for workers in the industry.[21]

FOOTNOTES

1. Ely Chinoy, *Sociological Perspective* (New York: Random House, 1954), p. 29
2. Charles Horton Cooley, *Social Organization* (New York: Scribner's, 1909), pp. 23-24.
3. Werner S. Landecker, "Group," in Julius Gould and William L. Kolb, eds., *A Dictionary of the Social Sciences* (New York: Free Press, 1964), pp. 295-297.
4. Harry M. Johnson, *Sociology: A Systematic Introduction* (New York: Harcourt, Brace, 1960), pp. 39-40. See also Manford H. Kuhn, "Reference Group," in Gould and Kolb, *op. cit.,* pp. 580-581; and Robert K. Merton and Alice Kitt, "Contributions to the Theory of Reference Group Behavior," in Robert K. Merton and Paul Lazarsfeld, eds., *Continuities in Social Research: Studies in the Scope and Method of "The American Soldier,"* (Glencoe: Free Press, 1950), pp. 53-81.
5. Robert F. Bales, "A Theoretical Framework for Interactional Process Analysis," in Dorwin Cartwright and Alvin Zander, eds., *Group Dynamics* (Evanston: Row Peterson, 1956), p. 30.
6. Scott A. Greer, *Social Organization* (New York: Random House, 1955), pp. 34-35.
7. Cooley, *op. cit.,* pp. 23-24.
8. Adapted from Edward A. Shils and Morris Janowitz, "Cohesion and Disintegration in the Wehrmacht in World War II," in *Public Opinion Quarterly,* 12:280-315 (Summer 1948).
9. Michael S. Olmsted, *The Small Group* (New York: Random House, 1959), pp. 46-62.
10. Merton and Kitt, *op. cit.,* pp. 59-70.
11. For a fuller discussion of this topic see Chapter 12 below.
12. Greer, *op. cit.,* pp. 33-39.
13. F. J. Roethlisberger and W. J. Dickson, *Management and the Worker* (Cambridge: Harvard University Press, 1939).
14. Robert F. Bales *et al.,* "Channels of Communication in Small Groups," in *American Sociological Review,* 16:461-468 (August 1951).
15. Talcott Parsons, *Working Papers in the Theory of Action* (Glencoe: Free Press, 1953), pp. 63-109.
16. Guy E. Swanson, "Pattern Variables," in Gould and Kolb, *op. cit.,* p. 487.
17. William Foote Whyte, *Street Corner Society* (Chicago: University of Chicago Press, 1943), pp. 251-263.
18. See Lewis Coser, *The Functions of Social Conflict* (Glencoe: Free Press, 1956).
19. Charles F. Marden and Gladys Meyer, *Minorities in American Society* (New York: American Book Company, 1962), pp. 92-94.
20. William Graham Sumner, *Folkways* (Boston: Ginn, 1906), p. 12.
21. Condensed and adapted from Dwight W. Chapman, "Industrial Conflict in Detroit," quoted in Logan Wilson and William L. Kolb, eds., *Sociological Analysis* (New York: Harcourt, Brace, 1949), pp. 727-740.

THE HELL'S ANGELS: AN "OUTLAW" SMALL GROUP

SMALL GROUPS — small collectivities of individuals with shared values and beliefs — are characteristic of associational societies. Members participate directly in the life of the group and each identifies strongly with the group. One illustration of small groups is the "chapters" of the Hell's Angels, an organization with an estimated total membership of 500, most of them in California. The organization was founded in 1950, but came to national notice when members unexpectedly roared astride their motorcycles into California's Monterey Peninsula on Labor Day weekend, 1964.

Each Hell's Angels chapter (formal small group) has a charter, elects officers, and collects dues. Members must wear uniforms, ride a certain kind of motorcycle, attend meetings, and do what the leader says. They constantly emphasize differences from outsiders, feeling that these differences give them status both within the organization and within the larger society. Through informal relations and personal experiences the small groups meet basic individual needs and condition attitudes and sentiments of sympathy, loyalty, cooperation, and competition. Thus, although members make a show of being free from social restraint, they are controlled by the group's own strict rules.

▼ *OUTSIDERS, called "citizens," silently watch Hell's Angels cyclists.*

◄ *DEVIANT SOCIAL AT-TITUDES are revealed by Angels' soiled, unkempt dress and bizarre behavior in public. Personal ornamentation reflects shared values, both uniting group into cohesive whole and separating them from outsiders. "Colors" include jacket with winged death-head and name of organization, name of chapter, and letters "MC" on back.*

▼ *GROUP LIFE takes precedence over family life for the Angels. Though some Angels have wives and children, the vast majority consider other Angels as their family. Two kinds of women affiliate themselves with the Angels. "Mamas," often as tough as the men with whom they associate, receive little respect from the Angels; "Mamas" are there to serve the needs of the group—to take care of the laundry, household, and sexual needs— and to keep their mouths shut. "Old Ladies"—wives and girl friends—are guarded jealously and treated with more respect.*

► THE "HOG," or motor-cycle, is the Angel's chief instrument for achieving freedom and power and consequently is his most important possession. Keeping bikes in perfect condition is a shared goal of the group. Here, a member gets bike ready for a "run"—a day-long or week-end ride to some sparsely populated area to have a party.

▼ THE DEVIANT VALUES AND ACTIONS that function to unify the Hell's Angels and set them apart from "citizens" also lead to strong disapproval by the larger community. The police, representing the larger community, call them "outlaws" (an antisocial out-group) and wage all-out war against them. The Angels respond by withdrawing further from the community, "defending" themselves, and "closing ranks"—typical manifestations of group conflict.

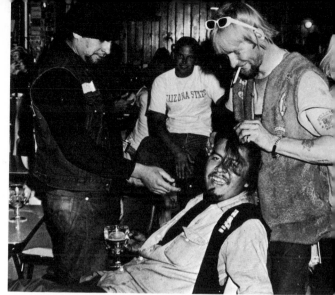

▲ *SHARED LEISURE activities include pool, dancing to a juke box, a great deal of drinking. The Angels are proud of their drinking ability— but usually stick to beer, which is inexpensive.*

▼ *CEREMONIAL ASPECTS of group life are illustrated by a funeral entourage of hearses and 125 roaring motorcycles bringing a Hell's Angel to his grave. The member was killed when his cycle collided with a car. Funeral services were held over a coffin draped by two black leather jackets.*

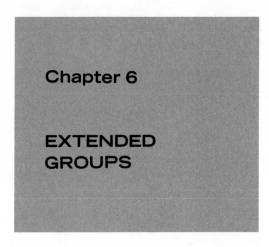

Chapter 6

EXTENDED GROUPS

By virtue of both size and social characteristics, the term small group excludes many important social collectivities. Such larger organizations may be called "extended groups." The small group is extended both in terms of the number and dispersion of members and in respect to the mode of organization. The very process of extension, however, radically alters the significant social characteristics of the collectivity. Scott A. Greer has stated the matter in the following way:

> The extended group may be thought of as nucleated, its basic working parts including (1) the small group, (2) the extended communication system which defines their relations to the total extended group, and (3) a system of control which causes these relations to persist in time. . . . It may be both primary and secondary, but its primary dimension will usually be more clearly revealed in the smaller subgroups.[1]

Extended groups, or large-scale associations, differ from other types of large social collectivities. Several types of large social collectivities are listed in Figure 6-1 and classified as structured and relatively unstructured. It will be seen that formal associations, secondary groups, or large-scale organizations are included in the category of structured units and are differentiated from other structured collectivities and from unstructured collectivities. The latter types of large social collectivities—both structured and relatively unstructured—are discussed elsewhere in this book.

It is now customary to stress the decisive characteristics of extended groups by calling them great associations, large-scale organizations, complex organizations, secondary groups, or the like. That is, reference is to a specialized kind of collectivity known as *association,* which Robert M. MacIver and Charles H. Page define as "a group organized for the pursuit of an interest or group of interests in common."[2] Modern large associations are characterized by formal organization, channeled communication, and rational control.

Some Types of Large Social Collectivities

Structured Collectivities	Formal Associations, Secondary Groups, or Large-Scale Organizations
	Racial and Ethnic Groups
	Societies, Nations, and Tribes
	Communities
Relatively Unstructured Collectivities	Social Categories, e.g., age, sex, income
	Social Aggregates, e.g., crowds, audiences, transient collectivities such as bargain-day shoppers
	Dispersed Collectivities, e.g., publics, mass-media audiences, mass migrations

FIGURE 6-1

The number of formal associations is determined by the range and variety of social ends that men seek to attain through collective action. Using collective ends as the criteria of classification, Figure 6-2 illustrates some of the variety of formal associations in American society. This exhibit at most can suggest only part of the vast number and great variety of large formal associations that characterize a modern associational society like the United States.

FORMAL ORGANIZATION

The decisive characteristic of large associations is formal organization. In this respect, large associations are sharply differentiated from small groups. Formal organization may be revealed by examining the nature of membership, the channeling of communication, the rationality of structure, and the centralization of control.

Formal Membership ❯ Large formal associations include two types of participants. One type comprises those who are members by virtue of their roles and statuses in the organized collectivity. The other type is composed of officials and employees who wield group power and execute group actions. The cadres of officials form the bureaucratic structure of the association, which will be discussed below. The roles and statuses that go with membership in large formal associations may be understood by examining the associated motivations, qualifications, rights, and obligations.

First, membership in formal associations is voluntary and is moti-

Some Illustrations of Formal Associations in the United States

1. *Political Parties*
   Democratic
   Republican
2. *Labor Union Federations*
   AFL-CIO
   Railroad Brotherhoods
3. *Protestant Denominations*
   Lutheran Church in America
   Southern Baptist Convention
   Presbyterian Church of the United States
   United Church of Christ
4. *Industrial Corporations*
   American Telephone and Telegraph
   General Motors
   General Electric
5. *Veterans' Organizations*
   American Legion
   Veterans of Foreign Wars
6. *Farm Organizations*
   American Farm Bureau Association
   National Grange
7. *Professional Associations*
   American Medical Association
   American Bar Association
8. *Business and Trade Associations*
   National Association of Manufacturers
   Chamber of Commerce of United States
9. *Welfare Organizations*
   National Welfare Council
   American Red Cross
   United Service Organization
10. *Pressure Groups for Citizen Defense*
    Anti-Defamation League
    American Civil Liberties Union
11. *Women's Organizations*
    League of Women Voters
    American Association of University Women
12. *Educational Organizations*
    National Education Association
    National Congress of Parents and Teachers

FIGURE 6-2

vated by specialized individual interests. An individual *joins;* in this respect the formal association differs decisively from some primary groups. The decision to join is determined by motives and interests of the individual and is related to the understood aims of the association. Thus, for example, a worker joins a labor union in order to get or hold a job or as a means of collective striving for the rights of the working class. He joins a church, a bowling league, or a political party for different reasons.

Next, membership in formal associations is conditioned by fulfillment of certain restrictive qualifications. These may include sex, age, race, nativity, occupation, religion, education, interests, talents, and achievements of many kinds. Application procedures or membership tests help to match the individual's personal characteristics with group requirements. For example, some organizations are for women only, others for Italian-Americans, and still others for elderly persons, Negroes, or bald-headed individuals. A symphony society may attract lovers of good music, while a social work association may restrict membership to holders of the Master of Social Work degree.

Third, formal groups also define minimal rights of members. These may include the right to attend meetings, to join in discussions and debates, to vote, to run for and hold office, to wear official uniforms, pins, and other regalia, and to receive the official publications of the association. Some associations also provide special facilities, special protections, or special services.

In addition, certain other rights and benefits accrue to members. By virtue of belonging they have the opportunity to associate with fellow members. Occasions are created for such contacts, and members are placed in favorable reciprocal relationships. Other benefits include the exchange of useful information, helpful influence, special consideration in crucial situations, and all the things referred to familiarly as "influence," "contact," or "pull."

Finally, formal membership also exacts certain specific obligations of individuals. As a condition of membership they must perform a series of overt duties and procedures, such as paying dues, attending meetings, and serving on committees. Members are expected to subscribe to the policies of the association and to champion its causes and enterprises. They must support it in public and defend it from critics. In short, to be a member of an association an individual must subject certain portions of his behavior to the regulations of the group. But since the formal association affects only a segment of his life, his obligations are limited.

For example, the member of a chamber of commerce or labor union would be required to carry out several quite similar patterns of overt activity. Although the two associations would make different ideological demands on their members, they would expect each member to espouse group aims and to defend group policies.

In sum, it can be observed that formal membership is functionally related to the overall aims of the association. However, as R. M. Mac-Iver and Charles H. Page point out, the average member has both an active and a passive formal role, which are often difficult to reconcile. Passivity tends to interfere w h fulfillment of the active membership role and thus tends to limit full attainment of collective ends. In this connection, MacIver and Page observe that when the active is subordinated to the passive formal role, "the great state tends to develop its spectator-citizens, the church its spectator-worshippers, the large corporation its passive stock holders, the political party its exploitable 'rank and file,' the union its 'paper dues-paying members.'"[3]

Formal Mechanisms ▶ Formality is typical of large associations. Activities of members are routinized and clearly related to collective aims. Spontaneity of action and individualization of goals are minimized and relegated to the small informal groups that flourish within the large associations. To ensure formality of goal-linked activity, large associations employ several social mechanisms.

First, organization is rationalized by means of an articulated hierarchy of the component small formal groups. Such component groups, or "building blocks," are variously called branches, chapters, locals, congregations, parishes, cells, and the like. The individual member belongs immediately to the small component local unit and, through this group, to the large association. The familiar "table of organization" portrays how the small units are arranged and articulated to produce the large organization.

Workers belong to union locals, lawyers to chapters of the bar association, civil rights workers to branches of the NAACP, and worshipers to congregations. The localized units of a labor union are joined with others into the city-county council, which in turn is a constituent of the state organization. The national or international union includes local, city-county, and state units as component parts.

Second, communication is channeled. Established routes are maintained for the transmission of standardized information. Considerable effort is directed toward assuring that the channels remain open and accessible. Flow and clarity are facilitated by reducing information to such standardized forms as organizational jargon, "governmentese," and red tape. Channeled communication is mediated by means such as the staff meeting, field representative, traveling inspector, house organ, memo, and directive. In large associations, official communication tends to be emotionally neutral. Further, under such circumstances communication is typically focused with relevance to collective aims. And finally, the extended communication system of large associations defines the relations of small component groups to one another and to the parent association.

Further, interaction of members in large associations takes place in terms of "participation." Thus, members pay dues and have their names entered in the official register. They attend meetings and ceremonies and give official service to the association. In meetings they may receive information, join in discussions and debates, and share in decision-making. Membership permits the individual to participate in voting on issues and candidates, to run for office, and to hold both elective and appointive offices.

For example, the member of a labor union has a card as evidence of dues paid, while a church or political party member simply has his name entered upon the register. The worker attends meetings of his local, pickets when the union is on strike, marches in the Fourth of July parade, or attends the annual picnic. As a political party member he attends election rallies, participates in the "grand debate" over taxes or medicare, and goes off on election day to cast his ballot.

Fourth, the aims of formal associations are rationally defined and consciously expressed. In terms of group process in such associations, Scott Greer calls these aims "social products."[4] They are manifest functions and are supported by the sanctioned values of the association. Often they are stated in writing in a constitution, a charter, a set of bylaws, or a public relations brochure.

Finally, large associations utilize incentives to motivate members to act on behalf of collective aims. For example, the organization rewards the faithful and stimulates the laggards by distributing promotions, prizes, honorific titles, private offices, and all the other trappings and paraphernalia of associational life. The association must transform individual motivation to attain individual ends into collective action on behalf of the aims of the association. Further, incentives function to create the sense of wider and fuller involvement than is ordinarily permitted by segmental roles and formal structure. Through the use of incentives, the association seeks to generate enthusiasm for aims and leaders and to foster comradeship among members who by virtue of their roles are only casually related and superficially involved. The task of individual motivation and control is facilitated when members are indoctrinated with the importance of participation and conformity. In *The Organization Man* William H. Whyte shows how material rewards, social prestige, acceptance, and the like function as incentives to associational conformity.[5]

Formal Power ◗ Large formal associations define important fields of power in associational societies. Power in such associations is formally organized and controlled. It may be dispersed among members in a democratic pattern or concentrated in cadres of decision-makers and officials in an authoritarian pattern. Democratic-authoritarian patterns form the extremes of a continuum along which large associations can be located in terms of their actual power patterns. Within this frame of reference the concept of bureaucracy, which is examined below, is relevant to the analysis of the organization and control of associational power.

In large associations of the *democratic* type, basic decisions are controlled by members. Leaders and officials are occupied primarily with policy administration. Familiar illustrations include most Protestant denominations; national, international, and federated labor unions; farm associations; veterans' organizations; most professional associations; many business and trade associations; and women's organizations.

For example, in a labor union with national coverage in an industry, delegated officials negotiate a contract renewal with management. Although the new contract may be approved by national officials, it does not become binding until the members in the various locals have ratified it. Or again, national officials may decide to call a strike. They cannot act until this decision has been ratified by the membership, voting in union locals. The power of members in many unions is so great that they can ignore or defy national action with impunity. For example, in the East and Gulf Coast dock strike of 1965, even after a new contract had been negotiated and ratified, some locals refused to be bound by the majority decision and remained on strike until their local and specific demands were satisfied.

In such large associations as religious denominations, labor unions, or veterans' associations, policy administration tends to become a subordinate field of power. Elected leaders and appointed officials develop an organization distinct from, yet linked to, the membership organization. As Seymour Martin Lipset shows in the excerpt quoted below, the technical demands of policy and service administration define a field of power and action beyond the understanding and control of members. This power-wielding, task-oriented organization of leaders and officials is attached to the formal membership association and reveals the characteristics of bureaucracy that are discussed below.

In large, formal, *authoritarian* associations, power is controlled and executed by cadres of elected leaders and appointed officials. The validity of their power is sustained by compliance of members with policy decisions. Familiar illustrations of authoritarian associations include the Roman Catholic Church, military organizations, and large governmental agencies.

In the Roman Catholic Church, the Pope is elected by the College of Cardinals. Other officials are appointed. Basic policies are enunciated by the Pope. Lesser officials, such as Cardinals, Archbishops, or Bishops, may formulate interpretations or policies of specific application within the framework of basic Church policy. Within the Church there are no meetings or conventions where members and their delegates debate and formulate policy, and parishes do not ratify organic policy decisions. Or again, in the Army enlisted men never attend decision-making meetings, send delegates to conventions, ratify military policy, or defy policy decisions with impunity.

In such large, authoritarian associations the formal membership has been absorbed into the formal power structure. Group members have become bureaucratic officials. The association is thus correctly described as a bureaucracy and must be analyzed in such terms.

FORMAL ORGANIZATION AND BUREAUCRACY IN LABOR UNIONS

In the following material, Seymour Martin Lipset illustrates the major characteristics, problems, and trends of large associations. The formal membership organization is delineated and the trend from democratic to authoritarian power arrangements is traced in relation to internal and external conditions. Lipset also differentiates the membership organization of labor unions from their collateral bureaucratic formality. In this respect the excerpt serves to introduce the discussion of bureaucracy that follows.

Bureaucracy. In addition to the usual tasks of collective bargaining, handling workers' grievances, and keeping basic records, a large local union may take care of workmen's compensation, apprentice training, pension plans, hospitalization, and insurance. As activities multiply, larger full-time staffs are hired. This growing officialdom, with its professional specialization, hierarchical structure, and complex procedures becomes increasingly remote from the rank and file. The member finds that his organization has lost its simple town-meeting character and is much like a government bureau.

While this process always accompanies increased size and the multiplication of activities, there are significant variations. These depend on the extent of centralization in the industries with which the unions must deal. The more centralized the industry, the greater is the development of union bureaucracy, because in order to deal effectively with management the union must adapt itself to the administrative pattern of the industry. A union such as the United Steel Workers of America, which bargains with a few gigantic corporations, must set up a union authority structure to parallel that of the corporations. . . .

Democracy vs *Authoritarianism.* A significant consequence of this adaptation is the great pressure for *responsible unionism.* In exchange for a general contract covering many thousands of workers management will demand that the unions control their constituent locals. Indeed, the possibility of offering a period of uninterrupted production is one of the union's most important bargaining powers. . . . This demand by management for "responsibility" often leads the unions to seek and exercise greater control over their members. The result is a potential conflict between the values of democratic unionism and "responsible" unionism.

"Responsible unionism" enhances organizational stability and strengthens the hand of the union at the bargaining table. But the price of union responsibility is often increased power at the top. This reënforces other tendencies toward the self-perpetuation of leaders.

By increasing the power of the top officials over local units, the sources of organized opposition are controlled or reduced. Some unions have given their executive boards the right to suspend local officials for violating policies of the central bodies. Such constitutional changes are usually defended as necessary for contract negotiations, but they also enable the national officials to eliminate potential oppositionists.

A somewhat different situation is found in highly competitive industries. Here the pressure for bureaucratization may come from the union. Large unions operate more effectively when industrial practices are uniform and predictable. Unions in the clothing industry have developed highly centralized structures and are able to persuade employers to establish similar collective bargaining procedures, sometimes by getting them to join industrial associations and to set up codes of business practice. In such highly competitive industries, unions are likely to prevent their local units from violating standard policy as are unions operating within highly centralized industries. Either extreme seems especially conducive to the development of trade-union bureaucracy.

The intervention of government in collective bargaining is another factor leading to more centralized decision-making in unions. Increasingly, local unions are yielding their powers to headquarters officials who deal with centralized government agencies.

Formal Membership. As control over decisions shifts away from the local levels, membership interest in local affairs declines. Policy disagreements become limited to conflicts over national issues, about which only the officials are really well informed. Conflicts occur more as administrative fights at national headquarters and less as political struggles among groups in locals. The implications of this shift were once expressed by a steel worker who said, "We don't have a union anymore, we have a contract. The economists and statisticians negotiate contracts—all we can do is vote yes or no on them."

When unions are small, or do not deal with large centralized industries or highly competitive ones, they may permit local units greater autonomy. The International Typographical Union, for example, which operates in an industry without large national companies, permits its locals considerable freedom in negotiations. Even this union, however, limits the freedom of its locals to strike or to make concessions to management on issues involving union security or jurisdiction over various mechanical processes.[6]

BUREAUCRACY

Bureaucracy may be defined as that specialized form of social organization that is characterized by (1) the rational arrangement of leadership, and official roles and technical processes; (2) the wielding of concentrated power; and (3) the attainment of stated goals with efficiency, economy, and expedition. We have seen that bureaucracy is either an associated or an integral feature of large formal associations. It was suggested in the foregoing chapter that such small formal groups as committees, boards, squads, work teams, and staffs tend to be bureaucratic in organization. The discussion in Chapters 8 and 9 will reveal that bureaucracy is also characteristic of such major social institutions as government, economy, and education.

Bureaucracy as a sociological concept must be distinguished from the popular usage of the term. In the jargon of the mass media and the street, bureaucracy refers to government by bureaus and implies excessive formalism, red tape, and pretentious officialism. A bureaucrat is a practitioner of such officious acts. In common parlance, both terms have a negative and unpleasant connotation. However, in sociology bureaucracy has a precise analytic meaning and important heuristic value.

Peter M. Blau points out that in historical perspective modern bureaucracy emerged from a syndrome of conditions.[7] In the context of transition from communal and parochial to associational and mass society, he identifies money economy, sheer size, the capitalistic system, and secularism as major factors. However, Blau notes that such historical factors fail to explain why bureaucracy develops in one large association and not in another. This kind of explanation is to be sought in the conditions and problems of the organization itself and within its milieu. Thus, as Lipset showed in the excerpt quoted above, bureaucratic formalization arose in some labor unions in the face of industrial centralization, and in others as a method of imposing centralization upon dispersed industries. Alvin W. Gouldner's study of a gypsum plant revealed that bureaucracy sometimes emerges to meet managerial needs where prior informal systems are no longer effective, or where such systems do not exist.[8]

Elements of Bureaucracy ▶ Max Weber, Robert K. Merton, and others have identified at least five elements of bureaucracy.[9] Together these elements form an ideal-type which appears as a variable characteristic of the organization of many small groups, large formal associations, and social institutions. Robert C. Stone says, "The characteristics of the ideal type are rationality in decision making, impersonality in social relations, routinization of tasks, and centralization of authority."[10] The five elements may be summarized as follows:

1. A series of carefully defined operational positions or offices.
2. A hierarchical arrangement of the offices with clear-cut lines of authority, responsibility, and communication.
3. Selection of personnel (occupants of the offices) on the basis of demonstrated technical or professional competence for the office.
4. Explicit codified rules and regulations, consistent with the authority system, governing actions and interactions of the office holders.
5. Security of tenure, the patterning of promotions in rank, and the possibility of a career within the hierarchy.

The elements of the bureaucratic type can be illustrated by reference to the faculty of a college or university. The system contains a series of precisely defined academic roles arranged in a hierarchy of ranks from instructor through assistant professor and associate professor to professor. The conditions of tenure are specified; a procedure for promotion is spelled out; and an individual can find a career within the system. A codified set of rules and regulations, sometimes set down in a manual, describes and governs the activities and relations of faculty members. Admission to each office and rank is controlled by definitions of required competence and examination of the qualifications of aspirants.

In empirical study, the elements of the bureaucratic type constitute analytic tools for revealing the degree of bureaucratization in a given large association. For example, Gouldner found limited evidence of bureaucracy in the gypsum plant before the death of the original manager.[11] Formal organization inhered in the division of labor, the definition of jobs, and the organization of authority; social relations, however, were traditional and informal, and cohesion was organized around loyalty to the manager. The new manager found it impossible to perform his task under such circumstances and was forced to initiate formality of rules, hierarchy of positions, and authoritarian control. However, bureaucracy developed gradually: first, installation of a system of written work reports; next, strict surveillance and enforcement of work rules by supervisors; then, replacement of some old supervisors by efficient bureaucratic officials; and ultimately, a thoroughgoing bureaucratic system.

One dimension of the transformation of communal into associational society is the pervasive spread of bureaucracy. In totalitarian systems like the Soviet Union, bureaucracy is revealed in extreme form. In an amusing but revealing experience, General Walter Bedell Smith, former U.S. ambassador to the Soviet Union, describes this bureaucracy at work. In the following excerpt note the pyramiding of authority, the formality of red tape, and the flow of routine business along the bureaucratic lines.

> . . .[We] all share in common, whether satellite communist or western capitalist, the same difficult problems of attempting to do business with a vast bureaucratic machine, where all policy emanated from the Kremlin and where a subordinate official, or even a Cabinet Minister, found it safer—both professionally and personally—not to give the slightest indication of his reaction or possible action until the most precise orders had been received *in writing* from the men at the top of this monolithic structure. I had interesting proof of the fact that even relatively minor matters, which with us would be handled directly by a junior officer, must in the Soviet Union, be passed on by a very senior official. One day, the Foreign Office replying to one of our memoranda on a routine unimportant matter, sent by mistake with their memorandum the carbon copy which was intended for file. The margin of this copy bore penciled notations of half a dozen Foreign Office officials, in increasing order of importance, and at the bottom an official OK by no less a person than Vice Minister Vishinsky.[12]

The pure type of bureaucratic official is neither an elected representative nor a voluntary member. Rather, he is appointed, either by a superior or by impersonal competition. The election of leaders and the existence of voluntary memberships determine the purposes of the organization. The technical operations for attaining these purposes, however, are carried out by continuing staffs of bureaucratic officials.

Figure 6-3 lists some of the familiar classes of bureaucratic officials, or, as William H. Whyte calls them, "organization men." Although many are found in government and economy, many others are located in churches, education, scientific organizations, and the like. In addition, there are the managers, foremen, supervisors, production workers, clerks, stenographers, secretaries, typists, receptionists, and so on who are found in office and shop.

Functions of Bureaucracy ◗ Inevitably, bureaucracy has important consequences for society. With the tool of bureaucratic structure people can manage the business of large-scale organization and complex, dispersed action. This is the social machine that goes with big cities, industry, mass communication, modern electronic systems, and the like. In short, it is possible for modern mass societies to exist and operate because they have access to bureaucracy as the method of organizing their social business.

Bureaucratic structure stresses efficiency, precision, and reliability. Wasted effort, conflict of personal interests, uncertainty of human conduct, improper or inadequate utilization of material and human resources, and the like are to be eliminated or at least minimized. Bureaucracy applies human beings and resources directly to the at-

Some Illustrations of Bureaucratic Officials

The junior executive in the large corporation

The minister in the church hierarchy

The sub-administrator in the governmental agency

The officer in the Army or Navy

The junior faculty member in the large university

The doctor in the large corporate clinic

The scientist—physicist, chemist, mathematician—in the government laboratory

The intellectual in the large foundation research project

The engineer in the large corporation drafting room

The young apprentice in the large law office

Source: *Adapted from William H. Whyte,* The Organization Man, *pp. 3-4.*

FIGURE 6-3

tainment of the social product. This is seen in national defense, the production of automobiles, and the implementation of religious activity. Charles H. Page observes of the Roman Catholic Church: "This great organization . . . enjoys their [great bureaucracies]—order, predictable action, dispatch of business [even when the "business" is soul-saving]."[13]

The bureaucratic pattern tends to spread from its stronghold in government and economy into almost every sphere of life. Behavior and relations become formalized, and life begins to lose its flexible primary-group character. This is one aspect of the disenchantment with the world that pains and frustrates many people and signals the transformation of remaining communal forms into true associational society.

Bureaucracy also has consequences for individuals. The fixed positions, clear rules, and regulated authority are sources of protection and security for office holders. The world of offices and the prospects of advancement open alternatives of individual achievement beyond those traditional ones in the risky world of social, political, and economic free enterprise. Thus the bureaucratic office holder can look forward to a steady income, a clear occupational and social status, regular increments of salary and rank, and ultimate retirement at a fixed and calculable pension.

Bureaucracy also offers its clients and customers democratic equality of treatment. The rationality of universalistic norms eliminates preference and promises efficient service to all. Equality is meted out by the social machine. Thus the customer at the check-out counter, the job applicant at the employment service window, the votary at the Pope's audience, or the freshman in a section of introductory sociology all appear the same size, are processed through the same machine, and are marked with the same stamp.

Some Dysfunctions ▶ At the same time, bureaucracy is related to the widespread alienation and disenchantment that characterize life in many modern associational societies. Perhaps most people at some time have experienced and protested against bureaucratic red tape, buck-passing, ambiguity, impersonality, intimidation, and poor service. Frustration and annoyance are commonplace, and social relations are distorted.

Alienation within the large-scale bureaucratic association is revealed in the transformation of active into passive members. With the growth of bureaucracy, the association loses its vibrant town-meeting character and participants become dues-paying, card-carrying "members on paper." In the office of the big bureaucratic industry or business, alienation is structured into the so-called "bureaucratic personality."[14] In response to the structural milieu, such individuals are said to become cautious, unimaginative, regular in work habits, devoted to the rules, obsequious to superiors—thoroughly colorless and uninspiring figures.

Another group of young people have made an accommodation to bureaucracy by leaving home to take the vows of organization, as William H. Whyte has put it.[15] Sensitive to the power process, they are rational and communicative and tend to maximize "togetherness" and "human relations." They possess disciplined minds and imaginations and retain few illusions about life in a world of power, prestige, and preferment.

The rank and file of workers at the bottom of the bureaucratic hierarchy in office, factory, farm, or mine also experience alienation. Their world is narrowly constricted by the official structure and by the repetitive and monotonous character of their work. These circumstances tend to make them dull, plodding, uncommunicative, and uninspired.

It is widely observed that bureaucracies tend to build inflexibility into their structure. Robert K. Merton has noted the tendency to exalt means rather than ends and to render the structure unadaptable.[16] For example, all forms must be completed and all functionaries consulted no matter how trivial the business or how irrelevant these activities to the business. Or again, an individual's application or claim may be denied, no matter how valid his case, because he ignored or violated a minor and inflexible rule.

At the same time, bureaucracies are disposed to become preoccupied with self-maintenance and self-perpetuation. This tendency is revealed in the time and resources devoted to defense of the public image, maintenance of the budget, protection of the hallowed program, and the like. Preoccupation with self-maintenance and self-perpetuation is most characteristic of governmental and other public and semi-public structures that are sheltered to some degree from the demands of competition and adaptive change. In time, social machines that once could boast of efficiency, rationality, and economy tend to become rigid and lose touch with changing social reality.

Many of the leading social problems of the time are in fact bureaucratic dysfunctions. Examples are such problems as chronic unemployment, poverty, agricultural imbalances, labor-management struggles, and waste of resources. Such dysfunctional consequences of bureaucratic systems have attracted wide attention and have been condemned by prevailing values; as a result, they are now targets of collective planning and social action.

Finally, bureaucratic systems function to permit or facilitate various types of deviant behavior. Prevented by organizational barriers from achieving culturally approved ends by culturally approved means, some individuals turn to culturally disapproved methods for the attainment of these goals. Sometimes fraud, collusion, unfair competition, misrepresentation, and the like are practiced on behalf of the organization. At other times individuals engage in these and other types of deviations for personal gain or advancement.

INFORMAL RELATIONS IN LARGE ASSOCIATIONS

Many social relationships within extended groups are informal and spontaneous. It is impossible, even if it were desirable, to fit all the varied activities of individuals into formal patterns.[17] In the industrial plant, for example, at lunch, in the restrooms, during the coffee break, and when going on and off the shifts, the workers exhibit an impressive panorama of informal social activity. Or, after the morning church service, the congregation breaks up into many little clusters of individuals informally chatting, visiting, or moving about casually.

The network of informal relations constitutes an essential part of the organization of the extended group. It fills out the interstices of the formal structure of roles, norms, and authority. On the other hand, the organization of informal relations is conditioned in substantial measure by the very nature of the formal structure. In the extended group, formal and informal organization are fused in the overall system of action.

Sources of Informal Relations ◗ Several circumstances of formal organization permit or favor informal relations. First, the extended group establishes numerous situations of social relationship for which no formal pattern is provided. Lacking explicit direction, the individuals turn to personal and spontaneous interaction. They become oriented to one another directly for definitions of the situation and for guidance in their behavior. Interpretations are formulated on the spot, and directives to action are perceived in the flow of interaction. The resultant flow of action and interaction tends to be personal, spontaneous, and relatively free of fixed form.

This situation can be illustrated in the context of the industrial plant. In the scramble of the change of shifts, individuals dash to and fro in cheerful haste. Freed from—or not yet confined by—the routines of the job, they pass in corridors and aisles or mill in lobbies and parking lots. The structure of the building or the flow of traffic impose some pattern and restraint, but there is a considerable realm of largely unstructured activity. The situation falls somewhere on the continuum between the impersonal formality of the large association and the unstructured informality of the small primary group.

In the lunch room or at the coffee break, relations are likely to develop informally within friendship groups. Friends gravitate together at the same table and take up a flow of relationships that has been only temporarily interrupted by the separation of the job. The situation is already defined and expectations are established. The flow of interaction is in terms of the small-group patterns analyzed in the foregoing chapter.

Second, the impersonality of social relations within the system of the extended group is often conducive to the development of informal

CHANNELING OF COMMUNICATION by long-established practice is illustrated in this large-scale organization, the Chicago Board of Trade—the world's largest commodity exchange. In the trading of commodity contracts, an out-turned palm signals an offer to sell, one turned inward an offer to buy. Fingers indicate the price. The Board is an example of a large formal organization held together by a common interest. Not all members have direct dealings with one another.

relations. Red tape, procedure, routine, regulation, chain of command, and all the other impersonal and formal mechanisms of the extended system appear as frustrating or deadening to some individuals. They are provoked to break through this dehumanizing wall to personal if not intimate relations with fellows. The breakthrough occurs not only in the structural interstices of the group, as noted above, but also within the very midst of formal and impersonal activity. That is, the individual renders the impersonal forms in some measure personal and informal by individual improvisations, adaptations, or additions.

The flow of red tape, for instance, provides occasions for informal personal improvisations. In the preparation of an official report, the individual may employ colorful language, add a humorous twist, or insert a personal note. During World War II a submarine commander reported laconically regarding an encounter with an enemy craft: "Sighted sub. Sank same." Sometimes individuals render the conformity to impersonal formality palatable by making jokes at the expense of themselves and the forms. In the factory, for example, workmen gather around a tool or piece of equipment, evidently examining it with care. Presently, they erupt into a burst of laughter following the joke that one of them has just told.

On the other hand, the formal prescriptions of the extended group are sometimes so general as to leave an individual to his own devices for specific direction. Rules cover classes of situations. The standard forms are set forth in general principles and broad directions. Hence no specific directions may be given for certain situations. Activity within the extended group may confront the individual with situations not heretofore experienced and therefore not yet anticipated by a rule. In this situation the individual is freed and forced to react on the basis of his judgment. He must formulate definitions of situations and make decisions regarding action for which there is indeed no form. His relations with others may then develop at the personal level without the guidance of established forms.

Fourth, substantial change in the large association and its situation may also produce informality. Installation of a new piece of equipment, occupancy of a new building, application of a novel procedure, modification of the formal organization, or shift of the basic group situation: all these and similar changes may render existing forms relatively inapplicable. Individuals have few clear and reliable guides to action, and thus make informal innovations.

Finally, informal relations spring up and flourish in the extended group around personal problems and interests. These are the subjects of attention and communication for which the extended group has made only limited provision. The range of such interests and problems is almost unlimited. They may include concerns about health, family relations, financial obligations, and housing accommodations. Personal interests may include, in addition to the problems enumerated above, such things as hobbies, extra-group activities, aspirations, and possessions.

Each such focus of individual attention and interest may become the basis of communication outside the formal structure of the extended group. Individuals are thrown together for prolonged periods, share such common interests, and have at their disposal occasions for communication. It is virtually inevitable that a complex series of personal and informal relationships will spring up and flourish around these foci of interest.

Nature of Informal Relations ❥ Informal relations within the confines of large-scale organization take a variety of forms. A multitude of small groups exist within all large-scale organizations. As shown earlier, the fabric of informal relations within extended groups can be analyzed by means of the pattern variables. Within the context of informality individuals may interact as equals or unequals. Or again, individuals may treat one another as ends or means. At times the response may be to the individual as a unique person by means of a nontransferable social role; or action may be controlled by regarding the individual as one of a class of individuals. Under certain circumstances, the informal relations will vary significantly in the degree of permissiveness in expression and in extent of participation.

The Bank Wiring Room: Informal Relations Illustrated ▶ The Bank Wiring Room of the Hawthorn plant of the Western Electric Company is a celebrated example of informal organization and relations within formal social structure. In this material one can see that informality not only arises within the interstices of formal structure, but also attaches to the sanctioned and explicit patterns. The material indicates how informal activity impinges upon the formal aims of the industry and reveals the extended organization as a fusion of explicitly patterned and spontaneously expressed social activity.

The Bank Wiring Room was a small sub-department where banks of connections for central office telephone switchboards, called "equipments," were assembled. It was separated by high partitions and all the work benches faced in one direction. Fourteen men worked regularly in the room, nine wiremen, three soldermen, and two inspectors. In addition, two other men were frequently in the room—a trucker and a group chief, the lowest grade of supervisor in the Western Electric Company. The section chief and foreman, higher supervisory officials, visited the room from time to time.

Informality in Work. Let us now turn to some of the activities over and above each man's special job, that were observed in the room. One of the commonest was helping another man out by doing some of his wiring for him when he had fallen behind. Although no formal rule of the company said that one man should not help another, helping was in practice forbidden, on the theory that the jobs were one-man jobs and that each man could do his own best. Nevertheless a good deal of help was given. The wiremen said it made them feel good to be helped. Donovan said in one of his interviews: "It seems like if a fellow is loafing and gets behind, nobody will help him out, but if he is making an honest effort he will be helped. Some people are friendlier than others, you know, and where that's the case you will find them helping each other out." Everyone took part in helping. Unlike some other activities, it was not confined to one social group.

Job trading between wiremen and soldermen was, like helping, forbidden in theory but tolerated in practice. An occasional change of job was enjoyed by the men in the room. But there was more at stake in job trading than a bit of variety in the work. In practically every case, the request for a trade came from the wireman, and the solderman traded without protest.

Informal Activity. Something of the same sort came out in the choice of the "lunch boy," as he was called, who went out of the room every noon to order and pick up, from the plant restaurant, the lunches for all the men. Cermak came into the room after the study was under way, and when he did, he took over the duties of lunch boy as a regular part of his job.

In the lunch hour and from time to time during the work, the men in the room took part in all sorts of games. Almost anything was an excuse for a bet: matching coins, lagging coins, shooting craps, cards, combinations of digits in the serial numbers of weekly pay checks. Pools were organized on horse racing, baseball, and quality records. In the games, the money at stake was not the important thing. Bets were small—one to ten cents—except in horse racing, which was a serious matter. The group picked out a "test room horse" and bet on him fairly consistently. The observer also included under the headings of games the practices the men adopted of "binging" one another and chipping in together to buy candy.

Small Groups. The pattern of participation in games indicates that the persons thus joined took part in one or more games, either as pairs or as members of a larger group. Participation in games occurred for the most part within two groups.

Interpersonal Patterns. The material collected could also be interpreted to show that friendships or antagonisms existed between men in the room. All friendships occurred within one or the other of the two groups already mapped out on the basis of participation in games. Several of the men were not particularly friendly with any of the others. The antagonisms of soldering unit 3, the selector wiremen, were more marked than those of any other unit. Their antagonism for Mueller is noteworthy.

Summary. Roethlisberger and Dickson sum up all this evidence by saying that, although the members of the Bank Wiring Observation Room were pulled together in some ways, for instance, in mutual help and in restriction of output, in others they were divided. In particular, there were two cliques in the room, whose membership was approximately that revealed by participation in games.[18]

FUNCTIONS OF LARGE-SCALE ORGANIZATION

Large-scale organizations of all types have important social consequences. Some of these were considered above in the discussion of functions and dysfunctions of bureaucracy. At this point it may be useful to call attention to some wider and more general consequences of large complex organization.

Societal Functions ▶ After a study of large voluntary associations, C. Wayne Gordon and Nicholas Babchuk identified three types of services.[19] They include (1) activity functions, i.e., immediate and continuing gratifications; (2) expressive functions, i.e., organized flow of symbolic gratifications in the present; and (3) instrumental functions, i.e., the social product of maintenance of conditions of effectuation of change outside the organization. The voluntary association is seen as an agency for the fulfillment of ends that have value for the society as well as for members.

In broad perspective, large-scale organizations are prime agencies for the achievement of basic societal ends.[20] Everywhere and under all societal conditions individuals are joined into large social units to modify and control the physical environment, transmit the culture, maintain internal social control, order relations with other societies, and regulate relations with the supernatural. For example, in primitive societies tasks like hunting, house building, maintenance of order, and warfare are organized and executed through the clan or village as the appropriate available extended group. In associational societies, however, political parties develop to facilitate the business of government. Economic functions take expression in such large formal associations as industrial corporations, labor unions, trade associations, and agricultural organizations.

The structure of various societies is conditioned by both the number and type of large organizations and the manner of their arrangement and articulation. As a consequence, societies tend to reveal variable organizational profiles. Some may appear to be flexible and pluralistic, while others are seen as rigid and monolithic. For example, the United States, with its multitude of diverse religious faiths, denominations, and sects, presents a profile of flexible pluralism in this respect. In countries with an established church, say Norway or Sweden, the profile is monolithic and rigid. Or again, the Soviet Union or Communist China, with a single inclusive political party, presents a different organizational profile from France, with its numerous splinter parties. These differences of profile and structure are significantly related to stability and process in the total social system.

The organization of a society is conditioned by its system of large-scale associations. Large-scale organization creates a field of interconnected areas of consensus, establishes the channels of basic communication, and structures the organization and exercise of authority. For example, in pluralistic societies like the United States or the United Kingdom these conditions issue from the clash and compromise of interests that are structured in large complex organizations. In the totalitarian societies consensus, integration, and stability are imposed through the concentration of authority in a single dominant association. The process and quality of social life are substantially different in these variable societal situations.

Services to the Individual ▶ Under the circumstances of modern life, action through large-scale associations constitutes the only—or at least the best—way in which the individual may attain many of his personal goals. Acting alone, he cannot achieve all the ends he has learned to desire. As noted, under conditions of bureaucracy the efficiency and economy of the large association in the performance of these tasks are substantially magnified. Life is therefore substantially better in many respects for the individual because of the existence and activities of large associations.

For example, the irrigation of deserts, the harnessing of water power, or the control of erosion can be achieved only by collective effort. Each individual can have a share in the satisfactions that accrue from the collective accomplishment. Under the conditions of urban industrial employment, the individual worker is virtually powerless to protect his interests in relations with the large economic association. The labor union has become the workers' organizational tool for managing these relations and achieving their economic goals.

The large association constitutes one means of integrating the individual into the formal structure of modern society. The statuses, roles, functions, and policies of his labor union, lodge, church, veterans' organization, business or trade association, and the like constitute anchors in the massive impersonal structure of the total society. They incorporate him, however much he may be estranged and disenchanted, within the purposes and processes of the larger society. Large associations give him a place, condition his viewpoint, and define his general role as a socially significant actor in the formal and impersonal social system.

Large associations function to protect individual members and participants. It was pointed out above that the small informal groups that flourish within large-scale organizations protect the individual as a unique person. Protection for the individual in the categoric sense as citizen, parishioner, or brother results from the actions of large formal associations. Such organizations establish buttresses against many of the risks that are structured into the social system itself. For example, it is only through formally organized collective effort that the individual can protect himself against unemployment, conquest by other societies, extermination by epidemic diseases, or exploitation by powerful individual interests. The coexistence of informal small groups within large formal associations ensures that the individual will be protected, to some degree at least, both as a unique person and as a member of a category of individuals.

The discussion of bureaucracy above drew attention to some of the dysfunctions of large-scale organization. These include the reduction of organizational efficiency, the growth of alienation, the trend toward organizational rigidity, and the development of conditions conducive to deviant behavior. In addition, as Robin M. Williams and others have pointed out, large complex organizations establish the structural framework for important areas of social conflict, e.g., labor-management, international, or racial.[21] In sum, although large, complex organization, especially of the bureaucratic type, is man's most effective social tool, it has some important limitations.

Sociological knowledge of the nature and functions of large, complex organizations is less complete than that of small groups, discussed in the previous chapter, or that of communities, to be examined in the following one. This is not strange, for the great complex bureaucratic structures of modern times are recent developments that emerged with the rise of industrial mass societies. Sociologists have only recently come to the study of this type of social phenomenon.

Systematic study in this field began with the sociological investigation of modern institutions like government, the economy, and education. Research was advanced by Max Weber's pioneer work on bureaucracy and his substantial contributions to methodology in this field. At present, large-scale or complex organization has emerged as a distinct field of sociological study. There are treatises and texts on the subject and it is recognized in courses and areas of specialization in the curricula of graduate departments of leading universities. What is even more important, the work thus far has defined a number of fundamental and continuing problems for research and theory testing.

FOOTNOTES

1. Scott A. Greer, *Social Organization* (New York: Random House, 1955), pp. 41-42.
2. R. M. MacIver and Charles H. Page, *Society* (New York: Rinehart, 1955), p. 12.
3. *Ibid.*, p. 320.
4. Greer, *op. cit.*, pp. 33-39.
5. William H. Whyte, *The Organization Man* (Garden City: Doubleday, 1957).
6. Condensed and adapted from Seymour Martin Lipset, "The Political Process in Trade Unions: A Theoretical Statement," in Morroe Berger, Theodore Abel and Charles H. Page, eds., *Freedom and Control in Modern Society* (New York: Van Nostrand, 1954), pp. 83 ff.
7. Peter M. Blau, *Bureaucracy in Modern Society* (New York: Random House, 1956), pp. 33-36.
8. Alvin W. Gouldner, *Patterns of Industrial Bureaucracy* (Glencoe: Free Press, 1954).
9. See H. H. Gerth and C. Wright Mills, *From Max Weber: Essays in Sociology* (London: Routledge and Kegan Paul, 1948), pp. 196-198; and Robert K. Merton, *Social Theory and Social Structure* (Glencoe: Free Press, 1957), pp. 195-205.
10. Robert C. Stone, "Bureaucracy," in Julius Gould and William L. Kolb, eds., *A Dictionary of the Social Sciences* (New York: Free Press, 1964), p. 61.
11. Gouldner, *op. cit.*
12. Walter Bedell Smith, *My Three Years in Moscow* (New York: Harcourt, Brace, 1949), pp. 108-109.
13. Charles H. Page, "Bureaucracy and the Liberal Church," in *The Review of Religion*, 16:144-145 (March 1952).
14. Merton, *op. cit.*, pp. 197-199.
15. Whyte, *op. cit.*, pp. 3-7.
16. Merton, *op. cit.*, p. 200.
17. Such relations constitute what Charles H. Page has called "Bureaucracy's Other Face." See *Social Forces*, 25:88-94 (October 1946).
18. Condensed and adapted from George C. Homans, *The Human Group* (New York: Harcourt, Brace, 1950), pp. 61-71 *et passim*.
19. C. Wayne Gordon and Nicholas Babchuk, "A Typology of Voluntary Associations," in *American Sociological Review*, 24:27 (February 1959).
20. See the inventory and discussion of societal imperatives in Chapter 3 above.
21. See Robin M. Williams, Jr., *American Society* (New York: Knopf, 1951), Chapter 6. Williams analyzes the conflicts between giant industry and giant labor in the American economy.

Chapter 7

COMMUNITIES

The community is another universal form of social organization. It is both a social collectivity and a way of structuring activities related to essential and important social functions. In one form or another, the community is to be found in every human society. As a form of social organization, the community differs from both groups and societies. It is more self-sufficient than a group but less self-sufficient than a society. The community is often one component of a society. On the other hand, groups constitute major components of communities. Both communities and societies are identified with definite and delimitable locales. Within these limitations a community may be thought of as a small society or as a special kind of large association.

Communities differ from one another in several ways. They may vary in size from the gigantic metropolis with millions of inhabitants to the tiny rural village with only a score or more of members. Although most communities are settled in one place, some are mobile, like the nomadic tribes of buffalo-hunting Plains Indians or the pastoral Kurds of the Arabian Desert. Some communities are based upon commercial or industrial activities, while others depend upon farming, mining, or governmental activities. Sometimes, social structure is relatively simple and consistent, but in other instances the community presents an exceedingly complex and heterogeneous system of social organization.

Many different schemes for classifying communities have been formulated. The accompanying figure indicates some of the referents of the term that are in current use. There is obviously considerable overlapping among the categories. At least two implications can be drawn from this array. First, community is a universal form of human social organization. Second, the term refers to units of organized life that vary enormously in size and scope.

NATURE OF THE COMMUNITY

In social science, the concept *community* has acquired two somewhat different though related emphases. Some students view the community as an area of consensus and a field of communication. Charles Horton Cooley wrote: "In its most general form it [the social ideal] is that of a moral whole or community wherein individual minds are merged and the higher capacities of the members find total and adequate expression."[1] Reference here is to a psycho-social field structure that both facilitates and harmonizes social action.

Several familiar phrases reveal this emphasis on consensus and communication. People often speak of "the business community," "the Catholic community," "the moral community," or "the community of free nations." Although a vague and unspecified geographic locale may be implied, specific reference in such usage is to value consensus and established communication.

On the other hand, some social scientists employ the concept com-

Common Uses of the Term Community

I. Primitive Communities
  A. Nomadic communities
    Food-gathering
    Hunting and fishing
    Pastoral
  B. Settled communities
    Agricultural
    Religious shrines
    Military forts or political centers
    Trading centers

II. Modern Rural Communities
  A. Communities classified on the basis of structure
    Open-country
    Village and hamlet
    Suburban
  B. Communities classified on the basis of functions
    Farming
    Extractive—mining, logging, fishing
    Storage and processing
    Residential (suburban)

III. Modern Urban Communities
  A. Communities classified by size
    Metropolis
    City
    Town
  B. Communities classified by function
    Industrial-financial
    Trading-financial
    Political
    Cultural—university, museum, observatory, laboratory
    Resort

IV. Some Extensions of the Community Concept
  A. World Community
  B. North Atlantic Community, other regions of the world
  C. Nation
  D. Region—New England, Southwest

FIGURE 7-1

munity to refer to a definite human collectivity located within a delimitable geographic area. The urban community is a case in point. While this mode of conceptualization emphasizes an area-based social collectivity, the social and psychic concomitants of consensus, communication, and systematic action are clearly implied as well.

This geographic emphasis is illustrated in much current community research. Three recent studies, chosen more or less at random, are *Middletown, Yankee City,* and *Black Ways of Kent.* Each title contains the fictitious name of a locale identified with a definite social collectivity which had, at the time of the research, an identifiable structure of consensus, communication, and action.

A working definition of community can be formulated by fusing the two emphases into a single statement: The concept *community* refers to a functionally interdependent human collectivity, residing and acting within a delimitable geographic area, persisting through time, sharing culture that establishes an area of consensus, and maintaining systems of communication and organized activities. In order to clarify further the nature of the community as a social form, we will present a short case and then later explain the elements of the definition.

BLANC SABLON: AN ISOLATED COMMUNITY

Blanc Sablon, situated near the headwaters of the St. Lawrence River at the foot of the Laurentian Mountain Range, contains the distinctive characteristics of community. Isolation enforces self-containment and self-sufficiency. Small size permits description of the total social system of the community. Prolonged stability of the community has perpetuated social and cultural integrity. The community way of life is inseparably fused with the forbidding locale that constitutes, perhaps, Blanc Sablon's most visible distinction.

Ecological Setting. In the Lower St. Lawrence region innumerable fishing villages have developed fringing upon the Gulf or the countless bays or inlets or river estuaries which empty into the St. Lawrence. It is almost needless to say that such natural geographic factors as these have determined largely the distribution of the population and have imposed at the same time a considerable restraint upon contact with the outside world. Clustered in rocky convolutions of the earth, these little settlements present an aspect forbidding to an extreme—especially to eyes more accustomed to the seemingly sculptured configurations of certain sections of the continent south and east. On one side toss the cold, foam-flecked swells of the Gulf, or of the Atlantic Ocean; on the other, swamps and bogs, terminating at the foot of hills or ridges of rock which rise to heights of about eight hundred feet, form what might aptly be called a backyard. There are relatively few settlements on the upland. Quite frequently promontories separate one village from its neighbor. Blanc Sablon is nestled at the head of a natural bay formed by two such promontories. Communication from one village to another is effected in summer and late spring by means of small water-craft; in winter, late fall, and early spring the *cométique,* drawn by dogs, is used. The paths leading over the mountains are used but infrequently, and then only in early fall and in winter, when the men foray north or northwest in search of firewood, or go hunting and trapping.

Outside Contacts. In Blanc Sablon is located a branch of the Hudson's Bay Company, and a small post office; and here the Clarke Steamship Company's "Sable I" casts anchor every fourteen days during summer, discharging and picking up mail and occasional passengers. In summer during the height of the fishing season, and following three days after the departure of the "Sable I" also appears the Newfoundland steamer "Sagona." Occasional sails likewise serve these far-flung communities. There is considerable communication constantly among Longue Pointe, Blanc Sablon, and Brador, mostly by water. In winter, fast dog-team *cométiques* pass between the villages over the mountain ridges.

Social Organization. The population of Blanc Sablon comprises 78 individuals in thirteen families, all of which are related by marriage. The community is made up of *habitants,* whose ancestors were born there, and who themselves are therefore inured to the soil. They would never consider moving away to some other locality. The women who go into or are assimilated by the group of the men they marry constitute the exceptions. It is seldom, however, that they marry outside their own locale.

Each community, though strongly integrated through residence and marriage, and possessing within its own confines a smoothly functioning local economic system, is also bound up directly with North Shore marketing and trading activities. The sea is really communal. Cod-fishing is carried on independently by each family unit, but each family's success in fishing depends to a considerable extent upon the direct cooperation it receives from other similarly integrated units. For example, one man may point out to his neighbors the better fishing locations; he may protect fishing gear other than his own, or refrain from disturbing the cod or salmon traps of others. All work harmoniously together in not permitting Newfoundland fishing schooners—the crews of which are considered foreigners or outsiders—to enter their fishing domain, except when the winds are unfriendly and the trespassers cannot with safety stand outside the harbor. Even then the schooner is only permitted to cast anchor: all rival fishing must itself be done away from the immediate territory in spite of dirty weather.

Although Blanc Sablon has a more direct contact with the city system than either Longue Pointe or Brador, Longue Pointe must be considered as the focal point for religious life of all three communities, for situated here is the Lourdes de Blanc Sablon, and here lives the parish *curé,* Père Gagne, and to here each Sunday come worshipers from Blanc Sablon, Greenley Island, and Brador. Longue Pointe and Blanc Sablon share therefore a mutual dependency; for while the former is the centre of religious life, the latter is a centre in itself of contact with the city system.[2]

Self-Contained Collectivity ▶ A community is a self-contained group. In the community, individuals depend upon one another for the discharge of many essential functions. Collective aims and individual activities relate to a wider range of needs and interests than are encompassed by large organizations. One result is the fact that the community exhibits a considerable degree of self-sufficiency. Robert MacIver has stated the matter succinctly.

. . . Wherever the members of any group, small or large, live together in such a way that they share, not this or that particular interest, but the basic conditions of a common life, we call that group a community. The mark of a community is that one's life *may* be lived wholly within it. One cannot live wholly within a business or organization or a church; one can live wholly within a tribe or a city. The basic criterion of community, then, is that all of one's social relationships may be found within it.[3]

The functional interdependence and self-containment of the community are admirably illustrated in Blanc Sablon. Within this village community virtually all needs of the members are satisfied and a self-contained way of life has developed. Communities, however, are seldom totally independent. Although an individual may live his whole life within an American metropolis, the metropolis itself is not a self-sufficient unit. Even Blanc Sablon must depend on other communities for some goods and services that it cannot provide for itself.

Delimitable Locale ◗ The community is identified with a definite and delimitable locale. It is located somewhere and its boundaries are fixed by the activities of the members of the collectivity. Even when the specific reference is to structures of consensus and systems of communication, e.g., the business or the Catholic community, a more or less definite geographic locale is implied. Ordinarily, however, the concept refers to a delimitable area that contains unique natural and man-made features to which a system of social organization has been adjusted.

Location is basic to the idea of community in several ways. First, it indicates the limits of the collectivity and social system that differentiate one community from another. As Dwight Sanderson has pointed out, the boundaries of a rural community can be located by plotting on a map the limits of shopping areas, mail and parcel-post deliveries, newspaper, department store delivery, and other service areas.[4]

Second, the locale serves as a locus of social and psychic orientation. The members' ties or roots are generally connected to the area defined by the community. This sociopsychic orientation is one meaning of the "address" or the "home" as these words are commonly used.

Third, location influences the organization of social activity. The facts of boundary and address draw members together and orient them in mutual and reciprocal relationships. At the same time, the locale always contains physical features, both natural and man-made, to which social accommodations must be made. Certain physical phenomena are woven into the way of life and serve to distinguish one community from others. For example, San Francisco is inconceivable apart from the hills and the Bay, while Los Angeles reflects the influence of its semitropical climate.

Social System ◗ Communities reveal variable though identifiable social systems. Expected behavior is organized into social roles articulated through the community structure. The actions of individuals are thus connected and meshed in an orderly fashion. This community system persists in time, fosters self-awareness, and permits distinctions between different communities.

Systematic social relations take place in such community organizations as the city government and school system, the United Fund and Council of Social Agencies, and the Merchants Association and Chamber of Commerce. Many other groups and subordinate organizations, such as labor unions, luncheon clubs, softball teams, department stores, and neighborhood clubs, also reveal the systematic character of social relations within the community. Moreover, research has shown that communities have their own class or stratification systems that further organize and systematize social relations. Rights, obligations, and authority are allocated to members in terms of community aims as these are embodied in prevailing values and norms.

Authority Structure ▶ The community develops a structure of authority that reflects both formal organization of control and the dimension of personal influence. By means of this structure it ensures effective conformity to its distinctive social norms, and thus maintains a necessary measure of order. In addition, the authority structure makes it possible to mobilize members for concerted action toward goals that are regarded as important for the collectivity as a whole. This topic is discussed more fully below.

Values and Norms ▶ The community is the locus of a distinctive system of values and norms. Certain ultimate and intermediate values of the society are reformulated in terms of the symbols and events that are meaningful in the community context. This value system produces an area of agreement and a field of communication that is both integrative and distinctive.

Community values foster the "we" feeling typical of the primary social relationships which predominate in the nonliterate community. In associational societies, however, community values are less cohesive and contribute to social integration rather through functional interdependence and structural articulation.

A normative order exists for carrying on essential and important activities. John A. Kinneman has noted that certain community folkways are connected with local associational groups and political and religious organizations.[5] The way of performing a given act that is *de rigueur* in one community may be *verboten* in another. Some usages are widely shared and tend to characterize entire communities. For example, Los Angeles is noted for its informality of dress and manners, while San Francisco is equally celebrated for its cosmopolitan formality. Again, part of the distinction among southern cities derives from different formulations of the "etiquette of race relations."

Self-Awareness ▶ One decisive characteristic of the community as an inclusive group is self-awareness. This involves mutual recognition among members and a sense of belonging. At the same time, mutual identification together with boundary-maintaining orientations produce a sense of distinction from others. Community awareness is revealed in attitudes such as community pride, loyalty, and defense. Rivalry with other communities and enthusiastic support of local enterprises give evidence of the mechanisms of individual and group identification. In this psychological and social process, boundaries of real significance may be established and maintained between communities where physical boundaries do not exist.

SPATIAL STRUCTURE OF THE COMMUNITY

Interaction among individuals, groups, and institutions leads to allocation of the land area of the community to industry, business, transportation, residence, education, recreation, and other uses. One consequence is a spatial structure that is functionally related to the social structure. Some forty years ago, from a study of Chicago, E. W. Burgess described community spatial structure as a system of concentric zones in which the center—the area of oldest settlement and most intensive business activity—was surrounded by successive zones of diverse use, increasing recency of settlement, and distance from the center. Two later formulations confirmed the general outlines of the Burgess model but introduced some important refinements. Empirical research and common-sense observation tend to confirm the general hypothesis, although numerous greater or smaller deviations have been noted. Each of the formulations is examined briefly below.

There is reason, however, to suggest that this model of spatial structure is typical, or at least most typical, only of American cities. In many European cities, especially those in Scandinavia, it is difficult to identify a single or main "central business zone"; and slums, where they exist, are not concentrated in the zone just surrounding the central area. These cities include districts or sections that have real meaning for people and permit a considerable measure of self-containment and self-sufficiency. In the large cities of India this dispersion in land use is even more pronounced. For example, recent land use maps of Madras show hundreds of little "slum" pockets scattered in every section of the city. There is little evidence of distinguishable zones, although a street of major business and shopping does exist. In reading the following material, then, the student is cautioned that the models of urban space are applicable typically to American cities.

Concentric Zone Pattern ♦ Burgess concluded that the urban community pattern can be portrayed as a series of concentric zones as shown in Figure 7-2.[6] The zones, idealized for simple graphic representation, constitute subdivisions of the urban space that are reserved for certain functions and occupied by the appropriate population types and social

Concentric Zone Scheme of Urban Ecological Structure

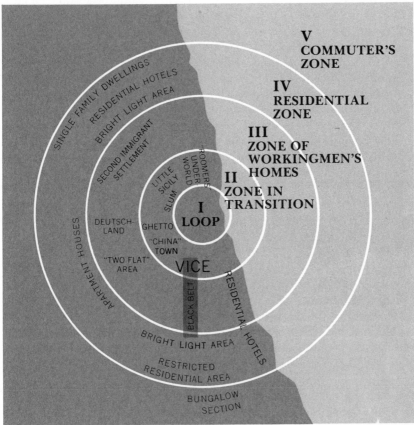

Source: E. W. Burgess, "Growth of the City," in The City by R. E. Park and E. W. Burgess, Chicago, University of Chicago Press, 1925, p. 55.

FIGURE 7-2

institutions. In this way the social and economic organization, the cultural milieu, and the population composition are shown to be related to the spatial pattern of the community.

The central business zone contains skyscrapers, department stores, cheap variety emporia, hotels, restaurants, theaters and motion picture houses, commercialized recreational facilities, office buildings, and light-manufacturing establishments. The district is thronged by day with workers and shoppers, but the nocturnal occupants are residents of transient hotels. The *zone of transition* lies in the line of expanding business and industry. This zone is heavily populated by lower-income groups, old-world immigrants, and rural migrants, unconventional persons, social failures, and social outcasts such as criminals, prostitutes, and the like.

The *zone of working men's homes* contains two-flat dwellings occupied by men who work in factories, with sons and daughters who have jobs in the central business area. These families can afford some of the comforts and luxuries of the city and their children plan to marry and invade the middle-class area. The *zone of middle-class dwellers* is occupied by professional people, owners of small businesses, the managerial class, clerical workers, and the like. Homes and physical surroundings combine some of the advantages of rural conditions with city living. The *commuter's zone* is composed of residential satellites and suburbs around the periphery of the city, and is occupied by upper-class (or middle-class) families who draw their livelihood from the central city.

Burgess employed a series of ecological processes to analyze the development of the urban community as well as its continuous change. The most important are segregation, invasion, and succession. Segregation refers to the constantly repeated tendency for land uses to differentiate and regroup into the basic types, so that the nature and relations of the zones remain constant despite growth and change. It was noted, for example, that heavy industry tends to concentrate around the periphery, large commercial establishments in the center, and poor immigrant, migrant, maladjusted, and antisocial groups in the transitional or slum zone of the city, even when the actual physical location of these zones shifts gradually with time.

The methods by which one type of land use, whether functional, institutional, or population, replaces a former, are analyzed by means of the paired concepts of invasion and succession. Thus the constant incursion of commercial, business, and light industrial activities into the slum zone is seen as an instance of invasion. When an identifiable sector of the transitional area has been fully taken over for some new use, succession is said to have occurred.

Burgess' formulation of urban zones has been employed fruitfully in the investigation of many aspects of urban life. By dividing the cities into zones differing markedly in many economic and social characteristics, it is possible to identify specific factors—such as slum housing, unemployment, or low income, for example—which may go together with the phenomena being studied. Two notable examples are the summary of studies of juvenile delinquency over a period of some twenty years in some twenty cities by Shaw and McKay, and the investigation of mental illness, chiefly in Chicago, by Faris and Dunham.[7] These—and similar—researches have made significant additions to the scientific understanding of important phases of social life.

Sector Pattern ▶ Some years after Burgess' study, Homer Hoyt formulated the hypothesis of urban space in different terms and stressed the importance of communication.[8] He employed the quadrant or sector rather than the concentric zone as the basic spatial design. In terms of its location within the various sectors, population was classified

Sector Scheme of Urban Ecological Structure

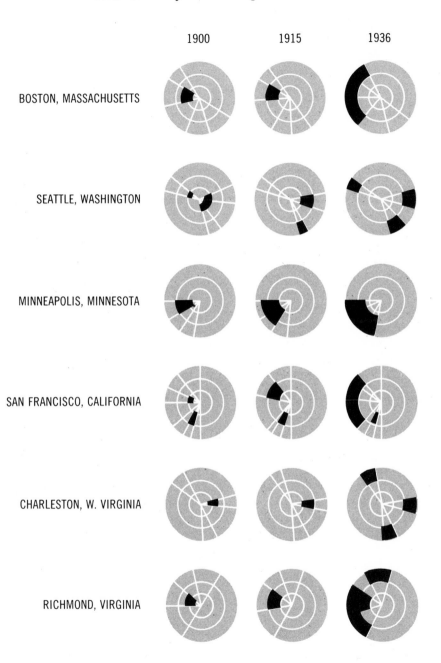

1900 1915 1936

BOSTON, MASSACHUSETTS

SEATTLE, WASHINGTON

MINNEAPOLIS, MINNESOTA

SAN FRANCISCO, CALIFORNIA

CHARLESTON, W. VIRGINIA

RICHMOND, VIRGINIA

Source: Homer Hoyt, Structure and Growth of Residential Neighborhoods in American Cities, Federal Housing Administration, Government Printing Office, Washington, 1939.
Shifts in location of fashionable residential areas in six American cities, 1900-1930. (The fashionable residential areas are indicated by solid black.)

FIGURE 7-3

as "high-rent" and "low-rent." Hoyt showed that the segregation, allocation, and organization of population into high- and low-rent areas
were influenced by such factors as topography, culture, the economy,
and social organization.

According to Hoyt's formulation, high-rent areas occupied by
middle-class families are located on the outer fringe of one or more
sectors of the city. With growth, as is shown in Figure 7-3, the high-
rent areas move out in one sector along a main street or highway. The
abandoned districts become obsolescent and deteriorated and change
into low-rent areas occupied by low-income families. In some sectors
the expanding low-rent district is shaped like a slice of pie, its broad
base at the center and tapering toward the periphery along an axial
line of communication. Industry tends to locate at the periphery of the
city along rivers, waterways, and rail lines. Because of the importance
of axial lines of communication, Hoyt argued that a space use map of a
city would look more like a giant octopus than a series of concentric
circles.

Hoyt believed that a community could grow according to three patterns. First, growth may be "vertical." That is, single-family dwellings
are replaced by multiple-family units. This pattern of growth is usually
consistent with the high-rent or low-rent population type already established in the area. Second, the community may grow by filling in
the vacant lots and blocks in the already settled sectors. Interstitial
growth of this kind maintains consistency with the high-rent or low-
rent population type already established. Or third, new settlements
may develop at the periphery of the community, or old suburbs may
grow together to form new areas. Hoyt called this pattern of growth
"centrifugal" and "lateral." Sometimes such new settlements grow
adjacent to industries that locate at the periphery of the city.

Multiple Nuclei Pattern ❱ C. D. Harris and E. L. Ullman point out
that in many cities the spatial pattern is built around several discrete
nuclei.[9] It is argued that the rise of separate nuclei and differentiated
districts reflects some combination of four factors: (1) Certain activities
require specialized facilities. (2) Certain similar activities concentrate
because they profit from cohesion. (3) Certain unlike activities are
detrimental to each other, hence they tend to locate separately. (4)
Some urban activities are unable to afford the high rents of the most
desirable city sites. A model of the multiple nuclei spatial pattern is
shown in Figure 7-4.

Harris and Ullman point out that although the number of nuclei
varies from one community to another, the following are found in
most large American cities. The *central business district,* nuclei 1 and
2 in the diagram, is located at the focus of intra-city transportation.
This district often includes specialized centers of retail trade, financial
activity, government offices, and the "automobile row." Second, the

Multiple Nuclei Pattern of Urban Space

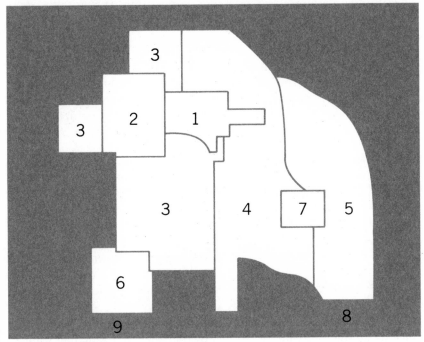

Source: C. D. Harris and E. L. Ullman. Op. Cit., p. 13.

FIGURE 7-4

wholesale and light *manufacturing district,* nulcei 3, includes two sub-concentrations and is conveniently within the city but near the focus of extra-city transportation.

The *heavy industrial district,* 4, is located near the present or former periphery of the city, accessible to large tracts of space and major intra-city transportation. The *residential district,* 5 and 6, often includes a middle-class subdivision, located on well-drained land away from the urban nuisances, and a low-income dwelling area situated in older sections of the city. Minor nuclei, 7, include cultural centers, parks, and outlying business and industrial centers. Finally, *suburbs* and *satellites,* 8 and 9, either residential or industrial, develop adjacent to or surrounding great cities.

SOCIAL STRUCTURE OF THE COMMUNITY

The social structure that emerges in the community reflects the functional accommodation of social life to the physical locale. The complexity of social organization varies considerably with the size of the community and the character of its geographical setting. It will be useful to analyze community social structure in terms of the dimensions of economic basis, sources of integration, groups, institutions, social classes, authority organization, and extended communication.

Economic Basis ◗ In the United States, nomadic food-gathering, hunting, fishing, and pastoral communities no longer exist to any great degree. In terms of our contemporary economic basis, three main types of communities are generally identified. They are *rural farm, rural nonfarm,* and *urban.* Such a classification recognizes the fact that social life is organized differently with variations in major economic enterprises.

Two general kinds of farm communities have emerged in the United States. One is the village community, where families reside within a limited locale and go out each day to work on their farms. This type of community structure was common in New England in the colonial and early national periods. However, it is relatively infrequent at present. The other type is the "open-country" rural community. Families reside on separate farms near their work and gather periodically in adjacent trading and social centers for a variety of common activities and services. In both types of communities, agriculture imposes the basic design on the structure of social life.

Rural nonfarm communities may be based on extractive activities such as mining, logging, or fishing, or they may be residential suburbs or satellites of large cities. The extractive nonfarm rural communities resemble farming places in many social respects. Rural suburban places, however, are more urban than rural in character. Suburban communities are discussed below.

A functional classification of urban communities can be made on the basis of the main type of economic activity. One economic typology of American cities is summarized in Figure 7-5. The nine categories include most of the typical urban economic activities; however, they omit governmental activity as in political capitals, and cultural pursuits as in art colonies or entertainment centers.

Sources of Integration ◗ Communities differ according to the main sources of social integration. At least two general sources of community integration have been distinguished.[10] Some communities are integrated by their identification with a strong unified tradition. Others, however, lacking such a unifying tradition, are functionally integrated by division of labor, interdependence, and social control. The difference between communities integrated in these ways tends roughly to correspond with the rural-urban dichotomy.

Integration by powerful tradition and deep identification is best exemplified in the nonliterate communal community. Many American rural localities, however, also exhibit this communal mode of cohesion. A population which is stable over a long period of time, the presence

An Economic Functional Classification of Cities

Type of City	Distinguishing Criteria
Manufacturing Predominant	Manufacturing employment equals 74 per cent or more of total in manufacturing, wholesaling, and retailing. Manufacturing and mechanical industries contain at least 45 per cent of gainful workers.
Manufacturing Mixed	Manufacturing employment equals at least 60 per cent of total in manufacturing, retailing, and wholesaling. Manufacturing and mechanical industries include between 20 and 45 per cent of gainful workers.
Retail	Retail employment is 50 per cent or more of total in manufacturing, wholesaling, and retailing and at least 2.2 times that in wholesaling alone.
Diversified	Employment in manufacturing, wholesaling, and retailing is less than 60 per cent, 20 per cent, and 50 per cent respectively of total in these activities. No other special criteria apply.
Wholesale	Employment in wholesaling is at least 20 per cent of total in manufacturing, wholesaling, and retailing and at least 45 per cent as much as retailing alone.
Transportation	Employment in transportation and communication is at least 11 per cent of all gainful workers, and they equal at least one third the number in manufacturing and mechanical industries and at least two thirds the number in trade.
Mining	Mineral extraction includes more than 15 per cent of all gainful workers (applicable only to cities of 25,000 and over for which data are available).
University	Enrollment in universities, technical, liberal-arts, and teachers colleges equals at least 25 per cent of the city population.
Resort and Retirement	No satisfactory criterion found.

Source: *Adapted from William H. Form and Delbert C. Miller,* Industry Labor and Community, *New York, Harper, 1960, p. 40, previously adapted from Chauncey D. Harris, "A Functional Classification of Cities in the United States,"* Geographical Review, *pp. 86-99, January 1943.*

FIGURE 7-5

of strong, primary mutual ties, and a considerable degree of isolation are all factors that tend to promote and strengthen the formation of a powerful tradition. The community of Blanc Sablon, described above, is an example.

Urban heterogeneity, on the other hand, inhibits the formation and transmission of a strong tradition. Population movement, social instability, status mobility, and ethnic heterogeneity foster diversity. Under such conditions, the systems of division of labor, mutual interdependence, and formal social control maintain functionally adequate solidarity.

Community as Constellation ▶ The community has been called a constellation of groups and institutions.[11] It is the locale of numerous small groups, extended groups, and institutional agencies. All are articulated into the community system to form a kind of social constellation. Thus systematized, they function to achieve a large measure of self-sufficiency.

The community is "home base" for small groups. Families, clubs, committees, subcommittees, and all manner of informal friendship cliques are nestled in the social order of the community. The community-based small group constitutes the individual's first line of connection with the total social order. What is more, within the community the countless small groups that include all the population are structured both spatially and socially with reference both to one another and to the elements of the larger social order.

The community is also the locale of many kinds of associations. Chambers of commerce, country clubs, labor union locals and federations, religious congregations, trade associations, professional association chapters, veterans' associations, service clubs, fraternal orders, councils, and the like are essential elements of the structure of the community. Such extended groups constitute further links between the individual and the larger society, and, as noted in the previous chapter, provide breeding places for many of the small formal and informal groups. Moreover, the community is home base for large-scale organizations whose memberships are distributed throughout the entire nation and even farther.

Some associations serve to articulate other groups, both small and extended. The council, or the constituent extended group, is an obvious case in point. Councils join, coordinate, and articulate separate groups in the community with reference to recognized interests and aims. Familiar examples include the council of social agencies, the United Fund, the merchants' association, the chamber of commerce, the trade union council, the council of churches, the federation of women's clubs, and the many *ad hoc* committees and commissions formed to cope with such problems as juvenile delinquency, recreation, housing, refugee assistance, and the like.

The community is also the natural locale of those formal structures of social function generally called institutions. The term institution calls to mind such areas of structure and function as government, education, religion, economy, family, recreation, and welfare. Within the community there exists a formal, powerfully sanctioned order of manifest and explicit social roles and norms for attaining ends that are universally accepted. The institutions, though universal forms of social structure, achieve their concrete manifestation within the community, where they provide a firm framework for relations among individuals and groups.

Social Classes ▶ In communities, individuals, groups, and institutions are separated, located, and ranked in terms of social class. The phrases lower class, middle class, and upper class are part of the ordinary vocabulary of community life. People recognize the existence of classes that serve to order and regulate their behavior.

In the concentric zone model of urban space, Burgess showed where the various social classes are located within the community. The lowest class of people are concentrated within the slum adjacent to the central business area in the zone of deterioration, crowding, and transition. Upper-class families live in the residential suburbs at the periphery of the city. Between these extremes, moving from center toward periphery, are found the residential areas of upper-lower-class, lower-middle-class, and middle-class families.

Since Burgess' pioneer work there have been many empirical studies of social classes in communities.[12] They all confirm both the existence of social classes in American communities and their geographic location generally along lines of the Burgess model. However, the number of classes found tends to vary from one community to another. In some small rural localities only two classes could be identified.[13] In others, especially in complex urban places, a large number and variety of social classes were observed. It has also been found that what people perceive as class distinctions are really differences in terms of three related variables: wealth, power, and community rank or standing.[14] The organization of power in communities is discussed in the following section.

The social classes of a community serve to order and regulate social behavior. Certain occupations are regularly associated with one or another social class. For example, lower-class workers are typically concentrated in the low-skill, low-paid, insecure occupations of industry and business. Middle-class persons, on the other hand, are engaged in managerial, professional, and technical occupations. One consequence is the familiar tags of "blue collar" and "white collar." At the same time, members of the various classes tend to live in different sections of the community and to have different styles of life. The organizations to which people belong, the contacts they have, and the activities they engage in are conditioned by their social class. Political attitudes, social philosophies, reading habits, and child-rearing practices are also determined by the individual's social class.

People tend to move up and down within the community class structure. For example, the son of a lower-class family may begin life in a slum neighborhood where his family lives. However, if he graduates from the local college or state university, he can get a white-collar job and move out into a better neighborhood. After some years, if he is successful, he may buy a home in an upper-middle-class residential suburb and fully enter into the life of this class. At the same time, a few individuals and families move downward in standing as a result of misfortune or misadventure—for example, from middle class to lower class.

Authority Structure ▶ Within the community, authority is organized in relationship to both spatial and social structure. Organized authority issues from the formal structures of bureaucratic institutions, organizations, and associations. Authority within the community also issues from the personal influence that belongs to some individuals because of family background, personal wealth, unique characteristics, or the like. The authority deriving from both these sources tends to be structured in relationship to recognized community functions.

One important sphere of community power is defined by the bureaucratic agencies of the community. This fact is illustrated in the chain of command in industrial plants, business concerns, school systems, and local governments. In large-scale membership associations, authority tends to be democratically organized. The formulation—or at least the validation—of policy decisions is controlled by members. Officials, though they wield great authority, are subject to the ultimate control of the membership. In small groups, both informal and formal, the organization and exercise of authority tend to be more informal and casual. Within the community, the spheres of authority in all such units tend to be more or less integrated and unified into an overall structure.

In Figure 7-6A William H. Form and Delbert C. Miller portray the organization of community authority in relationship to the institutional structure of the society and the community on the one hand, and to specific community projects and community leaders on the other. It is suggested that the foundation of community authority is the permanent institutional structure as it is concretely expressed in the community. Authority, however, remains latent until activated by community response to an issue. At this time the community influentials act to implement and mobilize the authority of the community complex.

Floyd Hunter conceptualizes community power as policy leadership and indicates how social authority and personal influence are fused in a structure.[15] He identifies two classes of leaders: a small group of

A Diagrammatic Portrayal of Community Power Structure

KEY
INFLUENTIALS
+
TOP INFLUENTIALS
+
COMMUNITY
POWER COMPLEX

INSTITUTIONALIZED POWER STRUCTURE OF THE COMMUNITY

INSTITUTIONAL POWER STRUCTURE OF SOCIETY

Explanation. *Institutional Power Structure of the Society* refers to the relative distribution of power among societal institutions. *Institutionalized Power Structure of the Community* refers to the relative distribution of power among local institutions. *Community Power Complex* is a power arrangement among temporary or permanent organizations, special interest associations, and informal groups emerging in specific issues and projects. *Top Influentials* refers to those persons who are reputed to be of most influence and power in community decision-making. *Key Influentials* are acknowledged leaders among the top influentials.

Source: William H. Form and Delbert C. Miller, Op. Cit., Figure 11.1 and text, pp. 437-438.

FIGURE 7-6A

Distribution of the Forty Top Policy-Making Leaders of Regional City by Principal Occupation or by Organizational Office

Occupation or Office	Number
President	13
Chairman of Board	6
Attorney	5
Social Leader	5
Vice-President, All Kinds	3
Manager, All Kinds	3
School Superintendent	2
Mayor	1
Treasurer	1
Dentist	1

Source: Floyd Hunter, Community Power Structure, Chapel Hill: University of North Carolina Press, 1953, adapted from Table 4, p. 76.

FIGURE 7-6B

"men of independent decision" and a more numerous category of "executors of policy." Hunter's list of the forty "men of decision" in a large southern city is shown in Figure 7-6B. Most hold positions as president, vice-president or manager of companies or organizations. A few, however, have no formal or vocational status and possess community influence by virtue of wealth, ancestry, or personal influence.

Hunter's findings imply the existence in the community of what C. Wright Mills has called a "power elite."[16] The term refers to a small number of loosely organized power leaders who exert crucial control in basic policy decisions. With reference to public opinion, Ralph H. Turner and Lewis M. Killian speak of an "elite public."[17] These observers admit, however, that the exercise of power is sensitive to the interests and feelings of subordinates and citizens in the total community.

Communication System ▶ The community acts as a field and system of communication. Shared values, mutual recognition, reciprocal orientations, and spatial juxtaposition facilitate and structure the flow of communication. In addition, the community contains a system of communication channels. This system is maintained both by the community structure and by the network of mass communication media.

The face-to-face contacts of small groups and the instrumental relations of extended groups facilitate communication on general issues. One illustration is found in community councils. In the constituent small groups, relations among individuals occur at the face-to-face level. Official representatives participate in the meetings and discussions of the council, relaying ideas and reactions to this general forum and returning other ideas and information to the grass roots of the community.

The bureaucratic institutions and large associations contain formal systems of communication within their structures. In addition, Ralph Turner and Lewis Killian point out that individuals perform the roles of "instigator," "mediator," and "receiver" in developing community opinion.[18] Individuals and groups mutually oriented by economic, educational, religious, political, and similar reference-group anchorages tend to form "discussion universes" within which communication proceeds freely and between which barriers to communication exist.

The mass media are agents of broad communication within the community and constitute communication links with the larger society. Members of the community sometimes make news which is purveyed by the press, telecommunications, or motion pictures. Letters to the editor, personals, meeting announcements, and the like are extensions at the mass level of the face-to-face contacts that occur at the primary and informal group levels of social interaction.

At the same time, the mass media link the community to other communities and to the larger society. This is most evident in the network radio and TV programs and the national and international press services. In this respect the motion pictures, TV, and national publications play a unique role, for they admit their audiences to a wide range of events lying outside the confines of the community.

ROXBURY:
RURAL VILLAGE AND URBAN COMMUNITY

Jesse F. Steiner's account of the growth and elaboration of Roxbury, Massachusetts, illustrates the distinctive characteristics of the community in both its rural and urban manifestations. From such a sketch it is possible to gain some insight into the processes of growth and change that have transformed the early rural places in the United States into teeming city communities. Even more significant, perhaps, is the fact that this graphic account sharpens the view of consensus and organization in small, simple, rural and large, urban communities alike.

The colony of "Rocksborough" was founded in 1630 largely by substantial farmers from Nazing and Essex parish twenty miles from London. They at once set about building houses, with a "meeting house" as a center of community life. The climate was harsh and in this section there is an outcropping of glacier-scarred conglomerate rock known as "pudding-stone." From the first, the problem of adapting their formal mode of life to the crude conditions existing in the new settlement proved to be difficult.

To offset the scarcity of money, grain and skins were bartered and wampum, the bead currency of the Indians, was in general use. Clothing was mostly of home-made woolen fabrics, though the cut conformed to prevailing English style. Dwellings were at first a square of logs chinked with mud and roofed with thatch. These gave way later to frame buildings, two stories in front, but with the shingled roof sloping to make one story at the back. At the end of the Revolutionary War, Roxbury was still a country village whose chief dependence was upon husbandry.

In the early days of the colony such industry as there was grew out of the needs of the community, existed for the sole purpose of supplying those needs, and was carried on by the colonists themselves, often in the intervals of farm work. In the first half of the nineteenth century industry increased, now being exploited for commercial profit, but producing useful articles. In this period there were rope, carpet, rubber, and lithograph factories. The operatives were from Northern Europe; largely Irish, Scotch, and German. Many of these newcomers were of a caliber to appreciate the traditions of the community, and since they came gradually enough to be assimilated, they made a real and lasting contribution.

Community Control and Cohesion. In the early days particularly, all control was exerted through the church, and an effective means it proved to be. Church attendance was enforced by fining and placing in the stocks all backsliders. The minister and officers of the church constituted a final court of appeal in most secular matters as well as in those pertaining to religion. The cost and labor of maintaining the church buildings was shared by all the colony, and the minister was supported at public expense. As civic means of control arose later, the control of the church diminished.

Primary social relations continued to a surprising extent until the middle of the nineteenth century. Although interest no longer centered about just one church, it was concerned chiefly with one faith, Congregationalist. All the male citizens congregated regularly in the Town House, and indeed on the least provocation. The Town Meeting was the main device of community solidarity for many years.

There were many other contributing causes of community cohesion. The chief of these, no doubt, was common blood and tradition, which still largely prevailed. Loyalty was also fostered by pride in a military organization which flourished for seventy years after the Revolution, latterly under the name of Norfolk Guards. Another important organization was Washington Lodge of Masons, founded in 1796 and exerting social value all through the nineteenth century.

Community solidarity also developed around pleasant unorganized social activity that centered in the taverns and reflected growing affluence. About 1830 there seems to have developed a marked interest in civic improvement. As wealth increased, interest began to focus upon intellectual and artistic expression, which provided a new basis of community solidarity.

Community Change. Transportation improved steadily. Road taxes were worked out by each property owner until 1816. In 1824 some of the streets were paved and a few sidewalks built, and the following year no less than forty streets were named. Four years later the "Mill-Dam" was opened. This was the first artificial road connecting Boston with the mainland. In 1832 Tremont Street was laid out, affording another connection with Boston. There was an hourly stage coach connecting Roxbury Town House with Old South Church in Boston for a fare of twelve and one-half cents. In another generation, railroad tracks were laid across the cherished meadows of the irascible farmers. In 1834 the Providence Railroad supplanted the coaches, and in 1856 horse-drawn streetcars were first used for local transportation.

Simultaneously with the great evidence of community solidarity we see the faint beginning of changes which appear one to three generations later as distinctly disorganizing factors. The town was rapidly becoming urban, or at least suburban. The increase of prosperity and growth of population caused a rise in land values, and while the real land boom did not come until later, there was considerable speculation in real estate, and in 1836 the Roxbury Land Company was formed.

Early in the nineteenth century the support of the minister and of the church became voluntary, and church attendance was no longer required. One of the signs of material prosperity in the crucial years around 1830 was the building of more and bigger churches. Not only were new denominations becoming entrenched, but other Congregational churches appeared, though in some instances the power of the church had so declined that only the old people were going to communion.

Growth was so rapid in the decade 1840-1850 that the population doubled. The City Charter was received in 1846. Industry underwent sudden expansion and change of character. In order to obtain more land for building sites, marshes were filled in, trees were cut, brooks and rivers disappeared, and farms were swallowed up. When Roxbury was annexed to Boston in 1867, it had very nearly lost its suburban character.

As factories were built the operatives sought homes nearby, in out-of-date wooden houses where rents were low. These were soon supplemented by apartment and tenement houses. The ledge hills provided new building room at different levels for the growing community.

The first immigrants had been Irish laborers brought over in 1818 to work on the Mill Dam. Each group at first had a fairly well-defined neighborhood as near as possible to its work, and brought traditions of thrift and religious belief. The Irish resisted efforts at Americanization, because they were discouraged from associating with people of faiths other than the Catholic.

Largely because of the good waters which underlay the soil, breweries increased in size and number until in 1875 there were twenty along the Stony Brook Valley. These were managed and operated chiefly by Germans who accumulated great wealth, did not plow back any of their gains into the district, and usually moved elsewhere to live.

By the end of the century the congestion already apparent was greatly increased by pressure from South Boston, which was reaching the saturation point of population and industry. Another current which flowed in as a result of the changed type of industry and cheap rents came from the North End, people driven out by the industrial occupation of that neighborhood. Many Southern Europeans, notably Italians, Greeks, Albanians, and Armenians had come in the last thirty years to work in the shoe factories. After the movement of population from South Boston, the torrent of immigration flowed in so fast that there could be no satisfactory solution of the housing problem, and no orderly racial grouping. Today no racial lines are drawn except a slight tendency to segregation of Jews and Negroes in some sections.

Except for the churches there have been few "centers of uplift" in Roxbury. For fifty years the Family Welfare Service has been an effective agency. There have been some Boys' Clubs and a Working Men's Institute. The Boston YMCA's facilities are available. The Roxbury Neighborhood House has served its immediate environs. The most effective interdenominational force is probably the Norfolk House Center in John Elliot Square. The most recent noninstitutional attempt to organize for community betterment was the Roxbury Improvement Society.[19]

THE MODERN METROPOLIS

Modern cities began to develop in the seventeenth and eighteenth centuries, when the growth of commerce and industry led to the concentration of population and economic activity.[20] Soon these cities came to be characterized by population heterogeneity, increased division of labor, and specialized land use. Urbanism emerged as the sociocultural system to order the new way of life.[21] In time this sociospatial system hardened into "central city" and new growth took the form of "suburbs." The most recent urban growth trend is expressed in such phrases as "suburbanization," "metropolitan explosion," "urban sprawl," and the like.

Central City ♦ The central city is the area of original urban settlement. It is delimited by political boundaries, defined by formal land use patterns, and distinguished by old and deteriorating business and residential buildings. The theories of urban space discussed above typically apply to the central city.

Population in the central city tends to be relatively stable in size though heterogeneous in composition. For example, between 1950 and 1960, the central cities of the 212 standard metropolitan areas increased by only 10.7 per cent.[22] In some instances these populations actually declined. Young, educated, aggressive, and upward-mobile individuals move from the central city to the new suburbs. Their places are taken by young migrants, principally southern Negroes, mountain whites, Puerto Rican workers, and Mexican laborers. Some elements, notably urbanized lower classes, nonmobile upper classes, and middle-class city enthusiasts, stay in the central city. As a consequence of all these trends, the central city tends to become progressively ethnically mixed, nonwhite, lower-class, and economically and culturally deprived.

The central city is the locus of the community's power system and institutional complex. Individuals participate impersonally in pageant-like enterprises through the mass media, mass transportation, huge auditoriums, and crowded streets. Purposeful individual activity is bureaucratically organized by economic, political, religious, educational, welfare, and other social institutions and associations. The extent of interpersonal voluntary activity shows substantial class differences within the central city. Some empirical research indicates that low-status and minority groups and new arrivals tend to maximize kinship contacts and to avoid voluntary associations.[23] As a consequence of all these factors, community cohesion tends to be limited in the central city.

Suburbs ▶ There have been two main periods of suburban development in the United States. The first period started late in the nineteenth century, concomitant with growing affluence, improved transportation, and increasing urban congestion. At this time, Milton outside Boston and the Main Line outside Philadelphia began receiving large numbers of wealthy people seeking to escape the congestion and squalor of the city. Today, such "old suburbs" constitute stable residential enclaves both inside and outside great central cities. They contain high-status, well-to-do families who have resided on spacious estates for two or more generations. The population includes greater than average proportions of women and older individuals. Long co-residence, similarity of status and taste, and intimacy of association promote inter-marriage and community cohesion.

"New suburbia" began to appear after the First World War and exploded nationwide following World War II. The new suburbs are typically tract developments of modest single-family dwellings in open country surrounding the city. Their rapid growth is shown dramatically by the fact that between 1950 and 1960 the suburban population (that outside central cities) of 212 standard metropolitan areas increased by 48.6 per cent, while that inside the central cities grew by only 10.7 per cent.[24] The Census Bureau reported that in April 1960 nearly 55 million individuals lived in the suburbs of the 212 standard metropolitan areas.

Two subtypes of new suburbs can be differentiated. The less numerous consists of middle-income, home-owning nontransient, family-centered neighborhoods that resemble old suburbs in important respects. The commoner type is peopled by young, transient, upwardly mobile home-renting "organization men" and their families. A fairly typical man in one of these suburban developments is between 25 and 30 years old, with a wife, one child and another on the way, and the salary of a junior executive.

In these "dormitory" suburbs people are "other-directed," devoted to "togetherness," and conformist in their studied casualness. They are superficially homogeneous and consciously well organized. Nevertheless, their transiency and social mobility tend to limit community cohesion.

Some Social Consequences ▶ The modern metropolis, which is itself a product of prior social changes, has important consequences for contemporary society. Historically and structurally, the central city emerges as the locus of some serious, even chronic, dysfunctions, most of which have been regarded as leading social problems. For example, rigid land-use patterns in relation to rapid growth and change produce such problems as social and population congestion, physical deterioration and squalor, and architectural and physical obsolescence and ugliness. In turn, these conditions are correlated with such social problems as crime and delinquency, family and community disorganization, personal maladjustment and deprivation, and the like. Actual and potential leadership is drained off by upward mobility and migration to the suburbs.

Meanwhile, the trends of change that produce and expand suburbs not only aggravate these problems; they also produce unique suburban difficulties. The transiency and mobility of the youthful suburban population act to limit community cohesion and a well-rounded way of life. The explosive growth of suburbia functions to defeat one of the major attractions of suburbs—their half-rural, half-urban character. The process of suburbanization seems to involve forces that are not yet subject to rational control and whose consequences are not yet fully understood.

THE REGION

In a world of growing and congested population and rapid transportation and communication, the region emerges as a reality of social life. It represents an extension of the community principle to larger populations and more inclusive geographic areas. A region is a social collectivity located within a contiguous territory and possessing a social system that is ordered by a normative pattern and defined by distinctive structure and functions. It is larger than a community but contained within a nation. In the United States the regional community has been conceptualized in three somewhat different ways.

Harris-Ullman Model ♦ On the basis of urban function, C. D. Harris and E. L. Ullman identify what can be called the "city service region."[25] Cities are central places in functionally connected surrounding areas for which they perform comprehensive services. Harris and Ullman state that this pattern constitutes a regional norm that may be varied in at least two ways.

First, transport cities performing "break-of-bulk" and allied services along transportation routes are tied to areas that may be remote in distance but close in communication. To the adjacent normal service region such cities as this add a wider and often noncontiguous territory. Such cities tend to be arranged in linear patterns along rail lines or at coasts.

Second, specialized-function cities performing a single service extend the normal service territory in another way. The city service region may be very large, and since the principal factor is often the location of a particular natural resource, such as coal, water power, or a beach, some regions are determined to a considerable extent by the natural environment.

The size and structure of the city service region are conditioned by the services performed by the central city. These may include, among others, trade, special services, religious and cultural activities, political functions, transportation breaks (e.g., from steamer to railway), and recreation. Systems of interdependence and communication develop to fuse the central city and its surrounding hinterland into a significant unit of social function.

Odum Model ♦ By analyzing some seven hundred different factors, Howard W. Odum was able to identify six major regions in the United States.[26] "The sixfold division basic to the study was evolved from a study of a large number of regional classifications and from many hypothetical groupings tested from various angles. . . . Allocation of states was made on the basis of the clustering of elemental indices, of which some seven hundred constituted the field of analysis."[27] Thus the regions appeared to emerge as functional divisions of the organized life of the nation. The six regions, together with the number of states in each, are shown in Figure 7-7.

Odum's analysis stressed the function of historical, geographical, and cultural factors in structuring constituent regions of the total

Regions of the United States as Defined by Howard W. Odum and the Census Bureau

ODUM'S CLASSIFICATION	CENSUS CLASSIFICATION
Northeast, 12 states	Northeast, 9 states New England, 6 states Middle Atlantic, 3 states
Middle States, 8 states	North Central, 12 states East North Central, 5 states West North Central, 7 states
Southeast, 11 states	South, 16 states South Atlantic, 8 states East South Central, 4 states West South Central, 4 states
Southwest, 4 states Northwest, 9 states Far West, 4 states	West, 11 states Mountain, 8 states Pacific, 3 states

Sources: H. W. Odum, Op. Cit., p. 6.
Census of Population, 1950, Op. Cit. The new states of Alaska and Hawaii and the territories of Puerto Rico and the Virgin Islands are omitted.

FIGURE 7-7

nation. Although the regions can be clearly delimited as geographic areas and populations, they are less sharply defined as self-conscious social collectivities. Each, however, represents the locale of an identifiable structure of activity in many areas of life. For this reason, Odum concluded that the six regions are natural bases for the analysis, planning, and administration of change and growth.

Rupert Vance and T. J. Woofter, Jr., applied similar methods in the investigation of the two main southern regions of the United States.[28] From this analysis Vance was able to identify 15 subregions in the South. Woofter was able to delineate twenty-seven subregions. In the view of these scholars, such subregions are smaller geographic areas where shared factors of geography, history, and economics have powerfully influenced and shaped social organization and cultural development.

Census Model ▶ To provide summary figures at levels between those for the United States and for individual states, the Census Bureau has established regions and geographic divisions. The latter unit represents a grouping of contiguous states, while regions are composed of groups of divisions.[29] The resulting four regions and nine divisions are shown in Figure 7-7; they constitute the spatial basis for reporting many kinds of data and for organizing many nationwide governmental programs and services.

PERSPECTIVE ON COMMUNITIES

In some societies most of the people live in small rural communities, although in others the population is concentrated in large urban places. For example, although some of the world's largest cities are located in India, three quarters of the Indian people still live in small rural villages. On the other hand, three fourths of the American population is classified as urban, and the proportion is even higher in some Western European countries.

Everywhere the number, size, and influence of urban communities tend to grow. For example, in 1790, when the first United States census was taken, less than 4 per cent of the population was classified as urban and there was not a single city with 25,000 inhabitants. Now nearly a dozen cities have a million or more inhabitants, and the Bureau of the Census has designated 212 places as "standard Metropolitan Statistical Areas." In Europe (including the Soviet Union) between 1800 and 1950 the percentage of people living in cities of 100,000 and over increased from 2.9 to 19.9.

More and more, large cities tend to dominate the way of life. Industry, trade and commerce, finance, and service activities provide economic bases. Values tend to become secular and rationalistic, and social organization becomes associational and bureaucratic. The extension of communication through the mass media and modern transport permits the great city to expand its dominance over more and more distant rural areas.

In advanced societies, some metropolitan centers tend to grow together to form "linear cities." One such linear city is said to extend from Boston to Richmond, another from Pittsburgh to Flint, Michigan, and a third from Los Angeles to San Diego. In these situations, urban dominance is reflected in "urban sprawl."

These trends are accompanied by persistent issues. In some societies rural and urban elements, old and new forces struggle for control of the social order. For example, in France the struggle was symbolized by *Poujadisme,** in the United States by the reapportionment controversy, and in India by the anti-cow slaughter riots. Wherever people in large numbers withdraw from village systems to migrate to burgeoning cities, severe and extensive social disintegration results. Often the society has few resources for managing change and disintegration. The growth of cities tends to tax the resources of some societies. Rural village institutions are undermanned, and urban resources are overtaxed by migration. These and other issues associated with world-wide urban trends present challenging issues for sociological research and constitute leading problems for social control and planning.

*A short-lived movement of the early 1960's among French small business and independent farming groups and their sympathizers against what they regarded as high taxes, price controls, and other government regimentation and urban domination.

FOOTNOTES

1. Charles Horton Cooley, *Social Organization* (New York: Scribner's, 1909), p. 33.
2. Condensed and adapted from Oscar W. Junek, *Isolated Communities* (New York: American Book Company, 1937), pp. 20-25.
3. Robert M. MacIver and Charles H. Page, *Society* (New York: Holt, 1955), pp. 8-9.
4. Dwight W. Sanderson, *Rural Sociology and Rural Social Organization* (New York: Wiley, 1942), pp. 276-277.
5. John A. Kinneman, *The Community* (New York: Appleton-Century, l947), Chapters 10 and 11.
6. E. W. Burgess, "Growth of the City," in Robert E. Park and E. W. Burgess, eds., *The City* (Chicago: University of Chicago Press, 1925).
7. See R. E. L. Faris and H. W. Dunham, *Mental Disorders in Urban Areas* (Chicago: University of Chicago Press, 1949); Clifford R. Shaw and Henry D. McKav. *Juvenile Delinquency in Urban Areas* (Chicago: University of Chicago Press, 1942); Bernard Lander, *Towards an Understanding of Juvenile Delinquency* (New York: Columbia University Press, 1954); and Roland J. Chilton, "Continuity in Delinquency Area Research: A Comparison of Studies for Baltimore, Detroit, and Indianapolis," in *American Sociological Review*, February 1964, pp. 71-83.
8. Homer Hoyt, *Structure and Growth of Residential Neighborhoods in American Cities* (Washington: U.S. Government Printing Office, 1939).
9. C. D. Harris and E. L. Ullman, "The Nature of Cities," in *Annals*, 242:14-16 (November 1945).
10. Blaine E. Mercer, *The Study of Society* (New York: Harcourt, Brace, 1958), pp. 190-194.
11. R. E. Park and E. W. Burgess, *Introduction to the Science of Sociology* (Chicago: University of Chicago Press, 1924), p. 493.
12. See Allison Davis *et al.*, *Deep South* (Chicago: University of Chicago Press, 1941); W. Lloyd Warner and Paul S. Lunt, *The Social Life of a Modern Community* (New Haven: Yale University Press, 1941); A. B. Hollingshead, *Elmtown's Youth* (New York: Wiley, 1949); and Wayne Wheeler, *Social Stratification in a Plains Community* (Minneapolis: University of Minnesota Press, 1949).
13. See John Useem *et al.*, "Stratification in a Prairie Town," in *American Sociological Review*, 7:331-342 (June 1942).
14. See Milton M. Gordon, *Social Class in American Sociology* (Durham: Duke University Press, 1958), Chapter 8.
15. Floyd Hunter, *Community Power Structure* (Chapel Hill: University of North Carolina Press, 1953).
16. C. Wright Mills, *The Power Elite* (New York: Oxford University Press, 1956), Chapters 2 and 3.
17. Ralph H. Turner and Lewis M. Killian, *Collective Behavior* (Englewood Cliffs: Prentice-Hall, 1957), p. 253.
18. *Ibid.*, pp. 235-254.
19. Condensed and adapted from Jesse F. Steiner, *The American Community in Action* (New York: Holt, 1928), pp. 106-133.
20. See Noel P. Gist and L. A. Halbert, *Urban Society* (New York: Crowell, 1948), pp. 19-20.
21. See Louis Wirth, "Urbanism as a Way of Life," in *American Journal of Sociology* 44:1-18 (July 1938).
22. *Statistical Abstract of the United States*, 1962, Table 10, p. 13.
23. See, among other sources: Hollingshead, *op. cit.*; Genevieve Knupfer, "Portrait of the Underdog," in *Public Opinion Quarterly* (Spring 1947); and Mirra Komarovsky, "The Voluntary Associations of Urban Dwellers," in *American Sociological Review*, 11:686-689 (December 1946).
24. *Statistical Abstract of the United States*, 1962, Table 10, p. 13.
25. Harris and Ullman, *op. cit.*, pp. 7-9.
26. Howard W. Odum, *Southern Regions of the United States* (Chapel Hill: University of North Carolina Press, 1936), pp. 5-7.
27. *Ibid.*, p. 7.
28. *Ibid.*, pp. 159-161.
29. Census of Population: 1960, *Characteristics of the Population*, U.S. Summary, Vol. I, Part 1, 1964, p. xxi.

"... *A SQUARE, THE COURTHOUSE in its grove the center; quadrangular around it, the store ... school and church and tavern and bank and jail each in its ordered place. ...*" In this way William Faulkner described the courthouse town, a community spatial structure characteristic of many areas of the country. Originating in colonial Virginia, where county government demanded a setting of importance, the courthouse town continues to provide a social and trading nucleus as well as a political center—a place of congregation for the surrounding county. The courthouse, which serves a judicial function, is frequently of Greek revival temple design, surrounded by grass, sidewalk, and parking places.

► *ECONOMICALLY, the courthouse town also performs important functions. On Saturday, farmers from the surrounding countryside bring their products to town, park their trucks in front of the courthouse, and sell their wares to the townfolk.*

▲ *CHURCHES to serve the community are an integral part of the square.*

▼ *PARK BENCHES are an important element in the social life of the town; here, men discuss community interests while their wives shop. Military memorial in the background is a constant reminder of the town's shared history.*

SOCIAL INSTITUTIONS, POPULATION, AND SOCIAL STRATIFICATION

In Part IV, stress is laid upon the structural aspects of social organization. The general framework of society is conditioned by the binding rules of social institutions, the changing make-up of populations, and the gradations of rank and prestige in stratification systems. From such a perspective, therefore, it is possible to describe and compare societies and to consider some important social trends and issues.

Social institutions are examined in the first two chapters of the Part. Their nature is delineated, a model for their analysis and comparison is constructed, and two main types are identified. Within this frame of reference the economy, government, the family, education, and religion are studied as leading social institutions. Chapter 10 treats the growth, size, composition, dynamics, and distribution of populations in relation to the structures and functions of societies. Chapter 11 examines the nature, sources, types, and consequences of social stratification. The discussion of social structure in this Part of the book brings to an end our study of social organization. The last two Parts will take up the study of social psychology and social change.

Chapter 8

POLITICAL AND ECONOMIC INSTITUTIONS

THE NATURE OF SOCIAL INSTITUTIONS

When people speak of social institutions, they may have different things in mind. Sometimes the term institution calls to mind a complex, bureaucratic organization like the Roman Catholic Church, the United Nations, or a great state university. The large-scale organization is symbolized tangibly by material objects like St. Peter's basilica, the United Nations building, and the halls, laboratories, and libraries of the university. At other times the concept institution refers to sanctioned rules of social action. This seems to be what people mean when they speak of the institution of marriage, money, or slavery. In this sense the stress is on rules of relationship rather than complex organizations.

These two images of social institution have a long and respectable history in social science literature. Some sixty years ago William Graham Sumner defined the structural image of social institution in the following way.

Institutions and laws are produced out of mores. An institution consists of a concept (idea, notion, doctrine, interest) and a structure. The structure is a framework, or apparatus, or perhaps only a number of functionaries set to cooperate in prescribed ways at a certain conjuncture. The structure holds the concept and furnishes instrumentalities for bringing it into the world of facts and action in a way to serve the interests of men in society.[1]

Thirty years later Walton H. Hamilton in a classic essay formulated the definition as follows.

Institution is a verbal symbol which for want of a better describes a cluster of social usages. It connotes a way of thought or action of some prevalence and permanence, which is embedded in the habits of a group or the customs of a people. In ordinary speech it is another word for procedure, convention, or arrangement; in the language of books it is the singular of which the mores or the folkways are the plural. Institutions fix the confines of and impose form upon the activities of human beings. The world of use and wont, to which imperfectly we accommodate our lives, is a tangled and unbroken web of institutions.[2]

After reviewing the various uses of the term, Louis Schneider in 1964 characterized social institution in the following way.

The term denotes an aspect of social life in which distinctive value-orientations and interests, centering upon large and important social concerns (e.g., education, marriage, property) generate or are accompanied by distinctive modes of social action. Its use emphasizes "important" social phenomena, relationships of "strategic structural significance."[3]

Institution is a concept for perceiving the organization of social life. Institutions are observed in all societies and transcend groups, large-scale organizations, categories, and communities. The term refers to the rules of behavior that have been developed to meet universal human problems. Social institutions are structured systems of instrumental, problem-solving norms attached to basic needs issuing from the biopsychic nature of man. Although basic needs are the same in all societies, institutions—or modes of solution—may vary.

For example, human beings are not only born without instincts, they are also almost completely helpless in infancy. Every society therefore must arrange for the care, protection, and training of infants and children. In many societies the mother meets most of these needs. In the upper classes of some societies many of these functions are performed by mother substitutes, e.g., nursemaids, "ayahs," or "black mammies." In some Israeli communities the functions of care, protection, and training of infants and young children are largely performed by the *kibbutz* nursery, the community child-rearing agency.

The universality of human problems and the variability of social solutions suggests the distinction between universal and particularistic institutions. The family, religion, and government, as structural systems of behavior designed to meet basic human needs and problems, are universal institutions. The specific clusters of usages and the types of solutions that are accepted as binding in a given society at a given time are particularistic institutions. Thus the medieval Roman Catholic Church, the Islamic family, or the totalitarian government of the Soviet Union are particularistic institutions.

The sociological study of social institutions is initially concerned with the question of what the rules of behavior are and how they are organized for meeting basic human problems in various societies. More than this, though, we also want an answer to the question "why?" That is, what are the functional consequences of these particular institutions? How well and in what way do they meet the needs they are intended to meet?

A Model for Institutional Analysis ◗ To facilitate the task of institutional description, we have constructed a model with four components: (1) ends, or social functions; (2) means, or normative systems; (3) structure, or role-status hierarchy; and (4) personnel, or implementing groups. With this tool it is possible to describe an institution, trace its changes through time, compare it with other institutions, and even project its possible course of development.

Institutional ends determine the particularistic version of basic human needs which are found in a given society at a given time. Institutional ends are established in the intermediate values of the society's value system.[4] When they are thus invested with value, the ends of an institution are its manifest functions. Some of the functions of institutions, however, are latent, for they are not intended and not recognized. Again, some of the consequences of social institutions are dysfunctional in terms of valued ends of the same or related institutions. When these consequences are recognized, they tend to be defined as social problems.

For example, it has been said that reproduction, protection, social placement, and socialization are universal functions of the institution of the family. In the United States, however, the small (nuclear) middle-class family also tends to encourage, or at least to permit, status striving, competition between the sexes, conspicuous spending, and emotional disturbance of members.

Institutional means are the sanctioned ways of attaining institutional ends. Institutional folkways and mores are integrated to form relatively stable normative systems. Time and rationalization tend to integrate institutional norms and lend them a quality of permanence and unquestioned validity. Learning and the gratification that comes from satisfying experience incorporate norms firmly into personality organization, thus making them largely self-enforcing.

For example, many religious practices have been enshrined as sacraments, and property relationships are often said to be sacred. In a mere twenty years the United Nations has developed and systematized a complicated fabric of usages that are now largely routine for participants. Apprenticeship, internship, and lecturing refer to normative systems that form integral parts of the institution of education in Western societies.

The ends of institutions are so pervasive and their normative systems so comprehensive that virtually all the social activities of a society exist as manifestations of social institutions. Walton H. Hamilton observed, "The range of institutions is as wide as the interests of mankind. . . . About every urge of mankind an institution grows up; the expression of every taste and capacity is crowded into an institutional mold."[5] The clustering and integration of social usage around social ends is a prime source of order in human society.

An *institutional structure* emerges when societal ends are subdivided into individual tasks, allocated to social roles, and ordered in relation to each other. The role-status structure is thus based upon institutional ends and defined by institutional norms. It is adjusted to such external factors as available personnel, the physical environment, other social institutions, and other societies. In form, as will be shown below, institutional structures may vary from the traditional, multifunctional kinship systems of primitive peoples to the instrumental, bureaucratic arrangements of modern associational societies.

For example, the roles and statuses of husband and wife, parents and children vary to produce polygynous and monogamous, patriarchal and democratic, and extended and nuclear family structures. The official titles of a government, industry, or university suggest the formal bureaucratic structure of institutions in the associational society. Every participant is, to use Sumner's words, a functionary set to cooperate at a certain conjuncture.

Institutional personnel are organized, deliberately or unconsciously, into a series of small and extended, formal and informal "implementing groups" which act to facilitate or to obstruct the attainment of institutional ends. The more obvious illustrations of the organization of institutional personnel are to be found in large bureaucratic organizations such as religious denominations and church congregations, nation states and political parties, labor unions and industrial corporations. As we have seen in Chapters 5 and 6, numerous unofficial, informal groups spring up and flourish within such formal institutional collectivities. From this perspective the organization within an institution may be viewed as the pattern of reciprocal arrangement among these constituent groups.

By reference to their relation to the ends and structure of institutions, implementing groups can be classified as *core, secondary,* and *interinstitutional.* Core groups are institutionally indispensable functional collectivities. The institution can neither exist nor function without a core type group. In the institution of the family, the core group is the family unit composed of parents and children; in religion it is the congregation of worshipers, with or without a leader; in education, the class of teacher and learners; in the political institution, the government or collectivity of rulers; and in the economy, the work group or team.

Secondary institutional groups are functionally and structurally relevant but not indispensable to institutions. They reflect the level of functional specialization achieved by an institution. Many of the unofficial formal and informal small groups within large bureaucratic organizations are secondary; the bowling team, the employees' grievance committee, and the volunteer charity group are a few of the more obvious examples. More significant are the secondary groups that typify associational societies. These are specialized groups clustered about all of our modern institutions. They include trade and professional associations, parent organizations, political parties, labor unions and farm associations, and so on almost without end.

Interinstitutional groups are attached to two or more separate institutions. They operate to bridge the gulfs between institutions that have developed in specialized isolation. The committee on Political Education of the AFL-CIO and the Parent-Teacher Association are familiar examples. As William H. Form and Delbert C. Miller demonstrate in Figure 8-1, many basically secondary institutional groups are functionally and structurally interinstitutional. For example, the industry groups and individual industries as well as churches and welfare groups work to influence policy and action of the city government.

Types of Institutions ◗ The institutions of communal societies differ basically in form from those of associational societies. The two types are called "traditional" and "bureaucratic." In contrasting the two, it must be remembered that traditional and bureaucratic are ideal-types and therefore do not fully correspond to actual institutions, which in fact always reveal some combination of features of both. The factor of variability along the power dimension, suggested by Max Weber, is indeed crucial, but other contrasts are equally significant.[6] The differences can be clarified by reference to the components of our institutional model.

Typically, traditional institutions reveal:

1. Multiple, nonrationalized, nonspecialized, implicit ends or functions.
2. Ritualistic, nonrationalized, uncodified, humanistic norms or means.
3. Informal, nonspecialized structures of inclusive kinship or locality roles and statuses.
4. Multiple-function, small, or extended kinship and locality core groups with few secondary and interinstitutional groups.

On the other hand, bureaucratic institutions typically reveal:

1. Unitary, rationalized, specialized, explicit functions or ends.
2. Systems of rationalized, expedient, codified instrumental norms or means.
3. Formal structures of activity specialties hierarchically arranged in explicit cadres of rank and authority.
4. Formal, single-function core groups with an abundance of secondary and interinstitutional groups.

The descriptive model and the ideal polar typology are employed in this and the following chapters in examining the basic institutions of government, economy, family, education, and religion. The materials are organized in four parts. First, the traditional institutional forms

Organizations in the Interinstitutional Complex of Business, Unions, and Government

ECONOMIC AGENCIES	GOVERNMENT
Industry	Mayor's committees
Individual firms	Council Commissions
Business associations	Planning
Chamber of Commerce	Library
Board of Trade	Traffic
Trade Associations	Administrative departments:
Labor	Public Works
Union Locals	Safety
AFL-CIO Council	Health
International and	Parks and recreation
regional representatives	(Board of Education)
Political arms	(Courts)
Committees on	
political education	
Professional	
Associations	
PARTIES	TANGENT ASSOCIATIONS
Central Committee	Municipal league
Ward Committee	League of Women Voters
Precinct Committee	Citizen's Association
Political clubs	Tax Association
Young Republicans	Institutional agencies:
Young Democrats	Church
Candidate clubs	Service clubs
	Welfare groups
	Recreational groups
	Youth agencies
	Veterans' groups

Source: William H. Form and Delbert C. Miller, Industry, Labor and Community, New York, Harper, 1960, Figure 5.1, p. 154.

FIGURE 8-1

of communal societies are described briefly. Next, by means of the analytic components, the transformation of traditional into bureaucratic institutions is traced. Third, modern bureaucratic institutional forms are examined in as much detail as space permits. And, finally, the functional adequacy of the institutions, especially in the United States, for meeting basic human needs will be considered. One brief, though incomplete, way of performing this task is to examine leading functional inadequacies and dysfunctions. However, before beginning the study of basic institutions, it may 'prove useful to examine some illustrations of traditional and bureaucratic forms.

Samoa: Traditional Institutions ♦ Before extensive contacts with the West, Samoa had its own system of traditional institutions. They tended to be diffuse and nonspecialized and structured through the inclusive kinship-locality system.

> Among the Samoans the major unit of social, economic, and religious organization is the "household," or large joint family. Under the leadership of a titled chief the household fulfills such functions as simple agriculture, celebration of religious ceremonies, and organization and management of ordinary social relations. Within the family circle, births, marriages, deaths, and burials are celebrated. The family owns the garden plot as well as both household and gardening utensils. Arrangements exist within the household for care of the sick, supervision and protection of children, organization and management of courtship, transmission of social skills and lore, and redress of minor personal injuries.
>
> Ten or more households combine to form a village or self-governing. political unit. Though held together by kinship and the need for mutual protection, the village fulfills other important social functions. The household chiefs form a village assembly which combines legislative and judicial functions and organizes all village-wide activities. The village owns and manages the fishing waters, carries on certain religious activities, and manages some relations among the constituent households.
>
> Occasionally several villages combine to form a larger political unit, or kind of district state. Its principal administrative agency is a council of village chiefs. The district manages such activities as war with other districts, relations among the constituent villages, district-wide religious ceremonies, and the punishment of heinous crimes.[7]

Harlan County: Institutional Transition ♦ Harlan County, Kentucky, in the years just prior to World War I revealed a pattern of institutional development in a society in transition from communal to associational. Some institutional structures, notably government and economy, were beginning to separate from the inclusive kinship-locality system and assume specialized form. The descriptive model constitutes a tool for bringing into view the areas and extent of institutional separation and specialization.

> Harlan County was inhabited by a group of mountain folk who constituted a large, self-contained communal society. Until the development of coal mining in 1911, this was an extremely isolated area. For more than a century the mountain folk had lived a self-contained life, their farms and household industries producing most of their necessities.
>
> In this stable society the family and the local community were the two basic units of social organization. . . . The heavy labor of clearing fields or building houses was done by neighbors working together on an informal basis of mutual aid. The people shared a common body of folkways and mores which came down to them from pioneer days. . . .

The people were independent and self reliant. There were no class distinctions and every man felt himself the equal of all others. . . . But Harlan had no active feud tradition. . . . On the whole the people were content to live a quiet, peaceful life following the traditions of their ancestors and paying little attention to what went on outside their narrow valleys.

In the realms of economic and political activity the Harlan County folk were being incorporated within the institutional structure of the larger surrounding society. A few manufactured articles were laboriously imported over the mountains. Cattle and lumber were shipped out, the latter being floated down on the flood waters of the Cumberland River. Some money was therefore in circulation in the county, but most economic relations were conducted by barter.

Meanwhile, the county and state governments ordered and regulated certain relations among the mountain folk as well as relations between the various communities and neighboring counties. Spirited political campaigning was common, and county government was, on the whole, honest though not always very efficient. The organization and control of private and personal relations, however, remained within the control of the family and community.[8]

The United States: Bureaucratic Institutions ‣ In Figure 8-2 Delbert C. Miller and William H. Form portray schematically the particularistic institutions and their relative dominance in the bureaucratic "institutional complex" of the United States in 1900 and in 1960. The length of the bars expresses an estimate of the relative dominance of the specific institutions within the total complex and reveals changes in these relations between 1900 and 1960. The figure shows that social behavior in a number of areas has become increasingly separated from the inclusive kinship-locality structure and organized into particularistic bureaucratic institutions. Many functions formerly fulfilled by informal organizations of kinsmen and neighbors have been incorporated into specialized institutions, thus increasing their dominance. At the same time, whole new areas of bureaucratic specialization have emerged, while others, such as the church, have declined in dominance.

POLITICAL INSTITUTIONAL ORGANIZATION

Traditional Political Institutions ‣ Every society must establish a system for maintaining order and for managing relations with neighbors. These functions can be discharged in many different ways. In most communal societies, social control occurs as an incidental aspect of living. As shown above, few specialized agencies are required to maintain order or to manage relations with other societies. Instead, the prevailing mores and the kinship-village structures are largely self-enforcing.[9]

Yet, even in the simplest society with the most rudimentary culture the mores and kinship-locality agencies cannot discharge all social control functions. Everyone is not fully acquainted with or committed to the societal values. Some problems cannot be handled in traditional ways. Occasionally it is necessary or desirable to organize certain social activities deliberately. These and other circumstances tend to foster the concentration of power. Robert Michels believes this tendency is universal in human society and calls it the "iron law of oligarchy."[10]

It is therefore possible to identify some social control roles in communal societies. They are indicated by such terms as chief, shaman, elder, warrior, and the like. The role of chief issues from kinship or locality organization. The authority of elders results from the prestige accorded age. Roles like shaman and warrior reflect the specialization of activities within the society. The number of such roles, their definition and degree of specialization, vary from one communal society to another.

Power Structuring of Bureaucratic American Institutions in 1900 and in 1960

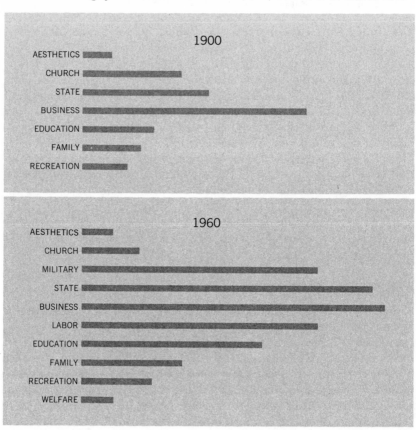

Source: Delbert C. Miller and William H. Form, Industrial Sociology, New York, Harper, 1951, Figures 127 and 128, pp. 853 and 854.

FIGURE 8-2

Often, too, rudimentary political structures are observed in communal societies. For example, in Samoa there was the village council of chiefs with legislative and judicial functions. Harlan County had its local governmental organization and spirited political campaigns. Yet, even where seminal political organization exists, most social control is still managed by kinship and locality units and issues from the power of the self-enforcing norms.

Transition of Institutional Forms ◗ The transitional process is illustrated in the situation of Harlan County described above. The intrusion of coal mining and improvement of transportation facilitated contacts with the outside society. The money nexus began to replace barter as the mechanism of economic activity. Formal state government entered the valleys through the mediation of county government and political parties. Thus we can see the self-enforcing mores and extended kinship-locality agencies giving way to the bureaucratic structures and explicit norms of modern political institutions.

With continued change, traditional institutional forms tend to give way to specialized bureaucratic arrangements. Conquest, mass migration, and population growth may change the situation to which society must adapt. Social and cultural contacts between societies tend to modify the forms of social control. Occupational, economic, cultural, and ethnic specialization foster diversity of social perspectives, interests, and backgrounds. Urbanization and industrialization place a severe strain on the control techniques of traditional political institutions.

Under the impact of these and other social changes, the communal institutions of control and societal relations become less and less able to regulate major areas of social life and to adjust the growing conflicts of individual and collective interests. Rising individualism and group autonomy require an external system of control. Conditions like these produce a need for explicit social norms and specialized authority structures to replace weakening communal expectations and kinship agencies.

Typically, the political society becomes a nation. Self-consciousness and in-group sentiment crystallize about the native language and home territory. The society creates a sense of its history and evolves a conviction of its destiny. This cluster of sentiments and ideas, known as nationalism, may be symbolized by "the fatherland," "zionism," "manifest destiny," or some other evidence of unity. Nationalism and the sense of nationhood are major forces in the transition of political institutions.

The State ◗ The specialized institution of social control is called the *state*. The state may be defined as that specialized social system and social structure that legitimately monopolizes the use of force of a collectivity within a specific territory for the discharge of recognized functions of maintaining internal order and managing relations with other societies.[11] The potential use of force as the ultimate sanction for maintaining internal order is expressed in the phrase "police power." The monopoly of force in external relations gives the state the unique right to make and terminate wars and to negotiate treaties with other societies.

Rudiments of the state may be seen in many communal societies, such as the village councils of household chiefs and the district councils of village chiefs in Samoa. Political forms are more specialized in the spirited campaigns and inept local government in Harlan County. Terms like mayor, board of aldermen, county commissioners, justice of the peace, governor, or state assembly are familiar symbols of the modern state in our daily lives. One image called up by the word "state" is that of a far-flung, complicated network of officials and public activities. In England this means the Queen, the Prime Minister, the Cabinet, and the Houses of Parliament set atop the "civil service," which is the British equivalent of our administrative bureaucracies.

Logan Wilson and William L. Kolb observe that the state exists in society wherever the following conditions are fulfilled.

1. Where there is a governmental system or ruling group.
2. Where a distinction is made between legal (explicit) norms and community (implicit, self-enforcing) norms.
3. Where a separation is made between the area of life controlled by law and those not so controlled.[12]

At least three other characteristics of the state merit attention. First, the exercise of legitimate power is based upon and conditioned by the consent of the society. Second, the exercise of legitimate power and the discharging of basic functions are regulated by a series of sanctioned norms. And finally, the state is superimposed upon a complex fabric of formal and informal nonpolitical groups and norms that both support and oppose its objectives. Therefore the state must both influence and be influenced by the overall societal consensus. The state is likely to be stable and effective when the general fabric of social organization and usage supports its functions and reënforces its sanctions. Instability, ineffectiveness, and change in political organization may issue from social situations where the state finds little support in the general nonpolitical social matrix.

MODERN POLITICAL ORGANIZATION

Modern bureaucratic political organization is varied and complex. Terms like monarchy, parliamentary democracy, totalitarianism, and republic suggest some of the variety in the organization of nation-states. Above this level the North Atlantic Treaty Organization, the Southeast Asia Treaty Organization, and the Organization of American States are examples of specialized international regional structures. The United Nations is the most inclusive worldwide political organization. Within the nation, region, province, county, and township are subordinate units of governmental organization.

Part of the complexity of modern American political organization results from the lack of coordination among a great many specialized administrative units. For example, over thirty years ago Charles E. Merriam and associates identified 1,642 governmental units in metropolitan Cook County, Illinois.[13] They included 240 cities and villages, 165 townships, 878 school districts, 70 park districts, 4 forest preserve districts, 11 sanitary districts, 190 drainage districts, 4 mosquito abatement districts, and one health district.

In the top half of Figure 8-3, some of the outstanding characteristics of modern complex political organization are summarized in terms of the institutional model. The figure indicates that the varied functions performed by modern governments are carried out by means of complex bureaucratic organizations. Although political behavior can be organized in many different ways, the table shows certain basic elements that are found in all modern states.

The lower part of the figure draws attention to some differences between modern democratic and authoritarian political institutions. Typically, democratic systems stress political functions, while authoritarian governments undertake a wide range of political, economic, and social operations. The formal structures required by these functions differ in both inclusiveness and rigidity. Thus, democratic systems grant citizens much wider areas of voluntary action than do authoritarian organizations. The values of democratic political institutions emphasize the welfare of the individual, while authoritarian systems tend to subordinate individuals to the service of the society.

The Politics of Developing Societies ▶ In the developing societies of Africa, Asia, Latin America, the Middle East, and Oceania the transition from traditional to bureaucratic political institutions is rapid and often precipitated suddenly by outside forces. The goal sought by most of these societies is some form of democratic organization. The transformation of their political institutions is just one dimension of the worldwide emergence of primitive society, with its simple technology, into modern complex civilization. The attendant problems of political instability are one of the signs of rapid social change.

The establishment of democratic political institutions in these societies presupposes the existence of a fully functioning pluralistic social organization.[14] Individuals still partly rooted in tribal organization are expected to pursue their various interests through specialized economic, religious, educational, recreational, and political associations. It is intended that the coalition and compromise of these clashing interests within democratic institutions will produce a stable democratic process. However, few individuals have had any experience or developed any skill for action outside the inclusive roles and patterns of the kinship-locality system.

In the Western nations, the majority of citizens are literate and can read about the issues and candidates. In the newly developing societies,

Components of the Political Institution

Ends-Functions, Intermediate Values
Maintain internal order and manage relations with other societies
Legitimately preëmpt force and expropriate individual wealth and labor
Render services to member groups and individuals
Conduct developmental planning

Means, Normative Systems
Legal, administrative, and judicial rules
Police, military, and diplomatic norms
Economic and social engineering patterns
Partisan political norms
Citizenship norms, e.g., jury duty, voting, tax paying, military service

Role-Status Hierarchies
Rulers (hereditary, elective, appointive) and the ruled
Legislative, executive, and judicial roles and statuses, e.g., the policeman, the soldier, the diplomat
Citizen roles, e.g., juryman, passport holder, licensee, constituent
Political party roles: e.g., leader, worker, member

Personnel, Implementing Groups
Core group: e.g., council of elders, the government, the presidium
Secondary groups: e.g., diet or parliament, political party, department staff
Interinstitutional groups: e.g., political action arm of labor union, League of Women Voters, American Legion

FIGURE 8-3

however, most individuals are illiterate, and mass communication via the press is thus impossible. As David Riesman has pointed out recently, though, in many developing countries the base of political participation is being greatly expanded by widespread use of radio and cinema in political communication.[15]

The rapid development of specialized political institutions often

Analytic Contrast of Democratic and Authoritarian Political Organization

Democratic	Authoritarian
Functions	
Maintain internal order	Maintain internal order
Manage relations with others	Manage relations with others
Supervise the economy	- -
Limited economic operations	Operate total economy
Essential planning and development	Inclusive planning for development
Many services for citizens	Rational utilization of citizens
Principally for the individual	Principally for the society
Norms	
Explicit codified legal	Explicit codified legal
Limited technical	Extensive technical
Voluntary citizen action	Citizen regimentation
Roles-Statuses	
Ranked cadres of explicit governmental	Ranked cadres of explicit governmental
Limited cadres of technical	Extensive cadres of technical
Many voluntary citizen	Few voluntary citizen
Citizen and alien (open categories)	Citizen and alien (closed categories)
Implementing Groups	
Government core group	Government core group
Numerous secondary associations	Few secondary associations
Many interinstitutional associations	Few interinstitutional associations

FIGURE 8-3 CONTINUED

taxes the limited indigenous leadership of developing countries. For example, when Belgium granted independence to the Congo, there were fewer than fifty university-trained Congolese in the country. The dearth of indigenous leadership accentuates the problems of communication, education, and organization already mentioned.

In the face of problems like these, it is difficult to establish viable democratic political institutions in developing or newly independent societies. In some large and important countries, successful and relatively stable democratic systems have been established. However, in many other instances the transition from traditional to modern political institutions is fraught with dangers. There is the chance that a leader or group of leaders may seize power from the uncertain democratic system and establish some type of authoritarian regime. At the same time, the opportunity exists for ideological antidemocratic forces to organize in opposition to the establishment of any type of democratic institutions. Again, new nations whose boundaries were often determined arbitrarily by colonial governments may lack any traditions or institutions of national unity. With the ending of colonial rule, many of these nations find their survival threatened by powerful regional and tribal conflicts and rivalries.

Structural Strains in the American Political System ▶ Political organization in the United States is composed of a complicated network of units. The superstructure is a federal republic of three basic parts, containing numerous administrative departments, agencies, commissions, and bureaus. There are fifty relatively independent governmental structures at the state level, plus two roughly equivalent territorial governments. The total system includes 3,058 county units, 17,202 townships, 17,118 incorporated places, and countless school, sanitary, and other administrative districts.

This complex structure is subdivided both vertically and horizontally. Vertically, four levels can be identified: the national, or federal; the state and territorial; the county; and the municipal-township levels. This hierarchical pattern is traditional and its subdivisions are organized on the basis of both territory and authority.

The hierarchical system tends to be rigid and is often out of touch with the changing realities of associational society. For example, the 1960 census of population reported 216 standard metropolitan statistical areas in the United States.[16] Although each of these areas approximates a single unit of social and economic organization and function, all are administered by numerous overlapping, quasi-independent, and relatively unchanging units of government. Another consequence of this structural rigidity is the continuing controversy over legislative reapportionment at both federal and state levels. Or again, the administration of many governmental services, e.g., the courts, public welfare, or traffic control, is limited by the fact that state and county boundary lines are no longer meaningfully related to population distribution and movement.

Horizontally, legislative, executive, and judicial functions are separated at all levels of government. The tripartite pattern is most clearly revealed in the federal and state systems; in local units the tradition is respected, even though it cannot always be observed.

The pattern of horizontal separation has tended to magnify some problems of government. The growing size, complexity, and instability of associational society require a degree of operational flexibility that is frequently impossible within the tripartite structure. The legislative process seems inordinately slow and cumbersome. In recent years administrative agencies have tended to exercise legislative and judicial authority.

This situation has provoked a sharp and continuing controversy both in and out of government. As suggested by the Hoover commission on governmental reorganization, some individuals advocate streamlining and further centralizing the federal government structure.[17] Others resist this suggestion and complain about the alleged encroachment of the executive and judicial branches upon the domain of the legislature.

Politics of the Mass Society ▶ Some have argued that large, complex industrial societies like the United States face political difficulties from another quarter.[18] The transition from "pluralistic" to "mass" society is said to threaten the integrity and adequacy of democratic political institutions. In pluralistic societies the interests of individuals are said to be organized and expressed through a variety of specialized associations. These associations provide the individual with anchorages of identity and permit expression and attainment of his various goals. The political process is viewed as the clash, coalition, and compromise of these various organized interests within the framework of democratic institutions. The resultant political society is seen to be essentially conservative and tolerant of differences of views and interests.

The advocates of the theory of mass politics argue that the rise of mass society tends to destroy, or at least to neutralize, the adequacy of the pluralistic system. Mass communication and extensive mobility detach the individual from the traditional organizations of the pluralistic society, e.g., family, community, class, ethnic group. New collectivities and aggregations develop to encompass participation in mass society, e.g., diffuse crowds, publics, mass audiences, fandoms. As a consequence, the traditional groups of the pluralistic society are said to disintegrate or atrophy, and the individual becomes alienated and incomplete. The institutions of democratic political organization, it is concluded, no longer express the interests of people or permit their involvement and commitment in the political process.

In mass society, it is said, masses of alienated individuals are swayed

BY VOTING, and sometimes
also by relating personally to
their elected representatives,
Americans enter directly into
the political process. By the
force of his personality,
presidential candidate John
F. Kennedy enabled people to
join him in breaking through
mass impersonality to a
warmer relationship.

aimlessly by propaganda appeals, or tend to withdraw from the political process in "apathy." Power tends to be concentrated in the control of large-scale organizations and power elites. Political process in the mass society, then, involves technical operations in mass persuasion.

Another political alternative of the mass society is called "ideological politics." This tendency refers to the emergence and organization of coercive antidemocratic forces that reject the pluralistic model and the process of compromise. The ideological extremists of right and left reject the idea of difference of views and interests, the compromise of differences, and the temporary acceptance of defeat. It is argued that the mass society provides fertile soil for the growth of such ideological extremist views and movements.

At least one observer disagrees with this gloomy theory of mass politics. Joseph R. Gusfield believes that factors in the mass society sustain democratic institutions and processes.[19] He writes: "Conditions of mass societies also provide support to democratic political norms through the consequences of mass communications, equalitarianism, and bureaucratization for national societies." That is, the mass society establishes the conditions and provides the mechanisms for including its masses in decision-making and collective action. The process is not less democratic than formerly because its structures, mechanisms, and orientations are new.

Expanding Functions of Government ♦ One of the most striking changes in modern political organization is the expansion of the functions of government.[20] This development results in part from the fact that some tasks can be performed adequately only by government, in part from the growing complexity of social organization and in part from ideological considerations. The growth of governmental functions necessitates extension and elaboration of political structures, and tends to limit the role of individual participation in governmental decisions and policies.

Maintenance of internal order and management of relations with other societies remain the fundamental functions of political institutions. Yet, even these traditional functions are taking on new meanings. For example, managing relations with other societies requires the United States and the Soviet Union to develop plans and rules for the exploration and occupation of the moon.

The older democracies of the West, e.g., the United Kingdom, France, and the United States, have tended to add new functions to government reluctantly and usually after other methods proved unavailable or unsatisfactory. For example, in the United States, radio and television were permitted to develop as free enterprises under governmental supervision. However, England and France established both as governmental monopolies.

In many of the newer democracies, e.g., India, Israel, or the African nations, and in the totalitarian countries, e.g., the Soviet Union, China, or Yugoslavia, government assumed from the outset many nontraditional functions. As a result, in the older democracies government tends to "supervise" the economic and social order, while in the newer democracies and totalitarian states government appears to "operate" or "control" the society.

In the United States the greatest expansion of governmental functions has occurred in the areas of public service, developmental planning, polar and outer space exploration, and military preparedness. Each new responsibility for government has provoked a serious policy debate and has been undertaken reluctantly. The new functions determine a large part of the activity of the federal government.

Trends and Issues ♦ When political organization is considered in broad perspective, it is possible to identify some leading trends and continuing issues. The dominant current trend in political life is the almost universal and irresistible push of the unprivileged masses as they force their way into the political process. Opposing this trend is the force of the authoritarian ideologies of right and left, which produces a struggle that conditions all relations among nations. The decay of empire fragments old units of political organization and permits the emergence of numerous small, often doubtfully viable, new nation states. On the other hand, the tendency toward empire building by the great totalitarian states, and the thrust toward international union by the free democracies, extend the areas and spheres of political unity.

At the same time, political institutions are confronted with some continuing issues. One of these is grounded in the society-individual antithesis that is structured in varying ways in all societal value systems. The proper balance and compromise of individual and collective ends challenges governments everywhere. The challenge of extremist ideologies is a major issue for political institutions of the democratic *genre*. The issue is both how to retain the values of diversity, tolerance, and compromise, and how to utilize these humanistic values in the mass societies that are developing in many parts of the world.

One final issue must be noted briefly. It is a consequence of the increase in size, the growth of bureaucratic complexity, and the spread of mass characteristics experienced by many societies today. These phenomena create their own dysfunctions and problems, and necessitate a reconsideration of desired ends and means of government. One aspect of the issue is the search for a means of involvement of vast numbers of dispersed and alienated individuals in the political process. Another aspect is the search for efficiency—for the size and form of governmental structure that is most favorable to rapid and efficient operations. While these two requirements may appear incompatible in the short run, it is more likely that neither can be fulfilled very long unless an adequate balance can be achieved between them. Governments everywhere continue to struggle with the problem and experiment with various forms of the basic bureaucratic model.

ECONOMIC STRUCTURE

Economic Organization of Communal and Associational Societies ◗ The members of every society must obtain food, clothing, shelter, and other necessities from their environment and organize their social relations for these purposes. A wide range of activities are incorporated in the different systems of economic organization. In most primitive societies, economic activity is only slightly differentiated from the ordinary business of living. Food gathering, fishing, hunting, simple agriculture, pastoral activities, and the processing and manufacture of materials and utensils are regular phases of family, clan, and community life. There are few specialized economic norms and but little material equipment.[21] The business of gaining a living is fused integrally into the process of living the traditional way of life.

Economic activities are closely integrated with the controlling ultimate values. Magic, recreation, art, or ancestor worship, for example, may be expressed in the manufacture of weapons and utensils, the cultivation of yam or taro patches, and the organization of hunting or trading expeditions.

With change, economic values of the intermediate order become separated from the ultimate purposes of the society. Figure 8-4 summarizes the changes that have occurred in the West along four dimensions of the economic institution. The production, control, and exchange of economic values were preëmpted by special groups or classes. The economic organization became itself specialized, and was used to advance and consolidate the power and prestige of the special classes or groups rather than to serve the whole society.[22] The resulting inequitable distribution of economic values, social power, and community prestige engendered and accentuated conflicts of interest among the various sectors and groups of society. While many non-Western nations are following different and often highly accelerated routes to economic development, some elements in the table are applicable to all industrializing societies.

Factors Basic to Modern Economic Institutions ▶ Modern economic institutions are uniquely characteristic of associational societies. Only in this societal situation can those conditions be found that permit and nourish such forms as the corporation, the bureaucratic industrial organization, and the labor union federation.[23] Five major factors seem to have determined the emergence of modern economic organization. In combination they differentiate between traditional and bureaucratic economic institutions.

First, there arose stable and calculable political and monetary systems. Government administration became subject to the control of law, and acquired steady predictability. Legal systems became rational, universally applicable, and predictable. A formally rational system of money was established and stabilized. A system of credit was established, and economic values could then be calculated, transferred, and managed.

Second, a high degree of control was achieved over the technical basis of production. This was in substantial part a result of the advance of science and its application to technology. Methods were developed for controlling and managing capital, raw materials, transportation, production, and labor, and were applied in the invention and exploitation of the factory system, mass production, the assembly line, and automation.

Third, raw materials, finished products, human services, managerial skill, and capital became available as resources for exclusive economic uses, and dissociated from other possible or socially important purposes. All of these factors were invested with an impersonal, determinate money value, and were structured into new forms of economic enterprise and activity. Just as economic factors were divorced from their traditional social context, so economic objectives of profit and production were dissociated from society's ultimate values. This phenomenon is intimately related to the other changes listed here, and

Phases of Development Along Four Dimensions of the Economic Institution

Phases of Technology

Traditional and non-
rationalistic processes;
hand tools

Machine power and
machine tools

Applied scientific and
technical processes

Phases of Economic Organization

I   Production organization

Kinship-locality groups

Individual enterprise
Individual/family units
Domestic workshops
Industrial factories

Collective enterprises
Church or state
Corporate enterprise

II Market Organization
Barter and direct
money exchange
Self-regulating market
Structured competitive
market system
Administrative market
system

Phases of Property

Communal ownership

Public ownership of
capital
Land capitalism
Industrial capitalism
Finance capitalism
Monopoly capitalism

Phases of Production

Food gathering, hunting
and fishing

Agriculture and herding

Domestic handcraft

Industrial machine craft

FIGURE 8-4

to the rise of secularism and scientific rationality occurring during the same period.

Fourth, the new type of society favored concentration of nonhuman means of production in the hands of owners and created a body of workers free from formal ties or obligations. Owner-worker relations were depersonalized and subjected to rational considerations of economic calculation. The worker no longer enjoyed a quasi-sacred claim upon a particular job, and the tools he used became the property of the employer. This system permitted a degree of control and manipulation hitherto impossible.

Finally, the system tended to glorify the free contract. The contract—a limited agreement between free individuals for the performance of specified tasks—became the indispensable link in all economic relations. The individuals involved were the sole determinants of the economic contracts they entered into, and there were no external restraints on economic activity. This situation was justified by the widespread belief that human conduct was rational and determined by enlightened economic self-interest. Economic activity was therefore thought to result from conscious, rationalistic, and enlightened agreements among individuals, and was believed to lead automatically to the welfare of the greatest number. As a consequence of these beliefs, there was little disposition to regulate production, prices, wages, or consumption, as typically occurred in communal Europe.

Transition of Economic Forms ◗ The transformation of economic organization along four dimensions is outlined in Figure 8-4.[24] Before the dawn of recorded history, food gathering, hunting, and fishing as major sources of livelihood gave way to agriculture and herding in many parts of the world. The domestic handicrafts of the Middle Ages were superseded in the Industrial Revolution by machines and rational processes. In our economic era, scientific technology and automatic machines are commonplace.

Through most of man's history, his major source of productive power was human labor, supplemented in part by animals, wind, and water. His tools were simple and, by modern standards, yielded little in return for the energy expended in making and using them. Primitive man had such tools as rude hoes, knives, arrows, spears, and boomerangs. Our recent ancestors employed spinning wheels, wooden plows, flintlock rifles, and two-edged steel axes. Processes of agriculture, animal husbandry, production, and management were a combination of tradition and common sense.

The rise of science and empiricism at the end of the Middle Ages transformed man's technology. The steam, electric, and internal combustion engines replaced human beings, draft animals, wind, and water as major sources of productive energy. New, powerful, and sophisticated tools were operated by the power machines. The spinning wheel and hand loom yielded to textile machines; and the wooden plow, hand pump, and other simple farm tools were replaced. Applied scientific processes of agriculture, animal husbandry, marketing, and management superseded the mixture of folklore, tradition, and common sense that had guided mankind for so long. Again, as shown in Figure 8-4, the discharge of economic functions through kinship-locality groups gave way to associational forms of economic organization. Individuals and families emerged as operators of businesses of many kinds, domestic handicraft centers, and later great manufacturing establishments. In the Middle Ages the Church, and often the state, had been collective agencies of economic enterprise. The decisive modern development in economic organization was the development and spread of the business corporation and its variants.

At the same time, the market changed and became elaborated. In communal societies the market was largely associated with a particular market *place,* and was restricted to barter and direct money exchanges of a limited range of goods.

In the late eighteenth and early nineteenth centuries, under the influence of the Industrial Revolution, the market tended to develop into an almost automatic self-regulating mechanism for free competition and exchange.[25] Later, as economic units became larger and competition came under more deliberate management, the market took on the tasks of regulating structured competition and rational exchange. At present, under "monopoly capitalism" and powerful governmental regulation, the market has been transformed into a series of interlocking and competitively cooperating spheres administering prices, competition, and exchange.

In many primitive societies, as suggested by Figure 8-4, land and major productive resources are held in communal ownership by kinship and locality groups. While group members have rights to the use or the fruits of these resources, exclusive individual ownership is rare. The notion of exclusive private ownership constitutes one key differential between communal and associational economic institutions.

Much property has been held publicly. For example, in the Middle Ages the Church owned great domains often containing thousands of manorial estates. At present the Soviet state owns the major "means of production," e.g., factories, mines, railroads, and banks. However, in most associational societies productive property is privately owned, often by individuals. This notion is basic to the ideology of capitalism and distinguishes all modern associational societies.

Some Distinctive Features of the American Economy ▶ The American economy has the tasks of raw material extraction, agriculture, manufacturing, transportation, communication, distribution of economic values, and financial operations. It fulfills many noneconomic functions as well. The broad societal functions are subdivided into innumerable specific services and activities. For example, Figure 8-5 illustrates this tendency in the advertised list of customer services provided by a small urban bank.

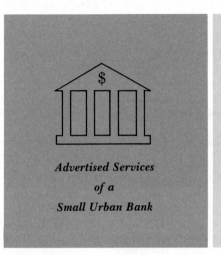

SAVING ACCOUNTS

BANKING BY MAIL

CHECKING ACCOUNTS

SAFE DEPOSIT BOXES

AUTO LOANS

BANK PERSONAL LOANS

TRAVELERS CHECKS

CHRISTMAS CLUBS

HOME IMPROVEMENT LOANS

BUSINESS LOANS

APPLIANCE LOANS

Advertised Services

of a

Small Urban Bank

Source: Advertising of Mechanics and Farmers Bank, Durham, N.C.

FIGURE 8-5

As we might expect, given its scope and almost infinite range of functions, the American economy includes a large number of units of varying sizes and types. For example, the *Statistical Abstract* of the United States reported in 1964 a total of 299,036 manufacturing establishments.[26] In 1961 there were 3,811,000 farms and 4,713,000 business firms in the United States.[27] In addition, there are thousands of local craft and industrial unions federated into national and international structures with city, county, and state echelons. Further evidence of complexity is seen in such business and trade-oriented organizations as the Chamber of Commerce of the United States, the National Association of Manufacturers, the American Bankers Association, and their state and local branches. Professional associations of physicians, lawyers, engineers, architects, and many more form an additional part of the complex whole. There are three large agricultural organizations—the National Grange, the American Farm Bureau Association, and the National Farmers Union—together with their state and local units. The economy also includes many governmental divisions, such as the Post Office Department and the United States Mint, quasi-independent corporations like the Tennessee Valley Authority and the Home Owners Loan Corporation, control instrumentalities like the Federal Reserve System and the Federal Deposit Insurance Corporation, service agencies like the Social

Security Administration and the Office of Education, and operating branches like the military.

Another aspect of the complexity of the economy is the variety of different modes in which units may be organized. The largest number of units is individually owned. The partnership remains a common mode of organization. The corporation, however, tends to dominate the economy, not because of the number of such units, but because of their great size and power. Corporate complexity is further increased by such devices of intercorporate coordination as the trust, the holding company, the interlocking directorate, and the cartel.

Industrial Organization ▶ In the United States, industry is the dominant type of economic activity, and the corporation is the leading form of industrial organization. Industry is characterized by mass production under the factory system with advanced technology. Extreme specialization and division of labor are coupled with mechanization and automation. These conditions permit standardization of manufacturing processes and require close integration of tasks.

Ownership of the industrial corporation has increasingly become diffused among large numbers of stockholders, but at the same time the actual control and management of ongoing operations and policies has become increasingly centralized. This centralization of control in the giant enterprises has brought with it ever-growing bureaucratization and has made intercorporate coordination increasingly feasible and attractive to management. As a counterweight to the industrial giants, opposing and balancing labor unions have developed with comparable power and centralization of control. The concentration of power in labor and industry, and the struggles between and within each faction, have led increasingly to a definition of the role of government as the rule-maker, arbiter, and compromiser functioning in the "public interest."

As far back as 1948, William N. Husband and James C. Dockeray could assert that "corporations today account for over 80 per cent of the total production of goods, workers employed, and wages paid."[28] Even before the Second World War, some 92 per cent of the total output of manufactured goods was produced by corporations. A generation ago the giant corporations had come to dominate the structure of American industry. Thus David Lynch noted in 1946 that the top five per cent of employers had 70 per cent of all workers.[29] Some large corporations control or condition the lives of hundreds of thousands of individuals. For example, the United States Steel Corporation reported an average of 273,562 employees during the second quarter, 1953. In recent years the General Motors Company has been referred to as the largest business corporation in the world.

A. A. Berle, Jr., and Gardiner C. Means point out that industrial corporations assume responsibilities and fulfill functions outside the sphere of pure economic activity.[30] Sometimes giant corporations wield as much social power as small states. In many instances an economic organization affects the structure and process of an entire community or even of a group of communities.

Economic activities which are organized bureaucratically, whether through the corporation or otherwise, tend to develop structural similarities. Thus, the economic organization in modern democratic and authoritarian societies reveals important institutional similarities. Our model of institutional organization helps to highlight many of these. Upon examination, the major differences between economic organization in modern democratic and authoritarian societies are seen to lie in the sources of control and the ends sought through economic activity.

The major components of economic organization under varying societal situations can be summarized as follows:

I. *Ends-functions, intermediate values*
   Obtain subsistence, i.e., food, shelter, etc.
   Produce, manipulate, exchange, and distribute material and non-material economic values
   Produce many kinds of services
   Organize and manage power
   Operate system for distribution of goods and services
   Many noneconomic functions, e.g., population redistribution, influences upon occupational and class structures, individual gratifications
   Various dysfunctions, e.g., unemployment, waste, labor-management conflict, etc.

II. *Means, normative systems*
   A. Property: principle of usufruct (no ownership), public ownership (by church or state), private ownership (exclusive, often individual)
   B. Management: by kinship-locality group, by other institutions, e.g., church or state, or by specialized economic institutions, e.g., corporation
      Management of ownership, production, research and development, sales and promotion, etc.
   C. Exchange: barter, money, market
   D. Technology: Hand tools and traditional processes, machine tools and applied scientific processes

III. *Status-role hierarchies*
   Sex-age division of labor
   Owners, managers, workers
   Collateral orders (staff principle), e.g., technicians
   Labor union organization
   Consumers

IV. *Personnel, implementing groups*
    Core group, work team
    Secondary groups, stockholders, labor union, trade association
    Interinstitutional groups, political action councils of labor unions, private nonprofit foundations

The Economics of Developing Societies ◗ A transition from traditional to bureaucratic economic forms is occurring in all the developing societies of Asia, Africa, Latin America, and Oceania. In contrast to the West, in these countries the process is officially controlled and carried forward with a sense of urgency. People attempt to make the jump from a communal, hoe and herding economy to modern urban technological economic organization in a single generation or less. Many such economies find it difficult to survive, and all confront severe problems of development and adjustment.

When the colonial peoples became politically independent they tended also to become more or less estranged from European economic organizations. Thus deprived of the leadership and resources formerly provided by the colonial power, and having few such resources of their own, these societies were obliged to turn to government to initiate and support the process of economic development. By force of historic circumstances, then, the economic systems of the developing societies were controlled by government from the outset. This situation was aggravated in the Communist countries, whose ideologies estranged them still further from the economic resources of the older capitalist countries.

The establishment of modern economic systems in the new nations presents some difficult problems. First, investment capital must be acquired, often at first by grants or loans from the West (and lately from the Communist bloc nations), but ultimately from the accumulation of savings.[31] However, capital accumulation is rendered difficult by inflationary pressures where the standard of living is very low, and by the pressure of rapid population increase. For example, many of the new nations of Africa have had to struggle against the inflationary effect of rising living standards, while India is threatened by explosive population growth.

In the developing nations, economic transition means a rapid shift from the technology and organization of a hoe economy under a kinship-locality system to advanced machine technology, bureaucratic organization, and complex accounting-marketing operations. In addition to capital, the emerging societies require indigenous resources of leadership, organization, and technical skill. One major initial resource to meet these needs has been technical assistance from the older industrial nations, often including the former colonial power. In time, leaders and technicians trained in the West or with foreign assistance at home increase in number and are able to train others.

Further, the developing economies must now operate within a world market system. This means that raw materials and manufactured goods must be sold, so that the foreign exchange thus earned can be used to purchase goods and services that the young society cannot produce for itself. But the developing society has had little experience in the world market system and does not have an established place in the market structure. Moreover, this new dependence on worldwide market processes tends to subject the society to forces completely beyond its control, and generally beyond the comprehension of the mass of workers. For example, peasant workers on coffee plantations in Brazil, tobacco farms in Rhodesia, or rubber plantations in Malaysia may suffer economic privations because of the vagaries of a world market quite foreign to their limited experience. Under colonial rule, many of these countries had come to depend on a single cash crop or mineral resource to provide the major part of their foreign exchange. As the old communal economy declines, subsistence agriculture is no longer adequate to meet the needs of the population, and new needs for goods and services continue to mushroom. In order to reduce their dependency on the fluctuating market for raw materials, most developing nations believe their best hope for economic self-sufficiency lies in a combination of diversified agriculture and rapid industrialization.

The American Economy ♦ All of the problems of transition and development mentioned above have long since been solved in the United States and the other older capitalist societies. The American economy has become incredibly vast, complicated, and inclusive. Today, the American economic system is so fully integrated into the total way of life that it is no longer possible to draw a clear line between purely economic and noneconomic organizations and activities.[32] For example, the United States government with its vast budget, staff, and expenditures is the largest economic organization in the society. In many communities a university or religious agency is the largest economic enterprise. Again, a man's occupation is not just an economic fact, but the key to his entire style of life. This integration of economy and society makes it meaningless to analyze economic organization in isolation.

It may well be that the most significant feature of the contemporary American economy is its close link with government. One interesting facet of this complex and growing relationship is the fact that it contradicts our hallowed tradition of *laissez-faire*. Nevertheless, close ties between government and economy are, as we have seen, characteristic of all modern systems. One justification for these ties is the fact that government performs certain economic functions that apparently cannot be fulfilled in any other way. For example, the United States government acts to sustain the rate of economic growth, takes measures to curb inflation, safeguards (as well as it can) the balance of payments, and acts from time to time to keep the sectors of the economy in balance and harmony.

Secular rationality is a key feature of our economic organization. The original application of this principle was in the utilization of science in machine and process technology. Other applications of rationality are seen in accounting, fiscal, and credit systems, in the social organization of ownership, management, and production, in the use and control of research and development, and in systems of sales and promotion. The manifest consequence of this primary reliance on rationality and control is the achievement of phenomenal levels of efficiency and productivity.

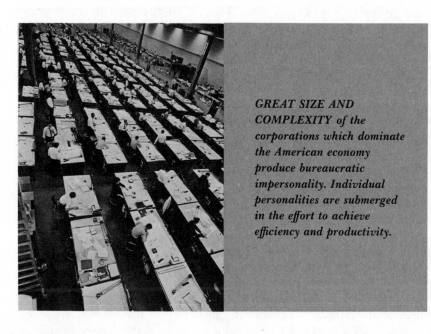

GREAT SIZE AND COMPLEXITY of the corporations which dominate the American economy produce bureaucratic impersonality. Individual personalities are submerged in the effort to achieve efficiency and productivity.

The emphasis on rationality tends to keep the system in a state of constant change. Every machine, every process, every operation is subjected to constant scrutiny by the tests of pragmatism, efficiency, and economy, and may be challenged by new inventions. Those that fail the tests or prove unable to meet the challenge are unhesitatingly swept aside. Yet, occasionally a new process or mechanism may gain the loyalties of many people and tend to acquire an almost sacred character.[33] It resists tests and challenges and stands as an island of cultural lag in a sea of relentless change. Such lags can produce strains and rigidities in the system that are partially involved in such undesired conditions as business cycles, waste of natural and human resources, widespread poverty, and central-city slums.

In one way or another, every American is involved in the economic system. Over 70 million of them (the largest number ever) are gainfully employed. At the same time, four to five million (enough to populate a good-sized state) are chronically unemployed. Of the 70 million workers, fewer than ten per cent, some six million, are engaged in agriculture. This phenomenally small proportion of farm workers can produce enough agricultural products for themselves, the rest of America, and many people in foreign lands.

Over nine tenths of the working Americans are occupied at manufacturing, commercial, and service occupations. One index to the affluence and productivity of the society is the fact that the number of workers in service occupations is increasing faster than the numbers in the two other categories. Of the 70 million American workers, less than twenty per cent are self-employed, a thoroughly deplorable state of affairs according to one of our treasured notions. Two fifths of all workers are women (the proportion continues to grow), and while the proportion of older workers increases, the percentage of under-14 workers declines. Mechanization, automation, and continuing technological change reduce the need for untrained and unskilled workers and expand the requirement for technically prepared people. As a consequence, the plight of the poor is exacerbated, the problem of unemployment is made more difficult to solve, and the occupational structure is further altered.

One aspect of the close integration of the economy into the total way of life is the significant influence it exerts on the general social system. It can be argued that in substantial part modern mass society is the consequence of such factors as impersonal bureaucratic organization, large size and complexity of structure, the mass nature of the modern market, the supremacy of secular rationality, and other features of the modern capitalist economy. David Riesman in *The Lonely Crowd* and William H. Whyte, Jr., in *The Organization Man* have examined some of the sociopsychological consequences of these economic and social phenomena. C. Wright Mills has shown that changes in the economic system have altered the traditional occupational structure and set in motion fundamental changes of the national class system.[34] Despite continuing controversy about causes and solutions, sociologists agree that our changing economic organization entails a number of crucial unresolved issues.

Trends and Issues ♦ In world perspective it seems fairly evident that traditional economic systems will be swept away in the face of the irresistible spread of Western-type bureaucratic forms. However, it is less evident that such new economies will evolve along the lines of free-enterprise capitalism typical of the older industrial societies rather than as politically controlled systems along authoritarian lines. At the same time, in the older industrial societies economic capability appears to be approaching that utopian state where want can be abolished and all people can enjoy the life abundant.[35] Yet, here again we cannot know for certain whether economic development will move toward this desirable end or veer off in another direction.

In the developing economies, whatever political direction they may take, the central issue is that of the establishment of viable and growing systems. The outcome is especially problematical for the ideologically authoritarian societies because of the economic isolation they experience. Some of these societies represent unstable and potentially explosive situations that constitute a threat to the rest of the world.

The American economy seems to present three major issues which, to one degree or another, are typical of all the older, advanced economies. First, as William H. Form and Delbert C. Miller have pointed out, the central issue continues to be the control of the economy.[36] This can be broken down into such component problems as the control of business cycles, the maintenance of adequate growth, the prevention of inflation, and the control and utilization of automation. The problem is one of finding the means to keep all the interrelated parts of the complex system operating properly.

Second, there is the issue of safeguarding the public interest against abuses by the economy. This is the other face of the issue of control of the economy. It is expressed in such concerns as the control of prices and wages, protection of the rights of consumers and workers, and care of irreplaceable natural resources.

Finally, another issue relates to the separation and balance of private and public control in economic affairs. That is, how far should government enter into economic activities, and where is the limit of the domain of private economic enterprise? This issue has been fought out in such cases as the "Dixon-Yates affair," the medicare program, and various aspects of the space program. The problem admits of no single, final answer, but will lead to new solutions and new difficulties as long as social and economic organization continue to change and grow.

FOOTNOTES

1. William Graham Sumner, *Folkways* (Boston: Ginn, 1906), p. 53.
2. Walton H. Hamilton, "Institution," in *Encyclopedia of the Social Sciences* (New York Macmillan, 1933), Vol. 8, p. 84.
3. Louis Schneider, "Institution," in Julius Gould and William L. Kolb, eds., *A Dictionary of the Social Sciences* (New York: Free Press, 1964), p. 338.
4. See the discussion of the organization of values in Chapter 4 above.
5. Hamilton, *op. cit.*, p. 84.
6. H. H. Gerth and C. Wright Mills, eds., *From Max Weber: Essays in Sociology* (New York: Oxford University Press, 1946), Chapter 8 *et passim.*
7. Condensed and adapted from George Peter Murdock, *Our Primitive Contemporarie* (New York: Macmillan, 1934), pp. 48-72. See also Ralph L. Beals and Harry Hoijer *An Introduction to Anthropology* (New York: Macmillan, 1963), pp. 549-553.
8. Condensed and adapted from Paul F. Cressey, "Social Disorganization and Re organization in Harlan County, Kentucky," in *American Sociological Review*, 14:389 392 (June 1949).

9. See Logan Wilson and William L. Kolb, *Sociological Analysis* (New York: Harcourt Brace, 1949), p. 516.

10. Robert Michels, *Political Parties* (New York: Hearst's, 1915), pp. 400-401.

11. See Gerth and Mills, *op. cit.*, p. 78; and William L. Kolb, "State," in Julius Gould and William L. Kolb, eds., *A Dictionary of the Social Sciences* (New York: Free Press, 1964), p. 690.

12. Wilson and Kolb, *op. cit.*, pp. 516-521.

13. Charles E. Merriam *et al.*, *The Government of the Metropolitan Region of Chicago* (Chicago: University of Chicago Press, 1933), p. xv.

14. See William Kornhauser, *The Politics of Mass Society* (Glencoe: Free Press, 1959), Chapters 7 and 8.

15. David Riesman, *Abundance for What?* (Garden City: Doubleday, 1964), pp. 418-442.

16. *Statistical Abstract of the United States, 1964* (Washington: U.S. Government Printing Office), Table 10, pp. 14-15.

17. Herbert A. Hoover, Chairman, Commission on Organization of the Executive Branch of the Government, *Concluding Report* (Washington: U.S. Government Printing Office, 1949).

18. In this connection see Hannah Arendt, *The Origins of Totalitarianism* (New York: Harcourt Brace, 1954); Erich Fromm, *Escape From Freedom* (New York: Rinehart, 1945); Karl Mannheim, *Man and Society in an Age of Reconstruction* (London: Routledge and Kegan Paul, 1940); Kornhauser, *op. cit.;* Robert Nisbet, *The Quest for Community* (New York: Oxford University Press, 1953); and Philip Selznick, *The Organizational Weapon* (New York: McGraw-Hill, 1952).

19. Joseph R. Gusfield, "Mass Society and Extremist Politics," in *American Sociological Review* (February 1962), p. 19.

20. Such expansion was recognized more than thirty years ago. See, in this connection, *Recent Social Trends in the United States*, by the President's Research Committee (New York: McGraw-Hill, 1933), pp. 1274-1330. For recent evidence, see any current textbook on government.

21. See Robert Redfield, "The Folk Society," in *American Journal of Sociology*, 52: 305-306 (January 1947); also Beals and Hoijer, *op. cit.*, Chapters 11 and 12.

22. This point is one central argument of Thorstein Veblen in *The Theory of the Leisure Class* (New York: Macmillan, 1899).

23. Robert L. Heilbronner, *The Worldly Philosophers* (New York: Simon and Schuster, 1953). See especially Chapter 2.

24. See, in this connection, Robert L. Heilbronner, *The Making of Economic Society* (Englewood Cliffs: Prentice-Hall, 1962); Max F. Millikan and W. W. Rostow, *A Proposal* (New York: Harper, 1957), especially Chapter 5; and Harry Elmer Barnes, *Society in Transition* (New York: Prentice-Hall, 1939), Chapter 1.

25. See Williams, *op. cit.*, pp. 156-162.

26. *Statistical Abstract of the United States, 1964*, Table 1107, p. 769.

27. *Statistical Abstract of the United States, 1962*, Table 839, p. 608, and Table 645, p. 487.

28. William N. Husband and James C. Dockeray, *Modern Corporation Finance* (Chicago: Irwin, 1948). See also Heilbronner, *The Making of Economic Society*.

29. David Lynch, *The Concentration of Economic Power* (New York: Columbia University Press, 1946), p. 114.

30. A. A. Berle, Jr., and Gardiner C. Means, "Corporation," in *Encyclopedia of the Social Sciences* (New York: Macmillan, 1933), p. 422.

31. Millikan and Rostow, *op. cit.*, discuss this issue at some length.

32. Karl Polanyi, *The Great Transformation* (New York: Beacon, 1957).

33. Alvin W. Gouldner, *Patterns of Industrial Bureaucracy* (Glencoe: Free Press, 1954).

34. See C. Wright Mills, *White Collar* (New York, Oxford University Press, 1951).

35. See Heilbronner, *The Making of Economic Society*.

36. William H. Form and Delbert C. Miller, *Industry, Labor, and Community* (New York: Harper, 1960), p. 3 ff.

Chapter 9

FAMILY, EDUCATION, AND RELIGION

FAMILY

To meet the universal need for replenishing its functional membership, each society makes arrangements to manage sexual expression, reproduction, care, socialization, and placement of the young.[1] In the fulfillment of these biological and social functions, dependency and affection emerge as primary social bonds. The associated social activities lead to common economic, legal, and social-control interests. One consequence of this complex of needs, functions, bonds, and common interests is the human family. Robert H. Lowie writes: "The total of sentimental, economic, and legal ties between spouses, parents and children, and between siblings, makes the family a very strong social unit."[2]

Variability of the Family ♦ As institution, the family is found in all societies, although it differs in many ways from one to another.[3] Variations of the family can be revealed along several dimensions. From a study of information about 250 "representative societies" deposited in the Human Relations Files at Yale University, George Peter Murdock identified "nuclear," "polygamous," and "extended" as major family types.[4] The nuclear family is the basic unit, composed of father, mother, their offspring, and occasionally one or more other relatives. In the United States nuclear families live typically as independent households.

In the polygamous family two or more nuclear units are joined by having one parent (either father or mother) in common. In the United States the Mormons used to have a family in which one man had two or more wives and sets of children. This kind of family, called polygynous, is still practiced by some Islamic groups of North Africa and the Middle East, some peoples of East Africa, and in many other places. Polyandry, plurality of husbands, is most often associated with Tibet.

The extended family joins nuclear units of two or more generations through the kinship bond. In many places sons remain with their parents, bringing wives from elsewhere to join them and adding children to the family complex.[5] Among the Zuni of Arizona and New Mexico the connection is through the daughters, who remain with their mothers and are joined by husbands from outside.

Families also differ on the basis of who wields primary authority. In Western Europe and the United States fathers have traditionally had major family authority, and the family is called "patriarchal." Recently, though, the father's dominance has declined while that of the mother has tended to increase, producing a type of family called "equalitarian" or "democratic." In some places, e.g., among the Zuni and in Southern India, women play a role of dominance in the family.[6] In some societies older people control the family. Ruth Shonle Cavan notes that in upper-upper-class American families, because of the concentration and control of inherited wealth, the senior members retain control.[7]

The rules of courtship, marriage, and divorce reveal great variations. In the United States young people typically choose each other as marriage partners after a courtship based on romantic love. Although this practice may appear to be quite "normal," it is neither universal nor traditional in all societies. The so-called "romantic complex" entered Western European culture in the late Middle Ages, developed rapidly, and spread to the United States and elsewhere.[8] It has now become so entrenched in American culture that it seems right and natural. However, in much of Asia, Africa, and Latin America, courtship as we know it in this country does not exist; instead, spouses are chosen by parents or official go-betweens. The relationship that leads to marriage is more like negotiation than courtship, and economic, familistic, class, or religious considerations influence the decisions. Even after the marriage, romantic love is at most only an incidental consideration.

Rules of "endogamy" (in-marriage) and "exogamy" (out-marriage) specify the groups within which spouses must be found and the appropriate groups where they may be sought. In the United States, custom and/or law prohibit the following matches: Negroes and whites, Jews and Roman Catholics, upper-class and lower-class, very old and very young, uncle and niece. People are urged to marry within their race, religion, class, and age, and to eschew the marriage of close relatives. In India the kinship and caste systems establish many complicated regional patterns of endogamy and exogamy.[9] In all societies incest, i.e., sexual union between close blood relatives, is tabooed, although the degrees of closeness and the specific relatives involved tend to vary. The rules of endogamy, exogamy, and incest, however irrational they may seem, are based on societal judgments about the welfare, hereditary, social-control, and other effects of the proscribed relationships.[10]

Every society has ceremonies to celebrate marriage. They range from the casual to the elaborate and costly. Such ceremonies indicate that marriage is regarded as one of the important events in the life cycle. In many societies rules also exist for terminating marriages. For example, a Hopi woman places her husband's personal possessions on the door sill to notify him that she has terminated the marriage. Roman Catholics prohibit complete dissolution of the marriage bond for any reason. In the United States divorce laws show great variety among the fifty states. Death of one spouse terminates a marriage, and in some societies widows may not remarry while in others both widows and widowers may do so. In some societies by the rule of the leverate a man's brother, or by the rule of the sororate a woman's sister, upon their death is required to assume the family role of the deceased spouse in order to produce children and continue the family line.

All societies sanction sexual activity between spouses and to one degree or another prohibit it elsewhere. Heterosexual activity is intended to lead to reproduction. To this end, many societies forbid or discourage birth control. However, some societies permit or sanction such extramarital institutions as concubinage and prostitution. In some instances extramarital sexual practices are associated with religious institutions, and in a few instances homosexual behavior is tolerated. At times, as in the United States today and in certain countries of Western Europe, sanctioned sexual activity between spouses has become relatively dissociated from reproduction. This development is associated with the birth control complex and reflects changes of cultural values and social orientations. Conscious programs of population control through "family planning," as currently practiced in India, sanction and promote the separation of sexual activity within the family from its traditional function of reproduction.

Societies vary as regards the attitude toward children. In some, for inheritance, economic, status, religious, and other reasons, they are highly valued. Boys (because most societies are dominated by men) are usually preferred to girls. In such societies the control of population by dissociating sex from reproduction and establishing family planning encounters difficulty. However, in some societies and in some situations, children are seen as a burden. This attitude may lead to infanticide, abortion, and various methods of birth control. Where sexual activity is dissociated from reproduction and established as an independent value, a relatively low value is placed on having many children.

There is also variability in the way children are reared. In middle-class American families early socialization is a family responsibility, and the mother has the central role. In many nonliterate tribal societies a large part of this task is performed by the women of the village with the assistance of older children.[11] Wealthy aristocratic and upper-class families in many societies utilize nursemaids, governesses, and tutors to discharge major child-rearing functions. Some tribal people assign training of boys to the mother's uncle, the avunculate, instead of to the father, who performs the same function for his sister's sons. In some parts of Israel the child-rearing agency of the "kibbutz" fulfills much of the socialization function of young parents who devote their time to work on agricultural and development projects. The aim everywhere, no matter how socialization is conducted, is to produce functionally useful members of the society.

During recent years child-rearing practices in the United States have changed.[12] A generation ago, strict control and discipline were regarded as proper. Lately, "permissiveness" has been fashionable. It used to be customary for women to rear their children in the traditional manner. Nowadays, especially among young middle-class mothers, so-called "scientific" child-rearing is the fashion. There is much ethnological material reporting variability among nonliterate peoples in regard to such practices as weaning, toilet training, handling, dressing, walking, and the like.[13]

Trends of Family Change ♦ The family institution has been in a process of continual change. In communal societies, both ancient and contemporary, it is a basic and inclusive social structure. In addition to reproduction, social placement, protection, and socialization, the family performs important economic, social-control, educational, recreational, and religious functions. Every individual lives a major part of his life within the context of his family.

The family is woven into the fabric of society through the inclusive kinship system. It serves as one major structural element of the local village or neighborhood. For example, a colonial New England town was organized around the family, the church, and the town meeting. An Indian village is structured by the "joint family," the caste system, and the temple.[14] In Nyasaland (now Malawi) Margaret Read notes that village organization was shaped by the family and the "kraal."[15]

The nature of the family in communal society is illustrated in two cases drawn from widely separated societies. In New England during colonial times, the Puritan family was a strong inclusive structure, although even at this early date it had emerged to a notable extent from an extensive kinship system, and individualism of members was a significant fact. The strong multifunctional family stood as one bulwark of the town community. In India, on the other hand, the family was enveloped into an inclusive kinship system and caste structure. Caste and kinship fully incorporated the individual and defined almost every aspect of his life by sacred ritual. Yet the joint family was a strong institution that helped to structure and unify the village. These cases also indicate that communal families enter the process of change from different starting points.

The New England Puritan Family. The family was undoubtedly the most important institution in colonial Puritan society. Both government and religion, though in some measure specialized, were subsidiary to the family. Religion and government were closely intertwined in the functioning of the Puritan family. While the individual received a "calling," the occupation was a family affair once it was entered. For the Puritans, both marriage and divorce were civil matters. The family derived its great strength from sources other than religious sacraments.

Because of English common law, secular practice, traditional sanctions, and religious doctrine, the father was clearly the head. The wife was subordinate in matters of property ownership, decisions, inheritance, and the like. Yet in the demanding New England setting women were forced by the exigencies of life to help in the heavier jobs as well as to carry on their usual arduous household routines—all this in addition to bearing many children. This extension of woman's family role led to modification of her status in both family and society. The assumption that the family rather than the state or some other secondary institution was the organizing center of society further modified the position of women in the Puritan social complex. The rugged northern frontier, Protestantism, and capitalism nurtured the growing individualism that still further advanced the status of Puritan women. Children were considered to be sinful, and were subjected to useful and arduous tasks as well as sternness and severe punishment. Many children helped augment the kingdom of God, provided useful workers, and insured the economic, religious, and cultural continuity of the family.

The self-sufficiency of this family system included economic, educational, religious, recreational, control, and other basic societal functions. The concentration was most marked in the economic realm. The village and city family was by no means as all-inclusive in self-sufficiency as the rural unit.[16]

The Indian Joint Family. In Hindu India the joint family is typical, although it varies somewhat from region to region and from caste to caste. It is headed by a patriarch and his wife and includes younger brothers and married sons, their wives and children, and unmarried sons and daughters. Sometimes there are other relatives and generally one or more servants. Daughters leave the family at marriage and sons bring wives into the family from outside. Choice of mates is controlled by variable and often complex patterns of endogamy and exogamy. Because of the mobility of girls by marriage into and out of the family, it has numerous kinship ties with other families and villages.

A decisive feature of the joint family is centralization of organization and control. Sometimes the entire family lives in a single dwelling, although the nuclear units may have separate sleeping and sitting quarters. There is a central kitchen and the whole family eats together. The household is a single operation under the control of the patriarch. The younger women, daughters, and daughters-in-law work in household activities under the supervision of the matriarch. All earnings of sons are placed in a central fund which, like property, is managed by the patriarch. Although he controls major family decisions, he considers the wishes and interests of all members. He controls family property, which is transmitted to sons under a variety of rules. The patriarch is the official representative of the family in business and public matters.

Social activities are collective affairs or under the control of the family. There is often a shrine where the family engages in religious rituals. Festivals, celebrations, ceremonies, and the like are inclusive family activities. Marriage is controlled by the family, the patriarch initiating inquiries and negotiations on behalf of son or daughter at the appropriate time. These negotiations are conducted with due account of the caste, kinship, endogamous-exogamous, economic, religious, and other conditions that are relevant and important.

Boys have high family status, and the eldest son stands next to the patriarch. Daughters, though cherished as persons, are expendable, since they will marry outside the family and require dowries. Daughters-in-law enter the family at a low status and must earn their place by obedience and respect to the matriarch, by diligent service in the household, and especially by bearing sons for their husbands. Children are cherished for their own sake and are regarded as belonging to the joint family.[17]

William J. Goode reported on the "world revolution in family patterns" after studying change in the West, Arabic Islam, Sub-Saharan Africa, India, China, and Japan.[18] He concludes that although all family systems are changing at varying rates and in different directions, nevertheless they reveal great stability. In the process of change, both society and family function reciprocally as cause and effect. The universal trend seems to be toward industrialization and urbanization in society, and toward some variant of the conjugal (based on marriage) system in the family. Industrialization, urbanization, and ideology establish the societal context within which family change occurs. When analysis focuses on the family, change may be conceptualized by means of the elements of our institutional model. The extended family tends to break up through fission releasing conjugal constituents. The emergent conjugal units, however, retain many attenuated ties with the extended kinship system. At the same time, societal changes function to limit the power of elders by removing control of economic and social opportunities from their hands. As a consequence, the status of women tends to improve *vis à vis* men.

Traditional relations within the family and between family and society are affected by change, some being buttressed and others being subjected to increased strain. Decline of the importance of land and rise of the importance of education as bases of opportunity tend to accentuate independence of the young, especially with reference to marriage choice and remarriage. Moreover, the proportion of the adult population living under concubinage and polygamy is declining.

The Changing American Family ▶ American families have developed within a complex context of change. Puritan families established themselves in New England. Quaker, Roman Catholic, Dutch, and other groups settled in the Middle Colonies. The South contained aristocratic slave-owning, poor white, and both free and slave Negro families. Major factors in the process of change include industrialization, urbanization, the frontier, mass immigration, the Civil War, universal education, emergence of social classes, and growing affluence. Major dimensions of the process of change were, first, diversification of family patterns and then, later, convergence toward a generalized type.

In change, family and society were linked in a process of mutual influence. The individualism of the sturdy colonial family was nurtured by life on the frontier and in the new industrial city, and in turn helped members of the changing family escape from formal and traditional bonds. The diversity of family patterns brought by the immigrants was eroded both in the school and the informal agencies of Americanization, and in the caldron of the agricultural frontier and the industrial city. In the middle of the nineteenth century, the steady course of family development was interrupted by the Civil War. A new rural and urban middle class arose to set the standard of family behavior. In the twentieth century, American families have been affected by war, depression, and recovery, and by the pressures of upward mobility and affluence in the face of hard-core poverty. Howard Beers studied an up-state New York farm family in the throes of change. In the following paragraph he describes the process of change and shows how the past is continued into the present and tends to affect the course of change.

THE CHANGING FARM FAMILY IN CENTRAL NEW YORK STATE

In many respects the portrait of today's farm family in Central New York could well hang on the same wall with needlework samplers and framed hair flowers. In other respects, it would not be out of place in a modern mural. It is a modification of old patterns, a partial acceptance of new patterns. It is smaller than the pioneer family, yet it is still among our chief sources of population increase. The rural social organization of the area is no longer familistic, but it is at least "semi-familistic." The roles of parent and child are less fixed in the mores. There is a definite heritage of paternal dominance, but the outlines of the heritage become progressively more dim. Obedience and subjection of children stand forth still as parental goals but with less and less filial recognition. Specialization and education have affected the division of labor, but shared work and shared leisure are still formative of the family pattern. Propinquity continues to foster solidarity, resisting the centrifugal effects of urbanization. There has been definite democratization in the changes of role and status. That is evidenced particularly in the joint executive function of mother and father. The rate at which this change occurs accelerates with the advance of business efficiency and industrialization in agriculture. Both the rate and direction of future change in the farm family pattern are, therefore, quite as likely to depend upon larger economic and social influences affecting agriculture as upon the dictation of tradition.[19]

In comparison with earlier types, the American family of the mid-twentieth century is changed in important respects, but retains striking similarity to its predecessor. The father is still the head of the family, but there are strong tendencies toward democracy and some families are matricentric. The institution is still grounded in religious sacraments and moral prescription, yet in some spheres family practice has become relatively secular and expedient. Sex has been legitimately dissociated from reproduction, and while births-out-of-wedlock occur, the family still retains moral monopoly over population replacement. While both the ease and rate of divorce have increased during the last century, the family continues to stand as a stable and durable institution.

Moreover, although it is said that change has fractured the extended family pattern, nevertheless so-called independent nuclear units are enmeshed in an intimate network of mutual aid and social relations with parental families. The modern family is called a "consuming organization," yet modern homes are likely to include a vegetable garden, storage freezer, workshop, sewing room, and numerous other "do-it-yourself" tools and facilities. In the changing family, members are freed from the control of the formal bonds of deference and duty, but find themselves deeply involved in the intimate obligations of affection and companionship.

Through change the many diverse threads of the American family fabric have been converging toward a generalized type that is best represented in the middle classes. This trend is to be expected in part because of the recent rapid expansion of the middle classes by mobility from the lower classes. In addition, representatives of the middle classes hold commanding positions in the major institutions, i.e., education, government, welfare, economy, religion, and communications, and can therefore set and diffuse standards of family organization and behavior.

From studies of American families, it is possible to construct an ideal-typical model of the middle-class family. While such a descriptive model may fit no family specifically, it typifies all in significant ways. Moreover, the background and elements of the ideal-type suggest the variations that are moving into conformity through change. Thus as a standard, the ideal-typical middle-class model indicates the nature and extent of variation found in emigrant, ethnic, and rural antecedents. By reference to specific patterns, e.g., parental roles, mate selection practices, or financial management, we can specify differences among the social classes. The model constitutes a mechanism for bringing into focus differences between urban and rural, central city and suburban, or young and mature families. It is not possible to present descriptions of all the variants around this generalized type, yet the model itself suggests the lines and directions of variation that still make up the whole complex American family fabric.

Middle-Class Ideal-Type. The middle class has developed its own culture, rooted in the family, supported by church and public school, and including belief in the goodness of the middle-class status. The unit is the small nuclear family, composed of husband, wife, unmarried adult and minor children. It begins with the marriage of a couple who typically move into an independent house or apartment while retaining important economic and social ties with parents and other relatives. It ends with the death of husband or wife and sometimes envelopment of the other in the family of a married son or daughter. The relationship circle may be considered a primary group rather than a true kinship system.

The middle-class family has a brief past, contacts rarely extending longer than two or three generations. The class suffers from the lack of cultural unity or tends to split into unified subcultural groups on ethnic or religious bases.

The income of such families is only to a slight degree based on inherited wealth, being derived mainly from white-collar and skilled occupations. Within the range of occupations of the class, each young person is free to choose, preferably for sons, one similar to or higher than that of the father. Such families are relatively free to move place of residence, for they are seldom bound by property or industry.

Children begin married life in small apartments, moving from one area to a better as resources increase, until they can live in the suburbs. Each generation and each child must prove its worth by establishing itself anew in the middle-class status.

Family organization tends to be paternal with a tendency toward equality in many areas. The husband is the economic and authoritarian head, producing major income and status and controlling major decisions. Unmarried grown daughters, young married women, and middle-aged women after the children are out of the way may work. Young children are not expected to work, but for boys, Saturday or vacation jobs are regarded as praiseworthy.

Husband and wife have differentiated but interlocking roles. He has many household duties while she has the triple role of wife-mother, housekeeper, and social arbiter. Only during the childless years do they place the sexual and social phases of marriage above the demands of parenthood. The middle-class woman has extensive community activities and is sensitive to social status.

Marriage occurs within sub-classes or adjacent classes where youthful cliques and limited parental control permit a wide range of choices. Children belong to both parents. The narrowness of the family circle both restricts and intensifies emotional ties. Middle-class persons are self-consciously parents and follow the dictates of "scientific child care" and early impose many routines upon children. In the imposition of controls, psychological and social rewards are stressed more than penalties, but penalties tend to be long-lasting and devastating. Except in periods of great social disorganization, the crises of middle-class families tend to result from interpersonal relations, are quickly resolved, and seldom involve outside help.[20]

Some Unresolved Issues ▶ Family change creates problems and raises issues in every society. In world perspective leading issues include the breakup of extended systems and the emergence of conjugal families, the decline of the power of elders, the changing relations both within the family and between family and society. Family change and its consequences stimulate a conflict of approving and disapproving value judgments.

In the United States, economic change has raised and sharpened some family issues. The dimensions of these changes have been captured by J. Kenneth Galbraith in *The Affluent Society* and Michael Harrington in *The Other America*.[21] The "working wife" is a symbol of the changing status of women and the altered pattern of family organization. The proportion of gainfully employed wives with children of all ages continues to increase. The working wife trend has both functional and dysfunctional consequences for the family. At the same time, rapid upward mobility of husbands in the affluent society raises other problems. The sensitive link between occupation and income on the one hand and family organization and behavior on the other ensures disruptive consequences of rapid widespread mobility. The extent of this change is documented in the growth of the new white-collar classes.[22] One unanticipated dimension of this problem is the impact of upward mobility, resulting from occupational desegregation, on Negro families. On the other hand there is a block of chronically poor and marginal families. The massive anti-poverty program is one response to recognition of this fact. However, the functional relationship between economic deprivation and family organization and behavior is not fully understood.

The young and the old are other foci of unresolved family issues. The weakening of some family mores and altered value orientations have encouraged or permitted many young people to marry in their teens and to engage in extensive premarital sexual activity with consequent alarming rise of venereal disease and illegitimacy rates. In spite of much empirical research and prolonged public discussion, cause and effect relationships in these issues are not fully understood. However, there is little room for doubt that these trends are having and will continue to have significant effects upon the family. On the other hand, the rapid growth of the older population, their altered position in the family structure, and their economic insecurity have raised other important issues. Current population projections suggest that this problem will increase in magnitude if not in severity. Although important efforts have been made to deal with the economic aspects of this problem, its institutional and personal dimensions remain largely unresolved.

Other family issues are produced by the existence of blocks of minority peoples in the nation's cities. These include Negroes, Southern Appalachian Mountain whites, Puerto Ricans, and Mexicans. Poorly adjusted to city life and isolated by color and culture, these minorities perpetuate or develop family patterns that deviate sharply from community norms, and their situation is aggravated by economic and cultural deprivation. The family issues are one facet of the acute problem of these minorities and of the American city.

Unresolved family issues are both sociological and social problems. They designate important areas of potential empirical research. The fact that they are unresolved suggests that sound empirical research can serve as the prelude and basis for informed social planning and action.

EDUCATION

The academic procession and graduation exercises at a leading university are a far cry from the puberty rites in a primitive tribe. Yet both are part of the institutional apparatus of education. Whatever its material and cultural circumstances, every society must transmit its culture. As Logan Wilson and William L. Kolb point out, "Education implies a number of . . . elements: something to be taught and learned, teachers and learners, and the activities of teaching and learning."[23] Yet, it will be evident that these elements may be combined in numerous ways. There is, consequently, great variety in educational organization. Three basic patterns, however, can be identified: (1) teacher to one learner, or the tutorial or apprenticeship system; (2) teacher to many learners, or the class-lecture system; and (3) learner to situation, or the system of learning by doing through direct experience.

Education in Communal Societies ◗ The organization and focus of education in communal societies is determined in substantial measure by the nature of the problem confronted. In primitive societies groups are small, relations are intimate, and the heritage is limited. In the main, social life is oriented toward maintenance of stability. The central educational problem therefore is transmission unaltered of the social heritage and involvement of new members in the whole life of the society. Robert Redfield observed of the ideal folk society: "Old people find young people doing, as they grow up, what the old people did at the same age, and what they have come to think right and proper."[24] As a consequence, what one individual knows and believes is the same as what all know and believe. This emphasis on similarity of knowledge and experience tends to inhibit social change.

Limitation of the cultural heritage is a crucial feature of education in primitive societies. In most, the individual can learn all that part of the total heritage that he needs to live as an adult by the time he reaches puberty. He therefore becomes a cultural adult as soon as he reaches biological maturity.

Education in communal societies is distinguished by at least two basic characteristics. First, socialization of the individual and transmission of the heritage are not formally dissociated from the ordinary functions and structures of group life. The school, if one may employ that term in reference to such societies, is the family and neighborhood. In daily play, Robert H. Lowie points out, "everywhere children mimic their elders and thus get painlessly educated for adult tasks."[25]

The research reports that some formal situations, occasions, and structures are reserved for education.[26] There are consequently a limited number of somewhat specialized educational roles and statuses. Elders in American and African tribes harangued the young, admonishing the boys to be brave in battle and decrying the evils of old age. To promote fortitude, youngsters of many tribes were often subjected to severe physical tests. Among the Hopi of Arizona and New Mexico, a man tutored his sister's sons in the behavior expectations and vocations of men. Many groups utilize outside agencies to supplement the activities of parents and other elders. The Ngoni of Nyasaland, now Malawi, maintained dormitories for the final education of teen-aged boys. Australian boys joined the bachelors' camp; Melanesian youths were isolated in dormitories of the clubhouse; southern Nigerian tribes conducted age classes for boys; while the Plains Tribes of Indians operated boys' military societies. Most primitive groups conduct puberty rituals of some degree of formality. In such experiences youths receive formal training in religion, folklore, vocations, sex, and moral conduct.

Second, these conditions foster simplicity of educational methods in communal societies. To carry out the functions of socializing new members and inculcating the values, norms, and models of the society, the teacher has only to engage in quite ordinary activities with the learners. The learners move in and out of learning experiences with no sense of their special character. To say that such educational processes are simple is not to claim that social organization or culture in communal societies are inherently simple. It is, rather, to point out that education within the communal complex is an integral phase of the ordinary business of living.

Education in Medieval Europe, the American colonies, or the western frontier revealed somewhat more specialization. Devices like indenture and apprenticeship formalized teacher-learner relations. Upper-class and wealthy families employed tutors and governesses for these educational functions. Some people could read and write, and part of the cultural heritage was therefore recorded. Some agencies developed to preserve, enhance, and transmit this part of the heritage. At first monasteries served as depositories of the accumulated literary wisdom. Some of these developed into universities for the enhancement and transmission of learning. In the cities, and in a few rural localities of Europe and America, schools, as specialized agencies with teacher, classes, appropriate buildings, books, and other equipment appeared.

Transition to Modern Educational Institutions ◗ In Europe and America the main trend of educational change has been the specialization of functions and the formalization of structures. In the way of life in Benjamin Franklin's time, still partly perpetuated in small towns and in the country, schooling, far from being the whole of education, was only one among a number of influences upon the growing child. The family was the center in which the child learned to become a successful adult. There was also the world of crops, animals, and wild nature. The way of life contained relatively settled and clear standards of conduct. The bond of the church undergirded and sanctioned the whole system.

In this situation, school signified a sort of extra-societal excursion into the "literary culture." At the lower level it was concerned with reading, writing, arithmetic, spelling, geography, history, and the like. For the older and more fortunate students the school promoted the study of literature, classical languages, logic, mathematics, philosophy, music, and art. These studies were deemed to have "cultural" and "spiritual" values and might prepare individuals for the professions and leadership. In its emphasis upon moral training and authoritarian discipline, the school was a projection of family, church, and neighborhood.

But this kind of schooling had relatively little to do with the everyday business of living and being trained for living. Most vocations, childhood and adult sex roles, social skills, morals, traditions, and the like were still inculcated in family, church, neighborhood, and natural environment. In this setting the school served other purposes, some of which survive in many localities today.

In time, however, both this way of life and mode of education changed.[27] Since 1790 the population has grown more than forty times, from fewer than 4 million to over 180 million. Stimulated by industrialization and rapid, inexpensive transportation, the population has become mobile, almost three fourths urban, and concentrated in great metropolitan areas. Industry has come to dominate the economic system and way of life. Popular democracy has flourished in the extension of the ballot to all adults; and growing dominance of federal and state governments has transformed the structure of local life. The population has become stratified and arranged in numerous large-scale organizations. Social relations are increasingly impersonal.

The characteristics of education in modern American society issue in part also from modifications of the cultural heritage. The accumulation of knowledge has become so enormous and complicated that no one individual could ever hope to comprehend it all. Much, perhaps most of it, is reduced to writing and stored in books, magazines, newspapers, and the like. Secular, achievement-oriented individualism has also entered the heritage as a major value. Meanwhile, the heritage has generated and incorporated positive orientations toward change itself.

Some conditions in the new way of life demand a specialized agency to discharge the functions of education. The changing "literary culture" can no longer be transmitted through play, parental guidance, and tutorship. The number of children to be inculcated has become far too large to be managed by these individualized and time-consuming methods. The society now includes areas of experience that fall completely outside the aegis of the family, neighborhood, and religious parish. Many aspects of the new culture and society are essential to such important realms of living as vocation, citizenship, and leisure. Meanwhile, the educational functions of family and church have been narrowed to initial socialization of children.

The sequence of historical events that culminated in the present American educational system is generally known. Religious organizations took the lead in establishing elementary and secondary schools and were responsible for founding the early colleges and universities. With the extension of the ballot and the growth of popular democracy, working-class people demanded tax-supported schools. The Reconstruction legislatures of the southern states established a pattern for government-financed and controlled free elementary and high schools. Soon thereafter public schools were established in every state. The Morrill Act of 1862 laid the foundation for a nation-wide system of some seventy land-grant, tax-supported institutions of higher agricultural, technical, and general education. By the beginning of the twentieth century, the foundations and outlines of the present American system of education had been established.

Education in the Developing Societies ▶ The course of educational change may be very different in the developing societies from that observed in Western Europe and the United States. In Latin America, and especially in Africa, the Middle East, and Asia, educational change is one aspect of the process of modernization. Developments in education are therefore often rapid, imposed by government, and dissociated from the traditional cultural heritage.

Peoples emerging from hoe and handicraft economies, tribal and village organizations, and nonliterate cultures must acquire and diffuse the scientific and technical elements of urban-industrial civilization. The process is promoted both by governments and by private agencies. Under these auspices young men and women from the developing societies study in the universities, industries, and organizations of the advanced countries. At the same time, professors, administrators, experts, and leaders go from the advanced societies to work in the developing countries.

To facilitate and continue the process of educational change and advancement, governments in the developing societies undertake to create and extend Western-style educational systems. Universities, technical schools, and teacher-training institutions are developed to prepare leaders, technicians, and teachers. Public school systems are established to introduce the masses of nonliterate people to the rudiments of the "literary culture" and to prepare them for later study in the institutions of advanced learning. Educational commissions, boards, and agencies of many kinds are developed to promote, co-ordinate, and facilitate the continuing process of educational change and advancement.

However, the developing societies cannot wait for the completion of this inclusive process of educational reorganization. Masses of adults must be readied quickly for life in big cities, participation in the process of democratic government, and work in modern industries and businesses. For this purpose agencies and programs of adult education that do not depend on a literate population must be established in all parts of the country. Insofar as they are available, radio, cinema, and television are employed. Photographs and graphic representations take the place of the printed word. Other means include demonstrations, exhibitions, variations of apprenticeship, in-service training, and the like. Everywhere direct verbal communication by teacher, leader, and demonstrator is the basic medium of education.

Such rapid, forced, and radical educational change has variable consequences for the developing societies. The traditional culture and modes of education are replaced. This change accompanies and in some measure undergirds the transition from communal to associational society. The nature and functionality of new educational institutions vary from one society to another. In some instances, e.g., Nigeria and the Congo, the new system cannot keep up with the demand for trained personnel, while in some others, e.g., India, the economy cannot absorb all the people who graduate from the universities and colleges. The actual requirements as well as the social demand for education tax limited resources. As a result, to one degree or another and from one perspective or another, education is a major problem in all the developing societies.

Modern American Education ▶ In the United States education has become a complex, bureaucratic institution. It specializes in preserving, accumulating, and transmitting the vast and increasingly literary and technical heritage. "The school" is its major working part, and tutorship, apprenticeship, learning by doing, and the like have been subordinated to ancillary methods. A bureaucratic structure and set of specialized norms have developed to fulfill ends, some of which did not exist at an earlier time.

With change and specialization, education has become differentiated from "socialization" and dissociated from family, religion, and community.[28] It stresses transmission of the academic skills (e.g., reading, writing, mathematics) and the social skills (e.g., communicating with, getting along with, and manipulating people). The major task of education is transmission of the vast and accumulating store of literary and technical knowledge, and development of the technical skills required for utilizing that heritage. A corollary task is the preservation and addition to that heritage through libraries, data storage, and research.

"The school" is the major instrument of education. Virtually every individual "goes to school" for a considerable part of his life. Figure 9-1 shows the number and types of schools in the United States at a recent date. There are three types by level (elementary, secondary, and higher education) and two types by support (public and private). In addition, there are tens of thousands of other less formally organized but officially recognized schools. These include voluntary classes and courses for children and adults on all kinds of subjects; in-service and on-the-job training courses for workers; institutes, workshops, seminars, and conferences of many kinds; radio and television courses; correspondence courses and lectures; demonstrations and exhibitions of an infinite number and variety.

Number and Per Cent of School Units in the United States
by Type and Means of Support

TYPE OF SCHOOL	PUBLIC		PRIVATE		TOTAL	
	NUMBER	PER CENT	NUMBER	PER CENT	NUMBER	PER CENT
ELEMENTARY	81,910	85.0	14,762	15.0	96,672	100.0
SECONDARY	25,350	86.0	4,129	14.0	29,479	100.0
HIGHER EDUCATION	721	36.0	1,316	64.0	2,037	100.0

Source: World Almanac and Book of Facts, 1965, p. 534.

FIGURE 9-1

In terms of the learner participants, American education is a vast and growing institution. For example, between 1899 and 1962 enrollment in all schools increased over two and one-half times (faster than the total population), from 17,198,841 to 48,273,198.[29] C. Horace Hamilton has estimated that between 1966 and 1975 enrollment in institutions of higher learning in the state of North Carolina will increase between 25 per cent (low projection) and 46 per cent (high projection).[30] These figures do not include those persons who participate in informal and unofficial educational activities nor the individuals who serve as policy-makers, administrators, and teachers.

As a bureaucratic structure, American education can be described by means of our model of institutional analysis. Educational ends emerged that challenged and supplemented the earlier societal functions.[31] With extension of the ballot and the flowering of popular democracy, it became necessary to produce citizens who could read, write, and understand the issues of the day. The Industrial Revolution required technically trained workers who could not be produced in family apprenticeship. Secular achievement-oriented individualism exalted personality growth and self-expression as legitimate aims of education. Increased stratification enhanced the value of education as both an index of status and an instrument of mobility. Expanded leisure called for training in activities and skills to be used off-the-job and outside the home.

Education employs four basic normative systems. First, the printed page as symbolized in texts, reference books, and libraries makes reading, along with writing and comprehension, the major skills of education. Second, the lecture-recitation-examination system assumes reading skill and joins teachers and learners in a formal structure of relationships. Third, problem-solving is the normative mode of education in laboratory and workshop and in such systems of professionalism as progressive education. And finally, the direct experience in internship, externship, the field trip, field work, home visitation, etc., is a way of selecting relevant aspects or sectors of the ordinary work-a-day or live-a-day world and incorporating them meaningfully into the educational process.

Educational roles are specialized and hierarchized. Policy-making functions are incorporated in the "board" member found in such groups as the board of regents of the state university or the advisory committee of a small rural school. Various series of administrative roles include president, chancellor, provost, dean, registrar, bursar, and departmental chairman in a university or superintendent, supervisor, or principal in a public school system. Third, members of the community are included in such roles as parent, voter, taxpayer, contributor, alumnus, "friend," and the like. The central educational roles include teachers, as specified in such ranks as professor, associate, and assistant professor; instructor; and lecturer; and learner as particularized in the statuses of pupil, student, apprentice, beginner, trainee, intern, extern; or freshman, sophomore, junior, and senior.

All participants are incorporated in various educational groups. The team of tutor and learner or class of teacher and learners constitutes the core group. There are numerous secondary groups, such as boards of education, alumni associations, professional associations, and student groups of many kinds. Some educational functions are implemented by interinstitutional groups such as the Parent-Teacher Association, the League of Women Voters, or the AFL-CIO.

Although American education tends to be bureaucratic in structure, specific units differ in many respects. Both features of organization are illustrated in the following brief description of high schools.[32] All fit the general bureaucratic model, yet they differ in size, location, source of support, degree of formality, clientele served, academic emphasis, type of curriculum, amount and quality of facilities, and so on.

Central-City Type. This is the large school in the metropolitan area, serving working-class families. Classes are big, facilities are limited, and sometimes there are two shifts of classes daily. An air of discipline and regimentation prevails. Equipment and art objects are usually locked up when not in use. The teachers are specialists, hold many classes, and use materials largely planned for them by state and local authorities. Such a school offers many different kinds of vocational training, and the great majority are enrolled in one of these, having made their choice more or less at random at the age of fourteen or fifteen since there is seldom adequate counseling service. Only a few students, perhaps a tenth, go on to college.

Suburban Type. In contrast is the high school in a middle-class suburb. Classes are smaller, teachers are better paid, and there is an active Parent-Teacher Association. There are many activities such as plays, athletics, and student publications. An atmosphere of relaxation and a concern for education prevail. A cleavage, based on differences of means and background, runs between the college-preparatory group and those who are taking vocational and business courses. But many able but less well-to-do pupils with sympathetic counseling take the college-preparatory course. About half the graduates go on either to college or to further education of some sort.

Some Other Types. Two other types are the private academy and the central high school in prosperous small towns. Although pupils in the academy come from upper-middle-class families, the small-town high school serves all types of residents. Both are well-equipped and taught with a sense of solidarity and pride. Personal relations between teachers and students, fairly thorough-going internal democracy, and a vigorous set of activities characterize the school. Most graduates of the academy and a substantial proportion from the small-town high school either go to college or otherwise further their education.

In rural communities two other types can be identified; the small traditional and the large consolidated schools. The traditional rural high school serves a limited area, is poorly equipped and taught, restricted in services and activities, rather authoritarian in organization, and dissociated from the home, work, and play life of the children. Only few of its graduates go to college or otherwise further their education. The consolidated school is large, often combining elementary and high school. It provides many of the facilities, services, and activities of the suburban or small-town high school. Children are transported to school by bus and there find a whole world of living. Effort is made to bridge the gulfs between school, home, and neighborhood. A fair share of the graduates enter college or university and in other ways advance their education.

School and Society ❯ Education is deeply embedded in society. Various often vaguely defined sectors of the society struggle for control of the schools. Education and the other institutions are interdependent. At every level and in all aspects the educational institution is conditioned by the class system. National policy and destiny influence and are influenced by education.

Under the American constitutional system, public schools are a responsibility of the several states. In actual fact, however, the states generally only supervise and coordinate public education, leaving operation to local units. Within this political tradition, the control of public education is supposed to rest with the citizens. In fact, though, they act directly only occasionally through elections to choose educational policy-makers, to approve tax rates or bond issues, to settle policy controversies, and the like. Day-to-day control is exercised by lay representatives on boards of education who make policy decisions and by professional educators who administer policies.

Struggle for control is expressed in competition among various sectors of the community for representation on boards of education.[33] Typically, industrial, business, and free-professional representatives outnumber others and tend to control policy. As a consequence, school systems are regarded as business enterprises, governed mainly by economic rather than by educational considerations, conservative in orientation, and committed to support of "free-enterprise" values. Opposition to such control comes from the educational professionals on ideological terms and from other sectors of the community, such as organized labor, religious interests, and minority groups, on power terms.

Federal aid for public education generates another struggle for control. Many individuals and interests believe that with federal financial assistance, the control of educational policy and operations will shift from the local community to the national capital. Although it is difficult to demonstrate that such fears are grounded in fact, they nevertheless foment a lively controversy and power struggle.

Although most secondary and elementary schools are publicly supported, most institutions of higher learning are private and were founded by religious bodies.[34] In other ways religion is involved in education. The federal aid to education issue, in terms of tradition of separation of state and church, has revealed the powerful lines of mutual influence and dependence between school and church. In addition, the economy is involved in education in many ways. Major sources of support for institutions, research, and specific activities are the big economic corporations and wealthy individuals. In a more subtle and indirect way also, through the heritage of values and value orientations, the economy influences both the process and content of education. We have noted in the foregoing section of this chapter some of the connections between family and education.

At the same time, the educational apparatus is conditioned by the class system. The literary, scientific, and technical heritage is typically associated with the middle classes. Educational organization and content are influenced by such middle-class values as individual achievement, the work ethos, status manifestation, personal freedom, and respectability. Policy-makers, administrators, teachers, and the other controllers and models are typically members of the middle classes. Moreover, the class structure functions to favor children from this class and to alienate lower-class children.[35] This issue is examined in Chapter 11. The class bias of American education is correlated with such social problems as cultural and economic deprivation, school segregation and desegregation, and hard-core slum conditions.

Sometimes directly, more often indirectly, national policy and destiny tend to condition and be conditioned by education. For example, one long-time ideological controversy in American culture is between the advocates of universal education for the masses and supporters of advanced education for the talented minority. When the Soviet Union launched *Sputnik I*, an animated debate over the content and functions of education was inaugurated. Some argued that education should stress basic knowledge and skill, i.e., communication, mathematics, science, and history, while others contended that these must be matched by emphasis on the social and humanistic elements of the heritage.[36] The issues of cultural deprivation and racial desegregation indicate another area where educational policy is tied up with national direction and emphasis.

Continuing Issues of Education ▶ Every society confronts unresolved problems of education. In the advanced societies some are associated with the rapid growth of knowledge and technology. In many places the population explosion increases the strain on overtaxed educational resources. The changing circumstances and atmosphere of the democracy-Communism confrontation has implications for education in many lands. Rapid and controlled modernization of the developing societies produces some unprecedented educational problems.

The developing societies are under pressure to acquire the literary, scientific, and technical culture of the West. However, everywhere the task is hampered by shortages of material and human resources. At the same time, the process of educational advancement tends to disintegrate traditional cultures and social organization. One consequence is a host of unfamiliar social problems. Since educational advancement is implemented by government, these societies face the possibility that the educational apparatus may be subverted or captured to support a party in power.

Some of the important issues of American society relate to education. Schools are the focus of a struggle for control. One dimension of this struggle is revealed in the federal aid to education controversy. At the local level it is expressed in competition between community sectors for domination of the board of education. At other times it is reflected in controversies over the content of education, the form of the curriculum, educational method, and so on.

Americans have not yet settled the issue of the aims of education. Many advocate universal education for the masses, through college now, as a basic right. Others favor advanced training for only the talented few. Along another front there is the debate between those who argue for basic education in science and mathematics, and those who believe that the humanities and social studies are of equal importance. The isolationism-internationalism controversy defines still another arena of disagreement over aims.

Inescapably, education is associated with orientations toward social change. The institution itself is caught up in the maelstrom of controversy and struggle over the desirability or undesirability of social change. For example, one agonizing issue relates to decisions and action on racial desegregation. The altered orientation toward poverty, persistent unemployment, and urban slums raises educational questions regarding the causes and consequences of social change. Many recent foreign policy debates reflect unsettled decisions in education with regard to the position and role of the United States in the changing world.

In spite of the unprecedented wealth of the nation, American education experiences continuing shortages of both material and human resources. There are continually inadequate funds, both public and private, for facilities, equipment, personnel, and activities. These shortages of educational resources are aggravated by the explosion of knowledge, rapid advances of technology, and the explosive increase of population.

RELIGION

The Pope blesses a hundred thousand of the faithful who assemble in St. Peter's Square. The Haitian natives engage in a tense voodoo ceremony in remote hills. Folks attend Sunday morning service in the First Methodist Church. Father Divine presides at a feast of his angels in the main heaven in Harlem. These situations are expressions of religion in the life of mankind. Logan Wilson and William L. Kolb describe the essentials of religion as follows.

> . . . Religious experience ranges from emotional ecstasy to highly rational speculation, from private contemplation to collective frenzy. Likewise, religious actions run the gamut from the spontaneous expression of private prayer to the complex ritual of a Zuni Indian rainmaking ceremony or a Roman Catholic Eucharistic Congress. Religious attitudes vary from those of propitiation, awe, and—if one's definition of religion includes magic—to those of manipulation and coercion.[37]

Variability of Religious Forms ♦ Figure 9-2 lists the major religions in the world and shows the approximate number of individuals identified with each. It is immediately evident that the population of the world is unevenly distributed among a considerable number of different religions. In addition, some of the categories include a large number of diverse religious groupings. For example, Protestantism is composed of several hundred denominational associations, and the term "primitive religions" is a catchall for a congeries of diverse forms of religious and quasi-religious behavior.

Estimated Membership of the Principal Religions of the World, 1965

Religions	Estimated Membership
ROMAN CATHOLIC	590,040,000
MUSLIM	465,237,000
HINDU	408,679,000
CONFUCIAN	357,855,000
PROTESTANT	227,670,000
BUDDHIST	165,094,000
EASTERN ORTHODOX	143,402,000
SHINTŌ	67,762,000
TAOIST	52,331,000
JEWISH	13,240,000
ZOROASTRIAN	150,000
OTHERS, INCLUDING PRIMITIVE OR NONE	752,801,000
GRAND TOTAL	3,244,261,000

Source: Britannica Book of the Year 1966, *Table p. 663.*

FIGURE 9-2

The religions vary in terms of inclusiveness and formality of organization. For example, Roman Catholicism, which includes almost a fifth of the world's population, is bureaucratically organized. Protestantism, on the other hand, reveals no such unitary structure. Yet, each of the various Protestant denominations is more or less bureaucratically organized. At the other extreme, most of the primitive religions are virtually unorganized. Religious behavior is individual action, and religious leaders are not connected to organized bodies of devotees.

On the basis of inclusiveness and method of origin, Leopold von Wiese and Howard Becker have formulated a fourfold classification of religious types.[38] The most inclusive type is the "ecclesia," or universal bureaucratic structure, such as the Roman Catholic Church. The "sect" is an informal, protesting, and emotional split from the ecclesiastical bureaucracy, like the early Protestant groups i ‧ Western Europe or some of the unorthodox bodies in the United Stat‧ . Next, the "denomination," i.e., Methodist, Presbyterian, Baptist, is ‧.e sect turned respectable and formal and accommodated to the surrounding culture and social organization. The "cult" is a loose collectivity of individuals, flung off centrifugally from ecclesia or denomination, who espouse similar philosophy or point of view.

Religions also vary in terms of the organization of behavior. Typically, in the Christian faiths and denominations, religious behavior is formal corporate experience. Devotees belong to a congregation or parish, and liturgical worship is a collective activity. However, in the "primitive religions" or Hinduism, religious behavior is individual action. For example, the Hindu devotee may be attached to a temple, but he does not belong to a congregation. Worship is a private and individual act and does not occur as an aspect of group activity. The individual is incorporated in the beliefs of the religion, not the collectivity or organization.

Finally, it is evident that the major and subordinate religions of the world reveal vast diversity of belief and practice. One dimension of this variety is expressed in the difference between religion and magic. Religion refers to beliefs about the nature of God and man that define the subordination of man to God and envisage worship as collective petition, adoration, propitiation, and so on. Magic, however, postulates gods that are much like human beings and defines religious activity as efforts and practices designed to control and manipulate the gods. Within the realm of true religion, there is infinite variety of belief and practice as one moves from faith to faith and from group to group.

In some modern associational societies the nature and variability of religious organization are conditioned by the state. For example, in the Soviet Union religion is prohibited by law, although a few churches are permitted to exist. On the other hand, some countries sanction a state church. For example, in little Finland the Lutheran Church is officially recognized in the Constitution. Although religious freedom is provided in the Constitution, some 95 per cent of the population belongs to the Finnish Lutheran Church.

Variability of religious organization is illustrated by two brief cases drawn from very different societies. Americans of whatever persuasion may find it easy to understand the pattern of Methodist organization presented in the first sketch. However, most Americans who visit India find the diffuse, casual organization of Hinduism hard to grasp. In both societies religious freedom is established by constitutional provision, although church and state are much more separate in the United States than in India.

The Methodist Denomination. An individual belongs to the denomination through membership in a congregation. Membership is a formal, voluntary, and individual status that is granted to those who fulfill certain qualifications. The members of each congregation are subdivided into "classes," assigned a leader, and given certain responsibilities. The congregation has an official structure of elected officers and boards directed by a minister who is appointed by the bishop. Although all members engage in worship, some religious functions are discharged by ancillary bodies like the Sunday School, the choirs, the deacon board, and the missionary society.

The congregations in a local area are united into a "district," which is supervised and coordinated by a "district superintendent" or "presiding elder" who conducts an annual conference to hear reports and transact district business. All the districts in a group of states are organized into a "conference" under the direction of a "bishop" who holds an annual meeting to hear reports, transact business, and appoint ministers. Ultimate authority of the denomination is vested in the general quadrennial conference. Each congregation, district, and conference is represented. All the major officers and many of the lesser officials attend the general conferences. This body establishes the policies, makes basic rules, and elects the bishops and other general officers. Between the quadrennial general conferences, the denomination is administered by the "college of bishops."

Organization in Hinduism. Hinduism is rather casually organized. The "temple" as the definitive unit of organization is an architectural structure, an organization of officials, and an indefinite number of "pilgrims" with a sense of community. A temple is identified with a definite local area, either a village or a section of a city.

The official organization of a temple includes one or more priests, a board of trustees, and various employees. The priesthood is a hereditary office, almost always filled by men of the Brahmin caste. Some trustees are hereditary; others are appointed. A large temple may employ one or more musicians, clerks, guides, bearers (porters), sweepers, and so on. The trustees manage the business and supervise the staff of the temple. Under federal law, each state has established a Religious and Charitable Endowment Board with a "Commissioner" who supervises handling of the funds of the larger temples and appoints some trustees.

A temple is visited by an indefinite and unrecorded number of "pilgrims." They worship, participate in festivals, consult priests, make financial contributions, and engage in other activities. They are, however, not members, for the temple is not a corporate group. An individual is a Hindu by ascription from birth and attached to a temple by preference and habit.

Each temple is fully autonomous, save for governmental supervision of finances. There is no district, regional, or national organization. However, all temples are casually linked into the Hindu religion through the priesthood which is Brahmin, through identification with the Hindu faith, through somewhat closer identification with the religious currents or "mutts" of Hinduism, and through the government, which supervises the administration of temple funds.

Religion in the Modern World ❯ The role of religion in the modern world is conditioned by several variables. Religion has largely been replaced by nationality as the major form of social organization. Conflict therefore is typically between nationality, not religious, groupings. The diffusion of Western civilization, though initially linked with religious activity, is now largely dissociated from the religious sector of the heritage. Religion thus occupies an ambiguous position in the process of modernizing the developing societies.

Western Europe and the Western Hemisphere are monopolized by Christianity, but the religious heritage of Asia and Africa is much more diverse. Christianity is associated with the Caucasian race, but the other major races are divided among many religious groups. Historically, the European branch of the Caucasian race and its descendants are typically Christian in religion and industrial in economy. These characteristics are associated with the history of rapid growth and expansion of Western Europe. On the other hand, the Mongolian and Negro racial categories of Asia and Africa are religiously diverse and typically nonindustrial. This cluster of conditions was associated with European policies of colonization, imperialism, and economic exploitation. Based on religious and economic differences, there developed in many of these areas what E. Franklin Frazier has called a "racial division of labor."[39]

Arnold Toynbee has noted that in the modern world religion has been replaced by nationality as the major basis of social organization and group conflict.[40] That is, religion no longer constitutes a major basis for the organization and mobilization of power, and religious ends seldom move people to violent struggle. The major exception to this generalization is found in the mechanisms of conflict that are structured into the aggressive ideologies of Russian and Chinese Communism, which may be viewed as forms of secular religion. The other significant exception is found in the perennial conflicts of Jews and Arabs in the Middle East and between Moslems and Hindus in the Pakistani-Indian subcontinent.

Christianity in Western Europe antedated the development of industrialism. Max Weber and R. H. Tawney have argued that changes of Christian doctrine as embodied in the Protestant Reformation were correlated with the rise of capitalism and industrialism.[41] However, the diffusion of the industrial complex from Western Europe and America to developing societies has followed a somewhat different course.

Three patterns can be identified in the contacts of advanced with developing societies. In the pre-industrial period of exploration and colonization, Christianity was fused with the politico-economic complex transported by the Europeans. The missionary was a teammate of the trader and the conquerer. Simultaneous effort was made (especially by the Spanish) to Christianize, rule, and exploit the people of the Western Hemisphere, Asia, and Africa. Later, when colonial regimes were well established, indigenous peoples were permitted to retain their aboriginal religions and Christian missionaries were admitted grudgingly.

In the developing Communist societies, i.e., the Soviet Union and mainland China, modernization has been dissociated from religion, which on ideological grounds has been rejected and suppressed. However, some argue that the politico-economic ideology has emerged as a modern secular religion to replace earlier orthodox forms.

In the other developing societies, modernization has proceeded in relative isolation from religious diffusion. The classic illustration is modern Japan. In India at the present time, modernization on all fronts proceeds with virtually no acquisition of Western religious forms in connection with the literary, scientific, and technical culture. In some developing societies, such as those of Africa, modernization tends to challenge and weaken indigenous "primitive" religions. The vacuum thus created is not filled by religious forms imported from the West along with the urban-industrial civilization.

Rise of Associational Forms in the U.S. ♦ The multiplicity of denominations and quasi-denominations in American society issued from the heritage of competing forms that existed in the colonies.[42] Dissociation of religious membership from general societal membership was predicated on separation of church and state and the doctrine of religious freedom. With change, the various communal forms tended to assume associational character.

Liston Pope was able to identify major dimensions of the process of change in a study of religious forms in a southern textile city.[43] He identified sects with the communal pattern of the mill workers and found denominations to be typical of religious organization among owners, managers, and other middle-class people. Pope's analysis of the transformation of sects into denominations can be summarized as follows.

1. Achieved membership in the sect, based on personal experience and unique status, was replaced by ascribed membership in the denomination, based on general qualifications and categoric status.

2. Casual organization of statuses and relations within religious primary groups was changed into formal organization of statuses and relations within formal associations.

3. Strong other-worldly orientation combined with rebellion or withdrawal from the surrounding social milieu was transformed into a this-worldly orientation and active conformity with the host social milieu.[44]

The structure of religion in contemporary American society can be described by our model of institutional analysis. First, new ends emerged to complement or challenge the functions of reaffirming ultimate values, intercession with the supernatural, and sanctioning of social control. The church espoused the causes of education, welfare, and international peace. There is evidence to indicate that religious institutions support the government and the economy.[45] More recently religious organizations have acted to advance such causes as human relations, family life, racial amity, labor-management accord, individual security, and civil rights. In a study of "the religious factor" Gerhard Lenski revealed that through the lives of members, religion tends to influence all the other institutions, and in the religious "sub-community" religious norms are extended beyond formal church associations.[46]

Religious norms reveal the variability and formality of associational society. The rituals of Sunday morning service in a metropolitan church are a far cry from the religious patterns in a southern mill town sect. Worship, administration, the ministry, and training of the young have been subjected to regularization and formalization. The social activity specialties of religion are therefore quite different from those of the market place, the arena of government, or the family circle.

Associational religious organization is characterized by formal cadres of statuses and roles. Membership became such a status-role and was dissociated from membership in the total society. Consider some of the status labels, such as minister, assistant minister, deacon, chorister, organist, elder, trustee, class leader, Sunday School superintendent, and teacher. In addition there are administrative offices such as bishop, presiding elder, moderator, or Pope. The hierarchizing of such religious offices is associated with the development of bureaucracy in the religious institution. The tendency toward bureaucracy is most advanced in the Roman Catholic Church, although it is evident in most of the Protestant denominations.

Institutionalization has issued in development of numerous specialized implementing associations. The parish, the congregation or body of communicants, is the core religious group. Terms like "connection" function to indicate the linking of many core groups into the extended association or denomination. Within the large formal organization are found numerous functionally specialized subassociations such as boards, clubs, councils, committees, societies, and the like. Further, modern religious institutions have sent out associational bridges to link with the other institutions. Consider, for example, the Young Men's Christian Association, the National Catholic Charities, and the Anti-Defamation League.

Religious Organization in the U.S. ▶ Religious organization is large and complex. An incomplete census, as shown in Figure 9-3, reveals 253 independent religious bodies, over 300,000 churches, and some 281,000 Sunday Schools. No account is here taken of other official organizations such as boards, choirs, classes, circles, and societies. In addition, there are the district, regional, national, and international echelons of organization.

Most individuals in the United States who are church members belong to one of the three leading faiths: Protestant, Roman Catholic, and Jewish.[47] In 1965 over half, about 55 per cent, of these persons were Protestants; more than a third, around 37 per cent, were Roman Catholic, and about 5 per cent were Jewish. The remaining 3 per cent are found in a variety of non-Christian faiths.

Units and Members of United States Religious Organizations

RELIGIOUS BODIES	253
NUMBER OF CHURCHES	321,449
TOTAL MEMBERSHIP	120,865,234
NUMBER OF SUNDAY SCHOOLS	281,593
TOTAL SUNDAY SCHOOL ENROLLMENT	45,805,074

Source: World Almanac and Book of Facts, 1965, p. 654.

FIGURE 9-3

Referring to religious organization in the United States, Ely Chinoy identifies three basic types.[48] In the "episcopal" type, authority is hierarchically ordered with supreme control over both ministers and laymen vested in a single supreme figure. The best illustration is the Roman Catholic Church, although the Anglican and some other Protestant denominations exemplify this form. The "presbyterian" type of organization is dominated by a group of preachers who form the governing body. In the "congregational" type, authority rests in the local group, which chooses its own minister and has an active role in church affairs. In the two latter types, local congregations are federated into denominational structures.

American religious institutions reveal some trends that are consistent with the social milieu. First, as Gerhard Lenski has shown, American churches will gain "in associational vigor and vitality in the foreseeable future" because first-generation immigrants and members of the working classes (elements least involved in religion) are declining, while third-generation Americans and the middle classes (those most involved in religion) are increasing in the population.[49] At the same time, as Will Herberg has shown, the alien faiths, denominations, and sects, most often associated with immigrants, have tended to become Americanized.[50] While growing larger and stronger, the whole religious apparatus therefore tends to conform to the American cultural ethos and to support national purposes.

Second, American religious organization becomes both more centralized and more proliferated. Large units merge into even larger units. For example, the Christian and Congregationalist denominations and sectors of Presbyterians and Lutherans have already merged, and still other denominational mergers are being negotiated. Or again, the Roman Catholic ecumenical movement is an exploration into doctrinal and organizational rapprochement with other faiths, especially the Protestant denominations.

On the other hand, new sects and schisms continue to proliferate.[51] Examples are the rural fundamentalist sects and urban store-front churches. Such new religious units are typically either isolationist, like Father Divine's Kingdom, or rebellious, like the Black Muslims.

Third, some forces in the American culture and social system tend to push religious institutions in the direction of secular rationalism. The assumptions of science, the pragmatisms of technology, and the rationale of bureaucracy tend to challenge traditional religious belief and practice. Consider, for example, the theory of evolution versus the doctrine of divine creation, propaganda appeals via the mass media versus personal religious confrontation, and professional qualification of ministers versus divine calling. The church is subjected to secular controls or pressures by government and the economy,[52] and required to confront such mundane issues as international war, economic poverty, class conflict, and racial discrimination.

Finally, the religious institutions are a prime locus of cultural and social lags. For example, there is the large central city church with its suburbanizing congregation left in what H. Paul Douglass has called "chronic crisis."[53] Doctrinal lags are illustrated in the inconsistencies between family canons and pronouncements and changing sexual morality and family organization. Or again, organizational lag appears in the reluctance of religious bodies to adopt bureaucratic forms and techniques in the face of growing size, dispersion of membership, impersonality of relations, and magnification of problems to be managed.

Social Issues of Religion ▶ The foregoing discussion has suggested some unresolved issues. The rise of ideological Communism in Russia and mainland China and their satellites has removed half the world's population from the aegis of orthodox religion. As a consequence, the evangelical religions are not only challenged by an aggressive secular gospel; but the mechanisms of expansion built into both systems establish one possible situation for massive conflict. At the same time, the leading systematic religions are confronted with the pressure to doctrinal and organizational rapprochement through ecumenism. Yet effort in this direction threatens to reactivate old quarrels and to have abrasive effects on relations among some great religious bodies.

Although, as noted, religion no longer establishes the structural setting of major social conflicts, some ancient feuds remain, smoldering and threatening. In addition to the Communist-Christianity confrontation mentioned above, there is the Arab-Jew vendetta in the Middle East and the Moslem-Hindu feud in the Pakistani-Indian subcontinent. One major issue of the modern world and its instruments for peace is how to contain the potential for massive violent conflict inherent in these situations.

The process of modernization has two significant religious consequences. On the one hand, economic change and urbanization tend to weaken and disintegrate indigenous religious systems. The vacuum thus created is not being filled by organized religions from either West or East. On the other hand, the developing societies do not acquire the moral and ethical systems of the advanced societies along with their literary, scientific, and technical complexes. There is therefore an absence of the moral controls and ethical patterns required for management of modern systems and for harmonious relations with the advanced societies of Europe and America.

In the United States, many people believe that a leading issue is lack of religious significance or loss of purpose. It is argued that religion no longer has a decisive impact upon social policy and national destiny. Some people claim that neither organized religion nor religious principles retain touch with the problems and issues of the society. From the point of view of religion in society, the issue is unresolved.

Another issue inheres in the process of rapprochement among the diverse faiths and groupings in the society. Although, as noted, a trend toward merger of denominational units is evident, doctrinal and power struggles still characterize religious relations. The most obvious examples are lingering anti-Semitism and anti-Catholicism. But new sects like the Black Muslims again touch off religious hostilities. Moreover, the great, powerful, and respectable faiths and denominations are vested interests with mechanisms of defense, conservatism, and collective integrity built into their structures.

Uneven change creates lags in the social structure that continue to plague organized religion. One index is the central city church whose congregation has moved to the suburbs, leaving a massive building and a large investment of sentiment behind. The thinning rural population faces problems of maintaining adequate organization of religious life. Meanwhile, with population growth, denominational mergers, and continued urbanization, religious organizations grow large, dispersed, and formal. It becomes increasingly urgent to adapt bureaucratic forms and techniques to mores, relationships, and sentiments that come from an informal agrarian past.

These and similar issues are coming under investigation by methods of sociology. One result is an accumulating body of theory, methods, and findings that are called the sociology of religion. This is one of the newer and promising subfields of sociology. One can expect that in time sociological research may serve as the prelude and basis for sound planning and action in the area of religion.

FOOTNOTES

1. Kingsley Davis, *Human Society* (New York: Macmillan, 1949), p. 395.
2. Robert H. Lowie, *An Introduction to Cultural Anthropology* (New York: Holt, Rinehart, and Winston, 1955), p. 252.
3. For brief descriptions of family systems in a variety of societies, ancient and modern, nonliterate and advanced, see Ruth N. Anshen, *The Family: Its Function and Destiny* (New York: Harper, 1959), especially Chapters 4 through 12; and Stuart A. Queen *et al., The Family in Various Cultures* (Chicago: Lippincott, 1961), especially Chapters 2 through 13.
4. George Peter Murdock, *Social Structure* (New York: Macmillan, 1949), pp. 1-2.
5. See Oscar Lewis, *Village Life in Northern India* (Urbana: University of Illinois Press, 1958); and C. M. Arensberg and S. T. Kimball, *Family and Community in Ireland* (Cambridge: Harvard University Press, 1940).
6. See Irawati Karve, *Kinship Organization in India* (Bombay: Asia Publishing House, 1965), Chapter 6.
7. Ruth Shonle Cavan, *The American Family* (New York: Crowell, 1963), Chapter 5.
8. See Dennis de Rougemont, *Love in the Western World* (New York: Harcourt Brace, 1940); and John Sirjamaki, *The American Family* (Cambridge: Harvard University Press, 1959), pp. 21-22.
9. Karve, *op cit.*
10. Davis, *op. cit.*, pp. 401-404.
11. See Margaret Mead, *Coming of Age in Samoa* (New York: Morrow, 1934).
12. See Robert R. Sears *et al., Patterns of Child Rearing* (Evanston: Row Peterson, 1957); and Daniel R. Miller and Guy E. Swanson, *The Changing American Parent* (New York: Wiley, 1958).
13. John J. Honigmann, *Culture and Personality* (New York: Harper, 1954).
14. See André Beteille, *Caste, Class and Power: Changing Patterns of Stratification in a Tanjore Village* (Bombay: Oxford, 1966); and Lewis, *op. cit.*
15. Margaret Read, *Children of Their Fathers* (New Haven: Yale University Press, 1960).
16. Condensed and adapted from Manford H. Kuhn, "American Families Today: Development and Differentiation of Types," in Howard Becker and Reuben Hill, eds., *Family, Marriage and Parenthood* (Boston: Heath, 1955), pp. 131-138.
17. Among many sources see Béteille, *op. cit.;* Karve, *op. cit.;* Lewis, *op. cit.;* and K. N. Pannikkar, *Hindu Society at Crossroads* (Bombay: India Publishing House, 1955).
18. William J. Goode, *World Revolution and Family Patterns* (New York: Free Press, 1963), especially pp. 366-380.
19. Howard W. Beers, "A Portrait of the Farm Family in Central New York State," in *American Sociological Review* (October 1937), p. 591.
20. Cavan, *op. cit.*, condensed and adapted from Chapter 7.
21. J. Kenneth Galbraith, *The Affluent Society* (Boston: Houghton Mifflin, 1957); and Michael Harrington, *The Other America* (New York: Macmillan, 1962).
22. C. Wright Mills, *White Collar* (New York: Oxford University Press, 1951).
23. Logan Wilson and William L. Kolb, *Sociological Analysis* (New York: Harcourt Brace, 1949), p. 620.
24. Robert Redfield, "The Folk Society," in *American Journal of Sociology*, 52:297.
25. Lowie, *op. cit.*, p. 162.
26. *Ibid., passim;* Thomas Woody, *Life and Education in Early Society* (New York: Macmillan, 1949); and Ralph L. Beals and Harry Hoijer, *An Introduction to Anthropology* (New York: Macmillan, 1965), Chapter 21.
27. See Don Martindale, *American Society* (New York: Van Nostrand, 1960), pp. 289-294.
28. See Chapter 12 below for an analysis of socialization and a fuller differentiation of socialization and education.
29. Kenneth A. Simon and W. Vance Grant, *Digest of Educational Statistics,* (U.S. Office of Education, 1964), Table 96, p. 112.
30. C. Horace Hamilton, "Projection of Fall Enrollment in North Carolina Colleges and Universities, 1966-1975," *University of North Carolina Newsletter*, Vol. LI, No. 3, September 1966, Table I.
31. Some of the new ends of education have been rationalized and stated as the

"Cardinal Aims." See Rudyard K. Bent and Henry K. Kronenberg, *Principles of Secondary Education* (New York, McGraw-Hill, 1955), p. 54.

32. Among various sources see Paul H. Buck *et al.*, *Education in a Free Society* (Cambridge: Harvard University Press, 1945), pp. 19-20; and James B. Conant, *The American High School Today* (New York: McGraw-Hill, 1959).

33. See Frederic W. Terrien, "Who Thinks What about Education," in *Public Opinion Quarterly*, 18:157-168 (Summer 1954).

34. See Martindale, *op. cit.*, pp. 289-294.

35. See Robert R. Bell, "Decreasing Student and Community Identification with the School," in *The Bulletin of the National Association of Secondary School Principals* (February 1961), pp. 117-120.

36. Conant, *op. cit.*; and Hyman Rickover, *American Education: A National Failure* (New York: Dutton, 1963).

37. Wilson and Kolb, *op. cit.*, p. 651.

38. Leopold von Wiese and Howard Becker, *Systematic Sociology* (New York: Wiley, 1932), pp. 624-628.

39. E. Franklin Frazier, *Race and Culture Contacts in the Modern World* (New York: Knopf, 1957), p. 159.

40. Arnold J. Toynbee, "Freedom's Religious Foundations," in *Bulletin of America's Town Meeting of the Air*, Vol. 21, No. 31 (November 22, 1955).

41. Max Weber, *The Protestant Ethic and the Spirit of Capitalism* (London: Allen and Unwin, 1930); and R. H. Tawney, *Religion and the Rise of Capitalism* (New York: Harcourt Brace, 1926).

42. Martindale, *op. cit.*, pp. 277-289.

43. Liston Pope, *Millhands and Preachers* (New Haven: Yale University Press, 1942).

44. *Ibid.*, pp. 122-124.

45. See William H. Form and Delbert C. Miller, *Industry, Labor and Community* (New York: Harper, 1960), Chapter 9.

46. Gerhard Lenski, *The Religious Factor* (Garden City: Doubleday, 1961), pp. 289-297 *et passim*.

47. National Council of the Churches of Christ in the U.S.A., *Yearbook of American Churches, 1965,* Table, p. 253.

48. Ely Chinoy, *Society* (New York: Random House, 1961), pp. 288-290.

49. Lenski, *op. cit.*, pp. 288-289.

50. Will Herberg, *Protestant, Catholic, Jew* (Garden City: Doubleday, 1966).

51. See Elmer T. Clark, *The Small Sects in America* (New York: Abingdon-Cokesbury, 1949).

52. See Form and Miller, *op. cit.*, Chapter 9; and Lenski, *op. cit., passim.*

53. H. Paul Douglass, "Some Protestant Churches in Urban America," in T. Lynn Smith and C. A. McMahan, eds., *The Sociology of Urban Life* (New York: Dryden, 1951), pp. 518-526.

THE SENIOR CITIZEN IN AMERICA

"SENIOR CITIZENS"—those over sixty-five years of age—have increased dramatically in number during recent years. In 1965, 16 million Americans were over sixty-five; by 1975 the figure will rise to 20 million. The prolongation of life

results from a number of factors, including better housing and working conditions and more effective medical care. Increased life expectancy raises important economic and social issues and leads to a re-evaluation of traditional American family structure. Where and how will the Senior Citizens of today and tomorrow live? Who will care for those who are not able, physically or economically, to care for themselves? Most fortunate are those retired couples and individuals who are able to maintain independent households. Those not so fortunate will spend the remaining years of their lives in various ways. Some will depend on their children for economic support. Some will experience the loneliness of the woman at right, who is cared for in an expensive rest home.

► *PHYSICAL CARE for the elderly—to be achieved most economically—necessarily takes on an impersonal quality, as at this pill distribution counter in a large state institution.*

▼ *HIDDEN TALENTS can be discovered by Senior Citizens who retain good health, like these participants in a Golden Age Club musicale at a public housing development. For those who need personalized physical or occupational therapy, an increasing—but still insufficient—number of community facilities are available.*

► *THOSE ALONE—without family, without pension plan or social security benefits— represent a growing proportion of the poverty-stricken in the United States. They present the greatest challenge to those who struggle to solve the problems of the elderly.*

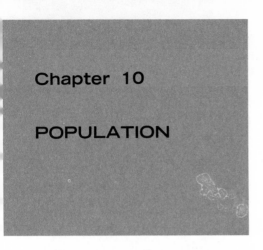

Chapter 10

POPULATION

The term "population" is a familiar language symbol that communicates meanings regarding many different aspects of life. For example, the term "population" refers to numbers of individuals when the Bureau of the Census reports that there are now some 190 million people in the United States, or that five U.S. cities have over a million inhabitants. The term stresses mobility when news reports note that California and Florida are growing faster than the other states. It denotes the kinds of characteristics of individuals when one speaks of the ratio of males to females, or of the percentage of Negroes, Catholics, or older persons in a given locality. The term population also symbolizes ways of acting, thinking, feeling, and believing. The United States has a formal policy on immigration that reflects the feelings of American legislators about the kind of individuals who should constitute our population.

The concept of population thus suggests some structural and dynamic aspects of human society that are of interest in sociological analysis. Logan Wilson and William L. Kolb observe that the characteristics and size of a population are not simple biological facts.[1] What is significant is the fact that the relation between them is reciprocal. They illustrate by pointing out that trade and industrial activity cannot flourish in sparsely populated areas; nor can a dense population be supported by a hunting or fishing economy.

A population may be defined as all the individuals of both sexes, all ages, and every characteristic, who occupy a specific geographic area at a given time. Particular or subpopulations may be differentiated by specifying appropriate distinguishing characteristics, such as location, time, age, sex, race, religion, or marital status.

Sociological analysis employs the data and concepts of population to further the understanding of structured functions in human society. For example, the institutional, class, and associational structure

of a society are affected by the size and composition of its population
In the southern region of the United States the arrangements of social
segregation developed and persisted because of the large proportion
of Negroes in the population. The institutions in logging, mining, or
frontier communities reflect the extreme excess of males. Or again,
when the American population was both smaller and younger than
now, there was little need for public programs of financial assistance
to needy older persons. The concentration of vast numbers of individuals in congested metropolitan areas raises the need for many
organized activities and services that were never thought of at an
earlier time in national history.

WORLD POPULATION

Growth and Size ♦ One of the most dramatic facts of modern life
is the rapid growth of world population. The almost irresistible
character of this increase has been captured in the phrase "population explosion." The consequences of this development have created
some of the most vexing and dangerous problems of modern life.
Evidence suggests that explosive growth of world population is both
cause and result of other important social and economic changes.

Figure 10-1 shows the size of the world population in 1965, together
with the amount and rate of growth by centuries since 1650 and projections to the year 2000. The table also shows mean reproduction rates
at selected dates. It will be seen that the total in 1965 was over six
times the total three hundred years earlier and is more than half the
total that is foreseen thirty-five years thence, in the year 2000. Rapidity
of growth is shown even more clearly by net reproduction rates as listed
in the last column of the table. Not only was the total in 1965 six
times greater than it was in 1650; the mean rate of reproduction
was almost ten times as great. Frederick Osborn observes that between 1650 and 1930 world population increased at an average of
0.5 per cent per year. Between 1930 and 1940, however, the rate was
1 per cent annually, and since the end of World War II it has been 1.6
per cent.[2] Whereas between 1650 and 1850 the total only slightly
more than doubled, at present rates of reproduction it will double in
about 50 years or less.

This picture of rapid growth of population parallels the birth,
flowering, and spread of Western civilization. The three centuries
since 1650 embrace the revolutions in thought, trade and finance,
technology, industry and communications, and the great era of
European expansion. The first impact of these changes, felt in Western Europe and the United States, contributed to the early population
increases. It was the initial phase of this population growth to which
Thomas Malthus reacted in the latter half of the eighteenth century.[3]
Since Malthus had access to only crude population data, and since he

Increase in the World Population, by Selected Dates, with Projections to 2000

YEAR	NUMBER*	AMOUNT OF INCREASE	PER CENT OF INCREASE	MEAN REPRODUCTION RATE (%)[1]
2000	5,965	897	17.7	—
1990	5,068	799	18.7	—
1980	4,268	961	29.0	—
1965	3,308	2,137	173.9	2.1
1900	—	—	—	0.6
1850	1,171	443	60.9	—
1800	—	—	—	0.4
1750	728	183	33.4	—
1700	—	—	—	0.3
1650	545	—	—	0.25

*Stated as thousands of millions.
Sources: Figures through 1850 from Encyclopaedia Britannica, 18:233, 1956. Figures for 1965 and estimates for succeeding years from Population Reference Bureau, Population Bulletin, "World Population Projections, 1965-2000," p. 96, Table 1 (Volume XXI, No. 4, October 1965). Projections are "medium" estimates. Projections for 2000 range from "continued trend" of 7,410 to a "low" of 5,296.
1. Adapted from Figure 1 of demographic materials prepared by Dr. Hermann Schubnell, Director, Division of Population, Federal Statistics Bureau of Federal Republic of Germany, for the Seventeenth International Conference on the Family, New Delhi, India, December 13, 1966.

FIGURE 10-1

did not fully recognize the implications of the new Industrial Revolution, his judgments and conclusions led him to gloomy predictions for the future.

However, as is shown in Figure 10-2, the rates of growth are not the same in all regions and countries. It will be seen that Latin America exhibits the highest rate of population growth. Asia and Africa, both developing continents, follow Latin America in the explosive rates of population expansion. Western Europe and North America, both with well-established urban industrial complexes, present low and declining patterns of growth.

The evidence indicates that rapid population increase characterized Western Europe and the United States in the late eighteenth and nineteenth centuries. Prior to the Industrial Revolution, birth and death rates were both high and tended to maintain a relatively stable population. Because of the new conditions, the death rate fell sharply, leading to increase of the survival rate and rapid population growth. In the twentieth century birth rates have also fallen, producing the low rates of increase shown in Figure 10-2.

Using such data, Frank W. Notestein refers to societies of "high" and "low" growth "potential."[4] The societies of low growth potential in general have had a long experience with urban industrial civilization. Those with high current rates of population increase and high growth potentials are only now acquiring modern economic, social, and cultural systems. Rapid growth at present and in the immediate future results from sharply declining death rates caused by improvements in medical care, sanitation, diet, and the like. Since most such societies still have hoe and handicraft economies, village social organization, and nonliterate cultures, rapid population growth strains or will soon strain resources.

The case of India, though extreme, is typical of the developing

Percent Estimates of Increase of World Population
by Major Regions, 1950 to 2000

World Regions	1950 to 1975	1975 to 2000
AFRICA	52	71
NORTH AMERICA (exclusive of Mexico and Central America)	43	30
LATIN AMERICA	86	95
ASIA (excluding USSR)	60	75
EUROPE (including USSR)	31	26
OCEANIA	62	38
WORLD TOTAL	53	64

Source: Population Reference Bureau, Population Bulletin, Vol. 16, No. 1, January 1960. Adapted from Table 3, p. 16, medium estimates only.

FIGURE 10-2

societies with high population growth potential. With a population of about 500 million, India occupies territory smaller than the United States. Its current rate and potential for growth are among the highest in the world. This large and exploding population, coupled with slow agricultural and economic development, recent droughts and crop failures, foreign exchange and managerial problems, and the like, presses at the limits of available resources, particularly food. The government, operating within the framework of state socialism and by means of national planning, is attacking this problem on two fronts. By direct action in the "public sector" and through encouragement of the "private sector" of the economy, effort is made to accelerate industrial development. At the same time, massive "family planning" (birth control) is pressed in all ways and in all sectors of the society. Under ordinary conditions, such approaches could possibly achieve a balance between population and resources. However, a series of extraordinary misfortunes have conspired to retard development and to exacerbate India's situation. In recent years the country has had to depend on foreign aid to support the exploding population. India's prospect for the immediate future is also bleak.

The population explosion has had other social consequences. Growing recognition of its catastrophic potential for mankind has generated activity on many fronts. In the developing societies, serious efforts are being made to increase food production to meet increasing demand. Because of many traditional and organizational difficulties, programs to control population growth have been less effective. The advanced societies of Western Europe and North America have increased assistance in the areas of industrial development, agricultural improvement, and population control to the developing societies.

Sex and Age Make-up ♦   Although there are about as many women as men in the world, the ratio of women to men varies considerably from one country to another. Figure 10-3 shows the number of women per 1000 men in selected developing and advanced societies. Some of these differences may result from differential male and female birth rates; yet it is doubtless true that variable social conditions are the leading influence. The other main impression conveyed by the exhibit is that there are typically fewer women in the populations of the developing countries than in the advanced societies.

The excess of males in the populations of the developing societies of the leading world areas is associated with their favorable position in the patriarchal structures of these societies. Sons are prized and given preferential care. Girls are regarded as burdensome, non-prestige-bearing, and expendable. They bring little honor to the family, will leave the family when married, and usually require dowries. There is little evidence of extensive female infanticide in these countries; however, girl babies and children are less well protected, cared

Number of Women Per 1000 Men in Selected Advanced and Developing Countries

Country	Number of Women
INDIA (1961)	942
IRAN (1956)	965
PHILIPPINES (1960)	983
UNITED ARAB REPUBLIC (1960)	988
BRAZIL (1960)	1,003
SWEDEN (1960)	1,005
KENYA (1962)	1,019
INDONESIA (1961)	1,028
UNITED STATES (1960)	1,030
JAPAN (1965)	1,035
UNITED KINGDOM (1961)	1,068
SOVIET UNION (1959)	1,220

Source: United Nations Demographic Yearbook, 1965, derived from Table 1, pp. 104 ff.

FIGURE 10-3

for, and preserved than boys. In adulthood, heavy work, continuous child-bearing, and general neglect tend to shorten their lives.

On the other hand, the fact that women equal or outnumber men in advanced societies seems to be associated with another set of social conditions. Patriarchal dominance has diminished, and women enjoy higher social value and status. At every stage in the life cycle, therefore, they receive better care and protection than do their sisters in the developing societies. As a consequence, as will be shown below, in the advanced societies there are substantially more persons in the upper age brackets, and most of them are women.

The age compositions of the populations of selected developing and advanced societies are shown in Figure 10-4. This exhibit differentiates children, work-age individuals, and older persons. The columns of figures show again that the developing societies are sharply distinguished from the advanced countries. In the developing countries 40 per cent or more of the populations are children, 14 years old and younger; but children constitute less than 30 per cent of the populations of advanced societies. Old persons, 65 and over, compose a tenth, more or less, of the populations of the advanced societies, but only half that proportion or less in the developing societies. As a consequence, that proportion of the population remaining in the work years, 15 to 64, is larger in the advanced than in the developing societies.

The sex-age composition of world population is connected to explosive growth and has some important social consequences. Although the immediate effect of declining death and high birth rates is seen in the high proportion of children, in succeeding years this bulge will be extended up the age ladder. Thus, in addition to the critical problem of food, these societies must draw upon limited resources to educate large numbers of children. The old, however, are a relatively light social burden, not only because they are few in number, but also because they do not regularly retire from the work force, as is customary in the advanced societies. *Vis-à-vis* the advanced societies, the work-age sector is not only relatively smaller; its efficiency is also limited by the traditions of hand labor and the extensive use of

Per Cent Distribution of the Populations of Selected Advanced and Developing Countries by Broad Age Categories

COUNTRY	UNDER 14	15 TO 64	65 AND OVER
PHILIPPINES (1965)	46.7	50.7	2.6
KENYA (1962)	46.0	49.2	4.8
IRAN (1959)	44.5	51.9	3.6
UNITED ARAB REPUBLIC (1960)	42.7	53.8	3.5
BRAZIL (1960)	42.6	52.5	4.9
INDONESIA (1961)	42.1	55.4	2.5
INDIA (1961)	41.0	55.9	3.1
SOVIET UNION (1961)	32.2	58.0	9.8
UNITED STATES (1965)	30.8	59.9	9.3
JAPAN (1964)	26.3	68.5	5.2
UNITED KINGDOM (1965)	22.8	65.0	12.2
SWEDEN (1963)	21.2	66.5	12.3

Source: United Nations Demographic Yearbook, 1965, *derived from Table 6, pp. 162 ff.*

FIGURE 10-4

women. On the other hand, the advanced societies not only have greater resources at their disposal; they also have relatively fewer children and young people to support and educate. At the same time, the work-age sector of the population is proportionately larger than in the developing societies and, because of technological advantages, is more efficiently occupied. However, the advanced societies must support a much larger number of older persons who, by law or custom, regularly withdraw from the productive work force. These population differences establish variable problems for the developing and the advanced societies. Because of increasing age and the withdrawal of older people from productive work, the advanced societies are faced with increasing problems of economic, social, and psychological maintenance for this sector of the population. On the other hand, the developing societies must establish modern educational institutions to serve their large youthful populations who are just now entering into activity in modern political and economic systems. At the same time they must rush forward with industrialization and agricultural development in order to occupy and support their growing populations.

POPULATION OF THE UNITED STATES

Growth and Size ▶ Growth of the population of the United States is an integral phase of the rapid expansion of world population. Figure 10-5 shows the size, amount of increase, and per cent of increase of the population of the United States by decades from 1790 to 1960. The present national population is more than 45 times greater than the total at the first census. Further inspection of the exhibit shows that the high growth rate, averaging over 30 per cent per decade in the early years, declined steadily though irregularly to a low point of 7.2 per cent in the 1930-1940 decade. Thereafter the growth rate rose sharply, reflecting America's own current population explosion. The United States has gained population from two major sources: by receiving persons from other societies, and by natural increase resulting from the excess of births over deaths.

The Bureau of the Census reports that between 1820 and 1963, 42,702,328 immigrants entered the country from all sources.[5] Negro slaves were smuggled from Africa and the West Indies prior to the Civil War. French, Spanish, and Mexican people were incorporated within the nation with the acquisition of Florida, the Louisiana Territory, and what are now Texas, Arizona, New Mexico, and California. Other population groups were included with the acquisition of Alaska, Hawaii, Puerto Rico, and the Virgin Islands. Immigrants entered the western part of the country from Asia, principally from Japan and China. When the growing nation occupied the territory to the Pacific Ocean, it acquired an indigenous Indian population estimated to number more than a third of a million.

Population Increase in the United States, 1790-1960

YEAR	TOTAL POPULATION	AMOUNT OF INCREASE	PER CENT OF INCREASE
1790	3,929,214	———	—
1800	5,308,483	1,379,269	35.1
1810	7,239,881	1,931,398	36.4
1820	9,638,453	2,398,572	33.1
1830	12,866,020	3,227,567	33.5
1840	17,069,453	4,203,433	32.7
1850	23,191,876	6,122,423	35.9
1860	31,443,321	8,251,445	35.6
1870	39,818,449	8,375,128	26.6
1880	50,155,783	10,337,334	26.0
1890	62,947,714	12,791,931	25.5
1900	75,994,575	13,046,861	20.7
1910	91,972,266	15,977,691	21.0
1920	105,710,620	13,738,354	14.9
1930	122,775,046	17,064,426	16.1
1940	131,669,275	8,894,229	7.2
1950	150,687,361	19,028,086	14.5
1960	178,464,236	27,766,875	18.4

Source: Statistical Abstract of the United States, 1964, Table 1, p. 5.

FIGURE 10-5

Only a few restrictions were placed on immigration.[6] In 1808 the importation of slaves from Africa and the West Indies was prohibited, although smuggling continued until the Civil War. The immigration of Chinese was prohibited by law in 1882, and Japanese immigration was terminated in 1908 by the so-called "gentlemen's agreement." In 1924, Congress restricted European immigration to some 375,000 annually by the National Origins Quota Act, which gave preference to persons from northern and western over southern and eastern European countries. During and following World War II, Congress modified this policy to permit refugees and displaced persons to enter the country. In 1965, Congress abolished the national origins quota principle and established limits upon free immigration from Canada and Latin America for the first time in national history.

Rapid growth of the diverse American population was part and parcel of the momentous events that were changing the world in recent centuries. The religious and political controversies of Western Europe drove millions to seek refuge in a new land. Virgin resources, the lure of freedom, the spirit of adventure, the urge for discovery, and policies of colonization and proselytism supported the migration to the new world. Once the young nation was established and stabilized, the business of settlement and growth required enormous resources of human population. The subsequent industrial, agrarian, communications, and financial revolutions maintained almost unlimited ceilings of population need. The impact of modern civilization upon virgin resources and the rapidly developing economy released the enormous reproductive potential of the virile young population.

In the foregoing chapters we have examined the consequences of population growth and diversification for the social system. Villages and frontier neighborhoods were transformed (through migration as well as growth) into cities and later into complex metropolitan areas. Patterns of primary relations that characterized the colonial and frontier systems were limited in scope and subordinated in importance as the growing heterogeneous population organized and acted through large, dispersed, and formal associations. As a corollary, the traditional culture of farm and village was superseded by formal systems of instrumental, specialized, literary norms. A further function, in part at least, of growth, diversification, and dispersion of the population, was the rise and magnification of bureaucracy in associational and institutional life. The institutions changed from traditional to bureaucratic and assumed new social functions. In the following chapters we will refer to some consequences of population growth, diversification, and dispersion for social stratification; personality development, organization, and function; collective behavior; and social change itself. Some consequences of population change are subjected to assessment by prevailing values and are classified as social problems.[7] For example, alarm over the large number of immigrants and hostility to the people from southern and eastern European countries contributed to the so-called "immigration problem."[8] The growth of cities and metropolitan areas is correlated with the development and crystallization of urban slums and deterioration. In these slums the processes of population change contributed to economic dependency, family and personal disorganization, crime and delinquency, and mental illness and illegitimacy. Robert K. Merton, William Foote Whyte, and others have shown that the growth of central cities through population change is functionally associated with criminal gangs, rackets, and vendettas as one accessible (though culturally disapproved) means to culturally approved ends.[9] And so it is to a greater or lesser degree with such other problems as racial conflict, labor-management strife, insecurity of the old, economic and cultural deprivation, waste of human and material resources, and so on. In Chapter 16 below we will examine how population, among a cluster of variables, can be managed in order both to remedy social problems and, hopefully, to prevent their occurrence.

Sex Composition ◗ Sex composition is numerically expressed as *sex ratio,* SR, or the number of males per 100 females. If the number of men and women is equal, the SR is 100. If there are more men than women, the ratio is larger than 100, and vice versa if the number of males is less than the number of females. The sex composition of a population differs in relation to such variables as locality, racial and ethnic make-up, occupation, and age. In 1910 the SR in the United States was 106; by 1960 it was only 97.8, and it continues to decline. This decline is associated with the curtailment of European immigration, two world wars, the Great Depression, and other internal factors.

Sex ratios vary from one place to another. In Alaska it was 162 in 1950, while in Washington, D.C. it was only 89. New England had the lowest SR of all regions, 96, while the ratio in the Mountain States was 104. The urban SR was 94, rural nonfarm 103, and rural farm 110.

These locality variations of sex ratios are correlated with variations of economic activities and occupational structure. Alaska and the Mountain States provide economic activities for men, while New England and most urban localities offer jobs and social opportunities to women. However, steel and heavy industry cities call for male workers, while commercial and governmental centers afford opportunities for women.

Sex ratios also vary in relation to age, race, and ethnic group. At birth there are about 106 white males to each 100 females, but the SR declines with increasing age. At all ages, the Negro population reveals a relatively low SR. Historically most immigrants were males, thus producing an unrepresentatively high sex ratio among the immigrant population. In 1950 the urban SR was 91 for persons 20-29 years of age, although for the total urban population it was 94. It is well known that there are more women than men over 65 years of age.

Sex Categories ◗ Social categories reflect the projection of population differentials into social organization. The resultant structural arrangements reveal several significant dimensions. Among the more important are: (1) the allocation of rights and obligations to social roles; (2) the ascription of roles (and hence of personnel) to positions in the status system; (3) the development of normative orders to regulate interaction and communication both within and between categories; and (4) the facilitation of grouping among individuals within the several categories.

In the United States a series of categoric roles for males and females has been defined and fixed at variable positions in the social structure. Sex roles are further differentiated on the basis of the age categories prevalent in the society. The categoric statuses of men and women in American social structure may be traced back to Biblical times, when the patriarchal family was the major institution defining roles and statuses.

The categoric status of women in the American social structure is revealed in the sex division of labor, existing legal restrictions, and persistent tendencies to sex segregation in education, play, social activities, and social organization. Females exceed male workers only in the clerical and service occupations. In some fields the proportion of women workers is almost negligible.

In many societies, however, the division of labor and status ascriptions of the sex categories differ radically from the familiar American pattern. The classic illustrations are the matriarchal societies. Among the Zuni and Hopi of Arizona and New Mexico, for example, women weave, make pottery, and work alongside men in home construction. They dominate the family, own the real property, and control many fetishes and secrets.[10]

Sex categories tend to prescribe appropriate normative modes of social action. Terms like coquetry, domesticity, and maternalism refer to typical action patterns of American women. Gallantry and chivalry designate the etiquette of male response to women. Dominant, aggressive, and competitive are words customarily used to describe expected behavior patterns of men in American social structure. Talcott Parsons has noted how the relevant categoric norms tend to facilitate the inculcation of female middle-class roles while impeding transmission of male roles.[11]

Sex categories constitute the basis of certain institutional and group units of social structure. Men's and women's colleges and preparatory schools are reminders of a time when sex segregation was widespread. Many activities in coeducational institutions are still organized separately for men and for women. Separation and status subordination is suggested by the women's auxiliary, which is a familiar adjunct of many organizations. Some important groups, such as press and service clubs, present parallel series of similar units for men and for women. There are multifarious independent groups exclusively for men or for women with no duplication or auxiliaries in the opposite sex category.

Age Composition ◗ The composition of the United States population is shown in Figure 10-6 by broad age periods. It will be seen that in 1960 over a fifth (21.8 per cent) of the total were children under ten years of age. On the other hand, almost one in ten (9.0 per cent) were elderly people 65 years old and over. Adolescents—persons 10 to 19 years old—constituted a sixth of the total. Slightly over half the popu-

Composition of the U.S. Population by Age Groups

AGE GROUPS	1910[1]	1940[1]	1960[2]
UNDER 5	11.6%	8.0%	11.4%
5 TO 9	10.6	8.1	10.4
10 TO 19	19.8	8.3	16.8
20 TO 39	33.3	32.2	25.8
40 TO 64	20.3	26.5	26.6
65 AND OVER	4.3	6.9	9.0
NOT REPORTED	0.2	0.0	0.0
TOTAL	100.0%	100.0%	100.0%

Sources: (1) Characteristics of the Population, *Bureau of the Census, 1950, Table 39, pp. 1-93;* (2) Statistical Abstract of the United States, *1962, Table 18, p. 26.*

FIGURE 10-6

lation were adult, between 20 and 64 years old. Almost equal proportions were young adults, 20 to 39, and mature or middle-aged adults, 40 to 64.

Figure 10-6 also reveals changes of the age composition in the half century from 1910 to 1960. The population of 1910 reflects the impact of mass immigration from southeastern Europe and the high pre-First World War birth rate. The 1940 figures, however, reveal the constricting effects of the Great Depression with lowered marriage and birth rates. The composition pattern of 1960 shows the effects of the wartime prosperity and the "baby boom" of the 1940's and 1950's.

It will be seen that the proportion of children under ten was high in both 1910 and 1960, although for somewhat different reasons. The 1940 child population was significantly low. The most striking fluctuation is among the proportion of adolescents, 10 to 19, at the three census periods. In 1910 over two fifths and in 1960 nearly two fifths of the total were under 20 years old, though in 1940 this age group made up less than a fourth of the total. The proportion of elderly persons has grown steadily, more than doubling in the half century. Although the proportion of young adults, 20 to 39, increased, the percentage of mature and middle-aged persons declined throughout the period.

Age composition also varies with differentials of sex, locality, nativity, etc. Among the old, females outnumber males, but among infants and children the reverse is true. In rural farm areas the proportion of young persons and in rural nonfarm localities the percentage of older individuals exceeds national averages. Foreign-born groups are now typically middle-aged and older.

Age Categories ❯ In all societies childhood, adolescence, young adulthood, middle age, and old age constitute socially significant age categories. They are fixed in the social structure and incorporated into the social system by distinctive status-role configurations. Figure 10-6 reveals how the American population is composed in terms of these age categories.

Leo W. Simmons has examined the category of old age in many different societies and times.[12] There is a voluminous literature reporting on the categories of old age and adolescence, although middle age has only recently attracted attention. In the remainder of this section age categories are illustrated with particular reference to the aged and middle-aged in the United States.

In contemporary American society, retirement formalizes 65 as the beginning of old age and institutionalizes the exclusion of the categorically old from productive work roles. The concept of the "scrapheap" age reflects the occupational rejection of this age category.

Census data show that although some male workers have begun to leave the labor force by their forty-fifth year, old age, as signified by 65, is characterized by a drastic withdrawal of these workers from productive occupations.[13] Less than a third of the men 65 years and older remained in the labor force in 1960. This figure is only 37 per cent of the proportion of male workers in the 55 to 64 bracket and almost 15 per cent less than the proportion of gainful workers 14 to 19 years old.

Entrance into the social category of the aged primarily signifies exit from productive work roles. It does not mark entrance into another clearly defined categoric social role, for no definite and generally acceptable role for the aged has been defined and sanctioned. The old, moreover, occupy an ambiguous collateral position in the social structure where social actions and social relations are neither clearly nor uniformly patterned by any stable normative order.

Categoric exclusion of the aged from the major organization of the society has fostered a number of collateral structures and functions. Old age insurance and assistance and a variety of pension systems have arisen to meet the economic needs created by exclusion of the aged from remunerative employment. For the same reasons, many types of housing arrangements have become necessary. Case-work and group-work services have had to be established to meet the social, emotional, and personal needs of older people who have been excluded from meaningful social participation. The common categoric status of old age constitutes one basis of many voluntary groups and associations.

Middle age, the span roughly between 40 and 65, between launching the children and retirement, constitutes a distinct age category in

American society. Robert J. Havighurst has characterized some of the role, status, and normative dimensions of middle age with particular reference to middle-class individuals in the United States.

As children leave, the parental roles become less demanding for parents who have become free. The home-maker role is reduced by moving to a smaller, less pretentious, and more efficient dwelling where the new leisure can be used in gardening, fixing up the place and the like. Released by children, spouses may spend more time together because they need each other more. At middle-age career peak, a man may relax and take his work more easily, or he may do just the opposite. Some women in middle age take up the worker role again. A person may drop out of certain organizations, such as the P.T.A., or join a social club for which he finds time and money. He may assume leadership or give it up. Combining wisdom with greater freedom, some middle-age persons take up the citizen role with distinction. Friendship roles increase because of more leisure and concern with people outside the family. Middle age brings variable use of leisure, ranging from full and constructive to dull idleness.[14]

POPULATION DYNAMICS

The discussion will now turn to an examination of the dynamic character of population, and an assessment of the relationship of these facts to organized social life. Populations change because human beings are both inherently dynamic and highly mobile. In the present discussion, attention is centered upon the inherent tendency of populations to expand, contract, and change in composition. The discussion of mobility is reserved for the following section.

Excluding migration, individuals may be added to a population only by birth and removed only by death. These episodic biological events of life are the sources of the inherent dynamic character of populations. The impact of these forces upon populations may extend over a considerable period of time and influence many aspects of composition and social life. Moreover, the rates at which new members are added or current members removed from populations both influence and are influenced by numerous social, economic, and psychological circumstances.

Measurement of Fertility ▶ Theoretically, a normal woman could become the mother of 40 children in the course of her reproductive life, roughly from age 15 to 44. As a matter of fact, however, perhaps no individual woman, and the females of no population have ever approached this maximum reproductive capacity, or fecundity. It has thus become necessary to devise measures of actual reproduction which do not assume that human beings reproduce as rapidly as is biologically possible. The most common measure is the birth rate.

Several kinds of birth rates can be computed. The simplest is the crude birth rate, or the total number of births in a single year divided by the total population in that year. When appropriate 1960 figures are used, 4,257,850[15] registered births divided by the population of 179,323,175[16] and multiplied by 1000 yields a crude birth rate of 23.7 for the United States.

The usefulness of this measure of fertility is seen when crude birth rates of several countries and regions are compared. Figure 10-7 shows actual and estimated crude birth rates for selected regions and nations of the world including the United States. Parts of Asia and Africa exhibit very high rates, while both northern and southern Europe fall below the United States and Canada. Some of the social and economic consequences of these differentials were examined briefly in earlier sections of this chapter.

Estimated Crude Birth Rates Per 1000 Population for Selected Areas of the World, 1954-1958

Region	Birth Rate
WORLD	35
AFRICA	45
North	45
Middle and South	46
NORTHERN AMERICA	25
LATIN AMERICA	41
ASIA*	40
JAPAN	19
EUROPE*	19
Northern and Western Europe	18
Central Europe	19
Southern Europe	21
OCEANIA	24
Australia and New Zealand	23
Pacific Islands	—
USSR, ASIAN and EUROPEAN combined	26

*Excluding the USSR
Source: Adapted from Table 1, p. 154, Population Bulletin, *World Population, 1960, Vol. 16, December 1960.*

FIGURE 10-7

As a measure of population dynamics, the crude birth rate has several significant limitations. The total population includes old persons, males, and young children, none of whom are capable of reproducing. Further, the crude birth rate fails to indicate the rate at which socially functioning new members are added to a population. Many of the babies born do not live long enough to become participating members of the society.

In order to measure the rate at which a population is renewing itself or changing in size and composition, it is necessary to combine some gauge of survival with the rate of reproduction. The result of this kind of computation constitutes an index of population survival and therefore of that part of total reproduction that significantly influences total population. If a baby survives until he is five, he has a good chance of becoming a mature member of his society. For these and certain statistical reasons the measurement of reproductivity is combined with the measurement of survival up to age five to produce an index known as *fertility ratio.*

A fertility ratio is computed by dividing the number of children under five years of age by the total number of women of child-bearing age, 15 to 44 years, in the year under consideration. When United States figures for 1960 are used, 20,321,000 children under five divided by 36,079,000 women 15 to 44 years old multiplied by 1000 produces a fertility ratio of 541. Such a measure recognizes the number of children surviving over a five-year period and thus indicates the rates at which new members are entering the population.

Variability of Fertility ▶ Fertility ratios vary in response to many different factors. Among the more important are customs relating to the rate and age of marriage and prevailing sex norms, particularly those determining coitus. The status of women, the evaluation of children, and group policies regarding family size are other influences. Policies—whether explicit or implicit—of population control, such as infanticide, abortion, and birth control, exert an influence upon fertility ratios. Still other influences, sometimes gross and sometimes subtle, issue from ideological considerations inherent in the structure and functioning of the institutional order.

Within the United States the fertility ratio varies from one subpopulation to another. The ratio is higher in rural than in urban localities; within rural places the farm ratio exceeds the nonfarm figure. Measures of fertility exhibit an inverse ratio to size of city, family income, and education. Manual workers have higher fertility ratios than white-collar workers, and Roman Catholics higher than Protestants.

In the United States the fertility ratio declined until around 1940, and thereafter increased.[17] The decline was most pronounced during the first four decades of the present century. By 1940 the fertility ratio, estimated to be about 1000 in 1800, had dropped to 343. During the next two decades the figure rose to 472 in 1950 and 541 in 1960, although since then the rate of increase has declined. The reversal of the long-term trend during these two decades is associated with the so-called war-time marriage and baby booms. Although ratios differ among subpopulations, the three classes of states—industrial, semi-industrial, and rural—have maintained their relative positions within the long-term trend.[18]

In order to eliminate or reduce the influence of temporary variabilities, say in age distributions, demographers (expert analysts of population) have developed some highly refined measures of fertility. These refinements, such as the Gross Reproduction Rate and Net Reproduction Rate, or Cohort Fertility Rates (the number of children born to women of approximately the same age as they move through the child-bearing period) will not concern us here. Students going on in the study of population will find some of the most sophisticated statistical techniques used in modern sociology.

Measurement of Mortality ▶ The measurement of mortality is simpler than the measurement of reproduction, since individuals of both sexes, all ages, and every social characteristic are subject to death. A death rate is computed by dividing the total number of recorded deaths in a year by the total number of individuals in the population. The accompanying figure 10-8 shows the downward trend of the United States death rates during the last forty years. It will be seen that, unlike fertility, the mortality rate has declined steadily. The figure also indicates that substantial reductions in mortality have occurred within the first year of life.

Another way to reveal the downward mortality trend is by the increase in the average length of life or longevity. It has been estimated that in the Roman Empire the average length of life was about 28 years. By the Middle Ages this figure had been increased to around 42 years. This same trend can be revealed by measures of life expectancy, or the average number of years a baby born at any given date can expect to live. In 1900 the life expectancy for males in the United States was 46.3 and for females 48.3 years. In 1962 the respective figures for total males and females were 66.8 and 73.4.[19] It has been estimated that by 1970 life expectations will be 69.8 for white males and 76.4 for white females.[20] Corresponding figures for nonwhites are regularly somewhat smaller.

The major evidence of the dynamic character of a population is expressed in the spread between its reproductive and mortality rates. When this spread is wide, the population is growing rapidly. When the spread narrows, the population loses some of its dynamic character. Frank W. Notestein's classification of populations as those in the stage of (1) high growth potentials, (2) transitional growth, and (3) incipient

Crude Death Rates and Infant Death Rates in the United States

CRUDE DEATH RATES [1]		INFANT DEATH RATES [2]	
YEAR	DEATH RATE	YEAR	DEATH RATE
		1915	99.9
1918 - 1922	13.5	1920	85.8
1928 - 1932	11.5	1925	71.7
		1930	64.6
1938 - 1942	10.6	1935	55.7
		1940	47.0
1946 - 1950	9.9	1945	38.3
		1950	29.2
1961 -	9.3	1953	27.8

Sources: (1) Warren S. Thompson, Population Problems, New York, McGraw-Hill, 1953, Table ii-4, p. 236; (2) National Office of Vital Statistics, Infant Mortality, Each State and Territory and Specified Possessions, 1953.

FIGURE 10-8

decline captures and conceptualizes the dynamic spread between re-productive and mortality trends.[21] The history of most societies shows that, as in the United States, fertility rates tend to fluctuate, declining generally, but sometimes increasing. Mortality rates, however, tend to decline steadily. One result is the acceleration of the dynamic character and growth of world population that was discussed earlier in this chapter.

Some Social Consequences of Population Dynamics ◗ Variations in the dynamic character of a population may function as cause or conse-quence of many diverse social conditions. Markets will be modified; unemployment may increase or a labor shortage develop; schools may become inadequate or superfluous; the family system may be dis-rupted; cities may swell or shrink; and so on almost without end.

In response to changes in population dynamics the population policy of a nation—whether explicit or implicit—may change, some-times eventuating in an ideology of over-population and expansion, and at other times resulting in doctrines of under-population, en-couraged immigration, and settlement. The consequences of such policies may be drastic and far-reaching. Maurice Hindus shows, for example, that in the Soviet Union consideration of militarism func-tioned to favor deliberate stimulation of rapid population growth.[22]

On the other hand, Japan's imperialistic claim on Manchuria or Fascist Italy's invasion of Ethiopia resulted in part from doctrines of overpopulation.

Variation in the dynamic character of a population may have other consequences. With change in the size or composition of population, the interplay between people of both natural and artificial resources will be altered. At the same time, important psychic or spiritual qualities of the society may also alter in response to variations in the dynamic character of the population.

POPULATION DISTRIBUTION

Man is a restless, mobile animal. He alone has occupied every inhabitable corner of the globe. The account of his migrations and movements constitutes a saga of unparalleled scope and heroism, and the drama of his restless movements is not yet ended. Although this heroic epic lies outside the scope of the present discussion, the consequences of human migration are crucial in the analysis of social relations. These migrations have brought human beings into significant contact with every type of geographic environment and have led to unlimited adaptations, combinations, and conflicts of cultures.

Intercontinental Shifts ▶ Perhaps the most significant chapters of human migration have been written since the revolutionary upheavals of the fifteenth to the eighteenth centuries shattered the communal societal cocoon of Western Europe and propelled its denizens into the modern era and into every quarter of the world. In these times and under these circumstances the distribution of world population altered profoundly. Figure 10-9 shows the present arrangement and redistribution of world population by continents for the period 1650 to 1950.

In this shifting and shuttling about, migrants transported the dynamic secular culture of Western Europe to every continent and precipitated a veritable frenzy of cultural conflicts and changes. The territorial aspirations that, in part at least, powered the dispersion of Europeans led to drastic changes of the political structures of the world and to extensive domination by the nation-states of Western Europe. Under these circumstances, races and cultures were fused and redefined and some of the seeds of present world problems were broadcast.

The most striking fact revealed by this exhibit is the phenomenal growth of population in the Americas. Although the population of Asia increased five times, it has remained about half the world total. Even though more than fifty million individuals left Europe during the eighteenth and nineteenth centuries, the population quadrupled between 1650 and 1950. Carr-Saunders shows that the immigrants to the Americas between 1846 and 1932 nearly equalled the number of individuals leaving Europe in that period.[23]

Estimates of World Population by Continents, 1650-1950

CONTINENT	1650	1750	1850	1950
EUROPE	100	140	266	395.4
NORTH AMERICA	1	1.3	26	216.3
CENTRAL AND SOUTH AMERICA	12	11.1	33	110.4
AFRICA	100	100	100	198
ASIA	250	406	671	1272
OCEANIA	2	2	2	12.9
TOTAL	465	660	1098	2207

Sources: A. M. Carr-Saunders, World Population, Oxford, The Clarendon Press, 1936, Figure 7, p. 30, for figures for 1650-1850; World Almanac and Book of Facts, p. 263, for figures for 1950. All populations stated in millions. Figures for Europe and Asia, 1950, exclude the Soviet Union, whose population in 1946 was reported as 193 millions.

FIGURE 10-9

It has been estimated that in the decade since World War II some 50 million individuals have migrated from one country to another.[24] About 20 million of these migrants are Europeans, and an equal number are Asians. Much of this recent movement of world population is connected with the recent war. Many individuals, however, continue to migrate from country to country for reasons not connected with the war.

World Urbanization ▶ Urbanization constitutes another important trend in the distribution of world population. For about a century large numbers of individuals have been involved in the movement to the city. Figure 10-10 shows the proportion of people in the world and in the various continents residing in large cities for selected dates between 1800 and 1950. It will be seen that in 1800 only a negligible proportion of world population was found in large cities, although by 1950 these individuals constituted almost one seventh of the total. The data also indicate that the rate of growth has accelerated during the last half century.

Urbanization of population began earlier and has proceeded further in Western Europe and North America than in Asia and Africa. Concentration of the population of Oceania in large cities is phenomenal, rising from none in 1850 to almost two fifths a century later. It seems likely that the cityward movement of world population will continue in the future, more slowly in Europe and America and more rapidly in Asia and Africa.

This exhibit also shows that in spite of their prestige and influence, large cities still contain only a minority of the world's people. There are only a few countries in Europe and America where the majority of the population can be classified as "urban." As will be shown below, the United States is one such country. Moreover, although some urban settlers are intercontinental and international migrants, most have remained within their native continent and country.

Like the explosive growth discussed above, urbanization appears to be one of the major trends of world population. As Kingsley Davis and Hilda H. Golden observe, "With the exception of Japan, the centers of urbanization today are the places where industrialization has gone hand in hand with the expansion of European civilization."[25] This trend will continue for a long time to produce some of the world's most difficult and dangerous social problems.

Distribution of the U.S. Population ▶ Attention may now be turned from the world population scene to a consideration of the American situtation. The United States was born and grew into mature nationhood as one phase of the growth of world population and the expansion of western Europe. The Bureau of the Census reports that between 1820 and 1963, 42,702,328 immigrants came to the United States from all countries.[26] Although most came from Europe, other millions came voluntarily or by force from Africa and Asia. Of this total, 80 per cent came from Europe, 14 per cent from American countries, and the remaining 6 per cent from Asia, Africa, and Oceania. The American Indian population was conquered, reduced in size, and herded into official reservations. A racially and culturally mixed population has occupied the territory that is the United States.

At this point we will direct our attention to the distribution and trends of redistribution of the present national population. Figure 10-11 shows the distribution of population within large regions of the United States. It is evident that the population is still concentrated in the eastern and northern part of the nation. The table also gives some indication of the rate and trend of redistribution. Between 1920 and 1960 all regions of the country except the West declined in percentage of total population, although the numbers continued to grow throughout the entire period. The most striking fact shown by the exhibit is the rapid growth of population in the states west of the Rocky Mountains. The proportion of population in this region almost doubled in the forty years covered.

The regions also differ as regards the composition of population. The Northeast and North Central regions contain higher proportions of urban residents than do the other regions. The South has the smallest percentage of foreign-born and the largest proportion of Negro population. It has already been noted that the South is the most fertile section of the nation and hence its population tends to be younger than that of other regions. Because of heavy in-migration,

Percent of Population in Cities of 100,000 and Over

CONTINENT	1800	1850	1900	1950
WORLD	1.7	2.3	5.5	13.1
ASIA	1.6	1.7	2.1	7.5
EUROPE*	2.9	4.9	11.9	19.9
AFRICA	0.3	0.2	1.1	5.2
AMERICA	0.4	3.0	12.8	22.6
OCEANIA	0.0	0.0	21.7	39.2

*Including USSR
Source: "The World's Great Cities," Population Bulletin 16, p. 119, adapted from Table 2 (September 1960).

FIGURE 10-10

Population of the United States by Region, 1920 and 1960

REGION	1920 NUMBER	1920 PER CENT	1960 NUMBER	1960 PER CENT
NORTHEAST	29,662,053	27.9	44,678,000	24.9
NORTH CENTRAL	34,019,792	32.3	51,610,000	28.6
SOUTH	33,125,803	31.4	54,963,000	30.6
WEST	8,902,972	8.5	28,053,000	15.9
TOTAL	105,710,620	100.0	179,323,000	100.0

Source: Statistical Abstract of the United States, 1962, adapted from Table 7, p. 10.

FIGURE 10-11

the Pacific Coast states—California, Oregon, and Washington— contain the largest relative proportion of young adults. Older persons, above 65, tend to be concentrated in New England and the Plains States. Orientals and Spanish-speaking persons remain largely concentrated in the West and Southwest. More detailed analysis will reveal other ways in which the populations of the four major regions differ.

The socioeconomic correlates of population distribution are of crucial importance in sociological analysis. For example, one variable factor in the traditional southern "race problem" is concentration of Negroes, although recent redistribution of the Negro population seems to be associated with intensification of the problem in the North and West. The various farm problems constitute decisive issues in the political and economic considerations of the agricultural South and Midwest. The low sex ratio in the urban and industrial Northeast has important consequences for marriage practices and family patterns. Traditionally, the Atlantic and Pacific Coast states have been more internationalistic in political and economic outlook than the states and regions lying in the interior of the nation. The dominance of urban population in the Northeast and North Central regions is related to the great economic and political influence of these regions. On the other hand, separation from the older centers of cultural activity in the East, rapid in-migration, and concentration of youthful population, combined with other factors, tend to foster unconventionality of behavior and outlook in the Pacific Coast States.

Internal Migration ❯ For many years the population of the United States has been redistributing itself. This internal movement has followed three main lines: east to west, rural to urban, and south to north. Beneath these broad patterns of migration may also be observed less consistent lines of population movement. As a consequence, the structures and functions of social life in the United States are being constantly modified.

The Frontier, as a historical symbol of the movement of population from east to west, disappeared statistically in the census of 1890 and politically by 1912, when the territories of Arizona and New Mexico were admitted to the Union. However, westward movement continues. In 1790, when the first census of population was taken, only the Indians inhabited that part of the continent west of the Mississippi River. By 1860 the Bureau of the Census listed a Western Region and reported that 13.4 per cent of the national population resided west of the Mississippi River. In 1960 over one third—34.2 per cent—of the national population lived west of the Mississippi.

It has been estimated that in 1930 some five million individuals born east of the Mississippi were living west of that river. This figure takes no account of those millions who, having migrated to the West, died prior to 1930. Nor does it portray the steadily moving wave of migration to the Pacific Coast and Mountain states. For example, between 1950 and 1960 the population of the Pacific Coast States increased by 40.2 per cent, while that of the Mountain States increased by 35.1 per cent.

The movement from country to city has been underway throughout the whole course of national history. As a consequence, the United States has become one of the modern urban societies. In 1960 nearly seven tenths, 69.9 per cent, of the total population was classified by the Census Bureau as urban according to the new definition. These figures contrast significantly with the 51.2 per cent urban in 1920, 15.3 in

1850, and about 5 per cent in 1790. Most of this astounding growth of urban population has come from migration.

The rural-urban migration is reflected in the increase in the number of cities of all sizes. For example, between 1930 and 1950 cities of 100,000 and over increased by 15 per cent (from 92 to 106), while those between 10,000 and 100,000 grew by 29 per cent (from 889 to 1115). However, in recent years—and particularly since World War II—urban growth has been concentrated in the suburbs.[27] Between 1950 and 1960 population growth in the "metropolitan areas" was altogether in the suburbs. The central cities in fifteen such areas lost population. Suburban growth resulted from migration from rural localities and especially from outward movement from the depopulating central cities, which alter even more phenomenally in population composition and density.

The movement from south to north has been associated with industrialization of the Northeast and North Central regions. A substantial part of this migration is composed of Negroes and is therefore related to other social and economic circumstances.

The Bureau of the Census has calculated the extent of south to north and north to south migration in the United States.[28] The north has shown a net gain of population each decade, and the rate of gain has tended to increase steadily. However, a small number of individuals have moved from north to south each enumeration period. Among other things, north to south migration is associated with continuing industrialization of the southern regions.

The redistribution of the Negro population constituted a significant thread in the south-to-north migration. In 1900 Negroes composed nearly one third of the total population of the South; but by 1960 this percentage had declined to about 20, or one fifth. During the same period the Negro proportion of the northern population had almost quadrupled, increasing from slightly over one per cent to more than five per cent of the total population.[29]

The full record of internal migration includes much movement aside from the three main streams described above. Some impression of the full scope of migration may be gained by considering the number of individuals who move from one state or county to another within a limited period of time. To be sure, some of these individuals migrate from east to west, from country to city, or from south to north and have been discussed in the foregoing paragraphs. Many others, however, are included in none of these major streams of migration.

The Bureau of the Census reports that between April 1954 and April 1955, 4,895,000 persons (3.1 per cent of the total population) migrated from one state to another. In the same period, 10,406,000 (6.6 per cent of the population) moved from one county to another. In 1960, 29,801,000 individuals were living abroad or in a county different from their residence in 1955.[30] These figures take no account of individuals who may have moved to a different state or county and returned within the enumeration period.

The consequences of internal migration for social life in the United States are numerous and far-reaching. Some aspects of these consequences that have been studied most extensively may be used as illustrations. First, the growth of cities is one obvious result of internal migration and population concentration. But perhaps even more significant is the fact that urbanism as a way of life has been formulated and diffused in large measure by mass internal migration.[31] In the wake of widespread population movement the social and psychological isolation that long characterized communal society has been destroyed. Subcultural differences have been lessened, and a national mass culture has emerged.

Many significant aspects of social organization have been modified by large-scale internal migration. The steady advance of industrialization in most regions of the country is functionally linked with these processes of population movement. The accessibility to raw materials and the character of markets have been altered by large-scale shifts of population. Furthermore, the organization of political power, the nature of religious structures, and the character of family organization—to mention some other aspects of social life—have all been measurably affected by mass internal migration.

At the same time, the very character of the various regions has been modified by heavy internal migration. The United States today is a significantly different society from that of a hundred years ago. The West is a reality, and the characteristics of New England or the "Solid South" are perceptibly different from what they were at the close of the Civil War.

FOOTNOTES

1. Logan Wilson and William L. Kolb, *Sociological Analysis* (New York: Harcourt Brace, 1949), p. 393.
2. Frederick Osborn, *This Crowded World*, Public Affairs Pamphlet, No. 306, 1960.
3. Thomas R. Malthus, *An Essay on Population* (New York: Dutton, 1914). First published in England in 1798.
4. Frank W. Notestein, "Population: The Long View," in Theodore W. Schultz, ed., *Food for the World* (Chicago: University of Chicago Press, 1945), pp. 36-57. See also "The Facts of Life" in Ruth Anshen, ed., *The Family: Its Function and Destiny* (New York: Harper, 1948), pp. 257-276.
5. *Statistical Abstract of the United States, 1964*, Table 117, p. 94.
6. See Robert A. Divine, *American Immigration Policy, 1924-1952* (New Haven: Yale University Press, 1957).
7. There is a voluminous literature on social problems which treats the role of population change. Also see Chapter 16 below.
8. The so-called "immigration problem" was once an important subject of sociological study. However, since the end of free immigration in 1924, this subject has declined in importance and interest.
9. See Robert K. Merton, *Social Theory and Social Structure* (Glencoe: Free Press, 1957), Chapter 4, "Social Structure and Anomie;" and William Foote Whyte, *Street Corner Society* (Chicago: University of Chicago Press, 1943).

10. See Robert H. Lowie, *An Introduction to Cultural Anthropology* (New York: Rinehart, 1955), Chapter 25.

11. Talcott Parsons, "Age and Sex in the Social Structure of the United States," in *American Sociological Review*, 7:604-616.

12. Leo W. Simmons, "Aging in Pre-Industrial Cultures," in Clark Tibbits and Wilma Donahue, eds., *Aging in the Modern World* (Ann Arbor: University of Michigan Press, 1955), p. 74.

13. See the *Statistical Abstract of the United States, 1964*, Table 290, p. 217.

14. Robert J. Havighurst, "Middle Age, The Prime of Life," in Tibbits and Donahue, *op. cit.*, pp. 36-38.

15. U.S. Department of Health, Education, and Welfare, Public Health Service, National Vital Statistics Division, *Natality, General Summary*, Vol. 1, 1960, Table 1-B, pp. 1-17.

16. Population figure is for the census enumeration date, April 1, 1960, instead of midyear. The difference in the computation is negligible.

17. See Warren S. Thompson and David T. Lewis, *Population Problems* (New York: McGraw-Hill, 1965), Chapters 9-11.

18. *Ibid.*, Figure 10-1, p. 276. The U.S. Public Health Service computes fertility as the rate representing the total number of live births per 1000 female population aged 15-44 years. "In 1961 this rate, computed on the basis of registered live births, was 117.3 compared with 118.0 for 1960. In 1950 the rate was 106.2 and during the 1930's it was as low as 75.8." See *Natality—General Summary*, Vital Statistics of the U.S., 1961, Vol. 1, Section 1, U.S. Public Health Service, pp. 1-7.

19. *Life Tables: Vital Statistics of the U.S.*, 1962, Vol. 2, Section 5, Public Health Service, National Vital Statistics Division, Table 5-4, pp. 5-10.

20. See *Abridged Life Tables: United States, 1957*, Vital Statistics, Vol. 50, No. 9, July 28, 1959.

21. Frank W. Notestein, "The Facts of Life," in Ruth Anshen, ed., *The Family: Its Function and Destiny* (New York: Harper, 1948), pp. 257-276.

22. Maurice Hindus, "The Family in Russia," in Anshen, *op. cit.*, pp. 111-124.

23. A. M. Carr-Saunders, *World Population* (Oxford: Clarendon Press, 1936), see Figure 9, p. 49 *et passim*.

24. Population Reference Bureau, *Population Bulletin*, "World Migration," 1946-1955, pp. 93 ff.

25. Kingsley Davis and Hilda H. Golden, "Urbanization and Development of Pre-Industrial Areas," in *Economic Development and Cultural Change*, Vol. 3, October 1954.

26. *Statistical Abstract of the United States, 1964*, Table 117, p. 94.

27. See, among other sources, Jean Gottman, *Megalopolis* (New York: Twentieth Century Fund, 1961), Chapter 4.

28. See U.S. Bureau of the Census, Sixteenth Census of the U.S., 1940, *Population, States of Birth of the Native Population*, PSR 11, Washington, D.C., 1944.

29. *Statistical Abstract of the United States, 1962*, Tables 6 and 24, pp. 10 and 30.

30. *Statistical Abstract of the United States, 1964*, Table 32, p. 33.

31. See Louis Wirth, "Urbanism as a Way of Life," in *American Journal of Sociology*, 44:1-18 (July 1938).

TODAY'S YOUTH: THE "NOW GENERATION"

*A SENSE OF IMMEDIACY pervades the lives of our nearly
100 million young people under 25. Living in the shadow
of the Bomb, they are no longer satisfied merely to prepare
for life; they attempt to compress a lifetime of experiences
into a day. Assertive, articulate, and independent, they
distrust what they consider adult deviousness. "Tell it like it
is" is a favorite slogan of the Now Generation.*

*Nearly 40 per cent of United States high school
graduates go on to higher education. Competition for good
grades, a choice college, and a good graduate school
is strong.*

◄ TRAVEL heightens the young person's awareness of the world and permits him to form new contacts, which in turn expand his awareness of differing goals and values. Physical mobility of the young has increased along with leisure time, economic means, and independence from parents.

IN DISCOTHEQUES all over the country members of the Now Generation dance to music written and performed by their contemporaries.

NATIONAL INCOME of teen-agers totals about $12 billion a year, giving them both considerable economic independence and influence on merchants and advertisers. Businessmen cater to teen-age fads and fashions and stress youth in their ads.

▲ *MOTORCYCLES represent independence to teen-age buyers.*

▲ *DISC JOCKEYS cater to teen music.*

▼ *CAR-STUFFING contest is sponsored by auto manufacturer to lure future patrons.*

▲ *CLOTHING in the latest style is main item of purchase by teen-agers.*

► *POLITICS is increasingly a matter of concern to youth today, but they are more inclined to support causes and issues than to follow ideologies and party lines.*

VOTE
SCOTT
ORR

▲ *THE BE-IN OR LOVE-IN is a happy, sometimes spontaneous gathering where flowers and dancing symbolize love rather than hate, peace rather than war. Buttons everywhere stating: "Don't trust anyone over 30" illustrate youth's reluctance to accept older generation's code.*

▼ *VOCIFEROUS SKEPTICS among the younger generation, in constructing their own moral codes, speak out for and experiment with formerly tabooed areas such as drugs and sex. This poster reads, "Mr. Public, don't delegate your morality."*

► *ALTRUISTIC CAUSES, represented by the Peace Corps and VISTA, attract students who feel a growing involvement with the world outside the campus. This youth postponed his studies to help with art restoration after the flood in Florence, Italy.*

▼ *IN VIETNAM men of the Now Generation have demonstrated their courage and patriotism. Though many question the conduct, rationale, and aims of the war in Vietnam, morale is high among fighting men. Many, in their off-duty hours, demonstrate a Peace Corps ardor in helping solve the problems of civilians.*

Chapter 11

SOCIAL STRATIFICATION

Social class is a familiar language symbol. It recognizes and refers to differences among people in power, prestige, and rewards resulting from variations of education, occupation, wealth and income, place of residence, dress, manners, and the like. Some people use the facts of social class differences—or social stratification—as the basis of invidious feelings and aggressive actions. For example, Karl Marx exploited such facts and feelings to rationalize the promise of a "classless" society to appeal to the poor and powerless of all lands. To the sociologist, however, the concept of social class provides simply another approach to the investigation of social organization.

In one way or another, class distinctions have been present in the organization of all known societies, ancient as well as modern, nonliterate as well as civilized. In the Roman Empire a vast gulf separated the patricians (aristocrats) from the plebs (commoners). The feudal system comprised a rigid and stable status structure with subdivisions of the aristocratic and serf categories. At the verge of the revolution of 1789, French society was divided into the *etats généraux*. In eighteenth-century England, just prior to the Industrial Revolution, clear lines of stratification separated nobility, gentry, and peasants. The present caste system of India, with its high and low hereditary social groupings, is well known.

The analysis of social stratification or class differentiation may be initiated by considering the two short illustrations below. Among the primitive Buin of Polynesia, in our first illustration, a class system developed after conquest of the aboriginal people by an alien group. Mutual rights and obligations were strongly influenced by an abnormal sex ratio among the conquering upper class. In Prairieton, U.S.A., the second case, the class structure issued from evaluation of such factors as ancestry, wealth, education, and occupation. This second account is particularly useful in illuminating how status distinctions develop within a changing community. The case is singular because it minimizes discussion of the middle class, which has come to play such a dominant role in American life.

Social Stratification Among the Buin. In the fertile, densely wooded district of Buin on Bougainville, one of the northwesternmost Solomon Islands, there live some 7,800 natives speaking a Papuan tongue. The occurrence of Papuan language here is remarkable because it is that of a subject population adopted by a conquering group. For the Buin of today are not a homogeneous people; only several centuries ago the indigenous population, short and broad-skulled, came to be periodically raided by the taller, long-headed island head-hunters, who enslaved the women and children and killed any men who offered resistance. Some of the pirates settled in Buin, rallied around them bands of the terrorized natives, and thus founded stratified societies with chiefs and bond-men.

In the course of time the sharpness of the cleavage was lessened. The conquerors had brought only a few women with them; hence their descendents were largely obliged to marry the daughters of the indigenous population. Because women of the higher class were so rare, endogamy could be enforced only for the successor to the chieftaincy, and broke down as a hard and fast principle. It continued to be applied to the first-born daughter but not necessarily to other aristocrats; a chief's widow might espouse a commoner, her second daughter a half-caste, and so forth. Naturally, the sons of such mixed marriages were favored above the common herd. Closely related to the chiefs, they were called their "pillars" and came to constitute an intermediate class of freemen, whose life and property were respected by the overlords. The contrast of ruling and subject class was thus materially lessened, so that we find no parallel here to the extravagant caste spirit of Polynesia.[1]

Social Stratification in Prairieton. The following case challenges the cherished myth that small towns and rural areas of the United States have no social classes. A South Dakota town, Prairieton, was selected for study. This is not a typical town in the sense of an average community, but it is typological because the nascent forms of social stratification are found in sharper focus. Prairieton today is primarily a farm trade center with a population of 3,500, largely of second-generation Scandinavian immigrants and families from Wisconsin, Minnesota, and Iowa. It is located in the heart of small grain agriculture, there are no industries in the immediate locality, and the nearest city is fifty miles away.

Prairieton contains three major strata: a low-status group consisting largely of ex-farmers, former farm hands, and unskilled laborers; a middle class made up of small shop-keepers, craftsmen, retired farmers, and professional people; and an elite composed of the locally successful entrepreneurs and large land holders. The elite, locally referred to as "the Tops," live on top of a bluff on the east side of town; the low-status group, called by Prairietoners "the Bottoms," are concentrated on the flats below the western portion of town.

The elite comprise a stable and integrated class with rigid criteria of membership. One important qualification for inclusion is coming from a family that has had high status in the community for a number of years. Newcomers with "good family background," or reputation of high status in another community, may be warmly welcomed but are rarely accepted immediately as functioning members of the class. Permanency of occupation is another requisite; persons who frequently shift their field of enterprise are regarded as on the fringe. To be seen with the "right" people and to engage in acceptable activities are important. Violation of expected roles subjects individuals to considerable comment until a redefinition is worked out. Deviant personalities, however, are not rejected, e.g., an eccentric old maid and a doddering man are highly respected members because of their family backgrounds.

Duration of residence, occupational history, and family background are not regarded by the Bottoms class as significant criteria for membership. Far more important to them are such traits as being neighborly and using simple, direct speech forms. Persons are excluded whose behavior is similar to that of the outgroup or who too often associate with them.

The development of classes is a comparatively recent phenomenon since both upper and lower classes stem from pioneer farm people not more than two generations ago. Younger members of the two classes, however, are children of parents with similar social positions in the community and there is no instance in the last generation of a person born in a Bottoms family becoming a member of the elite class, or the reverse. This low vertical mobility means that there is very little marked rearrangement of positions. Death and migration upon retirement are the principle unsettling factors among the upper stratum. Lower-class workers never voluntarily retire. They eventually become unemployable and continue to live at home with the help of grown children and public assistance.[2]

In modern large-scale societies, in contrast to primitive groups or small rural communities, the bureaucratic institutional structure is the principal agent of social stratification. Categories of roles, precisely defined and adjusted to expected individual competencies, are fixed at similar positions in associational hierarchies. That is, role categories that resemble each other tend to have roughly equal status and prestige. For example, mining engineers, civil engineers, and electrical engineers enjoy similar social positions and respect. Likewise, engineers, applied scientists, and middle-range industrial managers tend to share equivalent status and prestige. The resultant large role-status systems constitute social strata or levels in the stratification system.

NATURE OF SOCIAL STRATIFICATION

These preliminary remarks suggest some generalizations regarding the nature of social stratification. Melvin M. Tumin writes: "In the social sciences . . . the term has come to mean . . . the process by which or the resulting structure in which families become differentiated from one another and arranged in graded strata with varying degrees of prestige, and/or property, and/or power."[3] It has been said that age and sex differences are bases of social differences. So also are color, height, intelligence, special capacities, and certain other physical characteristics. Acquired characteristics like knowledge, social and mechanical skills and customs, and material possessions like property and weapons constitute still other bases of social differentiation.[4]

A stratification system facilitates allocation of the members of a society to the various social roles with some regard for role demands and individual capabilities and with reference to basic societal tasks. Kingsley Davis and Wilbert E. Moore observe that the stratification system must also "concern itself with motivation at two different levels: to instill in the proper individuals the desire to fill certain positions, and once in these positions, the desire to perform the duties attached to them."[5] The scarce values of the society—power, prestige, property, respect, etc.—function as both inducements for filling the positions and rewards for performing the associated duties.

Empirical research on social stratification, especially in the United States, indicates that individuals are differentiated in rank and tend to strive in terms of a series of variables.[6] Milton M. Gordon, after reviewing the scientific studies of social stratification in American sociology, wrote: "We have . . . outlined the nature of . . . three basic stratification variables—economic power, political power and social status. . . ."[7] It is now also recognized that status differentiations along these and other dimensions are not necessarily identical nor transferable.[8] For example, individuals or categories of individuals with political power do not for that reason also possess great wealth or enjoy high social prestige.

It is now possible to make some limited generalizations about social stratification. The population of every society tends to be differentiated into ranked categories. However, the names, number, characteristics, and social functions of such ranked categories vary significantly from one society to another. This variation is indicated by terms like social class, caste, and estate, which designate general types of stratification systems.

Whatever the method or variables used, the American population is shown to be stratified. Although the number of strata revealed tends to vary from study to study and from locality to locality, three is the number most often reported. The studies indicate two manifestations of stratification in the United States. One is found in a particular group, institution, association, community, or other limited social unit. The other is society-wide. Although the two types of stratification systems are interdependent, they are not identical and cannot be equated.

An example is in order. A man who works on the production line in a large factory, lives in a modest home in a working-class neighborhood, and has, say, a tenth-grade education, acquires only a modest amount of power in politics, prestige, and economic reward when compared to other people on a society-wide basis. He is located in a stratum below the one which includes professionals, managers, and some government officials, and perhaps below a stratum which includes foremen, skilled workers, lower white-collar workers, etc. But at the same time, he may be president of his lodge or local union, or an elder in his church, and within *those particular* institutions he is located in the very highest stratum.

Finally, status strata are more than mere statistical or logical abstractions. They reflect socially significant structures of the thought and actions of people. Joseph H. Kahl remarks: "A study of a particular American community, or even American society as a whole, that uses stratification as its focus provides an integrated and comprehensive view of social life."[9]

HAIR ARRANGEMENT and decoration, as well as dress, indicate social, sexual, and age status in many cultures. Warriors of the Masai tribe in Kenya and Tanzania proudly display their status by braiding their hair after smearing it with fat, red ochre, and mud. Masai women shave their heads.

Ascribed and Achieved Status ♦ During his lifetime each individual occupies many different statuses. One is his general position in the society-wide stratification system. His other statuses are his positions in the limited social units in which he is a participant. For example, in Prairieton, referred to above, one's community status was reflected by membership in the "Tops" or the "Bottoms." These terms suggest the groups that individuals belong to and the character of their activities, attitudes, and social experiences. Members of the "Tops" and "Bottoms" could be placed in the general American class system, although perhaps not at positions equivalent to those occupied in Prairieton.

An individual's statuses are gained in two different ways: they may be thrust upon him or bequeathed to him; or they may be sought and earned by him, either alone or by collective effort. Statuses that come to the individual through no effort on his part are called *ascribed*. These are his original positions in the society; they are determined by the physiological characteristics, social connections, and memberships for which he is not responsible and over which he had no control.

Family is the principal source of ascribed status. The class standing of a family, conditioned mainly by the father's occupation, is bequeathed to children at birth. Sex, race, and other physiological characteristics, insofar as they are evaluated, also function as sources of ascribed status. For example, in every society girls, and in the United States Negroes, are assigned a social rank on the basis of these physical characteristics.

Every individual is likely to occupy many statuses other than those that are ascribed. The stratification system may change, thus modifying any given individual's original statuses. As is more common, however, the individuals and groups may bring about changes of their ascribed statuses. Social positions that are acquired in this manner are called *achieved*. By definition they are different from ascribed statuses, since they result from conditions over which the individual has exerted some control. For instance, in college students and faculty earn promotions from one level to another. But in Prairieton it was noted that no member of the "Tops" had risen from the "Bottoms."

Many—though not all—stratification systems include both the possibility and the means for changing social status. Both individuals and groups may achieve modifications of social standing. In the college, for example, the faculty members may expect to gain promotions by evidence of successful teaching, advanced study, research, publications, community services, and the like. Some systems also provide regular procedures for demotion, or the loss of status. In the Army, for example, officers may be "busted" by procedure and with reason.

Individuals may achieve status as a consequence of group effort. Sometimes collective effort results in modification of the entire stratification system. More often, however, it eventuates in up-grading or down-grading of entire status groups. This fact is illustrated in some recent achievements of organized labor, farm groups, and Negroes in the United States. In the totalitarian countries, like Nazi Germany and Fascist Italy, the working classes were significantly degraded in status by suppression, dissolution, or control of the labor unions.

Ascription and achievement are integral dynamic aspects of stratification systems. First, the number, characteristics, range, and arrangement of strata in any system at any given time are consequences of prior processes of ascription and achievement. Each stratum is formed of the individuals whose positions have been ascribed or achieved. In

Prairieton and Buin, for example, the stratification systems ascribed positions to most individuals. In the college, on the other hand, most of the positions are filled by achievement. Both processes function to distribute and redistribute the available population.

Second, ascription and achievement constitute polar concepts of the dynamic character of stratification systems. When all or almost all the positions are assigned by ascription, the system tends to be relatively rigid. If, however, many social positions may be achieved by individual or group effort, the system is flexible, dynamic, and changing. As a matter of fact, every stratification system exhibits some combination of these rigid and dynamic characteristics.

Class and Caste ▶ Social class and caste are the two main contemporary types of stratification systems. They are differentiated principally by different degrees of structural rigidity. *Social class* refers to a flexible hierarchical system, composed of social categories of individuals (and groups) of both sexes, all ages, and various characteristics, who share similar socioeconomic circumstances and ranks, in which most statuses are *achieved*. On the other hand, *caste* refers to a rigid hierarchical system, composed of mutually exclusive categories of individuals and groups sharing many similar social, economic, and status characteristics, in which social ranks are *ascribed*.[10]

A social class is less organized and cohesive than a group, but more functionally significant than a mere aggregate. It constitutes a point of reference in social action and the basis of mutual orientation in thought and feeling. In limited measure, a social class is capable of concerted social action. The boundaries between social classes exist in the behavior and thoughts of people and may be revealed by objective criteria, social reputation, or self-identification, or by some combination of these variables.[11]

Most crucially, social classes are loosely structured and open-ended categories. Individual positions are neither rigidly nor precisely fixed. Membership is not lifelong and irrevocable. Movement within class boundaries is unrestricted and often encouraged. Movement from one class to another is normally permitted and sometimes facilitated. Marriage outside class boundaries, either up or down, is also normally permitted, though variously evaluated.

Avoidance of interstratum contacts and movement is the decisive characteristic of caste as a type of stratification. Status within the system is both ascribed and lifelong. Exogamy is severely prohibited, and rituals prescribe avoidance of contacts and relations between members of different castes. The system provides limited possibilities and means of achieving status within each caste.

Caste systems have existed or still exist in many parts of the world. In the excerpt on social stratification in Buin quoted above, Lowie alluded to the extravagant caste system that had developed in other parts of Bougainville. Racial stratification in South Africa is a striking contemporary instance of a caste system. Perhaps the best known caste system is the one that has existed in India for some 2000 years. Now legally abolished, vestiges of it continue to influence behavior, such as the choice of marriage partners.

MODELS OF STRATIFICATION SYSTEMS

Of the great variety of stratification systems to be found in human society, brief descriptions of four are presented here. These cases illustrate the various ways a population can be differentiated and ranked. They draw attention to the variety of factors that are utilized to differentiate and stratify the members of a population. The models described here also reveal variability in the rigidity of stratification systems. In the case of the Indian caste system particularly, some allusion is made to the social functions of stratification.

Social Class in American Society ▶ There have been many empirical studies of social stratification in the United States.[12] Such investigations have employed three major approaches and a large number of variables. Some studies have been limited to specific localities, while others apply to the entire society. The investigations have identified differing numbers of strata to which a variety of names have been assigned. However, all the studies tend to confirm certain basic findings about American society. The society is stratified and in spite of a good deal of variation seems to be divided into three major classes.

Figure 11-1 presents two models of the American class system as revealed in empirical research. By using the class titles and population percentages from the two studies, it was possible to construct diagrams that show sizes of the social classes and some relationships among them. What is striking about this figure is the fact that in spite of the apparent dissimilarity of the two diagrams, they actually reveal the same basic model of the American class system.

Richard Centers asked a national sample of some 1100 white men to locate themselves in one of the four classes shown in the upper diagram. By using the term "working class" he permitted the subjects to escape locating themselves at the lower end of the status system. One apparent result of this operation was near elimination of the lower class as a population category. At the other extreme, only three per cent of the subjects assigned themselves to the upper class.

If the bottom two categories are combined, then it is seen that 52 per cent of the subjects are lower class. Forty-three per cent of the sample reported themselves as middle class. These percentages reflect the traditional model of the American class structure, i.e., a tiny upper class and a significantly larger middle class, both resting upon the base of a large lower class.

W. Lloyd Warner and his associates studied the total population of some 17,000 inhabitants of a New England city. They secured data on a series of variables including education, occupation, income, wealth, and place of residence. They also secured from panels of judges evaluations of the subjects' reputations in terms of their social participation in the community. Although the Warner team used the traditional class titles, they were able to subdivide each stratum into an upper and lower level.

An inspection of the lower diagram in the exhibit shows that 3 per cent of the subjects fell into the upper classes. Over 57 per cent of the population was designated as lower class. The middle classes included just over 38 per cent of the total. Again we have a representation of the traditional three-tier model of the American class system. Although Centers and Warner distribute the population in the middle and lower classes somewhat differently, both show a tiny upper class of about the same size. Warner's distinction between upper-lower and lower-lower shows that there are relatively fewer persons at the very bottom of the structure than are to be found a little higher up.

Two Models of the American Class System

CENTERS[1]		WARNER[2]	
CLASSES	PER CENT	CLASSES	PER CENT
UPPER	3.0	UPPER-UPPER	1.44
		LOWER-UPPER	1.56
MIDDLE	43.0	UPPER-MIDDLE	10.22
		LOWER-MIDDLE	28.12
WORKING	51.0		
		UPPER-LOWER	32.60
LOWER	1.0	LOWER-LOWER	25.22

Sources: (1) Richard Centers, The Psychology of Social Classes, p. 77, 2.0% unclassified; (2) W. Lloyd Warner et al., The Social Life of a Modern Community, adapted from Table 2, p. 302, 0.84 per cent unclassified.

FIGURE 11-1

These diagrams cannot illustrate flexibility in the class system and mobility from one level to another. Mobility is, however, a characteristic feature of the American class system and is examined in a later section of this chapter. It is enough to mention here that movement is most pronounced in the upward direction and from the upper level of the lower classes into the middle classes.

Racial Stratification in the U.S. ▶ Sociologists are not agreed on whether to regard American Negroes as a social class or caste. For example, in recent studies of minority relations, Charles F. Marden and Gladys Meyer find that the concept of caste fits the situation of American Negroes, but George Simpson and J. Milton Yinger believe that the concept is inapplicable.[13] The research reveals that, whether called class or caste, the Negro population is excluded from the society-wide stratification system, relegated collectively to inferior status and internally stratified into two or more class levels.[14] Within the context of the American stratification system, and with reference to the Negro category, (1) membership is lifelong, (2) marriage is endogamous, (3) avoidance is ritualistic, (4) occupations are restricted, and (5) all of these are strictly enforced.

With only a few exceptions, the Negro individual enters the group at birth and leaves by death. Legally, in several jurisdictions "one drop" of Negro blood makes an individual a Negro. Children of mixed marriages are generally relegated to the Negro category. Although isolated individuals may escape, the group as a whole cannot. Group-wide inferiority is therefore altered only when and as the general stratification system is modified.

A few individuals escape lifelong membership in the Negro stratum by "passing." Estimates indicate that at almost any time some 110,000 individuals (about .5 per cent of the total) have entered the white population from the Negro category in this way. George E. Simpson and J. Milton Yinger assert: "Estimates of the extent of Negro 'passings,' which of necessity are very rough, range from a few thousands to tens of thousands per year in the United States."[15] Many other individuals pass segmentally, functioning as whites in certain realms and activities but retaining basic membership in the Negro category. For the vast bulk of Negroes, however, membership in the ethnic category is total and lifelong.

Ritual avoidance by segregation is the rule to which the exceptions are now increasing significantly. In many states, particularly the seventeen southern states, racial segregation in some institutions and spheres of life is required by law. In others ritual avoidance is a matter of custom. Although the legal support of racial segregation is weakening, it is still institutionalized to varying degrees in schools, churches, recreation, motion pictures, restaurants, hotels, hospitals, public conveyances, public washrooms, toilets and water fountains, waiting rooms, and residential areas.[16] In addition, etiquette of ritual avoidance and racial inferiority still governs Negro-white relations in many spheres of American life.[17]

The ethnic stratification structure implements occupational discrimination and inferiority for Negroes.[18] Job restrictions are accompanied by differentials in income, wealth, housing, food and clothing, luxuries, and leisure time. Some occupations have come to be widely regarded as "Negro jobs"; these include menial, low-skilled, low-paid, dangerous, and marginal jobs in industry, agriculture, and the service areas. These occupations lack or limit normal opportunities for promotion, training, up-grading, or transfers. They rank low in the prestige-authority hierarchy in industry, business, government, and the like.

Recent changes in educational policies, governmental programs, and practices of business and industry groups have expanded job opportunities for Negro workers. However, despite these changes, some occupations are, so to speak, still "off limits" for American Negroes. Job and wage discriminations persist, and unemployment remains disproportionately high.

Finally, the ethnic stratification structure is generally enforced. Some elements of the structure are still sanctioned by law or at least by the absence of appropriate laws and definitive public policy. Enforcement is achieved in part by custom and by the race relations etiquette which has made a deep imprint upon both white and Negro personalities. Violence and the threat of violence—though both are declining—remain as the extreme sanction. Change has been most extensive and significant in removal or weakening of both the legal and extra-legal sanctions of the stratification structure.

Social Stratification in the Soviet Union ♦ Russian society has been stratified for a long time.[19] Before the revolution of 1917 the hereditary aristocracy and peasants were the major classes. The revolution eliminated the aristocratic upper class and replaced it by a new ruling elite, derived in part from peasants. Moreover, the political ideology of the new ruling elite committed them to the doctrine of a "classless society."

In the fifty years since the Bolshevik Revolution, a new and relatively rigid stratification system has evolved and stabilized.[20] Figure 11-2 indicates the categories of the system and shows how they are ranked. The system developed through the concentration of political power, the closing of educational opportunities to certain categories of workers, the elaboration of an occupational prestige hierarchy, and the granting of special economic advantages to the prestige and power elites.

At the base of the structure are the forced laborers who, in addition to being denied any opportunity of upward mobility, are in fact not really members of the society. Just above these are the most disadvantaged rural and urban workers. These workers have few chances to escape by upward mobility to higher positions in the social order. Together these three categories may be regarded as the lower classes of Soviet society.

The middle range of status includes a broad spectrum of occupations and categories. In rural localities there are the well-to-do peas-

UPPER CLASS	*Ruling Elite:* Highest government, party, economic, and military officials, all educated Party members
MIDDLE CLASS	*Top Intelligentsia:* Politicians, engineers, managers, top military, upper bureaucracy *Ordinary Intelligentsia:* Doctors, lawyers, other professional, technicians, middle-range military and bureaucracy *Popular Heroes:* Writers, scientists, astronauts *Urban Workers:* Skilled workers, rank and file of industrial workers *Urban White-Collar:* Clerks, accountants, lower bureaucracy *Well-To-Do Peasants:* High producers, on best collective farms
LOWER CLASS	*Disadvantaged Urban Workers:* Low skill, minimum pay *Ordinary Peasants:* On ordinary or poor collective farms *Forced Labor:* Inmates of camps (outside of society)

FIGURE 11-2

ants on large, well-run collectives. In the cities are the rank and file industrial workers, skilled workers, and lower white-collar persons—the rank and file of the modern bureaucratic structure. Above these categories, forming a kind of upper-middle class, are the popular heroes, the ordinary intelligentsia, and the top intelligentsia. Members of this class have access to education and the other mechanisms of mobility. There is consequently some movement from one category to another of this middle class, and some members of the top intelligentsia move into the ruling elite.

The Soviet upper class is composed of the power elite. All are by ideological necessity members of the Party. The economic advantage of this upper class, as well as of the upper-middle class, is insured by the absence of inheritance taxes and an income tax system that levels off at about $6,000.

The Indian Caste System ◗ For many years the Hindu population of India was divided into several thousand mutually exclusive, non-overlapping, permanent social units known as castes and tribes.[21] Every individual was a member of the society in terms of membership in one of these castes. All the castes were integrated into the social structure and ranked in a rigid stratification system.

One major source of caste separation and cohesion was similarity of occupation. For example, there were castes of priests, merchants, money lenders, farmers, and many other occupations. Separation and cohesion were supported by powerful taboos against marrying, eating with, or associating with members of other castes. In addition, members of each caste tended to reside together in a separate section of the community.

Every individual's (except the Untouchables') status and role as a member of the society was determined by his caste. He was born into a caste, lived in it, and died in it. His world was his caste. In a sense, he was not an individual but only a caste member. As Professor S. Krishnaswamy observed: "If his caste fell on evil days he would fall with it, and so his caste *Dharma* was always to prevent it from falling, even if it meant fighting other castes violently.[22]

Caste membership, and consequently the individual's place in society, was revealed in many traditional ways. The leading caste indicators were occupation, place of residence, marriage partner, and social associates. Everyone performed the rituals of social action or avoidance associated with his caste. In addition, many people wore traditional caste costumes and insignia.

There were four hierarchically ranked orders of castes: Brahmin, traditional priests and scholars; Kshatriya, traditional warriors; Vaisya, traditional traders, businessmen, and money lenders; and Sudra, peasant farmers. Within these inclusive orders there were subcastes, or loose consolidations of specific castes, such as the Bania subdivision of the Vaisyas or the South India Nair subdivision of the Sudras. Since movement from one caste or inclusive caste unit to another was prohibited, the result was a rigid stratification system that revealed the meaningful distinctions of power, prestige, and privilege in the society.

Thousands of individuals lived outside the caste system as Untouchables or out-castes. Powerful taboos prohibited the Untouchables from having any contacts with members of the several castes. Moreover, they lived outside the community in classic Indian rural slums. As a consequence, although the Untouchables lived in the society and had important functions, they were really not members of the society, since they belonged to no legitimate castes. And yet, untouchability was itself a world of caste. Occupational groups of Untouchables, e.g., scavengers, cobblers, sweepers, or washermen, formed cohesive social units and practiced the traditional out-group taboos against other groups of Untouchables.

Interdependence and powerful ritual tended to bind the castes together and integrate them within the social system. Thus farmers needed merchants, cobblers and washermen depended on both, and all needed priests and scholars. The rituals of the system (and virtually every social act was specified in a ritual, whether of cooperation or avoidance) bound the castes together in a network of regular communication and understanding. One could not perform his role or live his ordinary way of life without depending upon the other castes. In time the whole system tended to become stable and harmonized and appeared to be a part of the natural order of the universe.

Moreover, the system was buttressed and sanctioned by Hindu doctrine. Caste was considered sacred and each individual was under religious injunction to support the practice and fulfill his obligations. Although the lower castes may at times have felt restive under the burden of their limitations, the Brahmins, with the support of religious injunctions and the power of their high position, defended the system.

Inevitably, though, with the passage of time and the impact of historic circumstance, the system tended to evolve and change. Each military invasion and cultural contact left its mark. Some individuals objected to the inequities of the system and urged modifications. With the change of geographic and economic conditions, elements of the system tended to become inefficient or dysfunctional.

After the establishment of British rule, change became more rapid and extensive. The British ignored the principle of caste inequality and declared all Indians to be equal before the law. At the same time they violated the tradition of occupational specialization in order to recruit Indian workers for lower echelon civil service positions. National independence brought the abolition of untouchability and improvements in the conditions of the "scheduled" or "depressed" castes. The steady march of industrialization, urbanization, technology, and secular rationality erodes traditional caste bonds and releases individuals for action and organization within associational forms. Yet, in the relatively isolated rural villages where 75 per cent of the Indian population lives, caste is still a fundamental force of social organization.

FUNCTIONS OF STRATIFICATION SYSTEMS

Stratification systems are utilitarian as well as universal. While some of their consequences are system-maintaining, others appear to be dysfunctional in character. Three general functions will be examined briefly: (1) contributions to social integration and structure, (2) regulation of individual and group participation, and (3) certain dysfunctional conditions, activities, and relationships.

Contributions to Integration and Structure ▶ The material on the Indian caste system illustrates the integrative function of a stratification system. It was pointed out that initially each individual is a member of a caste unit. All the caste units are fixed in the stratification system at a more or less definite position. Functional interdependence and inclusive rituals lace the castes together into a harmonious ongoing social system.

The stratification system also functions to harmonize and coordinate other social units within the general structure. For example, in the Soviet Union such organizations as youth clubs, trade unions, professional associations, and recreational clubs are integrated into the general social structure through the stratification system. Under the stratification umbrella these and other social units are fitted together and enabled to function with some measure of efficiency and harmony.

At the same time, the stratification system functions to influence the structure of various social units. For example, the members of each social class or status category tend to form organizations for leisure-time and recreational activities. The nature of such voluntary organizations, however, will vary from one class to another. Middle-class boys may form athletic teams at recreation centers or country clubs, while lower-class boys may congregate in unsupervised street gangs. Middle-class parents tend to join many voluntary leisure-time organizations, while their lower-class counterparts may not belong to any specialized leisure-time or recreational groups.

Studies of the American family reveal the influence of social stratification on social structure. Ruth Shonle Cavan has summarized much of this material in terms of family organization at various class levels. In the following short excerpts, organization in the upper-upper-class families is contrasted with that found among families of the lower classes. This material also serves to illustrate how these two family systems are differentially integrated into the general American social structure.

> *Upper-Upper-Class Family.* The family typically regards itself as a stage in the development of a historical family. It venerates the past generations whose accomplishments laid the foundation of present status. European ancestry of worth is respected, but real pride is felt for ancestors who establish themselves in America through individual energy and ability. Their early descendants consolidated the position and passed on to their children an impregnable prestige supported by adequate stable income based on inherited wealth.
>
> Since in a given community all upper-upper-class families tend to have established themselves at approximately the same period, they represent

the same ethnic stock and cultural traditions. Family income must be adequate to maintain the standards of the class, based primarily on inherited rather than newly acquired or currently earned wealth, and derived from certain sources in order to bring prestige. Since class prestige rests in part on the length of time the family has held a position of leadership and in part on inherited wealth, residential stability is common.

The great family consists of small nuclear units closely inter-connected by blood, marriage, history, and present ownership of property. It includes uncles, aunts, and cousins of various degrees of closeness. The tendency of members of the class to marry within the class, even within the great family—as cousins with cousins—has created a complicated system of relationships, so that it often may be truthfully said that the entire upper-upper class in a given community constitutes a kinship group. One is a member of the kinship family first, of the small family unit second. Organization tends to stress kinship rather than marriage ties, with headship resting in the oldest person or in a group of collateral elders. Since women frequently survive their husbands, the head of the extended family may be a woman. The small units tend to be patrilineal and male-centered. In general, marriages occur at a later age than in the other social classes. For several reasons, children are not only few in number but few in proportion to older people.[23]

Lower-Class Family. These families tend to abide by the common mores and meet such general expectations as family self support (except perhaps in times of great crisis), legal monogamous marriage, conformity to law, and participation in community institutions such as school and church. They have a very brief history. For most, the finite beginning is immigration of ancestors from Europe, often within the memory of a living member. Dispersion of members as they migrate from job to job breaks ties among related nuclear units. Correspondence is irregular, visits infrequent, and family records virtually nonexistent. For a minority at the bottom of the status scale, however, continuity exists in an almost unbroken experience of immobile dependence on public and private charities.

The family unit consists typically of husband, wife, and unmarried adult and minor children. Since the death rate among males is extremely high, the stable and continuing family unit tends to be mother and minor children. Ties with grandparents and collaterals are weak, although in crisis (particularly economic) such ties may strengthen, one branch giving sanctuary to a stranded one. Families in this class are culturally and ethnically variegated, including unsuccessful units with a long American background, newly arrived immigrants, remnants of early ethnic stocks who failed to adjust culturally, and economically and culturally deprived urban migrants—southern Negroes and "poor whites" from the Appalachian hills. Families with similar cultural and ethnic backgrounds tend to cluster together in distinct communities.

Income is derived principally from wages earned through semiskilled, unskilled, and seasonal labor. When savings are possible, they may go into the purchase of a home, although often they are swept away by emergencies. Regular or intermittent work of all employable members, children included, is common and believed to be normal and necessary. The most disadvantaged minority are supported by public and private assistance. These families exhibit slight residential stability, due largely to economic conditions.

Marriage, especially for girls, occurs at a very early age. Children come early, are numerous, and are accepted with little planning or preparation. As they grow up, they enter the life of the community with little parental supervision or restraint.

The father is head of such families, which are more patriarchal than families in the other classes. Nevertheless, it is the mother who rears the children and it is with her that the children remain if the family disintegrates. Husband and wife have a life of their own, centering largely about sex, and are relatively detached from and indifferent to the children who are clearly subordinated. Spousal roles are specifically defined and relatively dissociated. The frequency of homes broken by death, separation, and divorce reflects the instability of lower-class family organization. Frequent unemployment, illness, delinquency, occasional alcoholism, and aggressiveness toward neighbors and relatives along with the rapid arrival of children produce many crises for such families. Crises tend to be prolonged, sometimes chronic, and often seriously damage family organization. They frequently lead to contacts with welfare agencies.[24]

Regulation of Participation ▶ Stratification systems tend to regulate the approach of individuals and groups to participation in the total life of the society. Whatever an individual's position, high or low, some aspects of the whole spectrum of experience are inaccessible. For example, the upper-upper-class individual may have no chance to know about life in the city slum and the Untouchable can hardly be familiar with the intimacies of the Brahmin way of life.

What is more important, though, is the fact that in all stratification systems low-status individuals tend to be more or less excluded from the highly valued experiences. Thus the disadvantaged Russian peasant has little access to educational opportunities, and poor American Negroes cannot live in a suburb, attend the Metropolitan Opera, or vacation on the Riviera. Genevieve Knupfer observes: "The underprivileged person . . . has seen less, read less, heard about less, has in his whole environment experienced fewer changes than the socially privileged, and he simply knows of fewer possibilities."[25]

On the other hand, individuals who occupy high positions in the stratification system have access to these and the other highly valued social experiences. As a consequence, they have had a wider range of experience than low-status individuals and reveal this fact in differences of mode and pattern of social participation.

Differentials of social class rank in the United States have been significantly correlated with three categories of participation differentials: life chances and privileges, behavior, and attitudes. The reader is cautioned to remember that statements of correlation are not proof of causation; that two phenomena are significantly correlated does not prove that one causes the other. What is demonstrated in these data is the fact that variations of social class rank are regularly and significantly linked with differentials of social participation. It is possible and necessary to cite findings from only a few of the more than two dozen empirical studies that demonstrate the effect of social status on social participation. Albert J. Mayer and Philip Hauser reported that life expectation at birth was 59 years for lower-class individuals, while for upper-class persons it was 68.[26] According to Elmo Roper, 21 per cent of factory workers' children, 45 per cent of white-collar workers' children, and 73 per cent of professional and executive workers' children are applicants for admission to colleges.[27] Robert E. Clark's investigations indicated that rates of hospital admission for psychosis were significantly higher than average among the lower classes and significantly lower than average among the upper classes.[28] After an analysis of political attitudes, Arthur Kornhauser found that lower status individuals tend to favor Social Security measures, labor unions, and government regulation of business; high-status individuals tend to disapprove strong labor unions and an active government role in economic affairs.[29]

Joseph A. Kahl reported social class differentials in close friendships. He found that 30 per cent of unskilled workers had no close friends. For skilled small-business and white-collar workers the percentage was 13, and for professionals, top business, and government officials it was 10.[30] Genevieve Knupfer discovered that among the lower strata 35 per cent did not read magazines and 92 per cent read less than one book per month; among the higher strata the corresponding percentages were 7 and 59 respectively.[31] Eleanor E. Macoby and Patricia K. Gibbs investigated class differentials of child-rearing practices.[32] They found lower-class parents were more severe, used more physical punishment, and were less demonstrative with children, while middle-class families exhibited more permissiveness and warmth, made use of praise and reasoning, and allowed aggression of children toward parents.

Such variable life experiences, behavioral tendencies, and overt action patterns tend to become organized and stabilized into characteristic social class roles or styles of life.[33] The style of life is the ideal-typical social configuration that distinguishes more or less accurately the members of the various social classes. In ordinary social intercourse it specifies initial definitions of situations and indicates appropriate modes of social action. The readily accessible clues to the style of life include such items as type of clothing, personal grooming, mode of speech, manners and morals, content of conversation, work and leisure schedules, regular associates, and social utensils such as type of automobile, golf clubs, lunch box, or brief case. The style of life is less readily revealed by habitual modes of thinking, feeling, and believing.

The style of life as the ideal-typical social class role constitutes a basic model for socialization of children.[34] The child finds parents, siblings, relatives, neighbors, and other regular and familiar associates behaving in conformity with the class style. The models of the other social classes are less accessible to him and are supported by less immediate and powerful sanctions. He grows naturally into acting, thinking, feeling, and believing in conformity with the model presented by members and representatives of his own social class.

Part of the meaning of openness in open-class systems is the fact that life style models of the higher classes are to some degree, at least, accessible to members of the lower-status categories. Socialization occurs under conditions of effective cultural pluralism. The stratification system contains both the motivation and the means of social mobility. This situation is related to certain dysfunctional conditions.

Some Dysfunctions ▶ Four common dysfunctional effects of stratification systems can be examined briefly. First, status and role differentiations sometimes fail to match prescribed rights and duties with the demonstrated capabilities of the individuals who are assigned to the roles. This occurs particularly in rigid systems where all or almost all statuses are ascribed. Individuals inherit positions, responsibilities, and privileges for which they lack the requisite competence. Other individuals may be restricted to roles and statuses that fail to utilize their effective abilities and skills.

Hereditary aristocracies and caste systems present many illustrations of this dysfunctional effect of stratification structure. The French Empire just before the revolution of 1789 had seriously degenerated largely because the requirements of the monarchy far exceeded the capability of the last two rulers. The rigid caste system of India squandered incredible resources of human capability by narrowly restricting the rights and opportunities of the Untouchables. One implication of the Horatio Alger success theme is the existence of vast and undeveloped human talent in the lower status, underprivileged social categories.

Recent studies have demonstrated that the American class system wastes much talent by denying higher education and subsequent chances for useful service to children of lower-class, lower-income families.[35] The evidence indicates that attending college is a social-class-linked privilege. Higher education seems to be more significantly related to opportunities for social participation than to either the capabilities of individuals or the role requirements of the social system. Further evidence of this dysfunctional effect of the American stratification system is to be found in all the racial, religious, ethnic, and cultural discriminations that exclude many Americans from the rights, opportunities, and privileges of the society.

Second, sometimes the status component is dissociated from essential roles of a social system. Thus dissociated, status can be acquired and revealed by social activity that is marginal to the requirements of the system. Essential functions and adequate role performance tend to be neglected or subordinated. The diversion of essential effort and resources to functionally marginal or dysfunctional ends is thus legitimized or even maximized.

For example, the elaborate and stringent food and eating rituals of certain Brahmin castes served to affirm and reveal their high status *vis-à-vis* other castes. These rituals had little relation to their traditional functions as priests, scholars, and scribes. Later, when some of these Brahmins entered the British civil service, the rituals proved intolerably dysfunctional.

Some years ago Thorstein Veblen formulated the concept of "conspicuous consumption" to reveal the tendency to divert essential effort and resources to the public manifestation of status.[36] More recently, David Riesman, William H. Whyte, Jr., and others have studied similar tendencies in modern American society.[37] In a study of a middle-class Canadian suburb, John Seeley and his associates showed how clubs and associations were used to facilitate the acquisition, consolidation, exchange, and display of social status.[38]

Third, social stratification may establish one structural setting of social hostility and conflict. The elaboration and hardening of stratification systems may accentuate status-seeking and the probability of status frustration. Karl Marx perceived this possibility in his prediction of a universal "class war." However, subsequent historical events and empirical research have disclosed that status difference is not the sole cause of inter-stratum conflict.

Inter-stratum conflict often occurs in systems that are disintegrating. It is facilitated when depressed categories realize that substantive change is possible and when the inefficiency of the system and rising expectations combine to exacerbate the sense of collective frustration. Conflict may take the form of class effort for status advancement and is therefore an instance of conscious collective social mobility.

In flexible, open-class systems, struggle is expressed through interest groups and pressure associations that implement important areas of social conflict. In the United States, for example, labor-management, racial and ethnic, and farm-nonfarm designate important class-based areas of organized social conflict.

The struggles of former colonial peoples of Africa and Asia for independence have generally occurred within the structure of social stratification. Inter-stratum struggle in the Western nations has most often pitted labor against management, but not in the mode that Marx predicted. The American civil rights movement is a further instance of social conflict structured by the stratification system.

Finally, Robert K. Merton has shown that the stratification system may be linked with several types of deviant behavior.[39] Many individuals are in a position to conform to the culturally prescribed means (e.g., they can work) for attaining culturally approved ends (e.g., money, status, and power). Some others, however, especially members of the lower classes, find this more or less impossible. Merton classifies their deviance as "innovation," "ritualism," "retreatism," and "rebellion."

Innovation refers to the practice of improvising deviant means to legitimate goals. For example, to earn a profit, win a victory, gain prestige, or have a novel experience, an individual—if legitimate means are unavailable—may resort to crime, sharp transactions, rule violations, confidence tricks, misrepresentation, or the like.

Ritualism is the deviant adaptation of avoiding normal social risks by withdrawal behind the protection of a wall of normative routines. In this way the individual escapes possible frustrating experiences. This mode of adaptation is illustrated by the petty bureaucrat who refuses at any cost to "stick his neck out" and adheres doggedly to the letter of the rule.

Retreatism is deviant adaptation to frustration by disengagement from the society. This category of deviants includes psychotics, pariahs, outcasts, vagrants, vagabonds, tramps, chronic drunkards, and drug addicts. The retreatist is the true sociological alien, attached to the population but detached from the society.

Rebellion refers to the response to frustration in which the individual seeks to modify that part of the milieu to which he cannot conform. He would rewrite the rules so he can abide by them. Status-linked conflict, alluded to above, as well as conscious collective efforts for upward mobility, discussed below, fall into this category.

SOCIAL MOBILITY

Every stratification system recognizes the possibility that individuals and groups may alter their relative positions. Rigid systems are organized to reduce or prevent such changes. Flexible systems, however, are prepared to manage or facilitate modifications of social status. The foregoing discussion suggests that stratification in the United States is flexible and with some notable exceptions generally favors or permits considerable social movement. The management of status modification, or social mobility, is one function of the stratification system.

The term social mobility refers to the process of permanent movement that is socially significant. It envisages movement that is more lasting than a shopping trip, a visit to a neighboring community, or a vacation trip of two weeks duration. Social mobility involves the breaking or modification of old social ties and the establishment of new ones. The decisive dimension of the concept inheres in some modification of social status that issues from such movements. Social mobility may occur as an aspect of either individual experience or group experience. What is crucial is that the positions in which individuals and groups find themselves located are modified in socially significant degrees.

Horizontal and Vertical Mobility ◗ Within this perspective three types of mobility can be identified: geographical, horizontal, and vertical. When an individual or group moves its locus of social action from one place to another, the nature and content of significant social relations are necessarily altered. These changes may produce some modification of status and role. For example, if an individual changes his residence from a rural to an urban community, from the Southeast to the Midwest, or from the eastern seaboard to the Pacific coast, he has moved in both the geographical and social senses. This dimension of mobility is also illustrated in the mass migrations of populations within the United States or from Europe to the United States, and in the movement of organized groups like the Mollocans and the

RAPID MASS TRANSPORTATION, developed in the past half-century, enables individuals to make both temporary and permanent moves easily. Increased geographical mobility, often linked to establishment of new social ties, is symbolized here by aerial view of busy John F. Kennedy Airport in New York, where thousands arrive and depart each day.

Old Order Amish. Geographic mobility often has implications for social mobility in this way.

Geographical and vertical mobility are generally, though neither necessarily nor universally, interdependent. There are situations in which the change of geographical location is not accompanied by any significant alteration of social status. This may occur, for example, when individuals migrate from tenant or share-cropping farms in the Mississippi Delta Region to low-paid, unskilled, and service occupations, and slum residences in Chicago, Detroit, or Cleveland. It is observed in the peregrinations of managers of large corporations who are sent from one post to another.

Horizontal mobility has a somewhat different meaning from geographical or vertical mobility. Essentially, this refers to movement between positions which are roughly equivalent in status; that is, movement within a single stratum. Suppose that a man's father was a lawyer, placing his family squarely in the middle class. The son does not become a lawyer, but rather, say, a professor. The son remains in the middle class and at about the same level within the middle class that his father held. But by virtue of education, perhaps changed lifestyle and slightly reduced income, he has been mobile laterally or horizontally. Such positional or "situs" moves are quite frequent in our society and they are based on some interesting elements of the changing society.

Fewer men, including professionals, are "free" or "unattached." That is, more and more of us come, in one way or another, to work in large corporate, bureaucratic structures. A chemist working for a drug manufacturing firm is certainly in no position to "leave the business to his son." Children tend to inherit values of middle-class aspirations rather than businesses today. Consequently, they are more free to select occupations different from their fathers' but to remain within the same social class. This fact, plus a changing occupational structure which includes an increase in the professional, scientific, and technical occupations, has made horizontal or situs mobility quite common, most especially in the middle class.

Achievement of Status ▶ Social status is a social value. Each stratification system provides mechanisms for awarding initial statuses to members. In rigid systems initial statuses tend to be permanent. Few if any means and opportunities exist for modifying original ascribed statuses. Such systems also function to inhibit motivation for status change. The structure appears immutable. The value heritage stresses contentment and acceptance of one's allotted place. The individual's sacred duty is defined as fulfilling the obligations of his role in the traditional manner.

For example, under feudalism the peasants revealed little desire to move into the aristocratic class. The Indian caste system defined the individual's *Dharma* as defense of his caste, not as escape from its status limits. In the Soviet Union there is little evidence of status striving among members of the low-status categories.

On the other hand, flexible systems, like that in the United States, are characterized by both considerable movement and motivation to status modification. Figure 11-3 indicates the estimated extent of status modification in American society. It will be seen that movement occurs between each of the class layers and that at some points the extent of mobility is very considerable.

The system motivates individuals to status striving. There are many possibilities for advancement. The values stress improvement, not contentment. High status has been invested with social value. Thus mobility is a social force as well as a social process. The pressure for mobility is revealed in the demand for higher education, striving for advancement in the complex economic and political organization, and the flight to the suburbs.

At one time it was widely believed that the lower classes lacked the "American" motivation for advancement and improvement. They were said to be "lazy," "shiftless," and the like. However, recent research has disclosed that mobility motivation as an American value norm is shared by all classes.[40]

The achievement of status is conditioned by a variety of forces and circumstances in the social milieu. Among the more important variables are motivation to strive and the availability of opportunities. Research indicates that although motivation to strive exists in all social classes, it varies in intensity from one class to another. Moreover, actual upward mobility may be limited because of inadequate opportunities for adequately motivated individuals, faulty percep-

Social Mobility in American Society by Status

SOCIAL CLASS	PER CENT OF POPULATION	PER CENT OF MOBILITY FROM BELOW
UPPER	3.0	+7.7
UPPER-MIDDLE	9.0	+10.7
LOWER-MIDDLE	36.0	+28.2
UPPER-LOWER	35.0	+29.1
LOWER-LOWER	17.0	—
TOTAL	100.0	—

Source: Carson McGuire, "Social Stratification and Mobility Patterns," American Sociological Review, *adapted from Table 1, p. 200, Vol. 15, 1950.*

FIGURE 11-3

tions of available opportunities, actual lack of motivation, or some combination of these factors. In addition, it is revealed that low mobility rates in the lower classes are related to unrealistic aspirations and failure to perceive means of exploiting available opportunities.

It has been said that status differentials and striving are revealed along three basic dimensions: political power, economic achievement, and social status. Both the force and the process of social mobility are revealed along all three dimensions. Moreover, mobility striving may be either an individual or a collective expression.

Dimensions of Social Mobility ◗ Acquiring education is one method of achieving higher social status. A study of 998 Negro college students in North Carolina revealed that even before graduation, and including second-semester freshmen, three fourths had more years of formal education than their supporting parents or guardians.[41] The data also revealed that advancement through college tended to carry the students toward professional and white-collar occupations. However, only slightly over one fifth, 22 per cent, of the 998 parents and guardians were engaged in such occupations. As the students climbed the educational and occupational ladders, they were drawn to urban centers where these achievements had greater economic and prestige value. Thus educational advancement, vocational aspiration, and geographic mobility were manipulated in the achievement of social status.

C. Wright Mills has investigated certain aspects of social mobility in the American middle classes. He notes that small businessmen were considerably more mobile occupationally than either big business and professional or lower-class blue-collar workers. Mills draws attention to the manipulation of occupation, education, and marriage in the process of status achievement.

When we compare small business with other occupations of similar income level, we notice that they contain the greatest proportion of ascending individuals now in the higher income brackets; 18% of those who are urban-derived had wage-worker fathers and 9% low-income white-collar fathers. Thus 27% come from the lower groups. The free professional and big businessmen, on the other hand, do not include any individuals who derived from wage-worker or low-income white-collar.

Slightly more than half of these small businessmen have married girls whose fathers were in the upper half of the income occupation ranks. About 40% of them married daughters of wage workers; the remaining married into the lower income white-collar stratum.

The job histories of these little businessmen reveal the same basic pattern. Only one out of five of them was in a job as high as small business at the time of their marriage (their average age is now around 48) whereas almost half of them were working for wages at that time. Well over half (57%) did wage work for their first full-time job.

There is rigidity at the bottom and at the top—except among small businessmen who, related to comparable income groups, have done a great deal of moving up the line.[42]

Ultimate entrance of an individual or family into a higher social class involves at least five steps or phases. First, the individual must acquire the valued external characteristics of the new class. Second, he must associate himself in clique and formal association with members of the new class. Third, through these relationships he must internalize the subtle and intangible attitudes, values, and feelings of the new class. Fourth, he must identify psychologically with the new class and liquidate his identification with the old class. And fifth, ultimately he must be accepted by the new class as a "member."

It is evident that status achievement is functional since it contributes to fulfillment of the American value emphases on improvement, competition, and advancement. Nevertheless, it has some important dysfunctional consequences. To move from one status level to another, individuals and families must discard an established way of life and acquire another. Community and institutional structures are continually disorganized by widespread shifting of individuals from one geographic or social position to another. The resultant social instability impedes efficient allocation of individuals to societal functions with due reference to relevant capabilities and needs.

Collective Effort to Achieve Status ❱ Important modifications of the structure or shifts of internal relations of status systems frequently result from organized social effort. Successful revolutions destroy an existing stratification system and bring new classes of elites into power and prestige.[43] Social reform movements often modify important segments of institutionalized status arrangements, thus altering the relative positions of entire population sectors.[44] Interest groups and pressure groups implement social mobility by working for improved status for their members. While they seldom make serious attacks on the system itself, they seek to alter status relations within the existing stratification structure. An excellent illustration is the current American civil rights movement. It may prove useful to examine briefly another example of organized status modification in recent American experience.

The American labor movement commenced early in the nineteenth century with the beginning of urbanization.[45] The first successful national labor union federation was established in 1886, concomitant with the rapid industrial expansion that followed the Civil War. During the next half century the movement sought improved standing, recognition, and power of organized workers and the working classes as a whole. Specific aims included higher wages, shorter hours, improved working conditions, job security, certain "fringe benefits," and an increasing share in the decisions that conditioned the lives of wage-workers.

The working classes advanced slowly in status during these years. Major improvement resulted from passage of the National Labor Relations Act in 1935 and other federal legislation as part of the reform movement popularly known as the "New Deal." Minimum wages and maximum hours were written into federal law. Workers were protected in the right to organize and to bargain collectively for recognized objectives. Trade unions were protected against unfair labor practices. The labor unions grew rapidly in size, power, efficiency of organization, and self-respect. Organized labor came to be regarded along with management, agriculture, and government as one of the major elements of the economy. The public respect now accorded the working classes is symbolized by the prestige and power of their union leaders.

The working classes have risen significantly in social status. Some of the models of the American class system distinguish a working class from the traditional lower classes. In other models the most advantaged workers have been assigned positions in the middle classes. Mills, Kahl, and others point out that a substantial portion of the middle-class population is made up of blue-collar workers. At present a clear status distinction is made between the socially and economically adequate working people and what Lloyd Warner has called the "lower-lower class."

FOOTNOTES

1. Robert H. Lowie, *An Introduction to Cultural Anthropology* (New York: Rinehart, 1940), pp. 440-441.
2. Condensed and adapted from John Useem *et al.,* "Stratification in a Prairie Town," in *American Sociological Review,* 7:331-342 (June 1942).
3. Melvin M. Tumin, "Stratification," in Julius Gould and William L. Kolb, eds., *A Dictionary of the Social Sciences* (New York: Free Press, 1964), p. 695.
4. Talcott Parsons classifies such characteristics as "qualities," "performances," and "possessions." See "A Revised Analytical Approach to the Theory of Social Stratification," in Reinhard Bendix and S. M. Lipset, eds., *Class, Status and Power* (Glencoe: Free Press, 1953), pp. 122-125.
5. Kingsley Davis and Wilbert E. Moore, "Some Principles of Stratification," in *American Sociological Review,* 10:242 (April 1945).
6. See, for example, W. Lloyd Warner *et al., The Status System of a Modern Community* (New Haven: Yale University Press, 1942); A. B. Hollingshead, *Elmtown's Youth* (New York: Wiley, 1949); Richard Centers, *The Psychology of Social Classes* (Princeton: Princeton University Press, 1948); George Gallup, *The Pulse of Democracy* (New York: Simon and Schuster, 1940); and Milton M. Gordon, *Social Class in American Sociology* (Durham: Duke University Press, 1958).
7. Gordon, *op. cit.,* p. 248.
8. Leonard Reissman, *Class in American Society* (Glencoe: Free Press, 1959).
9. Joseph H. Kahl, *The American Class Structure* (New York: Rinehart, 1957), p. ix.
10. See H. H. Gerth and C. Wright Mills, "Ethnic Segregation and Caste," in *From Max Weber: Essays in Sociology* (New York: Oxford University Press, 1948), pp. 188-190. See also K. N. Pannikkar, *Hindu Society at Crossroads* (Bombay: Asia Publishing House, 1955).
11. See W. Lloyd Warner and Paul S. Lunt, *The Social Life of a Modern Community*

(New Haven: Yale University Press, 1941); and Centers, *op. cit.*

12. See Note 6 above. See, in addition, Kahl, *op. cit.*, and Reissman, *op. cit.*, for additional studies.

13. Charles F. Marden and Gladys Meyer, *Minorities in American Society* (New York: American Book Company, 1962), pp. 234-235; also George Simpson and J. Milton Yinger, *Racial and Cultural Minorities* (New York: Harper and Row, 1965), p. 244.

14. There is a voluminous and growing sociological literature on the American Negro group. Among other sources see Allison Davis and John Dollard, *Children of Bondage* (Washington: American Council on Education, 1940); W. Lloyd Warner *et al., Color and Human Nature* (Washington: American Council on Education, 1941); St. Clair Drake and Horace Cayton, *Black Metropolis* (New York: Harcourt Brace, 1945); Hylan G. Lewis, *Blackways of Kent* (Chapel Hill: University of North Carolina Press, 1955); Eli Ginzberg, *The Negro Potential* (New York: Columbia University Press, 1956); E. Franklin Frazier, *The Negro in the United States* (New York: Macmillan, 1957); and M. Elaine Burgess, *Negro Leadership in a Southern City* (Chapel Hill: University of North Carolina Press, 1962).

15. Simpson and Yinger, *op. cit.*, p. 159.

16. Legal support of the ethnic stratification structure has been challenged by a series of Supreme Court decisions and federal laws over a period of some thirty years, of which the most important are the Supreme Court decision in 1954 prohibiting segregation in public schools and the Civil Rights Act of 1964.

17. Bertrand W. Doyle, *The Etiquette of Race Relations in the South* (Chicago: University of Chicago Press, 1937).

18. In this connection see Robert C. Weaver, *Negro Labor* (New York: Harcourt Brace, 1942); Ginzberg, *op. cit.*; and Frazier, *op. cit.*

19. See, among other sources: S. V. Utechin, "Social Stratification and Social Mobility in the U.S.S.R.," in *Transactions of the Second World Congress of Sociology* (London: International Sociological Association, 1954), Volume II, pp. 55-63; Alex Inkeles and Raymond A. Bauer, *The Soviet Citizen* (Cambridge: Harvard University Press, 1960), pp. 67-100.

20. See Barrington Moore, Jr., *Soviet Politics: The Dilemma of Power* (Cambridge: Harvard University Press, 1950), pp. 239-246.

21. There is a voluminous literature on caste in India. See, for example: K. N. Pannikkar, *op. cit.*; Mills and Gerth, *op. cit.*, pp. 188-190 *et passim;* and André Béteille, *Caste, Class and Power: Changing Patterns of Stratification in a Tanjore Village* (Bombay: Oxford, 1966). In preparing this statement the author had the advice of Dr. S. Krishnaswamy, Professor of History, Madras Christian College; Dr. K. K. Pillai, Professor of History, Madras University; and Dr. D. N. Rao, Director, Madras Office, United States Educational Foundation in India.

22. S. Krishnaswamy, "The Emerging Class Structure in Modern India," unpublished paper presented at Seminar on "India and America: Cultures in Transition," Trivandrum, India, September 12, 1966, p. 1.

23. Condensed and adapted from Ruth S. Cavan, *The American Family* (New York: Crowell, 1958), pp. 119-147.

24. Condensed and adapted from *Ibid.*, pp. 171-187.

25. Genevieve Knupfer, "Portrait of the Underdog," in *Public Opinion Quarterly,* XI:114 (Spring 1947).

26. Albert J. Mayer and Philip Hauser, "Class Differentials in Expectation of Life at Birth," in Bendix and Lipset, *op. cit.*, pp. 283-284.

27. Elmo Roper, *Factors Affecting the Admission of High School Seniors to College* (Washington: American Council on Education, 1949), p. 17.

28. Robert E. Clark, "Psychosis, Income and Occupational Prestige," in *American Journal of Sociology,* 54:433-440 (1949).

29. Arthur Kornhauser, "Analysis of 'Class' Structure in Contemporary American Society—Psychological Bases of Class Division," in G. H. Hartmann and Theodore Newcomb, eds., *Industrial Conflicts* (New York: Gordon, 1939).

30. Kahl, *op. cit.*, pp. 137-138.

31. Knupfer, *op. cit.*, pp. 103-114.

32. Eleanor E. Macoby and Patricia K. Gibbs, "Methods of Child Rearing in Two Social Classes," in W. E. Martin and C. B. Stendler, eds., *Readings in Child Behavior and Development* (New York: Harcourt Brace, 1954), pp. 272-287.

33. Oscar Lewis has defined and popularized one version of a class-linked style of life as "the culture of poverty." See his *The Children of Sanchez* (New York: Random House, 1961). William H. Whyte, Jr., in *The Organization Man* (New York: Simon and Schuster, 1956), defines another life style.

34. In this connection see Joseph S. Himes, "Some Work-Related Cultural Deprivations of Young Lower-Class Negro Workers," in Louis Ferman *et al.*, eds., *Poverty in America* (Ann Arbor: University of Michigan Press, 1965), pp. 384-389. See also Chapter 13 below.

35. See, among other sources, W. Lloyd Warner *et al.*, *Who Shall Be Educated?* (New York: Harper, 1944); Eli Ginzberg, *The Negro Potential* (New York: Columbia University Press, 1956); and Michael Harrington, *The Other America* (New York: Macmillan, 1962).

36. Thorstein Veblen, *Theory of the Leisure Class* (New York: Macmillan, 1899).

37. David Riesman, *The Lonely Crowd* (New Haven: Yale University Press, 1950); and Whyte, *op. cit.*

38. John R. Seeley, *et al.*, *Crestwood Heights*, New York: Basic Books, 1956), pp. 292-339.

39. Robert K. Merton, *Social Theory and Social Structure* (Glencoe: Free Press, 1957), pp. 139-157.

40. Among other sources see: J. A. Kahl, "Educational and Occupational Aspirations of 'Common Man' Boys," in *Harvard Educational Review*, 23:186-203 (1953); W. H. Sewall *et al.*, "Social Status and Educational and Occupational Aspiration," in *American Sociological Review*, 22:67-73 (1957); Seymour M. Lipset and Reinhard Bendix, *Social Mobility in Industrial Society* (Berkeley: University of California Press, 1959); Fred B. Silberstein and Melvin Seeman, "Social Mobility and Prejudice," in *The American Journal of Sociology* 65:258-264 (1959); and Harry J. Crochett, Jr., "The Achievement Motive and Differential Occupational Mobility in the United States," in *American Sociological Review*, 27:191-204 (1962).

41. Joseph S. Himes, "The Factor of Social Mobility in Teaching Marriage Courses in Negro Colleges," in *Social Forces*, 30:439 ff., (May 1952).

42. C. Wright Mills, "The Middle Classes in Middle-Size Cities," in *American Sociological Review*, 11:520-529, especially 523 (October 1946). Also see Mills, *White Collar*, (New York: Oxford University Press, 1956).

43. See Lyford Edwards, *The Natural History of Revolution* (Chicago: University of Chicago Press, 1927); and Ralph H. Turner and Lewis M. Killian, *Collective Behavior* (Englewood Cliffs: Prentice-Hall, 1957), Part 4.

44. See Thomas Greer, *American Social Reform Movements* (New York: Prentice-Hall, 1949).

45. See Florence Peterson, *American Labor Unions* (New York: Harper, 1952).

Part V

PERSONALITY

The study of personality is a leading problem of social psychology, a field that unites sociology and psychology. To understand the concept of personality a student should have some background in both disciplines. The analysis of social organization in preceding Parts of this book provides adequate sociological background for this task.

In Chapters 12 and 13, personality is viewed as a leading social product. First, its development is traced within an established social system through the process of socialization. Next, Chapter 12 analyzes personality organization, both as a system of functionally integrated elements and as a creative system of social action. Chapter 13 discusses personality in relation to social structure and illustrates the relationship by reference to learning an occupation. Part V concludes with a brief discussion of deviant behavior and social structure.

Chapter 12

FORMATION AND ORGANIZATION OF PERSONALITY

It has been said that every society must train its newcomers, infant and older, to become useful operating members. This process is called *socialization* and constitutes an important part of the business of the society. *Social organization* constitutes the setting and apparatus for the management of socialization. The prelude to the study of socialization and personality is the analysis of social organization that occupied our attention in Parts II, III, and IV of this book. The appropriate sequel is the discussion of collective behavior and social change presented in the following part.

Early Approaches to Personality ▶ The Romans used the word *persona* to refer to the masks worn in ceremonies, pageants, and dramatic presentations. The mask made it clear that an individual represented someone or something other than himself. By derivation, the term persona came to mean also the role or part an individual assumed when he wore a mask. *Personalitas* was the spiritual essence or vital self that was thought to inhere in the role and attach to the mask. Assumed roles were thus clearly distinguished from the natural self, or *ego*. The ego was thought to reside in the body, from which it could not *naturally* be dissociated. The natural mask of the ego was the face, especially the eyes. The persona thus both concealed the individual's natural ego and indicated that he was representing another, or personalitas.

The distinction between the ego, or the natural role, and the persona, or the assumed role, raised the problem of the nature and source of the ego. The ancients solved this problem with a variety of theories. One view was animism, or the belief that the world was inhabited by spirits that resided in both inanimate and animate phenomena. Mountains, rivers, trees, rocks, and subhuman animals, as well as human beings, thus had egos. By masking himself an individual could acquire the spirit or ego, and assume the role of any of these phenomena.

In the early Middle Ages, it was widely believed that certain features of the ego, or powers, as they were called, resided in specific bodily organs and structures. Wit, shrewdness, or cunning was thought to reside in the brain, courage in the heart, and ill temper in the liver. People would sometimes eat the appropriate organ of a deceased relative or friend or of a slain enemy in order to acquire his powers of ego.

It was only a short logical step from these early notions of personality to the instinct theory that was accepted for a long time. This view held that personality was composed of a syndrome of hereditary elements called instincts. Each individual was thought to be born with a full set of completely·developed patterns of social behavior. The overt functioning of these automatic nonmodifiable patterns served to reveal the personality. The study of personality consisted in identifying, describing, and tracing the operations of the instinct elements. Maturation, the process of physical development, and not socialization was then the central process of personality formation.

Instinct theory presents at least three major problems. First, there seems to be no stimulus in the environment which triggers exactly the same response in all men everywhere. We all experience hunger, but the manner in which we satisfy our hunger differs greatly from culture to culture. Self-preservation is not instinctive either—if it were, how could we account for suicides or for men willingly going off to war? Culture, values, social structure—all of these seem to give better explanations for the behavior once called instinctive. Second, if one were to examine the lists of instincts compiled by earlier scholars, one would find great overlapping, but also considerable variation. Agreement was limited, and if instincts are as invariable as one would imagine, such variations as exist in these lists should not appear. Third, the instinct theorists used faulty logic. They abstracted from behavior a descriptive term and then used their description to explain the behavior. From observing sexual behavior, for example, an instinct theorist might abstract the idea of a sex instinct. Then, when asked for an explanation of sexual behavior, he would say it is due to the sex instinct—which explains nothing at all.

Under empirical scrutiny such early views of personality have been largely abandoned. Yet the differentiation of ego and persona foreshadowed some distinctions that are useful in sociological analysis of personality. First, such a differentiation expresses the separation that is often drawn between "real self" and "social self," or between what are sometimes called "authentic personality" and "status personality." Again, there is recognition that personality contains materials, some of which are inherited biologically and are unmodifiably inherent in the organism, and some of which are socially acquired, and so subject to modification. Less obvious is the implicit distinction between the typical and the unique personality. That is, both the ego and the persona dimensions are seen to contain elements that are characteristic of societies and groups as well as constituents that distinguish each individual uniquely.

Research during the past half century and more has provided empirical support for a social theory of personality. The theory holds that:

(1) Biological heredity, culture, and social organization constitute preconditions of personality.

(2) Personality develops through the interrelated processes of physical maturation and social learning.

(3) The members of every society manipulate and direct the process of personality development by means of the social organization.

SOCIALIZATION

Personality may be tentatively defined as (1) that dynamic system of individual action (both typical and unique) including motives, feelings, attitudes, habits, and ideas, (2) that is formed through interlocking processes of heredity, maturation, and learning, (3) that embodies the fusion of physiological, cultural, and social elements, and (4) that is revealed internally as self-consciousness and selfhood and externally as social roles and action system. Such a definition has the virtue of emphasizing the fact that personality is the product, taken at any point in the individual's life cycle, of a complex process of development and learning.

The Problem of Socialization ◗ Each society has to transform its new human personnel into functioning social members. This task implies "the existence of a 'system' in the upbringing of children, a system set up by a society and under its control, . . ."[1] Thus Clyde Kluckhohn writes: ". . . a definition of socialization in any culture is the predictability of an individual's daily behavior in various defined situations. When a person behaves most of the time as others do in following cultural routines, he is then socialized. . . ."[2]

To accomplish this societal end a society must fulfill three tasks, which may be called the dimensions of socialization. First, the biological appetites, drives, and processes of the human organism must be disciplined and confined within the patterns established in the culture. For example, the individual's physiological need to satisfy hunger, thirst, elimination, sex, etc., must be tamed and anchored to the gratifications approved by the society. Or again, his physical language capabilities must be subjected to the disciplines of the speech or dialect in use in the society.

Second, the individual must be taught that part of the cultural heritage needed for his functioning as a social member. That is, socialization focuses on transmission and inculcation of the essential and universal core of the culture, i.e., the part that enables him to behave most of the time as others do. For example, the individual must learn the values and norms required for gaining a living, protecting himself, living with others, supporting the group, and the like. It is just at this point that socialization differs from education, which stresses transmission of the specialized aspects of the culture.

Third, the individual must be integrated into the on-going social organization. To become a social member he must receive a place and a part in his social world. In one or more groups—family, peer group, neighborhood, kinship organization, or the like—he is given one or more statuses and one or more corresponding roles. He becomes child, sibling, playmate, and later worker, soldier, hunter, parent, or leader.

Aims of Socialization ▶ The system of socialization set up by a society and under its control must specify the aims and define the methods of operation. In every culture the aim of socialization exists, more or less explicitly, as a *model* of the kind of person the society wishes. In *Children of Their Fathers,* Margaret Read lists respect, honor, politeness, and courtesy toward others, especially elders, all leading to harmonious social relations and group solidarity and welfare, as the model of socialization among the Ngoni of Nyasaland.[3] Middle-class American parents want their children to be achieving, independent, poised, and "successful" in a way that will redound to the prestige and status of the family. Margaret Mead has shown that three primitive societies on the island of New Guinea—the Arapesh, the Tchambuli, and the Mundugumor—maintained sharply different models for men and for women.[4]

The process of socialization consists of presenting, interpreting, communicating, and inculcating this model. Parents and elders act it out. Stories and pictures portray it. School, church, the mass media, and the secondary institutions exemplify and reinforce the model. Rewards support conformity, and punishments discourage deviation. In time, naturally and inevitably, the individual becomes like the model and acts most of the time as others do in following the cultural routines.

PHASES OF SOCIALIZATION

The process of socialization is the first analytic problem of this chapter. It is useful to identify four phases in the analysis of socialization.[5] First, because of helplessness and extreme dependency, the infant is forced to accept group definitions in meeting his organic needs and in controlling his organic drives. The second phase is characterized by wider social contacts and the formulation of spontaneous definitions, which may or may not conform to those of the primary social structure. Third, by means of language symbols, definitions of the general social structure are acquired and internalized into the developing personality system. The fourth phase is distinguished by the emergence of self-consciousness and the development of a social self as the core of a self system.

Enforced Definitions ♦ Before the child can walk and talk, he has only slight control over his social experiences. Social definitions—meanings—are imposed upon him by those who manage his life. Nevertheless, even at this early age the child is a living, acting creature in dynamic interaction with his environment. Physiological needs and organic appetites propel the organism into action that impinges upon those around him. Experiences issuing from this interactivity produce general drives, attitudes, and feelings that further activate the organism.

Gordon W. Allport reports observations that demonstrate how an infant's organic needs and drives function to engage him in relations with others. The material indicates also that as the child develops, social motivations tend to support or supersede organic impulses.

(12th. day) When pushed by his shoulders away from the breast, A. shows active resistance, a contrary movement of body (specifically at shoulders) back toward breast.

(14th. day) As soon as he is lifted a little way toward the breast, but before he reaches it, A. stops crying, and makes vigorous sucking movements.

(3rd. month, first day) A notable feature of A.'s disposition is the relatively small amount of crying and large amount of smiling. He is easily amused by sounds, grimaces, wagging fingers, playful thrusts, etc.

(4th. month) Characteristics at four months: healthy, good natured, smiles readily, and is easily amused, coy (while nursing he withdraws, smiles at mother, aggressively returns to breast with a kind of divided attention that can only be described as coy).

(12th. month) Laughs readily in imitation, sociable but not affectionate, aggressive in friendships with other children, excitable; somewhat nervous. Regards people as agents for play; sociable, many inventions of games.[6]

At the same time, the organic functions of the infant draw parents and other adults into relations with it. The purposes of these relations can be classified as ministration to organic needs, control of physiological processes, and imposition of social definitions. These adults act toward the infant from the perspectives prescribed in the cultural and social definitions. The aim is to squeeze the infant's organic responses into the symmetrical models of the cultural patterns.

In the following engaging passage, Margaret Mead shows how ministration and control tend to pattern relations with the young Samoan child. The material and nonmaterial cultural elements are typically Samoan, yet the situation may appear familiar to many Americans. As Mead points out, the aim is to replace organic processes by social motives and definition.

Babies are always nursed, and in the few cases where the mother's milk fails her, a wet nurse is sought among the kinsfolk. From the first week they are also given other food, papaya, cocoanut milk, and sugar-cane juice; the food is either masticated by the mother and then put into the baby's mouth on her finger, or if it is liquid, a piece of bark cloth is dipped into it and the child allowed to suck it, . . . The babies are nursed whenever they cry and there is no attempt at regularity. . . .

The chief nurse-maid is usually a child of six or seven who is not strong enough to lift a baby over six months old, but who can carry the child straddling the left hip, or the small of the back. . . . Their diminutive nurses do not encourage children to walk, as babies who can walk about are more complicated charges. . . . The life on the floor, . . . encourages crawling. . . .

From birth to the age of four or five a child's education is exceedingly simple. They must be housebroken, . . . They must learn to sit or crawl within the house and never to stand upright unless it is absolutely necessary; never to address an adult in a standing position; to stay out of the sun; not to tangle with the strands of the weaver; not to scatter the cut-up cocoanut which is spread out to dry; to keep their scant loin cloths at least nominally fastened to their persons; to treat fire and knives with proper caution; not to touch the kava bowl, or the kava cup; and, if their father is a chief, not to crawl on his bed-place when he is by. These are really simply a series of avoidances, enforced by occasional cuffings and a deal of exasperated shouting and ineffectual conversation.[7]

In the first phase of socialization, by the very nature of the case, nonsymbolic interaction is maximized. Socialization cannot at this time be mediated by language or any other learned system of symbols. Adults act out the definitions and meanings that are directed to the infant. Thus, for example, mother lifts the infant toward the breast at feeding time or restrains his hand that is reaching for her glasses or earring. At the same time, the infant must act out his feelings and wishes and responses. Thus crying, suckling, wriggling, and other forms of overt and vocal activity initiate relations with adults.

Yet, action is always set within a context of symbolic and representational expressions. Among these are language, vocal tones and inflections, manual gestures, expressions of face and eyes, and a variety of bodily postures. These accompany action and constitute the setting of action. They are therefore meaningful parts of the total situation. Response of the infant to drive- and need-linked action also includes adaptive reaction to these peripheral elements of the situation.

It is evident from the foregoing discussion that even in the first phase, socialization involves two-way communication, i.e., between infant and adult. The actions of each impinge upon the other and communicate meanings. Each, infant and adult, is a stimulus to the other and acts in adaptive response to the actions of the other. Repeated intimate associations of mother with infant soon enable her to dissociate and identify features of his complex of behavior that indicate the pressure of specific organic drives and needs. Very early, also, the infant learns to differentiate those elements of his mother's action that are linked with his needs and drives.

Internally and at the psychic level the mechanism of identification implements communication and learning. The infant enters into the role of mother and thereby is able to reënact her actions toward him. This exercise, often called "taking the role of the other," facilitates communication by enabling the infant to understand mother's action as she meant it. From each experience of identification the infant tends to build up an accumulation of learned personality materials.

In the first phase of socialization the infant is forced to accept with little significant resistance the group definitions of social situations. He is required to learn to adapt his responses to those of adults. What he learns may be described at the level of overt action and at the level of feeling. On the one hand, the infant fixes attitudes in his personality which result in the repetition of actions producing satisfactions and pleasurable feelings. These attitudes issue into action when the appropriate specific situation presents itself.

On the other hand, he eliminates actions that either do not bring satisfaction or that produce unpleasant results. The inhibition of organic drives and related action is achieved by fixing attitudes of avoidance in his developing personality. These are linked to unsatisfying definitions. The attitudes and patterns of action thus developed are fused with his internal drives and expressed overtly in the content and pattern of his action.

At the level of feeling a lasting dichotomy of behavior is imposed in this phase of socialization. Experiences issuing from organically necessary interaction produce general drives, attitudes, and feelings of both affection and aggression. The separation is expressed in patterns of motivation, both inherent and learned, in the drive-linked attitudes that issue overtly into social action, and in the feeling-states that accompany experience and reinforce social action.

Later, these motives, attitudes, and feelings will be culturally patterned to focus upon various persons and groups in the individual's social world. The affectional tendencies are initially directed toward parents, relatives, and members of the individual's in-groups. Aggressive tendencies, on the other hand, are reserved for outsiders.

There is much empirical research that indicates that the content and pattern of socialization in this and later phases is conditioned by such variables as social class level, ethnic group identification, geographic region, parental personality organization, and the like.[8] The influence of some of these variables is examined at some length in the following chapter. At this point it will suffice merely to illustrate the fact of variation in the content and patterning of socialization.

Margaret Mead's sketch of early socialization among the Samoans presented above shows that management is permissive, casual, and not very demanding. As to content, stress seems to be limited to minimal patterns of participation within the family household setting. On the other hand, among some Plains Indian tribes, although the content of socialization may differ little from that observed among the Samoans, the pattern is rigid, demanding, and strictly enforced.

Research has revealed a number of socially significant differences of content and pattern in socialization among American lower- and middle-class families. Moreover, it has been shown that with the passage of time child-rearing patterns (socialization) among American middle-class families tend to change substantially.

Robert R. Sears and associates illustrate how personality differences of mothers affect the content and pattern of early socialization. Three mothers who were asked the following question gave characteristically different answers.

(Question) "Do you think babies are fun to take care of when they are very little, or do you think they are more interesting when they grow older?"

(First mother) "I don't know. I love little babies. I love to do things with little babies. I love to teach them things. I think it's a feather in your cap to see a little baby be able to do something and know that you taught them that, but at the same time, I think they are interesting when they grow up, too."

(Second mother) "Well, if I had been well and a little younger, I might have enjoyed him, but I will say frankly that it was just a hard job for me."

(Third mother) "They're more interesting as they grow older. Up until they're up to six months old, they're just a routine to take care of them." [9]

Spontaneous Definitions ◗ In time the child achieves a degree of independence in moving around and in handling objects. He learns to crawl and ultimately to walk. He is thus able to explore certain aspects of his environment without parental guidance or sibling intervention. At this time, also, the child gains a playgroup of agemates who are themselves just beginning to walk and have independent locomotion. Now, too, he can move out into the neighborhood and enter into relations with adults other than his parents and visiting relatives. All these persons join his parents as his mentors. Each new object, person, or group encountered is a novel episode of experience.

In this second phase, socialization reveals some new dimensions. First, the range, number, and variety of social experiences are enormously expanded. Second, situations are defined and redefined both in terms of remembered definitions and current social experience. And third, language becomes an increasingly important agency of communication.

Sometimes, novel experience does not involve relations with others, and therefore the child must make independent definitions of the situation. In this event definitions learned in prior situations are brought forward and adapted to the meaningful content of the new experience. Through such explorations and novel experiences he

PLAYING THE PART of the role model helps the child to learn that part of his cultural heritage needed for social functioning. Habits and capabilities thus acquired depend on the values and norms of the culture. The small girl above has not yet learned that shaving the face is practiced only by men in the United States. Role playing by the French boy below reflects the glorification of military tradition and values.

can and does develop new tendencies to action that do not issue directly from social relations with others. Jean Piaget illustrates the nature of spontaneous definitions in his account of the observations of children when first confronted with the game of marbles.[10]

Piaget reports that the first stage typically occurs among children of two or three. The child tends to make his own definitions of the marbles, or to bring forward apparently relevant definitions from earlier experience. He does not know or recognize any rules for playing with them. Although exhibiting regularities in detail and an early use of symbolism, his behavior shows little continuity or direction. The child seems to be trying to understand the nature of marbles and to adapt his motor patterns to this novel reality. He tries one mode of response after another: throwing them, heaping them into pyramids or nests, letting them fall, making them bounce, etc. Once he has gotten over the first astonishment, the game still remains incoherent, or rather still subject to the whim of the moment.

When spontaneous definitions come to the attention of parents or others, the consequences may be crucial for social learning. Sometimes, the spontaneous definitions are disapproved and extinguished since they conflict with those of parents as representing the general social structure. At other times, however, the child's definitions are reinforced by parents and others since they coincide with those of the controlling culture and society.

For example, he picks up the newspaper and brings it to Daddy; leaves the ash trays on the coffee table; or extricates himself harmlessly from the broom closet. His action issues from the adaptation of remembered definitions to the novel situation. A pat on the head, an affirmative nod, or an amused smile may convey parental approval and function to reinforce the child's original plan of action. Another day the exploring child discovers a cake in the kitchen. It is a soft, sweet, white object much like the food he is always urged to eat. Acting on this remembered definition, he stuffs himself. When Mother discovers what he has done, she scolds or punishes the exploring child.

Parental approval or disapproval may refer to a remembered episode or experience. Thus, when Mother scolded or punished, the cake had already been eaten. She conveyed a meaning and redefined a situation by reference to an imaginary and remembered experience. In this manner socialization acquires a new and important dimension in time. Past experience may thus overlap the present and be projected into the future.

Situations are also defined and meanings communicated in the flow of relations with playmates, neighbors, and others. Sometimes these experiences reinforce definitions learned in prior experience in the family situation. Sometimes they challenge and extinguish earlier learnings. Often, however, the experience in such group situations has no apparent connection with previous experience and cannot be interpreted by means of earlier definitions. Mates and associates, like parents in the family situation, communicate or impose definition of the situation. All the time the child is testing, altering, adjusting, and refining the behavioral tendencies, attitudes, and motives issuing from all sources.

In every phase the process of socialization is conditioned by the social structure. Some of these relationships are depicted diagrammatically in Figure 12-1. Primary and secondary groups of the traditional and mass society establish the social setting of the learning process. The developed personality system links the individual through both internal and external organization into the social structure as a functioning, contributing member of society.

Diagrammatic Portrayal of Socialization Process

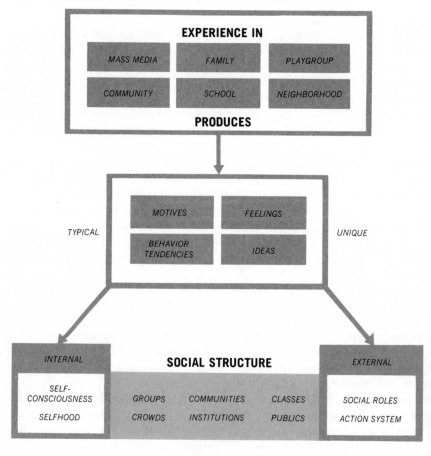

FIGURE 12-1

The Role of Language ♦ From the beginning, socialization involves both nonsymbolic and symbolic elements. At first,though, because the infant has no command of language or any other system of symbols, the burden of communication is carried by overt action, i.e., the non-symbolic elements. Yet each act is itself one element in a configuration of nonsymbolic and symbolic elements including language symbols, vocal tones and inflections, expressions of face and eyes, gestures of hands and head, postures of body, and the like.

As George Herbert Mead has noted, actions function as "gestures" to signal definitions of situations and other meanings, i.e., motives, feelings, ideas, etc. A connected sequence of action gestures is called a "conversation of gestures." Mead describes the conversation of gestures as follows: ". . . [T]he beginning of the act of one is a stimulus to the other to respond in a certain way, while the beginning of this response becomes again a stimulus to the first to adjust his action to the on-coming response."[11]

In time, as the child learns first to understand and then to speak language, the burden of communication shifts from the nonsymbolic to the symbolic elements of the conversation of gestures. The act is shorn of its communicational function and becomes mainly an episode of achievement. Definitions of situations, motives, feelings, ideas, and other cognitive elements are packaged and exchanged by means of language symbols, or, as Mead called them, "vocal gestures."

The acquisition of language tends to alter the process of socialization in at least two ways. First, it extends the range of social experience in both distance and time. Language permits the child to have imaginary or anticipatory experiences. Through such experiences parents can prepare the child for school, Sunday School, membership in the Boy Scouts, contacts with Negroes or Jews, his meeting with Aunt Minnie, the day when Daddy must go to the Army, the arrival of a baby sister, and so on.

Second, language facilitates the systematizing of internalized attitudes and feelings. This occurs through acting out internally and, in the fantasy permitted by language, the interlocking behavior of self and others. For example, Kenneth and Mamie P. Clark in a study of 253 Negro children aged three to seven, some from a segregated southern school and some from a mixed school in the North, found that a high proportion of the children (over 90 per cent) were aware of racial differences.[12] When asked to choose "the doll that looks like you," 20 per cent of the light-colored children selected the colored doll; 73 per cent of the medium and 81 per cent of the dark children identified with the Negro doll.

The role and impact of language in socialization is conditioned by such variables as social class, occupation, region, and the like. For example, lower-class and culturally disadvantaged people reveal what may be called a kind of "language poverty." Such individuals command only limited vocabularies and tend to be taciturn in vocal expression. As a consequence, a heavy burden of communication is vehicled by direct action and overt gestures.

On the other hand, in the professional and intellectual middle classes children are early launched into a sea of language. The rich vocabulary and universal language facility permits a range and subtlety of experience that is unknown among the culturally deprived lower classes. In this connection, child-rearing patterns are related in significant measure to the use and role of language.[13]

Such class-linked differentials of the role and impact of language in socialization issue into correlated differences of personality development and organization. Typically, the classes differ in the completeness of personality development and the sharpness with which personalities are differentiated. Some years ago Robert E. L. Faris and H. Warren Dunham showed that rates and types of personality disorganization and maladjustment are significantly correlated with social class level.[14] This may mean that personality problems are closely related to language development, although the issue has not yet been fully analyzed.

The role of language in socialization is also related to the variations of specialized vocabularies and jargons. One aspect of growing up in a region or ethnic group consists in learning the appropriate vocabulary or dialect. A decisive part of learning an occupation is acquisition of the technical jargon. Criminals, drug addicts, stereo fans, or teen-agers reveal a distinctive argot that internalizes definitions and facilitates communication with both self and in-group others. Speaking of the role of language in teen-age peer groups, David Riesman writes:

> It is used neither to direct the work economy, nor to relate the self to others in any really intimate way, nor to recall the past, nor yet as sheer word play. Rather it is used in the peer-groups today . . . as a set of counters by which one establishes that one is "in" and by which one participates in the peer-group's arduously self-socializing "work."[15]

Self-Consciousness and the Social Self ▶ The final phase of socialization is marked by appearance of mature self-consciousness and stabilization of a social self. Yet, as a matter of fact, both these aspects of personality organization have been developing throughout the socialization process. Self-consciousness is foreshadowed when the infant can differentiate self from not-self. That is, at an early time the infant learns to distinguish parts of his body, e.g., toes and fingers, from his blanket, his toys, or parts of his crib.

Differentiation of self from other is implemented by the mechanism of identification. Even as an infant the child enters the role of mother and others and therein is able to respond to himself. Though not yet fully conscious of himself as a person, he nevertheless senses, perhaps only dimly, a distinction between himself and the other person whose role he is taking.

The acquisition of language facilitates the development of mature self-consciousness. The language symbol, as Mead has pointed out, possesses the unique capability to arouse within the child a response similar to that it evokes in the other person. That is, the language symbol stimulates self and other in the same way. In this way the child becomes a social object to himself similar to the other persons with whom he interacts.

Charles Horton Cooley compared this process of self-awareness to the operation of a looking glass and referred to the image thus produced as the "looking-glass self."[16] The individual gains a conception of himself from the way he perceives that others see him. More than this, though, he evaluates the picture that he sees. The self-evaluation thus built into the looking-glass self is expressed in such self-referring attitudes as pride, self-assurance, shame, self-depreciation, and the like. Often, as is shown in the next chapter, the development of self-consciousness is a collective experience and leads to class-linked, ethnic-group-linked, regional, and other uniformities of self-conception.

Concurrent with these processes, a social self arises, integrates, and stabilizes. In infantile interaction the child begins to dissociate his responses from those of the persons with whom he identifies. The acquisition of language extends and facilitates differentiation of the individual's behavioral tendencies from those of the persons with whom he interacts. Such independent and partly independent behavioral tendencies are linked and fused together. New action elements resulting from expanding social experiences are continuously being added to the developing system.

Internally, the social self embodies the individual's capacity for independent social action. It is the source of his independent social existence and the basis of his sense of unique identity. Externally, the social self is revealed in the individual's consistent action pattern. It ties him into the social organization and keeps him in the strain of social interaction. The social self thus reveals the individual as both a typical and a unique member of society.

The social setting and nature of social experience determine in substantial measure the character of the social self. Ordinarily, this experience permits the developing individual to achieve separation from others and to become significantly independent. Arnold W. Green reveals this point in a perceptive analysis of neurosis among middle-class white male children.[17] Under the special conditions of life in the families being discussed, these children are subjected to "personality absorption." As a consequence, the development of self-consciousness is retarded and only a stunted and distorted self-consciousness can emerge. The result, argues Green, is a special kind of neurosis.

Continuing Socialization ❯ In varying degrees, each phase of socialization continues through childhood and adolescence into adulthood.

Although the rate of development may change with advancing age, the range of experiences becomes ever wider. Later socialization refers both to the acquisition of new behavioral elements and to the refinement, modification, and further integration of those already built into the personality system. The analysis of continuing socialization as conditioned by the social structure constitutes the major problem of the following chapter. Here we need only stress the fact that socialization is not completed in childhood.

In later socialization the setting of social experience changes. Family, playgroup, and neighborhood continue as important arenas of socialization. In later socialization, however, these groups are supplemented and to some extent replaced by the school, the church, specialized associations of the community, e.g., scouts, athletic teams, work associates, and labor and trade associations, and in broad perspective the media of mass communication.

Socialization continues through a series of age-linked stages. The child becomes an adolescent. Through a painful process the adolescent becomes an adult and, with the passage of time, middle-aged and then old. Entry into each age-linked stage requires learning new behavioral tendencies, social roles, modes of self-consciousness and the like, and subordinating or displacing those personality elements that fitted the person for life in the previous stage.

Movement in development and time through continuing socialization is seldom a smooth and continuous process. Often progression is marked by abrupt breaks, sharp turns of direction, or sudden changes in rate of development. The anthropological literature reports widespread evidence of these breaks, or "discontinuities," in the process of socialization.[18] For example, early socialization among the Hopi is marked by permissiveness, security, and relaxation. Suddenly, though, at around age four or five, the process becomes strict, demanding, and fraught with insecurity. In American society the transitions from childhood to adolescence and from adolescence to young adulthood are marked by such discontinuities.

Psychological concepts like fixation and regression testify to the unevenness of socialization in individual experience. Sometimes, the individual's experiences conspire to stop, or fixate, his development at a certain stage although he continues to develop physiologically and to grow older. Some other individuals, having tentatively achieved an age-linked level of development, move backward—regress—to an earlier level.

CONTRASTING PERSONALITIES: PRODUCTS OF SOCIALIZATION

The general pattern of socialization is the same in all cases. However, actual experience tends to vary from situation to situation and from individual to individual. Siblings, even identical twins who grow up in the same parental family, have different experiences and develop significantly dissimilar personalities. The study of such cases helps to illuminate both the process and the consequences of socialization.

The following account illustrates the process of socialization and shows how experience can be different even within the same family. Although the cultural setting of the family was not basically altered between the births of Millie and Sue, each girl brought different hereditary materials to socialization. The case is useful in illustrating certain aspects of the four phases of socialization. Little is said about the role of enforced definitions, since the narrative takes up each child's experiences after infancy. However, there is demonstration of how parents utilize spontaneous activities and definitions to direct learning. Loving and protecting parents make extensive use of language in guiding the development of the two sisters. The narrative brings the social looking-glass into clear view. Although the account ends in the midst of childhood, each girl had achieved self consciousness and had fashioned a distinctive system of social action.

The Burns lived in a modest bungalow-type house in a middle-class neighborhood. Both Mr. and Mrs. Burns looked forward to the first baby with enthusiasm, and, though Mr. Burns was disappointed that it was a girl, he accepted her with warmth and real affection. Mrs. Burns was enraptured and lavished love and attention on Millie. As soon as she could toddle, Mrs. Burns made Millie her helper and confidante. She encouraged little Millie to assist with household chores, took her on shopping and visiting trips, and permitted her to play with her ceramic materials and tools. Mrs. Burns showed Millie how to do things, corrected her mistakes, praised her successes, and reported her achievements to Mr. Burns when he returned home at day's end. Millie was an apt pupil and grew steadily into the tidy feminine ways of her mother.

When Millie was seven, her little sister Sue arrived. Mother's preoccupation with the baby gave Millie new opportunities, permitted her to assume some responsibility in the home, and brought more rewards of recognition and praise from both mother and father. Meanwhile, Mrs. Burns had got caught up more and more in her ceramic work and in various civic and service activities of the community.

When Sue was able to toddle about, she began to ask for things to do and looked for opportunities for expression. However, Mrs. Burns already had her helper and confidante and was preoccupied with other activities. She therefore had little time or patience to tolerate Sue's childish efforts, to teach her and to correct her mistakes. Whereas she used to encourage and reward Millie for little services and efforts, now she discouraged Sue, telling her to stay out of things and not to soil her clothes or disarrange the house. When Mr. Burns came home from the office, Mrs. Burns reported Millie's accomplishments and complained about the trouble Sue made.

Casually, almost inadvertently, one day Mr. Burns asked Sue if she would like to help him wash the car. She responded eagerly. This was something to do, something somebody wanted her to do. Mr. Burns thanked her gravely for her help and told her how useful she had been. Another day he enlisted her to help him with the flower bed. When he went out to fix the garage door, little Sue stood by, handing him the tools he needed and picking up nails and other things that he dropped. Soon Sue was Daddy's steady, dependable helper. Presently, he would suggest things that she might do alone, after she returned from kindergarten and before he came home from the office. She loved it and developed into Daddy's little outdoor girl. She never worried if her hands got dirty or if her dress was torn. When Mrs. Burns asked her to do anything inside the house, Sue tended to rebel, feeling that this was Millie's world and regarding any such task as an imposition.

INTERNAL ORGANIZATION OF PERSONALITY

Earlier it was said that personality may be viewed as an individual system of social action with both dynamic and stable aspects and including such behavioral patterns as motivations, feelings, attitudes, habits, and ideas, which is manifested internally as self-consciousness and selfhood and externally as social roles. The structure of the internal personality or self system can be analyzed as variable arrangements of overlapping and interdependent elements, of which the more important are (1) the self as actor, (2) an indefinite number of specific roles, (3) the self as object of action, (4) the moral self, (5) roles of an indefinite number of specific others, and (6) the generalized other. The system functions through self-conscious interaction among these elements in comprehending the acts of others and in creating appropriate responding acts.

This view of the internal organization of personality is depicted schematically in Figure 12-2. The concentric segments indicate the interdependent and overlapping elements. The arrows indicate the lines and directions of internal interaction among the various elements. The external expression of personality in social roles will be the subject of the following chapter.

Self as Actor ◗ George Herbert Mead has most adequately differentiated the self as actor from the self as the object of action.[19] He employs the pronoun *I* to express the self as the initiator of action and the objective or reflexive form *Me* to recognize that the self may be the object of action both to itself and to others. These two elements are thus interdependent even though clearly differentiated.

As actor, the self is the dynamic aspect of personality. Here are lodged and expressed the vital energies of the organism. The self is action, movement, process. In this way the energies of organic drives, social motives, reflexes, feelings, attitudes, and the like are channeled into the stream of social action.

Schematic Portrayal of Personality Organization

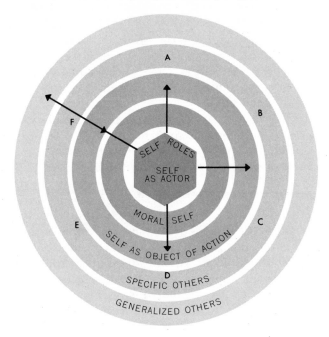

FIGURE 12-2

In this function the self is both initiator and respondent to social action. The behavioral energies of the organism may erupt independently into overt social acts. On the other hand, this element of the self is the answer of the sentient being to the psychically significant aspects of his environment.

As actor, the self is therefore variable and flexible. It expresses the adjustments of the individual to changing and unanticipated conditions. Personality is thus revealed as socially functional. For example, as Mead has noted, in walking, the situation is almost always in some respect different before each next step. The individual adapts to unforeseen circumstances in the very act of creating the step. By analogy, the self moves forward through action into the future, step by step, adjusting in the very act of advancing.

Finally, the active, creative self is seen to be in some measure unpredictable. Cultural conditioning and social sanctions tend to make individual action substantially typical and dependable. Yet the individual is a unique creator of social acts. It is possible to predict that he will react, and one can forecast the general type or class of his acts. Yet the very fact that social acts are created adaptively by a unique individual in response to partially unknown and unforeseen circumstances assures that social action will be in some measure unpredictable.

Self Roles ◗ The active core of the self system is fused into an indefinite series of individual social roles. As suggested by the diagram, these self roles constitute a kind of multi-faceted shell encasing the self as actor and representing the individual's *dramatis personae,* so to speak. They constitute the doors through which the active self enters the stream of social action. Or, to change the metaphor, the individual's roles may be thought of as masks that identify the part he is playing in the drama of social action.

An individual's self roles are formed of the behavioral materials derived through enforcement, spontaneity, identification, symbolization, and the other interactive mechanisms of socialization. Elements from this fund of materials are selected, fused, and integrated in adjustment to the groups and situations that constitute the individual's social milieu. In time, he develops one or more social roles, or more or less orderly systems of action, for each group and situation in which he regularly participates. He is baby, playmate, pupil, errand boy, and so on, depending upon the demands and potentialities of the situation.

Though basically unified, an individual's self roles are neither identical nor constant. They vary with the social situation. The family may require a child to play the submissive role of baby. In his play group, however, he may be the leader. With time and experience, a specific role may alter significantly. In adolescence an individual may play the baby role in his family very differently from the way he did as infant or child. Some roles may be substantially altered in content. The withdrawn person may develop into an extrovert, and the bully may become a democratically participating member of his groups.

The course of socialization is marked by a succession of age-situation-linked roles. This succession is the normal sequence of development from infancy through childhood, adolescence, and adulthood to old age. The roles that were appropriate at one stage are dropped from the self system and replaced by ones more appropriate to a later stage.

The individual acts out his repertory of self roles within the process of self-consciousness. He is always, therefore, watching and evaluating his performance. In the course of acting, or in anticipation of action, he will be modifying and adapting his performance to the terms of the social situation. Moreover, as will be pointed out below, the performance of a self role is affected by the self-image of which the individual is conscious. The actual performance is therefore likely to be creative and slightly unpredictable.

Finally, except in extreme cases, the self roles tend to be basically unified. They belong to the same individual and have been forged from a single fund of internalized behavioral materials. In action, the individual is recognizable, whatever the situation, as essentially the same person. His self roles issue into action from a single and relatively coherent self-image. The individual therefore is a single actor with many masks playing many different parts, yet playing them all in basically the same way.

The Moral Self ▶ In socialization the individual internalizes moral standards from the various cultures he has experienced. These moral standards form a qualifying shield around the core of action or a controlling medium through which action is projected. Acts of the individual, whether directed to self or to others, pass through this medium and are thus qualified, evaluated, and monitored by the self. In this way the individual passes judgment upon both his acts and himself. The standards of judgment, though integrally his own, are in final analysis derived by internalization from the social milieu. The self thus is a judging mechanism, or, as Howard Becker puts it, "man is a valuing animal."[20] Kimball Young analyzes the moral self and its functions in the following way.

> Like the other roles, those related to proper conduct begin in overt identification and gradually become introjected into the inner life organization as the conscience, or, as Sigmund Freud termed it, the "superego." . . .
>
> This conscience operates by the introduction of one set of roles which counteracts or blocks another. The psychological mechanism for this is the familiar one of inhibition. One role, the approved one, is first rewarded by others and later by the sense of self-righteous approval. The tabooed one is met with pain, deprivation, or other punishment, and later by personal shame and sense of guilt. The pleasant feelings and emotions are tied to acts which are morally approved, and unpleasant ones are those which are not. Shame and sense of guilt are degradations of the self, a reduction of one's sense of approved participation with others. In one form or another shame or guilt or both appear in all societies and are powerful devices of social control.[21]

The moral self is more than the constant self monitor. It is one decisive aspect of self-consciousness. An individual is not just aware of himself as a social object. He is conscious of himself judgmentally, evaluatively, comparatively as a certain *kind* of social object. It is only through this evaluation of self and others that the individual is able to create an image of self and fabricate responses to self and to others. Manifestly, if all self-consciousness were the same, all action would be the same, and this is clearly not the case.

By role-taking the moral self qualifies and permits the individual to evaluate acts directed to self from others, both individual and collective. The individual *understands* the acts directed to him by filtering them, so to speak, through the interpreting medium of the moral self. He thus comprehends not only what the other has said or done; he also understands what he *means*. This is how an individual knows whether a comment is a slight, a compliment, a pleasantry, or the like. It is rendered meaningful by interpretation in passage through the qualifying moral self.

Self as Object of Action ▶ It was noted above that the self-system includes a segment which is the object of action both to itself and to others. In contrast to the self as actor, the self as object tends to be stable and predictable. The individual has learned to see himself and to be prepared to respond to himself much as others do.

The objective self reveals at least two dimensions. The first dimension is the consistent self role that emerges from fusion and integration of motives, feelings, attitudes, and other behavioral materials. The action system to which an individual and others react is recognizably the same in various situations. On the other hand, this stable and predictable objective self is responded to in a variety of different situations. The self as object of action is observed to adapt to variable aspects of different situations.

For example, a man's friends may say of him that he is always the same. At least he is always enough the same to be recognized by himself and by others. But he is the same under very different circumstances. One time he is father in his family, another deacon in his church, still later manager in the chain store, operator of his automobile, plaintiff in a law suit, good fellow in the Saturday night poker game, and so on. In each situation he is both a same and a different social object both to himself and to his associates. In his living room he perceives himself and is recognized as urbane, gracious, clever, and so a delightful host. At the office, all agree that he is efficient, firm, tolerant, and astute. The wit must have had this multifaceted view of the objective self in mind when he observed that two men in conversation always involve at least six different persons: each man as he really is, each man as he thinks he is, and each man as the other thinks he is.

Specific Others ▶ A self system not only includes a stable self image to which the individual, and, he hopes, others regularly respond; it also incorporates an indeterminate number of role images of other persons. Such roles of specific others are derived from the whole context of socializing experience. As shown earlier, the roles of mother, father, and siblings are internalized rather fully and intimately from prolonged and close social contacts. Later, as contacts become more numerous, varied, and superficial, many other roles are internalized within the expanding personality system. From the secondary contacts of the great associations and the mass media still other specific roles are internalized and systematized. Together all these specific other roles form a sort of galaxy that constitutes part of the interactional repertory of the individual.

The self system thus appears as a social system. It embraces a constellation of social roles that are ordered, connected, and interacting by reference to the active and objective self as its core. An individual is, as the saying goes, not only all that he has seen and done; but also everyone that he has contacted and known.

This aspect of organization reveals an important difference of personalities in folk societies and complex urban systems. In the folk society the number and variety of specific others that an individual may internalize is very restricted. In complex heterogeneous societies, on the other hand, an individual may know a vast number of different persons and therefore may internalize a large number of specific other roles. Such a personality system tends to be complex and variegated like the social milieu within which it functions.

The galaxy of specific others in the self system fulfills at least two basic functions. First, by providing role-taking vantage points, it facilitates the process of self-consciousness. When playing these various roles of others, the individual responds to himself. He is thus able to be aware of himself from a variety of different perspectives.

Second, by means of these specific roles of others the individual can interact within himself. In this way he can understand the acts of others and create the appropriate responses. That is, the individual is re-enacting the acts of others or rehearsing responding acts by taking the roles of himself and others.

The Generalized Other ◗ George Herbert Mead has noted that the individual internalizes not only a congeries of specific roles of other persons; he also incorporates into the self system a role image of entire social collectivities. He called this internalized conception of social organization the "generalized other." In the following celebrated passage Mead delineates the essential characteristics of this segment of the total self system.

We get then an "other" which is an organization of the attitudes of those involved in the same process.

The organized community or social group which gives to the individual his unity of self may be called "the generalized other." The attitude of the generalized other is the attitude of the whole community. Thus, for example, in the case of such a social group as a ball team, the team is the generalized other in so far as it enters—as an organized process or social activity—into the experience of any one of the individual members of it.

If the given human individual is to develop a self in the fullest sense, it is not sufficient for him merely to take the attitudes of other human individuals toward himself and toward one another within the human social process, and to bring that social process as a whole into his individual experience merely in these terms; he must also, in the same way that he takes the attitudes of other individuals toward himself and toward one another, take their attitudes toward the various phases or aspects of the common social activity or set of social undertakings in which as members of an organized society or social group they are all engaged; and he must then, by generalizing these individual attitudes of that organized society or social group itself, as a whole, act toward different social projects which at any given time it is carrying out, or toward the various larger phases of the general social process which constitutes its life and of which these projects are specific manifestations.[22]

In this view the generalized other constitutes a stable point of internal action both to and from the individual. Holding it within the self, the individual can relate himself to others while following the rule of organized social conduct. Regarding the decisively social function of the generalized other, Mead writes: "The self-conscious human individual, then, takes or assumes the organized social attitudes of the given social group or community (or of some one section thereof) to which he belongs, toward the social problems of various kinds which confront that group or community at any given time, and which arise in connection with the correspondingly different social projects or organized cooperative enterprises in which that group or community as such is engaged; and as an individual participant in these social projects or cooperative enterprises, he governs his own conduct accordingly."[23]

In the larger sense the generalized other is the individual's internalized image of social organization; it embodies the systematic arrangement of the roles of specific others. In addition, as Jean Piaget pointed out, the generalized other includes the "rules of the game," or the intervening social norms. What is more particular, the individual sees himself as one integrally participating member of the generalized other.

In this sense the individual is a member, a part of society, since his conception of society is inextricably involved with his conception of himself. Indeed, his conception of himself as the object of social action is everywhere and always conditioned by the fact of his participation in an interlocking series of generalized others. Thus, within the self system of the individual, society and the individual are indistinguishable and inseparable.

The individual possesses many generalized others. He has a generalized other for every group, community, institution, or other social unit within which he participates. There is a generalized other for the work group and its rules, the religious organization and its beliefs and rituals, the family and its traditions, the school and its formal and informal patterns of action, and so on. These and many other "societies" are internalized in the self system and impinge upon the self as both actor and object of action.

Functional Organization of Self System ♦ The foregoing analysis has suggested some aspects of the functional organization of the self system. The leading functional processes are suggested by the double-headed arrows in Figure 12-2. The arrows indicate the sources, lines, and directions of internal interaction. Broadly, it may be said that the self system functions interactively in *understanding* social action directed to it and in *creating* responses to social action. All segments of the self system may be and usually are brought into play in these processes. A simplified description of functional organization of the self system may be sketched in the following way.

Suppose that Smith, the union steward, speaks of a minor grievance to Jones, the foreman in the bottoming room of a shoe factory. The situation is initially defined in terms of the official roles of the two men and of the frame of reference of the local union and factory management as reference groups. Internally, however, each man perceives the other in terms of previously established role images, or specific others, and the two reference groups have been internalized as interlocking generalized others.

But just what did Smith mean by this initiating act? How should Jones respond? Before Jones can answer either of these questions, Jones will have to work the matter out within his self system. That is, Jones must *think* about the matter and decide what to say or do.

First, to understand the meaning of the initiating act, Jones reënacts it by taking the role of Smith, the specific other in this situation. To do this the self as actor enters and animates the internalized specific other role and therein reënacts the act of the other person. Thus reënacted, the initiating act of the other is passed through the interpretive medium of the moral self. This process facilitates understanding in two ways: taking the part of the other and subjecting his act to interpretation. Now that Jones has acted to understand Smith's initiating act, he is ready to commence the process of creating an appropriate response.

At this juncture a series of alternative responses may suggest themselves to Jones. For example, he may answer directly and simply. He may repress the direct (and perhaps unpleasant) simple answer and be "diplomatic." He may temporize and stall for time to think up an appropriate answer. He may rationalize, giving a plausible rather than the true answer. He may become angry, frightened, amused, indifferent, or flippant. He may seek to ignore Smith's initiating act and turn the conversation to a different and less threatening topic. What is the appropriate response?

As actor in the self role, Jones rehearses internally, so to speak, these and other possible alternative responses, directing them toward his image of Smith's role. Each such rehearsed act is monitored through the moral self to judge and evaluate its meaning. Moreover, each such act must be interpreted in terms of its relevance to the two interlocking generalized others. Rehearsal and evaluation of action are also conducted in relation to remembered or anticipated events in Jones' experience.

But Jones must ask himself what these acts will mean to Smith. He can know this only as he did when seeking to understand the initiating act. By taking the role of the other, Smith in this case, he is able to reënact his own action. In this way he is able to understand the meaning of his own acts as seen by the other. In the posture of the other, Jones reviews each alternative of action that he calls to mind.

Presently Jones decides or concludes that one possible responding act is appropriate. "Appropriate" is the interpretation or judgment that issues from the moral self, the generalized other, and the standpoint of the other.

The act chosen for overt response may be one of the alternatives or some combination and fusion of alternatives. This behavior creation is then acted out overtly as Jones' visible social response to Smith. The other rehearsed alternatives are, for the moment at least, rejected or perhaps just held in reserve for future response building.

The Free Personality ◗ Stress on the creative process in the self system has led some students to argue that human personality is a "free" system. This viewpoint contrasts with some earlier deterministic formulations. One of these earlier theories held that personality was grounded in instincts. From this standpoint social behavior represented the expression of these inborn behavior patterns over which the individual had little if any control. The situational approach placed the deterministic forces outside the personality. Personality was conceptualized as a system of learned response patterns. Social behavior was interpreted as quasi-mechanical responses to the stimuli of social situations.

The view of personality as a free system does not deny the existence and influence of inherited and external factors. It places such factors into a perspective that is harmonious with the creativity of the self system. In the following illuminating passage, William L. Kolb interprets the free personality as a system functioning within a field of systems. The aspect of freedom that is essential in his argument issues from the fact that personality is viewed as a self-contained creative system involved with, yet detached in significant measure from, the supporting and interlocking field of systems. In Kolb's view the personality is a thoroughly social system and an independent variable in the social process.

> That the personality is a system and to some extent free . . . there can be little doubt. Human personality, as do all systems, emerges from a field of systems and is sustained throughout its existence by a field of systems. Hence personality in its very being is dependent upon the physical universe, the biological organism, society, and culture. . . . It is an emergent from the interaction of the biological organism with society and culture, but it cannot be reduced to any one of them or to any interactional combination of them. Many of the attitudes and ideas within the personality are internalized from the society and the culture, but to account for the behavior of the person in terms of these attitudes and the situation without discovering what has been going on inside the personality from the time that the attitudes were taken over until the behavior takes place in the particular situation is to reduce personality to the status of a purely dependent variable in the social process. The process of socialization viewed externally, the unique experiences of the person, the situation, all must be taken into account, but the personality is a system in its own right and can only be understood by studying it as such.

> Further, it is probable that personality is the most complex and dynamic system known to man. Once it begins to emerge as a system it is perhaps less

dependent for its behavior upon the sustaining and conditioning field than any other system. Not that it is in any sense completely free, but its organization, complexity, and capacity for thought, exploration of possibilities, analysis, fantasy, internal role playing, and symbolization give it the widest range of potentialities of response in most situations in which it finds itself. . . . Human personality is the only system which can respond to itself, view the future and the past, explore the most complex possibilities within its own organization, and then proceed to act. . . .[24]

Dimensions of Personality Organization ▶ Variations in the organization of personality may be analyzed along several dimensions. Such variations form a series of continua, the extremes of which are polarities of personality organization. Five dimensions of variation and the respective polarities can be stated as follows:

1. *Expression of the Active Self.* From unrestrained, spontaneous self-expression to severe control or repression; accompanied by full gratification and self-realization or serious deprivation and frustration.

2. *Integration of Self Roles.* From smooth internal harmony of self roles to deep systematic disjunctions of roles or role configurations; accompanied by relaxed poise, or tension and inner mental conflict.

3. *Moral Conformity.* From basic compatibility between the moral self and the sustaining moral codes to severe disjunctions and clashes between these two; tending to maximize cooperative social participation or to facilitate isolation and conflict.

4. *Self Conception.* From basic compatibility of self conception with the image held by others to serious disparity and inconsistency of these images; fostering easy communication and harmonious social participation, or limiting communication and hampering social relations.

5. *Conception of Social Reality.* From basic agreement of the social image with external social reality to severe skewing of the internalized social conception; accompanied by responses at the level of social reality, or behavior in terms of fantasy and wish-projection.

FOOTNOTES

1. Margaret Read, *Children of Their Fathers* (New Haven: Yale University Press, 1960), p.33.
2. Clyde Kluckhohn, *Mirror for Man* (New York: Whittlesey House, 1949), p. 197.
3. Read, *op. cit.,* pp. 36-37.
4. Margaret Mead, *Sex and Temperament in Three Primitive Societies* (New York: Morrow, 1935).
5. This organization of the socialization process is indebted to Logan Wilson and William L. Kolb, *Sociological Analysis* (New York: Harcourt Brace, 1949), Chapter 6.
6. Gordon W. Allport, *Personality: A Psychological Interpretation* (New York: Holt, 1937), pp. 122-126.
7. Margaret Mead, *Coming of Age in Samoa* (New York: Morrow, 1928), pp. 21-23.
8. Among other sources see Allison Davis and Robert J. Havighurst, "Social Class and Color Differences in Child Rearing," in *American Sociological Review*, 11:701 ff., 1946; Margaret Mead, *Childhood in Contemporary Cultures* (Chicago: University of Chicago Press, 1955); Robert R. Sears *et al., Patterns of Child Rearing* (Evanston: Row Peterson, 1957); and Daniel R. Miller and Guy E. Swanson, *The Changing American Parent* (New York: Wiley, 1958).

9. Sears, *op. cit.*, pp. 51-53.
10. Jean Piaget, *The Moral Judgment of the Child* (New York: Harcourt Brace, 1932), p. 41.
11. George Herbert Mead, *Mind, Self and Society* (Chicago: University of Chicago Press, 1934), pp. 14, 63, *et passim.*
12. Kenneth B. and Mamie P. Clark, "Racial Identification and Preference in Negro Children," in Eleanor Maccoby, *et al.*, eds., *Readings in Social Psychology* (New York: Holt, 1958), p. 608 ff.
13. Sears, *op. cit.*, pp. 427-432.
14. Robert E. L. Faris and H. Warren Dunham, *Mental Disorders in Urban Areas* (Chicago: University of Chicago Press, 1939).
15. David Riesman, *et al.*, *The Lonely Crowd* (New Haven: Yale University Press, 1950), pp. 84-85.
16. Charles Horton Cooley, *Human Nature and the Social Order* (New York: Scribner's, 1902), pp. 152-153.
17. Arnold W. Green, "The Middle Class Male Child and Neurosis," in *American Sociological Review*, 11:37-41 (1946).
18. John J. Honigmann, *Culture and Personality* (New York: Harper, 1954), pp. 180-181 and 232-234.
19. George Herbert Mead, *op. cit.*, pp. 173, 192, 209, *et passim.*
20. Howard Becker and Reuben Hill, *Family, Marriage and Parenthood* (Boston: Heath, 1955), p. 2.
21. Kimball Young, *Social Psychology* (New York: Appleton-Century-Crofts, 1956), pp. 129-130.
22. George Herbert Mead, *op. cit.*, pp. 154-155.
23. *Ibid.*, p. 156.
24. Condensed and adapted from William L. Kolb, "Social Psychological Conception of Human Freedom," in *Ethics*, 63:182-183.

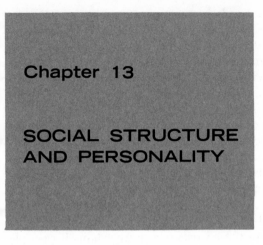

Chapter 13

SOCIAL STRUCTURE
AND PERSONALITY

SOCIAL STRUCTURE AND SOCIALIZATION

Social structure comprises those more or less durable arrangements within which systematic social relations take place. The more common forms include social groups, complex organizations, social categories, stratification systems, and social institutions. Culturally defined rights and duties are systematized and allocated to social roles. Coordinate orders of social roles are ranked and structured by attachment to social statuses. Authority is hierarchized by the status system and embodied in the social roles to produce a power structure. Channels develop among the orders and ranks of social roles to facilitate and pattern the flow of communication.

The social structure functions (among other things) to allocate available personnel to existing roles and statuses and to prepare individuals for the performance of these roles. Assignment of individuals to roles and statuses is accomplished through ascription and achievement. The preparation of individuals for existing social roles results from socialization. This chapter will examine the role of the social structure in the management of socialization.

Social Models ♦ The individuals who fill the various positions of a social structure may play their roles in different ways. It is, therefore, not enough to have them assigned to the positions of a given structure. They must also be instructed in the proper way to perform the accompanying roles. For this purpose, models of proper performance are established and individuals are urged to bring their conduct into compliance with these models. For example, the monogamous American family structure requires one woman to fill the role of wife-mother. There are, however, many different ways of performing this role. The woman may be submissive to her husband, authoritarian with her children, and limit her activities to homemaking and child care. On the other hand, she may act the dominant part, be permissive with her children, and engage in gainful employment outside the home. Ruth Shonle Cavan has shown that the American class structure establishes three major variants of the wife-mother model.[1] Other variants are associated with rural-urban, ethnic, institutional, and such other differences of the social structure.

It will be seen that a social role can be analyzed at two levels. At the first level it is conceptualized as an ideal-type. The behavior patterns that characterize various manifestations of the role and distinguish it from other roles are selected and assembled into a system of "typical" behavior. While this description fits all manifestations of the role, it does not portray any perfectly. In actual practice people tend to deviate more or less from the ideal-type. At this second level the role is a variant of the ideal-type. Some of these variants acquire validity for people and influence their behavior. Samuel Strong called these versions of the role "social types," and has analyzed their functions in the Negro community of Chicago.[2]

Management of Socialization ▶ Two aims of socialization are paramount in preparing individuals to perform social roles in approved ways. First, persons are encouraged or required to learn the knowledge and skills that constitute proper performance. At this level the aim is for overt conformity. Second, individuals are led to internalize a self-image consistent with the role model. Socialization at this level contributes to internal conformity.

Since all individuals are not assigned to the same positions in the social structure, they are expected to perform different roles. One aspect of preparations for proper performance is differential exposure to the various models. The role models to which an individual is likely to be exposed are consequently related to his position in the social structure. An individual in one position has ready access to certain models but finds others relatively inaccessible. The management of differential accessibility to role models is illustrated in the structure of industry. For example, in a factory, assembly workers have only limited access to the managerial models. Moreover, the industrial system disapproves of managers as the models of worker performance. The shop and the union hold up exemplary cases from the production line or the bargaining table as the proper models for workers.

The social structure establishes variants of the same general role. Socialization must therefore prepare the individual to perform in the way that is suitable to his position in the social structure. Guides are established to direct the individual toward the appropriate variant of the role model. For example, the authority of the middle-class husband-father is tempered by participation of wife and children in decision-making. The husband-father provides the family's main economic support, and his occupation determines its social status. He participates democratically in many family-centered activities and shares household duties, having full responsibility for certain ones. On the other hand, the lower-class husband-father exercises greater authority in decisions but has a smaller share in the family-centered activity and household duties. He may not be viewed as its major economic support, and his status-giving function is only vaguely defined. His sexual function is stressed, and he shares a private relationship with his wife from which the children are excluded. As they grow up, boys are directed to the variant of the role that is appropriate to their place in the social structure.

The meanings of social experience and the directives to action are embodied in the terms of the role models. Associated norms provide definitions and specifications of action that are sanctioned by the social structure. Alternative definitions and actions are discouraged by taboos and penalties. For example, in spite of legal changes, in many southern communities when it is time for the Negro mother to enter her six-year-old in school, she knows that the nearby white school may not accept her child. The racial structure defines the nearby school as unavailable and specifies that the child must attend the Negro school much farther away. The mother has learned the expected behavior associated with her place in the racial structure, and in time the child will learn the same patterns.

Finally, in time, the individual internalizes a self-image that is consistent with the social role he has learned. People have responded to him in terms of the role model that is compatible with his place in the social structure. Through socialization he learns to see himself as others see him, and so the internal and external dimensions of his role tend to become consistent. For example, when a man retires and becomes "categorically" old, he is assigned an ambiguous collateral position in the social structure. He is excluded from many useful activities and expected to play a role of helplessness, dependence, and social interference. Though many such persons rebel against this status and role, many others tend to learn the expected performance patterns and internalize the corresponding self-image.

Resocialization ❯ Socialization continues in an uneven course throughout the individual's lifetime. At various points he turns a corner, so to speak, and moves forward in a more or less altered direction. The child becomes an adolescent; the high-school graduate becomes a college student; young adults become spouses and parents; middle-aged persons become old people. These breaks in the process are called "discontinuities" and tend to vary significantly in their severity.[3]

If the discontinuity is fundamental and the individual is required to adjust to a new society or reorganize his personality, the ensuing process of learning is called "resocialization." The most obvious illustration is the Americanization of European immigrants. Resocialization is also illustrated in the experiences of plantation and Appalachian Mountain folk who migrate to northern industrial cities, and in the case of individuals who move up from the lower to the middle classes. An extreme instance is the practice of "brainwashing" or "thought control" as it has been conducted by some totalitarian regimes.

The process of resocialization involves at least three distinctive dimensions. First, a previously fully developed personality organization must be more or less completely liquidated. Second, the process of socialization is rationally managed with calculated use of relevant social structures. And third, learning progresses through a series of intermediate roles to a permanent pattern of personality organization.

Investigators have studied the process of resocialization in various structural settings. Much of the early research on assimilation of European immigrants is relevant to the discussion of resocialization. Recently Sanford M. Dornbusch studied the process as revealed in the experiences of cadets in the United States Military Academy.[4] Alan Gowman investigated the resocialization of the war blind in the American social structure.

In the following excerpt from Gowman's work, the process of resocialization is analyzed in sharp outline. Attention is directed to the liquidation of the former pattern of personality organization, to the control of experience by agents of the social structure, to the progression of the process through a series of intervening roles, and to the calculated use of various elements of the social structure.

Resocialization of the War Blind. The discussion will now shift to a consideration of how resocialization of the war blind is achieved in the ward setting. The reassimilation of the blind soldier into society may be analyzed as a three-stage process. The individual holds the successive positions of blinded soldier, blinded veteran, and blind man. Stages in orientation which represent the blinded individual's reintroduction to normal society can be best ordered in the framework elaborated by Parsons for the process of socialization and psychotherapy.[5] Like the child, the blinded individual is involved in an asymmetrical relationship which excludes the possibility of completely reciprocal interaction. This fundamental lack of equality has been phrased in terms of four components: support; permissiveness; denial of reciprocity; and manipulation of reward. They imply that the superior in the situation, the agent of society, exercises certain behavior mechanisms of a systematic nature when attempting to pull the immature or disordered individual into the major orbit of full societal functioning. He supports the dependent person and permits him to do things which would not be tolerated from an equal. As a price for these concessions, he rejects attempts to get the interaction on a symmetric basis, refusing to accord the other a full position by disengaging himself from straight-across-the-board relationships. In this atmosphere aggression will not be met by counteraggression, nor will inappropriate behavior be heavily condemned.

Finally, he manipulates rewards by withdrawing or manifesting his approval of the other's activities. The rewards are his to distribute and thus form the essential basis of his leverage as a teacher and agent of social control.

The role of blinded soldier is fulfilled primarily with the hospital ward as a stage. Here, the dramatic ebb and flow is centered in the process of socialization and little of the melodramatic can be found. In this insular environment the patient enjoys abundant support and permissiveness; his freedom is the more pronounced because it occurs in a military setting whose code is ordinarily the very obverse of individual idiosyncrasy. Oddities of dress, speech and other behavior are tolerated. Attendants are ever-present and aid the blinded soldier in countless ways, even to the extent of providing a variety of entertainments outside the ward. Additionally, the soldier periodically assumes the sick role following orthopedic, eye, or plastic surgery. These frequent respites woven into the re-education process allow for spasmodic release from the pressure exerted by orientation personnel. For mixed with this exaggerated license, described above, are the themes of manipulation, of reward and denial, of reciprocity. The protective shelter of the ward is double-edged. As it provides added increments of support, so it allows the application of control devices in a tightly-sealed system.

It is important to observe that the first step in successful reorientation of the blinded soldier is the collection of those so wounded into groups, where they have a common desirability and are isolated from other types of patients as well as from the larger society. The manipulation of reward, so essential to the maintenance of therapeutic leverage, might appear as cruelty in a less isolated context, so that special varieties of sanction could not be imposed. . . .

The blind individual at this stage does make random forays outside the ward as when he goes home on furlough or pass. It is something of a shock for him to return home, for there he finds a less structured system of expectations than those held by the ward personnel. The sanctions of the ward are no longer applied and he meets a liberality which constitutes, in effect, oversupport and overpermissiveness. He encounters too, a kind of overinteraction. At this early juncture, which takes place while the shooting war still excites the public, the blind soldier is almost by definition a hero. There is as yet no tendency to avoid him but rather to seek him out. Here civilian guilt flowers in the barroom as drinks are pressed on the blind person in a symbolic effort to redress what the sighted feel is an inequality of sacrifice.

When the blinded soldier is discharged from the hospital, he takes up the role of veteran. At first the situation is much like that just described. He still receives huge increments of support and permissiveness. However, as the postwar public euphoria levels off into a less frenzied mood, the blind veteran experiences a gradual withdrawal of support. Society's attitude becomes less guilty and less generous toward its defenders. Patterns of avoidance first appear and they connote an increasing use of social control. For the war blind, the full extent of the loss becomes slowly apparent.

At this point the blind veteran is classed with other veterans and takes part in the common period of postwar adjustment. There is a certain mutuality of relations between ex-soldiers, although in this case the blind have a degree of added leverage because of their obvious combat experience. No one can reasonably claim to have had a rougher war than theirs and a halo attaches itself to their words as the most real of veterans.

. . . The veteran stage is a level at which many blind fixate, trying to gain acceptance in a variety of historical roles which are defined by past events rather than present activities.

The final stage of resocialization is that in which the individual becomes a blind man. Shorn of the military referent, he merges with the total civilian blind population. The advantages in support and permissiveness are minimized, or may even become disadvantages for the blind individual who aspires to the main stream of American Society. In striving to conform to patterns of efforts and achievement the blind person must in fact renounce many of these gains because of the obligatory passivity involved in their acceptance. For if he desires the rights of mature role fulfillment, he must accept the correlative obligations of the role just as the sighted person does.[6]

Personality Integration and Strain ▶ The process of socialization is expected to produce personalities that are substantially integrated and consistent. Under such circumstances people appear to ,be adjusted, and social relations are harmonious. This is the intended consequence of socialization, and it is evident that it occurs in substantial measure. It is necessary to recognize, however, that in almost all situations socialization tends to build some elements of strain into personality systems.

Integration within a personality system can be revealed in terms of the harmony and consistency that are built into the behavior requirements of a major role. Ruth Shonle Cavan has analyzed the middle-class wife-mother role in a way to reveal basic integration. In the following short excerpt Cavan draws attention to the various behavioral requirements of this role and suggests how strains are managed.

The wife has a triple role: as wife and mother, as housekeeper, and as social arbiter. The maternal aspect of her interpersonal role tends to supersede the wifely aspect. . . . Only during the first few and childless years of marriage do husband and wife place the sexual and social phases of their own relationship above the demands and welfare of their children. . . .

The mother personally rears the children according to plans and standards of discipline and conduct agreed upon by husband and wife. Her personal care of the children creates a strong emotional bond to which the mother and children respond. In regions where inexpensive domestic help is lacking, she not only manages her home, but has designed and created it and it thus becomes an extension of her personality. She controls and manipulates the social activities and engagements of all members of the family with a view to preserving or enhancing family status. Her community activities in welfare and civic affairs, especially as her children grow up and leave her with free time, are extensive and provide her a great deal of satisfaction.[7]

Internal harmony in the mother role just described is achieved in part by balancing the various behavior demands, in part by a shift of emphasis with the passage of time. Socialization is also expected to produce consistency between the behavior tendencies of the personality system and the behavior expectations of the social system. In the following brief description of socialization in Hopi society, Kimball Young shows how this end is accomplished. He recognizes also that some elements of strain tend to become built into the system.

> The economic system is cooperative, and there is very little striving for individual success along economic lines. There is no system of social class, but some clans have more prestige than others. Any attempt on the part of an individual to gain wealth or power over his neighbor arouses suspicion. As a matter of fact, such striving is normally regarded as due to witchcraft and is highly disapproved. Conformity rather than social differentiation along class lines is highly emphasized among the Hopi.

> It would be a mistake . . . to assume that the Hopi show no hostility or aggression. On the domestic front, one of the means of social control is malicious gossip, especially concerning sexual deviations from the norm. Since women are in control of the household, if the wife gets tired of her husband she puts his personal things outside the Pueblo, indicating that she does not want him any more. He has to leave. Also there is much political intrigue. . . .[8]

Personality strain, like personality integration, is a consequence of socialization under most structural conditions. Some roles have elements of strain built into the contradictions of their behavior requirements. For example, the role of mother expects that a woman will be sympathetic, supportive, and loving with her children. At the same time, though, as mother she must exercise control, impose discipline, and occasionally administer punishment. The middle-class mother manages to reduce the strain in her role by being permissive with her children, avoiding physical punishments, and applying controls in a cooperative and constructive manner. However, in some instances it is impossible to eliminate or even significantly to reduce the strain that is built into a role. For example, the policeman who is a pal to the neighborhood boys is nevertheless required to enforce the law when one of them has committed a violation. The professor who develops friendly relations with his students still has to evaluate their work and sometimes make judgments that may be damaging.

Some strain issues from the inconsistency of behavior tendencies and behavior expectations. In one situation an individual may internalize a role that is inappropriate to his social position. When the individual's reference groups differ from his membership groups, he may learn inappropriate or conflicting social roles. Having learned a role in one situation, an individual may later find himself in another situation where the behavior demands of the role are inconsistent with prevailing behavior expectations.

In the following material Max Oppenheimer analyzes the strains that have been built into the role of the Soviet Man. In addition he draws attention to the compensations that are used to meet this dilemma and to some of the consequences of the total situation for mental health in the Soviet Union.

This spiritual dualism of the Soviet Man is revealed in the conventional outward acceptance of Soviet myths and their simultaneous inner negation with a resultant secret hatred of the Soviet order of things. He adjusts psychologically to this dualism by becoming either a cynic, an opportunist, or (in the opinion of some) just plain used to it. If he cannot adjust, he will become traumatized.

The Soviet Man lives inwardly in spiritual solitude, deprived of advisors, teachers, traditions. He consequently feels unstable, insecure, and has no control over his fate. Experience in the shifting Soviet scene is of little avail and every new problem requires a new decision, one that each man makes at his own risk.

Fear is a constituent element of the Soviet Man's psychology. This ever-present fear breeds incurable traumatic neuroses among all Soviet people. In as much as these neuroses must remain repressed in the subconscious of the Soviet Man, they increase the traumatic condition to the point of spiritual and mental diseases.

The Soviet Man suffers mainly from inability to assert or realize his "self," to satisfy his craving for personal dignity. He must constantly submit to degradations and can never divulge his inner feelings. The yearning for self-realization, which in other societies represents the normal sublimation of creative drives, is constantly suppressed or compelled to seek unsatisfactory compensations in the Soviet Man. There exists a constant conflict between what the man might consider a creative achievement or a morally worthy deed, and compliance with government orders, acquisitions, medals, prizes, recognition by the Party. The Soviet Man's personal dignity suffers from constant humiliation and he soon develops true or imaginary inferiority complexes.

Deep within himself this outwardly compliant individual harbors suppressed "dangerous" yearnings, labeled by the regime as survivals of capitalism. Such unpleasant psychological characteristics may erupt if the individual were to gain his freedom. The Soviet Man's conduct is consequently not determined by genuine principles, but by pseudo principles that are invented to justify his conduct. He develops a certain skill to operate, to fit the principle to the occasion.

The evident layer of the Soviet Man's consciousness comprises (1) thoughts concerned with trivial details of everyday life, e.g., worries over mere existence, job, fulfilment of norms, dominated by fear of reprisals, (2) constant awareness that he must unceasingly demonstrate and proclaim the correct and required attitude toward the regime and (3) the necessary rationalization enabling him to maintain this attitude. The Soviet Man's psychology may therefore be defined as willful self deception. The pseudo-consciousness is a sort of psychological superstructure peculiar to the Soviet Man, and comprised of the aggregate of all thoughts, feelings, viewpoints, tastes, and convictions considered by the regime as indispensable and sufficient. Ideally, the government would like to limit the inner world of the Soviet Man to his pseudo-consciousness.

By reference to the degree of internalization of Party ideology and norms, it can be said that every Soviet Man falls into one of three psychological types. (1) The average Soviet Man, (2) the active supporter of the regime, and (3) the "inner emigrant." The average Soviet Man typifies the spiritual dualism: on the one side the repression of his entire genuine spiritual life; on the other, his false life which exists only for show in the regime. The active supporter of the regime presents similar characteristics, but unlike the average Soviet Man, he actively supports the regime. The "inner emigrants" have accepted and internalized Soviet doctrine and norms. These mechanical citizens of the USSR are alone free from pseudo-consciousness, for internal and overt behavior is consistent.

Living conditions in the USSR and the Bolshevist theory have given the Soviet Man a bent toward practicality. His thinking has become rationalizing, expedient, and directed toward the specific end of achieving concrete temporary goals, thus contributing to a further narrowing of his consciousness. According to this manner of thinking, ideology is no longer concerned with truth, but becomes a weapon in the class struggle and only the criteria of practicality now prevail.[9]

Integration and strain are the polar concepts of an organizational continuum along which actual personality systems can be located. That is, every personality has elements of harmony and inconsistency built into its structures through socialization. However, in all social systems the individual has access to social and psychological mechanisms to minimize or at least to manage the impact of personality strain. For example, the middle-class wife-mother can separate contradictory demands of her role by compartmentalizing them or by putting them into a time sequence, and circumstances permit her to compensate for some frustrations and limitations. Hopi culture provided institutionalized outlets for hostility and aggression in a social system that discouraged competition, striving, and self-advancement. Although some severe strains were built into the role of the Soviet Man, nevertheless the system provided some mitigating compensations, rationalizations, and escapes.

OCCUPATIONAL STRUCTURE AND SOCIALIZATION

It may prove useful to examine the socialization process in some detail within the context of one sector of the social structure. For this purpose the occupational structure has been selected. The aim of this analysis is to reveal how the social structure is employed to prepare individuals for the roles and statuses to which they have been assigned in the world of work.

Some Popular Types ♦ The pageantry of American history and current life is animated by characters who typify various occupations. The reader will have little difficulty naming some of these characters. For many Americans the "Old West" survives in the daring and exciting exploits of the frontiersman, the prospector, the cattle man, and the cowboy. The plains and valleys throbbed and echoed to the endless struggle between the lawman and the outlaw. The turbulent, uproarious Westerners stood quiet, awkward, and reverent before the sky pilot or bellowed in adolescent glee at the misfortunes of the tenderfoot. These and other phrases capture, characterize, and distinguish the occupational types of an epoch of American history.

The modern city has its occupational types. Some are neatly tagged and distinguished by a descriptive cliché. The preacher and professor are familiar denizens of modern urban Americana. Often their manner or garb sets them apart. Their characteristics have been caricatured in cartoon and wisecrack. In the kaleidoscope of the American city they rub shoulders with the businessman, the factory worker, and the store clerk. There is Sinclair Lewis' "Babbitt" and the overalls-clad, lunch-pail-toting figure in the stock edition cartoon. And there are others—the promoter, the salesman, the politician, the scientist, the actor, and so on without end. The city also has its off-color occupational types. These are the characters whose occupations—or lack of occupation—deviate from the social norms. Among these are the hobo, the pan-handler, the racketeer, and the gangster.

The modern city has its female types as well. Some are traditional, like the teacher, the nurse, the secretary, and the social worker. Some traditional types are associated with industry and business. Women have long worked in textile mills, garment factories, and department stores. But with changes in the economic system and the occupational structure, women are entering many new jobs and vocations. Women are taking their place in substantial numbers in the professions, management, and the executive ranks of business and industry.

Perspectives on Occupational Socialization ▶ Occupations like those mentioned above and many others result from the division of labor through which major societal functions are subdivided into tasks that can be performed by individuals. In time, preferred ways of performance are culturally patterned and socially sanctioned. The occupations related to a given social function tend to become arranged and integrated to form an occupational structure. Occupational structure is illustrated by the hierarchy of systems of job titles to be found in a factory, a university, a hospital, the army, or a railroad.

Provisions must be made to recruit and prepare individuals to perform the tasks, or occupational roles, in each occupational structure. As shown earlier, recruitment is accomplished by the processes of ascription and achievement. For example, a monarch inherits his throne and the son of an upper-class family may automatically enter an executive position in the family business. In caste systems, virtually all occupational roles are filled by ascription. In open-class systems, however, most occupational roles are filled by achievement.

The nature and content of occupational socialization may be revealed from several perspectives. One is contained in the occupational role model and its inculcation. Regarding the character of occupational models, Phillip J. Allen writes: "Roles adopted may be found already tailored and may be put on as a ready-made suit (such as the more familiar institutional roles of policeman, U.S. Army Officer, clergy-man, judge, and physician whose expected behavior is clearly specified), or they may be personally tailored by one for his own individual use."[10] The socialization of individuals to perform institutionalized occupational roles is managed by such familiar institutional activities as vocational and professional education, indoctrination, apprenticeship, basic training, and on-the-job training.

The occupational role model may be illustrated in various ways. In a dictionary of occupational titles the technical and operational functions of jobs are summarized. The job description or job analysis specifies the rights, obligations, and technical skills of an occupational role as defined and sanctioned by the employing business or agency. Such a role portrait is likely also to include some of the social and non-technical institutional aspects of the occupation. The following description of a professional job in the Young Women's Christian Association illustrates this perspective on occupational socialization. In this description the technical and operational dimensions of the role are heavily overlaid with the philosophical sanctions of the institution.

A Job Description. I. A Statement on Professional Responsibility in the YWCA:

The professional worker in the YWCA has the responsibility of using her professional skills in the areas of work assigned to assist the Association to move forward in the accomplishing of its goals. The focus of all jobs is on people, for the YWCA is people and its job is working with people. This means persons of all ages, races, creeds, economic and social experience, for the YWCA tries to draw into its membership all kinds of people. It means working with members in a variety of relationships—as program participants, volunteer leaders of groups, as board and committee volunteers, and as fellow employed workers doing a variety of professional, clerical, house-keeping and maintenance jobs. The objectives of the Association are the outgrowth of faith in God, acceptance of all people as the children of God, and dedication to the building of a society where justice, goodwill, and freedom are the prevailing forces.

II. Title of Position: Adult Activities Program Director
To Whom Directly Responsible: Executive Director

III. Objectives For Job As Jointly Determined By Staff And Responsible Administrative Committee:

Long Range
a. To develop a program for young adults 18-35 years, which includes creative leisure-time activities, growth in citizenship responsibility, leadership development, thinking and action on social and economic problems.
b. To offer clubs and educational classes to adults.
Immediate
Surveying the present program of adult activities to determine direction of work for young adults and adults.
Restore adult classes.
Outline policies which will lead to more self direction for adult clubs.

IV. Areas Of Responsibility

A. Services to groups and individuals in groups
Give priority to program for young adults including clubs, and informal program through direct leadership and assistance of volunteers: offer clubs, classes, and interest groups for all ages with the aid of paid and/or volunteer help.

B. Services to Individuals outside the groups
Arrange for registration and interviews.
Plan for individual conferences and for referral if necessary.

C. Administrative Services
1. General: Serves as executive officer of the Adult Activities and Adult Education Committee.
Works with these to
    discover needs of group to be served.
    develop program for young adults and adults in line with available resources.
Plans with the chairman the agendas for committee meetings; makes necessary arrangements, attends and participates in discussion.
Sees that program is interpreted to the board, the total Association and the community.
Prepares and administers a budget with the help of the committee for the department in consultation with executive director.
Advises clubs and other groups in management of funds. Responsible for recording and reporting program.

2. Leadership: Recruits and develops adult leadership needed for program.
Works with chairman and executive director on recruiting committee members, assigning responsibilities and orienting new ones.
Recruits, trains and supervises program volunteers. Supervises paid program assistants. Sees that all leaders have opportunity for participation in total Association's work.
Develops leadership among participants by working in an advisory capacity with group officers, councils, committees and conference groups.
Insures that groups assume membership responsibilities, recruiting from them for participation in state, regional and national YWCA conferences.

D. Intra-Inter Association Responsibilities:
Responsible for integrating programs with the total Association program.
Participates in total Association planning.
Carries assigned responsibility for some all-Association programs or events.
Serves as a resource in the "Y" in area of specialization.
Consults with supervisor regularly on plans, methods, and evaluation of work.
Attends and serves on area, regional and national committees and conferences.

E Community Relationships
Works with other social agencies in referral of participants.
Responsible for YW interpretation to community through speeches and visitation to churches, etc.
Maintains contact with other outside groups which will have value for the YWCA and assigned program.

F. Professional Development
1. Scheduled conferences with supervisor.

2. Reading Association magazines and other available books and pamphlets.
3. Adjusting of work plans to allow study of three courses at neighboring college during first semester.[11]

Socialization for occupational roles may also be viewed in terms of typical consequences for classes of individuals. Analysis from this perspective focuses on the social type that is identified with certain kinds or classes of social occupations. The absent-minded professor, the school marm, and the long-hair artist illustrate such types. The classic empirical examples are the so-called "bureaucratic personality" and the "organization man." The following sketch of the bureaucratic personality stresses the consequences of occupational socialization.

The Bureaucratic Personality. The bureaucratic functionary is a product of modern complex, formal, and impersonal governmental and economic structure. William H. Whyte, Jr., writes: "The corporation man is the most conspicuous example, but he is not the only one, for the collectivization so visible in the corporation has affected almost every field of work. Blood brother to the business trainee off to join Dupont is the seminary student who will end up in the church hierarchy, the doctor headed for the corporate clinic, the physics Ph.D. in a government laboratory, the intellectual on the foundation-sponsored team project, the engineering graduate in the huge drafting room at Lockheed, the young apprentice in a Wall Street law factory."

The bureaucratic man is eminently practical, methodical, prudent, punctual, and disciplined in his job. He is concerned with day-by-day execution of orders, rules, and institutional regulations. He is unhappy and uncertain when he must make his own decisions and abhors the idea of responsibility involving the risk of failure.

The bureaucratic man prefers the power emanating from control of others within the narrow formal framework of office routine, inspection, or supervision. He is supported by strong sentiments which entail devotion to duty, a keen sense of the limitation of his authority and competence, and methodical performance of routine activities. He is likely to lack imagination and initiative and operates within the structure of institutional knowledge, skills, and authority.

Being timid, the bureaucratic man is motivated in his loyalty and actions by the desire for personal security. The routine technical functionary of business, of government, he wants none of the risks of business venture or political campaigning and election. He prefers a fixed tenure or civil-service security, a set of simple direct rules and a steady fixed salary and a regular system of promotions and retirement.[12]

Another perspective of occupational socialization is revealed in the process of internalizing the work role. Attention is directed to the self-system and self-consciousness as they reflect and support the scheme of external performance. The general occupational role is revealed as adapted to the unique characteristics of the individual. The following excerpt portrays some of the internal manifestations of the occupational role and suggests that "split personality" of a limited kind is one consequence of socialization.

> . . . The employees of the Stuyvesant understood rich clients and knew all the pains and drawbacks of being rich, although they were not rich men themselves. They had to deal familiarly, almost jovially, but always scrupulously with large sums of money, while living usually on modest salaries.

> If you were successful at the Stuyvesant you ended by developing a priestly, untouchable, ascetic attitude. You learned to think of your own financial life and your own problems as something apart from those other financial complications. If you did well enough to become an executive in the Stuyvesant, and this required a long time and an arduous apprenticeship, you found yourself solving the problems of individuals who had difficulty living within incomes approaching a hundred thousand dollars a year. You found yourself spending the working day discussing the investment of huge sums of money, only to get home yourself and to worry because the butcher's bill had risen some twenty dollars above the previous one. You had to debate the purchase or the sale of controls in business enterprises and then return home yourself to decide whether or not you could afford to buy a motor lawn mower, or a ready-made or a tailor-made suit. In time this gave you a split personality since you had to toss your own problems completely aside and never allow them to mingle in any way with those of clients and depositors when you reached your desk at the Stuyvesant. At your desk you had to be a friend and confidant, as professional as a doctor or a lawyer, ready with an intelligent perspective for almost anything. Anthony Burton had once said that this attitude was one's responsibility toward society. Though personally Charles had never felt like a social worker, he felt this responsibility. He was already forgetting Nancy and the children, already assuming his business character, when he said good morning to Gus, the doorman on the sidewalk outside the Stuyvesant.[13]

Management of Occupational Socialization ♦ The management of occupational socialization is institutionalized within the social structure. In the case of the self-conscious professions, socialization is organized as formal study in graduate professional schools. With the clerical occupations and some semi-professional pursuits, it is handled in the trade school or business college. In the trades, where theory and practice cannot be clearly dissociated, apprenticeship is perhaps less formal, though equally as controlled. With mass production, the assembly line, and the simplification of factory jobs, occupational socialization has been organized as on-the-job training or in-service and refresher education. Many variations of these and other basic patterns have evolved as the national economy and occupational structures have changed. It is possible to analyze the management of occupational socialization in terms of four aspects or dimensions.

First, the individual must be taught the appropriate skills of the occupation. These include a vast range of manual, intellectual, and social operations. For example, the brick mason must learn to handle such tools and materials as trowel, level, mortar, and bricks. A lawyer, however, has to be schooled to manipulate legal documents and court procedures. Some skills are related to proper and efficient behavior in the setting of the occupation. The assembly worker, for instance, must learn the decorum of the factory—how to punch in and out on the time clock, how to comply with orders of the foreman, and how to use the canteen and the first-aid station. A medical student, on the other hand, has to familiarize himself with the etiquette of the hospital, the doctor's office, and the patient's bedside.

Still other technical skills control and pattern the worker's relations with members of the occupational hierarchy. The factory worker's world includes such representatives of authority as the foreman, the union steward, the personnel representative, and the time and motion expert. These skills constitute a portion of what John S. Ellsworth, Jr., has called "factory folkways."[14] The young lawyer needs to learn to control or cope with senior partners, clients, judges, witnesses, police officers, and so on.

In the second place, the worker must be schooled in the appropriate manner and bearing of the occupation. He becomes familiar with the correct clothing and the proper way to wear it. For example, bellhops, streetcar conductors, baseball players, waitresses, nurses, and musicians regularly wear some type of uniform. For farmers, factory workers, and coal miners another type of dress is customary. The minister or priest is often distinguished by special garb, and the "business suit" has been named from its regular use by business and professional men.

Consciously and unconsciously, socialization in an occupation schools the worker in the appropriate manner and bearing. Often an individual's occupation can be inferred by observing his manner of speaking, walking, and conducting himself in public. This is frequently true of such pursuits as minister, factory worker, physician, business executive, and college professor. Sometimes appropriate manners and bearing are consciously inculcated as part of technical training. Often, however, the worker acquires the appropriate habits, attitudes, and sentiments through long and intimate association with mature fellow workers.

The following list of traits illustrates the characteristics that are said to distinguish a "good secretary." Such lists are used as teaching aids in business colleges and secretarial schools and are held constantly before secretaries on the job. Occupational skills, like shorthand, typing, filing, and handling mail, are basic and indispensable. Stress is also laid upon the skill of the secretary in complementing and adjusting to the responsibilities and habits of her employer. The list also includes general personality traits like the following.

Knows the value of self-appraisal. She can be objective about her work.

Knows how to accept praise and blame.

Is pleasant to all her co-workers.

Realizes the value of an attractive appearance. Knows that her crisp, white collar and just-shined shoes give her a well-groomed look.

Is alert, adaptable, and poised. Accustoms herself to all sorts of variations in dictation. She can meet the situation, whatever it may be. Is ready for changes her boss may make in his dictation.

Doesn't talk about her boss's idiosyncrasies.

Takes the initiative in appropriate situations, such as securing help, attacking all work assigned to her, following through on assignments, and the like.

Arrives at work a few minutes ahead of her boss.

Is a good secretarial housekeeper—keeps her desk straight, maintains the boss's desk in order, cleans and covers her typewriter before leaving at night.[15]

Third, occupational socialization promotes inculcation of relevant ideas and information. Some technical knowledge and information take the form of complicated theory or occupational ideologies. Legal theories, social work concepts, and engineering formulae are cases in point. The communication of such technical information constitutes a substantial part of technical training in professional schools.

Some occupational ideas are less theoretical. They are, however, nonetheless impressive in quantity and basic to performance. For example, an electrician may know little of the theory of electricity that constitutes an important portion of the knowledge of a physicist. The electrician, however, will exhibit a great fund of accurate and practical knowledge about its properties and behavior. Or again, a barber may be trained regarding the structures and functions of the human body. His apprenticeship, however, is not likely to include the study of biological theory.

Much of the special knowledge of each occupation is contained in a specialized vocabulary. Transmission of the occupational jargon constitutes an essential part of socialization. For example, a plumber must learn to communicate about Stillson wrenches, couplings, elbow joints, and valves. The divinity student's training will familiarize him with such terms as exigesis, the Moffett version, and the Immaculate Conception. Latin phrases constitute a large and impressive part of the special technical vocabularies of physicians and lawyers. A good deal has been said about the special argot of criminals, delinquents, and the so-called "beat generation."

Finally, socialization internalizes in the worker the appropriate sense of self-consciousness and self-image. These internal role segments are contained within the occupation-wide attitudes regarding self and others. High self-esteem and awareness of social responsibility, accompanied by carefully defined occupational rights and duties, are basic to the code of ethics in most professions. The young practitioner internalizes this profession-wide conception of self as the core of his professional role. In some professions the ethical codes and conceptions of the professional man have been detailed in lists of written specifications.

Occupational self-consciousness is less fully and formally developed in many occupational fields. Training places less stress on the transmission and fostering of occupationally oriented, self-conscious attitudes. This is evident in the case of those persons who work in factories with machines or are engaged in agricultural or service occupations. The growth of a vigorous, self-conscious trade union movement seems to be modifying this phase of occupational socialization. It now seems clear that the objective of American trade unions is the development and inculcation of self-consciousness and self-esteem among the so-called working classes. At present such developments are less specifically associated with particular occupations than is the case with the professions. Instead, it takes the form of a working-class development.

Many years are required to develop a mature occupational personality. This fact is illustrated in the following case. The decisive occupational models became influential even as early as high school. In high school, college, and graduate school the technical skills of the profession were acquired and refined. An occupational self-image was fashioned and supported by strong awareness of the professional generalized other. A work role has been organized and stabilized that conditions virtually every aspect of the man's total way of living.

The Research Chemist. . . . Baker's family had no specific goals for him. . . . Consequently, it was not surprising that the stimulation and the models for a career should come from sources outside the home—historical and fictional figures or real figures.

Baker says he always had a great deal of curiosity. . . . [O]ur subject read constantly—even the encyclopedia. As a result of this reading, he idolized two figures—Pasteur and Robinson Crusoe. Pasteur impressed him with his discoveries and versatility and in Robinson Crusoe he envied the solitude, lack of competition, and freedom. As he says: ". . . He didn't have to compete, he could be absolutely free and he could do whatever he wanted to do." A scientific research career would fulfill most of these conditions. He could avoid people in turning to his work and he avoided the anxieties of interpersonal competition by pitting himself against inanimate objects.

Those heroes were supplemented by more realistic models—professional men who took an interest in him and who aided and abetted him in his work and professional career. It was during high school that his professional interests began to take shape. The first significant figure in this regard was a pharmacist for whom he worked after school hours and who permitted Baker to watch him while he worked. At the same time he would play with a friend's chemistry kit, since his friend was not interested in it. Another outlet for his curiosity was the opportunity provided him by a biology teacher who lived close by and who permitted him to use his laboratory at home under supervision.

In college he again benefited from the guidance of a superior male. In one of his laboratory classes his bench was close to the front of the room where he came under the constant observation of his instructor. "He would come dashing over every few minutes and tell me what I was doing wrong. He was very exacting." It was this instructor who also suggested what specific branch of chemistry Baker should select for his career. . . .

Baker got a good deal of satisfaction out of his work in science. It gave him a sense of accomplishment, a means of gaining the approval of others, and an outlet for his curiosity. As he says, "It was actually showing my findings off to somebody else, showing I could do something and also discovering new things."

Baker had only one other real job experience before his present position. This was during his college days when he took on a part-time job in order to help support himself. His primary source of satisfaction in life is his job. He does not like unstructured situations and his field is "nice and exacting. It's clean-cut and when things happen it's right there. You don't have to dilly-dally around them." But there are other sources of personal satisfaction from his work. His profession sets him off from others and provides him with a good deal of prestige. He says, "I get some satisfaction in that chemists are quite rare. I mean there aren't too many chemists like there are butchers and bakers and what not." . . . He gains respect from others because of his accomplishments; so, too, does he gain respect from identifying with his profession which he evaluates highly. He holds scientists in very high regard. For him they are "the only saviors in the world at the present time. I believe they'll either make or break the world." The "theoretical" value is his highest in the values test.

He regards himself as a free agent on the job and in so doing it is obvious that he has realized his early fantasy of becoming a Robinson Crusoe. Not only that but he has also found himself a man Friday. He has one assistant who "does what I tell him without asking too many details, but yet he knows enough to go ahead when he knows he's right. . . ."[16]

Occupational Roles and Social Structure ♦ Occupational roles establish functional links between the individual and most sectors of the social structure. At the level of informal relations an individual's job provides the occasion of many friendships and small-group activities. Acquaintanceships based on similar work, common interests, and consciousness of kind extend beyond the factory or office and the trade union or trade association. Moreover, individuals with similar occupations tend to live in the same or similar neighborhoods, a condition that facilitates informal, off-the-job relationships.

An individual is thus likely to find that most of his close friends are fellow workers in his factory or office. For example, the fellows in Department 88 may go bowling together each Thursday night, or after union meetings each month a gang of good fellows stops off at Joe's place for a friendly beer. Friendships established in the factory tend to involve families who visit, picnic together, or belong to the same religious and social organizations. William F. Cottrell has shown how the rigid and meticulous time patterning of the railroader tends to influence relations in his family and neighborhood, and William

H. Whyte, Jr., has demonstrated that the managerial occupations of men react upon the personality organizations and social activities of their wives.[17]

In Figure 13-1 the relationships between occupational roles and social structure are indicated schematically. The worker, depicted by the central figure, may fill any of a series of occupational roles suggested by the titles in the inner circle. Each of these occupational roles will link him with the appropriate groups and institutions indicated by the titles in the outer circle.

Linkages of Occupational Roles with Elements of Social Structure

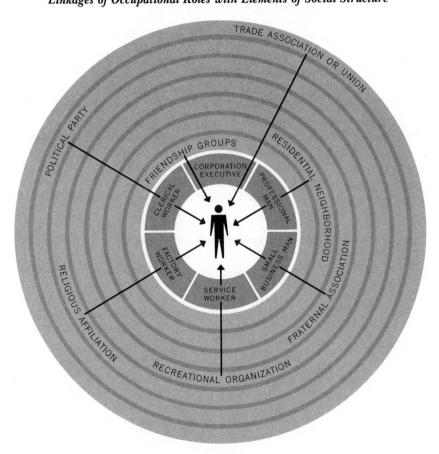

FIGURE 13-1

Many white-collar occupations permit or require contacts far beyond the confines of the office. Such workers therefore have a wide latitude for the formation of occupation-based friendships. Yet it will usually be found that the fellows who regularly play golf, eat lunch, or "roar" together at Lions Club meetings are engaged in similar types of occupations. As with factory workers, these friendships are likely to involve families in a wide range of friendship and social activities.

Occupational roles form the basis for many voluntary relationships and organization memberships. Among the more familiar organized occupational groups are the learned and professional societies, the trade and business associations, the trade unions, and the agricultural associations. Through such groups the individual has one important tie into the general social structure and gains, maintains, or loses statuses in his occupational world. Experiences in these organizations, moreover, tend to reinforce and extend personality patterning as institutionalized in basic job training and experiences. The struggle for recognition, leadership, and control in the occupational structure tends to support and reward those traits otherwise esteemed.

A professional man's income may be determined by his reputation in the community, but he is likely to prize his status and esteem among fellow practitioners more highly than community reputation. A worker's reputation as brick mason, riveter, or cement finisher has greatest importance within the construction industry and the building trades. A .403 batting average or a 2.17 earned-run average are indexes of occupational status among baseball players, league owners, and ardent fans. In a study of the public school superintendency, Ward S. Mason and Neal Gross stressed "function" as the major determinant of intra-professional prestige. They formulated the following working hypothesis for the investigation.

> . . . the prestige of one specific position will be higher than that of another to the extent that the position allows the incumbent to make a larger contribution to the "function." In general terms the function of formal public education is to socialize children in certain aspects of the culture. . . .[18]

The occupational role constitutes one main bond of the individual with the structure of large-scale organizations. In this way he is related to the significant functions of the organization and achieves a place in its status hierarchy and power structure. The organizational dimensions of the occupational role, however, extend far beyond the limits of the job. The organization constitutes a way of life and produces an occupational-based social type that William H. Whyte, Jr., has called the "organization man." Referring to the fundamental commitment of such white-collar workers to the organizational world, Whyte writes as follows.

> . . . They are the ones of our middle class who have left home, spiritually as well as physically, to take the vows of organization life, and it is they who are the mind and soul of our great self-perpetuating institutions.[19]

Finally, the nature and prestige rating of occupations helps to place individuals in the social class structure. The occupational role is extended into styles of life, value orientations, and social identifications. Such characteristics are integrated within the occupational complex to form a general class role. The resultant occupation-based role places the individual, and all those who depend on him for status, in a broad network of mutually recognized prestige, privilege, and relationships. This fact is illustrated by the conduct and contacts of a business or professional man in plane or pullman car en route to a convention. He might strike up an acquaintance with another business or professional man in the dining car and join a group of fellow spirits later for a cigar and a drink in the club car. While in the convention city he might attend the weekly meeting of Rotary International, join some newly made friends in a golf foursome, or go out with a group of recent acquaintances for dinner.

SOCIAL STRUCTURE AND DEVIANT BEHAVIOR

Nature of Deviance ♦ The amount of agreement between actual behavior and the standards of expected behavior is a variable that forms a continuum with social conformity as one extreme and social deviance as the other. Actual behavior falls somewhere on the continuum and reveals varying combinations of conformity and deviance. Variations of the amount of conformity and deviance present in the fabric of social behavior are of significance in sociological study, since the persistence of a social system requires that the elements of conformity exceed the elements of deviation.[20]

The deviant behavior of an individual or a subsystem may be classified along two dimensions in terms of its functional significance for an inclusive social system. Along one dimension it may be called adventitious or systematic in terms of degree of persistence and pattern. Along another, it may be classified as tolerated or nontolerated in terms of the collective estimate of its threat for the well-being of the system. Systematic and nontolerated social deviations are dysfunctional and are significant for sociological analysis.

Adventitious deviant acts occur as variants in an ordinary pattern of conformist behavior. They result from oversight, accident, ignorance, negligence, or the like. Such acts may never—or at least only seldom—be repeated. For example, a student of regular habits oversleeps and so misses an examination. Or again, a conscientious tax payer misrepresents his income tax return because he has made an error in arithmetic. When packing to return home at the close of school, a young man accidentally tosses his draft card into the rubbish container and it gets burned. Each of these is an adventitious act. Although all may have serious consequences for the actors, they have little sociological significance since they have only negligible consequences for the social system.

Systematic deviant acts are elements in a pattern of deviance. The individual or the group regularly behaves in a deviant manner. The deviance may not be intended, but recurs as part of a regular pattern of behavior. For example, parents are expected by legal and customary norms to send their children to school. However, the members of some religious sects refuse to comply with this norm because they are bound by overriding contradictory norms. The community is inclined to react vigorously against this type of deviant behavior, and some of these cases have become celebrated legal and judicial actions. Moreover, this type of deviance is sociologically significant because it has dysfunctional consequences for the inclusive social system. Such categoric violations of cultural standards are defined as social problems and set in motion remedial processes of social planning and action.

Social norms establish tolerated margins of deviation around the ideal standard. That is, the norms themselves recognize and permit limited digressions from the required pattern. For example, the norm of universal compulsory school attendance permits children to be taught at home (instead of at school) by parents or tutors, to be withdrawn from school for foreign travel, to remain at home when ill (sometimes for prolonged periods), to leave school to go to work with official sanction, and so on. Tolerated deviations enable the norm to accommodate to individual differences and to variability of social situations.

However, deviations beyond the limits of social tolerance tend to invoke the associated social sanctions. Deviations of this extent are socially significant for the community since they represent, or are considered to represent, threats to the general welfare. Because such deviations have important consequences for the social system, they are of sociological significance. Sociological study thus is interested in systematic nontolerated behavior.

In addition to having dysfunctional consequences for the social system, many types of deviant behavior are evaluated as socially undesirable. As such, they are regarded as social problems and constitute the objects of remedial planning and action. Some of the common illustrations are physical and mental illness, crime and delinquency, family disorganization and illegitimacy, racial and labor-management conflict, prostitution and drug addiction, and alcoholism and sexual deviation. The study of these types of deviant behavior as social problems constitutes an important area of sociological analysis.

Sources of Deviant Behavior ◗ Four sources of deviant behavior can be identified and examined. They include physical and psychological abnormalities, cultural pluralism, defective socialization, and adaptations to social frustrations. The term physical and psychological abnormality refers to those bodily and mental conditions that prevent individuals from performing social roles in the expected manner. This category would include persons with serious hereditary or congenital deformities, organic or structural disabilities, and mental defects and deficiency. For example, because of his position in the sex-age structure, a mentally defective man would ordinarily be expected to have a remunerative job and perform a productive occupation. However, his mental defect prevents his filling the position and performing the duties of an adult worker in the occupational structure. He may be able to perform a simple activity such as is usually reserved for children, or he may be excluded from the work force altogether. The study of the physical and psychological abnormalities that produce such behavior deviance lies outside the field of sociology. However, sociology is concerned with the behavior as an instance of systematic deviance. From this perspective it is possible to gain some insights into the behavioral requirements of social roles and the interactional content of the social system.

Much deviant behavior is a consequence of cultural pluralism. Behavior that is conformist within one culture system may be seen as deviant in terms of the criteria of another system. In complex, unstable social systems the phenomenon of cultural pluralism is a commonplace. What is at issue here is not a distortion or maladaptation of learned behavior, but rather the variability of moral criteria. An individual may have been socialized to the role expectations of his subgroup and subculture. Within this subgroup his behavior conforms to prevailing social expectations. It is only when his social acts are judged by the moral standards of the larger community that they are regarded as deviant.

Deviant behavior based on cultural pluralism is illustrated in the case of persons who migrate from one social milieu to another. For example, behavior that was appropriate in Puerto Rico or Mexico, in the Southern Appalachian Mountains or on a Georgia cotton farm, may be very much out of place in New York, Cleveland, or Los Angeles. Juvenile delinquency presents another example of deviant behavior that results from the plurality of normative standards. In the delinquency area and among his peers, the delinquent's behavior tends to conform to the relevant cultural norms. In terms of the criteria of the larger community, however, his behavior is deviant and unacceptable.

A third source of deviant behavior is defective socialization. That is, the socialization process has failed in some way to produce behavior tendencies in the individual that correspond with the behavior expectations of his social roles. The source of deviation inheres in the socialization process, not in the variability of moral standards nor in any physical or psychological abnormality. Three types of defective socialization can be identified.

From one perspective, socialization can be said to be defective when within his structural situation an individual is unable to learn the patterns that are expected of him. Though the models are relevant and approved, they are in some measure inaccessible. What the individual learns is only part of the expected behavior. He therefore is unable to fulfill some of the decisive expectations of the roles.

Deviance resulting from defective socialization is dramatic in the situation of children who have been cut off from contacts with others. Kingsley Davis studied the case of extreme isolation of a little girl and reported on the nature and extent of socially induced deviance.[21] When the girl was discovered, after some years of isolation, she could perform few of the behavior patterns normally expected of a child her age. The concept of "cultural deprivation" designates a similar, though less severe, type of deviance that results from defective socialization.[22] At home, in the neighborhood, at school, and elsewhere the deprived individuals have been more or less isolated from the models of expected social behavior. When tested by later experience, they are unable to perform the behavior that is expected of persons their age and in their situations. The deviation is described as ignorance of the norms of social intercourse, actual or functional illiteracy, lack of manual or mental skill, limitation of general information, and the like.

Defective socialization also refers to failure to perceive and learn all phases of the model. The full behavior pattern is not performed, since it was not learned. The part that is learned is consequently deviant in the context of the situation where it is performed. This type of defective socialization is illustrated in the experiences of some isolated lower-class individuals in the attempt to learn the middle-class role. The more dramatic and visible parts of the role are easily perceived and learned. Other parts, however, are subtle or relatively inaccessible and hence not easily learned. Performance of that part of the role that has been learned produces clearly deviant behavior. This is seen in the behavior of lower-class individuals who imitate the dress, recreation, or speech patterns of the middle-class role. These elements of the role are performed in detachment from other parts. The result appears as grotesque or pathetic.

Socialization to the models of a reference group that is different from an individual's membership groups is another source of deviant behavior. Roles learned in anticipation of joining a group that is admired may be deviant when practiced in the group situations to which one already belongs. Referring to data gathered in studies of the American soldier, Robert K. Merton and Alice S. Kitt have shown how anticipatory socialization to models of a reference group may induce deviant behavior within the individual's membership groups.[23] During the war, when the military organization was changing rapidly and promotions were numerous and easy, some soldiers, in anticipation of being promoted, tended to act with their peers like commissioned officers. Or again, adolescents and university students in many countries are influenced by youthful American models whom they learn about through films, magazines, radio, popular recordings, personal contacts, and the like. When practiced in the context of the indigenous culture, such behavior is deviant and provokes sharp criticism by adult members of the society.

A final source of deviant behavior is found in adaptations to social frustration. Robert K. Merton has shown that when structural barriers prevent people from attaining culturally approved ends by culturally approved means, they may turn to culturally disapproved means.[24] By prevailing standards such behavior is deviant, though the personalities of the actors may not be disorganized. Merton identifies four types of structurally adaptive deviant behavior which he calls "innovation," "ritualism," "retreatism," and "rebellion."

By innovation Merton means imaginative practices, in line with current usage but outside (and sometimes just outside) the margin of tolerance of the mores, designed to attain ends that are emphasized in the culture. The deviant improvises creatively on the theme of approved usage but strays beyond the line of morally tolerated behavior. In the business world the innovator engages in sharp and legally questionable practices of competition and financial manipulation. In athletics, players engage in activities which may not be specifically forbidden by the rules, but which are admittedly unsportsmanlike. Among the economically advantaged these deviations are called "white-collar crime," and among the poor they take the form of rackets, petty gambling, and the commercial vices.

Ritualism refers to the abandonment or scaling down of high cultural goals of success and rapid upward mobility to the point where the individual's aspirations can be satisfied with the means accessible to him. The individual conforms to the culturally approved means, but deviates (by reduction) from culturally stressed ends. Merton believes this pattern of deviation is most prevalent among the lower-middle classes, whose structural situation most typically limits chances of great success. The classic illustration of this type of deviation is the bureaucratic official. In the university the ritualist is the student who withdraws from competition for high grades and honors and settles for a "respectable" C or the professor who avoids scholarly striving and is satisfied with permanent tenure and a comfortable situation. Such behavior is deviant because the values expect that everyone will strive for the culturally defined symbols of success.

Retreatism designates adaptation to structural frustration by full withdrawal from the social system. Of the persons who practice this mode of adaptation, Merton writes: "They have relinquished culturally prescribed goals and their behavior does not accord with institutional means."[25] Such individuals can be said to belong to the population rather than to the society. In this category Merton places the adaptive activities of psychotics, autists, pariahs, outcasts, vagrants, vagabonds, tramps, chronic drunkards, and drug addicts.

In rebellion the individual *rejects* both the institutionalized means and the culturally approved ends of the social milieu. He is alienated from the society and becomes dedicated to a new and different set of valued ends that are to be attained by novel means. Merton notes that the spirit of rebellion is expressed in the myth of the social movement. Thus radical social movements constitute the clearest instances of this mode of deviant behavior.

FOOTNOTES

1. Ruth Shonle Cavan, *The American Family* (New York: Crowell, 1958), Chapters 5 through 7.
2. Samuel M. Strong, "Social Types in a Minority Group," *American Journal of Sociology,* 48:563.
3. John J. Honigmann, *Culture and Personality* (New York: Harper, 1954), pp. 180-181, 232-234.
4. Sanford M. Dornbusch, "The Military Academy as an Assimilating Institution," in *Social Forces,* 33:316-321 (May 1955).
5. Talcott Parsons, *The Social System* (Glencoe: Free Press, 1961).
6. Alan G. Gowman, *The War Blind in American Social Structure* (New York: American Foundation for the Blind, 1957), pp. 38-42.
7. Adapted from Cavan, *op. cit.,* pp. 156-158.
8. Kimball Young, *Social Psychology* (New York: Appleton-Century-Crofts, 1956), pp. 138-144.
9. Condensed and adapted from Max Oppenheimer, Jr., "The Soviet Man," in *Journal of Human Relations,* 7:427-448 (Summer 1959).
10. Phillip J. Allen, "Childhood Backgrounds of Success in a Profession," in *American Sociological Review,* 20:190.
11. Reproduced by consent of Harriet Tubman Branch, Young Women's Christian Association, Durham, North Carolina.
12. Adapted and condensed from Young, *op. cit.,* pp. 272-273; William H. Whyte, Jr., *The Organization Man* (New York: Simon and Schuster, 1956), pp. 3-4; and Merton, *op. cit.,* Chapter 6.
13. John P. Marquand, *Point of No Return* (Boston: Little, Brown, 1948), pp. 27-28.
14. John S. Ellsworth, Jr., *Factory Folkways* (New Haven: Yale University Press, 1952).
15. *Today's Secretary,* February 1952, p. 297. See also the detailed standards for lawyers in *Canons of Professional and Judicial Ethics* (Chicago: American Bar Association, 1947), pp. 1-43; and Orie L. Phillips and Philbrick McCoy, *Conduct of Judges and Lawyers* (Los Angeles: Parker, 1952), Chapter 3.
16. Adapted and condensed from Arthur Burton and Robert E. Harris, *Clinical Studies of Personality* (New York: Harper, 1955), pp. 737-739.
17. See William F. Cottrell, "Of Time and the Railroader," in *American Sociological Review,* 4:190-198; and William H. Whyte, Jr., "The Wives of Management," in *Fortune,* 44:62 ff.
18. Ward S. Mason and Neal Gross, "Intra-Occupational Prestige Differentiation: The School Superintendency," in *American Sociological Review,* 20:328.
19. Whyte, *op. cit.,* p. 3.
20. See Marshall B. Clinard, *Sociology of Deviant Behavior* (New York: Holt, 1957). Joseph Bensman and Israel Gerver, in "Crime and Punishment in the Factory: The Function of Deviancy in Maintaining the Social System," in *American Sociological Review,* 22:588-598, argue that deviancy sometimes has functional consequences in informal social systems.
21. Kingsley Davis, "Extreme Isolation of a Child," in *American Journal of Sociology,* 45:554-565. See also Kingsley Davis, "Final Note on a Case of Extreme Isolation," in *American Journal of Sociology,* 52:432-437.
22. See Frank Riessman, *The Culturally Deprived Child* (New York: Scribner's, 1954); and Joseph S. Himes, "Some Work-Related Cultural Deprivations of Young Lower-Class Negro Workers," in *Journal of Marriage and the Family,* 12:323-328.
23. Robert K. Merton and Alice Kitt, "Contributions to the Theory of Reference Group Behavior," in Robert K. Merton and Paul Lazarsfeld, eds., *Continuities in Social*

Research: Studies in the Scope and Method of "The American Soldier" (Glencoe: Free Press, 1950), pp. 53-81.

24. Robert K. Merton, *Social Theory and Social Structure* (Glencoe: Free Press, 1957), pp. 139-157.

25. *Ibid.*, p. 153.

THE CULTURALLY DEPRIVED CHILD

THE EXPERIENCE OF COMFORTABLE LIVING, parks, wide streets, and clean homes, is not possible for all our citizens. In economically and culturally deprived areas children internalize a self-image consistent with the social roles to which they are exposed. All too often their socialization is defective. Cultural deprivation leads to an ignorance of the norms of social intercourse; to some degree of illiteracy; and to a lack of productive skills.

But children are remarkably adaptable. Like the two boys below, they make do with the surroundings they have, improvising a place to play. Many assume responsibility early, like the small girl baby-sitting for a younger sibling. The two boys at top right are neatly dressed and probably experience careful parental supervision, but again the environmental limitations are obvious. Dependence upon a father figure is evident at lower left; the little girl at lower right, gripping a loaf of bread, seems to find a sense of importance in her own responsibility. For her, a simple chore brings satisfaction.

Part VI

MASS SOCIETY, COLLECTIVE BEHAVIOR, AND SOCIAL CHANGE

Human society is disorganized as well as organized, changeable as well as stable. This last Part of the book examines some of the problems that issue from the changing, unstable aspects of society. We approach this task from three different—though related— perspectives. Chapter 14 examines the alterations of traditional societies that have generated what is called a "mass" aspect. Mass societies and some of their social consequences are analyzed. In the next chapter crowds, public behavior, and social movements —that is, collective behavior—are studied as the leading forms of social activity issuing from the relatively unstructured character of associational and mass societies.

The final chapter discusses social change; social problems as one aspect of social change; and social planning as the approach to the solution and prevention of social problems. The book ends with some consideration of the role and potential of sociology and the other social sciences in man's eternal quest for the good society.

Chapter 14

MASS SOCIETY AND MASS PHENOMENA

The word "mass" is a common expression. People talk about mass communication, mass production, mass movements, and so on. In all such contexts the term seems to refer to large numbers, impersonal relations, and dispersed activities. The following list sets down some of the common expressions constructed around the word mass.

I. General descriptive terms
   Mass production
   Mass meeting
   Mass protest
   Mass movement

II. Modern communicational terms
   Mass media
   Mass communication
   Mass persuasion

III. Behavioral science terms
   Mass society
   The mass
   Mass culture
   Mass behavior

The first group of expressions represents popular usage and common-sense meanings. The second group of phrases is built around the process and consequences of mass communication. In the third category are listed some of the concepts that the behavioral sciences have developed to describe and analyze certain characteristics of modern society. To illuminate the core meaning of the term "mass" and to indicate the overlap between the common sense and scientific usages, it may help to examine a brief case.

THE MASS MEETING

"Mass meeting" is a colloquial expression used to designate any large public gathering called for the purpose of considering a popular issue. Such gatherings are fairly typical events of life in large, modern cities. The following account of a mass meeting reveals the salient characteristics of mass phenomena. The initial impression is one of large numbers of nameless individuals. Announcements in newspapers and on radio and television inform them of the meeting. They can assemble because they have access to rapid, easy transportation. Although they differ in social class, ethnic identification, educational achievement, religious affiliation, and so on, in the mass meeting they seem to be equal and alike. Sitting row on row, their eyes riveted on the rostrum, these people appear to be detached from their families, their jobs, their home communities, their friendship groups, and their labor unions or professional and other membership groups. Yet clearly they are unified by a common interest. No individual seems to know more than a few others, yet there is general conversation, friendliness, and mutual recognition even among total strangers. When the program ends, the meeting dissolves, and the nameless individuals separate, withdrawing from the ephemeral relationship.

The people came from all around. Buses and cars brought them from as far down on the peninsula as Palo Alto and San Jose. They came in across the Golden Gate Bridge and on the ferry from San Rafael and Santa Rosa up in Marin County. Some came from as far north and east as Sacramento and Stockton. From all the Bay communities—San Francisco, Oakland, Berkeley, Richmond, San Pablo, El Cerrito—they streamed into the Oakland Auditorium Arena through the bright Sunday afternoon. There was an air of expectancy and suppressed excitement in the crowd as the people milled in the lobby, chatted with friends, or hurried through a score of entrances into the high-vaulted arena. Ushers rushed back and forth with the appearance of busy importance. Vendors hawked souvenir programs. People streamed down the aisles, hesitating here and there in little clumps before disappearing into partially empty rows of seats. The murmur of cheerful, expectant voices swelled, rolled out and up toward the high ceiling, and lost itself in the vastness of the amphitheater. The bright spring sun made golden shafts across the walls, the aisles, the people, and the platform, giving promise of the brilliance and blue of the California sun and sky that summer would soon bring.

"Dat's him," a triumphant voice exclaimed as a grubby brown finger and eager eyes followed a chunky brown man surrounded by local dignitaries while he ascended the platform.

"Aw, no it ain't," a friend chided. "Man you mus' be blin'. Dat ain't Thurgood, dat's Rev. Smith."

All eyes scrutinized each new arrival on the gigantic platform trying to pick out Thurgood Marshall, "Mr. NAACP." This was the mass meeting and rally of the East Bay Branch of the National Association for the Advancement of Colored People to hear the report of Thurgood Marshall, Chief Legal Counsel, one year after the momentous Supreme Court decision of May 17, 1954 banning racial segregation in the nation's public schools.

The following day, the newspapers reported that the crowd was variously estimated to number between seven and ten thousand. It was a motley mosaic of colors, classes, ages, dialects, and costumes. Negroes of all hues and stations in life rubbed shoulders with whites, Chinese, Japanese, and Mexicans. By their voices, bearing, and behavior many persons could be identified as migrants from the tenant farms of Louisiana, Texas, Arkansas, and Oklahoma. There were doctors, lawyers, ministers, and other professionals. College professors mixed with public school teachers and housewives and shopkeepers. They were drawn by curiosity, deep emotional conviction, hero worship, the sense of obligation, intellectual interest, the desire to see and be seen, and many other more obscure and complex motives.

The program proceeded tediously through many singing groups, reports of the local staff, introductions of numerous local dignitaries, brief remarks and greetings from state and local government officials, and an old-fashioned money-raising rally.

The people laughed good-naturedly when the master of ceremonies misplaced his glasses and could not read his preliminary remarks. They applauded Byron Rumford, "the people's choice," local state assemblyman who had just engineered passage of a fair employment practices bill in the state legislature. They paraded to the front and gave their money in the rally. At times the din and confusion were appalling. But the crowd sat, patiently at first, and then doggedly after three hours of preliminaries, to hear "Mr. NAACP." That was why they had come.

The declining sun was making slanting bars of gold across the vast crowd when Thurgood Marshall was at last introduced. The crowd greeted him with a thunderous standing ovation that both released much of the crescendoing and pent-up excitement and welded them together into a cohesive focused mass. A tense, expectant hush fell like a mantle over the huge arena. People edged forward on their seats and craned their necks to see and hear better. This was the moment they had been waiting for, and they wanted to squeeze every possible ounce of experience from it.

Thurgood Marshall began speaking slowly, deliberately, and easily in a self-assured voice like a preacher who knows that his congregation is unified and devoted. He flattered the crowd for their loyalty and sacrifices. He stirred up hoarse, belly-jerking laughter with cruel and amusing episodes of race relations in the "deep South." He informed the crowd by reporting simply and objectively the developments in school desegregation during the first confused year following the historic Supreme Court decision. He excited and compensated the crowd by publicly excoriating the faithless, the hesitant, the disloyal, and the timid who let other more courageous and trustworthy souls fight their battles against oppression and humiliation. He evoked hoarse cries of "Amen!" "Here here!" "Tell 'em!" And he drew forth truncated blows of clenched fists as he struck down the enemies of freedom and decency in vivid verbal ritual and symbolic ceremony. Excitement mounted. The mood of the crowd rippled and varied as the speaker changed his attack.

When Thurgood Marshall finished speaking, the crowd exploded into a tumultuous ovation. They cheered and shouted and whistled and stamped their approval and the release of impounded feelings.

Within minutes, the crowd had disintegrated. Some people surged up to the platform to mix and mill with the dignitaries and to shake the hand of the "great man," or at least to get a closer view of him. From every exit they poured, animated, reassured, justified, laughing, and radiating high good feelings. And so they thinned out along the streets and into the parking lots.

MASS SOCIETY

Traditional Society ◗ We use the term "traditional society" to specify that form of organized social life that contrasts with mass society. Until very recently all of man's life was confined to traditional society. Indeed, a large part of mankind still lives in this ancient and ordinary state. This type of society is characterized by immobility of individuals, restriction of personal and cultural contacts, and direct primary relations.

In the traditional society the individual spent his life in the place where he was born. He did not "travel" because means of travel were inaccessible or limited and because the habit of travel was not established in the tradition. As a consequence, his social contacts were limited to the members of his community and the ideas and ways that they possessed and practiced. A "stranger," as both individual and experience, was a rarity. People did not communicate with individuals from afar because means of communication were inaccessible or limited and because the custom of communicating at a distance was not established in the tradition. Social relations, being restricted in number and scope, tended to be direct and primary. One *saw* his associates, often daily, and *spoke* to them by voice and eye. Such relations became stable, inclusive, and intimate. He did not engage in casual, nondirect relations with dispersed individuals because neither the means nor the practice of such communication existed.

The basic unit of traditional society was the kinship-locality, group-village clan, or tribe. But these kinship-locality units did not exist in isolation from one another. They tended to be aggregated and organized into more or less inclusive units, or societies. Sometimes clusters of villages or clans were aggregated and unified by extension of kinship bonds and by an inclusive tradition. The result was that type of society called "tribal." Tribal society is illustrated in the social organization of so-called nonliterate, "primitive," or pre-industrial peoples.

Sometimes kinship-locality groups were more formally aggregated and organized. For example, a powerful tribe might conquer neighboring tribes and bring them under its dominance. Occasionally rulers intermarried and merged their domains. Subject peoples revolted against domination and established a new system of organization and control. The result was political systems more formal and explicit than tribes. Yet the essential character of social organization was defined by the traditional complex and kinship-locality units.

Such societies are called traditional because they are organized by means of sacred, nonrational principles. Individuals are placed in the society, bound together, and assigned rights and obligations on the basis of kinship and location. A pattern of interpersonal relations and collective action is defined by a tradition of sacred norms and values. Being immobile, individuals who are bound together by kinship and tradition cluster into village or neighborhood units. Within such kinship-locality units individuals are categorized for functional purposes on the basis of such physical traits as sex and age. The sacred traditions, once established, become binding and acquire the character of social institutions. Kinship-locality groups were aggregated into societies by a sacred tradition or system of formal control, or both.

Modification of Traditional Forms ♦ Mass society became possible when ends of social action emerged that could not be attained by traditional means, and when therefore appropriate nontraditional means were created. These changes were noted in earlier chapters in the discussion of large formal associations and bureaucracy, modern metropolitan communities, population growth and concentration, modern social classes, and modern bureaucratic institutions. People recognized or created social goals in economics, government, education, recreation, and so on that could not be attained by kinship-locality organizations, or even by the formal structure of traditional political agencies. For example, the interplay of production innovations and rising wants created a demand for manufactured goods that could be met only by modern industrial economies. The steady growth and eventual explosion of knowledge produced a situation that required means beyond family and village apprenticeship for its accumulation, transmission, and utilization. The ancient fascination of the city and universal urbanization produced situations that could no longer be controlled by traditional kinship-locality systems.

At the same time, men developed new means for attaining these new ends. Sacred tradition tended to be replaced by the secular patterns of technical and social skills. All-purpose kinship-locality groupings were superseded by specialized associations. Specialized associations merged and aggregated into large-scale organizations that installed bureaucratic patterns of action. For example, the traditional ceremonies of the fishing village are in many places superseded by the "fishing industry." The ancient village where men went out to work in little plots with historic hand tools is swallowed up in the modern large farm and plowed under by modern tractor-drawn implements. Where once a few score of men huddled together in a village, now millions of their descendants wander more or less aimlessly through vast urban jungles.

Effects of Mass Media ♦ Mass communication has played a decisive role in the disintegration of traditional society and the emergence of mass society. In a later section of this chapter the nature, structure, and process of mass communication will be examined. Here we need only note three consequences of mass communication for traditional society. First, mass movement and communication broke the historic state of immobility and social restriction. With sail and steamboats, railroads, automobiles and good roads, and airplanes people could escape from the place where they were born. Now the means of movement were available; soon the habit of mobility entered the way of life. With mobility, restriction of personal and cultural contact was removed. An individual could see persons other than immediate neighbors. With mass communication—press, motion pictures, radio, television—he could contact persons far removed from his village and have experiences far beyond the possibilities of the locality. The new scope and range of personal and collective contacts permitted—indeed required—a new type of social relations. Now the individual could develop and practice indirect, casual relations. Such relations were not defined and patterned by the sacred tradition; they tended to change and fluctuate in an unprecedented manner.

Further, mass movement and communication enabled the new, large, formal, and specialized associations, organizations, and institutions to function and permitted many casually associated individuals to act within such social situations. The bus, the newspapers, and the radio made it possible for the villager to make a living in the great city. The giant industry, the mammoth sports arena, or city government could carry on their ordinary functions only by means of modern media of communication. At the same time, the worker, the sportsman, and the citizen could function only because of the services of the mass media.

Crucially for the development and existence of mass society, the mass media made possible communication, organization, and collective action at a level completely outside the confines of the traditional kinship-locality system. Traditional man could act in a clan, village, or tribe; but only modern mass-man can act as a participant in a national political party, space launching audience, or ideological social movement. In traditional society the people in one village may have virtually no conception of the existence—to say nothing of the characteristics or interests—of people in a village a thousand miles away. Modern mass-man, however, may know very much about people half the world away and is often significantly, even decisively, affected by their actions. The mass media enable people to communicate, to become mutually oriented, to organize, and to act with reference to issues, by collective patterns, and through social systems that uniquely distinguish mass society.

At the same time, as individuals became detached from the disintegrating kinship-locality system, they were rearranged into social classes. Economic differences were magnified and associated with distinctions in power and cultural accomplishment. Such differences tended to be revealed in differentials of social prestige and rank. The social class system that emerged and organized the dissolving traditional society functioned at first to reflect the individual's experiences and achievements; but in time it came to exercise control over his life chances and style. Loyalties to kin and identification with "home" place were replaced by allegiance to social class and sense (of either pride or shame) of social rank. Locality, as the place where an individual resides, was no longer a social anchor. Instead it became a symbol of social class and an indicator of social rank and group prestige.

Alienation and Homogeneity ▶ One consequence of the trends just discussed is the alienation of modern man. He has lost much of the steady anchorage, reliable direction, and inclusive security provided by traditional society. He operates increasingly in a world of numerous casual contacts, unreliable or ambiguous directions, and unrelieved insecurity. He experiences disturbing loss of identity, restriction of purpose, and sense of detachment. He thus experiences a dilemma: desire for the excitement, novelty, freedom, and expansiveness of mass society and need for the stability, direction, inclusive warmth, and security of traditional society.

The process of "massification" tends to weaken the ties of traditional society. In movement the individual breaks or weakens strong ties with the ancestral group. He withdraws, to some extent at least, from the pattern of intimate inclusive relations and gives up direction by the sacred traditional norms. At the same time he loses much of the social, psychic, and emotional support that resulted from participation in the total system of life. He becomes detached, isolated, alienated. As Hannah Arendt writes: "The chief characteristic of the mass-man is not brutality and backwardness, but his isolation and lack of normal social relationships."[1]

In his new world he is unable or unwilling to establish a new set of inclusive sacred ties. His urban residence may be a congested slum, a working-class neighborhood, or a middle-class suburb. But in none of these does he have the strong, intimate, inclusive ties that characterized his life in the traditional group. As Erich Fromm has said, he knows that "mode of experience in which the person experiences himself as an alien."[2] At work, on the streets, when shopping, at church, in the cinema, and so on, he establishes numerous contacts and associations. But they are all—or almost all—relatively transitory, casual, superficial, and instrumental. He learns to live in this kind of social milieu, partly because it is an exciting contrast to his old life, partly because in his new world he can establish no other way of living. He is left—or forced—much more than formerly to make his own decisions from among an unprecedented range of options. But lacking the reliable guide of a stable, traditional, normative pattern, he cannot choose; he is troubled by the need to decide. In this situation he experiences loss of social, psychic, and emotional security. He is troubled by a sense of loneliness, incompleteness, and malaise. He knows ennui, anxiety, and dissatisfaction.

Alienation is characterized by loss, to a greater or less degree, of identity. The self-image and sense of being, which in the stable, restricted traditional context were clear and strong, become blurred. The individual is not sure who he is, where he belongs, or where he is going. He is forced into the search for identity. Part of this search consists in the quest for significant social belonging; part of it is revealed in the effort to escape from reality. In this situation the individual experiences loss of purpose. If the nature of his being is not clear, then the reasons for being and for striving are not clear. Though the beginnings of his life may be remembered and treasured, they are removed in time and no longer accessible to him, not even in clear and inspiring recollection. By the same token, his sense of direction and destiny is even more blurred.

And yet it is evident that mass-man is not totally alienated, not completely atomized. He still lives a part of his life in the traditional primary and secondary groups, associations, and institutions—family, community, social class, ethnic identification, religious association, and so on. Traditional and mass then are the two faces of his world, the two sectors of modern society. But if alienation and atomization define modern man's relation to traditional society, then equality and homogeneity describe his involvement in mass society. For all individuals are equally and uniformly engaged in the structures, communication, and processes of mass society. No one asks the participant his social class, educational status, ethnic identification, religious affiliation, or the like. The keys to participation are interest, opportunity, facilities.

Primary Relations in Mass Society ❯ The disintegration of traditional society is characterized by enlargement of the spheres of non-primary social relations. As more and more sectors of life are brought under pattern by formal rational systems, the areas of informal primary association tend to be restricted and subordinated. The main remaining arenas of inclusive intimate experience are such independent informal groups as family and friendship clique and the informal constituents of large associations. When the individual leaves the personal haven of such groups, he steps into the impersonal formality of associational and mass society.

Yet, primary relations are no less essential to man now than previously, when they formed the whole context of life. The social self, self-consciousness, and the personality system are formed within a milieu of inclusive personal associations. The social and emotional—and indeed often the physical—well-being of the individual are strongly conditioned by the nature and extent of primary relations. In earlier chapters we examined some research that demonstrated the decisive importance of such experiences for modern man. For example, in World War II primary relations in friendship groups sustained German soldiers and kept them fighting even when they recognized defeat as inevitable. In "Cornerville" the "corner boys" almost instinctively formed informal friendship groups, and serious interruption of primary relations led to emotional or physical disturbances. In Crestwood Heights, a well-to-do middle-class suburb, people acted in clubs and associations, in part at least, to secure the warmth and security that had escaped from families which had become rather specialized associations.

The subordination of primary relations confronts mass-man with another aspect of his dilemma: how to experience the maximum opportunity for self-development, self-expansion, and self-realization made possible by mass society while ensuring the self-integrity, well-being, and satisfactions that flow only from the primary relations that typify traditional society. The response to this dilemma takes various forms. Some people strive to create islands of warmth and inclusiveness through the quest for "togetherness" or "belongingness." Another response is the tendency toward "conformity," or the effort to hedge against the threatening personal hazards of deviation by absorption into mass patterns. Other individuals seek to manage the dilemma by submerging themselves in the exaggerations of mass action, thus achieving a kind of desensitizing or narcotic effect.

Nature and Structure of Mass Society ▶ A society can become a mass society when the following conditions exist.

1. Great numbers of dispersed and mobile individuals.

2. Relative detachment of these individuals from the traditional social order and their involvement in the process of mass communication.

3. An unstable secular consensus that is defined around nontraditional values and norms and expressed in social policies.

4. Widespread psycho-social ambivalences issuing from splits and contradictions of the traditional and mass society and culture.

5. Collective action through such diffuse collectivities as publics, fashion, diffuse crowds, morale, and diffuse panic.

6. Widespread sanctioned participation of detached mobile individuals in the processes of decision-making and social action.[3]

These conditions form a syndrome. No one alone, nor indeed even two or three, can produce the mass character in a society. For example, large dispersed numbers of individuals cannot alone create a mass society. China and India in the nineteenth century had teaming millions, but neither was a mass society. In fact, it is doubtful that either society can even now fully qualify as a mass society. Or again, mass communication by itself does not produce a mass society. Many developing societies have installed systems of mass communication—press, cinema, radio, and television—but still lack the decisive characteristics of mass societies. All elements of the syndrome must be present in socially significant degree before a society fully acquires mass characteristics.

The concept of mass society refers to both a characteristic and a dimension of some modern complex societies. As characteristic, mass society is that state of detachment, secularism, impersonality, and anomie that alienates the individuals from traditional systems and creates superficial inclusive homogeneity. As dimension, it is a field of communication, organization, and action that falls outside the sphere of the traditional structures. Figure 14-1 is a diagrammatic representation of mass society as an extension of the traditional societal substructure. The wedges of the inner circle indicate the familiar forms of the traditional social order. The outer fringe suggests how this social system is extended by the structures and processes of mass society. We may further the analysis of mass society by examining

Schematic Representation of the Mass Dimension of Society

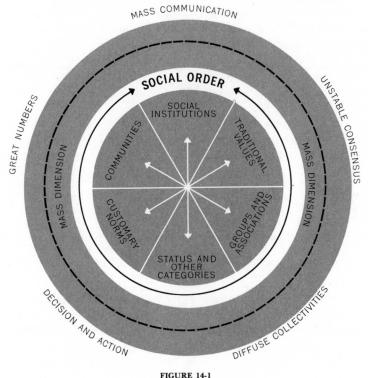

FIGURE 14-1

mass communication, mass behavior, and mass culture as its leading manifestations.

MASS COMMUNICATION

The term "mass media" is generally employed to refer to the press, motion pictures, radio, and television together with such supporting devices as the telegraph, telephone, and teletype. With the exception of the press, all these media of communication have been invented within the last seventy years. Including the press, all have become media of mass communication within this period. By a justifiable extension of meaning the term mass media may also be understood to include such means of rapid transportation as the railroad, the steamship, the automobile, and the airplane. These devices of movement and contact have been brought into widespread use during the last century and a half. It thus appears that the means of mass communication and movement have become a part of the setting of social life only within very recent times.

It is virtually impossible to ascertain precisely what proportion of mankind lives under the influence of these mass media and the consequent process of mass communication. It would seem evident, however, that a very large portion of the people on earth now have some degree of access to mass communication. Figure 14-2 indicates the extent and variability of press, radio, and motion picture coverage. These data are obviously only fragmentary and indicative and take no account of television, for which relevant figures are not available. Two inferences can be drawn from these data. First, an impressive number of individuals now come under the influence of mass communication. Second, some people are much more exposed than others to the process of mass communication. The effectiveness of the press, however, is contingent upon the variability of levels of literacy. In this connection Wilbur Schramm makes the following observations.

> The map of world literacy divides into three large areas. North America, Western Europe (except Spain), Australia, New Zealand, and parts of Southeast Asia have less than 10 per cent illiteracy. On the other hand, China, India, the Moslem countries, and practically all of Africa have more than 80 per cent illiteracy. Between these two extremes—in the band between 10 and 80 per cent illiteracy—are Central and South America, Spain, and the vast expanse of Eurasia dominated by the Soviet Union.[4]

Process of Mass Communication ♦ Mass communication subjects its receivers to a unique kind of social experience. Under quasi-isolated and impersonal conditions great numbers of dispersed individuals receive the same more or less standardized message from highly centralized sources. In this way they are admitted to a kind and range of social experience that lies outside the orbit of ordinary social life and

Availability of Newspapers, Radio, and Motion Pictures in Selected Countries

COUNTRY	NEWSPAPERS[1]	RADIO SETS[2]	MOVIE ATTENDANCE[3]
UNITED KINGDOM	580	288	22
FRANCE	250	237	10
WEST GERMANY	310	295	15
SWEDEN	486	507	9
U.S.S.R.	126	117	13
CHINA	14	3	2
POLAND	164	132	8
BULGARIA	171	5	5
INDIA	7	3	2
INDONESIA	10	5	LESS THAN 0.5
THAILAND	5	6	NOT AVAILABLE
PAKISTAN	9	2	LESS THAN 0.5
ARGENTINA	195	182	7
ECUADOR	6	15	NOT AVAILABLE
MEXICO	50	58	4
EGYPT	26	21	3
BELGIAN CONGO	2	1	LESS THAN 0.5
GHANA	24	5	1
JAPAN	394	148	10
AUSTRALIA	411	227	15
UNITED STATES	375	1000	15

Source: Wilbur Schramm, Mass Communication, Urbana, University of Illinois Press, 1960, Table Appendix A, p. 668.
1. Copies per 1000 people.
2. Per 1000 people.
3. Per year per capita.

FIGURE 14-2

primary communication. The mass communication process defines and allocates the categorical roles of message communicator and message receiver. It reduces or eliminates the dimension of interpersonal relations in the process of communication. It tends to detach individuals from the traditional sociocultural milieu. It extends the horizons of life at a level and in a realm beyond the orbit of ordinary social action.

However, both the participants and process of mass communication are grounded in the general social structure. John W. and Matilda White Riley have shown how mass communication constitutes an organically social process.[5] Communicator (C) and recipient (R) are engaged in a reciprocal process. Their relationship, however, extends beyond the simple one-to-one nexus; that is, it consists of more than a single communication which potentially elicits only a single reply. At the primary level, any given communication is rather one link in a chain of communications which extends over both space and time. When the communication takes on the mass dimension, emanating from a publisher, a film studio, or a broadcasting network, much of the C-R relationship is indirect, proliferating through the groups to which C and R belong. The message is thus transmitted from the members in C's groups to individuals in R's groups, who in turn reply. Moreover, each of these individuals has a definite position in the social structure which provides socially significant reference points. Beyond this, these several positions are related to one another within the social system. Thus the several communications which flow from one individual or group to another are not random or unrelated acts but are elements in a total pattern of on-going communication or interaction.

The content of mass communication can be classified and examined in terms of four broad categories.

1. *News.* Reportorial accounts and editorial interpretations of current events and outstanding personalities.
2. *Entertainment.* Presentations for immediate enjoyment and personal gratification.
3. *Propaganda.* Advertising and many types of noncommercial mass persuasion.
4. *Education.* Presentation of information and analysis for the purpose of increasing knowledge and skill.

The impact of the content of mass communication is conditioned by the variable cultural backgrounds and social identifications of recipients. Each recipient represents a syndrome of attitudes, sentiments, opinions, beliefs, and the like that prepare him for the broadcast message. His response tends to vary in ascertainable and predictable ways in terms of the nature of his cultural background and group identifications. Thus white, middle-class, suburban residents can be expected to react differently from poor Negro tenant farmers to a political appeal, an advertising statement, or a news report. The mass communication industry has responded to this situation in several ways. Studies have been conducted to identify specialized audiences and to specify their characteristics. Material for broadcast has been adjusted to the characteristics of such specialized audiences and beamed at them specifically. At the same time, material for general coverage is adjusted to the known characteristics of all types of audiences.

In audience situations, the stream of mass communication feeds into networks of social relations that facilitate the flow of personal influence. Usually, people go to the movies, watch television, or listen to the radio in the company of family or friends. They react to what they see and hear, both in terms of the mass communication message and in awareness of their associates. Individuals call each other's attention to items in the paper or articles in magazines, commenting about them, discussing them, and communicating their interpretations of what is read. This personal exchange has the effect of clarifying, validating, or reinforcing the mass communication message or of achieving the opposite effect. In the following excerpt from Hadley Cantril's study of the Orson Welles "Invasion from Mars" radio broadcast of some years ago, we see how the impact of the broadcast material was enhanced and diffused by personal contact and influence. Some people who were unaware of the program were persuaded to listen. Others who were amused or entertained were frightened by the reactions of friends. In most instances the individuals who exerted personal influence upon others neither intended nor fully recognized what they were doing.

On the evening of October 30, 1938, it has been estimated that at least six million Americans heard Orson Welles' famous dramatization of the invasion from Mars. The broadcast purported to describe a landing of Martians on a New Jersey farm. At least a million of these listeners were frightened or disturbed. If they paid attention, listeners first heard that a dramatization of H. G. Wells' *War of the Worlds* was to be presented. The program opened with a brief weather report which was followed by the music of "Ramon Raquello and his orchestra" from the "Meridian Room" of the Park Plaza Hotel in New York City. Shortly after the first selection had begun, an announcer interrupted, "Ladies and gentlemen, we interrupt our program of dance music to bring you a special bulletin from Intercontinental Radio News." He proceeded to read the first "report" about explosions on Mars. From then on the music was repeatedly interrupted for "announcements" concerning the "invasion."

The program was so realistic that for the first few minutes it was credible to even the relatively sophisticated and critical listeners.

But in many instances, normal critical abilities were overpowered by emotions generated in the listening situation. Some people listened with relatives or friends in their homes. Some individuals answered their telephones only to hear excited friends urging them to tune in on the broadcast. Some people heard the program in public places and others alone at home.

A person who was told to tune in by a frightened friend or relative listened under somewhat different objective conditions from one who tuned in alone for other reasons. One woman remarked, "My sister called up and I immediately got scared." "I was resting when an excited person phoned and told me to listen to the radio, that a big meteor had fallen. I was really worried." Though the total listening situation was doubtless somewhat different for each person, all tended to induce fear and heighten emotional contagion. The corroboratory effects of other people's behavior is decisive in most listening situations. Fear was often contagious. "I was getting worried," declared one listener, "when my friend came in and his face was ghastly white." He said, 'We're being invaded,' and his conviction impressed me."[6]

Content Control ▶ The broadcast of standardized messages from centralized sources makes mass communication particularly vulnerable to control. Publishers, managers, editors, producers, and other officials, operating in studios and editorial offices, determine what does or does not enter the stream of mass communication. The main techniques of content control are called censorship and propaganda. Because of the control of content, the process tends to be persuasive as well as merely communicational.

Censorship refers to the exclusion of certain material from the mass-distributed message. For example, a newspaper publisher may by policy prohibit the use of names and phrases that might offend minority groups or exclude material that could excite local antagonisms and incite to violence. Such censorship is a normal practice in the mass communication industry. In time of war or other national crisis, the practice of censorship may become official governmental policy and be enforced on behalf of the "general welfare." In such totalitarian countries as the Soviet Union or Communist China, where mass communication is a government monopoly, censorship is carried to the extreme.

Propaganda refers to the practice of manipulating the content of mass communication in order to persuade recipients to accept a predetermined viewpoint or follow a predetermined course of action. Material is injected, excluded, distorted, or used in a way calculated to achieve the desired end. As propaganda, the aim of mass communication is persuasion. The technique, however, focuses on the manipulation of content. Advertising is the familiar illustration of propaganda in mass communication. Yet, to one degree or another, most mass communication content is manipulated to achieve desired ends. In the totalitarian societies the main function of mass communication is propaganda.

Control permits focus and slant in the content of mass communication. Mass communication therefore does more than connect atomized individuals and facilitate consensus, interaction, and collective activity among them. It shapes their patterns of thought and feeling and determines their courses of effort and action. When large numbers of alienated individuals respond favorably to the persuasion of focused and slanted mass communication, they appear to be impotent, unconcerned, ill-informed, and apathetic. This situation is a cause for alarm for some observers and suggests to them the breakdown of democratic institutions.

By reference to the control of content and the role of persuasion, it is possible to differentiate propaganda from education. In ideal terms, propaganda manipulates communication for the purpose of persuasion. Education, on the other hand, utilizes communication, both primary and mass, to communicate information and to facilitate independent decision and action. As a matter of fact, however, this ideal distinction is seldom fully achieved in actual situations. Educators, even in the most ideal situations, seldom escape the inclination or the act of persuasion, and the propagandist must disseminate information and always contributes inadvertently to independent decision and action. Moreover, it must be recognized that propaganda, the deliberate use of communication to persuade, is regularly employed for ends that enhance the social system and are supported by the traditional values. When evaluated, then, propaganda must be considered in terms of its ends rather than its methods. Students interested in pursuing this subject will find a large and sophisticated literature. In many universities propaganda and mass persuasion are an area of graduate study and scientific research. Some aspects of this topic are examined more fully in the next chapter in connection with public opinion.

MASS BEHAVIOR

One consequence of the addition of the mass dimension to social life is to be found in the character of social behavior. The distinctive character of mass behavior inheres in the fact that individuals are alienated from the traditional social organization and that relations among them are mediated impersonally by mass communication. Yet mass behavior tends to precipitate interpersonal relations through "interaction chains," as Ralph H. Turner and Lewis M. Killian have put it.[7] It is possible to identify the following dimensions of mass behavior.

1. *Dimension of disagreement and debate.* Public behavior of all kinds, including the formation, manipulation, and expression of public opinion.
2. *Dimension of focused attention.* Diffuse crowd behavior including such familiar manifestations as radio and television audiences; various "fandoms"; and advertising-oriented markets.
3. *Dimension of social contagion.* Contagious and imitative behavior of which fashion, fads, and crazes are familiar types.
4. *Dimension of variable security.* Forms of mass behavior that are

characterized by feelings of security or insecurity issuing from variable confidence and enthusiasm for ends, means, and leaders, of which group morale and mass panic are polar types.

5. *Dimension of parallel action*. Similar or parallel action of dispersed and relatively isolated individuals in response to the same idea or event, sometimes referred to as "the mass."

6. *Dimension of social power*. Participation of alienated political "nonelites" through mechanisms of democratic decision-making in formulating societal policy.

Collective action in dispersed crowds and publics is examined in the following chapter. All the forms of social behavior considered here lie outside the sphere of the ordinary associational systems and depend upon the mechanisms and processes of mass communication. In such behavior individuals are mutually oriented in terms of values and consensuses that define them as participating units rather than as discrete persons. Yet, all such forms of social behavior tend to generate and utilize processes of interpersonal relations. For, even in mass society, modern man is only partially dissociated from the traditional societal substructure.

The nature of mass behavior may be revealed by an examination of the "craze." Turner and Killian assert that "a new idea which suddenly becomes important in the life of a community and which nevertheless does not appreciably disturb the preëxisting order can be called a craze."[8] Some familiar recent illustrations include hula hoops, the trampoline, the Madison, phone-booth jamming, sheath and chemise dresses, sit-in demonstrations, swastika painting, and beatnik styles of men's clothing. Some crazes are merely exaggerations of activities which are part of normal life in a society at a particular time. Sometimes the pattern of craze activity enters the general fund of mass culture. Turner and Killian find that the course of a craze appears to follow a pattern of five phases: (1) the latent period, (2) the period of rapid spread, (3) the saturation period, (4) the period of mental resistance or immunity, and (5) the period of stagnation or absorption into the mass cultural fund. The following case illustrates the character and phasic development of this form of mass behavior.

The use of thallium in the treatment of skin diseases as a preliminary measure to remove the hair developed as a craze in medical therapy. This practice was first advocated in 1914 both in Germany and in Mexico. The pioneers were careful to warn that poisonous effects might arise from an overdose. A survey of medical literature between 1914 and 1925 reveals that the drug was very little used during this period. This was the first or latent period of the craze. During the next two years, however, use of the drug became rapidly fashionable. Thousands of children were treated in centers widely distributed over the globe. In this period of rapid spread, a large body of literature was produced in which the results of treatment were described and commented upon, for the most part very favorably. The saturation phase was masked by the rapid growth of the realization of the dangers attached to the treatment. Several fatalities resulted from overdoses. The fourth phase of the pattern, which coincided with increasing immunity to the idea of this treatment, was reflected in the medical literature by a preponderance of writings which described experiments on laboratory animals and emphasized the poisonous nature of thallium compounds. At the same time, the total number of writings on the subject declined. From 1928 to 1940, this decline in interest was fairly continuous. Recent scientific publications on the use of thallium have, for the most part, been confined to experimental studies, to warnings against proprietary preparations, and to descriptions of instances where thallium had been used for attempted murder or suicide. Medical textbooks now accept the fact that the treatment has value in selected cases under very carefully controlled conditions. The fifth phase has been reached and the craze is over.[9]

MASS CULTURE

The concept of mass culture constitutes a further heuristic tool for analyzing the structures and functions of mass society. It provides a perspective for recognizing that all, or almost all, mass behavior is expressed in learned, shared, and variable patterns. In the aggregate, such patterns constitute an important strain in the total cultural heritage of mass societies. With reference to the nature and content of mass culture, John W. Bennett and Melvin M. Tumin write:

> It is composed of a set of patterns of thought and action which are common to the subcultures of a heterogeneous society. These patterns have common meanings and value for all or most of the members of the society and serve as points of mutual identification and recognition for these members. The mass culture thus can be seen as a kind of least common denominator, or as the overall configuration, or as a kind of film hiding the diversity beneath.[10]

Some parts of the mass culture are referred to as "popular culture" or "kitsch." Whatever the term used, the concept defines an area of consensus in mass society and indicates that the behavior that escapes from the traditional mores and social institutions is regulated. The distinction between the mass culture and the other major strains of the heritage can be illustrated by reference to music. Mass or popular music is differentiated from "classical" and "folk" music, neither of which depends upon mass communication for its development and continuation. Popular music, however, of which jazz, rock-and-roll, swing, blues, boogie, Dixieland, gospel songs, western songs, and hillbilly are the more familiar forms, is a creature of the mass media.

The concept of mass culture serves to reveal how extensively the processes of mass communication have invaded the life of modern man. Very few sectors of his life are left to exclusive definition and ordering by the cultural tradition. How extensive and pervasive mass culture has become is suggested by the incomplete listings of subareas in Figure 14-3. No attempt is made to classify the categories.

Advertising: press, billboards, neon signs, radio, TV
Architecture and home design
Art: commercial including advertising, cartoons, comics
Athletics and sports
Automobiles: styles and models
Conduct: morals, etiquette, posture, gaits
Diet: foods and cookery
Drama: films, radio, television, stage
Dress: women's and men's styles
Furniture and furnishings, home particularly
Language: slang, governmentese, jargons, space talk
Literature: westerns, detective, mystery, true love, science
     fiction
Love: the romantic cult, fashions in love-making
Music: generic jazz, western, hillbilly, gospel
Ornamentation: personal
Religion: crusades, gospel singing
Science: popular science and "scientism"
Vacations: location (e.g., as Atlantic City) and activity
     (e.g., as fishing)

FIGURE 14-3

Bennett and Tumin, however, point out that the variegated pattern of American mass culture is integrated around a core of basic values.[11] Secular individualistic pragmatism, including the materialistic bias, the distaste for the supernatural, the emphasis on practicality, the desire to build, succeed, and expand, and the desire to do all this individualistically "on your own" are the major threads in the fabric of mass culture. These central value threads function to weave all the variegated and diverse elements together into a loosely integrated cultural fabric.

The following document on taste-making illustrates the nature of mass culture and demonstrates its dependence upon mass communication. Russell Lynes' account of the rise and diffusion of styles in American taste also serves to indicate how mass behavior emerges in those realms of experience outside the cultural tradition and falls into the fluctuating patterns that constitute mass culture. It is evident that the mass production, diffusion, and consumption of taste are aspects of modern life.

TASTE-MAKING: MASS CULTURE ILLUSTRATED

The making of taste in America is a major industry, employing hundreds of thousands of people in editorial and advertising offices, in printing plants, in galleries and museums, in studios and laboratories, in shops and consultants' offices. The taste industry has gradually become essential to the operation of the American way of life. The economic system not only seeks to meet demand, but also to create it. One of the ways that demand is created is by changing people's taste, or at least inviting them to change, and by making the pressures to give up what seemed good yesterday for what should seem inviting today so strong that they are almost impossible to resist.

Periods of taste are never quite as neatly separated as they are sometimes pictured. They slide gradually from one into another, though occasionally there are upheavals that seem to set apart a vanishing era from a new style of taste. In the last years of the 1820's the long period of control over taste by a landed and intellectual aristocracy came to an end in the United States. When Andrew Jackson was elected to the presidency in 1828 on a wave of cocksure Americanism, there came with him a new "age of the common man."

In the 1830's mass production came to the whole furnishings industry. Suddenly almost everybody, instead of just a wealthy and cultured few, could buy "tasteful" carpets and chairs, wall papers and curtain materials. They were not only cheap but they were to be had in great variety. Inventions for manufacturing objects with which to decorate the home came in rapid succession, each more miraculous than the other. In 1837 William Compton patented a "fancy weaving loom" and seven years later the first wall paper printing machine was imported from England. In the same year Erastus Bigelow invented a power loom for making ingrained carpets and in 1848 a loom to make Brussels and tapestry carpets.

In the 1840's and 1850's Andrew Jackson Downing fashioned and disseminated a new style in home architecture and furnishings. Under the slogan "smiling lawns and tasteful cottages" Downing combined architectural, landscape, and furnishing themes into a design of the good life for the common man. He wanted everyone to live surrounded by tasteful objects with leisure to use their parlors and to cultivate their gardens. He wanted them to paint their houses in muted colors that harmonized with the tones of nature.

Downing's own house was a perfect example of the new taste that he so eloquently espoused. By the standards of its own day it was a "simple house," in what was then called the Elizabethan style, but which we now think of as Gothic revival. It was built of stone—neatly symmetrical, with slender, octagonal towers at either side of the peaked entrance and matching verandas whose roofs, decorated with ornamental wood work, were supported by slender columns and shallow arches. In executing his perfect house in its perfect landscape he set out to prove that "a beautiful, and durable and convenient mansion could be built as cheaply as a poor and tasteless temple."

By the middle of the 1870's, after a long period of "extremely tasty debauchery," the time seemed ripe to many people for a new maker of taste to usher in a brave new era. No one had added a dash of fresh spice to the aesthetic arguments about how people should live since Downing's death. At this juncture of historical events, Charles L. Eastlake, in 1872, published *Hints on Household Tastes*. This slim volume precipitated a veritable revolution in home furnishings. Households were completely refurnished to comply with its prescriptions. Furniture manufacturers and upholsterers were forced to scrap their old designs and patterns for new ones. Young brides declined to set up housekeeping with anything that was not certified as "artistic," and "sincere."

Like Downing, Eastlake was concerned not only with aesthetics and practicability, but also with morals. He was especially hostile to everything that he considered to be sham and showy rather than "sincere" or "honest." He was impatient with unnecessary curves which seemed to deny the essential functions of a piece of furniture—strength, forthrightness, and comfort. A chair or table or even a mantlepiece to be "sincere" should be put together with wooden pegs and dowls instead of nails and screws. It came to be believed that a whole house could be a poem by furnishing it artistically without following all the rules of high art. In an amazingly short time the American people hung their pictures and curtains, laid their carpets, colored their walls, procured solid wood, abjured veneering, and eschewed curves just as Mr. Eastlake said they should.

For half a century the Queen Anne style has been regarded as a monstrosity. But one needs only to look at the houses in nearly any long-established American city to see how extensively the good queen left her imprint on the way of life. Originally most of these houses were painted in somber tones of browns and reds, but many have been "vulgarized" by white paint. In the 1870's and 1880's the public took the Queen Anne style to its heart with an agility that surprised its protagonists. In the last quarter of the nineteenth century, the Queen Anne houses were as natural settings for Eastlake's furniture as a flat-roofed, glass-walled house is for the furniture that we call modern today.[12]

SOCIAL FUNCTIONS OF MASS PHENOMENA

By their very nature, mass phenomena are characteristic of advanced associational societies. Yet the consequences of these phenomena can be seen in the changes of traditional societies as well as in the characteristics of established mass societies. In many quarters there is an inclination to decry the evils of mass phenomena. These critics lament the vulgarization of culture, the alienation of modern man, the transiency of contemporary life. However, such a view of the matter stresses the evaluation of visible consequences and overlooks other important results. The foregoing discussion suggests that mass phenomena have at least three consequences for the total social system: (1) production of new areas of social integration; (2) limitation of traditional integration; and (3) facilitation of social change.

First, mass phenomena support the integration of a society. The traditional integration is extended by unstable consensus and functional cohesion in the realm of mass action. For example, the social solidarity based in the mores is supplemented and extended by the cohesion emanating from social policy that is grounded in public opinion and mass participation. Or again, all the cultural, ethnic, regional, and other subgroups find common social ground and a universe of discourse in the patterns and understandings of the mass culture.

Mass phenomena become crucial integrative mechanisms in time of societal crisis. In war, economic depression, or national calamity solidarity must be maximized and the society geared for concerted action. Such a situation requires subordination of subgroup and subcultural interests in favor of societal survival. Such total unity can be achieved and mobilized by means of mass symbols, values, organizations, and action programs. For example, in the Great Depression of the 1930's, the "New Deal" created blue eagles, alphabetical agencies, "the forgotten man," fireside chats, and a congeries of other mass symbols, modes of organization, and schemes of action to unify and mobilize the nation for the task of economic recovery. In World War II mass mechanisms were again utilized to subordinate political, labor-management, racial, religious, and other special interests to the requirements of the unified effort for national defense.

Second, at the same time mass phenomena tend to limit traditional integration. As noted, such phenomena tend to alienate individuals from the stable moorings of the traditional social order. These atomized and alienated individuals are significantly dissociated from the traditional consensus and solidarity. Total social cohesion and societal harmony therefore are restricted and weakened. This is doubtless the condition that many critics of mass society perceive.

In like manner, mass phenomena introduce a quality of instability and transiency into social life that many people find disquieting. Social arrangements and behavior patterns alter frequently. Usages that prevailed or worked at one time may soon be discarded or modified. For example, as recently as a generation ago, many people found that life tended to fall into a regular, dependable, and comfortable pattern. One knew what to expect and he could plan for the morrow. Today, many people perceive the forms and patterns of their lives as a kaleidoscope. They shift and alter rapidly and unpredictably. The whole design seems unstable, transient, and undependable. People often find it difficult to discover the organizing plan or the integrating principle.

Mass phenomena are also disintegrative because they function to feed change and instability into the on-going traditional system. Many now conventional modes of behavior originated as fads or crazes. For example, the wrist watch, initially a fad, has now largely replaced the pocket watch, and radio and television sets are now standard elements of life in American homes. Mass society constitutes a twilight zone between the realms of traditionally patterned social behavior and the sphere of fully unstructured and spontaneous improvisation. In this frontier of human experience, behaviors learned in the world of traditional life are brought forward and reshaped in the crucible of new demands and possibilities. The creative and changing role of mass phenomena is illustrated in the adaptations to radio and television in the recent past and to atomic fission and outer space in the present and future. Meanwhile also, improvisations from the frontiers of mass experience are fed back into the stable fund of the social heritage. The heritage is thus constantly modified and refreshed by a stream of new elements issuing from these latter-day frontiers of mass life.

Third, mass phenomena have important consequences for individuals. Through mass patterns and structures, vast numbers of detached individuals are admitted to participation and decision-making in the society. In rituals like athletic contests, parades, religious crusades, political campaigns, social movements, and the like, the individual gains the experience and feeling of solidarity and belonging.

At the same time, these mass phenomena function to release the tensions and produce the satisfactions that are characteristic of modern life. Such participation compensates for the frustration that is the lot of the atomized individual. It provides vicarious substitutes for people who feel hedged in by the limiting complications of their lives. For example, in soap operas, motion pictures, television dramas, the pulp magazines, comic strips, and the like, people can live out the aspirations and expend the energies and feelings that the routines and boundaries of daily existence repress.

We have said that mass society establishes the situation for mass behavior which tends to become loosely patterned in mass culture. The state of instability and widespread change produced by mass phenomena contribute to the general social situation of collective behavior. There is, therefore, a functional relationship between mass phenomena, discussed in this chapter, and collective behavior, which is examined in the following chapter. The student must be cautioned, however, that crowd behavior, public phenomena, and social movements— the main forms of collective behavior—are not restricted to mass societies.

FOOTNOTES

1. Hannah Arendt, *The Origins of Totalitarianism* (New York: Harcourt Brace, 1954), p. 310.
2. Erich Fromm, *The Sane Society* (New York: Rinehart, 1955), p. 120.
3. See, in this connection, the following: José Ortega y Gassett, *The Revolt of the Masses* (New York: Morton, 1932); Karl Mannheim, *Man and Society* (London: Kegan, Trench, Trubner, 1940); Erich Fromm, *Escape from Freedom* (New York: Rinehart, 1945); Louis Wirth, "Consensus and Mass Communication," in *American Sociological Review*, 12:1-15 (February 1948); Robert Nisbet, *The Quest for Community* (New York: Oxford University Press, 1953); Kimball Young, *Social Psychology* (New York: Appleton-Century-Crofts, 1956), p. 201; Ralph H. Turner and Lewis M. Killian, *Collective Behavior* (Englewood Cliffs: Prentice-Hall, 1957), Chapter 9; and William Kornhauser, *The Politics of Mass Society* (Glencoe: Free Press, 1959).
4. Wilbur Schramm, *The Process and Effects of Mass Communication* (Urbana: University of Illinois Press, 1954), p. 75.
5. John W. and Matilda White Riley, "Mass Communication and the Social System," in Robert K. Merton *et al.*, eds., *Sociology Today* (New York: Basic Books, 1959), p. 569.
6. Hadley Cantril, *The Invasion from Mars* (Princeton: Princeton University Press, 1940), p. 3 *et passim.*
7. Turner and Killian, *op. cit.*, pp. 165-166.
8. *Ibid.*, pp. 208-210.
9. *Ibid.*, p. 210.
10. John W. Bennett and Melvin M. Tumin, *Social Life* (New York: Knopf, 1949), p. 609. See also Bernard Rosenberg and David M. White, eds., *Mass Culture: The Popular Arts in America* (Glencoe: Free Press, 1957); and Max Lerner, *America as a Civilization*, Volume 2, *Culture and Personality* (New York: Simon and Schuster, 1957), Chapter 11.
11. Bennett and Tumin, *op. cit.*, p. 624.
12. Condensed and adapted from Russell Lynes, *The Tastemakers* (New York: Harper, 1954), Chapter 3 especially.

MASS MEDIA—the press, radio, movies, television—have, during the past half-century, extended the horizons of most of the world's people. Through these media are transmitted news of the world and of local areas; entertainment to help pass our increasing leisure time; propaganda to influence thought and action; and educational material to help increase literacy and expand general knowledge.

Television (above), with its tremendous educational and entertainment potential, is an increasingly widespread means of disseminating information about other areas and other peoples. In some parts of the world, however, information transmission is still primitive. In the remote Soviet territory of Chokotka (right), mail, magazines, and books must be brought in by helicopter for the reindeer herders.

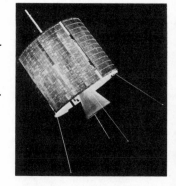

Present research in space, including the development of communication satellites, is binding the entire globe into a close-knit system in which events in one place will be known and transmitted just as fast as the world turns.

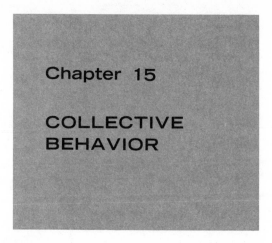

Chapter 15

COLLECTIVE BEHAVIOR

In earlier chapters we discussed the forms of organized social life. It was shown that culture, groups and associations, social institutions, and social categories are leading forms of social organization. However, equally typical of human social life are those situations in which change rather than stability, disorder rather than orderly structure, and uncertainty rather than predictability are distinctive.

In this chapter some of the manifestations of instability and change in human social life will be examined under the concept of collective behavior. Chapter 16 will discuss the sources, nature, and consequences of social change.

NATURE OF COLLECTIVE BEHAVIOR

The term "collective behavior" might be used to refer to the whole of human social relations that is the subject of sociology. Instead, however, by agreement, it has been reserved to describe a specific type of social relations. Ordinarily, collective behavior refers to crowds, publics, and social movements, which in the aggregate constitute the main areas of unstable and unstructured social activity. This concept provides a perspective for the study of those forms of social relations that lie outside ordinary social organization. Kimball Young and Linton Freeman write that "the concept collective behavior has usually been employed to refer to the relatively unstructured activities of aggregations such as crowds, mobs, audiences, followers of fashion and fads, and various publics."[1]

The unstructured nature of collective behavior is evident in a disaster such as a tornado, earthquake, or bomb attack. People will doubtless reveal intense feeling and random actions. However, their behavior will be relatively unstructured, since no cultural norms or social institutions exist (or are known) to control and pattern their behavior in such situations.

The decisive characteristic of collective behavior, then, is the fact that it is *relatively unstructured*. It gives free play to emotions, individual impulses, transitory opinions, and ephemeral allegiances. Yet such relatively unstructured behavior is not wholly dissociated from the order inherent in personal, cultural, and social organization. For example, the unstructured response to a disaster occurs within a society or community that possesses an established system of social and cultural organization. Thus, collective behavior is a two-edged concept— unstructured and structured, free-ranging and stable, spontaneous and conventionalized.

The concept of collective behavior as a perspective for the study of social relations focuses on the fringe of unstructured activity that issues from and surrounds the social order. It emphasizes change, not stability; innovation, not continuity; and reorganization, not organization.

Five underlying conditions of collective behavior have been identified and characterized.[2]

1. *Collective behavior is facilitated by absence, breakdown, or weakness of social control resulting from total lack or inadequacy of existing social organization.* Ordinary social forms fail to prescribe and sanction the appropriate ways of acting. Individuals are, therefore, left to their own decisions and devices.

2. *Collective behavior is facilitated by inadequate normative integration.* The cultural directives are inharmonious, inconsistent, or clashing. This condition invites the free play of emotion, personal rather than social responses, and decision on the basis of transitory impulses or opinions. For example, in a disaster people are not guided by well-established cultural norms. Or again, the shout of "Fire!" in a crowded theater may initiate unguided individualistic effort to escape the danger.

3. *Another condition that contributes to collective behavior is inadequacy of communication.* No commonly understood set of symbols, system of contacts, or channels of communication exist. Social signals fail to come through clear and strong to all participants. Some individuals fail to get the message at all, while for others it is weak, confusing, or garbled. They lack the proper cues to action and cannot, therefore, reciprocate in behavior by response to any commonly understood set of symbols.

4. *The sense of complexity, intricacy, and involvement inherent in the situation may also facilitate collective behavior.* Prevailing arrangements appear overwhelming, confusing, and threatening. The individual is dwarfed by the situation that appears unmanageable. He may feel no sense of loyalty or strong identification with the social organization. He may or must, therefore, follow his own decision.

5. *Finally, the foregoing syndrome of conditions functions to frustrate*

the individual and to predispose him to collective behavior. The individual's "legitimate" wishes for security, belonging, expression, and the like seem blocked, leaving him with a sense of deprivation and dissatisfaction. People tend to be restless and disenchanted. They seek release through crowds, fads, exotic movements, and the like.

These conditions often exist in rapidly growing, heterogeneous metropolitan areas. Sometimes, also, this syndrome of conditions may become general in an entire society. For example, during the mid-1960's crowd behavior has been widespread and intense in India. Crowd conditions have been sustained by rapid social change, political and economic instability, crop failures and food shortages, Hindu-Western culture conflict, population explosion, and rapid urbanization.

CROWD BEHAVIOR

The term "crowd" refers to collective behavior in many familiar situations. Some of them are listed in Figure 15-1. It will be seen that some, like lectures, religious services, or theater audiences, are relatively orderly and structured. Others, like athletic contests or auction sales, exhibit noticeably less structure. Beach gatherings or prison riots seem to exhibit only a negligible amount of structure. Most of the crowd situations listed appear to conform to prevailing social values. Some, however, like riots, lynch mobs, or adolescent gang fights, are clearly antisocial and structurally deviant. Most of the crowd situations are compact aggregations. Epidemic fashion and fad behavior, however, occur among dispersed populations where communication is secondary.

The situations listed in this figure provide a way of demonstrating that crowd behavior is numerically important. Consider, for example, professional baseball and football. In a single season, there are 1800 big league baseball games in 20 different cities before crowds that total nearly 20 million.[3] Professional football plays 72 games per season in 12 cities to crowds that are estimated to average 40,000 each.[4]

Characteristics of Crowd Behavior ▶ Although crowd situations are manifestly diverse and extensive, behavior in all reveals basically similar characteristics. Social relations are relatively unstructured and exhibit that quality of spontaneity, emotionality, and personalness that distinguishes collective behavior in general. Empirical research indicates that crowd behavior is distinguished by the following eight characteristics:

1. Social situations that are relatively unstructured and hence ambiguous.

2. Participants with different backgrounds, characteristics, and motivations, who, therefore, do not initially share common definitions and behavioral expectations.

Some Familiar Illustrations of Crowds

Athletic Contests
Professional—baseball, football, basketball, tennis, etc.
Academic—high school, college, university, all sports
Amateur—sand lot, recreation departments, all sports

Religious Gatherings
Regular services
Special services—revivals, crusades, etc.

Theater Audiences
Motion pictures—indoor and drive-in
Legitimate theater
Vaudeville—including night club shows

Rallies, Mass Meetings, Public Meetings
Political rallies (except nominating conventions)
Labor union rallies (except regular union meetings)
Protest mass meetings

Other Audience Situations
Lectures and concerts
Conventions—political, veterans, fraternal, etc.
Regular large-scale association meetings

Parties, Sociability Gatherings
Dances—both private and public
Receptions, especially large or public
Cocktail parties and other large parties

Other Large Gatherings
Parades or public welcomes for heroes and dignitaries
Demonstrations—student, ethnic group, political
Sales—auctions, bargain day, etc.
Beach crowd on hot summer days

Antisocial or Nonintegrated Collectivities
Lynching mobs
Riots—race, prison, etc.
Adolescent gang fights
Panic—theater, night club, etc.

Diffuse Epidemic Behavior
Swastika paintings, 1960
Phone booth crowding by college students, 1958-1960
Sit-in protests of Negro students, 1960
Sheath and sack styles of women's dresses

FIGURE 15-1

3. Existence of an atmosphere of crisis and uncertainty about the outcome of the situation.

4. A sense of urgency among participants who feel that they must do something immediately.

5. Initial restructuring of the situation by production and communication of common mood and image through processes of milling and rumor.

6. Crystallization of temporary crowd norms that reflect new cohesion and function to control participants.

7. Selective and variable suggestibility of participants in relation to processes of crowd mood and action.

8. Relatively permissive atmosphere with respect to attitudes and actions that are normally prohibited.

A Theory of Crowd Behavior ▸ The central problem of sociological analysis of crowd behavior is formulation of a scheme of explanation that fits the observed facts. A number of explanations have been constructed, applied, and rejected. For example, Gustave Le Bon postulated a "crowd mind," Sigmund Freud a version of the "Electra complex," and Everett Dean Martin the notion of "a social conspiracy" to render prohibited urges and actions respectable.[5] Utilizing a functional approach, Ralph H. Turner and Lewis M. Killian have constructed a theoretical model for the explanation of crowd behavior.[6] The basic proposition in this formulation is that crowd behavior constitutes one natural consequence of the circumstances of social life. It may, therefore, be explained and investigated by the same concepts and methods that are employed in the analysis of ordinary structures and functions of social life. The principal propositions of the theoretical model can be stated in the following way.

Crowd behavior is "built up" or generated through social interaction under certain specific conditions. The process is initiated when individuals who may differ in background, characteristics, motivations, behavior, etc., are aggregated by an arresting event or phenomenon. The relative structural vacuum in this situation creates an atmosphere of crisis, which functions to trigger the interactive crowd-building process of which milling is the preliminary stage. Milling (which heightens intersensitivity, develops shared symbols, and produces common mood and image) and rumor (which facilitates communication, transmits information, defines the situation, and structures behavior) are the principal mechanisms of initial crowd building.

If, at this stage, structure is imposed upon the situation by leadership of some kind—speaker, performer, presider, policeman, etc.—then the crowd-building process may be fixated. What is observed is conventionalized or controlled crowd behavior in an audience or a relatively structured situation. If the crowd-building process is not arrested, then the emotional dimension of interaction may further intensify in social contagion. In this event, high emotional or violently acting modes of crowd behavior may eventuate.

The crowd-building process has three social consequences. First, it produces common mood, image, and symbols that underlie crowd cohesion. Second, it facilitates temporary organization by generating crowd norms and by delineating and articulating social roles, among which the more obvious are leader, action hard core, rank and file participants, and ambivalent fringe or spectator-participants. And third, it generates a crowd process as revealed in intensification of emotional solidarity and distinctive overt action, either at the level of self-fulfilling social and emotional expression or goal-linked achievement.

The Sutler: Theory Illustrated ❧ Each step of the crowd-building process is illustrated in the following case. Men with divergent backgrounds and motives were pulled from the routines of camp life into a compact aggregate around a common focus of interest. In rumor and milling, they revealed their uncertainty about what was going to happen and their efforts to define the ambiguous situation. The jocose-angry ambivalence was resolved into social contagion that produced a uniformly ugly mood and defined the sutler (a man who followed the army and sold provisions to the soldiers) as unambiguously evil. A trivial symbolic incident—a little jet of blood spurting from the sutler's cheek—triggered intense contagion and overt action. The "regulars" as symbol of authority interrupted the contagion-action process.

We had fallen out and were lounging before our tents when a strange soldier from another regiment passed rapidly down the company street.

"There'll be some fun at the sutler's shack, just before taps," he remarked, to no-one in particular. Twenty paces further on he repeated his statement mechanically, and we heard him repeat it once more as he passed by the mess tent on his way to another company.

"Say, do you hear what that fellow said?" cried the cook, thrusting out his head from between the flaps of the mess tent.

"Oh shut up!" said the first sergeant. "You fellows have got to stay right here. Mind, I'm watchin' ye. The first fellow that leaves the company street'll get reported."

"What do you think?" murmured my tent-mate, Buck, an eager boy, enlisted under age. "They've been talking of running the sutler out."

"Nothing to it," I asserted. "They wouldn't dare. Anyway, you and I are going to keep out of it."

"Well, all right. But damn the sutler."

Until the pay ran out, the sutler was confronted from morning till night with thirsty and hungry soldiers, sometimes in ranks ten deep. And from morning till night an ugly quarrel was going on over his counter.

"Here, you damn dago, I gave you a dollar. Where's my change?"

"No, no, you gave me fi' cents."

"You're lying. Give me my change or I'll knock your damn head off."

The sutler would shrug his shoulders and serve another row of customers. If the trouble maker was very persistent, the sutler would shell out the change with poisonous gesture. He was an Armenian, and no doubt had learned in the trade with the Kurds how far one may defy, how far one must compromise with violence. Current report was that the sutler had made a regular practice of short change, but there was a strong minority opinion that this report was eight-tenths pure fabrication and one-tenth founded on mistake. Several men in my company boasted of their success in getting drinks for nothing and bullying the sutler out of change besides. Anyway, the sutler was bound to win out in the end; if his customers occasionally cheated him he nevertheless got the money back in trade. Inevitably he was cordially detested. . . .

The dusk was growing heavy. I was preparing to turn in, when Buck, who had been making a call on a neighboring company, thrust his head into the tent.

"Say," he whispered. "There aren't ten men in D company's tents. Our boys are all gone too. Let's get out before the officers catch on."

"They're all crazy," I grumbled. "They'll drill us to death tomorrow for this."

"Come on!" cried Buck, tugging at my belt.

I blew out my light and stepped out of the tent. Men from other companies were stealthily slipping through between the tents, headed for the sutler's. I caught some of Buck's eagerness and in a moment we, too, were slipping between tents in the darkness. Beyond the camp we issued upon a trail, now quite packed with dark figures.

"Hullo," sounded a strange voice in my ear. "Did he short change you?"

"No," I replied. "I never trusted him to make change."

"You were smart. I don't know another man he hasn't skinned. You're Peters, M company, aren't you?"

"No. C company."

"Oh, I mistook you. Gosh! Hear 'em?"

I caught the confused wave of sound, shouting interspersed with shrill whistles. We began to run.

In the clearing, under the flickering gasoline torch, hundreds of men were packed about the front of the sutler's shack. The Armenian stood in his doorway, pale but imperturbable, his eyes glaring fiercely, his thick lips curving in a nervous smile. The crowd was keeping its distance, as word had passed back from the front that the sutler had his finger on the trigger of a six-shooter. We were after fun, not shooting, and it was enough to hurl imprecations at him. When Buck and I arrived, the spirit of the crowd was good humored for the most part, but occasionally one could perceive a note of real hatred. What seemed a deliberate competition in imprecations got in motion, and the more violent curses gained rapidly over the milder ones. The character of the voices, too, began to change: the original miscellaneous clamor split into two well-defined currents of deep notes and high that would occasionally reinforce each other and make one thrill unaccountably. The crowd was pressing closer. The Armenian still kept his nerve, but the movements of his head were becoming spasmodic. It was still fun with us, but the idea that it was serious was visibly gaining on the Armenian.

"Poor devil," I thought, "this has been carried far enough." And then a new baying note rose from the mob, a note I had not supposed to be within the range of the human voice. I shivered, and as I glanced again at the Armenian darting his eyes from one quarter to another, in suppressed panic, I felt my pity slip from me. I began to exult, like a hunter who has found a wild animal in a trap, to finish at leisure. "Kill the damn thief! Kill the damn dago!" the crowd was yelling. It thrilled!

There was a lull: something was going on that we in the center could only divine. Above the mutterings, subdued for the moment, we heard a sound like the splitting of timber. Word passed from the flanks of the crowd. "They've pried out a plank behind." The Armenian turned to look back into his shack: his jaw dropped; his thin acquisitive profile quivered; the white of his eye seemed to glaze. A sharp pebble hurled from behind him struck him just below the cheek bone: it clung for a second, like a hideous black growth, then dropped, thrust out by a jet of blood. A mantle of frenzy fell upon the mob. An atrocious roar arose, carrying on its waves all the obscenities and blasphemies known to young America.

"Kill the damn Jew! Kill the God damn Nigger!"

The mob surged forward: all around me, men wedged between converging lines of force were crying out that they were being crushed. The Armenian darted into his shack, snapping the door in the face of a dozen men springing for him. They beat and pushed at the door while a hundred others thrust their weight against the counter shutters. The shack was rocking on its foundations: another thrust, and over she'd go. Suddenly I became conscious of a weakening of the pressure from behind me; of a subsidence of the volume of yells, of a subtle change in the quality of the sound. Did I merely imagine that I heard a sharp "Halt!" at my left? I stood on tiptoe, to look over the heads of the men about me. Through an opening produced by an accidental grouping of shorter men, I caught a glimpse of a long line of men in khaki, springing from the darkness to the rear, passing across the lighted circle, and into the darkness beyond, within which, by straining, one seemed to distinguish the dull gleam of rifle barrels and belt buckles, extending interminably.[7]

Crowd Structure ▶ In time, as the crowd-building process proceeds, individuals are mutually reoriented and engaged in reciprocating relations by fulfillment of a set of social roles that are uniquely typical of the crowd situation. Crowd cohesion and action facilitate articulation of these roles into an ephemeral structure. The center constitutes leaders who keynote the crowd process, either by symbolic communication of feelings and definitions of the situation, or by initiating, directing, and performing crowd actions. The leaders are fused with and supported by a hard core of dedicated participant followers. The main body of the crowd is composed of a less dedicated and more numerous but active body of participants. At this point, the crowd merges into an indefinite fluid fringe of ambivalent spectator-participants who are in continuous process of entering and leaving the crowd.

Milling and rumor in the amorphous situation of crowd-building facilitate the free flow of personal influence. In the example of the sutler, the mysterious soldier who passed through the camp reciting the announcement, the eager youth Buck, and the man encountered on the dark path to the sutler's shack perceptibly affected the narrator. In the developed crowd the flow of personal influence is conditioned by the role structure. Keynoters, agitators, and action leaders set the style for participants and spectators. Participants and spectators respond by approving or disapproving these suggestions or by sending up rival definitions and suggestions.

Crowds tend to vary in the following ways:

1. *Relation to social structure:* From that which is functionally integrated with the normative order and social structure to that which is structurally antithetical and largely dissociated from the prevailing values.

2. *Degree of formal organization:* From episodes which are conventionalized in place, time, and activity with substantial formal organization, to those which are almost wholly spontaneous and largely unstructured in both expression and activity.

3. *Level of action:* From activity of a wholly or mainly symbolic nature expressive of emotion and sociability to activity that is overt, sometimes violent, designed to attain definite and tangible objectives with the expression of emotion ancillary.

4. *Contiguity of participants:* From activity that aggregates individuals in compact units to collectivities that are loosely dispersed in both space and time.

Integrated Crowd Behavior ▶ Integrated crowd behavior is socially sanctioned and enjoys general approval. In this context of valuation, the terms crowd and crowd behavior are not sinister. Such crowd behavior constitutes either an extension or an instrument of the social structure.

Examples of integrated crowd behavior are numerous. Billy Graham's "Crusades" enjoy the support of local religious organizations and seek to advance generally approved ends. A political party nominating convention is a complex enterprise in sanctioned crowd behavior. At one time it may be a formal audience assembled to affirm the hallowed values and institutions of the society. Later, it becomes a public-opinion arena where issues are debated and decisions forged. The convention may be transformed into an uninhibited crowd indulging in a screaming, frenzied snake dance. Labor union rallies, Fourth of July orations in the park, jazz concerts in the Met or the Cow

Palace, athletic contests, and welcoming parades for homecoming heroes are other familiar illustrations. The Nazis, Chinese Communists, and Castro Cubans used the manipulated crowd as an instrument of government to sanction the liquidation of enemies, to enforce compliance with policies, and to generate enthusiasm for the party.

In terms of the supporting social order, integrated crowd behavior fulfills a number of social functions. With this instrumentality, churches save souls and conduct rallies, political parties nominate candidates, trade unions call or support strikes, athletic championships are decided, minority groups raise funds or morale, and civic and fraternal bodies formulate and execute policies. Parties, contests, rallies, and revivals provide socially approved occasions to ventilate feelings and relax tensions. Conventionalized crowds provide situations for revealing or enhancing social status. Through integrated crowd behavior social solidarity can be enhanced and participants can be supported or controlled.

Unintegrated Crowd Behavior ◗ Unintegrated crowd behavior opposes or violates sanctioned social standards. It is facilitated by social unrest, group conflict, ill-defined social change, widespread novel experience, and the like. It feeds upon unresolved anxieties, unrelieved dissatisfactions, and unsublimated hostilities. Unintegrated crowd behavior reflects cultural pluralism, for while it contravenes generally sanctioned standards and violates basic institutions, it is supported by subcultures and minority sectors of the population.

Unintegrated crowd behavior has many social consequences. Mobs, riots, gang fights, and the like destroy life and property, inflame passions, and render group conflict rigid and enduring. At the same time, however, they have been used as devices of social control and lead to emotional ventilation. Rioting has frequently been a method of popular revolt against political subjugation and tyranny.

The Chicago Race Riot: Unintegrated Crowd Behavior Illustrated ◗ A riot is a prolonged, dispersed, and destructive form of unintegrated crowd action. It involves mobs, rumor, panic, and certain other forms of collective behavior. In its direct-action phase, a riot involves a series of loosely linked and relatively uncoordinated aggressive crowds or mobs. They may spring up at widely separated parts of the community and carry out their depredations with little or no direct communication with one another. Many mobs form spontaneously from curious aggregations of spectators and loot, pillage, and murder until they spend their built-up fury. Some, however, are deliberately formed and directed. Later, on another day, the same or different individuals may join other mobs and commence the destruction all over again. In the following account of the famous Chicago race riot of 1919, these and other characteristics of unintegrated crowd behavior are illustrated.

The race riot broke out on Sunday, July 27. It was hot and humid, one in a series of 90 degree and more days. The lake beach flanks an area thickly inhabited by Negroes, yet it was used by both Negroes and whites. That section near Twenty-Seventh Street by tacit understanding had been considered as reserved for Negroes. The whites used the part near Twenty-Ninth Street.

Around four o'clock of the fateful July afternoon, Eugene Williams, a Negro boy, was swimming off shore around the foot of Twenty-Ninth Street. He had entered the water at a point used by Negroes and drifted south into the part ordinarily used by the whites. It was a hot day and white men, women, and children were congregated on the beach and in the water in that vicinity. Four Negroes passed through the group of whites and entered the water. They left when ordered away summarily by some of the white men. Soon, however, they returned with other Negroes.

Then there began a series of attacks, retreats, counterattacks, and stone-throwing that lasted for some time. Williams remained in the water during the fracas. He found a floating railroad tie and clung to it. Stones frequently struck the water near him. During the melee, a white boy of about his same age swam toward Williams. He let go the tie as the white boy neared, took a few strokes, and went down. Rumor held that Williams had been hit by one of the stones and drowned. But when examined later, his body showed no stone bruises. Several Negro witnesses blamed a certain white man for the stoning of Williams. They demanded that he be arrested by a white policeman who was on duty at the time. No arrest was made.

Awe in the face of tragedy gave way to excitement and whispers. "THEY" said he was murdered. The rumor circulated that the white policeman "REFUSED" to arrest the murderer. The Negroes began to mass dangerously. At this crucial point in the situation the accused white policeman arrested a Negro upon the complaint of a white man. The Negroes attacked the white officer. The riot was under way.

Reports of Williams' drowning and the alleged conduct of the white policeman fanned out into the neighborhood. Two hours later another death occurred. The crowd of Negroes moved up from the beach to the foot of Twenty-Ninth Street. As it grew more and more excited, a group of policemen was summoned by the officer who had been on duty at the beach. James Crawford, one of the Negroes, fired into the group of policemen. He was shot and killed by a Negro patrolman. Throughout the rest of that Sunday afternoon, many distorted rumors circulated rapidly through the neighborhood. The Negro mob from Twenty-Ninth Street swung into action attacking and beating white men that came into contact with it. As the rumors magnified and spread, new crowds gathered. Mobs spontaneously flared into activity and gangs commenced to join the lawlessness. It was reported that in all four white men were beaten, five were stabbed, and one was shot.

With the approach of darkness, white gangs farther to the west in the Stock Yard district joined the mob action. They attacked Negroes in white districts. It was estimated that from 9 p.m. until 3 a.m., twenty-seven were beaten, seven stabbed and four shot.

Few clashes occurred on Monday morning. But in the afternoon, white men and boys between the Stock Yards and the "Black Belt" amused themselves maliciously by directing mob violence against Negro workers as they returned home. White persons of all ages thronged the main thoroughfares, the street car routes, and especially the transfer points. Mob leaders brought street cars under control by pulling trolleys from wires. Negro passengers were dragged to the street, beaten, and kicked. Meanwhile, the police appeared powerless to cope with such numerous attacks. The reports showed that four Negro men and one white assailant were killed, and thirty Negro men were severely beaten in street car clashes on Monday afternoon.

At midnight Monday, the street car clashes ended because of a general strike that tied up the surface and elevated lines. The tie-up was complete and lasted the remainder of the week. By Monday night both whites and Negroes began to show signs of panic. Each group stayed to itself. Spontaneous mob violence gave way to deliberate terrorism by organized gangs.

. . . By Wednesday, July 30, the riot began to subside. At 10:30 p.m., the Mayor yielded to pressure and called out the militia which had been mobilized in nearby armories ever since Monday night. Rain on Wednesday and Thursday broke the heat wave and drove idle people into their homes. Thereafter, the violence and mob action declined steadily and rapidly until the riot was said to have ended completely by Saturday.[8]

Diffuse Crowd Behavior ♦ Through mass communication, crowd behavior can be extended beyond the limits of the localized collectivity. An extended communication system sustains the atmosphere of crisis and urgency over a wide area. Through mass communication, dispersed individuals can participate in the milling-rumor process and acquire the mood and image that emanate from a compact collectivity. Participants tend to develop the temporary crowd structure of norms, roles, and statuses that justify crowd behavior and counteract the control of traditional social norms.

The extended crowd communication system is illustrated in the telecast of an exciting athletic contest or of the racial incidents in Alabama in 1964 and 1965. When the event continues for days, as with a World Series or the assassination and burial of President John F. Kennedy, a diffuse crowd atmosphere is sustained and many dispersed individuals join the process of milling and rumor. Sometimes a crowd situation may be maintained in an entire nation for months. For example, in India during the fall and winter of 1966-1967 a nationwide situation persisted for months over the agitation against cow slaughter, which included several riots and dramatic fasts by *Acharyas* (fanatical leaders).

Diffuse crowd behavior is supported and renewed by a series of primary communication centers. Crowd participants form primary communication knots that tie them into the stream of mass communication. They animate and validate the standardized fare by giving it personal reference. Mass communication and interpersonal interaction are twin aspects of the same process. At the same time, the diffuse crowd is the source of new compact crowds. The existence of a diffuse crowd situation poses a continuing threat of the apparently spontaneous development of compact crowds.

PUBLIC BEHAVIOR

Louis Wirth suggests that public behavior in the technical sense was presaged by four developments in the history of Western societies.[9] First, the democratic revolutions admitted the mass of "nonelites" into the decision-making process. Second, mobility and urbanization detached them from the consensus of the mores and kinship society. Third, popular education functioned to admit the detached masses to aspects of the cultural heritage from which they had hitherto been excluded. And finally, mass communication mediated interaction at the secondary level.

Sociological analysis in this field has focused upon three main problems. The first problem is the structure and functions of public behavior. The second is the various methods of ascertaining the state and fluctuations of thought and opinion. And third, the very nature of this situation directs analytic attention to the control and manipulation of opinion and action as phases of the process of decision-making.

Nature of Public Behavior ◗ The term "public" may be used to refer to a dispersed collectivity that is (1) interested in, reacting to, and divided by an issue; and (2) seeking to formulate and express a collective opinion for the purpose of influencing some course of social action relative to the issue.[10] A public is, therefore, a form of social organization, a field of communication, and a system of social action.

The *issue* is the crucial element in the concept of the public. By its very nature an issue is a matter or subject that holds widespread importance and is at the same time both provocative and unsettled. It functions to legitimize disagreement and to structure interaction. The issue decisively defines the difference between public and crowd behavior. In the latter, disagreement is discouraged, dissent is suppressed, and emotional consensus is paramount.

Illustrations of issues may be found in the news stories of newspapers, radio, and television. Among others that have current importance are (1) testing nuclear weapons, (2) school desegregation, (3) tax reduction and reform, (4) Vietnam policy, and (5) the nature and content of high-school and collegiate education. The following case illustrates the nature of public behavior and the role of the issue.

Dispute in Dubuque ◗ Citizens of Dubuque, Iowa, have shown themselves to be interested in, reacting to, and divided by the issue of "obscene literature." Communication between the disagreeing parties takes the form of debate and controversy. Both disputants are seen to be trying to define a clear position on the issue and to win adherents from the uncommitted members of the community. Each side also is trying to sell its point of view to the responsible officials of city government.

All Dubuque was taking sides last week, either with the good ladies in church clubs or the lusty wenches of fiction.

It all began when the chief of police scooped up a lot of 25¢ reprints off newsstands, surveyed a collection of busty, flamboyant dames on the book jackets, and accused a distributor of peddling obscene literature. Then county attorney John Duffy, a Notre Dame graduate who takes his knowledge of literature seriously, looked over the evidence. The obscene books turned out to include best sellers by Somerset Maugham, McKinlay Kantor, and John Steinbeck, and a collection of art masterpieces which had in it nudes by Velasquez and Titian. He dismissed the charge and for doing so forthwith got the club women on his neck. They thought that such books should be barred from the newsstand and put out of reach of children. Duffy invited them to appear before the Dubuque grand jury and state their case, countered by sending two officers to the public library with a warrant for the seizure of copies of Boccaccio's *Decameron*, Fielding's *Tom Jones*, and some of Rabelais' works.

Both sides decided to state their position clearly. Duffy explained his library raid: "The action was taken so we will have something for the grand jury to use in making comparisons. I'm no expert on obscene literature and I don't believe the grand jury is either."

Mrs. Anthony Eberhardt, a mother of school-age children, was spokesman for the women's group, which included the Catholic Mothers Study Club, the Council of Protestant Churches, and the Dubuque Parent-Teachers Association. Said she: "We are not trying to influence adult reading or adult thinking. We are merely trying to remove what is objectionable to children. Of course, if this restriction is incompatible with freedom, then we agree that freedom is more important."

Duffy subpoenaed a couple of English professors from the State University of Iowa to tell the jury the difference between a classic and a dirty book.

After the session with the grand jury, Professor Paul Engle summed up his observations. "I didn't see a book there that I thought was really obscene. I think a lot of these novels are cheap, badly written books, and are a lot more likely to corrupt a child's prose style than his morals." Then Professor Engle got down to a point that really troubled the clubwomen of Dubuque: "I think if these books had come out in quiet jackets the whole controversy might not have started."[11]

Organization of Public Behavior ♦ The organization of public behavior may be analyzed from three perspectives. First, in the course of debating an issue, the conditions of public behavior facilitate the performance of a series of more or less specialized social roles. When articulated around an issue, such roles produce the transitory structure of public behavior. Ralph H. Turner and Lewis M. Killian have identified "instigator," "opinion leader," and "opinion receiver" as the principal types of public roles.[12] A schematic representation of the structure of public behavior in terms of such roles is shown in Figure 15-2.

Schematic Portrayal of Social Structure of Public Behavior

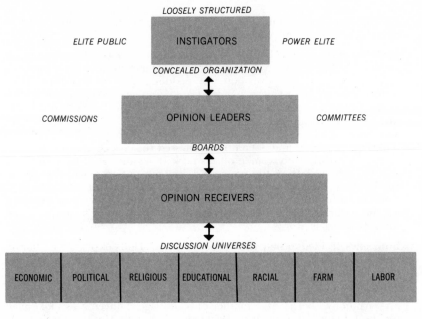

FIGURE 15-2

The instigators or originators of public opinion are members of the institutional power leadership. They constitute a kind of loosely organized, often invisible "elite public" which formulates and tests opinions or policies by reference to the mass of non-elites. Their conclusions are then transmitted to the opinion leaders for implementation. The opinion leaders are the visible members of such social structures as commissions, boards, and committees. In direct relations with the receiving non-elites they administer the policy decisions that are implicit in opinion creations of the instigators. The opinion receivers seldom originate interpretations of issues or formulate social policies. However, they constitute the ultimate decision-making referent of public opinion and social policy.

Public behavior is functionally related to the general social structure. Each participant, whatever his role in the structure of public behavior, in fact is initially a member of an institutional system and series of reference groups that Turner and Killian have called "discussion universes." This method of analysis suggests that public behavior is grounded in the general structure and is represented by the large block and its subdivisions that are shown in the bottom section of the figure. Discussion universes, with their established consensus, traditional mores, and social organization, equip the individual with basic attitudes and original orientations toward each social issue. The individual's final decision and course of action are likely to be influenced as much by the frame of reference of the discussion universes as by the facts and arguments of the public-opinion process.

Second, the organization of public behavior may be disclosed at the level of communication. By virtue of their membership in discussion universes and other reference groups, participants are committed initially to definitions of issues. Such initial definitions are, however, little more than general value positions prescribed by the institutional mores. Turner and Killian have shown that the ensuing debate consists principally in redefining and refining existing formulations of issues.[13] In this process a field of communication is structured by differentiating positions, indicating mutual orientations, and specifying roles of discussion and action. Public opinion consists of all the various definitions and actions that are relevant to a given issue at any time. The public-opinion process is contained in the definition-redefinition sequence that tends toward consensus regarding the issue or toward its ultimate disappearance.

Finally, public behavior is revealed as organized in terms of the action commitments of the variable definitions of the issue. This approach of analysis derives from the fact, noted earlier, that public opinion develops and is expressed with a view to influencing a course of social action or the process of decision-making relative to the issue. Nelson N. Foote and Clyde W. Hart propose that action can be analyzed in terms of an idealized series of phases.[14] First is the "problem" phase, when individuals recognize their situation as being problematical and therefore express discontent. Second is the "proposal" phase, when people are dominated by the sense that something must be done. They advance various proposals, some of which are rejected while others are adopted. In the third or "policy" phase, explicit discussion leads to group decision and responsible commitment to a course of action. In the final or "program" phase, the policy decision is translated into action. In this phase the public as a divided and disagreeing collectivity is supplanted by an organized group. It will be evident that all phases of the action process may, and in most instances do, occur simultaneously and repeatedly.

Managing Public Behavior ♦ In modern mass societies the social system functions largely on the basis of the open and transitory decisions that constitute social policy. Public opinion, then—not custom—is the significant prelude to collective action. In the formulation of social policy and the implementation of social action the decisions of the masses of non-elites are crucial. In these circumstances it becomes imperative to ascertain and manage public opinion.

The management of public behavior may be analyzed from two perspectives. The first focuses on the groups and associations that implement the opinion and action phases of public behavior. The second concentrates upon the methods of controlling the ideas and information that enter the stream of mass communication. The groups and associations that implement public behavior are called "vested interests" and "pressure groups." The content of mass communication is controlled by the methods of "censorship" and "propaganda."

Pressure groups include those associations and organized categories that engage in the effort to change or prevent the change of the status quo. When they favor existing arrangements (because of special advantages) such groups are called vested interests. Political parties, labor-union federations, industrial corporations, trade associations, religious associations, and ethnic or racial organizations are typical pressure groups. Such groups employ a variety of methods and tactics, including lobbies, propaganda, pressure politics, economic and social sanctions, public-relations techniques, and even bribery and intimidation to influence the formation of public opinion, the development of social policies, and the course of social action.

Control of the mass media (censorship) and control of the content of mass communication (propaganda) are two mechanisms for managing public behavior. In the contemporary totalitarian nations, censorship and propaganda have been carried to extremes. In the United States, however, no such complete control of mass communication is now possible. American public opinion is therefore less manageable and predictable than that in the Soviet Union.

In the U.S., government bureaus, party agencies, editorial offices, and other officials screen and select the content of newspapers and magazines, as well as radio and television programs.[15] The dispatches of American foreign correspondents are censored, to some degree at least, by officials of foreign countries. During the Second World War, the federal government exercised strict control over news and information that was vital to the war effort. Media of mass communication were placed under supervision of the Office of War Information. In ordinary circumstances, however, censorship is less severe and universal.

The term propaganda is used in many different ways.[16] In social science, however, it is now generally understood to refer to the conscious manipulation of symbols of communication to persuade individuals to accept a given point of view or opinion and consequently to act in a predetermined way. It is, therefore, by its very nature both deliberate and relatively rational. The essence of propaganda is the manipulation of symbols. These include, in addition to words and visual images—pictures, diagrams, signs, colors, etc.—auditory and other sensory symbols and various combinations of these. Perhaps the most important class of symbols is familiar and emotional collective representations. They express and draw upon such emotions as fear, hostility, security, love, hope, anger, distrust, disgust, friendship, and the like. They take many different forms—words, slogans, images, epithets, catchwords, nicknames, and so on.

Propaganda aims at influencing individual and collective opinion and the actions that issue from opinion. Its ultimate purpose is to persuade masses of people to engage in a predetermined course of action. It involves selection, organization, and dissemination of information regarding matters of widespread interest. Its content includes fact and fancy, truth and untruth, sound and erroneous interpretations, slanted and unbiased information.

One brief case is presented to illustrate the management of public behavior. The case is a summary of Robert K. Merton's analysis of Kate Smith's war-bond-selling campaign. This material portrays the process and method of propaganda and points out the major social symbols that were manipulated.

PROPAGANDA FOR WAR BONDS

September 21, 1943 was war bond day for the Columbia Broadcasting System. During the span of eighteen hours—from eight o'clock that morning until two the next morning—a radio star named Kate Smith spoke for a minute or two at repeated intervals. (Stardom implies a mammoth audience: it was estimated that in 1943 some 23,000,000 Americans listened to Smith's daytime programs in a week and some 21,000,000 to her weekly evening programs.)

On sixty-five distinct occasions in the course of the day she begged, cajoled, demanded that her listeners buy war bonds. Within the narrow borders of her brief messages, Smith managed to touch upon a variety of themes enshrined in American culture. She talked of neighbor boys from American towns and villages, now facing danger and death in other lands. And people listened. She told dramatic tales of generosity and sacrifices by soldiers and civilians alike. People continued to listen. She invoked themes of love and hate, of large hopes and desperate fears, of honor and shame. Apparently there was nothing here out of a cut-and-dry radio script. This was presented as a personal message, iterated and reiterated in a voice which often broke, it seemed, by deep emotion. And people did more than listen.

Before nightfall, Smith could begin to announce large totals of bond pledges. At one climactic moment, she reported that listeners in Los Angeles had that day subscribed several million dollars in response to her appeal. Each succeeding announcement acclaimed a swelling national sum of pledges. By the end of this, her third all-day drive, Smith had shattered her previous bond-selling records. During her first drive, she had amassed a million dollars in pledges and her second had netted two million. But this third war loan appeal far outstripped her earlier efforts, resulting in thirty-nine millions of dollars of bond pledges in the course of the one day. Here apparently was an extraordinary instance of mass persuasion.

. . . The content of Smith's broadcasts was analyzed into recurring themes and the proportion of time devoted to each of the themes was taken as a crude measure of comparative emphasis. As the following chart shows, she dealt almost exclusively upon six major themes.

What Smith Said: Time Distribution of Themes

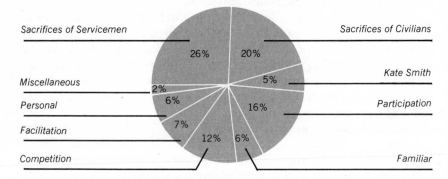

Sacrifices of Servicemen — 26%

Sacrifices of Civilians — 20%

Kate Smith — 5%

Miscellaneous — 2%

Personal — 6%

Participation — 16%

Facilitation — 7%

Competition — 12%

Familiar — 6%

Keynoting her appeals was the theme of sacrifice to which Smith devoted fully half her broadcast time. Twenty-six per cent went to stories of the sacrifices of servicemen; almost as much, 20 per cent, to the sacrifices of civilians and 5 per cent the sacrifices of one civilian in particular, namely, Kate Smith herself.

Sixteen per cent of all Smith had to say dealt upon the theme of participation, setting forth the view that the bond campaign was a common enterprise in which all of us could shuffle off our private egoisms and take part in a massive communal effort. Direct appeals to the families of service men accounted for 6 per cent of her broadcast time; a familial theme which defined war bonds as a means of getting the boys back home.

. . . Twelve per cent of her time was devoted to the competition theme, which urged listeners to help Smith surpass her earlier bond sales records and to help their own communities outdo others in purchasing bonds from her. The facilitation theme, accounting for seven per cent, reminded her hearers of the ease with which they could telephone their bond pledges. And the personal theme, in which Smith conversationally referred to her private feelings and aspirations, was casually interwoven into 6 per cent of her broadcasts.[17]

Ascertaining Public Opinion ▶ A great deal of effort is devoted to ascertaining and measuring public opinion. This is one consequence of the decision-making role of the non-elites in modern mass societies. Since public opinion is the prelude to action, it becomes imperative to know the state and changes of that opinion in order to understand, manage, and predict collective decision. Such activity, however, has little importance where consensus issues from the mores, where decisions are firm and universal, and where there are few disagreements regarding basic values and the actions issuing from them. In associational societies ascertaining the nature of public opinion is essential to rational and successful social action.

Some forty years ago, Arthur N. Holcombe reported twenty-three methods of ascertaining public opinion that were employed by political scientists.[18] He arranged the methods into four classes: (1) official election returns, (2) measuring fair samples of bodies of opinion,

(3) voluntary and spontaneous expressions, i.e., hearings, meetings, petitions, editorials, and (4) proceedings and remarks of legislative and other representative bodies of individuals. For present purposes, the methods of ascertaining public opinion most widely in use can be classified under three headings: (1) common-sense, (2) historical, and (3) scientific polling.

1. *Common-Sense Methods.* Perhaps the simplest and most direct way to ascertain the state of public opinion on any issue is to hold a referendum or election. If enough alternatives are presented and if all members of the group participate, it will be possible to obtain a relatively complete and accurate expression of opinion at the time. The periodic elections and referenda that occur in the United States and its subdivisions are common-sense measures of public opinion on a wide range of issues. Although such expressions are useful, they are never complete or final. All shadings of viewpoint are not represented. All members of the public never vote. The judgment expressed at one election is subject to change a short time thereafter.

Another common-sense device may be called "reading the pulse" of the public. A variety of pulse-reading techniques are in regular use. A newspaper or magazine may take a "straw poll" of its readers on a given issue. The summary of their answers serves as one common-sense measure of public opinion. Or again, a public official who wishes to know the state of public opinion on an issue before taking action may send up a "trial balloon." That is, he "leaks" a story and notes the reaction in newsprint, editorial comment, letters to the editor, mail from the people, and the like.[19] The amount, intensity, and nature of this reaction give a clue to the prevailing state of public opinion and may serve adequately as a working guide.

Further, prior to an election or during a "grand debate" on foreign or domestic policy, a newspaperman or public official may make a "swing around the country." He meets and talks with people from all regions, classes, and backgrounds, and attempts to summarize his observations and impressions. Somewhat similar is the survey of editorial opinion and mail. Representative newspapers in different regions and with different slants are selected and their editorial comment on the issue is digested and analyzed. Communications to the press and to members of Congress may similarly be summarized and analyzed. From such a survey a common-sense judgment can be derived of the prevailing state of public opinion.

2. *Historical Methods.* Historical methods are used to ascertain the long-range variations of public opinion. Short-run fluctuations constitute variations around long-term or secular trends. One historical approach employs the case method. The student investigates the variations in the development of public behavior in a single area of life or regarding a single issue. For example, Emory Bogardus presents two case studies of the development of public opinion extending over

a period of almost seventy-five years.[20] The investigations deal with the women's suffrage movement and prohibition.

As noted earlier, public behavior is grounded in the value commitments of the institutional structure, or as Turner and Killian put it, "discussion universes." The historical development of public opinion on any continuing issue can therefore be studied by examining trends and drifts in the content and expression of underlying values. Clarence Schettler notes that a variety of research methods may be employed in this task. He writes: "[A]n historical study can be a presentation of impressions, an interpretation and description of trends that are based upon statistical analysis, a compilation of illustrations, an experimental design of an ex post facto nature, a correlational analysis, etc."[21]

This author has noted that when interpreted in terms of the value heritage, some long-time issues tend to produce two extreme or polar definitions.[22] Public opinion tends to be crystallized and social policy and action are developed at many different positions between these polar extremes. In historical perspective, public behavior appears to oscillate in terms of definitions of the issue and correlated action between the two polar positions.

Harold Gosnell has identified certain trends or cycles in American life.[23] He notes that when the nation goes Democratic, certain states become far more Democratic than others, and when the swing is to the Republican Party, these same states go farther in this direction than other states.

3. *Public Opinion Polling.* The poll is now the best-known and most reliable method of ascertaining the state and changes of public opinion. The basic method of public opinion polling is not new. Newspapers and magazines have employed this technique for many years. For example, this device achieved notoriety in 1936 by the famous *Literary Digest* prediction of Republican victory in the presidential election.

The method of the public opinion poll consists of asking a "sample" of individuals their views on a given issue. The newness of current methods rests upon the scientific validity and refinement of the sampling technique and the procedures of analysis and interpretation. So important is this development that the application of scientific method for measurement of public opinion has become the major business of several national concerns. Rensis Likert characterizes public opinion polling methods as follows.

> The polling process can be conveniently divided into two major parts. One is the population sample used. The second is the questionnaire, the method of interviewing and the analysis of the replies. The accuracy of any poll depends upon the accuracy of each of these parts of the process.[24]

Many other scientific techniques may be employed in the measurement of states and changes of public opinion. Norman J. Powell states that "the manifold measurement devices available may be classified on the basis of objectivity, source of data, technique of collecting the desired information or other criteria."[25] Using method of gathering data as the criterion, Powell identifies the following alternatives to polling: (1) scales, (2) tests, (3) informal and depth interviews, (4) mail questionnaires, (5) mass observation, and (6) content analysis.

SOCIAL MOVEMENTS

In the two decades since the end of the Second World War, exotic place names and strange phrases have headlined leading stories in American newspapers. Readers have added names like Korea, Indonesia, Vietnam, Laos, Guinea, Algeria, Cyprus, and the Congo to their active vocabularies. They have become familiar with such phrases as Zionism, "cold war," Huks, Mau Mau, Eoka, Arab League, and Viet Cong. Most people are likely to associate these words and names with change, violence, and the danger of another world war. All these words and many others constitute the newsworthy name tags of social movements. In the aggregate they have provided a leading source of important news for nearly two decades. They refer to the most significant social events in the modern world.

There are no precise data on the number and extent of social movements in recent times. Rudolf Heberle cites liberalism, labor, socialism, conservatism, and fascism as the great social movements in the West since the eighteenth century.[26] Figure 15-3 lists some of the social

Some Typical Social Movements	International Communism
	German Nazism
	World Zionism
	Bahai World Faith
	Algerian Independence Movement
	Mau Mau of Kenya
	Castro's July 26 Revolution in Cuba
	National Liberation Front, Viet Cong
	Ghandi's Civil Disobedience in India
	French Poujadism
	Non-Partisan League in the U. S.
	The Townsend Movement of 1930's
	Industrial Labor Unionism

FIGURE 15-3

movements that have developed during the last generation or so. Some of the items in this list refer to movements that are international in scope. Others, however, consist of nationalistic revolts of subject peoples; the third group includes reform efforts or religious expressions that are limited to the territory of a single nation.

Nature and Classification of Social Movements ♦ Herbert Blumer observed that "social movements can be viewed as collective enterprises to establish a new order of life."[27] They arise out of a background that includes societal inadequacy, collective unrest, and personal dissatisfaction. A social movement is a complex, dynamic system of collective behavior whose most distinctive constituents are a social collectivity, a social ideology, and a social structure. In the course of its development, a social movement may encompass manifestations of all the other forms of collective behavior.

Ralph H. Turner and Lewis M. Killian define a social movement as "a collectivity acting with some continuity to promote a change or resist a change in the society or group of which it is a part."[28] They point out that the decisive characteristics of the social movement include (1) indefinite and shifting membership, (2) leadership determined by informal response of members, and (3) action that is continuous in several respects.

Social movements are classified in a variety of ways, depending upon the criterion employed. Figure 15-4 presents some systems of classification together with the main criterion upon which each is based. The types listed in the first three lines of the exhibit are primarily common-sense classifications, and they have only limited usefulness in empirical analysis. Blumer's system of types presented in the fourth line is well known as an attempt to construct a heuristic classification. The last line contains a system of three-fold classification that was developed and applied by Turner and Killian. Although the systems of classification vary in applicability, each has some use in the study of social movements. Turner and Killian differentiate the true social movement from "mass movements," "followings," and "cults," which they call "quasi-movements."[29]

Conditions of Social Movements ♦ Empirical research suggests that a social movement is properly viewed as a social product.[30] It arises and unfolds in response to a syndrome of conditions that may occur in any society. Although a large number of conditions tend to facilitate or support this form of collective behavior, the following four seem to be the most important.

1. *Societal inadequacy:* failure of existing institutions and agencies to gain the goals and ends of life that are defined and sanctioned by prevailing values, or inapplicability of existing values to the actual circumstances of life.

Some Systems of Classifying Social Movements Together with Main Criteria of Classification

Area of Activity:	political, economic, religious, minority group
Extent of Change:	reform, revolution
Direction of Change:	progressive, conservative, reactionary
Functional Scope:[1]	general, specific, expressive
Social Order:[2]	value-oriented, power-oriented, participation-oriented

1. Herbert Blumer, "Social Movements," in A. M. Lee, ed., Principles of Sociology (New York: Barnes and Noble, 1957), p. 199.
2. Ralph H. Turner and Lewis M. Killian, Collective Behavior (Englewood Cliffs: Prentice-Hall, 1957), p. 327.

FIGURE 15-4

For example, during the Great Depression of the 1930's "rugged individualism" appeared inapplicable to the circumstances of life when millions of people were unemployed and destitute and when a man could not find a job no matter how hard he tried or how good his reputation was. With increased outside contacts, with growing education, and with an increasing sense of power and nationalism, the native peoples of Africa south of the Sahara cease to accept themselves as the "white man's burden." The wretched, oppressed millions of seventeenth- and eighteenth-century Europe saw little in their lot to support the idea of "benevolent despotism."

2. *Social unrest:* a state of life characterized by widespread feelings of uncertainty, uneasiness, and insecurity, often tending to spiral downward from uncertainty to uneasiness, to insecurity, to bewilderment, to desperation. Social unrest is characterized by random seeking of meaning and by milling and social contagion. A German ex-serviceman writes the following description of the social unrest in the early days of the Nazi movement.

> Some thirty-five parties arose to confute the people, a very witch's Sabbath. Devoid of political training, sick of body and soul, the German people reeled giddily after the different will-o'-the-wisps. . . . There was a constant tension in the air. One government followed the other, the Marxists held huge mass meetings. The population was split up into tiny parties, the atmosphere was teeming with all sorts of plans. There was no unity of purpose anywhere. It was impossible to find one's way in the Hell's Kitchen of contradictory opinions. Divided by political views, interests, class and caste, the people were so many toys in the hands of the nation's enemies.[31]

3. *Personal dissatisfaction.* Unsublimated frustrations issue from widening gulfs between wishes and satisfactions, and the awareness of

the discrepancy between one's aspirations and his performances (between his ego level and his achievement level). The general tendency to depreciate the social worth of individuals and categories of individuals, and the widespread feeling that society has failed to give an innovator a fair and adequate hearing are also frustrating.

For example, under the Weimar Republic in post-First World War Germany, the salaried middle classes, seeing their prized status and prestige weakening and diminishing, became acutely dissatisfied. European businessmen and civil servants in colonial cities recognize the tendency of subject peoples to withhold status recognition as one of the early signs of "native trouble." One of the most disturbing indices of the Negro protest in the southern United States, from the viewpoint of the whites, has been the dissatisfaction of Negroes with traditional status-revealing symbols and patterns.

4. *Alternative proposals.* Another condition of social movements is the tendency of people to advocate alternatives to existing social values and institutional apparatus and transformation of these into rival programs. During the Great Depression of the 1930's, for example, a host of proposals arose to challenge the alleged effete social and economic order. Among the more familiar are the Townsend Movement, the National Farmers Union, the Political Action Committee, religious cults of many kinds, the Congress of Industrial Organizations, and the "New Deal" itself. In developing societies national independence emerges as an alternative to subordinate colonial status, and in seventeenth- and eighteenth-century Europe democracy arose to challenge declining benevolent despotism. Each of the conditions that underlie and precede social movements is illustrated in the following brief case.

THE NON-PARTISAN LEAGUE

For a number of years there had been signs of discontent in the upper Mississippi and Missouri valleys. Matters first came to a head in North Dakota. Resentment there was strong against the high interest rates of banks, the excessive charges of middlemen. Farmers of the state came to believe by 1915 that legislation was necessary to aid their demands. In that year they proposed the establishment of state-owned grain elevators, but the legislature refused to go along. Then they turned to a newly formed organization which promised to take political control away from the bankers and corporate interests and give political power to the farmers.

The Non-Partisan League was started in Bismarck, North Dakota in February, 1915. The idea of the organization was first presented to the North Dakota Union of the American Society of Equity, a group interested in cooperatives. The Union approved the idea and gave support to the man who "sold" them the idea. Organizers were sent out at once and by the end of that year the foundations of the League were firmly established.

. . . The league called for state ownership of terminal elevators, flour mills, packing houses, and cold storage plants. Other objectives, aimed at reducing the farmers' costs, included state-owned rural credit banks, exemption of farm improvements from taxation and state hail insurance. In a bid

for organized labor cooperation, the Non-Partisan league stood traditionally for basic workers' aims. . . .[32]

Ideological System of the Social Movement ❯ Social phenomena like
International Communism, French *Poujadism,* the Mau Mau of Kenya,
and the Non-Partisan League may appear more different than alike.
Yet as social movements, all are comparable by virtue of an underlying
ideological system. C. Wendell King has observed, "More than merely
stating its goals, the ideology of a movement encompasses most of what
is essentially its culture."[33] By means of this sociopsychological mechanism, individuals of many different kinds are fused together into a
more or less cohesive social collectivity. The ideology constitutes the
common emotional base, the intellectual arena, and the action orientation of the social movement. Herbert Blumer has identified the
following five functional elements in the ideological system.

1. A statement of the objectives, purposes, and promises of the
social movement.

2. A body of criticism and condemnation of the existing social order.

3. A collection of defense doctrines which serve as justifications of
the movement and of its objectives and methods.

4. A system of beliefs dealing with the policies, tactics, and practical
operations of the movement.

5. The myth, or societal goal of the movement, stated in utopian
terms and often captured in slogans, e.g., "the classless society," "Thirty
Dollars Every Thursday," or "First-class Citizenship."[34]

Development of Social Movements ❯ Social movements like crowds are
"built up." In the course of their development they encompass the
other major forms of collective behavior: mass reactions, crowd behavior, and public behavior. Rex Hopper has constructed a four-stage
model of the "natural history" of social movements that analyzes their
development and reveals the role of the other forms of collective
behavior.[35]

1. *Primary Stage: Mass Reaction.* Initially people are disturbed by
widespread unemployment, increased crime and delinquency, family
breakdown, housing evictions, mounting personal debts, and other
evidences of institutional failure. Frustrated and discontented, they mill
about restlessly looking for the source of their problems and the way
out of their dilemmas. Agitators and rabble rousers aggravate the situation with their propaganda of complaint and criticism. In this stage, behavior, though widespread, is typically nonfocused and individualistic.

2. *Secondary Stage: Crowd Behavior.* As the movement develops, individual reactions become socially cohesive. Individual discontent is
crystallized into collective resentment, and crowd-like excitement
intensifies. Milling tends to become contagious, producing a diffuse
crowd atmosphere and precipitating numerous compact crowds.

Leaders define collective villains and place blame, thus enabling collective feelings and action to become focalized. A rudimentary division of labor emerges as the agitator leaders attract followings of action-oriented individuals from the still discontent and aimless masses.

In this stage compact crowds appear spontaneously at many places. Some protest abuses in mass meetings, marches, strikes, and other demonstrations. Others go beyond the limits of protest into mob violence, riots, and gang fights. At this point the movement-building process can be arrested in two ways. First, ruthless police or military force can be used to suppress the people and their leaders. Or second, the steam may be let out of the developing movement by palliative reforms that meet major collective demands.

3. *The Formal Movement: Public Behavior.* In the third stage a social movement reveals aspects of public behavior. Collective discontent is crystallized into social issues. Individuals and groups take up positions around the issues and initiate a "grand debate." The disparate and unorganized elements of the crowd atmosphere—discontent, criticism, aspirations, goals, rationalizations—are gradually fused into an ideological system. As the movement takes structure, the crowd atmosphere and specific crowds tend to dissipate and become absorbed into the formal movement. The movement is now a collective enterprise engaged in struggle with the established social order to affect some course of social change.

4. *The Revolution.* The social movement may become a revolution if two further changes occur. First, participants define the central aim of the movement as shift of power from the class or sector in control to a class or sector that is seeking control. Second, members are willing to use violence, if that becomes necessary, as the method to accomplish the shift of power. As revolution, a social movement reveals certain distinguishing characteristics.

The revolution is initiated when the movement seizes power in the society. As noted, this may not require the use of force. At this point the intelligentsia, the moderates, and the reformers are superfluous—possibly even dangerous—and must therefore be removed or liquidated. Dissent or hesitation among the masses must be quieted, and for that purpose the revolutionary leaders may utilize the "reign of terror." The revolution is complete when "normal" or almost normal routines of life are reëstablished with the help of administrators, technicians, and workers who may or may not have had any active part in the revolution itself.

Social Movements and Social Organization ▶ Although a social movement is in revolt against the society of which it is a part, it is nevertheless firmly grounded in that host society. As a matter of fact, the social movement itself constitutes one important feature of the existing social order. The dominant orientation and the basic structure of the social movement are likely to be decisively conditioned by this reciprocal relationship. Four structural patterns of relationship between the social movement and its host society can be identified and examined briefly.

First, by means of its premises and objectives, a social movement tends to make differential appeals to the members of the society. It is, therefore, identified with particular strata or sectors of the society within which it develops. The movement is thus more firmly or clearly attached to one element or aspect of the social structure than to others.

For example, in France the Communist Party slants its appeal to working-class people, but *Poujadism* made its strongest claims upon small business and farm enterprisers. The Non-Partisan League drew its following from among grain farmers in the western Mississippi River Valley, but the National Association for the Advancement of Colored People is strong among Negroes and their sympathizers. The National Grange has great appeal for small farm owners in the United States, but the National Farmers Union recruits followers mainly among farm tenants and laborers.

Second, social movements constitute the institutional framework for aggregating and coordinating existing or new groups and associations. Sometimes a movement can incorporate, as active constituents, such old-line large-scale associations as trade unions, political parties, agricultural associations, religious federations, and professional societies. This mode of organization is exemplified in the "New Deal." The Anti-Saloon League had working agreements with some sixty thousand separate national, state, and local organizations.[36]

On the other hand, the social movement may develop by creating specialized subordinate divisions and task-force groups. It emerges as a multi-level and multi-cellular quasi-bureaucratic structure. For example, in addition to the mode of organization noted above, the Anti-Saloon League established state, county, and ward or precinct units. The Nazi movement fabricated a similar type of hierarchical organization. In the case of both modes of organization, the social movement tends to create a substantial area of institutional or quasi-institutional organization within the host society. In this way the movement tends to extend and diversify, for a time at least, the total social structure.

Third, social movements bequeath some measure of modification to the social organization of the host society. Sometimes the movement itself may become institutionalized and enter the social organization as a continuing constituent. This influence is illustrated by the trade union movement and the politico-economic reforms expressed in new political parties. Sometimes, however, the movement influences the social organization by forcing modifications of the on-going system. For example, the Negro protest movement in the United States has already produced some substantial modifications of educational, political, and economic organization.

On the other hand, the host society tends to affect the organization of the social movement. Some of these reciprocating influences have been suggested in the foregoing discussion. A clear illustration of the influence of host societies on a social movement is found in the ideological system, internal structure, and reciprocal relations of the Communist parties of countries as diverse in character as India, Italy, and Finland. This relationship is also exemplified in the history of radical religious sects in Europe and the new world.[37]

Fourth, social movements tend to facilitate development of a congeries of small informal groups and associations. They spring up spontaneously among friends, cohorts, and associates who live and work together in the career of the movement. Other small groups, like committees and task forces, are created by the movement. Such groups constitute the tough warp and woof of the movement and in the last analysis tend to condition its success or failure.

These small groups, together with the parent organization, add a net increment to the organization of the host society. For example, American social organization was significantly increased and proliferated by the complex social system of the Anti-Saloon League. The Mau Mau in Kenya, the Viet Cong in Vietnam, or the Huks in the Philippines added a new dimension to social organization in these societies. The variegated Negro protest movement in the United States has extended social organization in several ways.

Consequences of Social Movements ◗ Obviously, a social movement cannot continue indefinitely unchanged. One might legitimately ask, then, what happens to old social movements? Do they just fade away, leaving no trace of their existence, or do they impose some lasting imprint on the society within which they develop? Ralph H. Turner and Lewis M. Killian have formulated the answer to this question in terms of four social consequences.[38]

First, a successful movement may lose its zeal for change, become rigid, respectable, and institutionalized, and enter the permanent structure of society. Certain areas of competence and function become its field of action. Participation-gratifications diversify; individuals are attracted to the movement for prestige; and conventional motivations and behavior tend to replace the deviant patterns of the earlier phases. Institutionalization of social movements is illustrated in the transformation of sects into denominations, the growth of trade unionism, the evolution of new political parties, and the ultimate entrenchment of the New Deal in the American way of life.

Second, following a serious loss of program, power, or membership, a social movement may become reëstablished on a restricted basis. Leaders and functionaries have an interest in retaining the prestige, power, and income that the restricted movement affords. Participation-gratifications of the movement tend to perpetuate the organization even after chances of achieving significant changes have largely disappeared or become negligible. The movement assumes new criteria of success. Agitation for old age pensions, women's rights, and prohibition are typical cases in point.[39]

Third, a social movement may lead to some modification of the societal value structure. As it develops, whatever the movement's goals or methods may be, it condemns certain values and sanctions its demands for reform by reference to other values. Sometimes the modifications of the value structure occur as an inadvertent by-product of the movement. The fair employment practices movement, for example, advances the value of equal job opportunity at the expense of the value inherent in freedom from interference in running one's own business. Most popular movements for the reduction or control of crime advocate better law enforcement, improved crime detection, and stiffer penalties for violations.

Fourth, revolutionary movements tend to eventuate in some lasting modification of power relations, the distribution of wealth, and the form of the social structure. The revolution must achieve legitimacy and sanction for the new social order that it advocates. The necessary preoccupation with the control of power and protection from counter-revolution, however, sometimes jeopardizes the long-range reforms for which it works. As a consequence, although the revolution may bring about important changes in power relations and modifications of the institutional structure, it may fall short of its original objectives. This fact is illustrated in the record of every modern revolution. A current case in point is to be found in the July 26 Cuban revolution of Fidel Castro. Other illustrations of revolutionary impact on changing social systems are seen in nationalistic movements in Asia, Africa, and Latin America.

It has been said that the study of collective behavior focuses on unstable and changing aspects of social organization. The aim is to identify and analyze the forms of social behavior that emerge in this relatively unstructured sphere of social life. In the following chapter, our attention will be centered on change itself. The thesis in this discussion is that social change is not a "mindless" process and that man is not a helpless pawn of impersonal social forces. As is evident from the discussion of social movements, much social change is deliberate even if it is not always rational. It is proper therefore to consider the process, the consequences, and the control of social change.

FOOTNOTES

1. Kimball Young and Linton Freeman, "Social Psychology and Sociology," in Howard Becker and Alvin Boskoff, eds., *Modern Sociological Theory in Continuity and Change* (New York: Dryden, 1957), p. 556.
2. See Ralph H. Turner and Lewis M. Killian, *Collective Behavior* (Englewood Cliffs: Prentice-Hall, 1957), Chapter 2.
3. *World Almanac and Book of Facts*, 1962, p. 895.
4. *Official Encyclopedia of the National Football League* (New York: Barnes, 1959), table, p. 31.
5. Gustave LeBon, *The Crowd: A Study of the Popular Mind* (London: Unwin, 1897); Sigmund Freud, *Group Psychology and the Analysis of the Ego* (New York: Norton, 1960); and Everett Dean Martin, *The Behavior of Crowds* (New York: Harper, 1920).
6. Turner and Killian, *op. cit.*, pp. 102-103.
7. Alvin Johnson, "Short Change," *New Republic*, 14:381-383 (April 27, 1918), condensed from Robert L. Sutherland *et al.*, *Introductory Sociology* (Chicago: Lippincott, 1956), pp. 245-248.
8. Condensed from *The Negro in Chicago* by Chicago Commission on Race Relations (Chicago: University of Chicago Press, 1922), pp. 3-7.
9. See Louis Wirth, "Consensus and Mass Communication," in *American Sociological Review*, 13:1-15, February 1948.
10. In this connection, see Turner and Killian, *op. cit.*, p. 220.
11. Condensed from "Dispute in Dubuque," in *Time*, 56:21, April 2, 1951.
12. Turner and Killian, *op. cit.*, pp. 253-255.
13. *Ibid.*, pp. 225-226.
14. Nelson N. Foote and Clyde W. Hart, "Public Opinion and Collective Behavior," in Muzafer Sherif and M. O. Wilson, eds., *Group Relations at the Crossroads* (New York: Harper, 1953), pp. 308-331.
15. For a discussion of censorship, see Clarence Schettler, *Public Opinion in American Society* (New York: Harper, 1960), Chapter 14.
16. *Ibid.*, Chapter 15. See also "Propaganda" in Julius Gould and William L. Kolb, *A Dictionary of the Social Sciences* (New York: Free Press, 1964), pp. 547-548.
17. Condensed from Robert K. Merton, *Mass Persuasion* (New York: Harper, 1946), pp. 50-51.
18. Arthur N. Holcombe, "Round Table on Political Statistics: The Measurement of Public Opinion," in *American Political Science Review*, 19:124, 1924.
19. See Douglass Cater, *The Fourth Branch of Government* (Boston: Houghton Mifflin, 1959), for a discussion of such common-sense methods of ascertaining public opinion.
20. Emory Bogardus, *The Making of Public Opinion* (New York: Association Press, 1951), Chapter 14.
21. Schettler, *op. cit.*, p. 515.
22. Joseph S. Himes, *Social Planning in America* (New York: Random House, 1954), pp. 55-56.
23. Harold F. Gosnell, *Grass Roots Politics* (Washington: American Council of Public Affairs, 1942), pp. 7-18.
24. Rensis Likert, "Public Opinion Polls," in *Scientific American*, 179:7, December 1948.
25. Norman J. Powell, *Anatomy of Public Opinion* (New York: Prentice-Hall, 1951), p. 80. See also Schettler, *op. cit.*, Chapter 19.
26. Rudolf Heberle, *Social Movements* (New York: Appleton-Century-Crofts, 1951), pp. 32-37.
27. Herbert H. Blumer, "Collective Behavior," in Alfred M. Lee, ed., *Principles of Sociology* (New York: Barnes and Noble, 1957), p. 199.
28. Turner and Killian, *op. cit.*, p. 308.
29. *Ibid.*, p. 308.
30. See Hadley Cantril, *The Psychology of Social Movements* (New York: Wiley, 1941), Part I; Thomas H. Greer, *American Social Reform Movements* (New York: Prentice-Hall, 1949), pp. 3-6; Heberle, *op. cit.*, Parts II and III; C. Wendell King, *Social Movements in the United States* (New York: Random House, 1956), Chapter 1; Turner and Killian, *op. cit.*, Part IV; and Hans Toch, *The Social Psychology of Social Movements* (Indianapolis: Bobbs-Merrill, 1965), Chapter 1.

31. Theodore Abel, *Why Hitler Came Into Power* (New York: Prentice-Hall, 1938), p. 123.

32. Adapted and condensed from Greer, *op. cit.,* pp. 213-217.

33. King, *op. cit.,* p. 32.

34. Blumer, *op. cit.,* p. 210.

35. Rex D. Hopper, "The Revolutionary Process: A Frame of Reference for the Study of Revolutionary Movements," in *Social Forces,* 28:270-279, March 1950.

36. See Peter Odegard, *Pressure Politics: The Story of the Anti-Saloon League* (New York: Columbia University Press, 1928).

37. Pauline V. Young, *Pilgrims of Russiantown* (Chicago: University of Chicago Press, 1954).

38. Turner and Killian, *op. cit.,* Chapter 21; and King, *op. cit.,* Chapter 7.

39. See S. L. Messinger, "Organizational Transformation: A Case Study of a Declining Social Movement," in *American Sociological Review,* 20:3-10, February 1955.

Chapter 16

SOCIAL CHANGE, SOCIAL PROBLEMS, AND SOCIAL PLANNING

We noted in an earlier chapter that human society is unstable as well as stable, disorganized as well as organized, changing as well as established. For example, although family, work, leisure, worship, and education encompass the stable routines of daily life, each is also an arena of change and the locus of personal dilemmas and uncertainties. Government is organized traditionally at the federal, state, and local levels, but relations between these branches are shifting and confused. American families have always been monogamous and father-centered, yet the modern city family is very different from the farm family of a century ago.

In the study of mass society, crowds, and publics we drew attention to some aspects of instability and disorganization. Social movements were called collective enterprises in promoting or opposing social change. In the present chapter, the focus of attention is social change itself. We will examine the nature, sources, consequences, and control of social change.

THEORIES OF SOCIAL CHANGE

Man has the unique capacity to be a "participant-observer" of social change. While he performs the roles in the drama of social life, he is able to watch the action unfold about him. Fortunately for the behavioral sciences, man—the participant-observer—has reacted to his own show in at least three ways. Some individuals have described what they saw and thus produced the accumulating record of history. Others have sought to manipulate and utilize the on-going process by means of social control. And still others have striven to understand and explain the pageant of change by formulating theories of interpretation or schemes of analysis. The explanations of social change may be usefully classified as theories of causation, theories of process, and theories of functional analysis.

Theories of Causation ❯ The major theories of causation can be classified in terms of four factors. *Geographic determinism* is the term applied to those theories that explain social change in terms of one or more features of the natural environment. Arnold Toynbee, the distinguished British historian, and Ellsworth Huntington, the American geographer, are among leading exponents of this theory.[1]

Biological determinism refers to those theories that explain social change in terms of the effects of various traits or characteristics of the human organism. The most familiar form of this theory is contained in doctrines of racial superiority and inferiority. In the 1850's Count Arthur Joseph de Gobineau popularized this idea.[2] In 1899 Houston Stewart Chamberlain, an Englishman, and just after World War I Madison Grant and Lothrop Stoddard, American writers, restated and popularized the racial superiority theory.[3] In *Mein Kampf* and his speeches Adolph Hitler exploited the racist theory in extreme form.[4]

Economic determinism designates all those formulations that explain social change by means of economic forces and processes. The most influential statement of this theory is contained in the work of Karl Marx.[5] Charles A. Beard, the distinguished American historian, employed an adaptation of this theory, i.e., "the economic interpretation of history," to explain the orientations and compromises of the American Constitution and to illuminate subsequent developments in the American governmental system.[6]

Cultural determinism explains social change as the consequence of the influence of one or more elements of the cultural heritage. William F. Ogburn, a distinguished American sociologist, argued that there are two basic types of culture: "material" and "nonmaterial"; he stated that changes in the latter are caused by changes in the former.[7] Max Weber, the celebrated German sociologist, in the classic investigation of the impact of Protestant religious values on economic organization and behavior, stressed the dominant role of nonmaterial culture in causing social change.[8]

Although all these single-factor theories are now largely discounted, each has made some contribution to understanding social change.[9] The proponents of these theories have underscored the importance of the various factors in the empirical study and interpretation of social change. In a later section we will show how these and other factors tend to cluster in affecting specific instances of change.

Theories of Process ❯ Theories of the process of social change may be examined in three classes. *Linear* theories, though recognizing variations of rate, portray social change as unfolding in a line. The concept of evolution is the key to one of the most persuasive formulations of this theory. Writing just before the middle of the nineteenth century, Auguste Comte, the father of sociology, formulated a scheme of evolutionary stages through which human societies were said to develop.[10] Working among the Iroquois Indians, Lewis Henry Morgan, a pioneer ethnologist, constructed a system of fixed evolutionary stages in human development.[11] Herbert Spencer, the encyclopedic British sociologist, conceptualized human society as a gigantic organism that evolved from "militant" to "industrial" in type by becoming progressively more specialized, complex, and interdependent.[12] Karl Marx argued that the course of history was a continuous struggle between owners and workers in which the proletariat would eventually win.[13] Eventually the "dictatorship of the proletariat" would dissolve as class distinctions disappeared, as the state "withered away," and as a "classless" society of workers emerged and stabilized.

Cyclical theories of social change stress the undulating or fluctuating character of the process. Each phase of the cycle is viewed as the child of the former and the parent of the next. Arnold Toynbee fashioned a cyclical scheme of three phases: first, a state of social equilibrium or "integration of custom" called *yin*; second, the transition from *yin* to *yang*, or disequilibrium initiated by a dynamic act; and third, resolution of the crisis of creative differentiation and disequilibrium leading to a new state of equilibrium or *yin* in terms of the new societal conditions.[14] Wesley C. Mitchell constructed a cyclical pattern of economic change in which each phase of the business cycle emerged by dynamic transformation of the preceding one in an endless chain of cycles in which the phases recur regularly although the economic conditions are never altogether the same.[15]

The *trend model* is a more sophisticated way of stating the linear theory of social change. Ferdinand Tönnies described the trend as transition from *Gemeinschaft* (communal society) to *Gesellschaft* (associational society),[16] and David Riesman and associates constructed a master trend of social change.[17] The trend model was summarized in an earlier chapter and has been utilized in analysis throughout this book. The theory asserts that in spite of minor fluctuations and variations, social change is characterized by an overall trend. Inclusive kinship social forms tend to give way to numerous, specialized segmental units. The sacred traditional orientation toward life is replaced by the spirit of secularism, rationality, and pragmatism. Thus everywhere communal society tends to give way to the secular rationality of associational society.

Functional Theory ♦ Sociologists no longer engage in the construction and criticism of general theories of social change. Instead, social change, like social stability, is investigated as one class of social phenomena. The aim is to identify, describe, and measure specific instances of change and to specify the conditions of social structure and environment under which such change occurs. Social change is thus conceptualized as a social function.

One way of stating this functional relationship is to designate social change as a dependent variable associated with a cluster of factors that constitute the independent variable. From this perspective two problems of analysis emerge. First, it is necessary to define in sociological terms the characteristics of the specific change that is being investigated. Second, it is essential to identify and analyze the syndrome of factors with which the change under study is correlated. It will be seen that social change itself may serve as an independent variable tending to produce still other consequences, some of which are defined as social problems. This sequence of phenomena creates the motivation and rationale for social planning or the conscious collective effort to remedy social problems and manage social change.

DIMENSIONS OF SOCIAL CHANGE

Social change is described as variation of social systems through time. To study the change of a specific system it is, therefore, necessary to observe it at different times. For example, change of the human family can be revealed by observing the family at different times and under different circumstances. Social change is revealed simultaneously and can be analyzed along three dimensions of social systems: the structural, the cultural, and the interactional.

Structural Dimension ◗ The structural elements of social change are itemized in the first part of Figure 16-1. Structurally, change may occur as expansion or attrition of the behavioral and/or authority components of social roles. For example, George B. Baldwin and George P. Schultz point out that automation may lead to a reduction of work roles by compressing the behavioral components of several former jobs into a new occupation.

> ... When three or four different types of grinding operations, each now representing a separate job classification, are tied together by automation, one man will be able to operate the integrated grinding line. This man must have a generalized knowledge; and his changed broader job classification is likely to carry more pay than any of the old grinding occupations.[18]

Structural change may take the form of increase or reduction of the number of roles or role categories in a social system. Ruth S. Cavan has shown that the structure of the American family was altered by elimination of ancillary kinship and worker roles, leaving father, mother, and child as major role components of the nuclear family.[19] C. Wright Mills revealed that the American middle class changed by the addition of cadres of "new white-collar" individuals and families.[20]

Structurally, social change is revealed as up-grading or down-grading of roles or role categories within a social system. For example, as the American family evolved from patriarchal to democratic, the

STRUCTURAL DIMENSION

Expansion or attrition of role content

    Behavior aspect   Authority aspect

Increase or reduction of the number of roles or role categories

Shift of location of roles or role categories

Modification of communication channels among roles or role categories

Alteration of number and type of functions performed by the structure

CULTURAL DIMENSION

Cultural innovation   Invention, tentation, borrowing

         Diffusion   Conscious diffusion
                       Cultural drift

       Integration   Rejection of new forms
                       Duplication, old and new surviving
                           together in variable patterns
                       Replacement of old forms by new forms

INTERACTIONAL DIMENSION

Change of frequency: From frequent, numerous, or continuous, often also varied relations to infrequent, limited, or occasional; or the opposite.

Change of social distance: From intimate, informal relations through inclusive roles to remote, restricted, and formal through segmental roles (process of estrangement); or change in opposite direction.

Change of directionality: From interaction among status equals with horizontal directionality of relations to intercourse among status unequals with vertical directionality of relations; or change in opposite direction.

Change of instrumentality: From treatment of participants in a relationship personally as valued ends to relations that regard them as means, impersonally; or change in opposite direction.

Change of form: From the unifying solidary relations of cooperation, whatever its structural setting, to divisive and hostile experiences of struggle through rivalry, competition, and conflict; or change in the opposite direction.

FIGURE 16-1

role of wife moved up in status *vis-à-vis* that of husband. In the 1930's and 1940's, while the German working class was being degraded under the Nazi regime, the American working class was gaining status under protection of the National Labor Relations Act.

Structural change is also manifested in alteration of communication channels and modification of the functions fulfilled by a social system. With attrition of the number of roles and rearrangement of husband-wife roles in the American family went a reduction of the functions served and variation of the modes of intra-family communication. The addition of a managerial category to the structure of modern business and industry led to rearrangement of functions and alteration of traditional channels of communication. Administration was transferred from owners to managers and communication became more formal and mediated.

Cultural Dimension ▶ The second part of Figure 16-1 shows that while social structure changes, correlated cultural elements are also changing in three ways.[21] Cultural innovation occurs through invention, tentation, and borrowing. For example, the growth of technology and the Industrial Revolution (both complicated syndromes of inventions) led to the expansion of the managerial class in industry and the formalization of social structure in factory, office, laboratory, and sales room. This formal system of rational coordination of economic activity, called bureaucracy, constitutes one of the great inventions of modern times. Many features of industry and bureaucracy were borrowed (deliberately acquired) by Americans from countries of Western Europe. At the same time elements of technology, industry, and bureaucracy have been borrowed from societies in other parts of the world. George Peter Murdock has also called attention to the fact that cultural elements tend to vary through the creation of new ways by accident or trial and error, a process that he calls tentation.

Each cultural innovation causes adaptive changes of related cultural elements, which in turn necessitate still other adaptations, thus setting in motion a chain of cultural changes. For example, the development of commercial aviation altered manufacturing practices, changed business operations, modified travel patterns, changed governmental regulations, influenced family and vacation practices, and so on almost without end.[22] Cultural innovation thus must be viewed not as an act or series of discrete acts, but rather as a continuous process.

Cultural innovations diffuse (spread) from points and times of origin throughout an on-going cultural system. Much cultural diffusion occurs rationally and deliberately. This is the social meaning of advertising, education, and propaganda. For example, technology, industrial organization, democratic political ideas, and the "literary culture" are diffused to developing societies by teachers, foreign aid officers, engineers and technicians, governmental officials, and the agencies of news and propaganda. On the other hand, some cultural diffusion occurs unconsciously in the course of contacts among culturally different people. For example, European immigrants to the United States have contributed many elements to the developing American heritage. American tourists, soldiers, and public officials leave many American objects and customs in the lands they visit.

Finally, cultural change is complete when new elements become integrated into an on-going cultural system. Some innovations may be rejected completely, and occasionally an existing element is eliminated. For example, many inventions are never accepted, and patterns like lynching and "yellow dog contracts" have been excluded from the American cultural pattern. Often, the new cultural elements enter the system alongside the old ones that they challenge, and the two survive in varying patterns of relationship. For example, the city manager, commission, and mayor-council forms of city government exist side by side. The craft union form is not replaced by the newer industrial form, and airplanes, buses, and railroads exist side by side in a complex pattern of complementary relationship.

Sometimes the new form completely or largely replaces the old. Trial by jury has completely replaced trial by ordeal or pioneer jury trial, and the horse-drawn street car has disappeared from American city streets. But the corporation has not fully displaced the partnership, nor has democratic family organization replaced the patriarchal pattern. In ideal-typical terms cultural change issues into progressive normative reintegration. In reality, however, this is seldom the case, since the process of innovation and diffusion is continuous. Actual normative systems reveal varying combinations of disintegration and reintegration.

Interactional Dimension ♦ Modifications of a social structure and variations of a cultural system alter both the conditions and the expectations of social interaction. The accompanying changes of social relations may be analyzed along the five dimensions of frequency, social distance, directionality, instrumentality, and interactive form. Change of social relations is revealed as a shift of position on one or more of the continua that are defined by the extremes of the dimensions. The lower part of Figure 16-1 presents a schematic arrangement of the dimensions in terms of the polarities of the continua between which changes of social relations occur.

These categories indicate variables that are neither discrete nor exclusive aspects of social change. Rather they are analytic constructs to be employed in the investigation of concrete situations. Modifications of a social structure and its related normative order may be—and indeed usually are—accompanied simultaneously by change along several of these dimensions of social relations. For example, the experience of African and Asian peoples when they migrate to the cities to live and work under conditions of urban industrialism is accompanied by profound changes in the fabric of social relations. The individual establishes a far greater number and variety of relationships than he formerly experienced in his village or tribe. By contrast with his former life, also, the new set of social relations is typically superficial, impersonal, segmental, and instrumental. Forms of struggle are more characteristic of his life in the city than they were when he lived in the village or "bush."

SOURCES OF SOCIAL CHANGE

Research and speculation have failed to reveal the basic cause or a general theory to explain the complex process of social change. As a consequence, scientific thinking has turned to reliance on functional theory and correlational methodology as approaches to this problem. From this perspective, social change is regarded as a dependent variable that may be correlated with a syndrome of unequal and fluctuating independent variables. One task of sociological analysis becomes the attempt to identify those independent variables that are regularly and reliably correlated with social change, and, if possible, to measure the influence of each.

As noted above, almost every perceptible phenomenon has been cited as a cause of social change. The multitude of factors that have been identified as independent variables in the process of social change may be classified for discussion according to the scheme shown in Figure 16-2. This scheme makes no claim to indicate the variable and uneven influence of the categories; in fact, they always appear in combination. For example, writing of social change in tropical Africa, George H. T. Kimble states: "These pressures are both external and internal."[23] The inventory of major "causes" includes Western mechanical, industrial, urban, and military patterns; government and private initiative in providing better homes and services; Christian idealism; native incentive; and money as the symbol of wealth, power, and prestige.

Sociogenic Factors ▶ Some social changes are produced within the structure and action of societies. Those that are consciously initiated are called "manifest" and include such familiar enterprises as invention, social movements, social planning, and individual actions. Social movements were analyzed in the previous chapter, and the topic of social planning will be examined in the last part of this chapter. Illustrations of manifest sociogenic sources of social change are numerous and include, among other endeavors, the United Nations, the European Recovery Program, the Social Security system, and the Tennessee Valley Authority.

Individual action is a further source of social change. In terms of the sociogenic sources already mentioned, the individual may act as inventor, social movement leader, or social planner. He acts as leader or rebel, either in line with the development of the social system or in opposition to it. The role of individual action is illustrated in the careers of charismatic leaders—Jesus, Mohammed, Hitler, John F. Kennedy. Individuals initiate social change also by imposing unique styles on patterned social roles and usage. For example, the President, the professor, or the ordinary worker acts out his role and carries out his allotted action according to his own "style," in a way that he likes or finds comfortable.

The term "social drift" refers to social change that issues unconsciously and unintentionally from the accretion of minor variations of social change. This source of change is latent in the structure and functions of every society. Wilbert E. Moore notes the two main sources of social drift.

> On a strictly actuarial view of socialization, uniformities are somewhat more remarkable than variations. The uncertainties of socialization are given added point by the virtual impossibility of absolute role specification, even in a "tightly integrated" social system.[24]

Though almost imperceptible, such minor variations may aggregate into substantial alterations of the structure and usages in a society. Social drift is illustrated in the attrition of the American family system, the decline of local and the expansion of federal governments, the diminution of the role of the church in modern American society, and moral change in relation to youthful behavior.[25]

George Peter Murdock points out that "tentation" may occur in any situation in which established habits prove ineffective and individuals are so strongly motivated that they try out other modes of behavior in a search for an adequate solution to their problem.[26] This type of change arises most frequently from crisis situations such as famines, epidemics, war, economic depression, natural disaster, and the like. Scientific experimentation often takes the form of controlled tentation, where compounds, processes, or mechanisms are tested under trial-and-error conditions.

Strains within a social system constitute a further latent sociogenic source of social change. At least three types of change-producing strains can be identified. Sometimes strain issues from contrasting forms of social organization. Other inherent strains reside in the inconsistencies of normative and functional organization. Third, strain within a social system may arise from the impact of socially defined scarcities.

The role of the three types of strain in the process of social change is illustrated in the development of the labor union movement.[27] The growth of mass production processes and industries created a demand for large numbers of limited skilled workers. However, the labor unions confronted the new personnel scarcities and patterns of industrial organization with restrictive craft unions composed of highly skilled workers. The resultant lack of fit between industry and union organization produced strain in the economic system. One adaptive consequence was origination and diffusion of the industrial type of union organization.

The contrast of alternative forms of organization, craft and industrial, tended to produce strain within the labor union movement. Meanwhile, industrial organization was becoming centralized while union organization remained decentralized and localized, thus producing a further strain. These strains led to various adaptive changes in union organization, labor-management relations, and government control and supervision. In addition, as Wilbert E. Moore has pointed out, the introduction of unique individual performers into the generalized roles of formal structures produces a further type of strain.[28] Role specifications, interactional patterns, and authority systems are modified at the same time that the performer accommodates to the requirements of the system. This form of strain ensues when new workers enter the office or factory or when new members are taken into the union.

External Factors ◗ The earlier scholars perceived correctly that societies change in accommodation to forces outside themselves. Figure 16-2 classifies the external variables as (1) population changes, (2) alterations of the physical environment, (3) forceful impingement of other groups, and (4) cultural borrowing. A population may change in one or more of three ways: (1) by variation of its physiological traits through evolution or amalgamation, (2) by geographic redistribution, and (3) by modifications of its demographic composition.

The process of evolution requires a long time to produce physiological modifications that are socially significant. The mixture of different physical stocks, however, can occur rapidly and, as in recent times, may exert a powerful influence on the course of social change. Migration, fluctuation of density, and variations of composition occur constantly and constitute an important independent variable in the process of social change. Population changes are frequently the result of conscious social policy.

The role of population change in the determination of social change is illustrated by many events in the modern world. Perhaps the most striking example is the powerful effect of the current population explosion upon many aspects of structure and function in some societies. One of the major dynamic factors in the development of the acute problems of the Middle East is population redistribution and concentration in relationship to nationalism and national boundaries.

Almost any feature of the natural environment may alter because of either inherent or artificial forces. When this occurs, the depend-

A Classification of Factors That Function as Independent Variables

in Social Change

I. *SOCIOGENIC FACTORS*
   A. Manifest or intended
      1. Invention, social movements, social planning
      2. Individual action: leadership, rebellion

   B. Latent or unintended
      1. Drift, the accretion of minor unconscious variations
      2. Tentation, accidental, trial-and-error origination
      3. Strains within the social system, contrasting forms of organization, normative-functional inconsistencies, socially defined scarcities

II. *EXTERNAL FACTORS*
   A. Changes of population characteristics
      1. Evolution and amalgamation
      2. Variations of population density and migration
      3. Variations of population composition

   B. Alterations of the natural environment
      1. Natural changes
         Changes of topography
         Changes of natural resources
         Changes of flora and fauna
         Changes of climate
         Natural catastrophes—earthquakes, hurricanes, etc.
      2. Artificial changes
         Man-made modifications of any feature of natural environment

   C. Impinging groups
      1. Change resulting from application of collective force
         Conquest, colonization, merger, alliances, etc.

   D. Change through culture borrowing
      1. Diffusion of norms borrowed from a different culture system

---

FIGURE 16-2

ent social and cultural structures are forced into adaptive modification. Change of topography, natural resources, flora and fauna, and climate as a result of natural or inherent forces is generally a gradual process. The cumulative effect of long-term changes in these features of the natural environment may be socially significant. Natural catastrophes like earthquakes, hurricanes, tidal waves, or floods, strike suddenly and sometimes lead to radical social changes.

Man-made modifications of the natural environment are another source of social change. Flora and fauna, natural resources, and features of topography are most subject to human exploitation and alteration. The variegated programs of conservation of natural resources are cases in point. Unintentionally, however, human beings deforest mountains and plains, mine irreplaceable soil fertility, produce massive soil erosion, exhaust subsoil moisture, pollute rivers and lakes, exhaust valuable mineral deposits, destroy indigenous plant and animal life, and in other ways radically alter the natural environment.[29] All such changes of the supporting physical environment are likely to initiate or accentuate adaptive social changes. The influence of geographic factors is illustrated in the record of change and planning in the Tennessee River Valley, which is described below.

Modern means of transportation and communication make it virtually certain that groups will constantly impinge upon one another. Such contacts serve in several ways to initiate or facilitate social change. First, one society or group may produce change in another by the application of organized power or force. Perhaps the most obvious instances of forceful social change are conquest, colonization, and mergers. Second, the application of social force in societal contacts is associated with changes in other factors, such as alteration of population distribution and composition, and diffusion of alien culture. This source of social change is illustrated in the expansion of Europe by conquest during the seventeenth, eighteenth, and nineteenth centuries. The Soviet Union set about methodically reorganizing the social and economic structures of its satellite nations—East Germany, Czechoslovakia, Albania, and Hungary.

Finally, a further source of social change is the borrowing of norms and values from alien culture. As noted, this inevitably occurs under conditions of conquest, colonization, and merger. In the modern world, however, the media and process of mass communication are one great carrier of culture borrowings. Many dramatic instances of cultural borrowing are available. Countries like China, Cuba, and Poland have borrowed, diffused, and adapted Marxian socialist doctrines, theory, and methodology. The nationalism cultural complex has spread rapidly by borrowing all around the world, and most lately to the recently colonial peoples of Africa, Asia, and Oceania.

SOCIAL CHANGE IN HARLAN COUNTY

The following account of social disorganization in Harlan County, Kentucky, illustrates almost every aspect of the dimensions and sources of social change. It can be seen how changes of social structure, the normative order, and the system of social relations are inextricably interwoven. The material also reveals the operation of both sociogenic and external causal factors. By calling these changes "disorganization," Cressey not only focuses on the fact that they constitute alterations of previous social arrangements, but also notes that they are socially disapproved. Labor-management conflict, family breakdown, declining community health, and distortion of the sex ratio, as evidences of social change, also appear as social problems and suggest the organic connection between social change and social problems that is examined in the next section of this chapter.

Starting Point. Until the development of coal mining this was an extremely isolated area. For more than a century the people had lived a self-contained life, their farm and household industries producing most of their necessities. A few manufactured items were in use, but it was a two-day wagon trip over rough mountain roads to the nearest railroad and the volume of goods brought in from the outside was limited. Some money was in circulation, but most of the trade was carried on by barter. The chief sources of income were the sale of cattle and timber, the latter being floated out on the Cumberland River in the spring during periods of high water.

In this stable society the family and the local community were the two basic social units. A closely knit pattern of family kinship influenced all aspects of life. The heavy labor of clearing fields or building houses was done by neighbors working together on an informal basis of mutual aid. The people shared a common body of folkways and mores which came down to them from pioneer days. In this isolated primary society social contacts were so intimate that one elderly resident still recalls the days when he knew not only the people in the county but even the horses and to whom they belonged.

The people were independent and self-reliant. There were no class distinctions and every man felt himself the equal of all others. Although suspicious of unidentified strangers they were generally friendly and hospitable among themselves. The traditions of pioneer days lived on in intense individualism and resentment of personal slights and injustices. The use of liquor and firearms was another heritage of frontier conditions, resulting in a certain amount of violence and an occasional killing. But Harlan had no active feud tradition, there having been but one relatively brief family feud in the county's history. On the whole, the people were content to live a quiet, peaceful life following the traditions of their ancestors and paying little attention to what went on outside their narrow valleys.

Their culture was that of an arrested frontier society similar in many ways to that of the Boers of South Africa in the eighteenth and nineteenth centuries. The mountain culture had many characteristics of a folk society but it lacked the stability and class stratification found in typical peasant cultures. Pioneer attitudes survived in the exploitation rather than conservation of the soil and other natural resources.

Innovation. The industrial revolution came to Harlan with great suddenness in the summer of 1911. A railroad was built up to the headwaters of the Cumberland and mines were driven into the seams of coal which lay exposed along the sides of the valleys. The coal industry has come completely to dominate Harlan's life with 70 per cent of the men in the county in 1940 being engaged in mining.

Population growth has kept pace with this industrial development. From 10,566 people in 1910 the population reached a total of 75,274 in 1940. Most of these people came from nearby mountain counties bringing with them cultural backgrounds and personality traits similar to those of the older Harlan residents. In the early days some Negroes and foreign-born laborers entered the county. Since the majority of the immigrants travelled relatively short distances most of them brought their families with them, thus causing no major dislocation of the sex ratio as often occurs in new mining areas. Even so, in 1920 there was an average of 131 males 21 years of age and over for every 100 females, most of this excess being Negroes and foreign-born men who presumably had migrated from greater distances.

Disorganization. The development of coal mining and the enormous increase in population destroyed the stabilized frontier culture. The most immediate consequence was the disruption of the economic life of the county.

Instead of the security provided by the older self-sufficient agriculture there was substituted the instability of industrial employment. A man's livelihood now depended on fluctuations in the national economy which were entirely outside his control.

With this change in occupation money assumed a dominant place in the county's life. The friendly barter system disappeared and human relations came to be measured in terms of wages and profits. The insecurity of industrial employment and the occupational hazards of mining tended to develop a fatalistic attitude which mitigated against planning for the future. Thus there was little incentive to save, and wages were generally spent with reckless abandon as rapidly as received.

The most serious aspect of economic disorganization developed in the relations between mine operators and the workers. Instead of the older social equality a rigid class system was introduced. Men were now either bosses or laborers, with obedience expected from subordinates.

During the first World War, labor unions gained a temporary foothold but afterwards they practically disappeared. The depression of the 1930's together with favorable New Deal legislation, resulted in renewed efforts to unionize Harlan, first by the United Mine Workers and then by a Communist-influenced group. Violence flared up repeatedly with assassinations, pitched battles, and wide-spread suppression of civil rights of the miners.

More far-reaching was the breakdown of the older community structure. People who had always lived in stable primary groups were thrown together with masses of other uprooted individuals. The restraints of family clan and neighborhood ceased to be effective. The social values of the frontier society lost their meaning in the new community. Competition and exploitation replaced friendly mutual aid as social relations became casual and impersonal.

Even within the small family groups there was a serious readjustment of member roles. The father was now away all day in the mines. The care and discipline of the children thus fell almost entirely on the mother. Life in the company villages brought a loss to the wife of domestic handicraft and agricultural functions. The children had no farm chores or other duties and had little to do except to associate with other idle companions. The disorganizing effect of these changes is reflected in the rapid rise of the divorce rate.

With the disruption of the older community and family controls, crime and vice increased greatly. The miner found relaxation in drinking and continued his familiarity with firearms. Out of this combination grew many drunken brawls and shootings.

Prostitution and venereal disease were apparently unknown in the pre-industrial period. With the coming of railroads and automobiles there was a wide development of roadhouses which became centers of gambling, prostitution, drunkenness, and murder.

The political organization of the county has also been affected by the rapid social and economic changes. Before 1911 political campaigns were spirited and often involved intense rivalries, but they were essentially peaceful. There was some nepotism in the operation of the county government, but apparently no serious cases of graft or dishonesty. Recent years, however, have seen widespread corruption, killing of officials, stealing of elections, stuffing of ballot boxes with false votes, and many other forms of political dishonesty.[30]

SOCIAL PROBLEMS

Man is a "valuing" animal. That is, he is inclined to assess the facts and consequences of the change that he observes and to pass judgment upon what he sees. If he approves of what he perceives, he is disposed to call it "progress." If, however, he disapproves of what he sees, he tends to call it "problem."

Definition of Social Problems ♦ Paul B. Horton and Gerald R. Leslie define a social problem as "any condition affecting a significant number of people in undesirable ways about which it is believed something can be done through collective action."[31] Crime and delinquency, unemployment, racial conflict, and family disorganization constitute familiar illustrations. Any of these phrases refers to a condition that affects a significant number of people. In the case of unemployment, this fact is shown by the statistics of the jobless, their families, and all the other individuals and interests affected by them. Prevailing values in the United States define unemployment as undesirable, since the "right to work" is accepted as a basic value. Thus the condition is revealed as a social problem. Since American people generally do not accept such joblessness as inevitable, many collective efforts are formulated and executed to alleviate the problem. For instance, the reduction of unemployment is one reason for such national programs as poverty control, full manpower utilization, federal aid to education, the labor relations service, and so on.

Social Problems and Social Change ♦ This definition suggests that social problems are related to social change in at least three ways. First, the specific conditions that are evaluated as undesirable emerge, alter, and disappear with change. Second, the relevant values, as well as the specific conditions, tend to vary with the flow of social change. Thus the relationship between conditions and values is constantly altering. And third, people believe they can alleviate social problems by the control of social change through conscious collective action.

In the following schematic sketch of the development of the American family, Ruth S. Cavan illustrates the interplay between social change and social problems. She shows that the basis of valuation tends to alter more slowly than material and social conditions. Condemnation of current conditions issues in part at least from the resultant lag between unevenly changing conditions and values. In time, when the problem is recognized and defined, people are stirred to manage change rationally in order to close the gap between conditions and values and thus to eliminate the problem.

1. Relatively stable social situation: The rural situation of 75 to 100 years ago was relatively stable.

2. Integration of values, norms, and social behavior, with strong social approval of conformity and disapproval of violations: The rural family was a strong, semi-institutionalized organization, formed through legal marriage, lasting a lifetime, and performing many functions.

3. Change of social institution from rural to urban: In cities many institutions have taken over former functions of the family, thus weakening it; neighborhood controls are weakened; the family is less necessary for survival or fulfillment of needs.

4. Non-socialized or individualized behavior: When the old rural patterns and means of control break down, the way is open for individualized behavior, sometimes of a bizarre nature. Unmarried couples may experiment with premarital intercourse or trial marriage; marriage partners choose each other on a personal basis with little regard for the responsibilities of married life; contraceptives are used to avoid or limit the births of children; divorces are sought for personal reasons with little regard to the effect on children. . . .

5. Clash of old norms and individualized behavior (No. 2 versus No. 4): There has been and still is wide disapproval of types of behavior stated under No. 4. Attempts are made to enforce a waiting period between application for a marriage license and marriage, to tighten application of divorce laws, and to make the laws themselves more restrictive. Families are blamed for juvenile delinquency and for adolescent freedom that may lead to premarital intercourse. Well-organized religious and other groups exhort the family to hold fast to the older values and norms.

6. Modification of values, norms, and behavior to fit the new social situation: Gradually, responsible groups begin to examine the entire situation and to think through the problem of adjustment of the family to urban life. Instead of berating the family for not following the older rural pattern, they seek to formulate a new standard for the family adapted to the urban situation. American society is now entering this stage in the sequence of change. Family functions are being redefined, and other agencies are modifying their programs to aid the family: for example, to assist young people to meet companionable friends, to prepare them for marriage through courses in school or informal discussion groups, and to counsel confused husbands and wives. The value of permanent marriage is being asserted,

but with a new standard for stability—to give lasting happiness for the couple and a secure environment for children.

7. Reintegration of the family into society: This stage has not been reached in American society, partly because the modifications given above have not been uniformly accepted and partly because other institutions have not significantly modified their programs to give support to the new trend in the family.[32]

The Range of Social Problems ◗ A society's social problems are a product of its social life. There is never full agreement regarding which conditions are to be defined or classified as social problems. Moreover, the problems of one period or society are not necessarily the problems of another. Social problems tend to appear, alter, and disappear with the ebb and flow of social change. Each period and each society must therefore be carefully examined to identify the conditions that the people in that time and place regard as problematic.

The variability of social problems can be illustrated in several ways. In many of the developing countries of Asia and Africa the terms colonialism and modernization refer to important problems. Within the United States, however, there are no such problems. Again, child labor was once approved or at least accepted in the United States. Today, though, this is widely regarded as a social problem. Southern people are sharply divided over the issue of racial desegregation in public schools. For many this is a desirable condition, while for many others it is adjudged to be undesirable.

Perhaps the surest way to identify and inventory a society's social problems is to examine its value judgments. The negatively evaluated conditions would indicate the prevailing social problems. Such an inventory can be made in several ways. One is by means of the public opinion poll technique that was discussed in an earlier chapter. A common-sense inventory of the leading social problems of the United States can be made by examining the working agendas of Congress and the fifty state legislatures. The subjects on which legislation is proposed and debated indicate those social issues about which it is believed something should and can be done through legislative enactment. Figure 16-3 presents a list of some of the issues that have been before the United States Congress in recent years and therefore constitutes one inventory of American social problems.

Another census of the social problems current in American society can be made by surveying the topics treated in textbooks on the subject. Each author must decide what are the leading social problems of his time. A compilation of such lists constitutes a social science consensus of the leading social problems at a particular time. Figure 16-4 presents two such inventories. In the left-hand column are listed the problems recognized in the years prior to 1930. The right-hand

Some Issues Considered by the United States Congress in Recent Years

---

ISSUES AT HOME
National defense
Economic growth and unemployment
Problems of agricultural incomes and surpluses
Civil rights and internal security
Public education and public housing
Social security (health services for the aged)
Natural resources—off-shore oil and.
uranium deposits, water power, etc.

ISSUES ABROAD
Foreign military and economic assistance
Foreign cultural and technical assistance
Membership and participation in the United Nations
Foreign trade and balance of payments
Regional international policies—Western Europe,
Latin America, Southeast Asia, Africa, the Middle East

FIGURE 16-3

column lists the issues that were treated in books published after 1955.

World Problems ♦ Some social problems are world-wide in scope and implications. The specific negatively evaluated condition may not exist in all nations or regions of the world; nevertheless, the condition has world-wide implications. World problems resemble American social problems as regards the relationship to social change and the interplay between social value and social conditions.

Figure 16-5 presents a classification of world problems. The awareness and impact of these problems vary from one region or nation of the world to another; yet every society is involved in some measure and manner in the problems of international conflict, population explosion, and modernization.

Brief reference to some aspects of the problems of inter-societal conflict has been made in several places in the foregoing chapters. As noted there, some of these problems can be analyzed fruitfully by means of the concepts of social movements. The problems issuing from population explosion were touched upon in the consideration of population. The world's population problems are functionally linked with the issues of modernization of developing economies. Although fuller analysis of these problems is beyond the scope of this introductory treatment, there is research and a growing literature on each.

The tendency of human beings to react critically to social change issues from preëxisting psycho-social dispositions. As a consequence, any episode of change may elicit many varied responses. Such reactions tend to coalesce into two basic types that have been called (1) "boundary-maintaining," or change-resisting, and (2) "boundary-extending," or change-supporting.[33] The resulting efforts to manage social change constitute an expression of *social control* and are revealed as characteristic of all known societies.

Frequency of Treatment of Social Problems Categories
in Social Problems Textbooks

PROBLEM CATEGORY	1930 AND EARLIER[1]	1955 AND LATER[2]
THE FAMILY	7	7
CRIME AND DELINQUENCY	6	7
SOCIAL AND PSYCHOLOGICAL DEVIATIONS	7	6
RACIAL AND ETHNIC MINORITIES	5	7
POPULATION	5	4
INCOME DISTRIBUTION	6	2
IMMIGRATION	6	1
URBAN COMMUNITIES	5	2
RURAL COMMUNITIES	2	4
EDUCATION	3	3
LABOR-MANAGEMENT RELATIONS	3	3
GOVERNMENT	3	2
PHYSICAL HEALTH	2	3
RELIGION	2	2
WAR AND INTERNATIONAL RELATIONS	1	5

[1]*Sources: Henry R. Burch,* American Social Problems *(New York: Macmillan, 1918).*
Robert T. Dexter, Social Adjustment *(New York: Knopf, 1927).*
Grove Samuel Dow, Society and Its Problems *(New York: Crowell, 1920).*
Charles Ellwood, Sociology and Modern Social Problems *(New York: American Bk. Co., 1919).*
Ernest R. Groves, Social Problems and Education *(New York: Longmans, Green, 1925).*
Howard W. Odum, Man's Quest for Social Guidance *(New York: Holt, 1927).*
Ezra T. Towne, Social Problems *(New York: Macmillan, 1924).*

FIGURE 16-4

Social Planning as Rational Social Control ◗ The term social planning is reserved to designate rational methods of social control. Social planning is defined as the *rational collective process, combining investigation, proposal, discussion, and decision, for determining the proper means of social action to be employed to attain predetermined desirable ends of social structure and function through the management of social change.*[34]

Social planning contains two components, one social and the other instrumental. Socially, planning is an enterprise in communication, interaction, and consensus. The normal flow of social relations is consciously concentrated on the determination and evaluation of

Frequency of Treatment of Social Problems Categories

in Social Problems Textbooks

PROBLEM CATEGORY	1930 AND EARLIER[1]	1955 AND LATER[2]
OLD AGE	1	3
NATURAL RESOURCES	1	1
CIVIL LIBERTIES AND SUBVERSION	–	2
DISASTER AND CATASTROPHE	–	2
SOCIAL CLASS	–	3
MASS COMMUNICATION	–	2
LABOR UNIONS	2	–
BUSINESS AND INDUSTRY	2	–
PROHIBITION AND LIQUOR TRAFFIC	2	–
LEADERS	–	1
RECREATION	–	1
VESTED INTERESTS AND PRESSURE GROUPS	–	1
LOSS OF INDIVIDUALITY	–	1
MENTAL HEALTH	3	6
ADOLESCENCE	1	2

[2]*Sources: Jessie Bernard,* Social Problems At Mid-Century *(New York: Dryden, 1957).*
Mabel Elliott and Francis Merrill, Social Disorganization *(New York: Harper, 1961).*
Paul Horton and Gerald Leslie, The Sociology of Social Problems *(New York: Appleton-Century-Crofts, 1960).*
Elizabeth B. and Alfred M. Lee, Social Problems in America *(New York: Holt, 1955).*
Robert Merton and Robert Nisbet, Contemporary Social Problems *(New York: Harcourt, Brace, 1961).*
Earl Raab and Gertrude Selznick, Major Social Problems *(Evanston: Row, Peterson, 1959).*
S. Kirson Weinberg, Social Problems in Our Times *(Englewood Cliffs: Prentice-Hall, 1960).*

FIGURE 16-4 CONTINUED

A Suggested Classification of Worldwide Social Problems

Intersocietal Conflict
Conflicts based on ideological contradictions
Conflicts based on the extension of nationalism
Conflicts based on the competition
for limited natural resources

Population Explosion
The pressure of population on available
national or regional resources
The retarding impact of exploding population
on societal advancements

Modernization of "Underdeveloped" Societies
Problems attendant upon rapid, uncontrolled,
or unplanned societal change

FIGURE 16-5

social means and ends. The instrumental component consists of the application of social means in the management of the factors producing social change. This is essentially an administrative and engineering operation and need not concern us here.

Social planning is illustrated in the collective remedial approach to any of the social problems listed above. For example, the problem of aging has triggered massive research and investigation under both public and private auspices. The value judgments, the findings of investigation, and the proposals for remedial action have stimulated nation-wide discussions from which have come numerous specific proposals. Some of these, e.g., financial assistance, pension plans, medicare, and social services, have been implemented by programs of collective action.

The ends of social planning are revealed at three levels: (1) a predetermined series of substantive and qualitative experiences; (2) the social structure required to produce such experiences as their manifest functions; and (3) the management of social change required to assure establishment and stabilization of the appropriate types of social structure. The means of social planning consist of schemes of collective action for the management of social change. Management refers to the control of existing change and to the initiation or termination of change. The aim is to harness and focus the force of change in order to assure the desired ends of structure and function.

Social planning constitutes one method of doing what people believe can be done through collective action about social problems. R. E. Park and E. W. Burgess observe that "all social problems turn out finally to be problems of social control."[35] Through planning enterprises, people may act either to remedy existing social problems or to prevent their possible occurrence. Social planning is also employed to direct the course of change and to accelerate "social development." In many developing societies this type of planning, called "modernization," has become public policy and guides the transition from subsistence economies, traditional cultures, and kinship organization to technical associational forms. Developmental planning of this kind is examined in a later section of this chapter.

Finally, social planning is a social process. It is a repeated episodic version of the endless stream of social change. Every planning enterprise has unintended and sometimes unrecognized consequences which may themselves be evaluated as undesirable and adjudged to be new social problems. Thus the end of one planning enterprise may become the starting point of another.

TVA: Social Planning Illustrated ◗ The Tennessee Valley Authority program constitutes a familiar illustration of social planning in the United States.[36] The following sketch demonstrates the nature of social planning and reveals its relationship to social problems. The material also shows how social planning is employed as the policy instrument of social development. The TVA story provides an appropriate introduction to the discussion of the dimensions of social planning which follows.

> *Change and Problems.* The problems of the Valley were a consequence of its history. Antiquated farming and predatory lumbering methods had denuded many hillsides and plains. The natural balance of rainfall, protective vegetation, and river capacity was destroyed. Precipitation was very heavy in winter and spring, and the narrow rivers could no longer carry off the water that rushed down into them. Consequently the Valley was ravaged yearly by severe floods. Navigation on the Tennessee River and its tributaries was limited. Years of unchecked erosion had depleted soil fertility. Outmoded farming practices, inadequate transportation, inefficient business methods, and social isolation aggravated the problems and discontent of the people. Community and family life were disorganized and unrewarding. Individualism and conflict kept the Valley disunited. To economic poverty and social disorganization were added poor health and disease. News reports of disasters, accumulating research, widespread out-migration, mounting complaint and protest, and the like drew the conditions of the Valley and its people to public attention and served to define these conditions as problematic.

> But the region contained rich resources. There were important deposits of coal, nitrates, and other minerals. The rivers were potential sources of unlimited water power. A favorable growing climate and long growing season combined with ample annual rainfall to give the region great agricultural potential. The Valley contained large areas of potentially rich farming land. There was a vigorous, young, and growing population. The TVA region represented a large and as yet unexploited consumer market.

Adopting the Plan. Early in his first administration President Franklin D. Roosevelt proposed the giant TVA project as part of the New Deal. This action was the result of long and careful research by many individuals and groups. The plan involved a series of deliberate changes related to the natural and social features of the region and designed to accomplish certain desired adjustments through collective action. The proposal encountered many obstacles. Some people argued that it was "socialism," and therefore un-American. The private electric utilities opposed it as a threat to their business. To other persons it seemed visionary and wasteful. Some people saw in it another device of regimentation and a new scheme of poor relief. Many farmers in the Valley objected because their land would be taken to form the artificial lakes to be created by the navigation and conservancy dams. The program presented engineering problems of unprecedented magnitude and complexity.

TVA provoked a stormy controversy because powerful groups and forces both in and outside the Valley opposed it. The public controversy and clash of social values centered in a long and acrimonious congressional debate. Ultimately, however, major objections were overcome and the proposal was enacted into law in May 1933.

Structure and Objectives of the Plan. As provided in the new law, the Tennessee Valley Authority was a nonprofit federal corporation. As it developed, the corporation employed a huge staff of technicians of many kinds and organized them into a complicated bureaucratic structure. In time also the Authority acquired a large amount of property—dams, hydroelectric power plants, nitrate extraction facilities, etc. An intricate system of collaboration with the overlapping state and county governments was built up. An elaborate system of participation and cooperation with the people of the Valley evolved as the Authority carried out its work.

As defined in the basic law and as developed through experience, the objectives of the plan included:
1. Service to a region of 41,016 square miles embracing parts of seven different states.
2. Improvement of navigation on the Tennessee River and its tributaries.
3. Control of destructive floods in the Tennessee and Mississippi River valleys.
4. Development of new forms of artificial fertilizers.
5. Promotion of a practical system of agriculture utilizing these fertilizers.
6. Contributions to the national defense.
7. Development and distribution of hydroelectric power.
8. Studies, demonstrations, and recommendations that would assist in developing the natural resources and the social and economic welfare of the region.

Social and Instrumental Components. Some features of the social component of social planning in the TVA situation can be identified. Among others they include:
1. Social and engineering research stretching back over many years.
2. A many-sided dialogue of evaluations and definitions of the revealed conditions from which the social problems were identified and defined.
3. The offering, debating, and defense of proposals for remedial collective action.
4. The congressional debate of the TVA bill and the projection of this debate into the national public opinion arena.

5. Final enactment of the law by Congress as the symbol of a working consensus.
6. Programs of public relations and adult education that have evolved as parts of the plan itself.

The instrumental component of social planning in the TVA situation included the following minimal phases:
1. Vast engineering projects.
2. Population resettlement on an unprecedented scale.
3. The rational conservation and utilization of natural resources.
4. Economic, social, and political reorganization.
5. Organization and utilization of adult education techniques and programs.

Accomplishments of the Plan. The plan did not succeed perfectly. TVA has had its critics and its advocates. Many individuals and groups both in and outside the Valley sought to obstruct the program. For years the Authority was forced to carry on a rear-guard struggle with private power interests. Some of the specific projects and successive steps failed to work out as anticipated. Unforeseen engineering difficulties and obstacles were encountered. The solutions of some problems produced new and unexpected problems.

Yet, the physical accomplishments under the plan are staggering. The Authority has built or acquired an impressive series of dams, navigation and conservancy lakes, and hydroelectric plants. Since 1933 the Authority in cooperation with the Civilian Conservation Corps and the United States Forest Service dealt with erosion on more than a million acres of farm land. It has reclaimed many thousands of acres of marginal and submarginal land. More than 100 million trees have been planted, an increasing proportion with the aid of individual farmers. Cheap electric power has been furnished to the families, businesses, industries, and institutions of the Valley.

The social and economic accomplishments have been equally phenomenal. Studies, demonstrations, and recommendations have improved agriculture in terms of methods, equipment, processes, use of fertilizers, and plans of labor and economic organization. Health services, like the control of malaria, and education and demonstrations have been rendered to the people. In recreation, improvement has been made in facilities, programs, and leadership. Both rural and urban communities have been aided in solving problems of planning and development. Studies and recommendations have been made in order to improve transportation and communication. The authority has aided industries to locate at sites desirable in terms of labor resources, transportation, and power. A continuous program of studies and recommendations deals with the natural, human, social, and economic resources of the region.

STRUCTURE OF PLANNING ACTION

The structure of planning action in the United States is conditioned by democratic participation in the processes of decision-making and execution. Modes of social organization develop to harness and mobilize this diffuse social power and to focus it in the enterprise of deliberate social change.

Social Organization ❯ As noted, the multifarious reactions of individuals to social change tend to coalesce into the two polar boundary-maintaining and boundary-extending orientations. The social organization that issues from this dichotomy reveals the three levels of action that are depicted in Figure 16-6.

Analytic Levels of Social Organization for Social Planning

I. ORIENTATIONAL LEVEL
  A. Polar positions—boundary-maintaining
     and boundary-extending
  B. Intervening positions—semi-committed and neutral

II. ROLE LEVEL
  A. Decision-making—instigators, power leaders
  B. Decision-administering—executives, intermediaries
  C. Decision-complying—receivers, respondents, arbitors

III. ORGANIZATIONAL LEVEL
  A. Vested interest groups
  B. Other interest groups and institutions

FIGURE 16-6

Individuals tend to position themselves around a planning issue such as school desegregation or medicare. Such a deployment pattern is suggested schematically in Figure 16-7. As shown, relatively small numbers of individuals are strongly committed to action either for or against a proposal. Substantially larger numbers are passively involved in action. The largest sector, sometimes as many as half, are uncommitted and constitute a prime target of planning action.

When described in terms of action, as shown in the second part of Figure 16-6, individuals are seen to play three types of organizational roles. A few, usually persons of leadership and power in associations and institutions, make decisions about what is to be done and initiate planning action. Others, generally lesser officials of associations and institutions, execute the planning decisions and mediate between power leaders and the mass of planning compliers.

The majority of people are decision receivers, respondents, and compliers, and as such perform three decisive functions in the planning structure. First, they receive the planning decisions by attending meetings, paying attention to the mass media, and the like. Second, they respond to the plan either by accepting or by opposing it. And third, they bring the plan into reality—thus validating it—by acting out its prescriptions in daily conduct.

Schematic Portrayal of Orientational Structure of Planning Action

STRONG SUPPORTERS ——————   —————— STRONG OPPONENTS

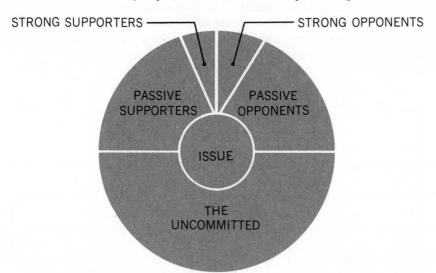

Suggested by Paul B. Horton and Gerald R. Leslie, The Sociology of Social Problems *(New York: Appleton-Century-Crofts, 1960), p. 388.*

FIGURE 16-7

Variability ◗ Social planning activities vary in several ways or dimensions. Variation is between extremes or polar types which establish a series of continua. Any given planning project represents some combination of the characteristics defined by the polar types and can therefore be located on the continuum at a point between the extremes. The following paired types represent the main dimensions of variability revealed in social planning.

1. *Dimension of authority.* From democratic (where planning compliers participate in decision-making) to authoritarian (where decisions are controlled by the power elite and compliers retain virtually no power of veto or validation).

2. *Dimension of auspices.* From public (governmental auspices) to private (nongovernmental or voluntary auspices).

3. *Dimension of scope.* From segmental (programs limited to subgeographic area or social sector of a society) to comprehensive (programs covering all geographic subdivisions or all social sectors, or both, of a society).

4. *Dimension of objective.* From remedial (programs designed to alleviate or prevent a social problem) to developmental (schemes aimed at managing and directing the total development of a society, often called "modernization").

Every actual planning enterprise represents some combination of these dimensions of variability. For example, the Tennessee Valley Authority program described above emerged from a democratic process of decision-making, although the Authority wielded considerable legitimate power under the law. The program was limited to a definite geographic sub-area of the United States; nevertheless, it affected all aspects of life within that area. TVA is a public plan, yet it utilizes the voluntary actions of thousands of groups and individuals. While the law specifies that the vast program of the Valley should be directed to the remedy of some acute and chronic problems, the plan was developmental in character so far as the Tennessee Valley is concerned. TVA is typical of American social planning—democratic, segmental, and mixed as to public and private and remedial and developmental. In the following section it will be shown that in the developing societies the approach to social planning is substantially different. In such societies comprehensive planning is basic public policy and constitutes the general method of modernization.

Social Planning in Developing Societies: The Process of Modernization ▶
In developing societies comprehensive planning is defined by public policy as the method to accelerate and coordinate the process of change in all sectors of the society.[37] Planning tends to be controlled by government, since this is the only agency with sufficient power and command of resources to mount and execute such a comprehensive program. However, since planning programs are initiated with a sense of urgency, and since in most instances the mechanisms of democratic decision-making are not well established, the planning process tends to be authoritarian.

Perhaps the most celebrated instances of comprehensive authoritarian planning for societal development are the successive five-year programs of the Soviet Union. Shortly after the Communist Party consolidated its control in Russia, the government projected a design for propelling the total society into the modern era. The plan synthesized all policies of the society, and the government became the overriding force in all spheres of life. The political fate of Party and government leaders was conditioned in significant measure by the success of the current plan. As one plan unfolded, its successor was being formulated. From one perspective, the history of the Soviet Union is told in the record of achievements of the series of comprehensive developmental plans.

Following the Soviet example, other emergent societies have utilized the device of comprehensive authoritarian planning to manage the process of modernization. The noteworthy case is China after the Communists captured control of the government in 1949. In some other societies the leaders have attempted to bring the process of comprehensive developmental planning under the control of mechanisms of democratic decision-making. One striking example of this approach to developmental planning is modern India. The case of India is instructive, not only because of its approach to planning, but also because its experience serves to bring into focus some of the crucial problems of social organization and social change in large complex societies.

When India acquired national independence in 1947, its leaders set out to establish a "socialist society" with state control of the economy and rational development under a parliamentary governmental structure. The key mechanisms of political democracy were a popularly elected parliament, the *Lok Sabha,* and a cabinet of ministers responsible to this parliament. A "public sector" was established in the economy and great effort was made to bring it to par with the "private sector" that was already in being. Some operations, e.g., radio and transport, became government monopolies. In addition, the government entered other fields of economic activity, such as industry, retail, and agriculture, and in some instances formed partnerships with private enterprises. At the same time, the private sector was respected and the government encouraged further development in this sector. All economic activity, both private and public, was brought under control of government policy and planning. Operating within this structural format, the government has formulated four successive five-year plans to manage the total development of the society.

In the third Plan, Prime Minister Jawaharlal Nehru described the aim of India's total developmental design as "to combat the curse of poverty, with all the ills that it produces, and to build up a technologically mature society and social order which offers equal opportunities to all citizens."[38] Since agriculture was basic to the economy, improvement in agricultural production was naturally the starting point. Improved agriculture required inputs from industry; therefore both sectors were developed simultaneously. This in turn depended upon irrigation and power, transport, and communications, all of which had to be modernized and expanded. Finally, the people had to be fortified with the necessary skills and attitudes for development. In order to carry out these aims, certain institutional reforms had to be inaugurated: land tenure had to be reorganized, a public sector in industry had to be created, the cooperative base had to be widened, and domestic savings and investment and foreign investment had to be increased.

Each five-year plan has stressed improvement of medical and welfare services as "investment in man." In the fifteen years from 1951 to 1965, medical institutions like hospitals and dispensaries increased, hospital beds doubled, and more than 5000 "primary health centres" (one for each 100 villages) were set up. Maternity and child welfare centres were increased and sources of safe water were established in many villages. Recently, to combat pressure of population explosion, a scheme of "family planning" under a government agency and applicable in all areas of the country has been established.

The principal aims of educational planning have been stated as: (a) to provide as early as possible a minimum of eight years of education to all children; (b) to relate education at different levels to the requirements of a developing economy; and (c) to ensure greater equality of opportunity among the various castes and other population segments for access to higher educational facilities. At the same time, rural community development has been considered central to overall planning. This program is organized in "block" units, each including approximately 100 villages and 65,000 inhabitants. It is claimed that in 15 years the entire country has been covered by some 5000 blocks.

Two distinct groups, "Scheduled Castes" and "Scheduled Tribes," have been recognized in the Constitution as the weaker sections of the nation. They suffer from certain specific disabilities, and the Constitution established schedules for their relief and imposed special responsibility on the State to protect and promote their interests. Planning for these depressed groups relates to educational opportunities, employment, representation in state and national government, land tenure, access to economic resources, and the like. Growth of cities and establishment of industries produced other problems for which plans had to be formulated. These problems demand the application of the principles of town and country planning, such as rational land use, regulation of land values, acquisition and development of sites, and dispersal of industries. The main features of India's policy on urban development are: (a) location of new industries away from the large and congested cities; (b) regional planning for large industrial or development projects, with the major industry serving as the focal point; (c) mutual reinforcement of rural and urban community development; and (d) diversification of occupational pattern within each rural area to replace exclusive dependence on agriculture.

In addition, Master Plans are being established for the metropolitan areas and coordinated with national programs of urban development.[39]

At present India has two types of social security schemes in operation. They are: (1) The Employees' State Insurance Schemes (for income maintenance and health and welfare protection); and (2) Provident funds (or employer-employee contributory retirement and survival benefit schemes). These programs have been improved and extended to cover more industries and workers in the course of the first three Five-Year Plans. In addition the government encourages state-supported and privately operated welfare and social work programs of many kinds.

The experiences of systems as diverse as the United States, India, and the Soviet Union suggest that large complex societies confront similar problems and tend to develop along similar lines. Change is universal and instability is endemic. Great size, dispersion, and heterogeneity exacerbate problems of organization and control. The total system has become so complex that events in one sector have repercussions in all sectors. It is no longer possible to rely on the working of natural laws or the process of evolution for stable, orderly development of the system. Control and direction of the system through comprehensive planning becomes a societal necessity. By the very nature of the societal situation, government becomes the planning agency and the process tends to be authoritarian.

At the same time, the problems that force large, complex societies to the approach of comprehensive planning tend also to foster similarity of method and ideology. With growing political maturity, decline of revolutionary zeal, rising levels of knowledge and aspiration, relaxation of economic stringencies, and so on, authoritarian systems tend to rely more upon democratic decision-making. On the other hand, in systems where democratic decision-making is traditional, the size and complexity of comprehensive planning tends to force substantial resort to authoritarian methods. Such developments are consistent with current theories of large-scale organization and suggest some new and promising lines of further research.

Social Planning and Utopia ♦ We have said that man is at the same time the cast, the audience, and the director of the drama of his social life. But man is also a dreamer. He keeps hoping he can make it all come out right in the end. He goes on tinkering—altering the action here, rewriting a line there, shifting the set about, always hoping that at last he has got it just right. Occasionally, in a fit of pique, he may scrap the whole show, rewriting the entire script and completely shifting the actors around. Often his efforts appear to be clumsy and inept, a grotesque travesty on the "human condition." Sometimes, though, he is luckier and manages to produce a really creditable show. Fail or succeed, man the dreamer goes right on trying to produce the perfect drama with the flawless plot and the happy ending.

Man's perfect society, the dreamer's utopia, has been called by many names and takes many forms. For some people the "golden age" existed in the distant past, while others dream of its realization in the remote future. The ancient Jews, a pastoral people, dreamed of the "promised land flowing with milk and honey," while many American Indian tribes, hunting people, longed for the "happy hunting ground." Plato called his dream society "The Republic," and Augustine wrote of "The City of God." Sir Thomas More invented the word "Utopia" for his dream world, and Karl Marx extolled the virtues of a "classless society." Henry George believed that utopia could be ushered in by a "single tax" on "ground rents," but Marx insisted that it would require class war, the victory of the workers, and establishment of a "dictatorship of the proletariat." Many groups of dreamers isolated themselves from the effete and hopeless world and tried to establish little utopian enclaves. Some men thought that the perfect society would come into being through the working of natural laws, but others were convinced that man would have to establish utopia on earth.

Although some of these schemes were actually tried, none ever succeeded to the extent or in the way that was hoped for. Something always went wrong with man's brightest dreams and best efforts. While it would be impossible to catalogue and analyze all the mistakes of man the utopian dreamer, it may prove illuminating and helpful to consider three. They are the errors of unrealistic judgments, the reliance on static models, and the handicap of inadequate control.

First, utopian schemes have been hampered by the fact that they are based upon unrealistic estimates of current conditions and future prospects. To justify the utopian dream and support the revolutionary effort, the surrounding world is depicted as evil and hopeless. Nothing less than escape to utopia can possibly save man and ensure the good life to which he is entitled. At the same time, utopia itself is painted in exaggerated terms of idealism. Thus from the very outset the utopians confront themselves with a set of unrealistic and often impossible conditions of action. They reject the surrounding world, which contains important resources and possibilities for effort, in order to strive for a situation that by its very nature is unattainable.

Second, to one degree or another, all utopian schemes constitute static models. It is assumed that once the halcyon state of being has been established, no further change would be required or could be anticipated. Some schemes attempt to hedge against the possibility of change by making social isolation one of the conditions of utopia. However, even in these circumstances, no mechanisms are built into the social systems for managing social change and its consequences. Inevitably, though, change flows over the utopian arrangements, increasing strain within the systems and making human experience fall short of idealistic expectations. For this very reason, disenchantment and discontent, when they come, are exacerbated and unrelieved.

Finally, utopian enterprises have been undertaken with inadequate control of the crucial environmental factors. By their social nature, utopians are usually impotent and impecunious minorities in established social systems. The tendency to dream and the necessity to struggle against the status quo dispose the dream builders to distort and misrepresent the surrounding world. The crucial factors therefore are often unrecognized and inaccurately described and estimated. As noted, the stream and force of change itself, a decisive factor, are generally overlooked or minimized in the specifications of the static utopian model. As a consequence, utopians are seldom prepared or equipped to manage the situational elements that influence the success or failure of their enterprise. Utopia construction is essentially an enterprise in social planning and thus requires realistic calculation of ends and means.

These dilemmas of man, the incurable dreamer, the utopian, present sociology and the other social sciences with some important and challenging opportunities. We said above that investigation is one basic element in the planning process. As the facts and insights of investigation illuminate and guide the discussion, decision, and action phases of planning, we can expect more rational calculation of means and ends. There is some chance that man can mitigate, if not fully overcome, the errors of unrealistic judgments, dependence on static models, and inadequate control of decisive factors. Yet, as Professor Moore cautioned in his Foreword, the social sciences are as yet limited in their ability to help man in his great dilemmas. Sometimes people neglect or refuse to call upon the social sciences for what help they can give. Sometimes—and this is a source of embarrassment for the social scientists—the social sciences do not know the answer and cannot provide the information or insight required. But substantial advances are being made in both respects, and this is both one bright hope for man the utopian dreamer and the great challenge and opportunity for the social sciences.

FOOTNOTES

1. Arnold Toynbee, *A Study of History* (New York: Oxford, 1954), Vol. II, pp. 271-299; and Ellsworth Huntington, *Civilization and Climate* (New Haven: Yale University Press, 1935), pp. 313-314.
2. Arthur Joseph de Gobineau, *Essai Sur L'inégalité des Races Humains,* quoted by Frank H. Hankins in *The Racial Basis of Civilization* (New York: Knopf, 1926), p. 34.
3. Houston Stewart Chamberlain, *Foundations of the Nineteenth Century* (London: Bodley Head, 1910); Madison Grant, *The Passing of the Great Race* (New York: Scribner's, 1918); and Lothrop Stoddard, *The Rising Tide of Color* (New York: Scribner's, 1920).
4. Adolf Hitler, *Mein Kampf* (Boston: Houghton-Mifflin, 1943).
5. Karl Marx, *Capital* (New York: Dutton, 1930).
6. Charles A. Beard, *An Economic Interpretation of the Constitution* (New York: Macmillan, 1935); and Beard, *The Economic Basis of Politics* (New York: Knopf, 1922).
7. William F. Ogburn, *Social Change* (New York: Viking, 1922).
8. Max Weber, *The Protestant Ethic and the Spirit of Capitalism* (London: Allen and Unwin, 1930).
9. All the single-factor theories of social change are summarized and criticized by Pitirim Sorokin in *Contemporary Sociological Theories* (New York: Harper, 1928).
10. August Comte, *A General View of Positivism* (Stanford: Academic Reprints, first published in 1845).
11. Lewis Henry Morgan, *Ancient Society* (New York: Holt, 1877).
12. Herbert Spencer, *The Principles of Sociology* (New York: Appleton, 1886), Vol. I, Part II, pp. 447-603.
13. Karl Marx, *op. cit.* See also Karl Marx and Friederich Engels, *The Communist Manifesto,* various editions.
14. Toynbee, *op. cit.,* pp. 293-294.
15. Wesley C. Mitchell, *Business Cycles and Their Causes* (Berkeley: University of California Press, 1941).
16. Ferdinand Tönnies, *Gemeinschaft und Gesellschaft* (1887), tr. and ed. by C. P. Loomis as *Fundamental Concepts of Sociology* (New York: American Book Company, 1940).
17. See David Riesman *et al., The Lonely Crowd* (New Haven: Yale University Press, 1950).
18. George B. Baldwin and George P. Schultz, "Automation: A New Dimension to an Old Problem," in *Monthly Labor Review,* 78:168 (February 1955).
19. Ruth S. Cavan, *The American Family* (New York: Crowell, 1963), Chapter 3.
20. C. Wright Mills, *White Collar: The American Middle Classes* (New York: Oxford, 1956).
21. George Peter Murdock, "How Culture Changes," in Harry L. Shapiro, ed., *Man, Culture and Society* (New York: Oxford, 1956), pp. 247-260.
22. William F. Ogburn, *The Social Effects of Aviation* (Boston: Houghton, Mifflin, 1946).
23. George H. T. Kimble, *Tropical Africa* (New York: Twentieth Century Fund, 1960), Vol. II, p. 54.
24. Wilbert E. Moore, "A Reconsideration of Theories of Social Change," in *American Sociological Review,* 25:814, December 1960.
25. John E. Nordskog, *Social Change* (New York: McGraw Hill, 1960), p. 327.
26. Murdock, *op. cit.,* pp. 247-260.
27. See Seymour Martin Lipset, "The Political Process in Trade Unions: A Theoretical Statement," in Morroe Berger, *et al.,* eds., *Freedom and Control in Modern Society* (New York: Van Nostrand, 1954).

28. See Wilbert E. Moore, *Social Change* (New Delhi: Prentice-Hall of India, 1965), pp. 53-54 *et passim;* and Wilbert E. Moore, *The Conduct of the Corporation* (New York: Random House, 1962), Chapter 7.

29. There is a large literature on this subject. For dramatic descriptions see such titles as Elspeth Huxley, *A New Earth* (New York: Morrow, 1960); and Henry Billings, *All Down the Valley* (New York: Viking, 1952).

30. Condensed and adapted from Paul F. Cressey, "Social Disorganization and Reorganization in Harlan County, Kentucky," in *American Sociological Review*, 14:389-394, June 1949.

31. Paul B. Horton and Gerald R. Leslie, *The Sociology of Social Problems* (New York: Appleton-Century-Crofts, 1960), p. 4.

32. Condensed and adapted from Ruth S. Cavan, *The American Family* (New York: Crowell, 1963), pp. 16-18.

33. See Talcott Parsons, *The Social System* (Glencoe: Free Press, 1951), pp. 36 and 482-483. Karl Mannheim identifies the orientations as "ideologic" and "utopian" in *Ideology and Utopia: An Introduction to the Sociology of Knowledge* (New York: Harcourt, Brace), 1936.

34. See an earlier formulation in J. S. Himes, *Social Planning in America* (Random House, 1954), p. 18 *et passim.*

35. R. E. Park and E. W. Burgess, *An Introduction to the Science of Sociology* (Chicago: University of Chicago Press, 1924), p. 785.

36. There is a voluminous literature on TVA. Among other things see Himes, *op. cit.,* pp. 44-45; David E. Lilienthal, *TVA—Democracy on the March* (New York: Harper, 1944); Billings, *op. cit.;* Phillip Selznick, *TVA and the Grass Roots* (Berkeley: University of California Press, 1949); and William Vogt, *Road to Survival* (New York: Sloan, 1948).

37. See Moore, *Social Change,* Chapter 5.

38. Director, Publications Division, Old Secretariat, *Social Development in India,* 1966, p. 7 *et passim.*

39. The most ambitious such regional plan formulated to date is *Basic Development Plan, Calcutta Metropolitan District 1966-1986,* Calcutta Metropolitan Planning Organization, Government of West Bengal, 1966.

OUR CHANGING RESIDENTIAL COMMUNITIES

AMERICAN CITIES AND SUBURBS have changed dramatically in the past half-century. Change has been both planned and unplanned. Attempts to rejuvenate the core of the city are illustrated below: over the years this Chicago neighborhood was transformed from low-density slum homes to modern, high-density housing. The construction of an expressway facilitated transportation.

INCREASING URBANIZATION has characterized the United States of the twentieth century. The compression of people into a relatively small portion of land has resulted in disorganized growth within, as well as disorganized sprawl around, our major metropolitan areas. Because of our long-standing beliefs that each man should choose his own manner of living and that government should not interfere in this realm, city planning was for years a controversial subject. In the last few years an ever-increasing amount of planned growth within and around our cities has had varying degrees of success.

▲ RIIS PLAZA, the central mall of a massive low-income housing project in the slums of Manhattan's Lower East Side, demonstrates attempts to improve recreation facilities within cities. Children enjoy play-pit, sunken amphitheatre, outdoor "room" with abstract fountain.

►TWIN TOWERS of Marina City apartments in Chicago attempt to encompass all living needs within a single complex of supermarket, restaurants, laundry, parking, drugstore, and a recreational boating facility.

▲ *ATTACHED RESIDENTIAL APARTMENTS clustering around landscaped patios, pools, and playgrounds constitute low-density urban renewal project in Sacramento, California.*

▲ *RESIDENTIAL REHABILITATION in Washington Square, Philadelphia, exemplifies the growing tendency of higher-income families to buy old buildings and turn them into townhouses located conveniently in or near the core of the city. Former inhabitants are displaced. This kind of rejuvenation is one of the city's answers to mass movements to the suburbs.*

◄CROWDING AND OTHER PROBLEMS created by the movement to the cities caused a second migration of families looking for the benefits of country living: solitude and their own small plot of land. Thus arose the suburban single-family subdivisions spreading around the inner city. Results have often been less than satisfactory. Transportation problems have become enormous, and according to some authorities the small backyard for each house is less satisfactory than one large play and recreation area would be.

►EXPERIMENTAL COMMUNITIES have been developed and constructed as the result of dissatisfaction with unplanned suburban sprawl. Reston, Virginia, a satellite city built complete with houses, apartments, schools, stores, churches, and even industries, sits in rolling woodlands just 18 miles from Washington, D.C. In a decade or so the city is expected to have a population of 75,000 living in seven villages, each a complete and self-contained community. This 15-story apartment building shares the shores of 30-acre Lake Anne with townhouses, shops, and other apartments.

SEVENTY PER CENT of Reston's residents will live in clusters of townhouses, the rest in high-rise apartments or in detached houses. Instead of private lawns, the community will offer 1600 acres of community recreational facilities, including two 18-hole golf courses. Ponds, hills, woods, and streams will be left unspoiled, within a short walk of any point. Despite the advantages of a planned community such as Reston, possible disadvantages are that close communal living—working and playing together—could be uncomfortably confining. In addition, although different income-level housing is supposedly represented, access to the development still falls largely within middle-class capabilities.

SUGGESTIONS FOR FURTHER READING

Chapter 1: Sociology as a Science

Berger, Peter L. *Invitation to Sociology: A Humanistic Perspective.* Garden City: Doubleday, 1963. (Anchor Book)

A gracefully written little book, addressed to the beginner, that seeks to explain what sociology is about and invites people to undertake the study of sociology as a humanistic discipline.

Chapin, F. Stuart. "Social Obstacles to the Acceptance of Existing Social Science Knowledge," *Social Forces,* 26:7-12 (October 1947).

Professor Chapin gives eight reasons why the findings of sociology and the other behavioral sciences are not more widely accepted and used.

Chase, Stuart, with Edmund D. S. Brunner. *The Proper Study of Mankind.* New York: Harper & Row, 1956.

A very readable treatment of the possible contributions of social science to the solution of human problems.

Chinoy, Ely. *The Sociological Perspective: Basic Concepts and Their Application.* New York: Random House, 1954.

A brief discussion of the basic perspective and concepts of sociology.

Davis, Kingsley. *Human Society.* New York: Macmillan, 1949. Chapter I.

An authoritative discussion of the sociological point of view, the hazards of social science, and the value of sociology.

Gee, Wilson. *Social Science Research Methods.* New York: Appleton-Century-Crofts, 1950. Chapter II.

In this chapter Professor Gee differentiates and compares the leading social sciences.

Gould, Julius, and William L. Kolb, eds. *A Dictionary of the Social Sciences.* Glencoe: Free Press, 1964.

A collection of brief essays by American and British scholars indicating the core meaning, the development, and current usage of the major concepts of sociology and the other behavioral sciences.

Hammond, Phillip E. *Sociologists at Work: Essays on the Craft of Social Research.* New York: Basic Books, 1964.

A collection of "anecdotes" or "chronicles" describing the methods and experiences of celebrated sociological researches and researchers.

Inkeles, Alex. *What Is Sociology: An Introduction to the Discipline and Profession.* Englewood Cliffs: Prentice-Hall, 1964.

This little book, written for the beginning student, is an introduction to some of the problems of sociology, a discussion of the significance of the discipline, and an overview of the present state of the profession.

Merton, Robert K. "Sociological Theory," *American Journal of Sociology,* 50: 462-473.

A sophisticated discussion of the nature and functions of theory in sociology by a competent authority.

Simpson, George. *Man in Society.* New York: Random House, 1954.

A discussion of the nature of sociology and social science, the inter-relations of the social sciences, and some important trends and problems of modern sociology.

Young, Pauline V. *Scientific Social Surveys and Research.* Englewood Cliffs: Prentice-Hall, 1966.

A useful guide for the beginning student on methods of collecting, classifying, and interpreting social data.

Chapter 2: Sociology as a Profession

Becker, Howard, and Alvin Boskoff. *Modern Sociological Theory in Continuity and Change.* New York: Dryden, 1957.

A scholarly symposium tracing the development of sociological theory, delineating some of the special fields, and describing sociological developments in several foreign countries.

Hinkle, Roscoe C., and Gisela J. *The Development of Modern Sociology.* New York: Random House, 1954.

A brief discussion of the development of sociology, its main assumptions, and its leading divisions.

House, Floyd N. *The Development of Sociology.* New York: McGraw-Hill, 1936.

An account of the antecedents and growth of sociology up to the mid-1930's.

Lewis, Myron F. "Careers in Sociology," in *Readings in Sociology,* eds. Edgar A. Shuler *et al.* New York: Crowell, 1960. Pp. 864-871.

A brief description of advanced education in sociology and some career opportunities for professionally trained people.

Roucek, Joseph S., and Roland L. Warren. "Some Men Who Influenced Sociological Theory," *Sociology: An Introduction.* Ames, Iowa: Littlefield, Adams, 1951. Chapter 23.

A collection of biographical sketches of leading sociologists from both Europe and the United States.

Sibley, Elbridge. *The Education of Sociologists in the United States.* New York: Russell Sage Foundation, 1963.

Known as the "Sibley Report," this is an empirical study of graduate departments of sociology, the education of graduate students, and the professionalization of sociologists in the United States.

Weber, Max. "Science as a Vocation," in *From Max Weber: Essays in Sociology,* eds. H. H. Gerth and C. Wright Mills. New York: Oxford, 1958. Pp. 128-156. (Galaxy Books)

A thoughtful comment by one of the great masters of sociology on the nature of science as a "calling."

Occupational Outlook Handbook: Career Information for Use in Guidance, 1966-67. Issued annually by the United States Department of Labor, Bureau of Labor Statistics.

A useful description of the types of jobs, place of employment, training requirements, prospects of advancement, types of employers, average earnings, and the future prospects of employment of sociologists in the United States.

Guide to Graduate Departments of Sociology, 1965. Issued by the American Sociological Association.

This little booklet lists university departments, graduate faculties, tuition and other costs, financial assistance available, and related information about graduate study of sociology in the United States.

The American Sociologist. "House organ" of the American Sociological Association. Published quarterly.

This magazine communicates news, announcements, comments, notes, and official information of the profession and professionals to the members of the Association and to other professional sociologists.

Scientific Journals. The research and discussion of theoretical and methodological issues are reported in scientific journals like the following:

American Sociological Review
American Journal of Sociology
Sociometry
Social Forces
Sociology and Social Research
Sociological Inquiry
Social Problems
Journal of Marriage and the Family
Journal of Educational Sociology
Health and Human Behavior

Chapter 3: Social Organization

Biddle, Bruce J., and Edwin J. Thomas. *Role Theory: Concepts and Research.* New York: Wiley, 1966. Especially Chapter I.

Biddle and Thomas present a summary of the history and present state of role theory in American social science.

Bram, Joseph. *Language and Society.* New York: Random House, 1955.

Professor Bram shows how organized social life among human beings rests upon symbolic communication.

Coon, Carleton S., ed. "The Pygmies of the Ituri Forest," *A Reader in General Anthropology.* New York: Holt, 1948. Pp. 323-325.

This well-known account shows how two groups in equatorial Africa developed a division of labor and meshed their social relations systematically while retaining their separate group identities.

Dahrendorf, Ralf. *Class and Class Conflict in Industrial Society.* Stanford: Stanford University Press, 1959. Pp. 157-165.

Dahrendorf discusses polar approaches to social integration under the delightful title of "the two faces of society."

Davis, Kingsley. "Societal Necessities," *Human Society.* New York: Macmillan, 1949. Pp. 28-31.

A succinct statement of the imperative problems confronted by every society.

Gould, Julius, and William L. Kolb. *A Dictionary of the Social Sciences*. Glencoe: Free Press, 1964.

This dictionary contains essay definitions of social organization and the subsidiary concepts discussed in this chapter.

Greer, Scott A. *Social Organization*. New York: Random House, 1954.

A brief analysis of the basic features of human social organization.

Johnson, Harry M. "Structure and Function," *Sociology: A Systematic Introduction*. New York: Harcourt, Brace, 1960. Chapter III.

A systematic, theoretical analysis of the essential elements of social organization.

Loomis, Charles P., trans. "Gemeinschaft" and "Gesellschaft," *Community and Society*. East Lansing: Michigan State University Press, 1957. Sections I and II. Pp. 37-102.

A translation of F. Tönnies' formulation of *Gemeinschaft* and *Gesellschaft*, the paired types of societies.

MacIver, R. M., and C. H. Page. "Primary Concepts," *Society: An Introductory Analysis*. New York: Rinehart, 1955. Chapter I.

This material defines and differentiates the elemental concepts of sociology.

Merton, Robert K. "Manifest and Latent Functions," *Social Theory and Social Structure*. Glencoe: Free Press, 1957. Chapter I.

The classic treatment of social functions in relationship to the structures of human society.

Redfield, Robert. "The Folk Society," *American Journal of Sociology*, 52:293-308 (January 1947).

A distinguished anthropologist defines folk or communal society as an ideal-type and differentiates it from urban or associational society as the polar opposite.

Whyte, William Foote. *Street Corner Society*. Chicago: University of Chicago Press, 1943.

A celebrated study of functional social organization among the boys and young men who inhabited the streets of a poor section of a large eastern city.

Chapter 4: Culture

"The American Way of Life," *Fortune*, February 1950, p. 63.

A comment on the goals, values, and regional subcultures of American society.

Bain, Read. "Our Schizoid Culture," *Sociology and Social Research*, 19:255-276 (January 1935).

This is now a classic description of the contradictions and clashes of American culture.

Chase, Stuart. "On Being Culture Bound," *Antioch Review*, 9:293-306 (September 1949).

A perceptive observer shows how the tendency of people to think ethno-centrically in terms of their own culture impedes communication with people from other cultures.

Davis, Kingsley. "Norms," *Human Society.* New York: Macmillan, 1949. Chapter III.

A clear delineation of the concepts of norms and their functions in society.

Gillin, John. "National and Regional Cultural Values in the United States," *Social Forces,* 34:107-113 (1955-1956).

A competent anthropologist inventories general American values and regional subsystems.

Hays, H. R. *From Ape to Angel.* New York: Knopf, 1958.

An informal history of anthropology written by a professional writer.

Kluckhohn, Clyde, and Dorothea Leighton. *The Navaho.* Garden City: Double-day, 1962. (Anchor Book)

A penetrating study of the cultural and social organization of a primitive people in the process of change and accommodation to a technically advanced culture.

Kluckhohn, Florence R., and Fred L. Strodtbeck. "Dominant and Variant Value Orientations," *Variations in Value Orientations.* Evanston: Row, Peterson, 1961. Chapter I.

A formulation of the concept of value orientation in terms of empirical research.

Kluckhohn, Richard, ed. *Culture and Behavior: Collected Essays of Clyde Kluck-hohn.* New York: Free Press, 1962.

Through these essays Kluckhohn makes important contributions to clarify the concepts of culture and to sharpen our understanding of values.

Sumner, William Graham. *Folkways.* Boston: Ginn, 1906. Chapters I and II.

In these chapters Sumner presents the pioneer definitions of the concepts of folkways, mores, and institutions.

"Teen Age Culture," *Annals,* 338 (November 1961).

This entire issue of *The Annals* is devoted to an examination of the teen-age subculture, principally in the United States.

Williams, Robin M. "Values and Beliefs in American Society," *American Society.* New York: Knopf, 1960. Chapter XI.

A systematic inventory of dominant American values by a perceptive student of American society.

Chapter 5: Small Groups

Bales, Robert. *Interaction Process Analysis.* Cambridge: Addison-Wesley, 1950.

A delineation of an approach to the study of small groups that emphasizes internal relations.

Cartwright, Dorwin, and Alvin Zander. *Group Dynamics: Research and Theory.* Evanston: Row, Peterson, 1956.

A collection of research papers arranged to probe the structures, properties, processes, and functions of small groups.

Cooley, Charles Horton. *Social Organization.* New York: Scribners, 1909. Chapter III.

This pioneer statement of the primary-group concept is still remarkable for its clarity and relevance.

Faris, Ellsworth. "The Primary Group: Essence and Accident," *American Journal of Sociology,* 38:41-50 (July 1933).

This article qualifies Cooley's formulation of the primary group concept and refines the analysis of primary relations.

Festinger, Leon, *et al. Social Pressures in Informal Groups: A Study of Human Factors in Housing.* New York: Tavistock, 1963.

A careful empirical study of the structures, internal relations, and functions of informal groups in a housing setting.

Hare, A. Paul. "Interpersonal Relations in the Small Group," in *A Handbook of Modern Sociology,* ed. Robert E. L. Faris. Chicago: Rand McNally, 1964. Pp. 217-271.

A summary from the interactionist point of view of research and findings on small groups together with an extensive bibliography.

Hare, A. Paul, *et al. Small Groups: Studies in Social Interaction.* New York: Knopf, 1955.

A collection of essays and research papers orientated in a psychological direction and including an annotated bibliography on small group studies.

Homans, George C. *The Human Group.* New York: Harcourt, Brace, 1950.

An analytic review of some of the important empirical studies of social groups containing summaries of research data and theoretical insights.

Olmsted, Michael. *The Small Group.* New York: Random House, 1959.

A summary of research and theory on small groups.

Shils, Edward A. "The Study of the Primary Group," in *The Policy Sciences,* eds. Daniel Lerner and Harold Laswell. Stanford: Stanford University Press, 1951. Pp. 44-69.

A review of developments in theory and methodology in the study of small groups by one of the leaders in the field.

Whyte, William Foote. "Small Groups and Large Organizations," in *Social Psychology at the Crossroads,* eds. Muzafer Sherif and John H. Rohrer. New York: Harper, 1951. Pp. 297-312.

Whyte points out that since small groups are components of large organizations, each should be studied in relationship to the other.

Chapter 6: Extended Groups

Blau, Peter M. *Bureaucracy in Modern Society.* New York: Random House, 1956.

A balanced summary of theory and research on bureaucracy.

——————. *The Dynamics of Bureaucracy.* Chicago: University of Chicago Press, 1955.

An empirical investigation of interpersonal relations in two governmental agencies with particular reference to the process of bureaucratic change.

Blau, Peter M., and W. R. Scott. *Formal Organizations: A Comparative Approach.* San Francisco: Chandler, 1962.

An analysis of the nature, types, structures, and functions of formal organizations.

Dornbusch, S. M. "The Military Academy as an Assimilating Institution," *Social Forces,* 33:316-321 (1955).

A study of the socialization of recruits into a bureaucratic organization.

Etzioni, Amitai. *Complex Organizations: A Sociological Reader.* New York: Holt, Rinehart & Winston, 1961. Especially Part IV, "Organizational Structures."

A collection of summaries of studies of various types of complex organizations.

Gouldner, A. W. *Patterns of Industrial Bureaucracy.* Glencoe: Free Press, 1954.

An empirical inquiry into the forces and processes that led to bureaucratization and its consequences in an industrial concern.

Lipset, Seymour Martin, *et al. Union Democracy: The Internal Politics of the International Typographical Union.* Glencoe: Free Press, 1956.

An empirical study of process and pattern in membership participation in a large formal association.

Merton, Robert K., *et al. Reader in Bureaucracy.* Glencoe: Free Press, 1952.

A collection of writings on the theory, causes, structures, personality implications, functions, and dysfunctions of bureaucracy.

Roy, D. "Quota Restriction and Gold Bricking in a Machine Shop," *American Journal of Sociology,* 57:427-442 (1952).

A study of the effects of small groups in obstructing goal achievement in a large organization.

Scott, W. Richard. "Theory of Organizations," in *Handbook of Modern Sociology,* ed. R. E. L. Faris. Chicago: Rand McNally, 1964. Pp. 485-529.

A summary statement of the sociological viewpoint on large-scale organization with an extensive bibliography.

Shils, Edward A. "Primary Groups in the American Army," in *Continuities in Social Research: Studies in the Scope and Method of 'The American Soldier,'* eds. Robert K. Merton and Paul F. Lazarsfeld. Glencoe: Free Press, 1950. Pp. 16-39.

One of the considerable number of studies of the roles and functions of primary groups in large formal organizations.

Turner, R. H. "The Navy Disbursing Officer as a Bureaucrat," *American Sociological Review,* 12:342-348 (1947).

A study of a bureaucratic type in a large formal organization.

Chapter 7: Communities

Blumenthal, Albert. *Small Town Stuff.* Chicago: University of Chicago Press, 1932.

A perceptive and sympathetic study of primary organization and life in a small town.

Foley, Donald L. *Controlling London's Growth: Planning the Great Wen, 1940-1960*. Berkeley: University of California Press, 1963.

A description and evaluation of the master plan designed to control and direct the growth of London and to limit or prevent some of the crucial problems of big cities.

Greer, Scott A. *Governing the Metropolis*. New York: Wiley, 1962.

A critical study of the problem of maintaining order in big cities in relation to their steady growth and spread.

_____. *Metropolitics: A Study of Political Culture*. New York: Wiley, 1963.

A study of the organization and process of community power in relation to a concrete issue in a metropolitan area.

_____. *Urban Renewal in American Cities*. New York: Bobbs-Merrill, 1965.

A sociological analysis of the nature and consequences of urban renewal as one massive approach to problem-solving and directed change in American cities.

Lowry, Ritchie. *Who's Running This Town?* New York: Harper & Row, 1965.

A study of the effective authority of a community in terms of its ideal functional structure.

Miller, Delbert C., and William H. Form. "Industry Shapes the Community," *Industrial Sociology*. New York: Harper & Row, 1964. Chapter IV.

An analysis of the impact of industrial growth on communities.

Orenstein, Henry. *Goan: Conflict and Cohesion in an Indian Village*. Princeton: Princeton University Press, 1965.

A study of village communities with specific reference to the factors making for integration and disintegration.

Thomertz, Carol Estes. *The Decision-Makers: The Power Structure of Dallas*. Dallas: Southern Methodist University Press, 1964.

A study of community authority structure using the so-called reputational method.

Vidich, Arthur J., *et al. Reflections on Community Studies*. New York: Wiley, 1964.

A collection of essays commenting on the flavor, methods, accomplishments, and consequences of sociological community studies.

Whyte, William H., Jr. "The Transients," *Prize Articles 1954*. New York: Ballantine Books, 1954. Pp. 39-112.

A perceptive comment by one of America's most distinguished sociological journalists on the people who occupy new suburbia.

Chapter 8: Political and Economic Institutions

Johnson, Harry M. "Institutionalization," *Sociology: A Systematic Introduction*. New York: Harcourt, Brace, 1960. Chapter II.

A clear but rather theoretical analysis of the nature of social institutions and the process of institutionalization.

MacIver, Robert M., and Charles H. Page. "Institutions," *Society: An Introductory Analysis.* New York: Holt, Rinehart & Winston, 1955. Pp. 15-18.

These authors formulate a meaning of institution and differentiate it from association.

Williams, Robin M., Jr. "Interrelations of Major Institutions and Social Groupings," *American Society: A Sociological Interpretation.* New York: Knopf, 1960. Chapter XIII.

This material delineates the interrelations of institutions and suggests an approach to empirical study.

Greer, Scott A. *Governing the Metropolis.* New York: Wiley, 1962.

A provocative analysis of the complex political problems created by the modern metropolis.

Key, V. O., Jr. *Politics, Parties and Pressure Groups.* New York: Crowell, 1958.

An analysis of the structures and functions of pressure groups and parties in the American political system.

Lipset, Seymour Martin. *Political Man.* Garden City: Doubleday, 1959.

A thoughtful analysis of the political process in modern mass societies.

Schermerhorn, Richard A. *Society and Power.* New York: Random House, 1961.

This little book summarizes theory and research on the issue of social power.

Tilman, Robert O., and R. Taylor Cole. *The Nigerian Political Scene.* Durham: Duke University Press, 1962.

A study of political and economic development in a new national society.

Heilbroner, Robert L. *The Making of Economic Society.* Englewood Cliffs: Prentice-Hall, 1962.

A popularly written description of the evolution of the modern industrial market economy.

Lipset, Seymour Martin, *et al. Union Democracy.* Glencoe: Free Press, 1956.

A study of formalization and bureaucratization of a large labor union in relations with a dispersed industry.

Millikan, Max F., and W. W. Rostow. *A Proposal.* New York: Harper & Row, 1957.

A brief, readable analysis of the economic problems of developing societies with a proposal for meeting these problems.

Polanyi, Karl. *The Great Transformation.* New York: Holt, Rinehart & Winston, 1944.

In this study Polanyi shows how in the process of transformation economy is absorbed into society.

Williams, Robin M., Jr. "American Economic Institutions," *American Society.* New York: Knopf, 1960. Chapter VI.

A sound interpretation of the complex American economic system.

Chapter 9: Family, Education, and Religion

Anshen, Ruth N., ed. *The Family: Its Function and Destiny.* New York: Harper & Row, 1959. Chapters IV through XII.

These chapters describe several varied family systems.

Cavan, Ruth S. *The American Family.* New York: Crowell, 1963. Parts I and II.

A lucid discussion of American families in terms of rural-urban, social class, ethnic group, and other variables.

Frazier, E. Franklin. *The Negro Family in the United States.* New York: Dryden, 1948.

This definitive study of American Negro families provides a background for many current racial issues.

Goode, William J. *World Revolution and Family Patterns.* Glencoe: Free Press, 1963.

An important study of the nature and trends of family change in major world regions.

Queen, Stuart A., *et al. The Family in Various Cultures.* Chicago: Lippincott, 1961.

This book contains descriptions of family systems of many types and in many times and places.

Beals, Ralph L., and Harry Hoijer. *An Introduction to Anthropology.* New York: Macmillan, 1965. Chapter XXI.

Educational practices and organization in the primitive world are here analyzed and illustrated.

Clark, Burton R. *The Open Door College: A Case Study.* New York: McGraw-Hill, 1960.

An empirical study of the administration, student population and movement, and teaching problems in junior colleges.

Conant, James B. *The American High School Today.* New York: McGraw-Hill, 1959.

A critical analysis of American public education, particularly at the high-school level.

Riesman, David. "The Oral Tradition, the Written Word and the Screen Image," *Abundance for What? And Other Essays.* Garden City: Doubleday, 1964. Pp. 418-442.

Riesman shows how people in developing societies can skip the stage of literacy in the process of modernization.

Woody, Thomas H. *Life and Education in Early Society.* New York: Macmillan, 1949.

A useful discussion of the nature and organization of education in earlier times.

Clark, Elmer T. *The Small Sects in America.* New York: Abingdon-Cokesbury, 1949.

A useful study of the proliferation and diversity of religious organizations in a society that is characterized by a strong trend toward bureaucratic centralization.

Form, William H., and Delbert C. Miller. "Religion: Moral Monitors," *Industry, Labor and Community*. New York: Harper & Row, 1960. Chapter IX.

This chapter examines the recent evolution of religion in Western societies and explores the relations between religion and the economy within a community setting.

Herberg, Will. *Protestant, Catholic, Jew*. Garden City: Doubleday, 1956.

In this imaginative book Herberg examines the differences, relations, and trends of the three great American religions, arguing that all are becoming typically "American."

Lenski, Gerhard. *The Religious Factor*. Garden City: Doubleday, 1961.

An empirical study of the role of religion in society with particular reference to the other institutions.

Pope, Liston. *Millhands and Preachers*. New Haven: Yale University Press, 1942.

A pioneer study of the organization and change of the modern American religious institution.

Chapter 10: Population

Cain, Leonard D., Jr. "Life Course and Social Structure," in *Handbook of Modern Sociology*, ed. R. E. L. Faris. Chicago: Rand McNally, 1964. Pp. 272-309.

An exploratory analysis of the influence of age categories on social structure and functions.

Davis, Kingsley. "The Unpredicted Pattern of Population Change," *Annals*, 305:53-59 (May 1956).

An analysis of population trends in the developing areas of the world.

Freedman, Ronald. *Population: The Vital Revolution*. Garden City: Doubleday, 1964.

A symposium by experts in demography, written in a popular style, dealing with the current world-wide population explosion.

Lenica, Jan, and Alfred Sauvy. *Population Explosion: Abundance or Famine*. New York: Dell, 1962.

A popular paperback with cartoon-like illustrations of the current world population crisis.

Malthus, Thomas R. *An Essay on Population*. New York: Dutton, 1914. First published in England in 1798.

This pioneer empirical study of population is regarded as the beginning of modern population science.

Osborn, Frederick. *This Crowded World*. Public Affairs Pamphlet, 306, 1960.

A brief, popularly written discussion of the world population dilemma.

Population Bulletin. Issued monthly by the Population Reference Bureau, Washington, D.C.

This little journal contains factual reports, interpretations, and commentaries on the population of the world, various regions, and nations and the United States.

Statistical Abstract of the United States. Washington, D.C.: United States Government Printing Office.

Issued annually by the Bureau of the Census, this is the official statistical record of the American population.

Taeuber, Irene B. "Population and Society," in *Handbook of Modern Sociology,* ed. R. E. L. Faris. Chicago: Rand McNally, 1964. Pp. 83-125.

A summary of population data, trends, and issues for the world and for the United States, with an extensive bibliography.

Thompson, Warren S., and David T. Lewis. *Population Problems.* New York: McGraw-Hill, 1965.

A comprehensive and authoritative textbook on population.

United Nations. *The Future Growth of World Population.* New York: United Nations, 1958.

An authoritative estimate of the growth of world population.

Wrong, Dennis H. *Population.* New York: Random House, 1956.

A brief analysis of the major aspects of the population issue.

Chapter 11: Social Stratification

Bendix, Reinhard, and S. M. Lipset. *Class, Status, and Power: Social Stratification in Comparative Perspective.* New York: Free Press, 1966.

In this reader, stratification theory is analyzed and stratification systems of many societies are described.

Broom, Leonard. "The Social Differentiation of Jamaica," *American Sociological Review,* 19:115-124 (April 1954).

An empirical study of social stratification in a West Indian society as conditioned by historical circumstances and ethnic differences.

Cavan, Ruth S. *The American Family.* New York: Crowell, 1963. Chapters V, VI, and VII.

This material describes family organization and behavior in the three American social classes.

Cohen, Albert. "Characteristics of the Lower Blue-Collar Class," *Social Problems,* 10:303-334 (Spring 1963).

An analytic description of one sector of the lower or working class in American society.

Gordon, Milton M. *Social Class in American Sociology.* Durham: Duke University Press, 1958.

This little book analyzes theory and conceptualization of social class in the recent history of American sociology.

Inkeles, Alex. "Social Stratification and Mobility in the Soviet Union," *American Sociological Review,* 15:465-479 (1950).

Professor Inkeles examines the phenomena of stratification and mobility in what the Communists like to refer to as the "classless society."

Lenski, Gerhard E. "American Social Classes: Statistical Strata or Social Groups," *American Journal of Sociology,* 57:139-144 (September 1952).

Professor Lenski examines the issue of the manner of conceptualizing American social classes.

Lewis, Roy, and Angus Maude. *The English Middle Classes.* New York: Knopf, 1950.

A study of the rise, functions, and characteristics of the English middle classes.

Mayer, Kurt B. *Class and Society.* New York: Random House, 1955.

This little paperback summarizes important theory and research on social class.

Mills, C. Wright. *White Collar.* New York: Oxford, 1956.

A well-known study of the American middle classes, both old and new.

Rosen, Bernard C. "Race Ethnicity and the Achievement Syndrome," *American Sociological Review,* 24:47-60 (1959).

An empirical study of achievement motivation of six racial and ethnic groups in relation to class standing and social mobility.

Srinivas, M. N. *Caste in Modern India: And Other Essays.* New York: Asia, 1962.

A penetrating though readable analysis of the Indian caste system by a knowledgeable Indian sociologist.

Vogel, Ezra F. *Japan's New Middle Class.* Berkeley: University of California Press, 1963.

An empirical study of social change and stratification in modern Japan, focusing on the organization and behavior of families in the new salaried middle class.

Wilensky, Harold, and Hugh Edwards. "The Skidder: Ideological Adjustments of Downward Mobile Workers," *American Sociological Review,* 24:215-231 (1959).

An empirical study of the social consequences and correlates of downward occupational mobility.

Chapter 12: Formation and Organization of Personality

Bandura, Albert, and Richard H. Walters. *Social Learning and Personality Development.* New York: Holt, Rinehart & Winston, 1963.

An analysis of socialization in terms of behaviorist learning theory that draws heavily upon empirical psychological findings.

Berkowitz, Leonard. *The Development of Motives and Values in the Child.* New York: Basic Books, 1964.

A summary and synthesis of empirical and theoretical knowledge about the growth of motives and moral values in children through socialization.

Brim, Orville G., Jr. "Personality Development as Role-Learning," in *Personality Development in Children,* eds. Ira Iscoe and Harold Stevenson. Austin: University of Texas Press, 1960. Pp. 127-157.

A clear statement of the sociological or role approach to the process of socialization.

Brim, Orville G., Jr., and Stanton Wheeler. *Socialization After Childhood: Two Essays.* New York: Wiley, 1966.

An analytical discussion of later socialization.

Child, Irvin L. "Socialization," in *Handbook of Social Psychology,* ed. Gardner Lindzey. Boston: Addison-Wesley, 1954. Pp. 655-689.

A summary of research and theory on socialization from the point of view of child development.

Cooley, Charles Horton. "The Social Self—1. The Meaning of I" and "The Social Self—2. Various Phases of I," *Human Nature and the Social Order.* New York: Scribners, 1902. Chapters V and VI.

Cooley's classic delineation of the "looking-glass" process, the social self, and its variants.

Elkin, Frederick. *The Child in Society.* New York: Random House, 1960.

A brief description of the socialization process in terms of role theory.

Mead, George Herbert. "Mind" and "The Self," *Mind, Self and Society.* Chicago: University of Chicago Press, 1934. Chapters II and III.

Mead's celebrated analysis of symbolic interaction, the emergence of self, and the structure and process of the self.

Miller, Daniel, and Guy Swanson. *The Changing American Parent.* New York: Wiley, 1958.

An empirical study of the variability of socialization in terms of the American class structure.

Sewell, William H. "Some Recent Developments in Socialization Theory and Research," *Annals,* 349:163-181 (September 1963).

An excellent summary of research and theoretical developments in socialization studies, especially for the five years prior to 1963.

Wylie, Ruth. *The Self Concept.* Lincoln: University of Nebraska Press, 1961.

A thorough summary and analysis of the empirical research on the self concept reported to 1960.

Chapter 13: Social Structure and Personality

Becker, Howard S., *et al. Boys in White: Student Culture in Medical School.* Chicago: University of Chicago Press, 1961.

An empirical study of the socialization of men into the medical profession.

Bronfenbrenner, Urie. "Socialization and Social Class Through Time and Space," in *Readings in Social Psychology,* eds. Eleanor E. Macoby *et al.* New York: Holt, Rinehart & Winston, 1958. Pp. 400-425.

Bronfenbrenner reviews the studies of socialization and social class that appeared over a quarter of a century, and synthesizes the findings and indicated trends in middle and working classes.

Gowman, Alan G. "Blindness in the Military Setting," *The War Blind in American Social Structure.* New York: American Foundation for the Blind, 1957. Chapter II.

A perceptive analysis of the structure and process of resocialization of the war blind.

Harris, Dale B. "Work and Adolescent Transition to Maturity." *Teachers College Record*, 63:146-153 (March 1961).

> This article discusses the significance of work experience in the socialization of adolescents and young adults.

Havighurst, Robert J., *et al. Growing Up in River City*. New York: Wiley, 1962.

> A study of the educational and social experiences, from childhood to young adulthood, of a sample of 500 young people in a midwestern city.

Mead, Margaret. *Sex and Temperament in Three Primitive Societies*. New York: Morrow, 1935.

> A study of how sex roles are differentially shaped in the social and cultural systems of three neighboring primitive tribes.

Parsons, Talcott. "The School Class as a Social System: Some of Its Functions in American Society," *Harvard Educational Review*, 29:297-318 (Fall 1959).

> A penetrating analysis of how teachers and peers tend to supersede family and parents as significant others in the process of socialization.

Prothro, Edwin P. *Child Rearing in the Lebanon*. Cambridge: Harvard University Press, 1961.

> An empirical study of variable patterns and consequences of socialization in a Middle Eastern society and culture.

Rabin, A. I. *Growing Up in the Kibbutz*. New York: Springer, 1965.

> A study of socialization practices in the unique child-rearing setting of the Israeli kibbutz.

Read, Margaret. *Children of Their Fathers*. New Haven: Yale University Press, 1960.

> An anthropologist presents a picture of structure and functions of socialization in a contemporary primitive society.

Rosen, Bernard C. "The Achievement Syndrome," *American Sociological Review*, 1956. Pp. 203-211.

> Classic analysis of variable socialization to achievement orientation within the American social structure.

Chapter 14: Mass Society and Mass Phenomena

Blauner, Robert. *Alienation and Freedom: The Factory Worker and His Industry*. Chicago: University of Chicago Press, 1964.

> An empirical study of worker alienation in relation to a number of variables in the industrial setting.

Fromm, Erich. *Escape from Freedom*. New York: Holt, Rinehart & Winston, 1941.

> A well-known analysis of the process of alienation in mass society.

Inkeles, Alex. *Public Opinion in Soviet Russia: A Study in Mass Persuasion*. Cambridge: Harvard University Press, 1958.

> A study of total governmental control of the content, process, and media of mass communication.

Kornhauser, William. "Theory of Mass Society," *The Politics of Mass Society*. Glencoe: Free Press, 1959. Part I.

An attempt to conceptualize mass society in terms of its conditions, structure, culture, and personalities.

Larsen, Otto N. "Social Effects of Mass Communication," in *Handbook of Modern Sociology,* ed. R. E. L. Faris. Chicago: Rand McNally, 1964. Pp. 349-381.

A summary assessment of research and findings, with an extensive bibliography, on the social effects of mass communication.

Lerner, Daniel. *The Passing of Traditional Society.* Glencoe: Free Press, 1958. Especially Chapters I and II.

An empirical study that shows how radios and roads function as mechanisms of mass communication to destroy traditional society.

Martindale, Don. "America as a Mass Society," *American Society.* Princeton: Van Nostrand, 1960. Part I.

This material examines the economics, taste, personalities, elites, and changes of American mass society.

Rosenberg, Bernard, and David M. White. *Mass Culture: The Popular Arts in America.* Glencoe: Free Press, 1958.

The pieces that are reproduced in this reader define the so-called popular arts as mass culture.

Schramm, Wilbur. *Mass Media and National Development: The Role of Information in the Developing Countries.* Stanford: Stanford University Press, 1964.

A description of the new roles and functions of the mass media in the process of societal modernization.

Wright, Charles R. *Mass Communication: A Sociological Perspective.* New York: Random House, 1959.

A brief discussion of the nature, content, and consequences of mass communication.

Chapter 15: Collective Behavior

Bates, F. L., *et al. The Social and Psychological Consequences of a Natural Disaster: A Longitudinal Study.* Washington, D.C.: National Academy of Science, National Research Council, 1962.

An empirical study of some of the social and psychological consequences of a hurricane.

Cantril, Hadley. *The Psychology of Social Movements.* New York: Wiley, 1941.

This book contains well-documented accounts and analyses of several social movements and similar collective enterprises.

Form, William H., and Charles P. Loomis. "The Persistence and Emergence of Social and Cultural Systems in Disasters," *American Sociological Review,* 21:180-185 (1956).

This study draws attention to the fact that social behavior is systematic even in highly disorganized situations.

Holtzman, Abraham. *The Townsend Movement: A Political Study.* New York: Bookman Associates, 1963.

A useful study of a recent American social movement.

King, C. Wendell. *Social Movements in the United States.* New York: Random House, 1956.

This little book summarizes and orders much of the sound sociological knowledge of social movements.

Lee, A. M., and N. D. Humphrey. *Race Riot.* New York: Dryden, 1943.

An empirical study of the 1943 Detroit riot.

Messinger, S. L. "Organizational Transformation: A Case Study of a Declining Social Movement," *American Sociological Review,* 20:3-10 (February 1955).

A useful comment and illustration of one class of consequences of social movements.

Petersen, William, and David Matza. *Social Controversy.* Belmont, Calif.: Wadsworth, 1963.

In this book the opposing positions of public opinion debates on a series of continuing issues are presented and evaluated.

"Races: Trigger of Hate," *Time,* 86:13-19 (August 20, 1965).

This graphic account of the riot in Watts, California, describes part of the background, the triggering event, the effective symbols, the process of contagion, and the structure and functions of violent crowd behavior.

Schettler, Clarence. "Public Opinion Groups in Action," *Public Opinion in American Society.* New York: Harper & Row, 1960. Part IV.

This material examines the operations and functions of pressure groups, lobbies, public relations representatives, censorship, and propaganda in the formation and manipulation of public opinion.

Schultz, Duane P. *Panic Behavior.* New York: Random House, 1964.

A brief analysis of the nature, manifestations, and consequences of panic behavior.

Smelser, Neil J. *Theory of Collective Behavior.* Glencoe: Free Press, 1963.

This book represents an effort to formulate a logically consistent and generally applicable theory of collective behavior.

Chapter 16: Social Change, Social Problems, and Social Planning

Billings, Henry. *All Down the Valley.* New York: Viking, 1952.

A graphic portrayal of physical and social deterioration in the Tennessee River valley and the nature and consequences of the TVA program as planned remedy.

Buckingham, Walter. *Automation.* New York: Harper & Row, 1963.

A study of the nature and consequences of automation with some attention to the possibilities of planned control of this innovation.

Cressey, Paul F. "Social Disorganization and Reorganization in Harlan County, Kentucky," *American Sociological Review,* 14:389-394 (June 1949).

A study of social disorganization and reorganization that can be read in terms of the concepts of social change and planning.

Cuber, John F., and Robert A. Harper. *Problems of American Society: Values in Conflict.* New York: Holt, Rinehart & Winston, 1951. Chapters II and III.

In this material social problems are said to issue from the value conflicts that are one consequence of social change.

Elliott, Mabel A., and Francis E. Merrill. "Social Disorganization," *Social Disorganization*. New York: Harper & Row, 1961. Chapter II.

This material conceptualizes disorganization as an aspect of social change and defines social problems as the evaluation of social disorganization.

Etzioni, Amitai, and Eva Etzioni. *Social Change: Sources, Patterns and Consequences*. New York: Basic Books, 1964.

A general treatment of the issue of social change.

Goldschmidt, Walter. *As You Sow*. Glencoe: Free Press, 1947.

This book examines the consequences of industrialization for the character and organization of rural life in the United States.

Goodenough, W. H. *Cooperation and Change: An Anthropological Approach to Community Development*. New York: Russell Sage Foundation, 1963.

An examination of community development as one technique of social planning.

Gross, F. "Some Social Consequences of Atomic Discovery," *American Sociological Review*, 15:43-50 (1950).

A review and analysis of the social functions of an important type of technological change.

LaPiere, Richard T. *Social Change*. New York: McGraw-Hill, 1965.

A general treatment of the issue of social change.

Murdock, George Peter. "How Culture Changes," in *Man, Culture and Society*, ed. H. L. Shapiro. New York: Oxford, 1956. Pp. 247-260.

A distinguished anthropologist summarizes and outlines the phases of the process of cultural change.

Rostow, W. W. *The Process of Economic Growth*. New York: Norton, 1952.

In this material Rostow constructs a model of economic growth that is, in his judgment, applicable to developing societies and that comprehends the impact of economic growth on general societal change.

Sindler, Allan P. *Change in the Contemporary South*. Durham: Duke University Press, 1963.

An analysis and estimate of recent change in the southern region of the United States.

GLOSSARY

ACCOMMODATION. *Process of achieving and resultant structure of status relations among groups or individuals that tends to maximize cooperation and minimize conflict.*

ACHIEVED STATUS. *Position of an individual or group which he (it) has gained by individual or collective effort.* Cf. *Ascribed status.*

ADVANCED SOCIETY. *Type of society that has achieved mature associational forms of social organization, culture, and economic organization and practice.*

ALIENATION. *Sense of social detachment and loss of personal identity associated with social change, instability, and anomie.*

ANOMIE. *Condition of ambiguity, indefiniteness, or confusion associated with breakdown or loss of organization, cohesion, and integration; sometimes referred to as normlessness.*

ASCRIBED STATUS. *Position given to an individual or group over which he (it) has no initial control and for which he (it) has not striven.* Cf. *Achieved status.*

ASSIMILATION. *Process through which culturally distinct groups subordinate differences, expand similarities, become fused, and lose their separate identities.*

ASSOCIATION. *A collectivity characterized by limited explicit objectives and formal organization and relations.* Cf. *Formal group, Secondary group, Complex organization.*

ASSOCIATIONAL SOCIETY. *Type of society characterized by formal specialized organization, rationalistic culture, and technical and mechanical economic arrangements.*

AUTHORITARIANISM. *Practice or condition of centralized authority for the control of decisions and action.*

AUTHORITY. *Power or force created, allocated, utilized, and regulated by a social collectivity.* Cf. *Sanction, Power.*

BORROWING. See *Cultural diffusion and borrowing.*

BUREAUCRACY. *Type of formal, efficient, instrumental structure, revealed in complex organizations and institutional arrangements, characterized by hierarchies of precisely defined roles (offices), rational rules, and graded authority and responsibility; providing career opportunities for office holders; and facilitating the development of supporting or obstructing small informal groups.* Cf. *Formal organization, Complex organization, Institution.*

CASTE SYSTEM. *Type of social organization composed of ranked, mutually exclusive units between which virtually no social mobility is permitted.* Cf. *Ascribed status.*

CENSORSHIP. *Deliberate exclusion of material from the stream of communication in order to influence ideas, decisions, or action.*

CLIQUE. *Small, intimate (primary) group based on friendship ties and shared interests.* Cf. *Primary group, Informal group.*

COLLECTIVITY. *General term to refer to a number (small or large) of individuals, whether aggregated or dispersed, organized or unorganized, as a recognizable unit without specifying characteristics or type.*

COMMUNAL SOCIETY. *Type of society characterized by informal social relations, kinship organization, traditional culture, and nontechnical practices.*

COMMUNITY. *A continuing, organized collectivity of individuals of both sexes and all ages, occupying a delimitable geographic area and sharing an inclusive sociocultural system.*

COMPETITION. *Continuous, impersonal, regulated process of struggle for ends that are external to the participants. When competition becomes personal, it is called rivalry.*

COMPLEX ORGANIZATION (or large-scale organization). A type of large, heterogeneous, dispersed unit of social organization characterized by formal or bureaucratic structure. Cf. Bureaucracy, Formal organization.

CONFLICT. Intermittent, direct, and sometimes unregulated process of struggle for advantage by limiting or annihilating the antagonist.

CONJUGAL. Conjugal specifies family forms in which the marriage nexus is the major basis of cohesion and organization and in which kinship (the consanguineal nexus) is subordinated. Composed typically of father, mother, and their offspring, conjugal families are often smaller and simpler than consanguineal units.

CONSENSUS. Condition of agreement or shared understanding within a social unit.

COOPERATION. Process of collaboration, working together for shared objectives.

CORRELATION. Dynamic relationship, often measurable, between two or more phenomena or variables. Correlation does not indicate either the fact or the direction of causation in the relationship.

CROWD. An unstructured collectivity, either compact or dispersed, characterized by sense of crisis, milling, temporary structure, and rejection of ordinary social norms.

CULTURAL COMPLEX. Functionally integrated unit of cultural elements that is adjusted to a social unit or situation.

CULTURAL DIFFUSION AND BORROWING. Spread of culture within or among systems; or acquisition of culture within or from another system.

CULTURAL EQUIPMENT. Material objects used in the practice of culture.

CULTURAL HERITAGE OR TRADITION. Body of cultural usage passed from one generation or group to another.

CULTURAL INNOVATION. Process of creating new items of culture, rationally or accidentally, individually or collectively.

CULTURAL LAG. Disjunction within a cultural system when one element changes faster than associated elements.

CULTURAL NORM. Sanctioned regularity of group behavior. Cf. Norm, Folkways, Mores, Taboo, Law, Culture pattern.

CULTURAL PRODUCT. Material object created by the application of cultural practices to raw materials.

CULTURAL RELATIVISM. Practice of interpreting and evaluating behavior and objects by reference to the normative and value standards of the culture to which the behavior or object belongs.

CULTURE. All the interrelated ways of acting, thinking, feeling, and believing that are created, shared, learned, and used by people as members of society.

CULTURE CONFLICT. Clash between unharmonious cultural elements or units.

CULTURE PATTERN. Regularity of group usage. Cf. Cultural norm.

CULTURE SYSTEM. Inclusive, integrated arrangement of cultural elements and complexes that is adjusted to a society; a culture, a "design for living."

DEFINITION OF THE SITUATION. Social meaning, i.e., a cluster of behavioral expectations, attaching to a social situation and embodied in the relevant culture.

DEMOCRACY. Practice and condition of decentralizing authority, of involving participants, for the control of decisions and action.

DEMOGRAPHY. The scientific study of population composition and dynamics.

DEVELOPING SOCIETY. Society in process of transition from communal to associational forms.

DISORGANIZATION. Process and resultant condition of loss or breakdown of a prior pattern of organization in any type of social unit.

DIVISION OF LABOR. *Scheme for subdividing a task or activity into components, allocating these as roles to individuals or groups, and synthesizing the resultant activities and relationships.*

DYSFUNCTION. *An unintended, often also unrecognized objective social consequence of the operations of a social system that is inimical to the system.* Cf. *Latent function, Manifest function.*

ECONOMY. *The economic system or economic order of a society.*

EMPIRICISM. *Method of acquiring primary knowledge by direct sensory observation, experimentation, and the testing of hypotheses.*

ENDOGAMY. *Practice of choosing marriage partners within specified groups or geographic areas.*

ETHNIC GROUP. *A large, dispersed collectivity whose criteria for membership may be national origin, religion, or race.*

ETHNOCENTRISM. *Practice of interpreting and evaluating behavior and objects by reference to the standards of one's own culture rather than by those of the culture to which they belong.*

ETHOS. *The emphasis, quality, or style of a culture that distinguishes it from other cultures.*

EXOGAMY. *Practice of choosing marriage partners outside specified groups or geographic areas.*

EXTENDED FAMILY. *Large family composed of several nuclear families joined by kinship, marriage, or mutual obligations.*

EXTENDED GROUP. *A group in which size and communications are extended beyond small-group limits, thus creating secondary and formal characteristics.* Cf. *Complex organization, Secondary group.*

FAMILY OF ORIENTATION. *The family unit of socialization; varies widely in composition from one society to another.*

FAMILY OF PROCREATION. *Reproductive family unit, usually father, mother, and their immediate offspring.*

FERTILITY RATIO. *Number of children under five years old per 1000 (sometimes per 100 or per 100,000) women of child-bearing age, 15 to 44 years.*

FOLKWAYS. *Patterns of social relations or ordinary usage of a group or society; the "habits of a people."* Cf. *Norm, Culture.*

FORMAL GROUP. *Group in which roles are segmented and relations are specified and explicit.* Cf. *Secondary group, Extended group, Complex organization.*

FORMAL ORGANIZATION. *The rational, explicit pattern of organization, often described in diagrams, charts, and written specifications.* Cf. *Bureaucracy.*

FUNCTIONAL ANALYSIS. *A version of the scientific method suited to the study of social systems, their operations and objective social consequences; the explanation of one social phenomenon in terms of the requirements or imperatives imposed by related social systems and structures.*

FUNCTIONAL ORGANIZATION. *The actual form of organization as revealed in the actions of people.*

GEMEINSCHAFT (German). *Condition of close integration, stable organization, and intimate relations characteristic of communal or traditional societies; opposite of* Gesellschaft.

GENERALIZED OTHER. *Internalized image of rules, and role expectations of groups and other social units.*

GESELLSCHAFT (German). *Condition of formality, impersonality, and disorganization characteristic of associational and mass societies; opposite of* Gemeinschaft.

GROUP. See *Social group.*

HIERARCHY. *Social structure composed of ranked orders of positions.* Cf. *Social stratification.*

HYPOTHESIS. *Tentative explanation or interpretation, offered in lieu of verification and available for testing by empirical methods.*

IDEAL-TYPE. *A model or construct composed of representative elements from different phenomena of the same category; it is typical of all phenomena of the category but identical with none.*

IDENTIFICATION. *Psychological mechanism of being another person by fully submerging oneself in the role of the other.*

IDENTITY. *Experience of involvement in society and attachment to self as action system and real person.*

IDEOLOGY. *System of thought and belief that serves to explain the past, interpret the present, predict the future, and justify current action.*

INCLUSIVE ROLE. *A social part, unique to one individual, engaging all aspects of his personality.* Cf. *Segmental role.*

INFORMAL GROUP. *Group in which roles are inclusive and relations intimate or casual.* Cf. *Primary group.*

INFORMAL ORGANIZATION. *The actual pattern of organization that is implicit in the actions of people.* Cf. *Functional organization.*

IN-GROUP. *A group with which an individual identifies; his membership and reference groups.*

INSTITUTION. *System of established, binding, and relatively sacred rules of collective action, implemented by social structures and collectivities, for the attainment of important societal ends.*

INSTITUTIONALIZATION. *Process through which social usages become established, binding, and relatively sacred.*

INTEGRATION *(or social integration). Condition of harmonious adjustment, both static and dynamic, among the parts of a social or cultural system. Process of increasing the degree of harmony within a social or cultural system.*

INTEREST GROUP. *An organized collectivity of any type united by and seeking to advance a collective interest.* Cf. *Association, Pressure group, Vested interest.*

ISSUE. *An interesting, important, problematical, and unsettled subject that people respond to, discuss, and disagree over.*

LARGE-SCALE ORGANIZATION. See *Complex organization.*

LATENT FUNCTION. *An unintended and sometimes unrecognized function.* Cf. *Dysfunction, Manifest function.*

LAW. *Collective usage, both unwritten and written, that is sanctioned by the authority of government.*

MANIFEST FUNCTION. *An intended and recognized function.* Cf. *Dysfunction, Latent function.*

MASS BEHAVIOR. *Modes of organization, communication, and action existing outside the sphere of ordinary social organization and behavior and facilitated by the media and process of mass communication.*

MASS COMMUNICATION. *Process of broadcasting or disseminating standardized messages from central locations to dispersed, unseen audiences.*

MASS CULTURE. *The norms and values expressing the consensus and the patterns of behavior and reflecting the instability of mass society.*

MASS MEDIA. *Instruments for broadcasting or disseminating standardized messages from central locations, including the press, motion pictures, radio, television, and certain ancillary devices.*

MASS SOCIETY. *Associational society*

with specific reference to widespread anomie and alienation and the accompanying forms of communication, organization, and collective action made possible by the mass media.

MEMBERSHIP GROUP. *A group in which an individual is a member by having one or more statuses and roles.*

MILLING. *Relatively unstructured social interaction, including random overt movements, facial and eye expressions, and verbalizations, that function to communicate ideas, images, feelings, etc.*

MORES. *Obligatory patterns of social conduct, considered right and strongly sanctioned; morals or moral norms.*

NATION-STATE. *A nationalistic society organized as a political state.*

NORM. *A pattern of social activity; what is socially required; what is generally expected; what is usually done.*

NORMATIVE ORGANIZATION. *The "ideal" form of organization as prescribed by the cultural norms.*

NUCLEAR FAMILY. *Small group composed of father, mother, and their immediate offspring.*

OUT-GROUP. *Any group with which an individual does not identify; a group which he refers to as "they."*

PERSONALITY. *The total changing system of internal and external action of an individual that has developed through socialization, heredity, and maturation as these processes are conditioned by physiological, social, and cultural factors.*

POLYANDRY. *Marriage pattern involving plurality of husbands.*

POLYGAMY. *Marriage pattern involving plurality of either wives or husbands.*

POLYGYNY. *Marriage pattern involving plurality of wives.*

POPULATION. *Number of individuals, either of all classes or by specific characteristics, in a specified place at a specified time.*

POPULATION COMPOSITION. *Relative proportions of component categories, e.g., sex and age, in a population.*

POWER. *The ability of an individual or group, resulting from either the authority inherent in a status or unique characteristics or circumstances, to enforce acquiescence and compliance from others.* Cf. *Authority, Sanction.*

POWER STRUCTURE. *Pattern of orderly allocation, arrangement, and exercise of authority and power within a social system.*

PRESSURE GROUP. *Organized collectivity acting to advance, enforce, or protect some interest.* Cf. *Interest group, Vested interest.*

PRIMARY COMMUNICATION. *Direct, nonmediated exchange of symbolic meanings.*

PRIMARY GROUP. *A small group in which roles are inclusive, relations intimate, and objectives general.* Cf. *Group, Informal group.*

PRIMARY RELATIONS. *Interpersonal interaction that is direct, informal, inclusive, nontransferable, and often intimate.*

PROPAGANDA. *Conscious manipulation of symbols of communication in order to persuade leaders and followers to accept a predetermined idea, decision, or action.*

PUBLIC. *Dispersed, indefinite collectivity interested in, divided by, and responding to an issue and expressing views in order to affect collective decisions and action.*

PUBLIC OPINION. *Views of a public, relative to an issue, including definitions, arguments, feelings, evaluations, proposals, programs, etc., for the purpose of influencing collective decisions and action.*

RACE. *A population sector distinguished*

by a cluster of presumably hereditary physical traits.

REFERENCE GROUP. *Any group that controls an individual's decisions and actions whether he is a member or not.*

REVOLUTION. *A social movement that radically alters the social structure and brings new groups or individuals into control of the social system.*

RIVALRY. See under *Competition.*

ROLE *(or social role). (1) Expected pattern or mode of behavior of an individual or group, attached to a social status and incorporated within a social system. (2) The unique, nontransferable way an individual or group plays his (its) part.* See also *Inclusive role, Segmental role.*

RUMOR. *Unverified symbolic communications serving to define unstructured situations and to indicate lines of action.*

SANCTION *(or social sanction). Refers to social actions and expressions that are perceived by individuals or groups as ratifications and/or deprivations issuing from actual or anticipated rewards and penalties, and that are intended to approve conformity with or to present deviations from social norms and other expectations.* Cf. *Social norm, Authority.*

SECONDARY GROUP. *Group with characteristics opposite to those of primary groups.*

SEGMENTAL ROLE. *A social part, applicable to a category of actors, engaging a segment—i.e., a behavior specialty—of an individual's personality.* Cf. *Inclusive role.*

SEX RATIO. *Number of men per 100 women in a population, usually stated as a per cent.*

SMALL GROUP. *A group in which each member has direct contact with all the others and is aware that they are members.*

SOCIAL CATEGORY. *Any number of individuals responded to as a social unit because they share in common one or more characteristics such as sex, age, amount of income, or status.*

SOCIAL CHANGE. *Variation through time of the structural, cultural, and interactional elements of a social system.*

SOCIAL CLASS. *A social category in a system of categories ranked in relative wealth, power, and prestige in which social mobility is permitted.*

SOCIAL COHESION. *Condition of unity, conjunction, or harmony among the constituents of a social unit or social system. Social solidarity is a common synonym.*

SOCIAL CONTAGION. *Rapid, uncontrolled spread of feelings, images, and ideas through an unstructured collectivity.*

SOCIAL CONTROL. *(1) Actions of a collectivity to constrain members and participants to comply with the sanctioned rules and standards. (2) Collective efforts of every type to manage the process of social change.*

SOCIAL DIFFERENTIATION. *Process of evaluating perceived differences among individuals and categories of individuals and of patterning social relations in accordance with such evaluations.*

SOCIAL DISORGANIZATION. See *Disorganization.*

SOCIAL DISTANCE. *Relative degree of intimacy or aloofness among participants within a social system.*

SOCIAL ECOLOGY. *The study of reciprocal influence between the natural and artificial environment and the deployment, organization, and relations of human society.*

SOCIAL FUNCTION. *An objective social consequence of the operations of a social system that is beneficial for the system.* See also *Dysfunction, Latent function, Manifest function.*

SOCIAL GROUP. *A collectivity (two or more) of individuals who are mutually oriented, sharing common values and beliefs,* *engaging in social relations with each other, and aware of their distinction from other such collectivities.*

SOCIAL INSTITUTION. See *Institution.*

SOCIAL INTEGRATION. See *Integration.*

SOCIAL INTERACTION. *(1) Continuous sequence of actions and reactions, both physical and nonphysical, by individuals and groups through which symbolic meanings are expressed, comprehended, and responded to. (2) Common equivalents are association, social relations. (3) Social behavior, social action, and social activity stress the action aspect of social interaction. (4) Communication refers to the exchange of symbolic meanings that is the decisive element of social interaction.*

SOCIAL MOBILITY. *Process of individual or collective change of rank in a stratification system, sometimes accompanied by change of geographic location.* Cf. *Achieved status.*

SOCIAL MOVEMENT. *Complex social enterprise, combining both crowd and public behavior, to initiate or obstruct social change.*

SOCIAL ORDER. *The stable, inclusive, systematic pattern of social life, society, the social system.*

SOCIAL ORGANIZATION. *Variable arrangements of roles and statuses, means and ends, and authority and communication patterns as revealed in social units of varying size and type.*

SOCIAL PLANNING. *Conscious social process, combining investigation, discussion, decision, and action, to achieve predetermined types of social structure and social experiences through the management of social change.*

SOCIAL POLICY. *Relatively rational agreements and decisions of the ends and means of collective effort.*

SOCIAL PROBLEM. *A widespread social condition, regarded as undesirable by a con-siderable number of individuals, about which it is believed something can be done by collective effort.*

SOCIAL PROCESS. *(1) Generalized stream of patterned interaction in human society. (2) Specific form of the stream of interaction among groups and/or individuals, e.g., cooperation, conflict.*

SOCIAL ROLE. See *Role.*

SOCIAL SELF. *An individual's self-image and action system with which he identifies.*

SOCIAL SOLIDARITY. See *Social cohesion.*

SOCIAL STATUS. See *Status.*

SOCIAL STRATIFICATION. *Process of forming and the resultant structure of ranked social categories reflecting differentials of wealth, power, and prestige and controlling many social experiences and life chances.* Cf. *Hierarchy.*

SOCIAL STRUCTURE. *The stable framework of a social system; often used as a synonym of social system.*

SOCIAL SYSTEM. *Any unit of social organization viewed as a functioning mechanism composed of a set of working parts and a complex pattern of operation.*

SOCIALIZATION. *Complex process of development and learning through which an individual acquires a personality and becomes a member of society.*

SOCIETY. *The most inclusive unit of social organization. The social system, locus of a culture, the arena of a way of life.*

STATUS *(or social status). (1) Position or place of an individual or group within a structure of positions in relation to other such positions. (2) Rank of a position, for either an individual or group, in a hierarchy of graded positions.* See also *Achieved status, Ascribed status.*

SUBCULTURE. *Variation of a culture,*

including both general and specialized elements, and adjusted to a subdivision of a society.

TABOO. *Strongly sanctioned prohibitions, negative mores, rules designating what is morally wrong or societally threatening.* Cf. *Sanction.*

THEORY. *A statement of relationship or explanation, based in part on empirical knowledge, in part on logical inference, which it is predicted will ultimately be verified.*

TOTALITARIANISM. *Type of social organization that concentrates power in the government and utilizes all sectors of the society to achieve ends which are determined by the government.*

TRADITION. *Cultural usage, sanctioned by association with revered predecessors or past events.*

TRADITIONAL SOCIETY. *Equals communal society. The term stresses non-modern social and cultural forms.*

VALUE. *Relative worth or preference, vis à vis available alternatives, of an idea, experience, action, person, group, or object.*

VALUE ORIENTATION. *Emphasis of interpretation of a value at a particular time or place.*

VARIABLE. *Changeable factor or element of a social situation, capable of serving as either cause or effect.*

VESTED INTEREST. *A collectivity deriving special advantage from and hence dedicated to the defense of the status quo.* Cf. *Interest group, Pressure group.*

Conjugal family, 217, 220
Consensus, 46
Conspicuous consumption, 299
Contrasting personalities, (case) 324-326
Cooley, Charles Horton, 12, 25, 26, 28, 100, 104, 106, 107, 108, 113, 149, 323
Cooperation, 118
Core groups, 183
Corner boys, (case) 113-116; see also *Street Corner Society*
Corporations. *See* Industrial organization
Correlation
    as method of explanation, 14-15
    with stratification, 296-298
Coser, Lewis, 27
Cottrell, William F., 13, 354
Courtship, 85, 213
Crawford, James, 404
Craze, (case) 384-385, 389
Cressey, Paul F., 437
Crestwood Heights, (case) 49-50, 59, 61, 376
Crime and criminology, 26, 27, 423, 444; *see also* White-collar crime
Crisis situations, 434
Crowd behavior
    (cases) 399-401, 403-405
    characteristics of, 396-397
    cohesion, 401
    compact, 405
    diffuse, 383, 405, 419
    in India, 396
    integrated, 402-403
    manipulated, 403
    mind, 398
    social functions of, 403
    social roles in, 399
    structure, 401-402
    theory of, 398
    unintegrated, 403
    variations in, 402; *see also* Collective behavior
Cultural borrowing, 435, 437
Cultural complex, 81-82
Cultural determinism, 427
Cultural diffusion, 431
Cultural equipment and products, 73-74
Cultural innovation, 431, 432
Cultural norms, 79-84
    types of, 79-81
    universals and alternatives, 81;

see also Social norms
Cultural pluralism, 359
Cultural relativism, 76
Cultural values, 86-94
    (cases) 87-89
    characteristics of, 86-89
    social organization, 94
    types of, 89-91
    variations in, 91
Culture, 72-97
    characteristics of, 74-75
    and communication, 75-77
    conditioning, 327
    defined, 72, 82
    literary, 431
    mass, 385-388
    nature of, 72-81
    organization of, 81-82
    pattern, universal, 82-84
    of Rampur, (case) 77-78
    and social organization, 94-97; *see also* Subculture
Culturally Deprived Child, (p.e.) 364-365
Custom, integration of, 428
Cyclical theories of social change, 428

Dahrendorf, Ralf, 30, 56
Darwin, Charles, 10
Davis, Kingsley, 16, 56, 268, 283, 360
Decision-making and -receiving, 406, 409, 450
Democracy, 132-133, 191-193, 227, 383, 406, 418
    in associations, 132
    in family, 213
Developing societies
    economics of, 206
    educational institutions in, 225
    modernization in, 442, 447, 451, 452
    politics of, 191
    social planning in, 452
Deviant behavior
    adaptive, 361
    adventitious, 357
    and bureaucracy, 139
    nature of, 357-358
    nontolerated, 357
    psychological, 444
    and social stratification, 299-300
    and social structure, 357
    sources of, 358
    systematic, 357
Dexter, Robert T., 444

school, 442
doctrines, 427
incidents (Alabama), 405
minorities, 444
organizations, 410
relations, 73, 121
segregation, 289
stratification, (case) 289-290; *see also* Chicago, race riot in; Negro and Negroes
Radio, 410; *see also* Mass communication; Mass media
Rallies, 403
Rampur, (case) 77-78, 82
Rationality, 59, 96-97, 208, 240, 428
Read, Margaret, 215, 313
Rebellion, 300, 361
Redfield, Robert, 58, 62, 222, 355
Reference groups, 102, 360, 409
    and the individual, 118-119
    and membership groups, 102-103
Region and regions, 171-173
Reign of terror, 420
Religion, 232-241
    in America, 238-240
    associational forms of, 237-238
    denominations, (case) 234
    in developing societies, 236-237
    forms, variability of, 232-235
    and nationality, 235-236
    new units of, 240
    organizations, 238, 410
    as social institution, 52
    social issues of, 240
Republic, The, 455
Resocialization, 339-342
    (case) 340-342
    and thought control, 340
    U.S. Military Academy study of, 340
Retreatism, 300, 361
Revolution, 420, 423
Riesman, David, 94, 193, 209, 299, 322, 428
Riley, John W., 380
Riley, Matilda White, 380
Riots, 396
    (case) 403-405
Ritualism, 300, 361
Rivalry, 117
Roethlisberger, F. J., 108, 144
Role and roles, 54, 100, 101
    assumed, 310
    defined, 45
    down- and up-grading of, 433

hierarchies, 205
inclusive, 101
in large-scale societies, 282
natural, 310
occupational, 349, 355
organizational, 450
segmental, 101
status hierarchies, 205; *see also* Social role and roles
Romantic complex, 213
Roper, Elmo, 297
Ross, Edward Alsworth, 25
Roxbury, (case) 167-169
Rumford, Byron, 370
Rumors, 398, 402
Rural communities, 149, 444
    open-country, 160

Samoa, (case) 186, 189, 315, 316
Sanderson, Dwight, 152
Schettler, Clarence, 414
Schneider, Louis, 181
School desegregation, 442
School and society, 229
Schramm, Wilbur, 378, 379
Schubnell, Hermann, 249
Schultz, George P., 429
Sears, Robert R., 317
Secondary groups. *See* Associations
Secondary institutional group, 183-184
Secularism, 59, 91, 240, 428
Security, loss of, 375
Seeley, John, 49, 299
Segmental role, 101
Segregation, as ecological process, 156
Self
    as actor, 326-327
    -consciousness, 189, 322, 349, 375
    -control, 84
        internalization of, 339
    -image
        and social role, 339
    moral, 329
    as object of action, 330
    -roles, 328-329
    social, 375
    -system, 330-331
        functional organization, 332; *see also* Ego and persona; Looking-glass self
Selznick, Gertrude, 445
Senior Citizen in America, (p.e.) 244-246
Sex
    categories, 257

Universal culture pattern, 82-84
Universal norms, 81
Universal reference, knowledge of, 7-8
Upper-upper-class family, (case) 294-295
Urban communities, 444
Urban ecological structure, 155-157
Urban industrialism, 433
Urban society, 62
Urban sprawl, 169
Urbanization, 169-170, 174, 372, 396, 406
 and religion, 241
 world, 267-268
Utopia and social planning, 455-457

Value, 86-94
 shared, 100; *see also* Cultural values
Value orientations, 91-94
Vance, Rupert, 173
Veblen, Thorstein, 299
Velasquez, 407
Vested interests, 410
Viet Cong, 415, 422
Village community, 160, 372, 373
Violence, 420
Vishinsky, Andrei, 136
Vocabulary, specialized, 352
Vocational education, 347

Wallin, Paul, 13
War blind, (case) 340-342
War-bond-selling campaign, (case) 411-412

"War of the Worlds," 381
Ward, Lester F., 25
Warner, W. Lloyd, 3, 12, 288, 306
Weber, Max, 12, 28, 135, 147, 184, 236, 427
Weinberg, S. Kirson, 445
Welles, Orson, 381
Wells, H. G., 381
Westie, Frank R., 10, 11, 12, 31
White-collar crime, 361
White-collar workers, 355; see also *Organization Man, The*
Whyte, William Foote, 4, 113, 114, 256
Whyte, William H., Jr., 131, 137, 139, 209, 299, 349, 355, 356
Wiese, Leopold von, 29, 233
Wife-mother role, 338, 342, 345, 431
Williams, Eugene, 404
Williams, Robin M., Jr., 92, 146
Wilson, Logan, 190, 222, 232, 247
Wirth, Louis, 406
Wolf, Kurt, 27
Women, 338, 345
Woofter, T. J., Jr., 173
Working class, American, 43

Yale University. *See* Human Relations Area Files
Yang. See *Yin* and *yang*
"Yankee City," 3, 12, 150
Yellow dog contracts, 432
Yin and *yang*, 428
Yinger, J. Milton, 289
Young, Kimball, 329, 343, 394